Fundamentals of
Management
Science

Efraim Turban

School of Business and Organizational Science
Florida International University

Jack R. Meredith

College of Business Administration
University of Cincinnati

Fundamentals of
Management
Science

1981   Revised edition

BUSINESS PUBLICATIONS, INC. Plano, Texas   75075
Irwin-Dorsey Limited   Georgetown, Ontario   L7G 4B3

ISBN 0-256-02393-X
Library of Congress Catalog Card No. 80-68036
Printed in the United States of America

1 2 3 4 5 6 7 8 9 0   D   8 7 6 5 4 3 2 1

To Rocha
    E. T.

To my parents, Blanche and Joyce Harvey
    J. M.

Preface

Today, the techniques of management science are known to businessmen, urban planners, farmers, military strategists, space scientists, and public administrators in a host of fields. Words such as "systems," "models," "optimization," "simulation," and "cost-benefit" are now common in the public vocabulary. The need, thus, is great for an introductory text that explains, with a minimum of mathematics, how to *formulate* decision problems, how to *solve* them using management science concepts, and how to *apply* the solutions obtained.

As more complex models were developed in the field, relatively more attention was paid to the task of solving the models while less emphasis was placed on the important phases of formulation and application. This book attempts to correct that deficiency by providing a comprehensive discussion of these two crucial phases.

This revised edition tackles these phases in much the same manner as the first edition but with increased emphasis on a managerial viewpoint. In particular, the linear programming simplex solution procedure has been revised and expanded, and sensitivity analysis of the LP solution has been significantly expanded. Furthermore, cases and glossaries have been added to all the "tool" chapters of Part II and a detailed analysis of a complex case has been added as Chapter 16. The book remains organized in three parts: Foundations, The Tools, and Applications.

In Part I of the book the foundations of the field are outlined. The reader is introduced to the topic of management science in Chapter 1. Its characteristics and processes are then outlined in Chapter 2, which focuses on the relation of management science to decision making.

Part II, The Tools, is concerned with formulating managerial problems from many different fields and finding solutions to them using management science models. The chapters are intentionally written to be independent of each other so the instructor may cover only the topics desired for the course. Chapters in this part of the book are divided into two sections: "Basics" and "Extensions." The essence of each topic is presented in the former at a minimal level of mathematical sophistication—typically, only algebra or elementary statistics is needed. The sections in the "Extensions" elaborate on some of the basic models at a somewhat higher level of sophistication. These sections are typically also independent of each other and may thus be selected at will by the instructor for further class study. The mathematical and statistical background needed for the book, as well as a few additional topics (such as "present value"), are included in Appendix A, Mathematics, and in Appendix B, Statistics. Appendix C includes requisite tables for the text and, lastly, the *answers* (not solutions) to the even-numbered problems are given in Appendix D.

Each chapter in Part II begins with a brief episode showing the student how a particular decision problem arises. When possible, this example is carried throughout the chapter to illustrate the concepts being developed. We have attempted to present a variety of decision situations from a number of fields to emphasize the flexibility of the management science approach. In lieu of presenting the mathematical theorems and proofs that form the basis of many of the models, we appeal to intuitive reasoning and logic. All of these chapters include a case to help the student apply the tools and techniques learned in the chapter to a realistic situation. The chapters then conclude with a glossary of chapter terms.

The sequence of the chapters progresses from general decision models (Chapters 3 and 4) through mathematical programming (Chapters 5, 6, 7), networks (Chapter 8), dynamic programming (Chapter 9), Markov chains (Chapter 10), game theory (Chapter 11), and inventory models (Chapter 12), and ends with the stochastic models of queuing (Chapter 13), and simulation (Chapter 14). Each chapter is as independent of the others as possible to provide the instructor with the flexibility of using selected chapters at will.

Part III, Applications, begins with an examination of the problem of implementing the decision. In Chapter 15 the implementation problem is viewed as having two primary sets of issues: those peculiar to the specific project itself and those concerned with the organization and how its overall climate affects implementation. A detailed case study is then given in Chapter 16 to illustrate how to integrate the tools and techniques in a more realistic framework than the problems of Part II alone allow. The book concludes with an assessment of the future directions and areas of application of management science (Chapter 17).

The book was written with the express aim of allowing coverage in a course ranging from one quarter (if only the "Basics" sections are covered) to two quarters if the entire text is to be covered).

The number of persons to whom we owe thanks for their contributions to the development of this book defies enumeration. Of great value were the comments and criticisms of our students regarding sections that were still written at too technical a level, even after multiple revisions. Of particular help were the suggestions and advice offered to us by John C. Anderson, University of Minnesota; Vance Etnyre, University of Houston; Israel Brosh, Tel Aviv University, Tigineh Mersha for the Chapter 16 simulation; and the editing of Sara and Ben Ettinger. We wish to acknowledge the following reviewers: Billy M. Bagwell, Mississippi State University: John C. Carter, Pace University; Richard D. Legault, Southeastern Massachusetts University; and Arthur Reitsch, Eastern Washington University. Special recognition should be given to the ideas and constructive suggestions of Carol Meredith, many of which distinguish both the previous and current editions of this book. Also, thanks go to Gale Harkins, who provided useful input both to the manuscript and to the Instructor's Manual, to Beaty Cancela for laborious proofreading, and to Julie Menchen, a typist and can-do secretary *extraordinaire*.

EFRAIM TURBAN
JACK MEREDITH

Contents

PART I

In this initial part of the text our aim is to provide a foundation upon which to develop the topics in the rest of the book. We do this in two stages:

- Chapter 1 introduces the topic of management science and its wide applicability to decision making. The chapter then concludes with an overview of the plan of the text.
- Chapter 2 is directed toward the management science process itself. The use of models to describe managerial problems is the essence of this approach and thus the focus of the chapter. The chapter then relates the management science tools to prototypal managerial problems and discusses their applicability.

FOUNDATIONS

1

This book is about the application of the scientific method to an area basic to all managers and administrators: decision making. Management science can be a tremendous aid to the manager faced with decisions. It can sort out the complex array of data, show what is relevant and what is not, focus on the lack of certain crucial information, provide an objective basis of choosing the best solution, and even quantify the manager's feelings and preferences for solution outcomes.

This chapter begins with a definition of management science. It then presents its major characteristics and a description of its historical development. The chapter ends with a discussion of the applicability and limitations of management science.

Introduction

1.1 WHAT'S IT ALL ABOUT?

Before we delve into management science—what it is, what it can be used for, and what it cannot be used for—let us briefly look at the word "management." "Management" is the planning and integration of effort, judicious use of resources, motivation of people, and provision of leadership in order to guide an organization toward its goals and objectives in an efficient manner. To carry out the above functions, managers are engaged in a continuous process of making decisions. Therefore, *management* is considered by many as equivalent to *decision making.*

For years, managers have considered decision making a pure art—a talent acquired over a long period of time through experience (learning by "trial and error"). It has been considered an "art" because a variety of individual styles can be used in approaching and successfully solving the same type of managerial problems in actual business practice. These styles are often based on creativity, judgment, intuition, and experience rather than on the systematic methods of science.

However, the style of management is changing. Man has already landed on the moon, and technological advancement dictates the pace of our life. Such advances in technology cannot possibly be made or sustained without concurrent advances in the systems of management. Such unusual strides have been made possible only because the "art" of management has increasingly been supplemented by science.

If one examines the reasons for bankruptcies of small and even large corporations, one frequently finds that the bankruptcy is the result of a single wrong decision. For example, many corporations expanded too fast during the economic boom of the early 70s and then collapsed during the mid-70s recession. A good example was the giant W. C. Grant discount chain. Lack of cash flow caused its bankruptcy. Similarly, excess inventories caused huge losses and bankruptcies for many agricultural machinery manufacturers.

Business and its environment are more complex today than ever before, and the trend toward increasing complexity is continuing. Figure 1.1 shows the changes in the major factors (on the left) that have an impact on managerial decision making. The results (on the right)

Management—the efficient use of resources

Decision making—art or science?

The importance of a single decision

Greater complexity and cost of errors

FIGURE 1.1
Factors affecting decision making

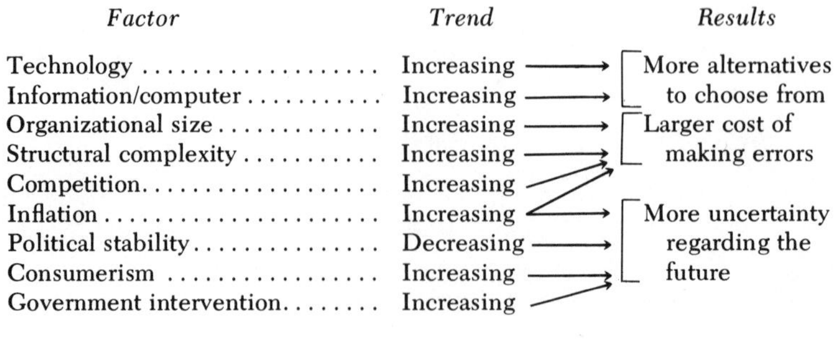

Factor	*Trend*	*Results*
Technology	Increasing ⟶	More alternatives to choose from
Information/computer	Increasing ⟶	
Organizational size	Increasing ⟶	Larger cost of making errors
Structural complexity	Increasing ⟶	
Competition	Increasing	
Inflation	Increasing	More uncertainty regarding the future
Political stability	Decreasing ⟶	
Consumerism	Increasing ⟶	
Government intervention	Increasing	

indicate that making decisions today is much more complicated than in the past for three reasons. First, the number of alternatives is usually much larger. Second, the consequences of the decisions are more difficult to predict due to increased uncertainty. Finally, the cost of making errors has become larger and larger, mainly due to mass production and a resulting chain-reaction situation in which the impact of an error may be felt in many places due to complex interrelationships.

To illustrate how critical the impact of a single error can be, consider the following example.

In the early 70s the management of Polaroid decided to invest *Polaroid's SX–70* millions of dollars in developing a new camera, SX–70. The justification for the huge investment was the anticipation of large profits from the sale of *film* for the camera. On July 2, 1975, the Dow Jones industrial average plunged almost 16 points and closed at a low for the year of 790. The major contributor to the fall was the drop in Polaroid, a once highly priced glamour issue, that fell 11⅜ points, a decline of 32 percent, in a single day! The drop was attributed to an announcement that the sales of SX–70 film were only one third of the company's projections. The plunge reduced the value of Polaroid shares by more than $360 million overnight!

As a result of these trends and changes it is very difficult to rely on a trial-and-error approach to management. Managers must become more sophisticated—they must learn to utilize new tools and techniques that are being developed in their field. No one can imagine a successful physician using the medicines and equipment of the turn of the century. Yet, in management one can find executives using management tools of that time.

The management science approach adopts the view that a substantial portion of decision making consists of (1) analyzing phenomena that can be measured, (2) determining relationships that can be represented quantitatively, and (3) isolating causal chains whose internal consistency can be tested experimentally. Thus, the objective of this approach is to bring as many management phenomena as possible into the domain of standard or "programmed" decisions where solution techniques are *Programmed decision* already available. Programmed decisions then can be solved quickly *making* with the aid of scientific tools so that the manager can devote a larger portion of time to the qualitative aspects of the problems as well as to more complex decisions.

1.2   DEFINITIONS OF MANAGEMENT SCIENCE

Management science has had almost as many definitions as it has had practitioners. Indeed, it is practically an annual occurrence for the retiring presidents of the professional societies to give their personal definition in presidential addresses.

Two classical definitions, for example, are:

1. "Operations Research [management science] is the application of scientific methods, techniques, and tools to problems involving the operations of systems so as to provide those in control of the operations with optimum solutions to the problems."[1]
2. ". . . the application of the scientific method to the study of the operations of large, complex organizations or activities."[2]

Other names

In this text, *management science* is defined as: *The application of the scientific method to the analysis and solution of managerial decision problems.* Note that *operations research* is another term used almost interchangeably with management science. Other names often used to connote more or less the same general area are: operational research, operations analysis, quantitative analysis, quantitative methods, systems analysis, decision analysis, and decision science. The reason for so many names (most of which have their own professional societies) is that the entire field is relatively new and there is no general agreement yet on what body of knowledge it includes.

In addition to the formal definition of management science, and sometimes instead of such a definition, it is customary to list the special characteristics of the field.

1.3 THE CHARACTERISTICS OF MANAGEMENT SCIENCE

The major characteristics of management science are:

1. A primary focus on managerial decision making.
2. The application of the scientific approach to decision making.
3. The examination of the decision situation from a broad perspective; that is, the application of a *system's approach.*
4. The use of methods and knowledge from several disciplines.
5. A reliance on formal mathematical models.
6. A dependence on electronic *computers.*
7. *An appraisal resting on criteria of economic effectiveness.*

These characteristics will be discussed in detail in Chapter 2.

1.4 THE TOOLS OF MANAGEMENT SCIENCE

The characteristics of management science established the foundation upon which the tools and techniques developed. The role of the management scientist can be viewed as that of a consultant who is called upon to diagnose a problem, propose a treatment, and sometimes to perform the treatment. In this capacity, the management scientist works

---

[1] Churchman, Ackoff, and Arnoff ([2], page 9).

[2] The Committee on Operations Research of the National Research Council in Great Britain.

with tools that enable him or her to analyze a problem (diagnosis), to predict the future development of the problem (prognosis), and to suggest the best treatment via an analysis of the possible consequences.

As management science developed, a number of decision-making tools were constructed. These tools were developed to cope with those managerial problems which appeared over and over again. For example, a recurring managerial problem is the allocation of scarce resources. For certain types of allocation problems, a tool named linear programming was developed. For more complex allocation problems, the tools of integer programming and dynamic programming were developed. (The entire spectrum of tools is presented in Chapter 2 and is discussed in detail in Part II of this text.)

Tools for recurring decision situations

In addition to such tools, management scientists also use tools borrowed from other disciplines. For example, statistical tools are used in determining significant differences between proposed solutions, and forecasting models are used in predicting the consequences of proposed treatments. Similarly, econometric, financial, marketing, and organizational behavior models are frequently incorporated into the analysis.

Borrowed tools

1.5   HISTORICAL DEVELOPMENT

It is difficult to mark the "beginning" of management science. The scientific approach to management can be traced back to the era of the industrial revolution and even to much earlier periods. In the late 19th century, Frederick W. Taylor formalized his *scientific management* approach, which marked the beginning of industrial engineering. There is evidence of the use of mathematical models at the turn of the century (e.g., Erlang's work on waiting line problems, Edison's work on war games, and the development of the inventory management Economic Order Quantity formula by Harris).

F. W. Taylor's scientific management

The use of math models

It was not until World War II that management science began to establish itself as a separate discipline, both in England (termed operational research) and in the United States (termed operations research). In order to maximize their war effort, the British government organized teams of scientific and engineering personnel to assist field commanders in solving perplexing strategic and tactical problems. They found that technically trained men could solve problems outside of their normal professional competency. They asked biologists to examine problems in electronics, physicists to think in terms of the movement of people rather than the movement of molecules, mathematicians to apply probability theory to improve soldiers' chances of survival, and chemists to study equilibria in systems other than chemical. Teams of specialists studied problems ranging from the evaluation of cost and effectiveness of complete military systems (such as the defense system of a country) to the best allocation of depth charges in antisubmarine warfare.

Cross-fertilization in science

The success of the British operational research teams led the

United States to institute a similar effort in 1942 (small-scale projects dated back to 1937). The initial project involved the deployment of merchant-marine convoys to minimize losses from enemy submarines.

From wartime use to industry

Following the war, operations research extended into industry—first into the process-type industries such as oil refineries, steel and paper mills. These industries are characterized by large volumes of relatively few products. The savings were high since even a penny a unit on a large volume could total up to millions of dollars. In addition, a high capital-to-worker ratio in these automated industries meant relatively fewer employees whose duties were mainly in supervision, control, and maintenance. Therefore, the employees showed little resistance to change.

The 35-year period after World War II saw a dramatic development and refinement of techniques with a corresponding expansion to almost all industries and services. Furthermore, the complexity of managerial problems attacked by management science increased significantly, especially with the introduction of the technique of simulation and large, efficient computing systems. As the field grew, the name management science increased in popularity.

Management science today

The development is evident in the management science departments that emerged at many universities, several of which grant a doctoral degree in the field. In the United States alone there are about 10,000 members in the professional societies. About 15 English-language periodicals deal with theories and applications of management science.

Trend toward public sector decision making

The latest trend is a penetration into large social and urban systems such as criminal justice, health care, and education. This trend is discussed in Chapter 17, "The Future of Management Science."

1.6 EXTENT OF USE AND LIMITATIONS

Dollar and other benefits surveyed

While relatively few studies have been published on the extent and success of using management science, the research that has been published reveals impressive results. A detailed survey reported by the American Management Association [1]* gives some indication of both the possible savings and the difficulties of measuring them. For example, of the 324 responding companies using management science, 130 reported "considerable improvement" and "appreciable net savings." Actual figures of $100,000 or more were reported by 17 companies; anticipated savings of $300,000 or more by 18 companies. Many indicated that directly measurable dollar savings were only a *small part* of the benefit obtained. Only two of the 324 companies indicated an

---

* The number within the brackets refers to a listing in the Reference section of each chapter.

intention to decrease management science activities, and not one indicated plans to discontinue using it.

Other surveys [3, 8, 9, 11], while failing to give savings figures, indicated that virtually all practitioners were satisfied with management science and planned to continue its use. Evidence of its benefits may also be seen in the constantly increasing rate of application of management science in industrial firms; some of the more common areas of application are shown in Table 1.1. Another survey ([11]) revealed that

Area of application	Survey		
	AMA [1] 1957 n = 631 firms (percent)	Hovey and Wagner [6] 1958 n = 90 firms (percent)	Schumacher and Smith [9] 1964 n = 65 firms (percent)
Production	24	32	68
Long-range planning	23	39	55
Advertising, sales, and marketing.	25	14	20
Inventory	21	31	68
Transportation	15	18	41
Top management	15	No data	No data
Research	14	No data	No data
Finance	13	No data	No data
Accounting	11	11	13
Purchasing	8	No data	No data
Personnel	8	No data	No data
Quality control	No data	22	38
Maintenance.	No data	11	24
Plant location	No data	10	24
Equipment replacement	No data	10	20
Packaging	No data	9	5
Capital budgeting	No data	7	29
Percent of companies using management science.	No data	42.6	61.5

TABLE 1.1
A comparative table of areas of application of management science techniques

44 percent of the largest U.S. industrial and service corporations[3] have a management science unit at their corporate headquarters.

Although most surveys indicated satisfaction with the techniques, there was some dissatisfaction with the wide gap that exists between theory and application in management science (e.g., see Grayson

[3] As determined by a sample taken from *Fortune* magazine's list of the 500 largest corporations.

[4]). Chapter 15 of this text deals with some of the reasons for the unsuccessful use of management science.

Management science, like any other management tool, is no substitute for good management. The manager must still decide what to investigate, what to do about the factors that cannot be quantified, and how to interpret the results of scientific analysis. Management science requires capable, well-qualified, and experienced personnel. It also frequently consumes a great deal of time and may become very costly. Attempting shortcuts by superficially examining the problems, using inappropriate models or inaccurate data, may produce results that, if applied, will be far more costly than simply using the dictates of subjective judgment.

Only a costly tool?

The results of management science cannot be guaranteed; the potential benefits, however, may be enormous and well worth all the time, effort, and expense required. The main arguments for and against its use are:

Management science—pro and con

For

1. Systematic and logical approach to decision making.
2. Helps communication within the organization through consultation with experts in various areas.
3. Permits a thorough analysis of a large number of alternative options.
4. Enables evaluation of situations involving uncertainty.
5. Allows decision maker to judge how much information to gather in a given problem.
6. Increases the effectiveness of the decision.
7. Enables quick identification of the best available solution.
8. Allows quick and inexpensive examination of a large (sometimes infinite) number of alternatives.

Against

1. Time-consuming.
2. Lack of acceptance by decision makers.
3. Assessments of uncertainties are difficult to obtain.
4. Evaluates the decision in terms of a sometimes oversimplified model of reality.
5. Can be expensive to undertake.
6. Studies may be shelved for various reasons (see Chapter 15) resulting in an unproductive expense.

One question that managers frequently ask in discussions after lectures on management science is "Where have these techniques been applied consistently?" The list of applications is growing continuously. Examples of typical managerial problems where management science techniques have been applied are:

- Inventory control.
- Facility design.
- Product-mix determination.
- Portfolio analysis (of securities).
- Scheduling and sequencing.
- Merger-growth analysis.
- Transportation planning.
- Design of information systems.
- Allocation of scarce resources.
- Investment decisions (new plants, and the like).
- Project management—planning and control.
- New product decisions.
- Sales force decisions.
- Market research decisions.
- Research and development decisions.
- Oil and gas exploration decisions.
- Pricing decisions.
- Competitive bidding decisions.
- Quality control decisions.
- Machine setup problems in production.
- Distribution decisions.
- Manpower planning and control decisions.
- Credit policy analysis.
- Research and development effectiveness.

Some uses itemized

1.7   PLAN OF THE BOOK

The text is divided into three parts (Figure 1.2): *Foundations, The tools,* and *Applications.*

The *foundations* part consists of two chapters. Here in Chapter 1, the characteristics, the basic philosophy, and the history of management science have been presented. Chapter 2 provides the theoretical background of managerial decision making and the methodology of management science.

Part I: Foundations

Part II presents the prototypal management science *tools.* In Chapters 3 and 4, the quantitative approach to decision making is considered, laying the basis for the management science tools and techniques presented in Chapters 5–14.

Part II: The tools

The last part of the book has been reserved for a discussion of the *application* of management science. Chapter 15 deals with the problems of implementation, both for a particular project and in general. The text then introduces a detailed case study in Chapter 16 and concludes with a general assessment of the future of management science in Chapter 17.

Part III: Applications

12

FIGURE 1.2
Organization of the book

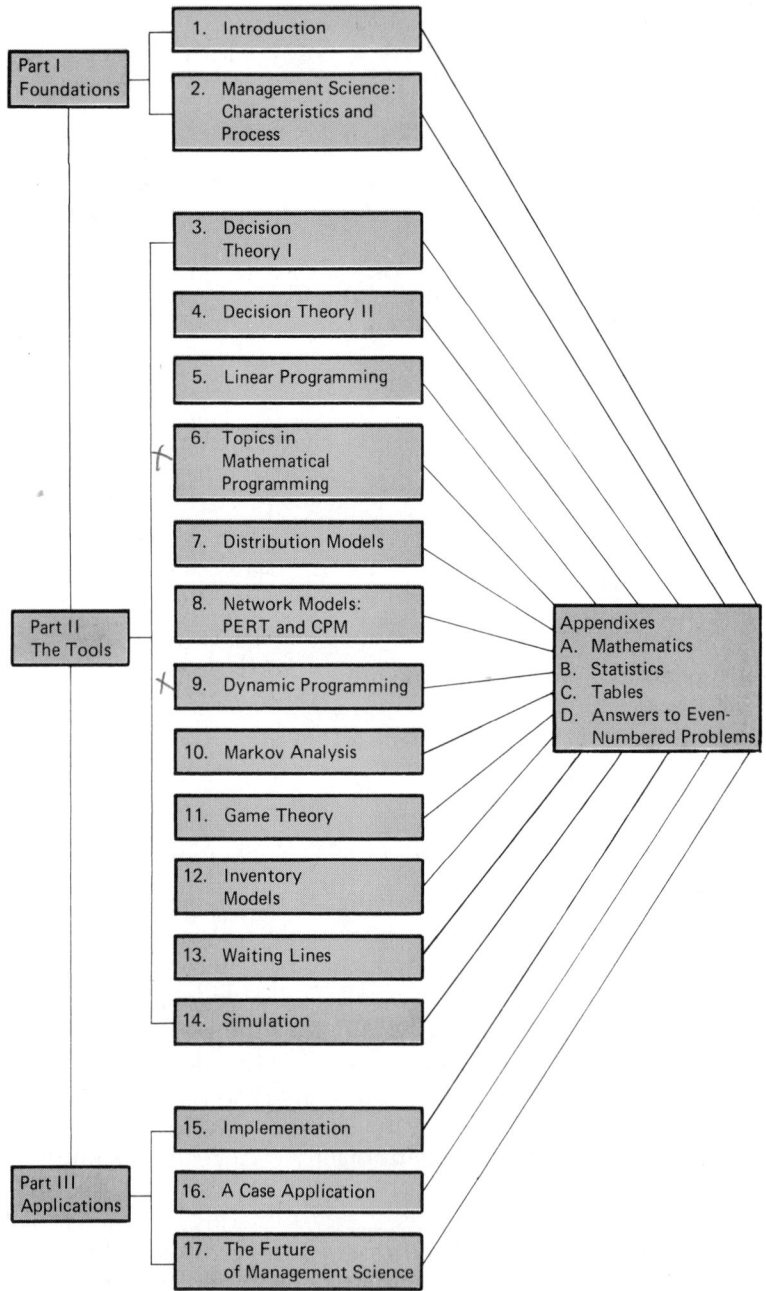

1.8   REVIEW QUESTIONS

1. Give an example which will illustrate the equivalence of management and decision making.
2. Explain why the management style of "trial and error" is becoming less and less attractive.
3. Explain why decision making today is more complex than 30 years ago.
4. Examine the definitions of management science. Can you give a personal example of a management science situation that will fit these definitions?
5. Explain how the standard tools of management science were developed.
6. Discuss the major advantages of management science.
7. Discuss the major disadvantages.
8. List some managerial problems that would seem amenable to management science techniques. List some that would *not*.

1.9   GLOSSARY

Management   Mobilization of resources in order to attain the organization's goals.

Management science   The application of the scientific approach to the analysis and solution of managerial decision problems.

Operations research   Basically the same as management science (used interchangeably in this text).

Programmed decisions   Standard or repetitive decision situations for which solution techniques are already available.

Prototypal managerial problems   Common organizational decision situations such as a "resource allocation" problem.

Techniques (tools) of management science   Mathematical models specially developed to deal with prototypal managerial problems.

Scientific management   A school of management thought headed by F. Taylor that focused on economic efficiency as the productive core of the organization.

1.10   REFERENCES AND BIBLIOGRAPHY

1. AMA Management Report No. 10. *Operations Research Considered.* New York: AMA Inc., 1958.
2. Churchman, C. W.; Ackoff, R. L.: and Arnoff, E. L. *Introduction to Operations Research.* New York: John Wiley & Sons, Inc., 1957.
3. Gaither, N. "The Adoption of Operations Research Techniques by Manufacturing Organizations." *Decision Sciences* 6(1975): 797–813.
4. Grayson, C. J. Jr. "Management Science and Business Practice." *Harvard Business Review* 51 (1973):41–48.
5. Hillier, F. S., and Lieberman, G. J. *Introduction to Operations Research.* 3d ed. San Francisco: Holden-Day, Inc., 1980.
6. Hovey, R. W., and Wagner, H. M. "A Sample Survey of Industrial Operations-Research Activities." *Operations Research* 6 (1958): 878–81.
7. Kenna, C. K. *Quantitative Methods for Public Decision Making.* New York: McGraw-Hill Book Co., 1980.
8. Ledbetter, W. and Cox, J. "Are OR Techniques Being Used?" *Industrial Engineering,* pp. 19–21 (Sept., 1977).
9. Schumacher, C. C., and Smith, B. E. "A Sample Survey of Industrial Operations-Research Activities II." *Operations Research* 13 (1965):1023–1027.
10. Simon, H. *The New Science of Management Decisions,* Rev. ed. Englewood Cliffs, N.J.: Prentice-Hall Inc., 1977.
11. Turban, E. "A Sample Survey of Operations Research Activities at the Corporate Level." *Operations Research* 20 (1972):708–721.

2

Decision making, which is of prime interest to management science, can be viewed as a systematic process. Such a perspective enables the development of quantitative tools with which managers can make better decisions.

Chapter 2 reviews the general decision-making process and then discusses the characteristics which are common to the quantitative tools. Throughout the exposition of these topics, the foundation for the entire book is laid. Therefore, the material presented here should be considered as the backbone upon which management science is constructed.

Management science: Characteristics and process

2.1   INTRODUCTION

In this chapter management science is going to be examined from three perspectives: its *characteristics*, its *process*, and its *tools*.

The characteristics

1.   A primary interest in managerial decision making.
2.   The employment of a scientific approach.
3.   Problems and decisions are viewed from a systems perspective.
4.   An interdisciplinary framework is attempted.
5.   Mathematical models are used.
6.   Computers are very frequently employed.

These characteristics, which are exhibited to a greater or lesser degree by all management science projects, are discussed in Sections 2.2–2.7.

The process

Management science employs a systematic approach to decision making. This process is discussed in Sections 2.8–2.11.

Decision making as a process

The tools

The tools of management science were created basically as a response to certain repetitive managerial problems. These problems, the appropriate tools, and the relationship between the problems and the tools are discussed in Section 2.12.

2.2   DECISION MAKING: A PRIMARY FOCUS

A *decision* is the conclusion of *a process* by which one chooses between two or more available alternative courses of action for the purpose of attaining a goal(s). The process is called *decision making*. According to Herbert A. Simon [12], managerial decision making is synonymous with the whole process of management. To illustrate the idea, let us examine the important managerial function of *planning*. Planning involves a *series of decisions* such as: What should be done? When? How? Where? By whom? Hence, planning implies decision making. Other functions of management such as organizing and controlling can also be viewed as composed of making decisions.

Planning: A series of decisions

Decision making and problem solving

A major premise of management science is that decision making, regardless of the situation involved, can be considered as a general process, consisting of the following major steps:

The general steps of decision making

16

(handwritten: problem solving) 1. Defining the problem.
2. Searching for alternative courses of action.
3. Evaluating the alternatives.
4. Selecting one alternative.

(handwritten: 2.15 ①) Much confusion exists between the terms *decision making* and *problem solving*. One way to distinguish between the two is to consider the entire process (steps 1–4 above) as *problem solving*; the specific step of "selecting an alternative" (step 4 above) is the *decision* or the *solution* to the problem.

However, in the interest of consistency with many other texts, the terms decision making and problem solving will be considered as equivalent in this text and will be used interchangeably.

Regardless of its name, the process is similar to the general process of scientific analysis. This similarity provides the basis for the management science approach to decision making, as will be shown in the following section.

2.3 THE SCIENTIFIC APPROACH

The scientific approach (also known as the "scientific method") is a formalized reasoning process to which many of the scientific discoveries since Descartes[1] must be credited. It consists of the following steps:

Step 1. The problem for analysis is defined, and the conditions for observation are determined.

Step 2. Observations are made under different conditions to determine the behavior of the system containing the problem.

The steps of the scientific method

Step 3. Based on the observations, a hypothesis that describes how the factors involved are thought to interact, or what is the best solution to the problem, is conceived.

Step 4. To test the hypothesis, an experiment is designed.

Step 5. The experiment is executed, and measurements are obtained and recorded.

Step 6. The results of the experiment are analyzed, and the hypothesis is either accepted or rejected.

The six steps of the scientific method can be applied to decision making. For example, the *evaluation* of alternatives is done scientifically through *experimentation*. The overall relationship of the scientific approach to the decision-making process is shown in Figure 2.1.

Using the scientific approach to solve problems

Management science employs this scientific approach for the purpose of solving problems. For each of the steps outlined in Figure 2.1, certain methodologies have been developed. These management

---

[1] A French philosopher and mathematician of the 17th century, considered the father of modern philosophy. Descartes emphasized the use of reason as the chief tool of inquiry.

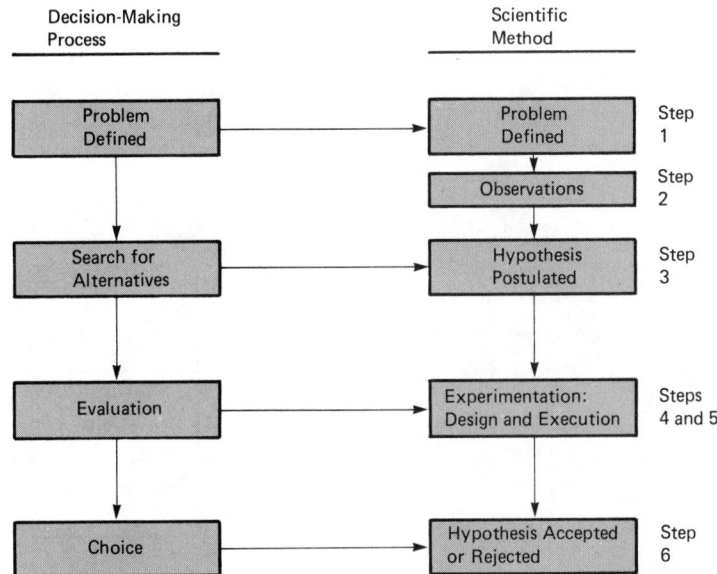

Decision-Making Process

Scientific Method

FIGURE 2.1
Relationship of the scientific approach to the decision process

science methodologies are centered around the idea that problems should be viewed as systems.

2.4   THE SYSTEMS POINT OF VIEW

The third characteristic of management science is its use of systems theory and analysis. A *system*[2] is a collection of people, resources, concepts, and procedures that is intended to perform some identifiable function, or to serve a goal. A clear definition of that function is most important. The *purpose* of an air defense system, for instance, is to protect the targets on the ground, not just to destroy attacking aircraft or missiles.

A system defined

The notion of *levels* (or a *hierarchy*) of systems reflects the fact that all systems are subsystems, since all are contained within some larger system. For example, a bank would include within itself *subsystems*, such as: (1) the commercial loan department, (2) the installment loan department, (3) the savings department, and (4) the operations department. Also the bank itself may be a subsidiary of a chain of banks, such as the Bank of America, which is a subsystem of the California banking system, which is a part of the national banking system, which is a part of the national economy, and so on.

A hierarchy of systems

---

[2] In the remainder of this book the term system is going to be used to describe an organization, a part of an organization, or a problem under study.

The structure of a system

Systems as inputs,
processes, and outputs

Systems are divided into three distinct parts: *inputs*, *processes*, and *outputs*. They are surrounded by an environment (Figure 2.2) and are frequently connected by a feedback mechanism.

FIGURE 2.2
The system and its
environment

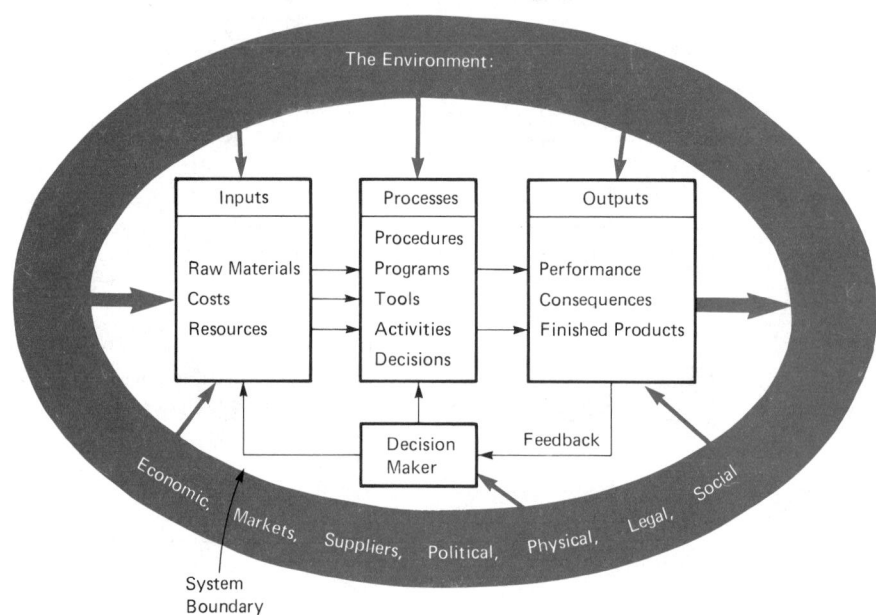

Inputs   Inputs include those elements that enter the system. Examples of inputs are raw materials to a chemical plant, or students to a university.

Processes   All the elements necessary to *convert* the inputs into outputs are included in the processes. For example, in a chemical plant a process may include energy, operating procedures, materials handling, and the use of employees and machines. In a university a process may include teaching, learning, examinations, and the use of faculty, laboratories, and libraries.

Outputs   Outputs describe the finished products or the consequences of being in the system. For example, fertilizers are one output of a chemical plant and graduates are the output of universities.

Feedback, the essence of control

Feedback   The flow of information to the decision maker concerning the system's output is called feedback. Based on this information the decision maker can modify the inputs or the processes, or both.

What is the environment?

The environment   There are several elements that lie outside the system in the sense that they are not inputs, outputs, or processes. However, they have an impact on the system's performance and consequently on the attainment of its goals. These are termed the *environment*. One way to identify the elements of the environment is by answering two questions as suggested by Churchman [4]:

1. Is it possible to manipulate this element? *no,*
2. Does the element matter relative to the system's goals? *yes*   ⟩ *environment.*

If and only if the answer to the first question is "no" but to the second is "yes," the element should be considered part of the environment. Environmental elements can be social, political, legal, physical, economic, and the like. For example, in a chemical plant the suppliers, competitors, and customers are elements of the environment. In a university the neighboring universities, the community, and the newspapers represent some elements of the environment.

The systems approach

Management science recognizes that a decision made in one segment of the organization may have a significant effect, not only on the operation of that particular segment but on the operation of other segments as well. Therefore, when possible, the overall organizational point of view is adopted. Such an approach is termed a *systems point of view* or a *systems approach*. Further discussion of the systems approach is given in Section 2.9 where the concepts of optimization and suboptimization are presented.

A systems viewpoint

The boundaries of a system

Since every system can be considered a subsystem of another, the application of a systems approach may never end. Therefore, it is necessary, as a matter of practicality, to confine the analysis to a defined area. Such confinement is termed "closing the system," that is, setting the *boundaries*, however difficult, within which the impact of a decision is going to be checked. The boundaries may be determined after preliminary investigation, but they *must* be determined before a model of the system can be constructed. A system can be bounded by a physical area or it can be bounded in terms of time. An example of the latter is made by considering a period of only one year, neglecting long-range effects.

Closing the system

System's effectiveness

Effectiveness is defined as the *extent to which goals are achieved.* As such, effectiveness is synonomous with performance. Effectiveness is evaluated by *measures of effectiveness* (also known as measures of performance).

Effectiveness is frequently confused with *efficiency*. Effectiveness measures the degree of a goal's attainment; efficiency measures how well resources are being utilized (ratio of output to input). Therefore, effectiveness does not necessarily imply efficiency. A system may be effective but very *inefficient* if it attains its goals but at tremendous expense. On the other hand, a system may be *efficient* (make best use of resources) but *ineffective* (not achieve its objectives). Management science is concerned with both effectiveness and efficiency.

Effectiveness versus efficiency

Measuring effectiveness and efficiency

In many managerial systems, and especially those involving the delivery of human services (such as education, health, or recreation), the measurement of the system's effectiveness and efficiency constitutes a major problem. The reason for the difficulty is due to the existence of several, often nonquantifiable, goals, as well as the indirect costs and benefits that are involved. In recent years, several methodologies have been developed under the names of *"cost effectiveness," "cost-benefit analysis," "benefit-cost ratios,"* and *"systems analysis"* which attempt to measure the effectiveness and efficiency of such systems. For further discussion and references see Van Gigch [13].

The examination of a problem from a systems point of view enlarges the scope of the analysis and creates encouraging conditions for an interdisciplinary approach.

Cost-benefit analysis

2.5 AN INTERDISCIPLINARY APPROACH

Many managerial problems have physical, psychological, biological, mathematical, sociological, engineering, and economic aspects. By bringing together a team with a variety of backgrounds, new and advanced approaches to old problems are often obtained. The scientific mind from each discipline attempts to extract the essence of the problem and relate it structurally to other similar problems encountered in one's own particular field. Having drawn some analogies, the researcher can then determine if the problem under study is amenable to solution methods traditionally successful in his or her field. When scientists from several disciplines do this collectively, the pool of possible approaches is large enough to reinforce individual disciplines.

The team approach

Therefore, many management science problems are attacked by teams (the average size is three persons). A team approach, however, has some potential dangers. Working as a committee, the team approach may suffer from the potential defects and weaknesses of committees such as inefficiency, compromised decisions, lack of leadership, and poor communication.

The problems of committees

Frequently, however, there is no economic justification for a team in which case the "one-person show" is appropriate. Many problems are simple enough to be handled by a single qualified researcher, especially one with an interdisciplinary training. Also, thanks to the advance of computers, it is easier and cheaper than ever before to retrieve information about other disciplines, thus enabling even a person with minimal training in several disciplines to employ an interdisciplinary approach.

2.6 MATHEMATICAL MODELS

A model defined

A *model* is a simplified representation or abstraction of reality. It is usually simplified because reality is too complex to copy exactly and because much of the complexity is actually irrelevant to the specific problem.

The representation of systems or problems through models can be done at various degrees of abstraction. Models are classified, according to their degree of abstraction, into several groups:

Iconic (*scale*) An iconic model, the least abstract, is a physical replica of a system, usually based on a different scale than the original. These may appear in three dimensions such as airplane, car, or bridge models to scale, or a production line. Photographs are another type of iconic scale model but in only two dimensions.

Analog An analog model does not look like the real system but behaves like it. These are usually *two-dimensional* charts or diagrams; that is, they are physical models, but their shape *differs* from that of the system. Some examples are:

- Organization charts which depict structure, authority, and responsibility relationships.
- A map where different colors represent water or mountains.
- Stock market charts.
- Blueprints of a machine or a house.
- An oil dipstick.
- An hourglass.

Analog models are more abstract than iconic models.

Mathematical The complexity of relationships in some systems cannot be represented physically, or the physical representation may be cumbersome and take time to construct or manipulate. Therefore a more abstract model is used with the aid of symbols. Most management science analysis is executed with the aid of *mathematical models* which utilize mathematical symbols. These are general rather than specific and can describe diverse situations. Furthermore, they can be manipulated easily for purposes of experimentation and prediction.

Too small for detail explanation.

Management science uses mathematical models

The components of mathematical models = *variables*

All mathematical models are comprised of three components: *result variables*, *decision variables*, and *uncontrollable variables*. These components are connected by mathematical (logical) relationships, as shown in Figure 2.3.

The result variables These reflect the *level of effectiveness* of the system. That is, they tell how well the system performs or attains its

Three types of model components

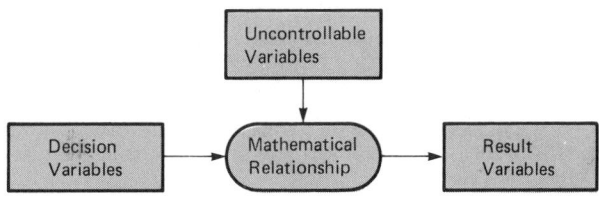

FIGURE 2.3
The general structure of a model

TABLE 2.1
Examples of the
components of models

Area	Decision variables	Result variables	Uncontrollable variables
Financial investment	Investment amounts Period of investment Timing of investment	Total profit Rate of return Earnings/share Liquidity	Inflation rate Prime rate Competition
Marketing	Advertising budget Number of models Zonal sales reps	Market share Customer satisfaction	Disposable income Competitor's actions
Manufacturing	Production amounts Inventory levels Incentive plan	Total cost Quality level Spoilage	Machine capacity Technology Materials prices
Accounting	Audit schedule Use of computers Depreciation schedule	Data processing cost Error rate	Legal requirements Tax rates Computer technology
Transportation	Shipments	Total transport cost	Delivery distance Regulations
Services	Number of servers	Customer satisfaction	Demand for service

goals. Some of the more common result variables which are used in organizations to measure effectiveness are shown in Table 2.1. The result variables are *dependent* variables.[3] They also have other names which are often used in management science:

- Measures of performance.
- Measures of effectiveness.
- Payoffs.
- Outcomes.

The decision variables The decision variables are those factors where a choice must be made. These variables are *manipulable* and *controllable* by the decision maker. Examples are the quantities of products to produce, the number of units to be ordered, and the number of tellers to use in a bank (others are shown in Table 2.1). Decision variables are classified mathematically as *independent* variables or *unknown* variables. They are denoted by the letters x_1, x_2, and so on, or by x, y, z. The aim of management science is to find the best values of these decision variables.

The uncontrollable variables In any decision situation there are factors which affect the result variables but which are not under the control of the decision maker. Examples are the prime interest rate, building codes, tax regulations, and prices of supplies (others are shown in Table 2.1). Most of these factors are uncontrollable because they

---

[3] A dependent variable means that for the event described by this variable to occur, another event must occur first. In this case the result variables depend on the occurrence of the decision and the uncontrollable variables.

emanate from the environment surrounding the decision maker. These variables are also independent variables since they affect the dependent result variables.

The structure of mathematical models

The components of a mathematical model are expressed as variables. These are then tied together by sets of mathematical expressions such as equations or inequalities, thereby forming a system. Figure 2.4 is an example of such a model of a manufacturing system. In management science, however, the arrows in the picture are replaced by mathematical expressions.

Mathematical expressions to tie the components together

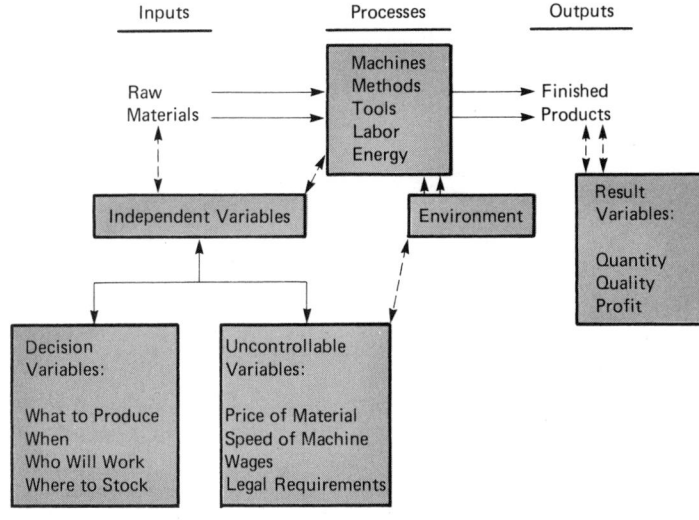

FIGURE 2.4
A manufacturing systems model

The mathematical relationships in the model

The mathematical relationships in a management science model may include two major parts: the *objective function* and the *constraints*.

Two types of relationships

The objective function   The objective function expresses the dependent variables in the model as they relate to the independent variables. For example, an objective function may look like:

$$R = p_1x_1 + p_2x_2$$

where R symbolizes the total revenue to a manufacturer (dependent variable); x_1 and x_2 are the quantities of the two products that are sold (uncontrollable variables); and p_1 and p_2 are the prices set by the company (decision variables). The objective, or goal, is to maximize the revenue. Such an objective is usually limited by *constraints*.

The constraints   The constraints express the limitations imposed on managerial systems due to regulation, competition, scarcity of resources, technology, or other uncontrollable variables. For example, a marketing constraint might be represented by:

$$x_1 + x_2 \le 50$$

That is, the total quantity of the two products that can be sold is 50 or less.

Figure 2.5 illustrates this manufacturer's model. The model can be interpreted as: Find the value of the decision variables p_1 and p_2 such

FIGURE 2.5
A model of a
manufacturing situation

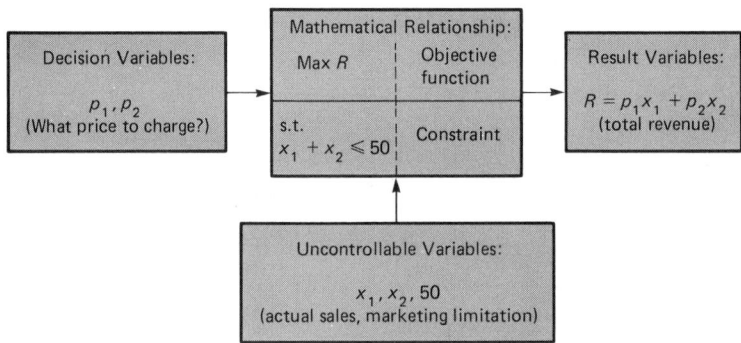

that the total revenue R (result variable) is maximized, subject to the marketing limitation and the level of sales, which are uncontrollable by the manufacturer.

2.7   USE OF COMPUTERS

The last characteristic of management science is its reliance on computers. Many managerial problems are rather complex, involving numerous interrelated variables. The search for and evaluation of alternative solutions, even when sophisticated models are involved, may become a gigantic computational project. In many cases a manual or a hand calculator approach to the analysis is impractical or even impossible, since it may take more than a lifetime to solve the problem. Thus, many problems are solvable only with the aid of high-speed computational devices. The use of computers has become closely associated with management science. Computers have the important advantage of being a relatively inexpensive means of rapid calculation and possess the accuracy and flexibility invaluable in experimenting with and solving managerial decision models.

**The need for high
speed computers**

**Faster, cheaper,
more accurate**

The computer has provided a means for solving those problems which have long been quantifiable but computationally too complex or time-consuming for human calculation. Problems which would take months to solve manually can be solved in seconds using computers. Production and personnel scheduling, allocation of resources, blending of raw materials, investment, ordering materials, and other managerial activities can be reevaluated daily in light of current information. Previously, such activities could be reevaluated only weekly, monthly, or even annually. By the time decisions were made, the information on which they were based was often obsolete so that poor consequences occurred.

Obsolete analyses in the past

As time passes, the availability of computers will increase and the cost of processing data and computing results will decrease. Thus, more and more use will be made of computers in management science.

The extent of the use of computers in management science can be shown by the results of several surveys. For example, in 1958, only about one third of the U.S. companies with management science departments used computers in their operations. In another study, conducted only six years later (1964), every one of the reporting management science units used computers in some aspect of their program.

The growth of computer use

It is therefore safe to say that the development of management science goes hand in hand with that of computers.

Summary of the management science process

It was demonstrated earlier that management science employs a scientific approach, and that rather than dealing with the organization or the problem itself, it deals with a representative mathematical model. In addition, the analysis is done from the perspective of a system, possibly by an interdisciplinary team. The question of exactly *what* this representation consists of and how it is conducted will be addressed in Chapters 3–14. In this chapter some general discussion of the *process* that management science follows will be presented as it relates to mathematical models.

The role of mathematical models in the management science decision-making process is shown in Figure 2.6. The manager with the real-life problem is on the left. On the right is the management scientist. The first step is defining the problem. This step necessarily includes the analysis of organizational goals. Following this, modeling of the problem can begin. By use of the model, alternative courses of action are generated and evaluated in order that a final choice may be recommended to the manager. These steps are discussed in Sections 2.8–2.11.

Modeling the problem

FIGURE 2.6
The role of mathematical models in decision making

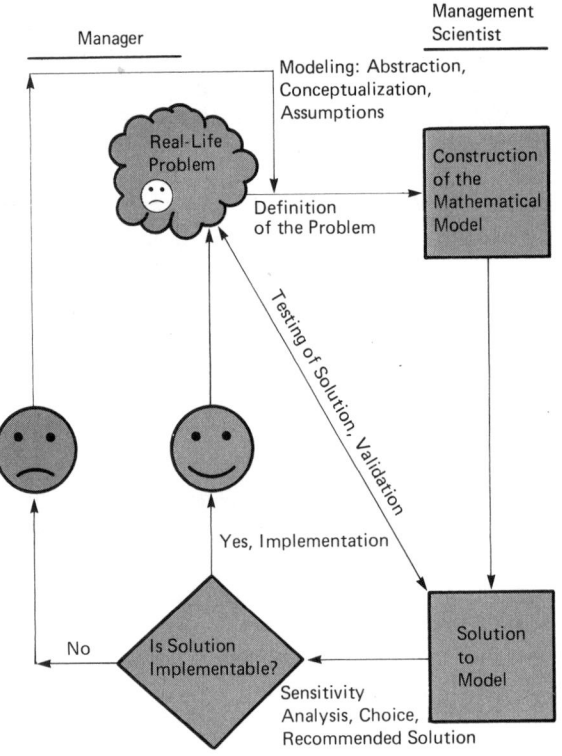

2.8 DEFINITION AND CLASSIFICATION OF THE PROBLEM

Since management science is a quantitative discipline, it is necessary to employ numerical analysis from the beginning. By the "definition of the problem" we mean recognizing that a problem exists, determining its magnitude, defining it precisely, and noting what its symptoms are. The so-called real-world problem is usually complicated by many interrelated factors.

The existence of a problem in an organization can best be appraised by comparing the desired level of goal attainment to actual performance. Management science attempts to measure these quantitatively. The following are some notes regarding the study and quantification of goals.

A problem exists when desired performance is not achieved

Goals as desired activity outcomes

The study of goals Simply stated, goals are the desired outcomes of organizational and/or individual activities. In this sense, goals include objectives, purposes, missions, and targets. These terms are sometimes used (as in this text) interchangeably.

Goals can be considered from three primary perspectives: (*a*) the organization, (*b*) the individual, and (*c*) the environment.

a. The organizational perspective Organizations may be defined as specific goal-seeking entities. One way to view their goals is via the classical economic theory of the firm which considers the organization as a single entrepreneur seeking profit maximization. However, the situation in reality is more complex, involving several participants whose goals may shape the activities and components of the organization. It is for this reason that organizations usually have *several* or *multiple* goals.

> **Multiple organizational goals**

b. The individual's perspective Organizational goals are affected by (and sometimes composed of) individuals' goals. For example, people join organizations to secure employment. To keep their jobs, they must produce some product or service which helps the organization in achieving one or more of its goals such as that of profit maximization. The study of individuals' goals is rather complex because it includes psychological and social factors that extend beyond the scope of this book. (For a discussion, see McGuire [8].)

> **Individual desires**

c. The environmental perspective Every firm constantly interfaces with the environment which may have an impact on its goals. The study of goals from the perspective of the environment involves, basically, the study of the goal constraints imposed by the marketplace and society. An example of such a constraint is wage and price control imposed by government.

> **Outside constraints**

Once the study of goals has been completed, it is possible to determine whether a problem really exists, how significant it is, and where it is located. In other words, it is then possible to clearly define the problem. A major factor that will determine the shape of the management science model is the *classification* of the problem. In general, managerial problems can be classified as either *programmed* or *nonprogrammed.*

Programmed versus nonprogrammed problems

Herbert A. Simon [12] has distinguished two extreme situations of decision problems. At one end of the spectrum are the well-structured problems that are *repetitive* and *routine* and for which a standard model has been worked out. These problems are called "programmed" because the method used to handle them is embodied in a series of consistent steps that can routinely be repeated. They are listed as *prototype managerial problems* at the end of this chapter. Examples of such problems are weekly schedules of employees, monthly determination of products to produce, and selection of the best quantity of materials to be purchased. At the other end of the spectrum are the *ill-structured* or *nonprogrammed* problems that are novel and nonrecurrent. For example, acquisition and merger decisions, undertaking a research and development project, expanding a freeway, and opening a university are all nonprogrammed problems.

> **Programmed models for recurring problems**

> **Ill-structured problems**

After the problem has been properly defined, the modeling of the problem can begin.

2.9   MODELING (FORMULATION)

Modeling, or *formulating*, the problem involves the conceptualization of the problem and its abstraction to a mathematical form. The dependent and independent variables are identified and the equations describing their relationships established. Simplifications are made, whenever necessary, through a set of *assumptions.* For example, a relationship between two variables may be assumed to be linear so that the problem will fit the model of linear programming. It is necessary to find a proper balance between the level of simplification of the model and the representation of reality. The simpler the model, the easier are the manipulations and the solutions, but the less representative it will be of the real problem.

The task of modeling is one of the most delicate and intricate in management science. It is a combination of art and science and involves a multitude of interrelated activities and methodological issues. The most important of these activities are:

1. Search for alternative courses of actions.
2. Selection of a principle of choice.
3. Making the choice.

Search for alternative courses of action

The decision-making process as presented in Section 2.2 involves a search for alternative courses of action that are candidate solutions to the problem. In management science such alternative courses of action may be either given or they may be generated by the model. In the first case the model is used to *evaluate* the given alternatives; in the second case it is used to generate and then evaluate alternatives.

There are several methods of searching for alternatives; some require a greater, some a lesser, degree of creativity and ingenuity (e.g., see Harrison [7]). At the very least, the search process requires resources such as money, labor, and time. Since these are usually finite, the search must be terminated sooner or later. In some cases, the search may continue while an *evaluation* is proceeding. Consider, for example, the selection of a person to fill a position. Typically, candidates are evaluated and compared while the search continues.

Selection of a principle of choice

The search for alternative solutions, and especially their evaluation, depends on the principle of choice used.

A *principle of choice* refers to a decision regarding the acceptability of a solution approach. Is the best possible alternative sought, or will a "good enough" solution do? Are we willing to assume risk or do we

The role of assumptions

The need to simplify the problem in the model

The delicate art of modeling

Modeling to generate and/or evaluate alternatives

The choice of a solution approach

prefer a conservative approach? Of the various principles of choice, the following are of prime interest:

Optimization   An optimal alternative is one which is demonstrably the *best* of *all* possible alternatives. To find it one should examine *all* alternatives and prove that the one selected is indeed the best. The principle of the "systems approach" must be used in order to achieve optimization.

The *best* way

In operational terms, optimization can be achieved in one of three ways:

a.   Get the *highest level* (maximum) of goal attainment from a *given* set of resources (or at given cost).
b.   Find the alternative with the *lowest cost* (minimization of resources) which will fulfill a required level of goals.
c.   Find the alternative with the highest *ratio* of goal attainment to cost (e.g., profit per dollar invested), or in other words, maximize efficiency.

Optimization *prescribes* the course of action that the decision maker should take in order to achieve goals most efficiently. Therefore, models designed to optimize an objective are referred to as *normative* models. Such a model must possess a decision criterion for selecting the *best* (optimal) available alternative and proving that the selected alternative is indeed optimal.

Normative models

Normative decision theory is based on the following assumptions:

The "economic man" assumptions

1.   Man is an economic being whose objective is to maximize personal goals; that is, the decision maker is *rational*.
2.   In a given decision situation, all alternative courses of action and their consequences, or at least the chance of the consequences, are known.
3.   The decision maker has an order of preference that enables him or her to rank the desirability of all consequences of the analysis.

Suboptimization   By definition, the use of optimization requires that the decision maker consider the impact of each alternative course of action on the entire organization. The reason for this is that a decision made in one area may have significant effects in other areas. Take as an example a production department that plans its own schedule. For that department it would be beneficial to produce only a few products but in large quantities to reduce manufacturing cost. However, such a plan may result in high and costly inventories and marketing difficulties due to lack of a variety of products.

Using a systems point of view affords consideration of the impact on the entire system. Thus, the production department should make its plans in conjunction with other departments. Such an approach, however, may require a complicated, expensive, and time-consuming effort.

Therefore, as a matter of practice, the management scientist may "close" the system within narrow boundaries, considering only part of the organization under study. Such an approach is called *suboptimization*.

Optimal or suboptimal?

If a decision is made in one part of the organization *without paying attention* to the rest of it, then a solution which is *optimal* from the point of view of the part may be *suboptimal* from the point of view of the whole, producing inferior or even damaging results.

The practicality of suboptimization

Suboptimization, however, may still be a very practical approach and therefore many problems are first approached from this perspective. The primary reason for this is that analyzing only a portion of a system allows some tentative conclusions to be made without bogging down in a deluge of details. Once a solution is proposed, its potential effects on the remaining departments of the organization can be checked. If no significant negative effects can be traced, the solution may then be considered optimal from a systems point of view.

Advances in management science models and computers may ultimately allow an analysis of the complex *whole* readily and effectively in one evaluation; that is, to use an optimization approach. Until then the use of suboptimization will continue as a very practical approach.

Good enough or "satisficing" According to Simon [12], most human decision making, whether organizational or individual, involves a willingness to settle for a satisfactory alternative, "something less than the best." In a "satisficing" mode the decision maker sets up an *aspiration* (desired) level of goals and then searches the alternatives until one is found that achieves this. The usual reasons for satisficing are lack of time or ability for optimization as well as an unwillingness to pay the price for the required information. An example of selecting a satisfactory alternative can be seen in a company that wants to sell some property. According to the optimization approach, the company should examine *all* offers and select the *highest* offer, assuming that their objective is to maximize the profit from the sale. In reality, this process is not followed. What the seller normally does is assess the market and set up a desired price (the aspiration level), say $55,000. The first buyer to offer $55,000 (or more) will get the property. If the seller is unsuccessful in getting a bid of $55,000 within a certain period, he or she will change the asking price, say to $53,000, which in essence means reducing the seller's level of aspiration or goal. If the seller then sells the property for at least $53,000, the seller is satisficing a new goal.

Satisficing to an aspiration level

Satisficing as a principle of choice is used in those management science tools which are labeled *descriptive*.

Descriptive models

Descriptive models describe things *as they are*. Their major use in management science is to investigate the outcomes or consequences of various alternative courses of action, as reflected by the system's performance or effectiveness. However, since the descriptive analysis checks the effectiveness of the system for given conditions (or given alternatives) rather than for *all* conditions, there is no *guarantee* that an alternative selected with the aid of descriptive analysis is optimal.

Descriptive models are used in decision situations when normative models are not applicable. They are also used when the objective is to define the problem or to assess its seriousness rather than to select an alternative. Descriptive models are especially useful in *predicting the behavior* of the system under various assumptions.

Predicting behavior with descriptive models

Other principles of choice In addition to optimization and satisficing there are several other, less common, principles of choice. They are discussed in Chapter 3.

Making the choice

Once the principle of choice is determined, the comparison among the alternatives may begin in an attempt to make a choice. In general, this activity involves four steps:

1. Predict the outcome of each alternative.
2. Relate outcomes to goals.
3. Compare the alternatives.
4. Select an alternative according to the principle of choice.

1. Predict the outcome of each alternative In order to evaluate an alternative it is necessary to predict its outcome. One of the greatest contributions of management science to decision making is that it can reduce the time and associated cost of the search for alternatives by predicting which alternatives may have infeasible outcomes.

Eliminating the infeasible outcomes

Several potential solutions to a managerial problem may not meet all the conditions or requirements of the problem. For example, there are many ways of getting dressed. As a matter of fact, there are $n!$ (n factorial) different ways of getting dressed with n pieces of clothing. With $n = 10$ there are 3,628,000 different ways of getting dressed. Suppose you want to determine the fastest way of getting dressed; do you have to check all 3,628,000 alternatives? Of course not! You can start with your socks, then shoes, then shirt and so on. But you cannot put your socks on after your shoes are on—this is obviously an *infeasible* solution. By identifying the infeasible solutions early, it is possible to narrow down the number of alternatives requiring evaluation.

Infeasible solutions

2. Relate outcomes to goals The quality of a decision is judged in terms of the goal's attainment. Sometimes an outcome is expressed directly in terms of a goal. For example, *profit* is an outcome while *profit maximization* is the goal, and both are expressed in dollar terms. In other cases an outcome may be expressed in terms other than those of the goal. For example, the outcome may be in terms of machine breakdowns while the goal can be expressed in terms of dollars. In such cases it is necessary to transform the outcome so it is expressed in terms of the goal.

Outcomes versus goals

3.   Compare the alternatives   Once the previous activities have been completed, the decision maker can compare the alternatives and select one. Some of the difficult issues considered in this stage are:

- *Multiple goals.*   The models described in this book are frequently based on the analysis of one goal, such as "maximization of profit." In reality, several goals may exist simultaneously. Methods for overcoming this difficulty are discussed in Chapter 4.
- *Sensitivity to change.* The dependent variables may be particularly sensitive to changes or errors in some of the independent variables. The evaluation should check this sensitivity to avoid highly sensitive alternatives or exploit unexpected opportunities as will be explained later in this chapter.
- *What constitutes a significant difference between alternatives?* In comparing alternatives one may find that alternative A will bring $323,200 while alternative B will bring $323,150. Is alternative A superior to B? In general, it is important to determine when an alternative is indeed superior. Since we deal with models, we simplify reality. Alternative A will bring 50 extra dollars but might make some employees unhappy. In this text a choice is made based on quantitative factors only. In reality other factors must be considered, especially when the difference seems to be small. (Statistical tests can be employed in certain cases to determine if a significant difference exists.)
- *What principle of choice to use?* The selection of a principle of choice must precede the actual decision. Should the decision maker attempt to find an optimal solution, or should a "satisfactory" solution be accepted if it can be derived much faster (and/or cheaper)? The principle of choice reflects the attitudes and objectives of the decision maker.

4.   Select an alternative   The process ends with a choice, namely the selection and recommendation of a solution (or an alternative course of action). The decision is based on the "principle of choice" determined earlier.

2.10   SOLUTION TECHNIQUES

A *solution* to a management science problem means the *identification* of a specific set of values of the decision variables that result in a desirable output of the model. This desirable output can be an optimal solution, good enough solution, or a prediction of the level of goal attainment. This depends on the objective of the analysis and on the principle of choice selected earlier. Generally speaking, solution techniques can be classified into two major categories: *numerical* and *analytical.*

Numerical techniques

Numerical techniques consist of a trial and error comparison of several proposed solutions. Each solution can be distinguished by its set of decision variables. The specific method to be used depends on the principle of choice and on the nature of the problem under consideration. Numerical techniques can yield either optimal or nonoptimal solutions.

The numerical techniques that yield optimal solutions consist of those which are based on *complete enumeration* and those which are based on *algorithms*.

Enumeration or algorithm?

Complete enumeration When one checks *every possible* solution (or values of the decision variables) he or she performs a complete enumeration. This technique is useful only when the number of alternatives is small; otherwise, it is a lengthly, tedious, or even impossible approach.

Algorithms An algorithm is a step-by-step process of searching for the optimal solution by *gradually* improving each solution. Thus, in contrast to a complete enumeration where an exhaustive trial and error process is performed (*all* solutions are checked), an algorithm is a progressive trial and error process that checks only a *portion* of all feasible solutions.

The numerical techniques that yield nonoptimal solutions are basically those of *simulation* (Chapter 14).

Simulation does not guarantee optimal solutions

An illustration

To illustrate the use of numerical techniques, one might consider a control box. The box has knobs on it representing different independent controllable variables, and dials (gauges) representing the dependent variables which measure the system's effectiveness. The uncontrollable variables are built into the operation of the box through internal wiring. When the decision maker wants to explore the consequence of a given alternative course of action, he or she merely turns the knobs (each combination setting of the knobs represents an alternative course of action) and watches the dials.

The illustration in Figure 2.7 represents a control box for an inventory model. The box has only one dial representing the cost of inventory. This is the measure of the system's effectiveness. The knobs represent two controllable variables: x_1 is the number of orders placed each year and x_2, is the quantity of safety stock the company keeps. The decision maker, sitting in front of this box, would manipulate the knobs. For example, the decision maker may set $x_1 = 2$ orders per year and $x_2 = 400$ units of safety stock. Then the dial which shows the resulting cost can be observed.

An inventory control box

FIGURE 2.7
A control box for an
inventory problem

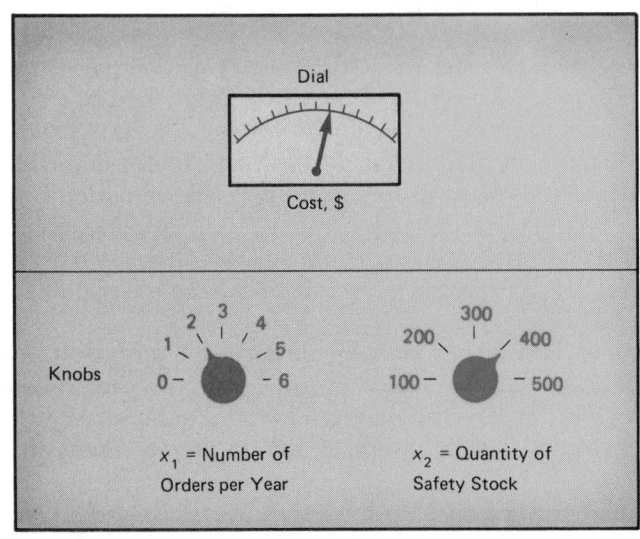

FIGURE 2.7
A control box for an
inventory problem

Complete
enumeration or an
algorithm?

In the case of *complete enumeration* one will have to experiment with *all* combinations of the knobs. For example, $x_1 = 2$ and $x_2 = 400$ is one combination shown in Figure 2.7. Each time a combination is attempted, the cost is recorded. When *all* possible combinations have been tried, the *optimal* solution can be identified.

In the case of using an *algorithm* there is no need to check *all* alternatives; through previous experience, or a certain theory, one attempts to generate new combinations of knobs such that their cost is *continuously decreasing.* The time and cost of using an algorithm will be less than that of complete enumeration since fewer combinations of knobs will be checked. Unfortunately, there are not many cases where algorithms can be used.

Finally, management can decide not to check all combinations of the knobs, but only some of them. In this case the choice will be the best of those alternatives checked, but not necessarily the best inventory policy. This case is typical of the technique called *simulation* where the solution is not guaranteed to be optimal.

Analytical techniques

Analytical approach
for direct result

Analytical techniques use mathematical formulae to directly (in one step) either *derive* an optimal solution or *predict* a certain result. As such, analytical models are *deductive* in character in contrast to the numerical procedures which are essentially *inductive* in character.

The management science tools which are discussed in this text are classified in Figure 2.8, according to the solution techniques discussed above.

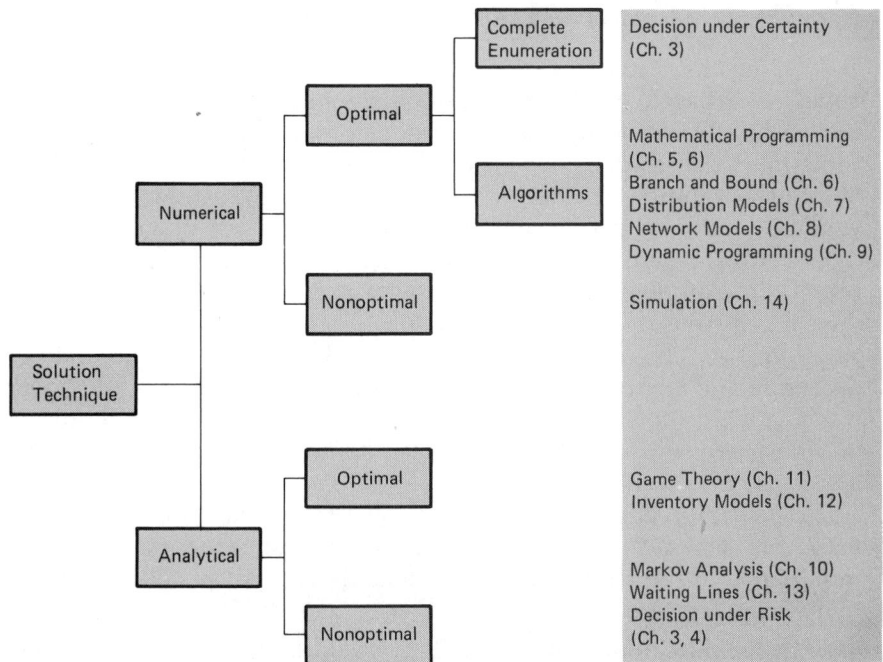

FIGURE 2.8
Model classification by
solution technique

Other classifications of solutions

Solutions can be classified as being *feasible* or *infeasible, optimal* or *nonoptimal,* and *unique* or *multiple.*

Feasible and infeasible solutions A *feasible* solution is one which satisfies *all* the requirements and constraints imposed on the problem. Violating one or more of these requirements results in an unacceptable, *infeasible* solution.

Feasible

Optimal and nonoptimal solutions An *optimal* solution is the *best* of all feasible solutions. For a solution to be declared optimal there must be proof that *all* feasible solutions were checked and that the proposed solution is better than any other solution. A feasible solution that cannot be classified as optimal is considered nonoptimal.

Optimal

Unique and multiple solutions If there exists only one solution it is called *unique.* If two or more solutions can be identified, then there exist *multiple* solutions. The latter case is usually preferable to management since it gives them greater flexibility in implementing a solution. Mathematical models may not include some behavioral and qualitative factors. In comparing multiple solutions management may include consideration of these variables, thus making the solution more acceptable.

Unique

2.11 TESTING AND VALIDATION OF THE MODEL

Model validation is
necessary

A solution for a model is only as good as the information upon which it is based. Since assumptions are made and relationships are established based on various sources of information whose accuracy is sometimes uncertain, it is necessary to check the validity of the model before the solution can be recommended to management. One way to validate a model is to try it with different possible sets of data and see if the solutions resemble the historical behavior of the system. For example, if a model describes sales behavior as a function of interest rates, then it can be tested by "plugging in" several values of interest rates, say, 4, 5, . . . , 19 percent, examining what level of sales is predicted in each case and comparing this to historical data. Obviously, if the model was unable to successfully describe historical occurrences, it should not be considered valid for making future predictions; therefore, adjustments are necessary in the model.

Sensitivity analysis for insight

Sensitivity analysis Sensitivity analysis is an attempt to help managers when they are uncertain about the accuracy or relative importance of their information. In sensitivity analysis the information in question is altered to find what effects, if any, changes will have on the output of the proposed solution to the problem. In other words, the purpose of sensitivity analysis is to determine the effect of *changes* in the independent variables on the values of the dependent variables. For example, an optimal soution that was based on an assumed prime interest rate of 7 percent may have prescribed an investment in real estate rather than in stocks or bonds. Suppose the interest rate is 6 percent or 9 percent—is real estate still the best investment?

Of special interest are questions such as:

*Questions a
sensitivity analysis
can answer*

1. What change can occur in a certain independent variable before a change occurs in the recommended solution?
2. What is the magnitude of a change in the proposed solution resulting from a change in an independent variable(s)?
3. Which independent variables are most sensitive? That is, which variables will, when changed only slightly, cause the value of the dependent variables to change significantly? Which independent variables are insensitive?
4. Is a proposed solution highly sensitive? That is, does the solution include sensitive variables which, when changed slightly, will alter that solution so that it will no longer be optimal? Conversely, insensitive solutions will hold with a wide range of variations in the independent variables.

Insensitive solutions are usually easier to implement since their predicted results are more certain to occur and since management can modify the proposed solution with a small loss in effectiveness of the system.

2.12   MANAGERIAL PROBLEMS AND THE TOOLS OF MANAGEMENT SCIENCE

Throughout the history of management science, certain types of problems have been encountered repeatedly. The structure of these has been abstracted and analyzed so as to yield "prototype" problems. To handle these prototype problems, a set of standard solution procedures (also called *tools* or *techniques*) has been developed. Thus, whenever a management problem is recognized as a prototype problem, it can be molded into a standard format and the appropriate tool can be applied for its solution.

Models for prototypal managerial problems

The prototype managerial problems

Some common managerial problems discussed in this text are:

Allocation problems   These problems arise when (1) there are a number of activities to be performed, (2) there exist two or more different ways to perform these activities, and (3) resources or facilities are scarce. The problem then is to find the best utilization of resources; namely, which activities to pursue and in what magnitude, so that effectiveness will be maximized.

Distribution problems   Moving a commodity (e.g., oil or corn) from several sources to several destinations at minimum cost constitutes a *transportation problem*. Several types of problems (e.g., production scheduling) can be viewed and solved as transportation problems. A related topic is the *assignment problem*, in which certain items, such as a person or an activity, are to be assigned, on a one-to-one basis, to other items such as facilities or services. The objective is to minimize the cost or to maximize the effectivensss of the assignment.

Network problems   Network problems describe flows of commodities, activities, information, or other resources between locations. For example, in the construction of a bridge, many activities, information, and resources flow as time passes. The problem is to find the best activity plan for such systems.

Competitive situations   When the results of a decision are determined not only by one's own course of action but also by that of another decision maker, a competitive situation exists. This situation may be viewed as a game which each party attempts to win.

Inventory control   The proper level of inventories of materials, money, finished products, or persons is a major problem in many organizations. The costs of carrying inventories are high, but inventories can result in large savings by preventing shortages, providing discounts on large quantities purchased or produced, eliminating changes in the level of production, and reducing ordering and setup costs. The problem is to find the proper level of inventory, which is determined by the decisions "when" and "how much" to order, that will minimize the total cost.

Waiting line problems Whenever persons or objects that require service arrive at a service facility, a waiting line is likely to occur, especially in rush periods. Typically, in such situations there is a waiting line during certain periods, but the facility may be idle during other "slack" periods.

In general, the larger the facility, the costlier its operation but the smaller the waiting time for service. The problem is to find the appropriate size of the facility as well as to determine its operating procedures (e.g., give priority to certain customers) in such a way as to minimize the sum of the relevant costs.

Predicting the behavior of a system Management is frequently interested in predicting the behavior of a system under different conditions. While this is not classified as a prototype problem by itself, it can be used in constructing prototype procedures and/or evaluating solutions.

Other problems Several other managerial problems are of interest to management scientists. The most important are:[4]

- Sequencing (which task to do next) and routing (what part minimizes travel time between points).
- Maintenance (how often to repair) and replacement (which items, how often).
- Search (which items to consider first).
- Bidding (what strategy, how high or low).

The tools of management science

As indicated earlier, certain managerial problems were singled out for intensive study as they appeared more and more frequently in practice. These studies resulted in a body of tools and techniques developed specifically for solving certain managerial problems. Listed below are those tools of management science that are discussed in this text.

Decision tables Allocation and investment problems involving a relatively small number of possible solutions can be presented in a tabular form known as a decision table.

Decision trees The extension of decision tables for situations involving several decision periods takes the shape of a "tree."

Mathematical programming Mathematical programming attempts to maximize the attainment level of one goal subject to a set of requirements and limitations. It has extensive use in business, economics, engineering, the military, and public service, mainly as an aid to the solution of allocation problems. In this text, the following models

---

[4] These are not discussed in the text. The interested reader is referred to Wagner [15].

will be covered: *linear programming; transportation* and *assignment* models; *integer* and *goal* programming.

Branch and bound   Branch and bound is a step-by-step procedure used when a *very large* (or even infinite) number of alternatives exist for certain managerial problems.

Network models   This is a family of tools designed for the purpose of planning and controlling complex projects. The best known models are *PERT* (Program Evaluation and Review Technique) and *CPM* (Critical Path Method).

Dynamic programming   Dynamic programming is an approach to decisions that are basically sequential in nature or can be reformulated so as to be considered sequential. It is a very general and powerful tool.

Markov chains   Markov chains are used for predicting the outcome of processes where systems or units change their condition over time (e.g., consumers change their preferences for certain brands).

Game theory   Game theory provides a systematic approach to decision making in competitive environments and a framework for the study of conflict.

Inventory models   For certain types of inventory control problems, special models that attempt to minimize the cost associated with ordering and carrying inventories have been developed.

Waiting line (queuing) models   For certain types of problems involving waiting lines, special descriptive models have been developed to predict the performance of service systems.

Simulation models   For the analysis of complex systems when all other models fail, management science uses descriptive-type simulation models. Specifically, five types of models are presented in this text: (1) artificial intelligence, (2) heuristic programming, (3) management games, (4) systems simulation, and (5) Monte Carlo simulation.

The relationships between managerial problems and the tools

The one-to-one matching of a problem to a technique does not always hold. In some instances, a particular tool can be used for several prototype problems; and in other situations, one problem can be addressed with several tools. Although selection of a specific tool may depend on the specific problem, there are certain relationships that *usually* hold true. These are presented in Table 2.2.

2.13   CONCLUDING REMARKS

Decision making is a complicated process consisting of certain steps and elements common to all decision situations. Such generalization makes it a potential subject for scientific analysis. The importance and complexity of the decision-making process has attracted investiga-

TABLE 2.2
The major relationships between problems and tools

Chapter	3	4	5,6	6	7	8	9	10	11	12	13	14
Problem area \ Tools	Decision tables	Decision trees	Mathematical programming	Branch and bound	Transportation, assignment	PERT/CPM	Dynamic programming	Markov chains	Game theory	Inventory	Waiting lines	Simulation
Allocation	X	X	X	X			X					
Distribution			X	X	X							
Network						X	X					
Competitive decision making									X			X
Inventory			X				X			X		X
Waiting lines											X	X
Predicting a system's behavior	X	X						X			X	X

tors from several disciplines resulting in various approaches to the study. One of these approaches is management science.

This chapter concludes the first part of the book in which many concepts were described. In Part II, the various tools and techniques of management science will be presented.

2.14 PROBLEMS*

1. A manufacturer of solar energy devices has two models available: Alpha, which costs $800 and sells for $1000, and Beta, which costs $1150 and sells for $1500.
   a. The company's objective is profit maximization; write the objective function.
   b. The company's objective is to maximize sales in units; write the objective function in this case.

2. Express, mathematically, the following requirements and constraints for the preceding problem.

   a. The market for the Alpha devices is limited to no more than 400 units a month.
   b. The total number of devices will be at least 540 produced per month.
   c. Production capability is limited to no more than 720 units per month.
   d. The capital available for production is $50,000 per month.

3. A company has a $55,000 fixed cost in their Model T product. This model sells for $1000 while its variable cost is $740. The company's goal is profit maximization. Write the objective function.

---

* Answers to the even-numbered problems are given in Appendix D.

2.15   REVIEW QUESTIONS

P16   1. What is the difference between making decisions and solving problems? Give an example.

2. Apply a scientific approach process to the following problems:
   a. Can vitamin C cure colds?
   b. Will a new product be accepted in the market?
   c. Should an airline add an additional flight between Chicago and New York?

3. Analyze a managerial system of your choice and identify the following:
   a. The components.
   b. The environment.
   c. The inputs.
   d. The system's goals.
   e. The decision variables.

4. What are some of the "measures of effectiveness" in a manufacturing plant; in a restaurant; in an educational institution; in the U.S. Congress?

5. Give an example of a managerial problem where an interdisciplinary team is desirable. Explain why.

6. Give an example of a mathematical model used by management.

7. What are some of the controllable and uncontrollable variables in the following systems: automotive manufacturer, hospital, courthouse, airline, restaurant, hotel, bank, oil refinery, atomic power plant?

8. What is meant by an objective function?

9. Why are computers an integral part of management science? Under what conditions should computers *not* be used by a management scientist?

10. Give examples of three programmed decisions in an organization with which you are familiar.

11. Give examples of two nonprogrammed decisions in an organization.

12. Apply the management science process to the problem of deciding whether to open a new fast-food outlet. What should the principle of choice be?

13. City A is debating whether or not to build a public transportation system. What should the principle of choice be?

14. Compare and contrast normative versus descriptive approaches to decision making.

15. Give an example that illustrates the difference between optimization and suboptimization.

16. Distinguish between numerical and analytical solution techniques. Between an algorithm and a simulation.

17. Give an example to illustrate the simultaneous existence of several goals in organizations.

18. How can a model that predicts the movement of the stock market be validated?

19. Describe a situation that will demonstrate the meaning of sensitivity analysis.

20. Give an example of an infeasible solution.

21. Define a "unique" solution.

2.16   GLOSSARY

Algorithm   A set of logical steps to follow to reach a solution.

Analog model   A physical model in a different form from the actual system being modeled.

Analytical   Considering the individual subparts of a system to deduce a result.

Constraints   Limitations on actions.

Dependent variables   System measures of effectiveness.

Descriptive   Nonoptimizing; describes how a system operates.

Effectiveness   The degree of goal attainment.

Efficiency   Ratio of output to input.

Enumeration   Listing of possible items to consider.

Environment   Uncontrollable elements outside the system which affect it.

Iconic Model   A physical, scaled replica.

Infeasible   Not acceptable; can't be done.

Inputs   The forms of resources introduced into a system for transformation into outputs.

Mathematical model A system of symbols and expressions to represent a real situation.

Model An abstraction of reality.

Normative Prescribes how a system *should* operate.

Numerical Trial and error comparisons.

Optimization The best solution possible.

Outputs The result of a transformation process in a system.

Principle of choice The criterion for basing a choice among alternatives.

Programmed problems Repetitive, routine problems for which standard models have been developed.

Satisfice A solution that is acceptable.

Sensitivity analysis Effect of a change in one variable on a proposed solution.

Simulation An imitation of reality.

Suboptimal Best for a subsystem of the total system.

System A set of elements that are considered to act as a single, goal-oriented entity.

2.17 REFERENCES AND BIBLIOGRAPHY

1. Ackoff, R. L., and Emery, F. *On Purposeful Systems.* Chicago: Aldine Publishing Co., 1972.

2. Aronofsky, J. S., ed. *Progress in Operations Research—the Relationship between Operations Research and the Computer.* New York: John Wiley & Sons, Inc., 1968.

3. Bonczek, R. H., et al. "Computer-Based Support of Organizational Decision Making." *Decision Sciences,* vol. 10 (April 1979).

4. Churchman, C. West. *The Systems Approach.* New York: Delacort Press, 1968.

5. _____. *The Design of Inquiring Systems.* New York: Basic Books, Inc., Publishers, 1971.

6. Gass, S. I. "Evaluation of Complex Models." *Computers and Operations Research,* vol. 4, no. 1 (1977).

7. Harrison, E. F. *The Managerial Decision-Making Process.* Boston: Houghton Mifflin Co., 1975.

8. McGuire, J. W., ed. *Contemporary Management: Issues and Viewpoints.* Englewood Cliffs, N.J.: Prentice-Hall, Inc., 1974.

9. Mitroff, I. I., et al. "On Managing Science in the Systems Age: Two Schemes for the Study of Science as a Whole Systems Phenomenon." *Interfaces,* vol. 4, no. 3, 1974.

10. Newell, A., and Simon, H. A. *Human Problem Solving.* Englewood Cliffs, N.J.: Prentice-Hall, Inc., 1972.

11. Rivett, P. *Principles of Model Building.* London: John Wiley & Sons, Ltd., 1972.

12. Simon, H. A. *The New Science of Management Decisions.* Rev. ed. Englewood Cliffs, N.J.: Prentice-Hall Inc., 1977.

13. Van Gigch, J. P. *Applied General Systems Theory.* 2d ed. New York: Harper & Row, Publishers, 1978.

14. Verma, H. L., and Gross. C. W. *Introduction to Quantitative Methods—A Managerial Approach.* Santa Barbara, Calif.: Wiley/Hamilton 1978.

15. Wagner, H. M. *Principles of Operations Research,* 2d ed. Englewood Cliffs, N.J.: Prentice-Hall, Inc., 1975.

PART II

In Part I of this text the foundations of management science were outlined. The management science process was described as centering around the formulation of managerial problems as mathematical models. In this part of the text we will present the most common standard models, which are termed the "tools" or the "techniques" of the management scientist. Each chapter in Part II is divided into two sections: Basics and Extensions.

The Basics sections—

- Start with an illustrative example.
- Discuss the nature of the situation presented.
- Generalize the situation.
- Present the logic and methodology of the tool.
- Show, through example(s), how the tool is applied to the managerial problem.
- Summarize the material.
- Present problems for solution.

The Extensions sections usually include the theory behind the tool, other advanced topics, other applications, and more difficult problems.

At the end of each chapter there is a case study to illustrate the application of the tool and a comprehensive bibliography for further study.

THE TOOLS

3

This chapter begins the presentation of the tools and techniques of management science. Thus, the general procedure of problem analysis, presented in Chapter 2, will now be put to work. The major content of this chapter is the use of *decision tables* as a tool for enumeration. Managerial problems are then classified and the appropriate tools and techniques are divided into three major classes: decisions under certainty (deterministic), decisions under risk (probabilistic), and decisions under uncertainty. These three classes are discussed in detail here. Additional topics and concepts are discussed in Chapter 4.

Decision theory I

PART A: BASICS

"The Dow Jones industrial average failed to hold above the 1,000 mark" the ticker tape calmly proclaimed. Mary Golden, vice president of Friendly Trust Company, read the message on the ticker tape over and over again. She moaned to herself: "This is the sixth time in the last four months that the famous indicator has penetrated the magic 1,000 mark but could not hold above it more than a few days." The major reason cited by most analysts, for the weakness of the market, was fear of an upcoming inflation and climbing interest rates. Mary was still in shock when the ticker tape brought another message: "City Bank of New York raised the prime rate by ¼ of 1 percent." This was too much for one day.

Mary was in charge of the Trust's investment department. She had just been authorized to invest a large sum of money in one (and only one) of three alternatives: corporate bonds, common stocks, or certificates of deposit (time deposits).

The Trust's objective is to maximize the yield on the investment over a one-year period. The problem is that the economic situation seemed to be uncertain and no one was able to predict the exact movements of the stock or even the bond markets. It was rather obvious to Mary that the yields (in percent of return on investment) depend on the state of the economy. Therefore, she consulted the economic research department. The researchers were not sure what the exact state of the economy would be after one year. However, they told Mary they expected the economy to be in one of three possible conditions (or states): solid growth, stagnation, or inflation. When asked for the likelihood of each condition, the researchers estimated a 50 percent chance for solid growth, a 30 percent chance for stagnation, and a 20 percent chance for inflation.

Mary examined the relationship between the yield on the possible investments and the state of the economy and concluded that past experience indicated the following trends:

1. *If* there is solid growth in the economy, bonds will yield 12 percent; stocks, 15 percent; and time deposits, 6.5 percent.
2. *If* stagnation prevails, bonds will yield 6 percent; stocks, 3 percent; and time deposits, 6.5 percent.
3. *If* inflation prevails, bonds will yield 3 percent; the value of stocks will drop 2 percent; and time deposits will yield 6.5 percent.

Mary examined all the above information and realized that the investment decision would not be simple at all.

3.1   DECISION ANALYSIS WITH DECISION TABLES

Characteristics of the investment problem

Mary's dilemma is a typical managerial investment problem. Mary, the *decision maker* in this case, must make a *choice* among several *courses of action.* She will attempt to evaluate the alternatives based on their future yield, since the Trust's goal is to maximize their yield. The difficulty is that there is *uncertainty* with respect to what is going to happen in the future. No matter which choice Mary makes, she is going to *assume some risk* that the future she has hoped for is not going to materialize. What is the degree of risk that she is assuming? How does it relate to the available alternatives? Can the risk be reduced? Can the risk be eliminated? *Decision theory,* a quantitative analysis procedure applied to decision making, attempts to answer such questions.

Decision theory for risk and uncertainty

The use of decision tables

The quantitative data of many decision situations can be arranged in a standardized tabular form known as a decision table (or a *payoff* table). The object of doing so is to enable a systematic analysis of the problem. While not all decision situations are explicitly amenable to a tabular presentation, many concepts used in decision tables are common to all decision situations.

The payoff table for analyzing data

Decision tables typically contain four elements:

1. The alternative courses of action.
2. The states of nature.
3. The probabilities of the states of nature.
4. The payoffs.

Let us return to Mary's problem and arrange the information there as a decision table.

(1) *The alternative courses of action*   Decision making, by definition, involves two or more *options*, or *alternative courses of action,* called "strategies" or "alternatives." One, and only *one,* of these alternatives *must* be selected. The alternative courses of action are generally designated as $a_1, a_2, \ldots, a_n$, where n is the number of available possibilities. For example, the decision to select a textbook for a particular class may involve numerous, but finite, alternatives. If, however, one were producing beer, the quantity of water to add to the mix may include, at least in theory, an infinite number of combinations. For example, one can add 2.1 gallons, 2.11 gallons, 2.111 gallons, and so on.

A finite number of alternatives

In most operating circumstances, however, not all possible alternatives are considered, but only those within a limited range. This range may still leave an infinite number of alternatives to select from in beer making. There are, however, enough rules of good brewing to estabish that the water added ought to be within the range of, say, 7 to 7.5 gallons

Only feasible·
alternatives

to a 10-gallon barrel. This is the range of *feasible* solutions. It still leaves an infinite number of points between 7 and 7.5, but one might decide to structure the alternatives in only tenths of gallons, thus reducing the number to only six (7, 7.1, 7.2, 7.3, 7.4, 7.5). Decision tables are then used when the number of alternatives is *finite* and usually small (e.g., less than 100).

In the investment problem there are three alternatives. They are listed on the left-hand side of the decision table (see Table 3.1). It is assumed that Mary will choose one of the given alternatives.

TABLE 3.1
Decision table (payoffs
in percentage yield)

can not be controlled / Alternatives — *Controllable choice* / States of nature	p_1 .5 Solid growth s_1	p_2 .3 Stagnation s_2	p_3 .2 Inflation s_3	←Probabilities
a_1 Bonds	12	6	3	$= p_1 s_1 + p_2 s_2 + p_3 s_3$
a_2 Stocks	15	3	−2	
a_3 Time deposits	6.5	6.5	6.5	

Finite *(handwritten above table)*
infinite (handwritten left of table)

(2) **The states of nature**   At the top of the table, the possible "States of Nature" (also called "events" or "possible futures") are listed. They are generally labeled $s_1, s_2, \ldots , s_m$. A state of nature can be a state of the economy (inflation), a weather condition (rain), a political development (election of a certain candidate) or other situation which the decision

Uncontrollable futures

maker cannot control. In the investment example there are three states of nature, which are the possible states of the economy, namely: solid growth, stagnation, and inflation. The states of nature are usually *not* determined by the action of a single individual or an organization. They are basically the result of an "act of God," or the result of many forces pushing in various directions. The number of states of nature in decision tables is finite and usually not large. Only one state of nature may occur at a time.

(3) **The probabilities of the states of nature**   A question may be asked: "What is the likelihood of these states of nature occurring?" Whenever it is possible to answer this question in terms of explicit chances (or probabilities), the information is recorded at the top of the table. The probabilities are given either in percent or in percentage fractions; for

One and only one
state of nature will
result

example, 50 percent = .5, 30 percent = .3. Since it is assumed that one *and only one* of the states of nature will occur in the future, then the sum of the probabilities must always be one. This is expressed as:

$$p_1 + p_2 + \cdots + p_m = 1 \tag{3.1}[1]$$

---

[1] Alternatively the equation can be written as $\sum_{j=1}^{m} p_j = 1$.

where p_1 = probability of s_1 occurring, p_2 = probability of s_2 occurring, and so on. In Mary's example, p_1 = .5, p_2 = .3, and p_3 = .2. The subscript m designates the fact that m states of nature are considered.

(4) **The payoffs**   The payoff (or the *outcome*) associated with a certain alternative and a specific state is given in that cell within the body of the table located at the *intersection* of the alternative in question (given by a row) and the specific state of nature (given by a column). The payoff is designated by u_{ij} where i indicates the row and j the column. For example, in Table 3.1, if the decision maker selects alternative a_1 and future s_2 occurs, then the outcome of the decision is estimated as a payoff (yield) of 6 percent. The payoffs can be thought of as *conditional* since a specific payoff results from a specific state of nature occurring but after a certain alternative course of action has been taken. An important point to remember is that the payoff is measured within a *specified* period (e.g., after one year). This period is sometimes called the *decision horizon.* Payoffs can be measured in terms of money, market share, or other physical measures.

The general structure of a decision table

Table 3.2 shows the general structure of decision tables.

Alternative courses of action	States of nature				
	p_1	p_2	$\cdots$	p_m	Uncontrollable variables
	s_1	s_2	$\cdots$	s_m	
a_1	u_{11}	u_{12}	$\cdots$	u_{1m}	
a_2	u_{21}	u_{22}	$\cdots$	u_{2m}	
.	.	.	$\cdots$	.	Result variables
.	.	.	$\cdots$	.	
.	.	.	$\cdots$	.	
a_n	u_{n1}	u_{n2}	$\cdots$	u_{nm}	

Decision variables

TABLE 3.2
The decision table—general structure

In terms of the elements of mathematical models the decision table can be described as:

The decision table as a model

alternative courses of action = independent, decision variables
state of nature = independent, uncontrollable variables
payoffs = dependent, result variables

3.2   CLASSIFICATION OF DECISION SITUATIONS

Decision situations are frequently classified on the basis of what the decision maker knows about the situation. It is customary to divide

FIGURE 3.1
The zones of decision making

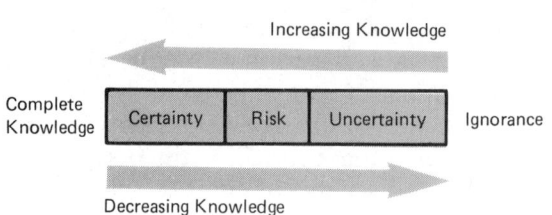

Increasing Knowledge

Complete Knowledge

| Certainty | Risk | Uncertainty |

Ignorance

Decreasing Knowledge

Decision zones

the degree of knowledge (information) into three zones (see Figure 3.1), ranging from complete knowledge, on the left, to ignorance on the right. Specifically, these zones are:

1. Certainty (complete information).
2. Risk (partial information).
3. Uncertainty (limited information).

Deterministic decisions

① **Decision making under certainty**

In decision making under certainty, it is assumed that complete information is available so that the decision maker knows exactly what the outcome of each course of action will be. The decision maker thus becomes a perfect predictor of the future. For example, the question of whether to invest in U.S. Savings Bonds is one in which it is reasonable to assume complete availability of information about the future return on the investment. Such situations are also termed *deterministic*. They occur most often with short time horizons. For example, with decisions whose impact will be felt after three months it is more reasonable to assume certainty than in a decision whose impact will be felt after two years. A substantial amount of knowledge and understanding of the behavior of the system under consideration is required to assume a state of certainty.

The decision table describing certainty is composed of a single column since only one state of nature is assumed to occur.

② **Decision making under risk**

Probabilistic decisions

A decision under risk (also known as a *probabilistic* or *stochastic* decision situation) is one in which the decision maker must consider several possible states of nature with given probabilities of occurrence. Thus, in risk situations, it is assumed that the long-run probabilities of occurrence of the given states of nature (and their conditional outcomes) are known. A classic example of such a situation is roulette. The roulette board is divided into 37 equal parts: 18 are black, 18 are red, and one is marked with 0. The player knows the probabilities of each state of nature represented by parts of the roulette field (e.g., 18/37 for red, 1/37 for 0). In making a decision, the player knows the long-run probability of winning the bet and therefore can assess the degree of risk assumed.

Less information is available than in decision making under certainty since it is not definitely known which outcome will occur. The actual outcome depends on which *state of nature* occurs. For example, the number of umbrellas a store sells in a month depends on how much rain falls during the month.

③ Decision making under uncertainty

In decision making under uncertainty,[2] the decision maker considers situations in which several outcomes are possible for each course of action. However, in contrast to the risk situation, the decision maker does not know the probability of occurrence of the possible states of nature. For example, it may be impossible to assess the probability of the success of a brand-new product. Thus, uncertainty situations contain even less information than risky situations.

Uncertainty or risk?

The relationship between these decision situations and the different management science techniques, which were briefly introduced in Chapter 2 and which are discussed at length in Chapters 3–14, is shown in Table 3.3

Chapter	Management science techniques	Decision situations		
		Certainty	Risk	Uncertainty
3, 4	Decision tables	X	X	X
4	Decision trees	X	X	
5	Linear programming	X		
6	Branch and bound	X		
6	Integer programming	X		
7	Distribution (transportation, assignment)	X		
8	CPM	X		
8	PERT		X	
9	Dynamic programming	X	X	
10	Markov chains		X	
12	Inventory	X	X	
13	Queuing		X	
14	Simulation	X	X	

TABLE 3.3
The relationship between decision situations and management science techniques

3.3   DECISIONS UNDER CERTAINTY

In decision under certainty the situation can be mapped as a table with one payoff column (one state of nature). Therefore, in making a decision, all one has to do is to compare all the entries in the payoff column and select the alternative with the highest profit or lowest cost.

[2] The definitions of the terms *risk* and *uncertainty,* as presented here, were suggested by Professor F. H. Knight of the University of Chicago in 1933. Several other definitions can be found in the literature.

The logic for such a choice is simple: there is no reason for doing otherwise. In executing such a comparison, one distinguishes between two cases:

Enumeration or search

1. When the number of alternatives is relatively small. In this case, an approach known as *complete enumeration* is used.
2. When the number of alternatives is large. In this case a comparison and search for the best solution is conducted with the aid of mathematical models.

① Complete enumeration

Complete enumeration means examining every payoff, one at a time, comparing the payoffs to each other (e.g., in pairs), and discarding inferior solutions. The process continues until *all* payoffs are examined.

Example: Assignment of employees to machines A maintenance crew of three machinists is to be assigned to the repair of three machines on a one-to-one basis in a manner that minimizes repair time. Based on historical data, the supervisor knows the exact repair time, which varies with each person-machine match. The repair times, in hours, are shown in Table 3.4. (For example, if Jack works on machine A it takes him three hours to fix it; the repair time is the payoff in this case.)

TABLE 3.4
Repair times

Machinist \ Machine	A	B	C
Jack	3	7	4
Gene	4	6	6
Mel	3	8	5

Solution All alternative assignments with their appropriate total repair times are shown in Table 3.5. Note that the decision table has only one column.

TABLE 3.5
Assignment payoffs

Alternatives	Payoff (total repair time)	
a_1 Jack—A, Gene—B, Mel—C	3 + 6 + 5 = 14	
a_2 Jack—A, Gene—C, Mel—B	3 + 6 + 8 = 17	
a_3 Jack—B, Gene—A, Mel—C	7 + 4 + 5 = 16	
a_4 Jack—B, Gene—C, Mel—A	7 + 6 + 3 = 16	
a_5 Jack—C, Gene—B, Mel—A	4 + 6 + 3 = 13	← Best
a_6 Jack—C, Gene—A, Mel—B	4 + 4 + 8 = 16	

By comparing the total repair times for *all* possibilities, it is found that alternative a_5 is the best, since the repair time is the smallest. Larger assignment problems have an extremely large number of possible solutions and are therefore solved by algorithms (as will be shown in Chapter 7) rather than by enumeration.

Comparison with analytical models

While complete enumeration is an effective approach in many situations, there are two cases in which it does not work at all or works very poorly. The first is the case of an *infinite number of alternatives.* Managerial problems such as the allocation of resources or the setting of an optimal inventory level are examples of such situations. To cope with these problems, models such as linear programming (Chapter 5) and deterministic inventory models (Chapter 12) have been developed.

Why use models?

The second case involves problems with *a finite but very large,* sometimes astronomical, number of alternatives. Such problems are frequently referred to as *combinatorial problems.* Several scheduling and sequencing problems are of this nature. In these cases, it is possible to enumerate all the alternatives, but it may take years to do so, even with the aid of high-speed computers. Special models such as branch and bound (Chapter 6), assignment (Chapter 7), and dynamic programming (Chapter 9) have been developed for effective solutions.

Combinatorial problems

Summary

Decision making under certainty[3] involves the following steps:

1. Determine the alternative courses of action.
2. Calculate (or assess) the payoffs, one for each course of action.
3. Select the one with the best payoff (e.g., largest profit or smallest cost), either by complete enumeration, by using an algorithm, or by the use of an analytical model.

3.4   DECISIONS UNDER RISK

Decision situations in which the chance (or probability) of occurrence of each state of nature is known (or can be estimated) are defined as decisions made under *risk*. In such cases the decision maker can assess the degree of risk that he or she is taking in terms of probability distributions. For example, a decision not to purchase fire insurance means that the decision maker takes a chance of perhaps one in 10,000 of losing all of his or her property in a fire.

Calculated risk

---

[3] For an extended discussion of decisions under certainty, see White [11].

Objective and subjective probabilities

There are two approaches to the assessment of the probabilities of the states of nature: objective and subjective.

History or experimentation for probabilities

Objective probability Objective probabilities can be derived either based on historical occurrences or based upon experimentation. Alternatively they can be derived with statistical formulas. For example, the probability of a "head" in the toss of a coin is computed statistically as ½ because only two states of nature (a head or a tail) can occur; and assuming the coin is fair, there is an equal chance for each (i.e., 50 percent). Thus, the use of objective probabilities narrows the scope for judgment. Unfortunately, the use of objective probabilities requires several of the following crucial assumptions that restrict its use:

1. Objective probabilities are based on observation of past events or experimentation, or both. Therefore, in using objective probabilities for decision making it must be assumed that future conditions will follow the same pattern as past conditions (or that a clear trend for future events has been established); otherwise, predictions of the future would be meaningless.
2. A necessary result of the assumption above is that the process observed must be stable.
3. It must be assumed that if a sample was observed for determining past behavior, it was large enough (statistically) and representative of the process under study.

Belief about the probabilities

Subjective probability The subjective probability approach measures the *degree of belief* in the likelihood of the future occurrence of a given outcome. Thus, such probabilities are a subjective appraisal of the nature of reality, in contrast to objective probabilities which must be an actual, countable, observable fact. Subjective probabilities are intuitive judgments about the probabilities of the states of nature, made by an individual(s) possessing experience with the phenomena involved. Subjective probability is used in cases in which objective probabilities cannot be used. The major problem with subjective probabilities is that different decision makers may give different estimates of the probabilities, and even change their estimates as a result of psychological, emotional, or other such factors.

Solution approaches to decision making under risk

Three criteria

The most acceptable approach to decision making under risk is the use of *expected value* as a criterion of choice. Alternatively, the *expected opportunity loss* criterion may be used. Both lead to the same result. Other criteria are the "most probable state of nature criterion" and some of those used for decision making under uncertainty (such as minimax), which are discussed in Section 3.8.

An example of decision making under risk: How to beat inflation At the beginning of this chapter an investment problem was presented. In that problem, Mary Golden was considering an investment for a trust fund in one of the following alternatives: a_1 = corporate bonds, a_2 = common stocks, or a_3 = time deposits. Suppose the Trust wants to invest in only *one alternative* with a declared objective of maximizing the yield over a one-year period. The yield (in percent of return) will depend on the state of the economy, which can be either solid growth, stagnation, or inflation. The estimated yields under each alternative and state of the economy are shown in Table 3.6. The problem is to find the best investment alternative.

TABLE 3.6
Yields (in percent) of investment alternatives

States of nature / Alternatives	.5 P_1 Solid growth S_1	.3 P_2 Stagnation S_2	.2 P_3 Inflation S_3	←Probabilities Expected value (percent)	
a_1	12 u_{11}	6 u_{12}	3 u_{13}	8.4	←Maximum
a_2	15	3	−2	8.0	
a_3	6.5	6.5	6.5	6.5	

$$\frac{12}{.5} \quad \frac{6}{\times .3} \quad \frac{3}{\times .2}$$
$$6 \quad +1.8 \quad +.6 \quad = 8.4.$$

Solution approach A: The use of the expected payoff criterion
This approach prescribes that the decision maker select the alternative with the best expected (average) payoff. This alternative should be selected each time the decision maker confronts this situation. Over the long run the average yearly yield will be the same as the expected payoff.

> The expected payoff of an alternative is the sum of all possible payoffs of that alternative, weighted by the probabilities of those payoffs occurring.

How to find the expected payoff The expected payoffs are computed, one by one, for each alternative.

Maximizing expected yield

Step 1. Multiply each payoff by its corresponding probability. For example, in alternative a_1 of Table 3.6: $12 \times .5$; $6 \times .3$, and $3 \times .2$.

Step 2. Sum the results of the multiplication of step 1; the total is the expected payoff.[4]

[4] In mathematical terms, let:
 a_i = alternative i.
 s_j = state of nature j.
 p_j = probability that state of nature s_j will occur.
 u_{ij} = payoff resulting from the selection of alternative a_i when s_j occurs.
Then, the expected value $E(a_i)$ is:

$$E(a_i) = p_1 u_{i1} + p_2 u_{i2} + \cdots = \sum_j p_j u_{ij}$$

For alternative a_1 in Table 3.6 the results are: $E(a_1) = 12 \times .5 + 6 \times .3 + 3 \times .2 = 8.4$ percent, where $E(a_1)$ is the symbol designating expected value, E, of alternative a_1.

Repeating the process for alternatives a_2 and a_3, one gets:

$$E(a_2) = 15 \times .5 + 3 \times .3 - 2 \times .2 = 8.0 \text{ percent}$$
$$E(a_3) = 6.5 \times .5 + 6.5 \times .3 + 6.5 \times .2 = 6.5 \text{ percent}$$

The selection of an alternative Once the expected payoffs for all alternatives are determined, only the newly formed column of expected payoffs need be considered (see the right-hand column of Table 3.6). If the problem is one of maximization, then the *highest* expected payoff is searched for, using complete enumeration. In minimization, the alternative with the *lowest* expected payoff is sought. In the investment (maximization) example, alternative a_1 has the highest expected yield and therefore investing in corporate bonds is recommended. The meaning of this choice is that the decision maker should invest in a_1, and only in a_1, each time that he or she is confronted with the decision. Furthermore, the average yearly yield, over the long run, per decision, is 8.4 percent. Note: The use of this criterion, when the payoffs are expressed in dollars, is called the *expected monetary value* or the EMV criterion.

Solution approach B: The expected opportunity loss (EOL) criterion (also called the regret criterion) The basic idea of this criterion is that people frequently act to minimize their anticipated average (expected) regret. Opportunity loss is defined as the relative loss resulting from selecting an alternative, given that a particular state of nature occurred, as compared with the best alternative that could have been selected. For example, if Mary Golden invests in bonds (a_1) and solid growth occurs, she will regret not having invested in stocks (a_2), which would have been the best alternative. Since she will make 12 percent with the bonds versus 15 percent that she could have made with stocks, her regret, or opportunity loss, is 3 percent. Table 3.7 shows the complete opportunity loss data. Once the table is constructed, the *expected* regret is computed by the same method

Minimizing regret

TABLE 3.7
Opportunity loss table (percent yield) of Table 3.6

States of nature / Alternatives	.5 Solid growth	.3 Stagnation	.2 Inflation	←Probabilities Expected regret	
a_1	$15 - 12 = 3$	$6.5 - 6 = .5$	$6.5 - 3 = 3.5$	$3 \times .5 + .5 \times .3 + 3.5 \times .2 = 2.35$	←Sma regre
a_2	$15 - 15 = 0$	$6.5 - 3 = 3.5$	$6.5 - (-2) = 8.5$	$0 \times .5 + 3.5 \times .3 + 8.5 \times .2 = 2.75$	
a_3	$15 - 6.5 = 8.5$	$6.5 - 6.5 = 0$	$6.5 - 6.5 = 0$	$8.5 \times .5 + 0 \times .3 + 0 \times .2 = 4.25$	

used in computing expected payoffs and the alternative with the *smallest expected regret* is selected. This rule is true for *both* profit and cost tables as regret is always bad and to be avoided.

Note also that alternative a_1 was selected under both the opportunity loss criterion and the expected payoff criterion. This is *not* a coincidence. Both will *always lead* to the *same choice* since the mathematical operations are basically the same. The difference is only philosophical. These are merely two different explanations of why people make certain choices.

Solution approach C: The "most probable state of nature" criterion   This criterion prescribes that as the decision maker confronts the various possible states of nature in a decision under risk, he or she ignores all but the most probable state. By doing so, the decision maker changes the situation to a decision under assumed certainty. Some nonrepetitive decisions are based upon this principle. For example, decisions to embark on new ventures are sometimes made only on the basis of what will happen if the venture succeeds (assuming the chance for success is .8 or more), although there is almost always some chance for failure. The deficiency of this solution approach is that it uses only part of the available information, making assumptions which may be incorrect.

Ignoring less likely outcomes

Example   Consider the investment decision of Table 3.6. According to the most-probable-state-of-nature criterion, the decision maker assumes that solid growth will occur since it has the largest chance of occurring. The other states of nature are ignored. Therefore, she will select a_2 since it will give her the largest yield (15 percent) in the event that solid growth will occur. However, if the decision maker is wrong, she may end with a yield of 3 or even lose 2. If this is a repeating situation, she will make 8 (the expected value) over the long run.

Solution approach D: Criteria of choice for uncertainty   In Part B of this chapter we introduce five criteria of choice for the case of uncertainty. These could be used for the case of risk as well. However, with the exception of nonrepetitive decisions it is very unlikely that these criteria will be used since they possess too many deficiencies and do not quantify the risk.

Notes on application

Nonrepetitive decisions   The expected value approach is based on achieving the best over the long run. For example, if the decision maker of Table 3.6 selects alternative a_1, he or she will make *either* a 12, 6, or 3 percent yield, each time the decision is made. Only over the *long run* will these yields average out to 8.4 percent. The question may thus be asked: Is there any justification in using an expected value approach for a one-shot, nonrepetitive decision?

There is at least one case in which the answer to this question is clearly yes. If a company is making several one-shot decisions whose payoff is more or less of the same magnitude, then the overall impact of using an expected value approach is similar to that of a repetitive decision. In cases where an expected value cannot be justified, the criteria discussed in Section 3.8 (such as minimax) can be used, or the use of utilities, as shown in Chapter 4, may be a good approach.

Use of mathematical models The evaluation of decisions under risk is made by comparing (complete enumeration) *all* expected payoffs and selecting the best one. However, this may be a long and costly procedure if many alternatives and payoffs are considered. For these types of situations probabilistic mathematical models (such as those presented in Chapters 12–14) are available.

The use of utilities as payoffs This subject will be discussed in Chapter 4.

Dominance In certain cases it is possible to eliminate some alternatives from evaluation because they are *inferior to* or *dominated by* other alternatives. For example, assume that alternative a_4 is added as an investment alternative to Table 3.6, where the yields are: 10 in the case of solid growth, 6 in the case of stagnation, and 2 in the case of inflation. If we compare this alternative (a_4) to a_1, we get:

	Solid growth	Stagnation	Inflation
a_1	12	6	3
a_4	10	6	2

It can clearly be seen that the decision maker should not consider a_4 at all, because no matter what state of nature occurs, the decision maker will be as well off or better with a_1. Thus, it is said that a_1 *dominates* a_4.

Summary

The use of the expected payoff criterion for making decisions under risk enables the decision maker to calculate the risk involved in the decision. The expected payoff is the sum of individual payoffs weighted by their probabilities of occurrence. Other criteria of choice may be used, especially in nonrepetitive situations.

3.5 CONCLUDING REMARKS

Most managerial decisions are made in one of two decision environments which are presented in this chapter, namely *certainty* or *risk*. In decisions under certainty, the payoff, or the outcome of selecting an alternative, is known with certainty. In decisions under risk, it is possible to assess the chances of various outcomes occurring but it is not possible to predict exactly which one will occur.

Decision theory has developed a methodology of analyzing managerial decisions. It uses a standardized format, known as a decision (payoff) table, for arranging all the pertinent data of the situation.

In the case of certainty, the selection of the best alternative is made either by a comparison process called complete enumeration or with the aid of mathematical models. Mathematical models are used to conduct an efficient search among given alternatives, or sometimes even to generate the alternatives themselves. In either case, the choice is based on a rational selection of the *best* payoff.

In the case of risky decisions, the decision maker may use one of several available criteria for making a choice. Most acceptable is the search (again conducted by complete enumeration or mathematical models) for the alternative with the highest expected payoff.

Part B of this chapter discusses the third decision situation, that of uncertainty. The value of acquiring additional information about the states of nature is also discussed. Additional related topics are discussed in Chapters 4 and 11.

3.6 PROBLEMS FOR PART A

1. The demand for a certain product is estimated as:

    *Number
    of units   Probability*

Number of units	Probability
20	.15
21	.20
22	.36
23	.19
24	.10

    Find the expected revenue if the product sells for $399.

2. An $800,000 property has a $1/10$ of 1 percent chance of catching fire that will cause damages of $100,000; and $1/20$ of 1 percent chance of catching fire that will completely destroy the property. Management decided to insure the property and it is reviewing two possible insurance policies:

    a. A policy with $50,000 deductible: i.e., the insurance company covers all damages except the initial $50,000. The annual premium for such a policy is $750.

    b. A no-deduction (fully paid) policy with an annual premium of $1,000.

    If the company's objective is cost minimization, which policy should it purchase? Build both an expected opportunity loss table and a decision table for the situation and solve them.

3. The table below shows the length of stay distribution in a hospital, in days.

Days	Probability (percent)	Days	Probability (percent)
2	3	6	15
3	5	7	25
4	5	8	20
5	10	9	10
		10	7

    The hospital makes $120 net profit per day during the first four days of patients' stay, and $40 a day for the fifth day or more of stay. How much profit will a hospital make in one year (365 days) if it admits 20 patients per day, on the average?

4. Lemon Auto kept detailed statistics on car sales during the last year. The dealership operated 300 days. During 15 days there were no sales; during 30 days one car was sold; each day during 87 days two cars were sold; during 141 days three cars were sold; and during 27 days four cars were sold.
   a. Find the frequency distribution of the sales.
   b. Find the average number of cars sold daily.
   c. Find the yearly profit of Lemon Auto if the average profit per car is $237.

5. Fire insurance for a plant valued at $1,000,000 is $150.
   a. Should the company take the insurance if the chance of a fire that will destroy the plant is one in ten thousand (base your answer on expected value)?
   b. What factor(s) may change the decision?

6. You have been offered the chance to play a dice game in which you will receive $10 each time the point total of a toss of two dice is 4. If it costs you $1 per toss to participate, should you play or not?

7. A survey conducted over the last 20 years indicated that in 8 of them the winter was mild, in 7 of them it was cold, and in the remaining 5 it was very cold.
   A company sells 1,000 fur coats in a mild year, 1,300 in a cold year, and 2,000 in a very cold year.
   Find the yearly expected profit of the company if a fur coat costs $85 and it is sold to stores for $123.

8. Find the best alternative in the following decision tables: *a* and *b* are *profits*, and *c* is *cost* data. Use both an expected value and an expected opportunity loss (EOL) approach.

a.

Alternatives \ States of nature	.3	.5	.2
	s_1	s_2	s_3
a_1	5	8	3
a_2	6	5	7

b.

Alternatives \ States of nature	.6	.1	.2	.1
	s_1	s_2	s_3	s_4
a_1	3	5	8	−1
a_2	6	5	2	0
a_3	0	5	6	4

c.

Alternatives \ States of nature	.1	.6	.3
	s_1	s_2	s_3
a_1	5	2	1
a_2	4	3	3
a_3	2	6	1

9. A marketing agent frequently flies from New York to Boston. She can use the airport bus, which costs $3; but if she takes it, there is a .08 chance that she will miss the flight. A hotel limousine costs $7, with a .96 chance of being on time for the flight. For $15, she can use a taxi that will make 99 of 100 flights. Each time she catches the plane, she will conclude a business transaction, which will produce a profit of $1,000; otherwise, she will lose it.
   Which mode of transportation should the marketing agent use in order to maximize her profit?

10. The yearly demand for a seasonal item follows the distribution below:

Demand (units)	Probability
1,000	.20
2,000	.30
3,000	.40
4,000	.10

The manufacturer of the item can produce it by one of three methods:
   a. Use existing tools at a cost of $6 per unit.
   b. Buy special equipment for $1,000. The value of the equipment at the end of the year (salvage value) is zero. The variable cost, per unit, is $3.

c. Buy special equipment for $10,000, which can be depreciated over four years (one fourth of the value each year). The variable cost using this equipment is $2 per unit.

Which method of production should the manufacturer follow in order to maximize profit?

Hint: Compare annual costs.

Assume: Production must meet all demand.

11. A firm needs temporary business space. It can lease the desired space for $5,000 for one year or $9,000 for two years (all rent is paid in advance). Alternatively, it can rent the space for one year for $5,000 and then if it wishes to re-rent, pay $5,500 on the first day of the second year as rent for the second year. The firm estimates that there is a 25 percent chance that they will have to depart from the city after one year. In that case, if they have rented the space for two years, they can sublet it for the second year. The chance of subletting is 60 percent, and they would receive $5,500, paid on the first day of the second year. If they are unable to sublet the space, it will remain empty for the entire second year. The interest rate that the company uses for evaluating such decisions is 10 percent.

Should the company rent the space for one year or two? Why?

12. ABC Groceries buys fresh fruit daily for $1 a crate. Crates sold the same day bring $1.50 profit contribution, each. Crates which are not sold in a day are sold later as animal food for 25 cents, each. The demand for fruit fluctuates, according to the following distribution (data collected over the last 300 days):

Demand	Number of days
10	120
11	90
12	75
13	15
Total	300

a. How many crates should the store order if ABC wants to maximize profit from selling fruit? Use an expected value approach.
b. What will be the average daily profit?

13. An apartment building has eight washing machines. The probability of these machines failing in any given year is:

Number of machines failing during the year	Probability
3	.15
4	.30
5	.50
6	.05

Once a machine has failed, its repair will cost either $30, the minimum service charge, $70 for a moderate repair, or $120 for a major repair. The chance for a major repair is 36 percent while for a moderate repair is 44 percent for any washer.

Sears offers a prepaid one-year maintenance policy that costs $45 per machine.

a. Should the owner of the apartment building buy the maintenance insurance?
b. Assume that the cost of repair is evenly distributed over the year while the insurance premium is prepaid. How is your analysis affected by this assumption?

14. A consultant plans to work in a foreign country where the exchange rate is 100 units of the foreign currency for $1. He plans to be there for several months, and his expenses for the period are estimated at 250,000 units of the foreign currency. A sky-rocketing inflation is temporarily in check while the government attempts to get a loan, the effect of which will be to lower the exchange rate by 10 percent (i.e., $1 = 90 units). If the loan is refused, the exchange rate will increase by 20 percent ($1 = 120 units). Suppose it is known that the probability of the government receiving the loan is .80. The consultant considers the following alternatives:

a_1 Immediately convert enough dollars into foreign units to meet expenses for the entire period.
a_2 Wait until the loan is either granted or refused; in the meantime hold dollars.
a_3 Hedge by converting part of the dollars to 125,000 units of foreign currency now and holding enough in dollars until the loan is

either granted or refused, and then buy 125,000 additional units of the foreign currency.

Assume the decision on the loan is to be made prior to his arrival in the foreign country. Assume also that after the change in the exchange rate, the consultant will still need 250,000 units of the foreign currency (regardless of the exchange rate).

If the consultant wants to minimize his dollar expense, which course of action should he take?

15. A common scene in many casinos is an old lady simultaneously playing two slot machines at a rate of 30 plays on each machine per hour. Assume that she plays the "dime" machines. The winning chances are given below (per play, per machine):

Winning prize	Chance
$10 (jackpot)....	1 out of 400
$1.............	1 out of 100
50¢.............	1 out of 50
20¢.............	1 out of 10

a. Find the net gain (loss) of the old lady during a four-hour period.

b. Compute the profit (loss) of the "House" from each machine in an hour.

c. The total cost of operating such a machine (including maintenance and depreciation) is $6 per day. The machine is played an average of ten hours a day. Is the machine profitable?

d. How many plays per hour will have to be made for the Casino to break even on each machine?

PART B: EXTENSIONS

3.7 THE VALUE OF PERFECT INFORMATION

In decision making under risk, the decision maker operates with less information than in the case of decision making under certainty. One may ask the question: Suppose that additional information can be obtained; what will its value be to the decision maker? This discussion will be confined to the case where the obtained information changes the situation from one of risk to one of certainty. That is, the decision maker is assumed to acquire information describing precisely which state of nature will occur next. (The basic distribution of the states of nature does not change—one just learns with certainty *which* state will occur next.) The information involved is called *perfect information.*[5]

A crystal ball . . .

The decision maker faces two decisions when perfect information is involved. First, if the perfect information were available which alternative should be selected? Second, should the perfect information be acquired? The second decision is based on the comparison of the benefit of the perfect information with its cost.

. . . for a price

Example

Let us analyze the investment decision presented in Table 3.6 as reproduced in Table. 3.8.

Alternatives	States of nature	.5	.3	.2	Expected value
		Growth	Stagnation	Inflation	
a_1 Bonds		12	6	3	8.4
a_2 Stocks		15	3	-2	8.0
a_3 Time deposit		6.5	6.5	6.5	6.5

TABLE 3.8
The investment decision (in percent yield)

The problem, solved by the expected value approach, indicated that the best alternative was a_1, yielding an average of 8.4 percent. Let us now assume that each percent of yield equals $10,000; that is, a decision maker who uses the expected value as a criterion will make, over the long run, $8.4 \times 10,000 = \$84,000$.

---

[5] Cases involving *imperfect* information are more complicated to analyze since the problem remains that of decision making under risk, with revised probabilities. Bayes' theorem (see Chapter 4) is used in such cases to compute the revised probabilities.

What alternative course of action given perfect information? Assume that we deal with a repetitive situation; e.g., a decision is made every year. Suppose that in advance of making a decision, a market research firm is able to predict, with certainty, the state of the economy that will prevail. Thus, the decision maker can make a choice with complete certainty. The choice depends on what the research firm predicts:

- If the research firm predicts "growth" the best choice is stocks (a_2).
- If the research firm predicts "stagnation" the choice will be time deposit (a_3).
- If the prediction is for "inflation" the choice will again be time deposit (a_3).

A varying choice

Note that, in contrast to the regular expected value situation where one alternative is selected, here the choice may vary among alternatives.

The expected payoff with perfect information Assuming that the frequency distribution of the states of the economy does not change over the long run, then 50 percent of the time the research firm will predict that growth is the next state. The decision maker, now knowing in advance what is going to happen next, will select a_2 and realize a 15 percent yield. Similarly, 30 percent of the time stagnation will be predicted and the decision maker will make 6.5 percent by selecting a_3, and 20 percent of the time inflation will give 6.5 percent by selecting a_3. The decision maker's average (expected) yield will be:

$$.5 \times 15 + .3 \times 6.5 + .2 \times 6.5 = 10.75 \text{ percent}$$

Using the $10,000 per 1 percent equivalence, the average return per decision will be $107,500.

Should the perfect information be acquired? If we compare the expected yield with perfect information ($107,500) with the expected yield under regular conditions ($84,000) we see an improvement of $23,500. In general, decisions with perfect information yield much better results than decisions without it. The difference of $23,000 is called the *expected value of perfect information*[6] (EVPI) and is used to

EVPI

---

[6] The mathematical expression of the expected value of perfect information in the case of maximization is:

$$\text{EVPI} = \underbrace{\sum_{j=1}^{n} p_j \left(\max_i u_{ij} \right)}_{\substack{\text{Expected yield with} \\ \text{perfect information}}} - \underbrace{\max_i \sum_{j=1}^{n} p_j u_{ij}}_{\substack{\text{Expected yield} \\ \text{without perfect} \\ \text{information}}}$$

where:

p_j = probability of state of nature j.
u_{ij} = the payoff when action a_i is taken and state of nature j occurs.

answer the question of whether or not the perfect information should be acquired.

Note that EVPI is the average improvement in the objective function, per decision. If this figure is compared against the cost of acquiring the information, management can make a decision regarding the acquisition of the information. For example, if the research firm charges $15,000 per prediction, the investor stands to gain $23,500— $15,000 = $8,500, on the average, by using the service. But if the marketing firm charges $23,500 or more for this service, then the arrangement would not be profitable.

Thus, the EVPI tells the decision maker the *upper limit* one should be willing to pay for "perfect predicting information"; information which is 100 percent reliable.

What's the ✓
info worth?

If the decision maker decides to buy the perfect information, the decision maker should, of course, wait for the (perfect) prediction and then make a choice.

Summary

To determine whether or not to purchase perfect information one should:

1. Compute the expected yield without perfect information and select the best alternative.
2. Compute the expected yield with perfect information, assuming the best selection of alternatives is made.
3. Compute the EVPI by subtracting 1) above from 2). (Reverse order for cost minimization.)
4. If the difference is larger than the cost of the information, it should be purchased; otherwise, it should not.
5. The value of EVPI *must* be ≥ 0.

Note: The equivalence of EVPI and EOL

The expected value of perfect information (EVPI) in the investment example was $23,500 or 2.35 percent of yield. Examining Table 3.7, the reader will find that the expected regret or expected opportunity loss (EOL) of the *best alternative* is also 2.35 percent yield. Is this a coincidence? The answer is: No! As a matter of fact the EVPI is *always equal* to the best EOL.

EVPI = EOL

In the case of minimization:

$$\text{EVPI} = \begin{bmatrix} \text{Expected cost without} \\ \text{perfect information} \end{bmatrix} - \begin{bmatrix} \text{Expected cost with} \\ \text{perfect information} \end{bmatrix}$$

3.8   DECISIONS UNDER UNCERTAINTY

In the condition of uncertainty, the decision maker recognizes different potential states of nature but cannot confidently estimate the probabilities of their occurrence. This is an undesirable but often unavoidable situation. It may occur when one faces a completely new phenomenon (é.g., the 1973 energy crisis) or when a completely new product, process, or state of nature is under consideration.

Example

The Palm Tree Hotel is considering the construction of an additional wing. Management is evaluating the possibility of adding 30, 40, or 50 rooms. The success of the addition depends on a combination of local government legislation and competition in the field; four states of nature are being considered. They are shown, together with the anticipated payoffs (in percent of yearly return on investment), in Table 3.9.

TABLE 3.9
Payoff table (percent of return on investment)

| | | | $1/4$ | $1/4$ | $1/4$ | $1/4$ |
Alternatives	States of nature	Positive legislation and low competition s_1	Positive legislation and strong competition s_2	No legislation and low competition s_3	No legislation and strong competition s_4
$a_1 = 30$ rooms		10	5	4	-2
$a_2 = 40$ rooms		17	10	1	-10
$a_3 = 50$ rooms		24	15	-3	-20

Management cannot agree on the probabilities of the states of nature. The problem is: how many rooms to build in order to maximize the return on investment.

No "right" answers

At the present time, decision theory does not provide a single best criterion for selecting an alternative under conditions of uncertainty. Instead, there are a number of different criteria, each with its justifications and limitations. The choice among these is determined by organizational policy or the attitude of the decision maker, or by both.

Criteria of choice

Five criteria of choice are presented:

Laplace

1. The criterion of equal probabilities (Laplace)   The user of this criterion assumes that all states of nature are *equally likely* to occur. Thus, equal probabilities are assigned to each. The expected values are then computed and the alternative with the highest expected payoff is selected.

Example.   Using the example given in Table 3.9, probabilities of ¼ are assigned to each of the *four* states of nature. The expected payoffs are:

$$E(a_1) = ¼ \times 10 + ¼ \times 5 + ¼ \times 4 + ¼ \times (-2) = {}^{17}/_4$$
$$E(a_2) = ¼(17 + 10 + 1 - 10) = {}^{18}/_4 \text{ (largest expected yield)}$$
$$E(a_3) = ¼(24 + 15 - 3 - 20) = {}^{16}/_4$$

Thus, the best alternative is a_2, with an expected payoff of ${}^{18}/_4$. The major argument against this criterion is that there is absolutely no reason to assume the probabilities are all equal. Such an assumption is as erroneous as assuming one outcome in particular will occur.

2. *Criterion of pessimism (maximin or minimax)* The user of this criterion is completely pessimistic, since he assumes that the worst will happen, no matter which alternative he selects. To protect himself, the decision maker should select the alternative which will give as large a payoff as possible under this pessimistic assumption.

Example   Let us reproduce Table 3.9 as Table 3.10 (payoffs in percent yield).

States of nature / Alternatives	s_1	s_2	s_3	s_4	Worst (minimum)	Best of worst (maximum of minimums)
a_1	10	5	4	-2	-2	-2
a_2	17	10	1	-10	-10	
a_3	24	15	-3	-20	-20	

TABLE 3.10
Pessimistic approach in the case of profit

Assume that the decision maker selects a_1; then the *worst* than can happen is a loss of 2 percent when s_4 occurs. Similarly, the worst for a_2 is −10, and for a_3 is −20 (the lowest number in the row is selected in the case of maximization, the highest number is selected in the case of minimization). This information is entered into a new column labeled "worst." From this column, the best entry is then selected (−2 in the example). The decision maker maximized the minimum payoffs, and therefore this criterion is labeled *maximin.*[7] The use of this criterion will guarantee the decision maker that in the *worst possible case* the loss will be 2.

One drawback of this criterion (which is also a common drawback of all the remaining criteria) is that the decision is based on only a *small*

---

[7] In the case of cost minimization, the decision maker will minimize the maximum possible costs; that is, the decision maker will *minimax.*

portion of the available information. Thus, valuable information is completely disregarded as shown in Table 3.11 which illustrates a deliberately exaggerated case (maximization).

TABLE 3.11
Profits under two alternatives

States of nature / Alternatives	s_1	s_2	s_3	Minimum	
a_1	40,000	20,000	500	500	
a_2	550	520	510	510	←Maximum

According to the criterion of pessimism, a_2 should be selected. The decision is based on the "Minimum" column which includes only one entry from each row. The rest of the data is ignored. In reality, most decision makers will pay attention to the remaining information and consequently not use this approach and select a_1. The pessimistic decision maker acts in a superconservative manner, paying attention only to the risks and completely neglecting the opportunities.

Maximax

Larry Lucky

3. *Criterion of optimism* (*maximax or minimin*) An optimistic decision maker assumes that the very best outcome will occur and selects the alternative with the best possible payoff.

To do so, the decision maker searches for the best possible payoff for each alternative. These are placed in a new column to the right of the decision table. The alternative with the best payoff in this newly added column is then selected (best of bests).

Example Reproducing the data of Table 3.9 in Table 3.12, the "best" column is created.[8] According to the maximax criterion, alternative a_3 would be selected.

TABLE 3.12
Maximax choice

States of nature / Alternatives	s_1	s_2	s_3	s_4	Best	
a_1	10	5	4	−2	10	
a_2	17	10	1	−10	17	
a_3	24	15	−3	−20	24	←Best of bests

---

[8] If the data were costs, then the optimistic decision maker would select as best the *lowest* cost payoff for each alternative and then select the *lowest* of these lowests. Such an approach is labeled *minimin*.

Notice again that no attention is paid to most of the available information; only the highest payoff is considered. Thus, an optimistic decision maker is a gambler who disregards the risks and looks forward only to the opportunities.

4. Coefficient of optimism (Hurwicz criterion) Most decision makers are not completely optimistic or completely pessimistic. Therefore, it was suggested, by Hurwicz, that the degree of optimism (or pessimism) labeled alpha, α, be measured on a 0 to 1 scale (0 = completely pessimistic, 1 = completely optimistic). Hurwicz suggested that the best alternative is the one with the highest (in maximization) weighted value, where the weighted value, WV, for each alternative (row in the decision table) is expressed by:

(margin note) Middle-of-the-road types

(margin note) Hurwicz

$$WV = \alpha \text{ best } u + (1 - \alpha)\text{worst } u \qquad (3.2)$$

(handwritten: degree of optimism)

Example   Examining Table 3.12, with α given as .7. We get:

$WV(a_1) = .7 \times 10 + (1 - .7) \times (-2) = 6.4$
$WV(a_2) = .7 \times 17 + (1 - .7) \times (-10) = 8.9$
$WV(a_3) = .7 \times 24 + (1 - .7) \times (-20) = 10.8 \leftarrow$ (maximum)

Thus, alternative a_3 is the best. Note: In the case of minimization, select the alternative with the *lowest WV*.

The major difficulty in applying this criterion is the measurement of alpha.[9] Note that use is made of more information than in minimax, yet only the two extreme payoffs are considered and the remaining information is ignored.

5. The criterion of regret (Savage's criterion) The concept of regret is equivalent to the determination of *opportunity loss*, discussed in Section 3.4. Both concepts represent the important economic concept of *opportunity cost* which indicates the magnitude of *the loss incurred by not selecting the best alternative*.

(margin note) Savage's "regret"

(margin note) I wish I had done . . . ,

Savage argued that the decision maker should attempt to *minimize the largest anticipated regret*. That is, employ a *minimax* approach to the regret data (in a basically pessimistic manner).

Example   Let us use the hotel example of Table 3.9.

Solution:

Step 1.   Build a regret (opportunity loss) table. This is done according to the method exhibited in Table 3.7. The result is shown in Table 3.13.   *(P. 66).*

Step 2.   Minimax the regret. This is done by finding the worst (largest) regret in each row, and then selecting the lowest regret in the . newly formed column.

---

[9] One way to determine it has been suggested by Luce and Raiffa ([6], page 283).

TABLE 3.13
Regret table for Table 3.9

States of nature / Alternatives	s_1	s_2	s_3	s_4	Largest regret	
a_1	24 − 10 = 14	15 − 5 = 10	4 − 4 = 0	−2 − (−2) = 0	14	
a_2	24 − 17 = 7	15 − 10 = 5	4 − 1 = 3	−2 − (−10) = 8	8	←Minimum
a_3	24 − 24 = 0	15 − 15 = 0	4 − (−3) = 7	−2 − (−20) = 18	18	

In the example the lowest regret is for alternative a_2. This selection guarantees that regardless of what happens, the decision maker will never have a regret larger than 8. Note that use is made only of a small portion of the available information.

Note: The value of regret, by definition, can never be negative.

Summary

Decision making under uncertainty is more difficult than it is for risk or certainty. All five different criteria presented here have some deficiencies and will usually point to different selections of alternatives. In management, decision making under uncertainty should be avoided since the results can be disastrous. Instead, enough information should be acquired so that decisions are made, at worst, under risk or, at best, under certainty.

3.9 PROBLEMS FOR PART B

16. Find the expected value of perfect information in Problem 8 (a), (b), and (c). Compare the results to the EOL.

17. Review Problem 12. Assume that the store can buy information which will enable it to predict, with certainty, the daily demand. How much should the store be willing to pay for such information?

18. Review Problem 14. Find the value of perfect information and comment on it.

19. Given two decision tables below, find the best alternative in each by the following criteria:

a. Laplace (equal probabilities).
b. Pessimism.
c. Optimism.
d. Coefficient of optimism (Hurwicz) with α = .4.
e. Regret (Savage).

TABLE 1—cost data

	s_1	s_2	s_3	s_4
a_1	5	8	3	1
a_2	7	4	5	2
a_3	3	6	6	4

TABLE 2—profit data

	s_1	s_2	s_3
a_1	7	2	−1
a_2	3	6	2
a_3	0	3	8

20. Consider a decision in which the possible outcomes can be classified as either acceptable (x) or not acceptable (y). Given below is a payoff table.

Alternatives \ Futures	s_1	s_2	s_3
a_1	x	x	y
a_2	x	y	x

a. If the probabilities of the futures, s_1, s_2, and s_3 are unknown (call them p_1, p_2, and p_3), which alternative would you select? Why?
b. Describe under what conditions the two alternatives would be of equal value to the decision maker.

   Hint: Naturally, the utility of x is larger than that of y. Use the "expected value criterion." Assume a repetitive situation.

21. The manager of an advertising agency has to make a decision between three available programs (a_1, a_2, a_3). There are three possible futures that can be expected: s_1 = market rises, s_2 = market falls, s_3 = no change in the market. The manager can estimate the yields in each case (given in the table below, in percent of return) but cannot estimate the probabilities of the various futures occurring.

Programs \ Futures	s_1	s_2	s_3
a_1	3	6	−1
a_2	8	5	4
a_3	−4	7	12

Which program would you suggest the manager select if he uses the following decision approaches:

a. Laplace (equal probabilities).
b. Pessimistic approach.
c. Optimistic approach.
d. Hurwicz criterion with $\alpha = .55$.
e. Minimax regret (Savage).

22. American Investor's Bank is evaluating two investment proposals involving $3,000,000. The first is to buy class A bonds with a 7.3 percent return. The second is to buy some land in Easton, Pennsylvania. The land is intended for development into an industrial park in which case a 17 percent return is expected. However, the land is close to a planned new highway, and the government may purchase the land to build a rest area. In this case, the government will pay the bank 4.5 percent above the purchase price.

    Assuming a one-year decision horizon, what would you advise the bank to do if the probability of the government action is unknown?

23. The probability of the government action in Problem 22 is unknown. However, there exists a theoretical probability which will make the two alternatives *equal*. Find that probability.

24. Review a decision made by an organization. Describe how the decision was made. Was the decision a case of certainty? Uncertainty? Risk? Could a decision table approach be applied? Why or why not?

25. It is said that managers will avoid making decisions under uncertainty. Why?

3.10 CASE

THE CONDOMINIUM

It was a hot summer day in Miami and Dave Greenhouse was trying to make a decision before 5:00 P.M. Dave was in the business of buying repossessed condominium apartments from lending institutions such as savings and loan associations and banks. In the summer of 1980, during the recession, there were many such repossessions. The lending institutions' objectives were to get rid of the property as soon as possible. Dave would buy the apartments and then sell them, hopefully with a nice profit.

This time the Blue Key Savings and Loan Association offered him three units (he must take all of them or nothing at a nonnegotiable price of $72,000. It was the last day that the offer was valid, and Dave knew that he must make a fast decision. Dave had already had the assets appraised. The estimated selling price that he could get for the units is shown below:

Unit 1. $26,900
Unit 2. Twenty-five percent chance of $25,000, 50 percent chance of $26,000, and 25 percent of $27,000.
Unit 3. Thirty percent chance of $25,000, 40 percent of $26,000, and 30 percent chance of $27,000.

There was also a selling cost of $1,000 per unit (advertising, legal, financial, and so forth).

Dave hoped to sell the units within 60 days. This was the time limit the savings and loan association gave him to pay the $72,000; Dave estimated there was a 70 percent chance that he could do it. Any unit which was not sold within 60 days would be sold, for certainty, within the next 30 days. However, in that case there would be a financial charge for late payment of $440 per apartment.

Present the situation in a decision table and advise Dave on what to do.

3.11 GLOSSARY

Alternative course of action An alternative of choice which is open to the decision maker.

Certainty The decision environment when there is only one possible payoff for a decision. This situation occurs when only one state of nature exists.

Coefficient of optimism, α A measure of willingness to assume risk. There exist two extremes: $\alpha = 0$, completely pessimistic; $\alpha = 1$, completely optimistic (gambler).

Complete enumeration A listing of all possible combinations and the comparison of their results.

Conflict A decision situation where the payoff is conditioned upon the decisions made by two or more decision makers with conflicting objectives.

Criterion of optimism A criterion of choice under uncertainty that assumes that the best is going to occur (maximax).

Criterion of pessimism A criterion of choice under uncertainty that asumes that the worst is coming. Thus, trying to select the best of the worsts (maximin).

Dominance When one alternative is preferred to another because it is at least as good as the other and, in some outcome(s), better.

Equal probabilities (Laplace's) criterion of choice Criterion for decision making under uncertainty that assumes that the probabilities of all states of nature occurring are equal.

Expected monetary value (EMV) Expected value when the payoffs are given in monetary terms (dollars).

Expected opportunity loss (EOL) The average opportunity loss, or regret, per decision.

Expected value (EV) A weighted average (mean), found by weighting each possible payoff by its probability (relative frequency) of occurrence.

Expected value of perfect information (EVPI) The difference in expected payoff between making a decision under risk with an expected value approach and making a decision having perfect information about which state of nature is going to occur.

Minimax regret A pessimistic criterion for decision making using the regret figures as payoffs; using this criterion one minimizes the maximum regret values.

Most probable state of nature A criterion of choice for decision making under risk which assumes that the state of nature with the highest probability will occur.

Objective probability Probability estimate based on hard data obtained from history or through experimentation (contrast with subjective probability).

Opportunity loss (or cost) The amount of loss attached to each possible outcome of an alternative, due to *not* selecting the best alternative.

Payoff The result of selecting an alternative course of

action, given a specific state of nature occurring (also called outcome).

Perfect information   The prior knowledge of exactly which state of nature will occur.

Regret   See "Opportunity loss (or cost)."

Risk   A decision situation where several states of nature exist and their likelihood (probability) of occurrence is known.

State of nature   Future event that impacts the result of a decision and is *not* under the control of the decision maker.

Subjective probability   The probability estimate of a knowledgeable person which is based on judgment and intuition.

Uncertainty   The decision environment in which several states of nature exist, but their chances of occurring are not known.

3.12   REFERENCES AND BIBLIOGRAPHY

1. Brown, Rex V.; Kahr, Andrew S.; and Peterson, Cameron.   *Decision Analysis for the Manager.* New York: Holt, Rinehart and Winston, Inc., 1974.

2. Harrison, E. F.   *The Managerial Decision-Making Process.* Boston: Houghton Mifflin Co., 1975.

3. Holloway, C. A.   *Decision Making under Uncertainty.* Englewood Cliffs, N.J.: Prentice-Hall, 1979.

4. Huang, C. L., et al.   *Multiple Objective Decision Making, Methods, and Applications: A State of the Art Survey.* New York: Springer/Verlag, 1979.

5. Lindley, D. F.   *Making Decisions.* London: John Wiley & Sons, Ltd., 1971.

6. Luce, R. D., and Raiffa, H.   *Games and Decisions.* New York: John Wiley & Sons, Inc., 1957.

7. Oxenfeldt, A. R.   *A Basic Approach to Executive Decision Making.* New York: AMACOM, 1978.

8. Raiffa, H.   *Decision Analysis.* Reading, Mass.: Addison-Wesley Publishing Co., Inc., 1968.

9. Starr, M. K.   *Management: A Modern Approach.* New York: Harcourt Brace Jovanovich, Inc., 1971.

10. Thomas, H.   *Decision Theory and the Manager.* London: Pitman Publishing Corporation, 1972.

11. White, D. J.   *Decision Methodology.* London: John Wiley & Sons, Ltd., 1975.

12. Zionts, S.   *Multiple Criteria Problem Solving: Proceedings in Buffalo, 1977.* New York: Springer-Verlag, 1978.

4

Extending the exposition of Chapter 3, this chapter now delves into additional topics and concepts of decision theory. It begins with the use of utilities as a measure of payoffs and then moves to a discussion of the quantitative handling of multiple goals in decision situations. Part A of the chapter ends with the presentation of the graphical tool of decision trees.

In Part B an exposition of Bayes' theorem for revising the probabilities of the states of nature is presented with an application to a decision analysis involving decision trees.

Decision theory II

PART A: BASICS

> Paul sensed he was caught in a dilemma. All month he had planned to take his girl to the school's annual prom. He had even saved up the usual $20 per couple admission fee. But at the last minute the student council raised the fee to $30 to cover the unexpected costs of hiring a well-known dance band. That seemed to doom Paul's plans. Then one of his friends, knowing his dilemma, jokingly offered him a coin-toss gamble. If the toss showed heads, Paul must pay him the $20 he had saved, but if it showed tails, he would pay Paul $12. At the time, Paul had laughed off the gamble since it was so obviously unfair. But now, Paul wondered—perhaps it wasn't such a foolish gamble after all.

4.1   UTILITY AND DECISION THEORY

Let us attempt to analyze the above situation with the expected value method presented in Chapter 3, as shown in Table 4.1. The payoffs represent the money left after the gamble.

TABLE 4.1
The expected monetary payoff

Alternatives \ States of nature	.5 Heads	.5 Tails	Expected payoff	
Accept offer	0	32	16	
Reject offer	20	20	20	← *Maximum*

Solution   Using an expected payoff approach, Paul should reject his friend's offer, since the expected value of rejection is higher.

Analysis   Before Paul rejects the offer, he should do some thinking. He should consider the enjoyment he will have at the prom, and about his date's possible reaction. He probably should accept the offer. The reason for this is that the $20 is of very little use to him, since it cannot get him to the prom; but if he wins the gamble, he will have enough money ($20 + $12 = $32) to pay the admission fee and even buy a drink or two. What should actually be compared in this case are not the monetary values but the benefits or *utilities* that it has for Paul.

Expected value or expected utility?

Discussion   In the analysis of decision making under risk, the best alternative is usually selected by calculating and comparing the expected monetary values (EMV) of the various alternatives. However, there are at least three situations in which EMV is *not* likely to be a valid criterion. First, as in the school prom case, if the decision maker finds difficulty in expressing the values of some of the outcomes of his or her

EMV not valid in three cases

decisions in terms of monetary payoffs, then EMV cannot be used. Second, EMV assumes that the decision maker is willing to risk losing money in the short run as long as he or she is better off in the long run. In reality, however, decision makers frequently act to *avoid* risk in the short run, particularly if there is any possibility whatsoever of incurring a large initial loss. Finally, EMV assumes a linear relationship between the amount of money and its value (or utility). For example, it is assumed that the value of $20,000 is twice that of $10,000. In reality, however, it has been observed that with an increase in the amount of wealth accumulated, the value of additional money decreases. (For example, the value of a dollar added to $10 is larger than that of one added to $1,000.)

For all these situations there is a need for a measure other than money which better describes how decision makers value possible outcomes.

The application of *utility* as a measure for the value of an outcome was proposed by von Neumann and Morgenstern [11]. They suggested that each individual has a measurable preference among various choices available in risk situations. This preference is called *utility* and is

Utiles

measured in arbitrary units called "utiles." By suitable questioning (an example will be given later), it is possible to determine a person's utility for various amounts of money. This is called a person's *utility function*. The graph of this function offers a picture of the individual's attitude toward risk-taking. Von Neumann and Morgenstern hypothesized that in any decision involving risk, a person will choose *that* alternative which maximizes his or her expected utility.[1]

This idea is based upon the following assumptions:

Utility a cardinal measure

1. Utility can be measured on a cardinal scale. That is, cardinal numbers (1, 2, and so on) can describe how many utiles constitute a payoff. For example, if a certain consequence, say a 5 percent share of the market, is twice as important as another consequence, say 6 percent profit, we describe the 5 percent share of the market as having twice as many utiles as the 6 percent profit.

Utilities are additive

2. Utilities of different objects can be added together (this is called the "additivity assumption"). For example, if object A is worth 10 utiles and object B is worth 5 utiles, then objects A and B together are worth 15 utiles.

Solution of the school prom case using utilities

Let us examine the problem in utility terms: Since the $20 will not get Paul to the prom, it is of little value to him. We may arbitrarily

---

[1] The mechanics of computing *expected utility* are the same as the mechanics of computing any expected value; namely, multiply the probabilities by the corresponding payoffs (this time given in units of utility called utiles) and add them up.

assume that the $20 is worth 100 utiles. Losing the $20 will leave him with no money, a situation which is worth 0 utiles. However, the additional $12 is crucial since he will have $32 and will then be able to go to the prom. Therefore, the $32 is extremely valuable, worth say, 500 utiles. Now the decision situation can be reviewed (see Table 4.2) in terms of utilities.

States of nature / Alternatives	.5 Lose (heads)	.5 Win (tails)	EU	
Accept	0	500	250	← *Maximum*
Reject	100	100	100	

TABLE 4.2
Expected utility (EU)

Using utility, Paul should *accept* the offer, since the expected utility in the case of "accept" is: .5(0) + .5(500) = 250 utiles, which is higher than the expected utility of "reject," which is .5(100) + .5(100) = 100.

The above example can explain why people gamble; that is, why they are willing to spend money to assume risk. The next example of utility will show why people insure themselves; that is, why they are willing to spend money to avoid risk.

Gambling versus insurance

Example: To insure or not to insure?

Suppose management is about to make a decision concerning fire insurance on a plant valued at $2,000,000. There is a chance of 1 in 2,000 (.0005) that a fire will destroy the plant during a one-year period. The annual premium for insurance is $1,500. Should the company insure or not? The situation is shown in the decision Table, 4.3.

Insure or not?

States of nature / Alternatives	.0005 Fire	.9995 No Fire	Expected cost (EMV)	
Insure	$1,500	$1,500	$1,500	
Do not insure	$2,000,000	0	$1,000	← *Minimum cost*

TABLE 4.3
Fire insurance, EMV outcomes

According to the EMV, management should not insure. In the long run it will cost much more to insure than not to. However, since the situation is in the realm of uncertainty, there is a chance, although very

small, that fire will occur during the very first year. The loss of
$2,000,000 would probably bankrupt the company—a situation that
management could not afford. Therefore, they will buy the insurance
even though it has a larger expected monetary cost. If the same situation
is analyzed in utility terms, it might look like this:

The $1,500 premium is worth -1 utile to the company; zero dollars
is worth zero utiles. A loss of $2,000,000 is worth $-10,000$ utiles. This
information is entered in Table 4.4.

TABLE 4.4
Fire insurance, EU
outcomes

Alternatives \ States of nature	.0005 Fire	.9995 No fire	Expected utility (EU)	
Insure	−1	−1	−1 utile	← Maximum utility
Do not insure	−10,000	0	−5 utiles	

The results show that the expected utility of insuring is higher than
that of not insuring; thus, the company will elect to insure.

Utility curves

The EU

From the discussion so far it is evident that the mechanics of using
utilities as payoffs are similar to using money (or any other objective
value such as yield) as payoffs. The only difference is that the expected
value is expressed in terms of expected utility (EU), instead of the
expected monetary value (EMV). The biggest problem, however, is the
assignment of utility values as a replacement for monetary values. The
relationship between money and utility can be described graphically
with the help of a curve termed the *utility curve* or *utility function*.

Utility curves

If a utility curve can be constructed, then one can read off the curve
the utility values that correspond to any desired monetary values. The
construction of the curve, therefore, is the key to the analysis. According
to the von Neumann-Morgenstern proposal, a curve can be constructed
by measuring the attitude of the decision maker toward risk. Several
such curves are shown in Figure 4.1. The shape of each curve is a
function of the individual's attitude toward risk. For example, money
has a lot of value when a risk averse person is poor but monetary
increases have less and less value as the amount of money increases.
Once a person's utility curve is known, then it is possible to replace
any monetary value by its utility equivalent for that person.

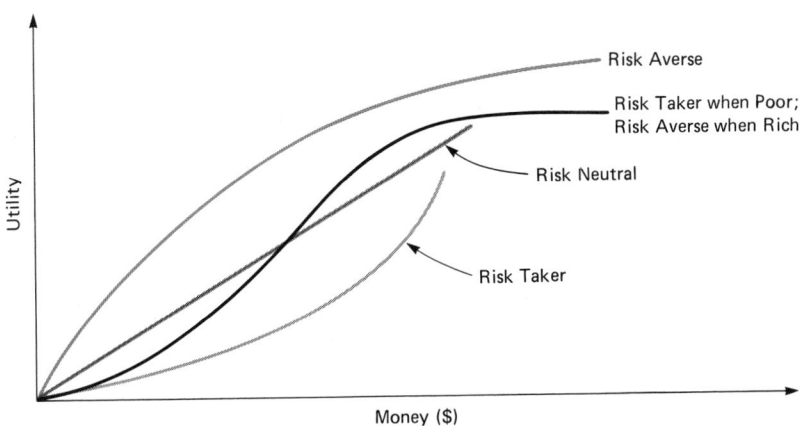

FIGURE 4.1
Different utility curves

Example

A decision table with three alternatives and three states of nature is shown in Table 4.5 (with payoffs given in dollars). The objective is to maximize profit. The problem is to select the alternative that will do so.

	States of nature	.2	.5	.3	EMV	
Alternatives		s_1	s_2	s_3		
a_1		12	6	4	6.6	← Maximum
a_2		15	3	−2	3.9	
a_3		6.5	6.5	6.5	6.5	

TABLE 4.5
Decision table with profit figures ($)

Solution by EMV Using expected monetary value, alternative a_1 with the largest EMV of $6.6 is selected.

Solution by expected utility In order to evaluate the decision table in terms of utility, it is necessary to express *all* nine entries in the table in utiles. The question of how to do this can be answered with the aid of the decision maker's utility curve.

How to construct a utility curve

To illustrate how the decision maker's utility-of-money curve is obtained, let us first arbitrarily assign the value of 100 "utiles" to the highest outcome, $15, and 0 utiles[2] to the worst possible outcome −$2.

---

[2] One can use any other pair of numbers instead of 100 and 0; for example, 1 and 0.

FIGURE 4.2
The utility-of-money
curve

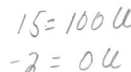

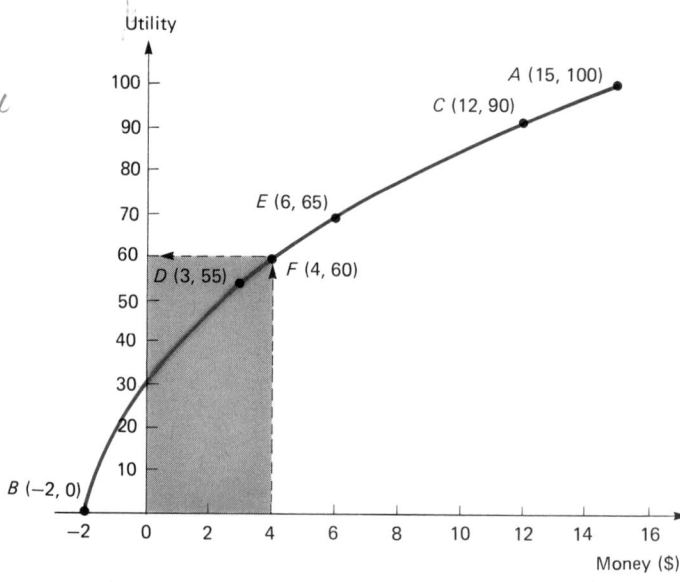

This data is graphed in Figure 4.2 (see points A and B). To build the utility curve, additional points are needed. The utility for $12 will be derived in order to illustrate how to obtain additional points on the curve.

Constructing the utility curve

One way of doing this is to ask the decision maker, whose utility curve is to be constructed, to visualize a hypothetical gambling situation in which the decision maker has the option of investing:

a. Either in a lottery ticket with two possible outcomes: winning $15 (the highest outcome) or losing $2 (the worst outcome).
b. Or in a project that is sure to yield $12.

A gamble

(The situation is similar to the popular TV program "Let's Make a Deal.")

"Let's Make a Deal"

The decision whether or not to take the lottery ticket clearly depends on the chance of making the $15; and it is a personal, subjective decision. Some people will prefer the lottery only if the odds of making $15 are very high; others will take it with lower odds. The management scientist attempts, by trial and error, to find the "*chance* of making $15," to be labeled "*p*," which will make the decision maker *indifferent* between the two options.

Gamble or take the "sure thing"?

This is done in the following manner:

First, the decision maker is asked if he or she *prefers* the $12 certain return over the lottery ticket with an arbitrary probability of, say, *p* = .80. If the decision maker says "yes," *p* is *increased* slowly to *p* = .81, *p* = .82, and so on, until the point that the decision maker is *indifferent* between the sure return and the ticket. If the decision maker

A point of indifference

says "no," the value of p is decreased slowly to the point where the decision maker expresses indifference.

Suppose that the analyst finds that at a probability of $p = .90$, the decision maker is indifferent between the two options. Given this information, the analyst can now find the decision maker's utility for $12, using the indifference Equation 4.1.

> Utility of a Certainty = Expected Utility of the Lottery   (4.1)

In our case:

$$U(\$12) = pU(\$15) + (1 - p)U(-\$2)$$

The assigned values of 100 utiles to $15 and 0 utiles to $-$2 are now introduced into Equation 4.1, as are the predetermined probability values:

$$U(\$12) = p(100) + (1 - p)0 = .9(100) + .1(0) = 90 \text{ utiles}$$

(margin handwritten notes:)
$U = 100$).
$P = .90$
$\$12 = 90 u$

Thus, the utility of $12 is 90 utiles (point C in Figure 4.2).

Similarly, by the use of further hypothetical gambling situations (e.g., $6 for certain versus a lottery with a probability, p, of gaining a yield of $15 and $1 - p$ of $-$2), it is possible to obtain other values for the curves. Let us assume that the utility values for the additional points of $3 and $6 were found to be 55 and 65 respectively. These results are plotted in Figure 4.1 (points D and E). Next, a continuous curve is constructed by connecting all computed points (marked with a dot). This curve describes the decision maker's utility for money. Note that this decision maker is somewhat risk-averse; more money has less utility for him than it has for a risk-taking decision maker (see Figure 4.1).

(margin:) Risk taker or risk averse?

From this graph in Figure 4.2 it is possible to read the utility values for all the monetary payoffs of Table 4.5. These utility values are shown in Table 4.6. For example, to read the utility value of $4 in Figure 4.1, go from point 4 on the horizontal axis up (follow the arrows) to point F; then turn 90 degrees to the left and go to the utility axis (reaching it at 60). The coordinates of point F are thus 4 and 60 which means that $4 is equivalent to 60 utiles.

TABLE 4.6
Utility values for the profits of Table 4.5

Alternatives	States of nature	.2		.5		.3		EMV	Expected utility (EU)
		s_1		s_2		s_3			
		$	Utiles	$	Utiles	$	Utiles		
a_1		12	90	6	65	4	60	6.6	68.5
a_2		15	100	3	55	-2	0	3.9	47.5
a_3		6.5	70	6.5	70	6.5	70	6.5	70 ← Maximum EU

It is now possible to compute the expected utility value (EU) of the various alternatives.

$$EU(a_1) = 90(.2) + 65(.5) + 60(.3) = 68.5$$
$$EU(a_2) = 100(.2) + 55(.5) + 0(.3) = 47.5$$
$$EU(a_3) = 70(.2) + 70(.5) + 70(.3) = \boxed{70} \vartriangleleft$$

The third alternative has the highest expected utility, and is therefore recommended.

A nonlinear relationship

Note that the alternative with the highest EMV, (a_1), does not have the highest EU. This is not surprising due to the nonlinear relationship that exists between monetary values and utility for this decision maker. Alternative a_1 is more speculative than a_3. The decision maker indicated, through personal preferences, that he or she is less likely to gamble. The shape of the utility curve tells us that this decision maker is averse to risk.

Summary

Utility theory has been found to be a useful instrument in explaining decision making under risk.

While the theoretical value of the utility concept is apparent, its implementation is no simple task. Besides the frequent skepticism expressed by managers, there are several measurement problems that must be overcome to obtain utility curves; for example, resolving issues of whether or not the curves remain stable over time.

4.2 MULTIPLE GOALS

The analysis of management decisions aims at evaluating, to the greatest possible extent, how far each alternative advances management towards its goals. Unfortunately, managerial problems are seldom evaluated in terms of a single goal such as profit maximization. Today's management systems are becoming more and more complex, and a single goal is rare. Instead, managers want to attain simultaneous goals, some of which conflict with each other. Therefore it is often necessary to analyze each alternative in light of its potential impact on several goals.

No single goal

For example, consider a profit-making firm. In addition to making money, the company wants to grow, to develop its products and its employees, to provide job security to its workers, and to serve the community. Managers want to satisfy the shareholders and at the same time enjoy high salaries and expense accounts, while employees wish to increase their "take-home" pay and fringe benefits. Needless to say, some of these goals complement each other while others are in direct

Complementary and conflicting goals

conflict. Add to this social, legal, and ethical considerations and the system of goals begins to look quite complex.

    The normative approach in decision theory is based on comparing a single measure of effectiveness. Therefore, it is necessary to transform, mathematically, the multiple goal problem into a single goal problem prior to the final comparison.

A transformation is required

    Before presenting a methodology for dealing with the multiple goal situation, it will be worthwhile to discuss some of the difficulties involved.

1. It is usually difficult to obtain an explicit statement of the organization's goals.
2. Various participants assess the importance (priorities) of the various goals differently.
3. The decision maker may change the importance assigned to specific goals with the passage of time or different decision situations.
4. Goals and subgoals are viewed differently at various levels of the organization and in various departments.
5. The goals themselves are dynamic in response to continuous change in the organization and its environment.

Some difficulties

    In spite of these difficulties, it is instructive to examine some methods that can be used to resolve the multiple goal situation.

Expression of goals as requirements (constraints)[3]

    One approach is to express all goals, except the most important one, in terms of system *requirements*.

Goals as system requirements

    Example The ABC Corporation expresses its goals in the following manner: major goal—cost minimization. All other goals are expressed as constraints:

1. Maintain *at least* a 15 percent market share.
2. Profit should be *no less* than $2 per share.
3. Sales volume should top last year's by *at least* 6 percent.
4. Consumer complaints should *not increase*.
5. Product quality should *not decrease*.
6. Employee turnover should *decrease* by 1 percent.

Conversion to a single external scale

    Multiple goals can sometimes be expressed by a single measure such as dollars. In this case, all of the outcomes, as well as the costs of the alternatives, should be expressed in the same measure.

A single external scale

---

[3] This approach is used in the application of linear programming (Chapter 5).

Example: Change in maintenance policy   Assume that a company is considering a change in their maintenance policy from weekly to biweekly preventive maintenance. The maintenance policy primarily affects breakdowns but also has an impact on maintenance costs, product quality, and spare parts inventory. In this case it may be possible to express the effect of the two alternatives on the various goals (or measures of effectiveness) directly in dollar terms. For example, total weekly cost = $3,000 for maintenance + $600 for product quality losses + $280 for breakdowns = $3,880.

Expressing one goal in terms of another

Goal tradeoffs

Sometimes it is possible to express several goals in terms of one, thus again arriving at a single measure of effectiveness as in the single-external scale conversion above.

Example: Sales and profit increases   The projected outcomes of two alternatives are shown in Table 4.7. The question is: Which

TABLE 4.7
Two outcomes

Alternatives \ Outcomes	Sales increase	Profit increase
a_1	$50,000	9%
a_2	$80,000	4%

alternative is better if both cost the same? To answer this question it is necessary to find a single measure of effectiveness.

Suppose management decides that each 1 percent increase in profit is worth a $10,000 increase in sales. Then $50,000 and $80,000 sales increases are equivalent to a 5 percent and 8 percent increase in profit, respectively, as shown in Table 4.8.

TABLE 4.8
Combined outcomes

Alternatives \ Outcomes	Sales expressed as percent profit	Profit	Total	
a_1	$\dfrac{\$50,000}{\$10,000} \times 1\% = 5\%$	9%	5 + 9 = 14	←*Maximum*
a_2	$\dfrac{\$80,000}{\$10,000} \times 1\% = 8\%$	4%	8 + 4 = 12	

Once the two outcomes are expressed in one measure, we can combine and compare them (14 for a_1, 12 for a_2), then select the most effective (a_1 in this case).

Using a utility or point system

The value of one goal in the previous example was expressed in terms of the other. Another similar method is to express all alternatives in terms of utiles.[4]

A utile scale

Example Two alternatives are considered in light of the attainment of the four different corporate goals shown in Table 4.9. Table 4.10 gives management's personal utility valuation of these goals.

Alternatives \ Corporate goals	Profit	Market share	Sales*	Cash reserves*
a_1	5%	18%	23	.6
a_2	3%	20%	30	.3

* In millions of dollars.

TABLE 4.9
Multiple outcomes

Alternatives \ Corporate goals	Profit	Market share	Sales	Cash reserves	Total utility
a_1	40	60	20	40	160
a_2	25	80	28	30	163 ← *Maximum*

TABLE 4.10
Utility valuation of Table 4.9

Relative weights In the example just presented, utiles were assigned and totaled, assuming that all goals carry the same weight. However, in many organizations, objectives may carry different weights and priorities. Therefore, it is appropriate to adjust the utiles before totaling them.

One way to treat such situations is to compute the weighted total of utiles. For example, Table 4.11 shows the problem of Table 4.10 with weights put on each goal.

A weighted sum

Goals	Profit	Market share	Sales	Cash	Total weighted utility
Weights	2.0	1.2	.4	.8	
a_1	40	60	20	40	192 ← *Maximum*
a_2	25	80	28	30	181.2

TABLE 4.11
Weighted utilities

---

[4] The approach presented in Section 4.1 can be used for assigning utiles. For other methods, see Fishburn [2].

The total weighted utility is then computed, similar to the way that expected value is computed. Each utile is multipled by its relative importance, and the results are totaled.

For a_1: 40(2) + 60(1.2) + 20(.4) + 40(.8) = 192.
For a_2: 25(2) + 80(1.2) + 28(.4) + 30(.8) = 181.2.

Thus, alternative a_1 is superior.

A major problem in such an approach is assessing the relative importance, or priorities, of goals. Various methods such as ranking, pairing, allocating 100 points among the alternatives, and the like can be used. Also the use of experts is recommended (e.g., via the DELPHI method [4]). The interested reader is referred to Fishburn [2] and to Turban and Metersy [10].

A well-known variation of the use of utility is the *point system*. A point system is used by many universities in admission decisions. For example, in order to be admitted into an MBA program the university may require a minimum of 750 "points." These "points" are computed by multiplying the student's grade point average by 100 (e.g., a "B" average is 3.0, or 300 points) and adding the result achieved on the Graduate Management Admission Test (GMAT). Banks also use a point system to determine loan eligibility, and some employers use a point system in their annual performance evaluation to consider several performance variables.

Delphi

The point system

Goal programming

A special method of treating certain multiple goal situations involving problems of linear programming is termed *goal programming*. According to this technique, goals are ranked in order of their importance. For example, profit may be more important than the share of the market. Then allocation decisions are made such that deviations from the goals are minimized. This topic is treated in more detail in Chapter 6.

4.3 DECISION TREES

Decision making as discussed thus far has been limited to a single period: A decision was made at the beginning of the period, and the future consequences were estimated for the end of the period. All the information was presented in the form of a decision table. There are many times, however, when a decision cannot be viewed as an isolated, single-period occurrence, but rather as something that will have an impact during several future periods (e.g., years).

Due to the fact that consequences are measured several times in the future, additional decisions may have to be made before the full impact of the initial decision is known. Therefore, the decision maker must consider the whole series of decisions simultaneously. Such a situation is called a *sequential* or *multiperiod* decision process. Using decision tables to analyze these decisions becomes too cumbersome. The tool that was developed instead is called a *decision tree*,[5] which is basically a graphical exposition of decision tables in the form of a tree.

Decision trees for sequential decisions

Advantages

Decision trees provide a graphical presentation of sequential decision processes. They show, at a glance, when decisions are expected to be made, what the possible consequences are, and what the resultant payoffs will be.

Decisions at a glance

Another advantage is that the results of the computations are depicted directly on the tree, simplifying the analysis.

The composition of a decision tree

A decision tree is composed of the following two elements (see Figure 4.3):

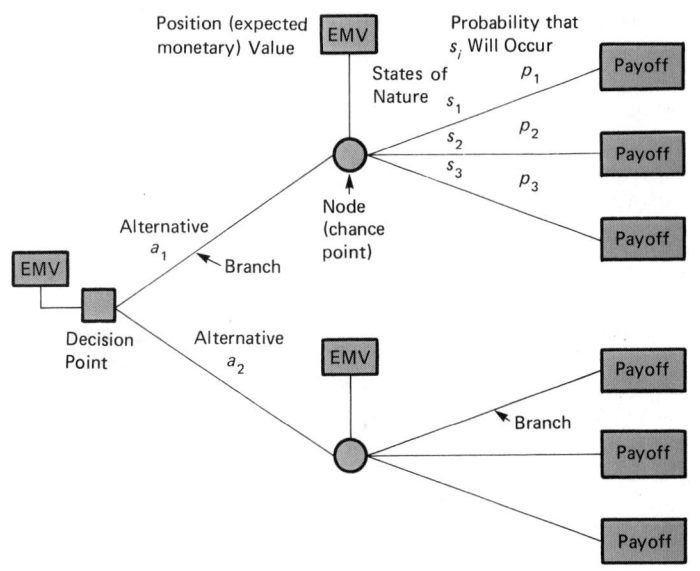

FIGURE 4.3
The general structure of a decision tree

1. *Decision points* At a decision point, usually designated by a square, the decision maker must select *one alternative course of action* from a finite number of available ones. These are shown as branches emerging out of the right side of the decision point. When there is a cost associated with the alternative, it is written along the

Decision and chance points

---

[5] A similar but more complicated tool, *dynamic programming*, will be described in Chapter 9.

branch. Each alternative branch may result in either a payoff, in another decision point, or in a *chance point*.

2. **Chance points** A chance point, designated by a circle, indicates that a chance event is expected at this point in the process. That is, one of a finite number of *states of nature* may occur. The states of nature are shown on the tree as branches to the right of the chance points. Since decision trees depict decision making under risk, the probabilities of the states of nature are assumed to be known and are written above the branches. The states of nature may be followed by payoffs, decision points, or more chance points.

Constructing a tree

A tree grows to the right

A tree is started at the *left* of the page, with one or more decision points. Once the decision point is constructed, all possible alternatives are drawn branching out to the right. Then, a chance point or other decision points are added, corresponding to events or decisions that will occur after the initial decision. Each time a chance point is added, the appropriate states of nature with their corresponding probabilities branch out of it to the right. The tree continues to branch from left to right until the final payoffs are reached. Figure 4.3 shows the general structure of a small tree. Larger trees involve a sequence of several decision and chance points, representing several decision periods, as shown later in both this section and in Section 4.6. The tree shown in Figure 4.3 represents a single decision and as such is equivalent to a decision table.

Example of the equivalence of decision trees and decision tables

Table-tree equivalence

Consider the situation in Table 4.12. (This problem was solved in Chapter 3 by computing the expected value of each alternative. Alternative a_1 was recommended with the highest expected value.) This table is presented as a decision tree in Figure 4.4.

TABLE 4.12
Table 3.1 reproduced

Alternatives	States of nature	.5 Solid growth s_1	.3 Stagnation s_2	.2 Inflation s_3	Expected value
a_1 Bonds		12	6	3	8.4
a_2 Stocks		15	3	−2	8.0
a_3 Time deposits		6.5	6.5	6.5	6.5

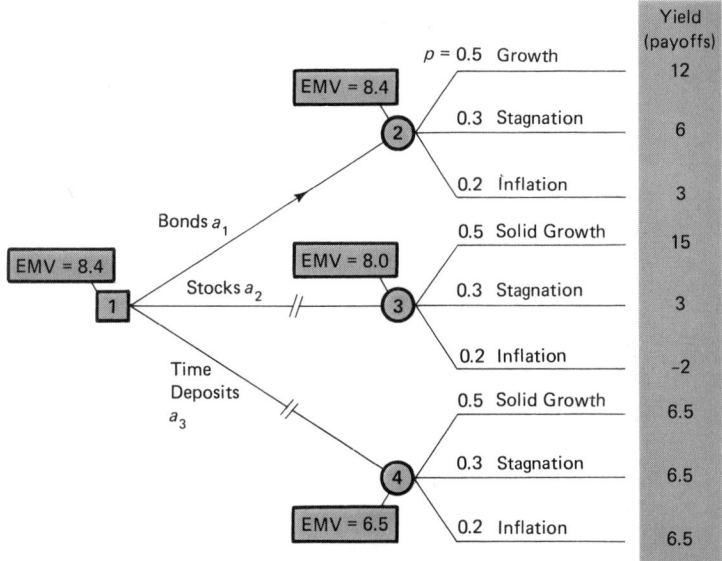

FIGURE 4.4
A decision tree for Table 4.12

Solving a tree In order to solve a tree, it is customary to divide it into segments. Two types of segments are considered: *decision points* with all their alternatives (Figure 4.5a), or *chance points* with all their emerging states of nature (Figure 4.5b).

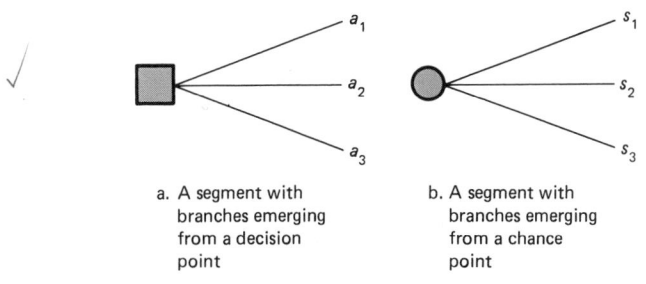

FIGURE 4.5
Segments of a tree

a. A segment with branches emerging from a decision point

b. A segment with branches emerging from a chance point

The solution process starts with those segments ending in the final payoffs, at the *right side of the tree*, and continues to the left, segment by segment, in the reverse order from which it was drawn.

Chance segments

1. *Chance point segments.* The *expected value* of all the states of nature emerging from a chance point must be computed (multiply payoffs by probabilities and sum up the results). The expected value is then written above the chance point inside a rectangle (labeled a *position value* in Figure 4.3). These expected values are considered as payoffs for the next branch to the left.

Position value

Decision segments

2. *Decision point segments.* At a decision point, the payoffs given (or computed) for each alternative are compared and the best one is selected. All others are disregarded. A disregarded alternative is marked by the symbol ‖ directly on the branch (see Figure 4.6).

Solving the tree of Figure 4.4

Computations at a chance point   The segments at the right are considered first. They are all chance points, and therefore *expected values* are computed: The expected values (designated in Figure 4.4 as EMV) are:

For point 2   EMV $= 12(.5) + 6(.3) + 3(.2) = 8.4$.
For point 3   EMV $= 15(.5) + 3(.3) - 2(.2) = 8.0$.
For point 4   EMV $= 6.5(.5) + 6.5(.3) + 6.5(.2) = 6.5$.

Payoffs

The EMVs are entered, above each chance point, inside a rectangle. They are now considered as *payoffs* for the next step.

Computations at a decision point   Figure 4.6 shows the situation in Figure 4.4 after EMVs for all chance points have been computed. At decision point 1, all alternatives are compared with the EMVs considered as payoffs. Alternative a_1 with the highest payoff is recommended.

FIGURE 4.6
Computation at a
decision point

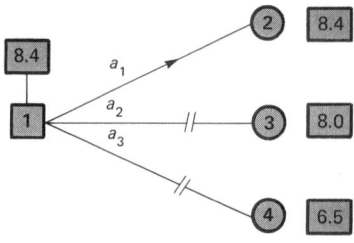

The example just presented showed a decision tree for a single-decision period (equivalent to a decision table). However, decision trees are especially useful in multiperiod situations involving sequential decisions.

The multiperiod case

The multiperiod tree

Decision trees involving a sequence of decisions are nothing but a collection of smaller decision trees, each representing a single time period. All grow horizontally from left to right; the trunk is at the left and the branches at the right. The tree can be extended to the limit of forecasting ability.

Example   The Microflange Company is facing heavy demand for one of its flanges. The existing manufacturing facility is presently working at full capacity on normal shifts. The firm has two options to meet the heavy demand: either instituting overtime, an option that will cost $2,000, or installing new machinery at a cost of $20,000. The choice between the options depends mainly on what happens to sales over the next two years. During the *first year* there is a 70 percent chance that sales will rise and a 30 percent chance that they will fall.

The information given so far is sufficient to start building a decision tree (Figure 4.7 points **1, 2,** and **3**). After one year of operation, management will be faced with another decision (among four possible) which will depend on the action taken initially and on the projection of second year sales.

The decisions after one year

First decision (*point* **4** *in Figure* 4.7)   If a new machine had been installed and sales had risen, then management could either install a second machine or institute overtime. The decision at point **4** depends on the anticipated payoffs after two years. These depend on sales forecasts which can be either high (20 percent chance), medium (70 percent), or low (10 percent). In the event that a second machine is installed, then the anticipated payoffs are $80,000, $60,000, and $50,000, respectively.[6] This information is entered on the right side of the tree. The expected value is then computed ($63,000) and entered above chance point **8**.

Decisions, decisions, decisions!

However, if overtime is instituted, the profits will be $60,000 for high sales, $50,000 for medium sales, and $40,000 for low sales. This information is used to compute the expected value which is then entered at chance point **9** in Figure 4.7 ($53,000).

Second decision   If a new machine had been installed initially and sales had fallen, then the decision maker would be at point **5** after one year. At that point, management would have no choice but to use the existing capacities to the fullest extent. Anticipated results are shown on the tree at point **10**.

Third decision   If overtime had been instituted initially and sales had risen, then management would be at decision point **6** with two alternatives open: install a new machine, or install a new machine *and* use overtime. The anticipated payoffs are shown at points **11** and **12**.

Fourth decision   If overtime had been instituted initially and sales had fallen, then management would be at decision point **7** where only one alternative is assumed to be available: institute overtime. The anticipated results are shown at point **13**.

The problem is to find the best course of action the company should take *initially* and at *intermediate* stages, knowing all the information above.

---

[6] We assume that these figures are, as are the rest of the payoffs and costs in this problem, given in present values, so they can be combined and compared.

FIGURE 4.7
The Microflange Company decision tree

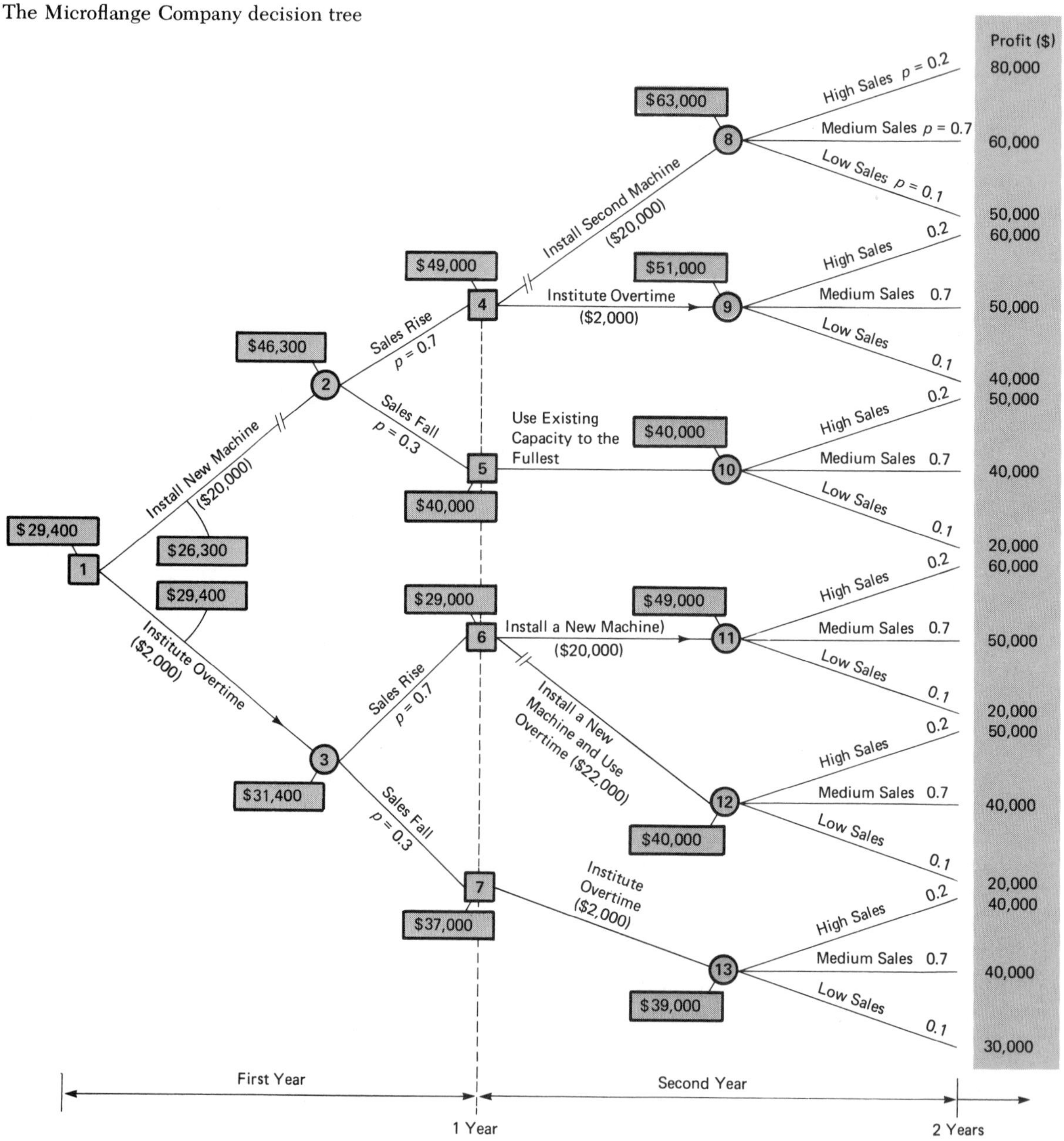

	Profit ($)

High Sales $p = 0.2$ — 80,000

$63,000 — (8) — Medium Sales $p = 0.7$ — 60,000

Low Sales $p = 0.1$ — 50,000

Install Second Machine ($20,000)

$49,000 — |4| — Institute Overtime ($2,000) — $51,000 — (9) — High Sales 0.2 — 60,000

Medium Sales 0.7 — 50,000

Low Sales 0.1 — 40,000

Sales Rise $p = 0.7$

$46,300 — (2)

Sales Fall $p = 0.3$

Use Existing Capacity to the Fullest — $40,000 — (10) — High Sales 0.2 — 50,000

$40,000 — |5| — Medium Sales 0.7 — 40,000

$40,000 — Low Sales 0.1 — 20,000

$29,400 — |1|

Install New Machine ($20,000)

$26,300

$29,400

Institute Overtime ($2,000)

$29,000 — |6| — Install a New Machine) ($20,000) — $49,000 — (11) — High Sales 0.2 — 60,000

Medium Sales 0.7 — 50,000

Low Sales 0.1 — 20,000

Install a New Machine and Use Overtime ($22,000)

$40,000 — (12) — High Sales 0.2 — 50,000

Medium Sales 0.7 — 40,000

Low Sales 0.1 — 20,000

Sales Rise $p = 0.7$

(3)

$31,400

Sales Fall $p = 0.3$

|7| — Institute Overtime ($2,000)

$37,000

$39,000 — (13) — High Sales 0.2 — 40,000

Medium Sales 0.7 — 40,000

Low Sales 0.1 — 30,000

First Year — Second Year

1 Year — 2 Years

Solution

Using the procedure previously outlined, the expected values at all chance points are computed (starting from the right).

For point **8**:

$$\text{EMV} = .2 \times 80{,}000 + .7 \times 60{,}000 + .1 \times 50{,}000 = \$63{,}000$$

For point **9**:

$$\text{EMV} = .2 \times 60{,}000 + .7 \times 50{,}000 + .1 \times 40{,}000 = \$51{,}000$$

Similarly, for the other points the EMV's are:

Point	⑩	⑪	⑫	⑬
EMV	$40,000	$49,000	$40,000	$39,000

Next, the computation moves leftward, thus reaching decision points **4, 5, 6,** and **7.**

Point 4. At this decision point the alternative of a second machine ($63,000 − $20,000 = $43,000 profit) is compared with the alternative of overtime ($51,000 − $2,000 = $49,000 profit). Since the latter is more profitable, it is selected and the EMV of $49,000 is entered above point **4.**

Point 5. There is only one alternative. The expected value of point **10** is thus recorded at point **5.**

Point 6. At this decision point there are two alternatives: install a new machine ($49,000 − $20,000 = $29,000) or overtime plus new machine ($40,000 − $22,000 = $18,000). The first one is better, and so an EMV of $29,000 is recorded at point **6.**

Point 7. There is only one alternative at this point. The EMV from point 13, $39,000, is recorded (less the $2,000 expense) at point **7.**

At this stage only the left side of the tree is considered. This information is presented in Figure 4.8.

Computation of the left side (*Figure 4.8*)

$$\text{EMV of point } 2 = .7 \times \$49{,}000 + .3 \times \$40{,}000 = \$46{,}300$$
$$\text{EMV of point } 3 = .7 \times \$29{,}000 + .3 \times \$37{,}000 = \$31{,}400$$

Finally, decision point **1** is considered:
The expected value of installing a new machine is:

$$\text{EMV} = \$46{,}300 - \$20{,}000 = \$26{,}300$$

The expected value with overtime is:

$$\text{EMV} = \$31{,}400 - \$2{,}000 = \$29{,}400 \quad \leftarrow \text{best}.$$

Thus, it is better to plan now on overtime, for an expected net gain of *$29,400.* The final decision, therefore, is to use overtime this year and, *if*

FIGURE 4.8
Left side of Figure 4.7

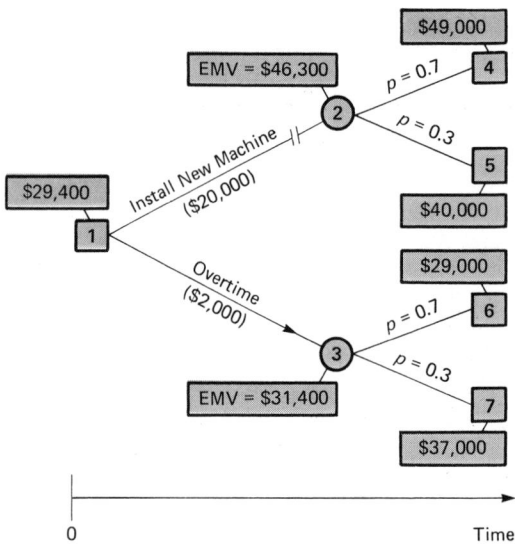

sales rise, install a new machine the second year. If sales fall, however, the overtime should be continued.

Summary

The unique feature of decision trees is that they allow management to view the logical order of a sequence of decisions. They show a clear graphical presentation of the various alternative courses of action and their possible consequences. Using decision trees, management can also examine the impact of a series of decisions (multiperiod decisions) on the objectives of the organization. The graphical presentation helps in understanding the interactions among alternative courses of action, uncertain events, and future consequences.

The computations required in decision trees can usually be done manually; a computer is required only when extremely large and complicated trees are analyzed. For some practical aspects of implementation, consult Magee [5] and [6].

4.4   CONCLUDING REMARKS

The material presented in Part A of Chapter 4 is based upon and supplemental to that of Chapter 3. Three topics were discussed. First, the use of *utility* theory was introduced, permitting subjective assessments of payoffs and the additivity of different payoffs. Second, the difficulty of measuring attainment level when *multiple goals* exist was emphasized, and some techniques of solving this problem were suggested. Finally, the use of a *tree diagram* for decision under risk was shown and evaluated. In Part B of this chapter the use of decision trees will be expanded and Bayes' theorem will be presented.   Bayes' theorem

4.5   PROBLEMS FOR PART A

1. A manager expresses indifference between a certain profit of $5,000 and a venture with a 70 percent chance of making $10,000 and a 30 percent chance of making nothing. If the manager's utility scale was set at 0 utiles for $0, and 100 for $10,000, what is the utility index for $5,000?

2. The manager in Problem 1 is indifferent between a venture that has a 60 percent chance of making $10,000 and a 40 percent chance of making $1,000, and a sure investment that yields $5,000. Find the value of $1,000 in utiles for this manager.

3. Below are the results of a preference test given to an executive:

   a. The executive is indifferent between an investment that will yield a certain $10,000 and a risky venture with a 50 percent chance of $30,000 profit and a 50 percent chance of a *loss* of $1,000.

   b. The executive's utility function for money has the following shape:

Money ($)	−1,000	0	5,000	20,000	30,000
Utility	−2	0	10	20	30

   A new risky venture is proposed. The possible payoffs are *either* $0 or $20,000. The probabilities of the gain cannot be determined. Find what probability combination of $0 and $20,000 would make the executive indifferent to the certain $10,000.

4. A manager has an opportunity of investing $3,000 in a venture that has a .2 chance of making nothing, a .3 chance of making $2,000, a .2 chance of making $4,000, and a .3 chance of making $6,000. Her utilities for each of the outcomes are 0 for $0, 25 for $2,000, 35 for $4,000, and 40 for making $6,000. Draw the manager's utility curve and advise her on making the investment.

5. A plant manager has a utility of 10 for $20,000, 6 for $11,000, 0 for $0, and −10 for a loss of $5,000.

   a. The plant manager is indifferent between receiving $11,000 for certain and a lottery with a .6 chance of winning $5,000 and a .4 chance of winning $20,000. What is the utility of $5,000 for the manager? Construct the manager's utility curve.

   b. Using this curve, find the "certainty equivalent" for the following gamble (i.e., the amount of cash that will make the manager *indifferent* to the game):

Payoff	Probability
$−2,000	.2
0	.3
3,000	.4
10,000	.1

   c. What probability combination of $0 and $20,000 would make the manager indifferent to the certain $11,000?

   d. The manager is facing a decision about buying a new production machine that can bring a net profit of $15,000 (80 percent chance) or a loss of $1,000 (20 percent chance); alternatively, the manager can use the old machine and make a $10,000 profit. Use the utility curve to find which alternative the manager should select. Specify all necessary assumptions.

6. A survey of 10 physicians, 50 patients, and 20 nurses shows that each group allocated 100 "units of worth" among the four stated objectives of a hospital as follows:

Objectives	Physicians	Patients	Nurses
A.............	10	30	20
B............	20	20	20
C............	50	30	20
D	20	20	40
Total ...	100	100	100

a. Assuming that all participants are considered to be equal, find the relative importance of the various objectives.

b. Assume that physicians are considered twice as important as nurses and nurses are three times as important as patients. Find the relative importance of the various objectives.

7. EDX Electronic Corporation can produce either product A, which will result in a 23 percent share of the market and a net profit of 7 percent, or product B which will result in increasing the company's share of the market to 27 percent and a net profit of 5.5 percent. If the company considers each percent of net profit as important as a 2 percent share of the market, which product should the company produce?

8. Given below are the results of three years of operations at Computer Services Corporation:

Measure	1978	1979	1980
Sales (in million $)	6.0	6.6	7.2
Share of market (%).......	15.0	13.5	16.5
Net profit ($ per share)	2.0	1.8	1.4
Equity per share ($).......	4.0	4.2	4.8

The company's stated policy is that the relative importance of the objectives is as follows:

a. Net profit is the most important objective.
b. Equity per share is half as important as net profit.
c. Sales are 1.2 times more important than equity per share.
d. Share of the market is .4 times as important as net profit.

Which year was the most successful for the company's operations? Use 1978 as the base year.

9. International University uses a mathematical model for the initial screening of law school applicants. The variables considered are:

a. The Law School Admission Test (LSAT), which has a possible score between 200 and 800.
b. Grade point average (GPA on 0–4 scale).
c. An essay score on the LSAT that can vary from 0 to 80.
d. The undergraduate school attended by the applicant which is evaluated between 1 (poor) and 5 (excellent).
e. The applicant's involvement in extra curricular activities which is valued from 0 (nothing) to 10 (extremely active).

The weights for the variables are: LSAT = .4, GPA = .4, essay = .1, undergraduate school = .05, extra curricular activities = .05.

John and Mary applied to the school; the information available on both is given below:

	LSAT	GPA	Essay	Under-graduate school	Extra activities
John ...	500	3.8	60	2	6
Mary...	600	3.0	72	4	6

Use a single measure of performance to evaluate the two candidates. Which candidate is better?

10. a. Write the following decision table in tree form:

Alternatives \ Futures	Fire	No fire
Insure	$ 100	$100
Do not insure	$8,000	$ 0

These figures are cost data.
There is a .01 chance for a fire.

b. What action should an individual take to minimize cost?

11. Given the decision tree below, find the best alternative and its expected value. The outcomes shown are *costs* and the investment expenses are in parentheses.

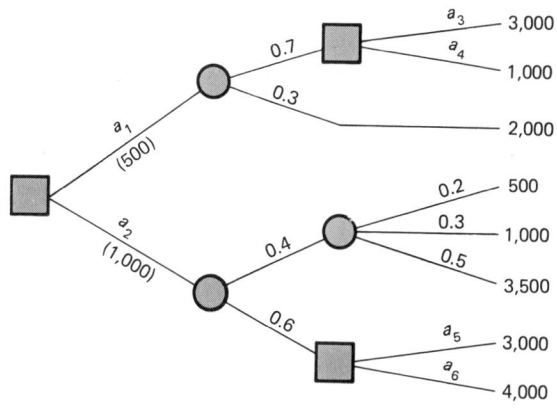

	Oil price		
	High	Very high	Extremely high
Sun I.......	−50,000	73,000	500,000
Sun II.....	138,000	−100,000	60,000

The company economist estimates that the chances that oil prices will be high are 60 percent, very high 30 percent, and extremely high 10 percent. What device should the company develop if it is interested in maximizing profit?

a. Present as a decision tree.

b. Solve the tree; find the best alternative.

14. If you attend all class sessions, your probability of passing the course is .8; but if you only attend randomly, your probability of passing the course is .5. If you fail, you may take a makeup exam where the probabilities of passing are .6 if you attended in full and .1 if you attended at random. If passing the course is worth 5 utiles, but, in terms of energy, attending full time "costs" 3 utiles and attending randomly "costs" 1 utile, which attendance pattern should you adopt?

Note: Assume that all failing students will take the makeup exam. The utility of failing is zero.

15. An oil explorer, commonly called a wildcatter, must decide whether to drill a well or sell his rights to a particular exploration site. The desirability of drilling depends upon whether there is oil beneath the surface. Before drilling, the wildcatter has the option of taking seismographic readings which will give him further geological and geophysical information. This information will enable him to deduce whether subsurface structures usually associated with oil fields exist in this particular location. However, some uncertainty about the presence of oil will still exist after seismic testing because oil is sometimes found where no subsurface structure is detected and vice versa.

The wildcatter estimates that the cost of drilling a well would be $250,000 (in net present value terms, after making allowance for all taxes). The yield that would be expected

12. Given a decision tree, as shown in the figure below:

a. Write the equivalent table form.

b. Find the action that will minimize total cost (assume data are present values; use the tree presentation).

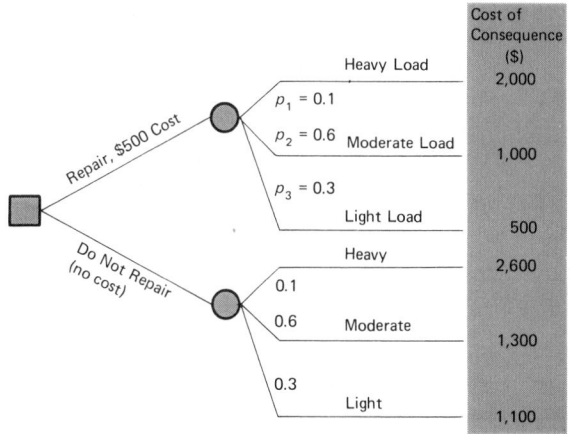

13. The future of solar energy depends on oil prices. The ABC Company is considering the development of one of two possible home solar energy devices: Sun I and Sun II.

The anticipated profits as they relate to oil prices are shown in the table below:

from a typical oil well is estimated to be $1,200,000 (in net present value terms, net of all taxes and operating costs but excluding drilling costs). Seismic tests would cost $50,000 per test.

The wildcatter could sell his rights for $230,000 before either drilling or testing. However, if he should decide to carry out seismographic readings and no subsurface structure is indicated, the site will be considered almost worthless by other wildcatters, in which case he will barely be able to sell the rights for $10,000. If substructure is indicated by the test, he can sell his rights for $300,000. If no oil is found, the value of the exploration site is considered to be zero.

The probability of getting oil from the site without any test is 30 percent. If he carries out the seismic test, he feels that the test will indicate subsurface structure with a 40 percent probability. In case of structure, he can drill with a 65 percent chance of finding oil. In the case of no structure, he can drill with a 75 percent chance of finding the well dry.

What should the wildcatter do? Draw a decision tree to solve the problem.

16. ABC's growth rate in past years has been slower than the average for the industry. The company is considering two alternatives to rectify the situation: (1) expand the number of product lines and (2) increase inventories for better service.

There is a 70 percent chance that the economy will go into a growth stage, in which case there is an 80 percent chance for increased demand. If demand increases, a profit of $1,000,000 is expected; however if demand does not increase, only $800,000 profit is anticipated. If inventories are increased, a profit of $900,000 is anticipated in case of high demand; otherwise, $600,000 will be realized.

In the event the economy does not grow, a mild recession is anticipated. In this case, there is a 50–50 percent chance for either high or low demand. The profits are then estimated to be:

Expansion and high demand	$750,000
Expansion and low demand	600,000
Inventories and high demand	550,000
Inventories and low demand	400,000

Profit figures are forecast for after one year of operation.

A product expansion policy requires $100,000 in cash now. Keeping inventories will cost $12,000 for the year, payable at year-end.

The company is using an interest rate of 10 percent for its analysis.

Should the company expand its products or work with inventories?

17. ABC Corp. operates two complex production lines on an eight-hour per day basis. These lines fail frequently due to the extensive work load. The daily probability of line no. 1 failing is .10 and that of line no. 2 is .15. When any line fails, the cost if $100 each hour; when both lines are down, at the same time, the cost is $140/hour.

The company is trying to decide whether to hire one or two repair persons. The time for one person to repair a machine is five hours. If two are hired they can work either as a team or individually on separate machines. If they work as a team the repair time reduces to three hours. If a repair person costs $10 per hour, what would you recommend ABC do?

18. A machine shop received an order for 2,000 units to be made on one of its automated machines. This is a multi-station operation and once it is started it runs without interruption. The machine shop makes $2 profit on each part of acceptable quality. Each unit which is classified as "defective" needs rework at a cost of $3.50 before it is considered "acceptable."

Historical data indicates that if the machine is used without any special preparation it produces either 1 percent defectives (this happens 50 percent of the time), 2 percent defectives (this happens 30 percent of the time), 3 percent defectives (this happens 12 percent of the time), or 5 percent defectives in the remaining cases. With a minor adjustment that costs $42, the defective rate above 2 percent is reduced to 2 percent; with a major adjustment (cost $100), the defective rate is 1 percent.

What adjustment policy should the machine shop adopt in order to maximize profit?

PART B: EXTENSIONS

4.6   BAYES' THEOREM

The key to the management science approach to decision making under risk is the assessment of the probabilities of the states of nature. In today's complex world, management may find this task more and more difficult.

In evaluating a decision under risk, the decision maker may come up with an *initial* assessment of the probabilities (called the "prior" probabilities) of the states of nature and solve the problem using these. However, the decision maker may question the accuracy of the probabilities, especially if they were subjectively derived. At this stage the decision maker has the option of getting *additional information* (via research, survey, experimentation, or even spying) which should be considered in the decision process.

Additional information can result in one of two events: *either* the uncertainty is *completely removed*, in which case the decision will be made under certainty (perfect information), *or* the additional information is *imperfect*. That is, the decision maker cannot predict with certainty the state of nature that will occur, but the decision maker can *revise* his or her initial (*prior*) assessment of the probabilities. The revised probabilities are then called the *posterior* (after) probabilities. The statistical tool used to perform such an analysis is termed *Bayes' theorem*. A schematic presentation of such an analysis is shown in Figure 4.9. The revision process is demonstrated next.

Additional information

Imperfect information

Prior and posterior probabilities

Bayes' theorem

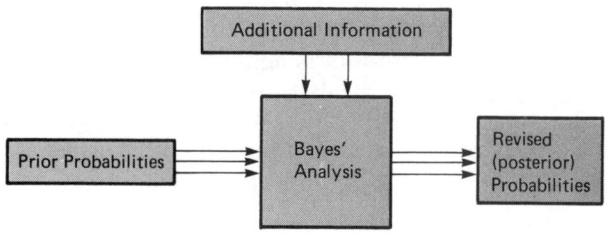

FIGURE 4.9
The Bayes' analysis

How to revise probabilities

Example   American Ecology, Inc., estimates that their new product, E-3, has a .8 chance (80 percent) of being a "winner." Thus, there is a .2 chance of its being a "loser." However, before the company makes a production commitment it would like to further investigate the situation. Hence, the possibility of calling upon a market researcher to conduct a special survey of the market is being evaluated.

From previous experience it is known that such a special survey can either *predict success, predict failure,* or be *inconclusive.* Statistically, it is known that of all the new products that were successful, 70 percent of the time the surveys correctly predicted success (*S*), 10 percent of the time they falsely predicted failure (*F*), and 20 percent of the time they were inconclusive (*I*). On the other hand, an examination of all the cases that were failures (losers) indicated that in 85 percent of these cases the surveys correctly predicted failure, in 10 percent they were inconclusive, and success was incorrectly predicted in the remaining 5 percent. This information is summarized in Table 4.13.

TABLE 4.13
Reliability of the surveys

	Actual state of products	
Results of Survey	Winners (*W*)	Losers (*L*)
Predicted success (*S*)	.70	.05
Inconclusive (*I*).	.20	.10
Predicted failure (*F*).	.10	.85
Total.	1.00	1.00

Conditional
probabilities

The probabilities in Table 4.13 are *conditional probabilities*[7] and indicate the *reliability of the surveys to prospective customers.*

Formulation Let *P(W)* be the prior probability of the product being a winner. Given:

P(W) = .80.
P(L) = .20 (the probability of the product being a loser)

The conditional probabilities of Table 4.13 are:

1. *In the event the product is actually a winner:*
    $P(S/W)$ = probability of the survey predicting success, given the product is actually a winner. $P(S/W)$ = .70.
    $P(I/W)$ = the probability of the survey being inconclusive, given the product is actually a winner. $P(I/W)$ = .20.
    $P(F/W)$ = the probability of the survey predicting failure, given the product is actually a winner. $P(F/W)$ = .10.
2. *In the event the product is actually a loser:*

    $P(S/L)$ = probability of the survey predicting success (given . . .) = .05.
    $P(I/L)$ = probability that the survey is inconclusive (given . . .) = .10.
    $P(F/L)$ = probability of the survey predicting failure (given . . .) = .85.

---

[7] A conditional probability is the probability of a certain event occurring *given* the occurrence of some other event (see Appendix B).

The point to remember here is that all this information is known *before* the survey is actually taken.

Revision of the probabilities of the states of nature   Suppose the survey is taken and it predicts success. The prior probability of $P(W)$ will be changed now to a posterior probability, $P(W/S)$, which is the probability of the product being a winner *given* that the survey predicts success. This probability can be computed by using the Bayes' formula for two variables as given in Equation 4.2:

$$P(W/S) = \frac{P(W)P(S/W)}{P(S)} = \frac{P(W)P(S/W)}{P(W)P(S/W) + P(L)P(S/L)} \qquad (4.2)$$

This formula is adapted from the general formula for Bayes' theorem, Equation 4.3:

$$P(N_i/B) = \frac{P(N_i)P(B/N_i)}{P(B)}$$

$$= \frac{P(N_i)P(B/N_i)}{P(N_1)P(B/N_1) + P(N_2)P(B/N_2) + \cdots + P(N_n)P(B/N_n)} \qquad (4.3)$$

where:

B = outcome predicted by the research (or new information) which is, in our example, either success (S), inconclusive (I), or failure (F).

N_i = A possible state of nature (e.g., either a winner (W) or loser (L) in our example).

i = 1, 2, 3, . . . n, where n = the number of states (two states here, winner and loser).

Equation 4.3 states that the posterior probabilities of the states of nature (N_i: winner or loser), after observing some survey evidence (B: success, inconclusive, or failure), is proportional to the product of the prior probability of N_i and the conditional probability of B given state N_i.

Computing the revised probabilities

A. *In the event the survey predicts success:* Using Equation 4.2 we get:

$$P(W/S) = \frac{.8 \times .7}{.8 \times .7 + .2 \times .05} = \frac{.56}{.57} = .9825$$

That is, the probability of a winner is increased from 80 to 98.25 percent due to the fact that the additional information predicted success. Similarly:

$$P(L/S) = \frac{P(L)P(S/L)}{P(L)P(S/L) + P(W)P(S/W)} = \frac{.2 \times .05}{.2 \times .05 + .8 \times .7} = \frac{.01}{.57} = .0175$$

It is possible to compute $P(L/S)$ in a shorter manner. Since the product can be either a winner or a loser, then $P(W/S) + P(L/S)$ must sum to 1.0. Therefore:

$$P(L/S) = 1 - P(W/S) = 1 - .9825 = .0175$$

An important question that one may ask is: What is the probability of the survey predicting success? This probability is designated $P(S)$ and is computed from Equation 4.4.

$$P(S) = P(W)P(S/W) + P(L)P(S/L) \qquad (4.4)$$

Note that this value is exactly the denominator in Equation 4.2. In our example:

$$P(S) = .8 \times .7 + .2 \times .05 = .57$$

B. *In the event the survey is inconclusive:* Using Equation 4.3 we get:

$$P(W/I) = \frac{P(W)P(I/W)}{P(W)P(I/W) + P(L)P(I/L)} = \frac{.8 \times .2}{.8 \times .2 + .2 \times .1} = \frac{.16}{.18} = .8889$$

Similarly,

$$P(L/I) = 1 - .8889 = .1111$$

Also, the probability of the survey predicting inconclusiveness, $P(I)$, is computed as .18 (the denominator of the $P(W/I)$ equation).

C. *In the event the survey predicts failure:*

$$P(W/F) = \frac{P(W)P(F/W)}{P(W)P(F/W) + P(L)P(F/L)} = \frac{.8 \times .1}{.8 \times .1 + .2 \times .85} = \frac{.08}{.25} = .32$$

(Notice the drastic revision, from 80 percent to 32 percent!) And similarly,

$$P(L/F) = 1 - \frac{.08}{.25} = \frac{.17}{.25} = .68$$

The chance of the survey predicting failure, $P(F) = .25$ (the denominator of the $P(W/F)$ equation).

What will the survey predict? We showed that it is possible to revise the initial probabilities *without actually taking* the survey. Of course the answers that we received are *conditional, depending on the outcome of the survey.* For example, *if* the survey predicts success, then the probability of having a winner, $P(W/S)$, is 98.25 percent, and so on. In decision making it is important to find out, *before* the survey is taken, the chance that they survey will predict success, failure, or will be inconclusive. In deriving the solution above it was found that:

Revision without the survey

$P(S)$ = probability that the survey will indicate "success" = .57.
$P(I)$ = probability that the survey will be inconclusive = .18.
$P(F)$ = probability that the survey will indicate "failure" = .25.

Note that since these are the only possible survey outcomes, they must sum to 1.0.

Figures 4.10 and 4.11 summarize the process and the results obtained in the example above.

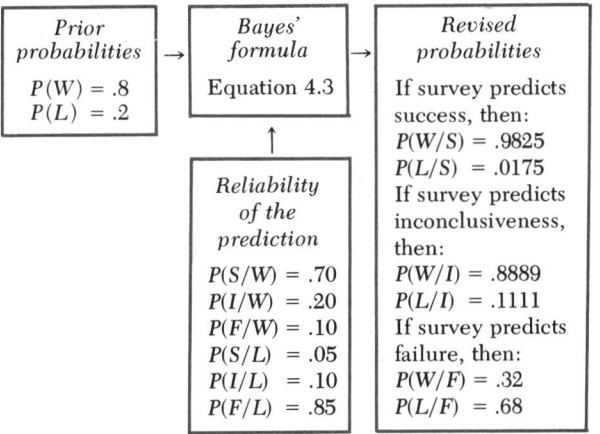

FIGURE 4.10
Summary of the Bayes' process

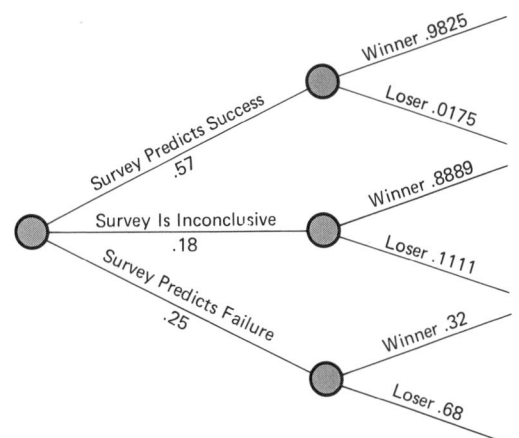

FIGURE 4.11
Tree representation of the Bayes' process

Managerial application of revised probabilities—Decision policy

Bayes' theorem is a procedure that is used for revising the probabilities of the states of nature through the acquisition and manipulation of additional information. The revised probabilities, however, depend on the nature of the additional information, which is known only after the information is acquired. For this reason, if we analyze a situation prior to the actual acquisition of the information, we cannot prescribe the best alternative. Instead, we derive a *decision policy* or *strategy*.

A *decision policy* does not recommend a particular alternative as best. Instead, it recommends several specific alternatives, one for every

A policy; a strategy

possible outcome of the additional information. Then the decision policy can be presented in the form of a decision tree.

The use of revised probabilities in a decision policy involves 8 steps. These steps are:

Step 1. The decision situation is evaluated with the prior probabilities.

Step 2. Assuming that it is impossible to obtain perfect information, the possibility of acquiring reliable partial information is checked.

Step 3. Revised (posterior) probabilities are computed, one for each possible outcome of the research.

Step 4. The probabilities of each of the research outcomes are computed.

Step 5. All information is entered on a decision tree. Expected values are computed accordingly.

Step 6. A decision is made regarding whether or not to acquire the additional information.

Step 7. If the decision is *not* to acquire the additional information, then a choice is made immediately on the best alternative.

Step 8. If a decision is made to acquire additional information, then the research is undertaken. Only after that, based on the result of the research, is the selection of an alternative made.

Example The marketing department of Production Unlimited, Inc., is considering whether or not to develop a new product. All the relevant information is shown in Table 4.14.

TABLE 4.14
Marketing payoffs (dollars)

Alternatives	States of nature	.2 A	.5 B	.3 C	Expected value	
a_1 Develop		300,000	200,000	−600,000	−20,000	
a_2 Do not develop		0	0	0	0	← Best

Solution

Step 1. Initial evaluation Using the prior probabilities, the expected values can be computed. Accordingly, the product *should not* be developed since a loss of $20,000, on the average, is expected if the product is developed.

Step 2. Acquiring partial information Since Production Unlimited is unable to obtain *perfect information*, they have decided to settle for less than perfect information. Thus, a consultant has been called upon to predict, through a survey, what state of nature, in the consultant's opinion, will occur. The consultant asks $50,000 for the survey. The past record of the consultant indicates that the consultant's surveys have the prediction reliabilities shown in Table 4.15.

TABLE 4.15
Consultant's reliability

	Actual state of nature		
	A	B	C
Survey predicted A (call this prediction, A_p)	$P(A_p/A) = .80$	$P(A_p/B) = .10$	$P(A_p/C) = .10$
Survey predicted B (call this prediction, B_p)	$P(B_p/A) = .10$	$P(B_p/B) = .90$	$P(B_p/C) = .20$
Survey predicted C (call this prediction, C_p)	$P(C_p/A) = .10$	$P(C_p/B) = 0$	$P(C_p/C) = .70$

For example, of all the past cases in which A actually occurred, 80 percent of the time the survey correctly predicted that A would occur, 10 percent of the time the wrong prediction of B was made, and 10 percent of the time the wrong prediction of C was made.

Should the consultant be used? Management must now decide whether or not to use the consultant. Then they must decide about the new product (a_1—develop, a_2—do not develop). The situation is shown in the form of a decision tree in Figure 4.12.

Two decisions

The upper part of the tree shows the information presented in Table 4.14. The lower part of the tree presents the situation of using the consultant. There exist three branches: branch A_p for when the survey predicts A, branch B_p for when the survey predicts B, and branch C_p for when the survey predicts C.

Step 3. Revision of the probabilities Given (in Table 4.14) the prior probabilities, and the reliability of the survey (Table 4.15), the revised probabilities can be calculated with the aid of Equation 4.3:

For branch A_p:

$$P(A/A_p) = \frac{P(A)P(A_p/A)}{P(A)P(A_p/A) + P(B)P(A_p/B) + P(C)P(A_p/C)}$$

$$= \frac{.2 \times .8}{.2 \times .8 + .5 \times .1 + .3 \times .1} = \frac{.16}{.24} = .667$$

$$P(B/A_p) = \frac{.5 \times .1}{.5 \times .1 + .2 \times .8 + .3 \times .1} = \frac{.05}{.24} = .208$$

$$P(C/A_p) = \frac{.3 \times .1}{.3 \times .1 + .2 \times .8 + .5 \times .1} = \frac{.03}{.24} = .125$$

FIGURE 4.12
A decision tree for
Bayes' analysis—general
structure

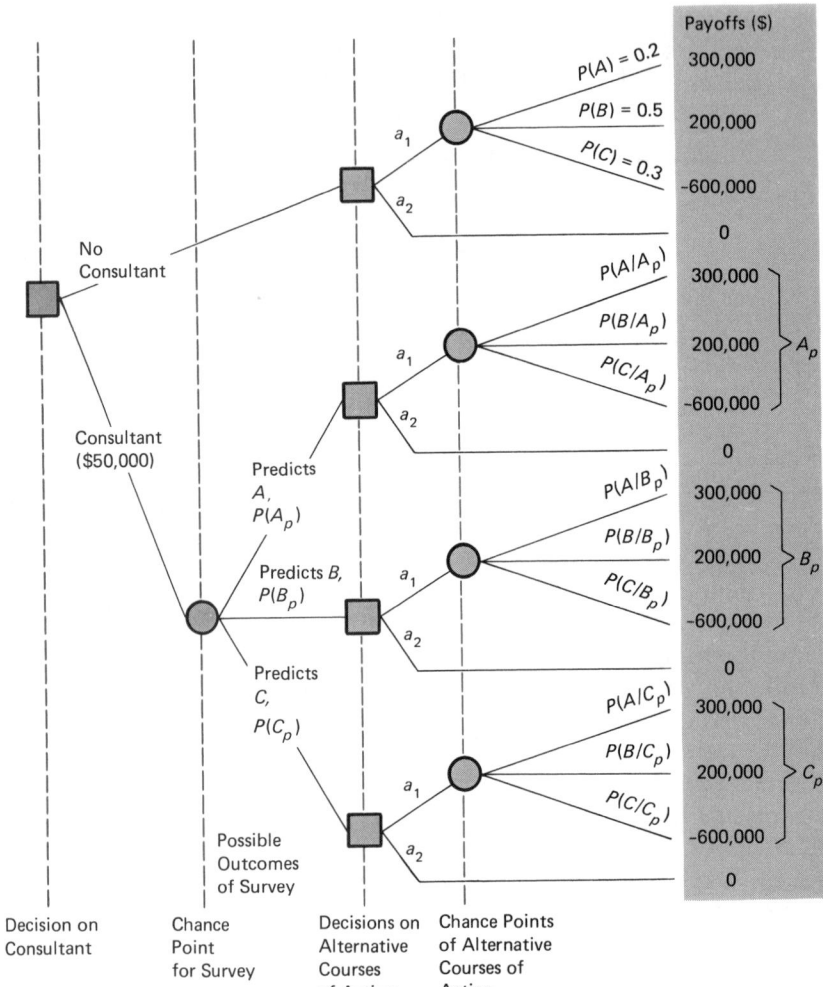

For branch B_p:

$$P(A/B_p) = \frac{.2 \times .1}{.2 \times .1 + .5 \times .9 + .3 \times .2} = \frac{.02}{.53} = .038$$

$$P(B/B_p) = \frac{.45}{.53} = .849$$

$$P(C/B_p) = \frac{.06}{.53} = .113$$

For branch C_p:

$$P(A/C_p) = \frac{.2 \times .1}{.2 \times .1 + .5 \times 0 + .3 \times .7} = \frac{.02}{.23} = .087$$

$$P(B/C_p) = 0$$

$$P(C/C_p) = \frac{.21}{.23} = .913$$

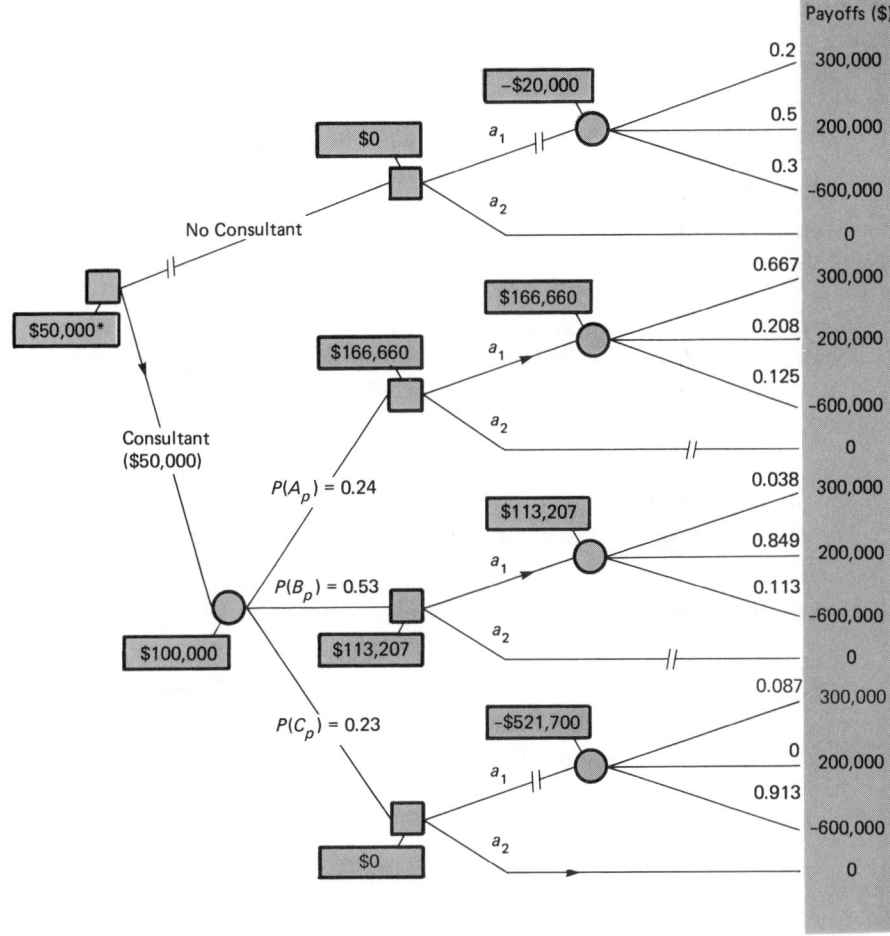

Payoffs ($)

FIGURE 4.13
Decision analysis with revised probabilities

* Use of consultant is recommended.

This information is entered on the appropriate chance points of the decision tree in Figure 4.13.

Step 4. Predicting the result of the survey In order to determine whether or not to use the consultant, it is necessary to use the probabilities that the consultant's survey will actually predict events A_p, B_p, or C_p. These probabilities (derived above as the denominators of the Bayes' equations) are:

$$P(A_p) = .24$$
$$P(B_p) = .53$$
$$P(C_p) = .23$$

This information is entered on the left side chance point of the tree in Figure 4.13. It is now possible to analyze the decision tree in order to decide whether to use the consultant or not.

Step 5. Compute expected values The expected values at all chance points are computed. Then the best alternative at every decision point is selected. If the consultant is not used, the expected value (top branch) is zero. If the consultant is used, the expected value (*after* paying $50,000 for the consultant's services) is:

$$.24(\$166,660) + .53(\$113,207) + .23(\$0) - \$50,000 = \$50,000.$$

Step 6. Decision about the consultant Since the expected value of using the consultant will increase profits by $50,000, the survey should be undertaken.

Step 7. (Not applicable here.)

Step 8. Selection of an alternative course of action The selection of a final course of action depends on what the survey indicates. The decision policy is:

If the survey indicates A_p, alternative a_1 should be taken.
If the survey indicates B_p, alternative a_1 should be taken.
If the survey indicates C_p, alternative a_2 should be taken.

The value of imperfect (sample, or partial) information

The value of imperfect information

The information collected in Bayes' analysis is less than perfect, since its prediction reliability is not 100 percent. Therefore, it is interesting to determine the value of such information. The expected value, per decision, of the imperfect information (EVII) is computed (for the case of maximization[8]) as:

EVII

$$EVII = \begin{bmatrix} \text{Best expected value of} \\ \text{the decision } with \text{ the} \\ \text{imperfect information} \\ \text{(revised probabilities)} \\ before \text{ payment is made} \\ \text{for this information.} \end{bmatrix} - \begin{bmatrix} \text{Best expected value of} \\ \text{the decision using the} \\ \text{prior probabilities.} \end{bmatrix}$$

In our example:

Expected value with imperfect information (revised probabilities)
$= 100,000$
Expected value with prior probabilities
$= 0$

Thus, EVII $= \$100,000 - 0 = \$100,000$. Since the information in this case costs only $50,000, it should be acquired. As in the case of EVPI, here too we get an indication regarding the upper limit that management should be willing to pay for the additional information. Note that the expected value of imperfect information is *smaller than* the expected

EVII < EVPI

---

[8] In the case of minimization:

$$EVII = \begin{bmatrix} \text{Best expected cost} \\ \text{using prior} \\ \text{probabilities} \end{bmatrix} - \begin{bmatrix} \text{Best expected cost} \\ \text{using revised} \\ \text{probabilities.} \end{bmatrix}$$

value of perfect information. The reason for this is that the imperfect information is less reliable. The value of perfect information serves as an *upper limit* for the value of imperfect information. The ratio of EVII/EVPI is called the *efficiency* of the imperfect information.   Efficiency

Note: All the EVPI and EVII discussion assumes the decision maker uses the expected value criterion of choice.

4.7 PROBLEMS FOR PART B

19. Management is considering replacing an energy-saving device with a new one. The new device has a probability of 60 percent of being superior to the old one. A testing service is called upon to test it.

From experience it is known that when a new device was actually superior, the testing service predicted this superiority in 80 percent of the cases. However, when the new device was really inferior, the testing service predicted it to be superior 50 percent of the time.

a. Suppose a test is undertaken and superiority for the new device is predicted. What will management's revised probabilities be of the device being superior?
b. Suppose the test indicates that the device is inferior. How would the probabilities be changed now?
c. What is the probability that the test will indicate a superior device?

20. A patient calls her doctor complaining that she is sick. Based on the described symptoms and the knowledge of the kind of diseases currently epidemic in the city, the physician suspects that there is a 40 percent chance that the patient has disease D_1 and a 60 percent chance that she has disease D_2.

Upon arrival at the physician's office the patient is subjected to a test which has either a *negative* or a *positive* result.

The physician knows that there is a .6 likelihood that the results discovered in the test are associated with D_1. That is, in all past cases of D_1, the test was positive 60 percent of the time. Also, the physician knows that there is only a .2 likelihood that the results are associated with D_2.

a. Find the revised probabilities of D_1 and D_2. Assume that the patient has either D_1 or D_2.

b. What is the probability that a test will yield negative results?

21. Given a decision matrix ($000)

	S_1	S_2
a_1	5	8
a_2	9	3
a_3	−1	10

The probability of S_1 is .35 and that of S_2 is .65. A research company's track record showed that they had three predictions (P_1, P_2, and P_3) with respect to the states of nature as shown below.

	S_1	S_2
P_1	.8	0
P_2	.1	.1
P_3	.1	.9

1. Draw a decision tree for the situation, including the decision regarding the employment of the research company.
2. Show all revised (posterior) probabilities.
3. What is the probability of predicting P_3?
4. The research company charges $2,700 per prediction; would you advise using it?

22. The following is the payoff profit matrix for two alternate plans:

Alternatives \ Futures	$p = .75$ Market receptive	$p = .25$ Market unfavorable
Plan *a*	$20,000	$6,000
Plan *b*	$25,000	$3,000

a. Which plan do you recommend adopting using the expected value criterion?
b. What is the expected value of perfect information?
c. It is known from past experience that of all the cases when the market was receptive, a research company predicted it in 90 percent of the cases. In the other 10 percent they predicted an unfavorable market. Also, of all the cases when the market proved to be unfavorable the research company predicted it correctly in 85 percent of the cases. (The other 15 percent of the cases they predicted it incorrectly.) Find the posterior probabilities of all states of nature.
d. Using the posterior probabilities, which plan would you recommend now?
e. How much should one be willing to pay (maximum) for the research survery?

4.8 CASES

CASE I—MAINTAINING THE WATER VALVES

With the 1978 passage of California's Proposition 13, local governments across the country became very cost conscious. Sharon Brown, Evergreen's city manager, was under continuous pressure to contain costs.

The city of Evergreen owns and operates its own water system. A major expense item is water valve repair. These valves are currently repaired by the city's maintenance department. In preparing next year's budget, the water system manager, Bill White, was faced with the following situation.

The average number of valves repaired in one year is 4120. The average time needed to repair a valve is 42 minutes. It is estimated that the labor cost next year will be $14 an hour. Parts and supplies are estimated at $3 per valve. Overhead shop expenses are computed at 40 percent of the total labor and parts cost. Some of the valves being repaired also need reworking, because of poor material or mistakes made by employees. Historical data indicate that the percentage of repaired valves that need reworking varies according to the following distribution:

Reworking needed (percent)	Probability
3.0	.50
4.0	.40
4.6	.10

A reworked valve is 100 percent reliable because such valves go through a special quality control check. The reworking cost is estimated to be $20 per valve.

Last month, the city manager called in all her assistants and advised them about some cost containment programs that were soon to be implemented. Specifically, she requested they each check on the possibility of eliminating inefficient in-house services that could be contracted out. Accordingly, Bill White advertised the valve repair job on a contractual basis. Western Maintenance Corp. (WMC), a reputable company, came up with the lowest bid: a $38,000 flat yearly fee plus $5 a valve with all reworking done at no additional charge.

City manager Ms. Brown requested that Mr. White evaluate WMC's proposal in terms of possible dollars savings. Mr. White's response is given in the following memo:

TO: Sharon Brown, City Manager
FROM: William White, Manager, Water System
SUBJECT: WMC's Proposal on Valve Repair Jobs

After careful evaluation of the proposal, I recommend that the contract be awarded to WMC. However, due to the budget squeeze, I will not be able to reassign the employees involved to any other jobs. Therefore, I recommend that the contract be awarded to WMC if and only if they will hire all displaced employees.

Upon receipt of this memo, Sharon Brown called the president of WMC. His response was as follows:

WMC is currently fully staffed, so hiring the city employees, some of whom are not highly skilled, will increase our cost. Therefore, WMC will be able to hire them only if the terms of the contract are changed to a flat fee of $40,000 plus $5 per valve, or else a $38,000 flat fee and $5.50 per valve.

Use a decision tree approach to advise Sharon Brown what to do.

a. Construct a decision tree and include the alternative of WMC not hiring the city employees.

b. Solve the tree; discuss the results.

c. Suppose the city agrees to the $40,000 flat fee and $5 per valve proposal, provided that the $40,000 is paid in four quarterly payments. The first payment is made with the signing of the contract. If Evergreen's cost of capital is 10 percent compounded quarterly, how will this impact the decision?

CASE II—THE AIR FORCE CONTRACT

ABC Aviation, Inc. is considering its bidding strategy for a U.S. Air Force contract. Because of the specialization of this job, there is only one other contractor currently approved to bid on it, XYZ Aircraft. The Air Force determines bid eligibility after lengthy investigation, and is, therefore, unlikely to approve of any additional contractors in the near future.

Due to the repetitive nature of such bids, ABC usually has special meetings to consider bidding strategy. They are considering two options: bidding "high" or bidding "low." Marketing Director Ella Jones explained the logic behind these options as follows:

"Our company's policy is to bid every time, while XYZ's policy is to bid only 60 percent of the time. And we have only two choices: a high bid or a low one. If we bid high and XYZ doesn't bid, we get the job and make $1,100,000 profit. But if XYZ bids, then we might get the contract or we might not, depending on their bidding level. All in all, our profit on a high bid averages out to zero when XYZ bids. If we place a low bid, our per bid profit averages out to $500,000 *regardless* of XYZ's action."

Steve Green, ABC's Director of Finance, thought for a few moments: "If what you say is true, it seems that we should bid 'high'

whenever our competitor doesn't bid and 'low' whenever they do."

"Exactly," replied Ms. Jones. "But," said Steve, "how can we find out what XYZ might do? We could try to buy this information from someone at XYZ, but not only is that unethical, but probably illegal as well."

"Wait a minute," said Ms. Jones, "Suppose it were legal; how much should we offer for such information assuming it were 100 percent reliable?"

"That's a good question," replied Mr. Hunt, the company's president. "It seems to me, however, that we're getting off the track. What do you propose to do, Ella?"

"We could use an expected value approach to solve this problem," said Ms. Jones, "but that approach would assume that our competitor will behave in the future as they behaved in the past, and how can we make such an assumption? How can we know what they'll do?"

"Well," said the president, "we've tried before to predict their moves. Aviation Research Co. has provided such information before, at $100,000 a shot. Their track record isn't bad: of 30 times that XYZ bid, Aviation Research predicted it correctly 24 times. On the other hand, of the 20 times that XYZ didn't bid, Aviation called it right 17 times."

"What you're saying, Mr. Hunt," said Steve, "is that this research company isn't 100 percent reliable."

"You may infer that, but Aviation Research is still considered the best research company available in this market. Now it's getting late, and we have to make a decision."

You are Steve Green. Prepare a short report advising your boss how to handle this decision. Specifically use the concepts of the value of perfect and imperfect information and decision policy. Work out the actual numerical values.

4.9 GLOSSARY

Additivity assumptions (of utilities) The utility of two or more items equals the sum of the utilities of the individual items.

Bayes' theorem A statistical process of revising prior probabilities based upon additional information.

Branches (of a decision tree) Lines or arcs that emerge either from a decision point to designate alternatives, or from a chance point to designate states of nature.

Chance point A circle on the decision tree designating that states of nature follow.

Decision point A square on the decision tree that indicates that a choice is to be made (selection of an alternative course of action).

Decision tree A graphical representation of a sequence of interrelated decisions to be made under risk.

DELPHI method A forecasting technique which attempts to reconcile differences of individual judges using a series of questionnaires.

Expected monetary value (EMV) The average gain/loss for each alternative course of action. It is computed by weighing the payoffs by their probabilities of occurrence.

Expected utility (EU) The long run average utility per decision.

Expected value of imperfect information (EVII) The difference between the best expected value with posterior probabilities and the best expected value with prior probabilities. It is a measure of the maximum (or upper limit) value of the additional information.

Multiple goals A situation in which the impact of a decision is evaluated for several goals simultaneously.

Utile A unit of measurement of utility.

Utility The subjective value of the outcome to the decision maker.

Utility curve The relationship between the quantity of money and its benefit to the decision maker.

Prior probabilities The original probabilities of the states of nature prior to adjustments made as a result of acquiring additional information.

Revised probabilities The probabilities of the states of nature after being adjusted with the aid of Bayes' theorem.

4.10 REFERENCES AND BIBLIOGRAPHY

1. Brown, R. V. et al. *Decision Analysis: An Overview.* New York: Holt, Rinehart and Winston, 1974.

2. Fishburn, P. C. *Utility Theory for Decision Making.* New York: John Wiley & Sons, Inc., 1970.

3. Jones, J. M. *Statistical Decision Making.* Homewood, Ill.: Richard D. Irwin, Inc., 1977.

4. Linstone, H. A. and Turoff, M. (ed.) *The Delphi Method.* Reading, Mass.: Addison-Wesley Publishing Co., Inc., 1975.

5. Magee, J. F. "Decision Trees for Decision Making." *Harvard Business Review* 42 (1964): 126.

6. ———. "How to Use Decision Trees in Capital Investment." *Harvard Business Review* 42 (1964): 79.

7. Oxenfeldt, A. R. *A Basic Approach to Executive Decision Making.* New York: AMACOM, 1978.

8. Raiffa, H. *Decision Analysis.* Reading, Mass.: Addison-Wesley Publishing Co., Inc., 1970.

9. Starr, M. K. and Zeleny, M. (ed.) *Multiple Criteria Decision Making*. New York: Elsevier-North Holland, 1977.

10. Turban, E., and Metersky, M. "Utility Theory Applied to Multivariable System Effectiveness Evaluation." *Management Science* 19 (1973): 817–28.

11. Von Neumann, J., and Morgenstern, O. *Theory of Games and Economic Behavior*. Princeton, N.J.: Princeton University Press, 1944.

MATHEMATICAL PROGRAMMING

Mathematical programming is the name for a family of tools designed to help solve managerial problems in which the decision maker must allocate scarce (or limited) resources among various activities to optimize a measurable goal. For example, distribution of machine time (the resource) among various products (the activities) is a typical allocation problem. Allocation problems usually display the following characteristics and necessitate making certain assumptions.

CHARACTERISTICS

1. A limited quantity of economic resources (such as labor, capital, machines, or water) is available for allocation.
2. The resources are used in the production of products or services.
3. There are two or more ways in which the resources can be used. Each is called a *solution* or a *program*.
4. Each activity (product or service) in which the resources are used yields a *return* (or reward) in terms of the stated goal.
5. The allocation is usually restricted by several limitations and requirements termed *constraints*.

ASSUMPTIONS

1. Returns from different allocations can be compared; that is, they can be measured by a common unit (such as dollars, utility, or share of the market).
2. The return from any allocation is independent of other allocations.
3. The total return is the sum of the returns yielded by the different activities.
4. All data are known with certainty.
5. The resources are to be used in the most economical manner.

The allocation problem can generally be stated as: find the way of allocating resources to various activities so the total reward will be maximized. Allocation problems, typically, have a large number of possible alternative solutions. Depending upon the underlying assumptions, the number of solutions can be either infinite or finite. Usually, different solutions yield different rewards. Of the available solutions, one (sometimes more than one) is the *best* in the sense that the degree of goal attainment associated with it is the highest (i.e., total reward is maximized). This is referred to as the *optimal* solution.

The field of mathematical programming that is covered in this text includes:

Linear programming (**Chapter 5**) Linear programming deals with allocation problems in which the goal (or objective) and all the requirements imposed on the problem are expressed by linear functions (see Appendix A).

Integer linear programming (**Chapter 6**) When the requirement that some or all of the decision variables must be integers (whole numbers) is added to a linear programming problem, it becomes one of integer (linear) programming. Integer programming can also be used as an auxiliary tool for solving a host of difficult managerial problems.

Nonlinear programming (**Chapter 6**) Mathematical programming problems where the goal and/or one or more of the requirements imposed on the problem are expressed by nonlinear functions (see Appendix A) are referred to as nonlinear programming problems.

Goal programming (**Chapter 6**) This is a variant of linear programming that is used when multiple goals exist.

Distribution problems (**Chapter 7**) The transportation of a commodity from sources of supply to destinations, at minimum cost (or maximum profit) and the assignment of workers (or equipment) to jobs are examples of what are termed distribution problems. These are also a special case of linear programming.

The uses of mathematical programming, especially of linear programming, are so common that "canned" computer programs[1] can be found today in just about any organization that has a computer. A glance at almost any issue of a professional or trade journal reveals the increasing rate of applications of mathematical programming. To date, thousands of examples of successful applications have been published. For instance: the petroleum industry makes extensive use of linear programming techniques, and integer programming is increasingly applied to the complex problems of scheduling operations. Process industries such as chemicals, food, steel, and rubber are known as especially heavy users of mathematical programming.

---

[1] Canned computer programs are preprogrammed computer routines to help solve specialized problems, requiring only the input data peculiar to the problem at hand.

5

Linear programming (LP) is one of the best known tools of management science. Perhaps the most general statement of its objective is that it is used to determine an optimal allocation of an organization's limited resources among competing demands. There are many managerial problems that can be considered allocation problems. These range from product-mix and blending problems to bus scheduling and dietary planning.

Linear programming deals with a special class of allocation problems; namely, those in which all the mathematical functions in the model are linear.

Part A of this chapter presents the general formulation of the LP problem, the graphical technique for its solution, and some examples of formulation. In Part B the simplex method of solution, a most efficient algorithm of linear programming, is presented.

Linear programming

PART A: BASICS

> Suji Okita and his wife Keiko were heartily enjoying their dinner of fresh shrimp, their first unhurried meal in days. Final tests had just been successfully completed on the new "slit matrix" television projection system Suji had developed, and the outlook was encouraging. "They'll be installing the system on two models for initial sales next week," he was saying to Keiko. "I wish we had a larger work force, more machine time and better marketing capabilities; I'm sure we could make considerably more profit. But even as it is, we don't know how many of each model to produce."
>
> Keiko was thinking about her problem at the Toshida Paint Company. A new expensive, special purpose paint, Sungold, was becoming very popular, and the production manager asked Keiko to see if she could find a combination of two new ingredients, code-named Alpha and Beta, that would result in an equivalent brilliance and hue but at less cost than the original ingredients. She felt confident she could.
>
> Keiko did not realize that her problem, a typical *blending* problem, was in many ways equivalent to Suji's, a typical *product-mix* problem.

5.1   THE NATURE OF LINEAR PROGRAMMING PROBLEMS

Two LP problems

Allocation problems appear in several forms. Two of the most common are the *product-mix* problem faced by Suji and the *blending* problem faced by Keiko.

The product-mix problem

Product-mix type problems are among the most common in linear programming. They are especially important in planning and scheduling situations. In a product-mix problem there are two or more *products* (also called *candidates* or *activities*), such as TV models in the previous **Maximize profit with** example, competing for limited resources, such as limited production **fixed resources** capacity. The problem is to find out *which products* to include in the production plan *and in what quantities* these should be included (product mix) in order to maximize profit.

Allocating scarce resources

Although a solution to a product-mix problem does specify the quantities to be produced, what it tells more generally, in effect, is *how to allocate* scarce resources. This is because the technology of production is given and once a decision has been made on the products and quantities to produce, a determination is made of what resources to use (allocate) and in what quantities.

The blending problem

Blending problems involve the determination of the *best blend* of available ingredients to form a certain quantity of a product under strict specifications. The best blend means the least-cost blend of inputs required to meet a designated level of output or given specifications. Blending problems are especially important in the process industries such as petroleum, chemicals, and food, and in fields where a certain level of service is desired at minimum cost. The decision maker must determine the ingredients to use and in what quantities.

In this respect the blending problem is similar to the product-mix problem. However, the objectives usually differ. In the product-mix problem, the profit derived from selling the products made from the given amount of resources is to be maximized. In blending, the cost of the ingredients is to be minimized, while adhering to certain specifications and using certain ingredients (resources). In the *blending* problem an attempt is made to use *as few resources as possible to provide a given product* (or service) level.

Therefore, a blending problem is also considered a problem of allocating resources in the best manner.

Minimize resource use to obtain a fixed output

Solution to allocation problems

Allocation problems such as product-mix, blending, and others which will be presented in Chapters 5 and 6 can be structured in an identical manner. The general structure of the allocation problem includes, as can be seen in the product-mix and the blending examples, two parts:

1. The problem has only one goal which is either to maximize (as in the product-mix case) or to minimize (as in the blending case) some measure of effectiveness.

   A single goal

2. The attainment of the objective is *limited* by one or more constraints. For example in the blending problem, the specifications of the final product are limiting factors.

   Limiting constraints

An allocation problem may not initially appear to be difficult to solve. The fact is, however, that allocation is considered in many organizations as the most difficult problem of management. The reason for this is that there are an infinite or a very large number of possible solutions. Of all these solutions the *best* is sought. Linear programming is basically a tool for conducting a systematic and efficient search for the optimal solution.

5.2   FORMULATION: TWO EXAMPLES

Let us return to the product-mix and blending problems and present both with the relevant data. Then, we will formulate both problems in the general structure of the linear programming model.

Example: The product-mix (maximization) problem

The two models of color TV sets produced by the Sekido Corporation, Suji's employer, will be designated as A and B. The company is in the market to make money; that is, its objective is profit maximization. The profit realized is $300 from set A and $250 from set B. Obviously, the more A sets produced and sold, the better. The trouble is that there are certain limitations which prevent Sekido Company from producing and selling thousands of sets. These limitations are:

constrain

1. Availability of only 40 hours of labor each week in the production department (a labor constraint).
2. A weekly availability of only 45 hours of machine time (a machining constraint).
3. Inability to sell more than 12 sets of model A each week (a marketing constraint).

Sekido's problem is to determine *how many sets of each model to produce each week so that the total profit will be as large as possible.* In solving this problem, the above limitations and the known technology of manufacturing must be taken into consideration.

The linear programming approach is divided into two steps: first the problem is set up or *formulated,* and then the model is solved.

Formulation

The problem's variables   The formulation of linear programming, as that of any other mathematical model, requires the identification of certain variables and their interrelationships.

Decision variables

The *decision variables* in this case are:

x_1 = the number of sets of model A.[1]
x_2 = the number of sets of model B.

The *dependent* (or *output*) *variable* in this case is the total profit. All linear programming problems have only one dependent variable which is called the *objective function.*

Objective function

The objective function   The profit realized from selling sets of model A is $300x_1$ (i.e., the profit per unit times the number of units). Similarly for model B, a profit of $250x_2$ will be realized. The total profit, z,

---

[1] The decision (unknown) variables are usually denoted by x_1, x_2, . . . , x_j, . . . , x_n. However, other notations of variables such as x, y, and z are also acceptable.

is, therefore, $300x_1 + 250x_2$. This total profit is called the *objective function*.

Remember that Sekido wishes to maximize the total profit; i.e., they want to maximize the objective function z.

The constraints on the system The limitations on the system are given as:

1. Labor constraint The production department has only 40 hours of labor available each week to manufacture both models. It is known that each set of model A, being of higher quality, requires two hours of labor whereas each set of model B requires only one hour. This limitation can be expressed as:

Constraints

Demand for labor		Supply
Total labor for model A	Total labor for model B	Total labor available
$2x_1$	$+ \quad 1x_2$	$\leq \quad 40$

Note that the "less than or equal to" sign ($\leq$) is used. That is, 40 hours is the *available* capacity which does not necesarily have to be used in full.

2. Machine time constraint There are up to 45 machine-hours available per week. Machine processing time for one unit of model A is one hour and for one unit of model B, three hours. This limitation can be expressed as:

$$1x_1 + 3x_2 \leq 45$$

3. Marketing constraint It is only possible to sell *up to* 12 units of model A each week. This can be expressed as: $1x_1 \leq 12$; that is, x_1 is smaller than or equal to 12.

4. Nonnegativity constraint Finally, it is impossible to produce a negative number of sets; that is, both x_1 and x_2 must be *nonnegative* (zero or positive). This constraint is expressed as:

Nonnegativity

$$x_1 \geq 0, \quad x_2 \geq 0$$

In summary, the problem is to find the best weekly production plan[2] (or program) so that the total profit will be maximized.

> The problem, then, can be summarized as follows. Find x_1 and x_2 that maximize z, the objective function, subject to constraints.

---

[2] Since production continues week after week, it is not necessary to complete all sets at the end of the week; that is, a fractional number of sets is permissible (e.g., 5.7 sets). However, had it been necessary to complete all sets by the end of the week, additional constraints limiting x_1 and x_2 to whole numbers would have been added. Such an addition changes the problem to one of *integer programming*.

$$\text{maximize } z = 300x_1 + 250x_2$$

subject to:
$$2x_1 + 1x_2 \leq 40 \quad \text{(labor constraint)}$$
$$1x_1 + 3x_2 \leq 45 \quad \text{(machine time constraint)}$$
$$1x_1 + 0x_2 \leq 12 \quad \text{(marketing constraint)}$$
$$\left. \begin{array}{rcl} x_1 & \geq & 0 \\ \\ x_2 \geq & & 0 \end{array} \right\} \text{(nonnegativity constraints)[3]}$$

We shall return to the solution of this problem later.

Example: The blending problem (minimization)

In preparing Sungold paint it is required that the paint have a brilliance rating of at least 300 degrees and a hue level of at least 250 degrees. Brilliance and hue levels are determined by the two ingredients Alpha and Beta. Both Alpha and Beta contribute equally to the brilliance rating, one ounce of either producing one degree of brilliance in one gallon of paint. However, the hue is controlled entirely by the amount of Alpha, one ounce of it producing three degrees of hue in one gallon of paint. The cost of Alpha is 45 cents per ounce, and the cost of Beta is 12 cents per ounce. Assuming that the objective is to minimize the cost of the resources, then the problem is to find the quantity of Alpha and Beta to be included in the preparation of each gallon[4] of paint. The problem is shown graphically in Figure 5.1.

Formulation

Decision variables

The *decision variables* are:

$x_1 =$ quantity of Alpha to be included, in ounces, in each gallon of paint.
$x_2 =$ quantity of Beta to be included, in ounces, in each gallon of paint.

The *dependent variable* is the total cost of the ingredients in one gallon of paint.

Since the cost of Alpha is 45 cents per ounce, and since x_1 ounces are going to be used in each gallon, then the cost per gallon is $45x_1$. Similarly, for Beta the cost is $12x_2$. The total cost is, therefore,

---

[3] Throughout the remainder of this book we *shall not* write these constraints in the formulation of problems. However, they are always implied, and the reader should remember their existence.

[4] An optimal answer for one gallon will remain optimal for any number of gallons as long as the relationships are linear. The total quantity of paint to be produced is of course larger than one gallon, and it is determined mainly by the demand and the manufacturing technology.

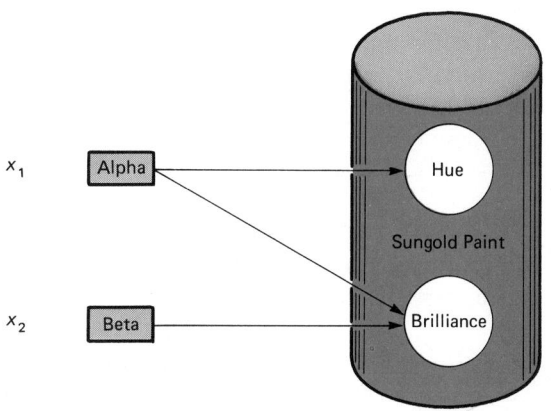

FIGURE 5.1
The blending problem

$45x_1 + 12x_2$, and it is to be *minimized* subject to the following specifications:

1. To provide a brilliance rating of at least 300 degrees in each gallon. Since each ounce of Alpha or Beta increases the brightness by one degree, the following relationship exists:

$$\underbrace{1\,x_1}_{\text{Supplied by Alpha}} \quad + \quad \underbrace{1x_2}_{\text{Supplied by Beta}} \quad \geq \quad \underbrace{300}_{\text{Demand}}$$

2. To provide a hue level of at least 250 degrees. The effect of Alpha (alone) on hue can similarly be written as:

$$\underbrace{3\,x_1}_{\text{Supplied by Alpha}} \quad + \quad \underbrace{0x_2}_{\text{Supplied by Beta}} \quad \geq \quad \underbrace{250}_{\text{Demand}}$$

> *In summary*, the blending problem is formulated as follows. Find x_1 and x_2 that:
>
> minimize $z = 45x_1 + 12x_2$
> subject to:
> $1x_1 + 1x_2 \geq 300$ (brightness specification)
> $3x_1 + 0x_2 \geq 250$ (hue specification)

As mentioned before, the nonnegativity requirement will not be restated.

The blending problem is going to be solved later in the chapter. At this time the reader may note that the blending problem is very similar in structure to the product-mix problem. Two differences can easily be seen: one is in the objective (minimum versus maximum) and the other is in the sign of the inequalities: $\geq$ in minimization versus $\leq$ in maximization. The latter difference is common but not essential. Several maximization problems have $\geq$ constraints and vice versa.

5.3   GENERAL FORMULATION AND TERMINOLOGY

In the previous section two classical managerial problems were formulated. Let us now generalize the formulation.[5]

Formulation of a linear programming (LP) problem

Every LP problem is composed of:

LP components

Decision variables   The variables whose value is unknown and are searched for. Usually they are designated by $x_1, x_2, \ldots$

Objective function   This is a mathematical expression, given as a linear function, that shows the relationship between the decision variables and a *single goal* (or objective) under consideration. The objective function is a measure of effectiveness of goal attainment. Examples of such goals are total profit, total cost, share of the market, and the like.

Optimization   Linear programming attempts to either maximize or minimize the objective function.

Profit or cost coefficients   The coefficients of the variables in the objective function (e.g., 300 and 250 in the product-mix example or 45 and 12 in the blending problem) are called the profit (or cost) coefficients. They express the *rate* at which the value of the objective function increases (profit) or decreases (cost) by including in the solution one unit of each of the decision variables.

Constraints   The maximization (or minimization) is performed subject to a set of constraints. Therefore, linear programming can be defined as a *constrained optimization problem*. These constraints are expressed in the form of linear inequalities (or, sometimes, equalities). They reflect the fact that resources are limited (e.g., in a product-mix problem) or they specify the product requirements (e.g., in a blending problem).

Input-output coefficients   The coefficients of the constraints' variables are called the *input-output* coefficients (or *technology* coefficients in a product-mix problem). They indicate the rate at which a given

---

[5] The problem area has been of interest to economists and mathematicians for a long time. The pioneering work in formulating the LP problem was done by the Russian economist L. V. Kantorovich. Several other economists, such as T. C. Koopmans, R. Dorfman, W. W. Cooper, A. Charnes, H. W. Kuhn, and A. W. Tucker, were important contributors to the area. But the person who should get most of the credit for the breakthrough in solving linear programming is George B. Dantzig (in 1947).

resource is depleted or utilized. They appear on the left side of the constraints.

Capacities The capacities (or availability) of the various resources, usually expressed as some upper or lower limit, are given on the *right-hand side* of the constraints.

Nonnegativity It is required that only nonnegative (zero or positive) values of the decision variables be considered. This requirement merely specifies the fact that negative values of physical quantities do not exist.

Example These major components of a linear programming model[6] are illustrated for the blending problem (discussed in the previous section).

Find: x_1 and x_2 which will minimize the value of the linear objective function: Decision variables

cost coefficients

$$z = 45x_1 + 12x_2$$ Objective function

decision
variables

---

[6] The general linear programming problem can be presented in the following mathematical terms. Let:

a_{ij} = the input-output coefficients.
c_j = the cost (profit) coefficients.
b_i = the capacities (right-hand side).
x_j $\doteq$ the decision variables.

Find a vector $(x_1, \ldots, x_n)$, which minimizes (or maximizes) a linear objective function $F(x)$ where:

$$F(x) = c_1x_1 + c_2x_2 + \cdots + c_jx_j + \cdots + c_nx_n \qquad (5.1)$$

Subject to the linear constraints:

$$\left. \begin{array}{l} a_{11}x_1 + a_{12}x_2 + \cdots + a_{1n}x_n \leq b_1 \\ a_{21}x_1 + a_{22}x_2 + \cdots + a_{2n}x_n \leq b_2 \\ \cdots \quad \cdots \quad \cdots \quad \cdots \quad \cdots \\ a_{i1}x_1 + a_{i2}x_2 + \cdots + a_{in}x_n \leq b_i \\ \cdots \quad \cdots \quad \cdots \quad \cdots \quad \cdots \\ a_{m1}x_1 + a_{m2}x_2 + \cdots + a_{mn}x_n \leq b_m \end{array} \right\} \qquad (5.2)$$

and the nonnegativity constraints:

$$x_1 \geq 0, x_2 \geq 0, \ldots \qquad (5.3)$$

subject to the linear constraints:

$$1x_1 + 1x_2 \geq 300$$
$$3x_1 + 0x_2 \geq 250$$

input-output   capacities or
coefficients   requirements

and subject to the nonnegativity of the decision variables: $x_1 \geq 0$; $x_2 \geq 0$

Advantages of linear programming

Linear programming is a tool that can be used to solve allocation-type problems. Such problems are very common and extremely important in organizations. Their solution is difficult due to the fact that an infinite number of possible solutions may exist; thus it is practically impossible to find an optimal solution. Linear programming not only provides the optimal solution but does so in a very efficient manner. Further, it provides information concerning the value of the resources that are allocated.

Limitations of linear programming due to assumptions

The applicability of linear programming is severely limited by several assumptions. As in all mathematical models, assumptions are made for reducing the complex real-world problem into a simplified form. The major ones are summarized below.

Certainty   It is assumed that all data involved in the linear programming problem are known with certainty.[7]

Linear objective function   It is assumed that the objective function is linear. This means that per unit cost, price, or profit are assumed to be unaffected by changes in production methods or quantities produced or sold.

Linear constraints   The constraints are also assumed to be linear. This means that all the input-output coefficients are considered to be unaffected by a change of methods, quantities, or utilization level.

Nonnegativity   Negative activity levels (or negative production) are not permissible. It is required, therefore, that all decision variables take nonnegative values.

Additivity   It is assumed that the total utilization of each resource is determined by adding together that portion of the resource required

---

[7] In problems under risk, the expected value of the input data can be considered as a constant, thus enabling the treatment of risky situations by linear programming. (For details, see Dantzig [3].)

for the production of each of the various products or activities. The assumption of additivity also means that the effectiveness of the joint performance of activities, under any circumstances, equals the sum of the effectiveness resulting from the individual performance of these activities.

Divisibility Variables can, in general, be classified as continuous or discrete. Continuous variables are subject to *measurement* (e.g., weight, temperature), whereas discrete variables are those which can be counted: 1, 2, 3, ... In linear programming it is assumed that the unknown variables x_1, x_2 . . . , are continuous; that is, they can take any fractional value. If the variables are restricted to whole numbers and thus are indivisible, a problem in "integer programming" exists. (Chapter 6)

Independence Complete independence of coefficients is assumed, both among activities and among resources. For example, the price of one product has no effect on the price of another.

Solving linear programs

All solutions to a linear programming problem which *satisfy all the constraints* are called *feasible*. The collection of feasible solutions is called the *feasible solution space* or area. Any solution which violates one or more of the constraints is termed *infeasible*.

Feasible or infeasible?

The major task in applying linear programming is the formulation of the problem. Once a problem has been formulated, one of several available methods of solution can be applied. Normally, this is done with the aid of a computer. Of all the solution methods, only two have a significant value. They are: the *graphical method,* and the general, powerful *simplex method* and its variants. In the next section the graphical method is illustrated; the simplex method is presented in Part B.

The simplex

Another process for solving linear programming problems has recently been reported [4]. This method, developed by a Russian mathematician, L. G. Khachian, involves shrinking an elliposid which surrounds the feasible solution space until it converges upon the optimum solution. This revolutionary approach is currently being evaluated to determine its potential.

5.4 THE GRAPHICAL METHOD OF SOLUTION

The graphical method is used mainly to illustrate certain characteristics of LP problems and to help in explaining the simplex method. The only case where it has a practical value is in the solution of small problems with two decision variables (such as x_1 and x_2) and only a few

A graphical solution

constraints, or, problems with two constraints and only a few decision variables.[8]

Example: A maximization problem

In order to illustrate the graphical method let us reproduce the product-mix problem discussed previously:

$$\text{maximize } z = 300x_1 + 250x_2$$
subject to:
$$2x_1 + 1x_2 \leq 40 \quad \text{(labor constraint)}$$
$$1x_1 + 3x_2 \leq 45 \quad \text{(machining constraint)}$$
$$1x_1 + 0x_2 \leq 12 \quad \text{(marketing constraint)}$$

FIGURE 5.2
The first constraint

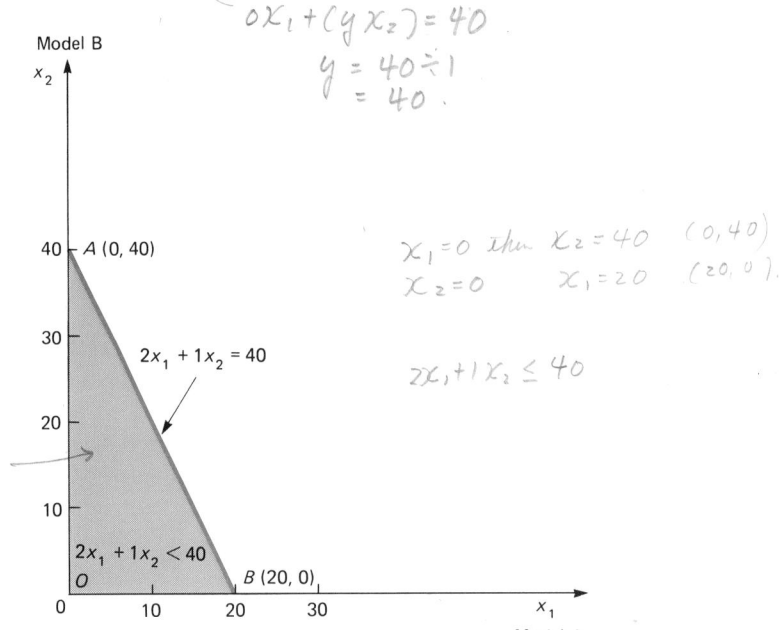

$$0x_1 + (y x_2) = 40$$
$$y = 40 \div 1$$
$$= 40.$$

$x_1 = 0 \text{ then } x_2 = 40 \quad (0, 40)$
$x_2 = 0 \qquad x_1 = 20 \quad (20, 0).$

$2x_1 + 1x_2 \leq 40$

area in which meet the Labor limitation constrain

Since there are only two decision variables, the problem can be graphically treated in a two-dimensional space.

Graphing the constraints

Graphing the feasible area   The graphical method starts with the graphing of a *feasible* area within which a search for the optimal solution is to be conducted. The feasible area is established through graphing all of the inequalities and equations that describe the constraints.

Graphing the first (labor) constraint (*Figure 5.2*) This is expressed as $2x_1 + 1x_2 \leq 40$. The steps in constructing the constraint are:

[8] In the latter case duality theory (Chapter 6) is used to transform the problem into one with two decision varibles prior to the use of the graphical method. Problems with three decision variables can be solved graphically, but it is a cumbersome process.

Step 1: Build the x_1 and x_2 axes. Only the quadrant[9] where both x_1 and x_2 are nonnegative is of interest.

Step 2: Since an inequality of the type *less than or equal to* has in effect two parts, we will first consider only the equality part of the constraint. In our example, it will be $2x_1 + 1x_2 = 40$. Since an equation can be shown graphically as a straight line (linear function in a two-dimensional space), it is sufficient to find two points to graph the entire equation. To do so, x_1 is first set to zero (i.e., do not produce TV model A). This will yield a point where the equation $2x_1 + 1x_2 = 40$ intersects the x_2 axis (point A in Figure 5.2).[10] When $x_1 = 0$, then $2(0) + x_2 = 40$, or $x_2 = 40$. This solution means that only model B sets are produced, at a rate of 40 per week. Thus, point A will have the coordinates of $(0, 40)$[11]. Similarly, if x_2 is set to zero, then:

$$2x_1 + 0 = 40$$

or

$$x_1 = 20 \text{ (produce 20 units of model A)}$$

This is shown as point B (20, 0) in Figure 5.2.

Step 3: Joining points A and B by a straight line is a representation of the equation $2x_1 + x_2 = 40$. However, it is not just the equation which is of interest but also the inequality $2x_1 + x_2 \leq 40$. This inequality is represented by an *area* below and to the bottom left of the equality (Figure 5.2).

This area would normally include negative values of x_1 and x_2 except for the fact that in linear programming negative values are excluded by the nonnegativity constraints $x_1 \geq 0$ and $x_2 \geq 0$. The end result is a feasible area inside (and including the boundary of) the triangle O-A-B in Figure 5.2 (shaded). Note that this shaded area includes an infinite number of solution combinations of models A and B, all of which meet the labor limitation.

Graphing the second (machine time) constraint Similarly, the shaded area O-C-D in Figure 5.3 represents the area of feasible solutions for the machining constraint $1x_1 + 3x_2 \leq 45$. This area is constructed as follows:

First, the equation portion of the inequality is considered:

$$1x_1 + 3x_2 = 45$$

Second, x_1 is set to zero. Then:

$$x_2 = 15 \text{ (point } C)$$

Inequality represents an area

Nonnegativity

---

[9] A two-dimensional space is divided into four quadrants by the two axes, x_1 and x_2.

[10] The equation describing the x_2 axis is $x_1 = 0$; that is, any point *on* the x_2 axis will have a coordinate of $x_1 = 0$ and an appropriate x_2 coordinate.

[11] Any point on a two-dimensional space is described by two numbers. For example, A (0, 40) means that $x_1 = 0$ and $x_2 = 40$.

130

FIGURE 5.3
The second constraint

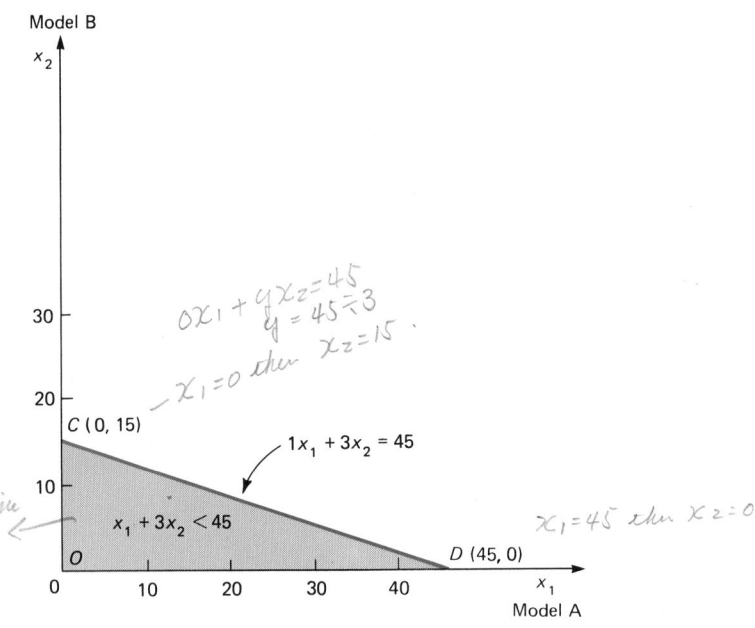

Third, x_2 is set to 0. Then:

$$x_1 = 45 \text{ (point } D)$$

Finally, points C and D are connected by a straight line, and the feasible area is then to the *left* of the line.

Graphing the third (marketing) constraint Next, the equality part

FIGURE 5.4
The third constraint

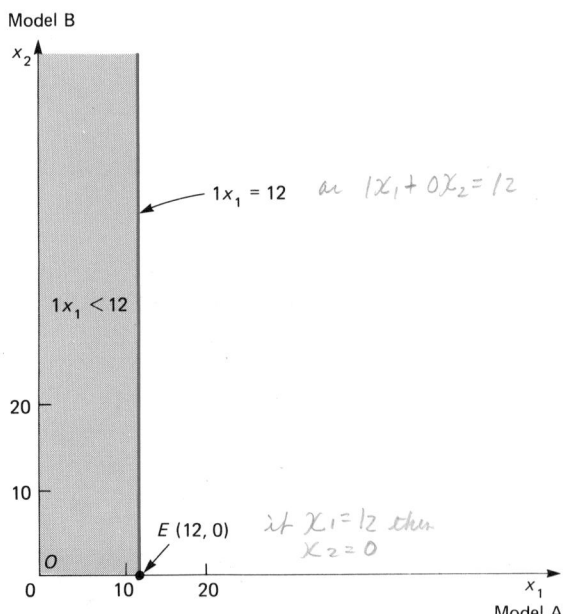

$x_1 = 12$ of the marketing constraint $x_1 \leq 12$ is plotted, as a straight line, vertically from point E and parallel to the x_2 axis (Figure 5.4). Again, the feasible area is left of the line.

Combining the constraints   Once all the constraints have been drawn, they can be put on one graph. As a matter of practicality they can be built on one graph from the beginning. We used the three graphs of Figures 5.2, 5.3, and 5.4 for instructional purposes only. The combination of all constraints is shown in Figure 5.5. The shaded area O-C-G-E is

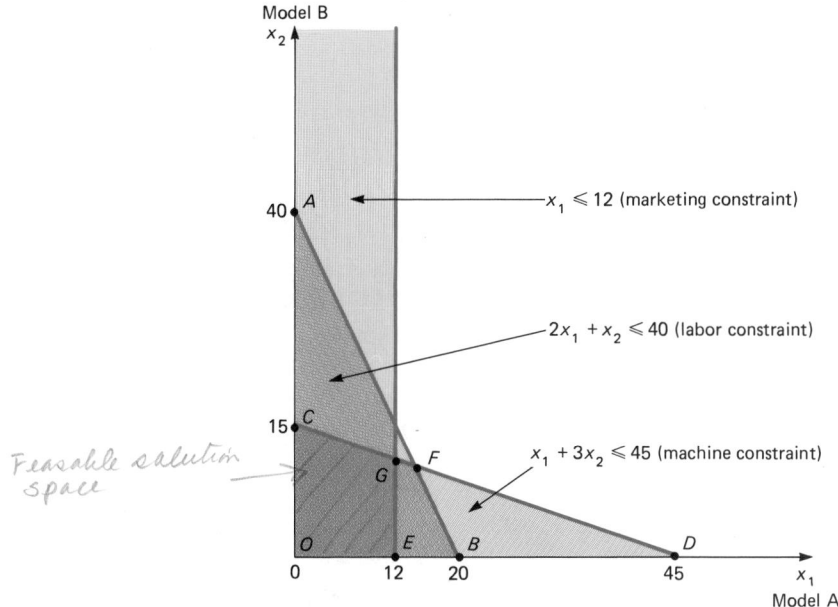

FIGURE 5.5
All three constraints
simultaneously

the area which is to the lower left of all equations simultaneously. Therefore, any solution in this area is *feasible* with respect to *all* the constraints. To put it another way, solutions in this area do not violate any of the constraints. This area, including the boundary, is called the feasible solution space and is reproduced in Figure 5.6.

Feasible—the area within *all* constraints

Identifying an optimal solution   Any point in the shaded area of Figure 5.6 and its boundary is a feasible solution. Since there are an infinite number of points in this area, there are an *infinite number of solutions* for this problem. To find an optimal one, it is necessary to identify a solution (point) in the feasible area which maximizes the profit (objective) function.

Infinite number of possible solutions

How can this task be accomplished? Let us examine a feasible solution inside the feasible area of Figure 5.6; say, point H. This point is a solution plan that calls for five sets of model A ($x_1 = 5$) and three sets of model B ($x_2 = 3$). This solution is not optimal since production of x_1 can be increased from point H to point K (12 units of x_1 and 3 of x_2), resulting in a higher profit. Notice that such an increase may continue only until

FIGURE 5.6
The feasible area

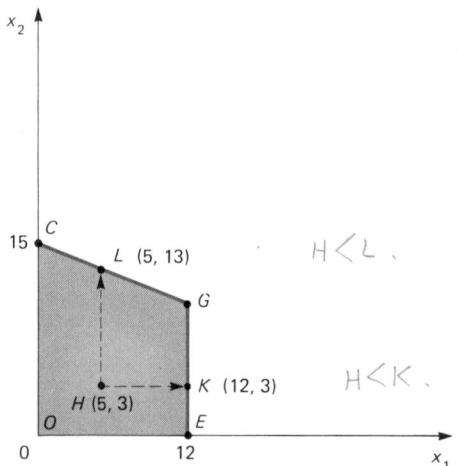

we are limited by a constraint. Similarly, point L, where more x_2 is produced than at H, will result in a higher profit than point H.

The reason that both point K and L are better than point H is because both yield a higher profit since the coefficients of the objective function are positive (more units, more profit). It can, however, be shown that no matter what sign the coefficients of the objective function have, there will always be at least one point somewhere on a boundary of the feasible area which is *superior* to a point inside the area. Therefore, an optimal solution to a linear programming problem can *never* be inside the feasible area but must be on a boundary. Furthermore, it can be shown that an optimal solution must be at a corner (called a *vertex*) where two (or more) constraints intersect.[12] Therefore, an efficient search for an optimal solution need only consider corner points (O, C, G, and E in our case). Two methods can be used for such a search.

On the boundary

To a corner

Enumeration

1. Enumeration of all corner points   In this method the solution values at all the corner points are compared. This is done by determining the coordinates of all corner points and then computing and comparing the values of the objective function at these points. Let us demonstrate: For points O, C, and E the exact coordinates can be read directly from Figure 5.6, as given below:

Point	x_1	x_2
O	0	0
C	0	15
E	12	0
G	? =12	? =11 ← optimal point

[12] If only one optimal solution exists, it must be on a vertex. If more than one optimal solution exists, then *at least* one optimal solution *must* be on a vertex, the others will be on the boundary.

For point G the approximate coordinates can be read from the graph, or exact coordinates can be computed as follows: Point G is at the intersection of two straight lines. Therefore, the value at point G (as given by x_1 and x_2) must be the same for the two intersecting lines. Such a value can be found by simultaneously solving the two intersecting linear equations,[13] one of which describes the marketing constraint and the other the machine time constraint. In this case:

Equation 1: $1x_1 = 12$ (marketing constraint).
Equation 2: $1x_1 + 3x_2 = 45$ (machine constraint).

The solution is simple in this situation since the value of one decision variable, x_1, is already known to be 12. This value is introduced into Equation 2 which can then be solved.
We get:

$$1x_1 + 3x_2 = 12 + 3x_2 = 45, \quad \text{or} \quad 3x_2 = 33, \quad \text{or} \quad x_2 = 11$$

Therefore, the coordinates of point G are (12, 11).

Now the profits at each corner point can be calculated using the objective function $300x_1 + 250x_2$. The results are shown in Table 5.1.

Identify the best corner

Point (corner)	Solution coordinates	Total profit $300x_1 + 250x_2 =$
O	(0, 0)	300 (0) + 250 (0) = 0
C	(0, 15)	300 (0) + 250(15) = \$3,750
E	(12, 0)	300(12) + 250 (0) = \$3,600
G	(12, 11)	300(12) + 250(11) = \$6,350 ← *Maximum*

TABLE 5.1
Profit values at corner points

The point which yields the greatest profit is point G. The optimal solution, therefore, is to produce 12 units of A and 11 units of B. The total profit is \$6,350.

The process of comparing profits at all corner points may be very lengthy, since in larger linear programming problems many corners exist. The second graphical method that can be used for the search of the corners is more efficient.[14] This method is presented next.

2. The use of isoprofit lines According to this procedure the optimal solution can be found by using the *slope* of the objective function as a guide. Let us illustrate.

Slope of the objective function

In examining solution H (5, 3) in Figure 5.6 it was indicated that better solutions are available (e.g., K (12, 3)). The question is: In what direction should one move to find better solutions? The answer to this

---

[13] For methods of solving simultaneous equations, see Appendix A.

[14] The simplex method (see Section 5.8) is a nongraphical procedure for efficiently conducting such a search.

question is found from the objective function. If the objective function (a profit function in our example) is graphed and the direction of increasing profit is identified, then when one starts moving the profit function in that direction, the profit will increase and increase. The limit to the increase is reached when the function touches some point(s) on the boundary of the feasible area (if the feasible area is bounded).[15] This point is then an optimal solution. The graphical method accomplishes this task in a systematic fashion.

Graphing an objective function   The graphing of the profit function may at first appear difficult, for profit functions (such as $z = 300x_1 + 250x_2$) describe an infinite number of equations which depend on the value of z and therefore, cannot be presented as a single line. To overcome this difficulty, *a family* of linear equations, called *isoprofit lines*,[16] is built by assigning various values to z (where z is the total profit). Graphically, such a family can be plotted as many lines *parallel* to each other (see Figure 5.7). The location of each line depends on the value of z.

Isoprofit lines

FIGURE 5.7
Family of isoprofit equations $z = 300x_1 + 250x_2$

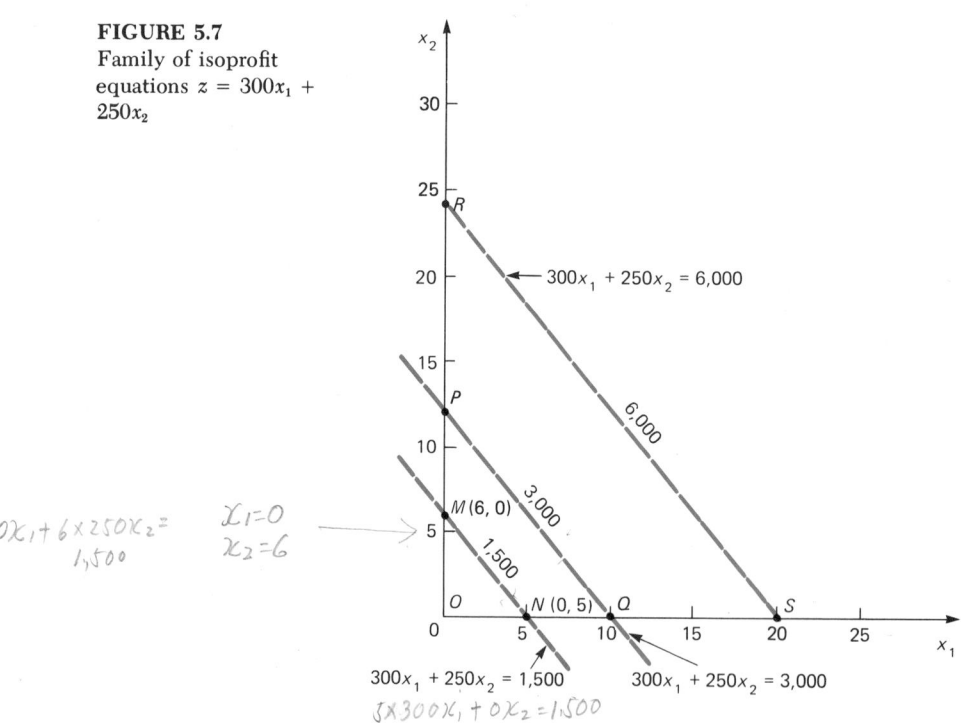

$300x_1 + 250x_2 = 6,000$

$300x_1 + 250x_2 = 1,500$ $300x_1 + 250x_2 = 3,000$

(handwritten left margin): $0x_1 + 6 \times 250x_2 = 1,500$ $x_1 = 0$ $x_2 = 6$

(handwritten bottom): $5 \times 300x_1 + 0x_2 = 1,500$

---

[15] A feasible area may be unbounded from one or more sides. For a treatment of such cases, see Dantzig [3].

[16] An isoprofit line is a line each of whose points (a line is a collection of points) designates a solution with the *same* profit.

Let us assume that $z = 1,500.$[17] In this case the profit equation, $300x_1 + 250x_2 = 1,500$, can be drawn as a straight line exactly in the same manner as the equality constraints were drawn. This line intersects the x_1 axis at N in Figure 5.7 (where $x_2 = 0$ and $x_1 = 5$) and the x_2 axis at Point M (where $x_1 = 0$ and $x_2 = 6$). Point N tells us how many units of product x_1 *alone* are required to produce a profit of $1,500. Since the profit contribution per unit of product x_1 is $300, the answer is $1,500 \div 300 = 5$ units of x_1. Similarly, since the per unit profit contribution of x_2 is $250, it takes 6 units of x_2, if only x_2 is produced (as indicated by point M), to produce a profit of $1,500. All points on the isoprofit line MN are within the shaded area, representing feasible solutions, each giving a total profit of $1,500 (see Figure 5.8).

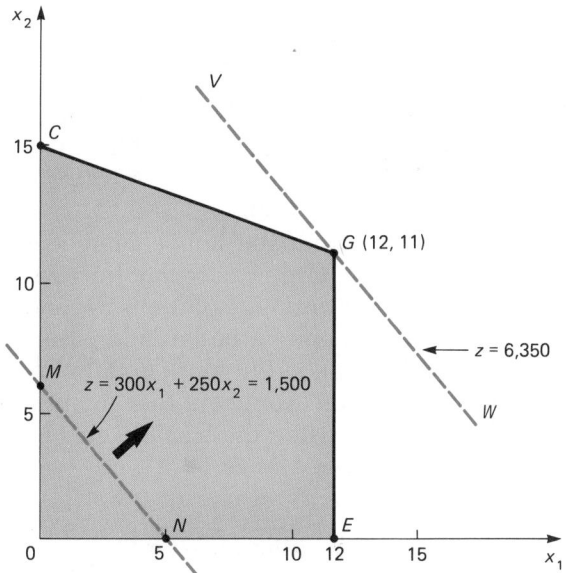

FIGURE 5.8
Moving to an optimal solution

In a similar fashion, other isoprofit lines could be drawn, yielding different levels of profits. For example, line PQ in Figure 5.7 represents a $3,000 isoprofit level, and the line RS represents a $6,000 isoprofit level. An examination of lines MN, PQ, and RS shows that they are *parallel* to each other. Note also that the line RS with the highest profit is located *farthest away* from the origin (point O).

A little reflection will show that an even higher profit can be achieved if additional isoprofit lines can be drawn farther away from the

Moving parallel

Farthest from the origin

---

[17] Any arbitrary profit figure will work. However, it is simple to pick a profit number which gives an integer as an answer to x_1 when we set $x_2 = 0$ and vice versa. A good choice is to use a number that is divided easily by the coefficients of both variables. For example, $1,500 \div 300 = 5$, and $1,500 \div 250 = 6$.

origin. The question is: Where is the farthest *isoprofit* line? Let use see how this question can be answered.

Finding the optimal solution(s)   The feasible area is reproduced from Figure 5.6 as Figure 5.8. Superimposed on the figure is the isoprofit line *MN*.

Now, if one starts building parallel isoprofit lines in the northeast direction (see the arrow), these lines will represent higher and higher profits. We shall now show how to build such parallel lines and how to find the farthest possible isoprofit line.

> *To build parallel lines to MN take a ruler and a 90-degree triangle. Hold the ruler perpendicular to line MN and keep one side of the triangle on the line MN. To find the farthest isoprofit, move the triangle slowly to the northeast until the point where it is about to leave the feasible area (shaded in Figure 5.8).*

In our example the farthest isoprofit line (*VW*) hits point *G* which is declared the *optimal solution*. The coordinates of this point were previously computed as 12 and 11.[18] The value of the objective function at that point is $300(12) + 250(11) = 6,350$. Therefore, line *VW* designates an isoprofit line $z = 6,350$.

A vertex or a
boundary?

When employing the above method, one of two cases may be expected. First, the farthest isoprofit line may intersect one corner point providing a single optimal solution. Second, the farthest isoprofit line may coincide with one of the boundary lines of the feasible area. (This second case is discussed in more detail in Section 5.9.) This procedure reaffirms the previous comment that an optimal solution must be on the boundary and not inside the feasible area and that the optimal solution must always occur at a vertex.[19]

Example: A minimization problem

Minimization

The graphical method can be used for minimization problems in a manner similar to the maximization case. To illustrate, let us examine the *blending problem* discussed earlier.

The problem is reproduced below:

$$\text{minimize } z = 45x_1 + 12x_2$$
$$\text{subject to:}$$
$$1x_1 + 1x_2 \geq 300$$
$$3x_1 + 0x_2 \geq 250$$

---

[18] Note that if the optimal values of x_1 and x_2 are introduced into the inequality constraints, the solution will fully utilize only the second and the third resources. That is, the labor constraint is not binding. This can be clearly seen in Figure 5.5 where the labor constraint does not intersect at the optimal point. In general, any constraint which does not intersect on the optimal vertex is *not* fully utilized.

[19] If only one solution exists.

To begin with, the inequality constraints are considered equations. They are drawn in Figure 5.9. Since the inequalities are of the *"greater-than-or-equal-to"* type, the feasible area is formed by considering the area to the *upper-right* side of each equation (away from the origin, the shaded area in Figure 5.9). Next, a family of lines that represents various levels

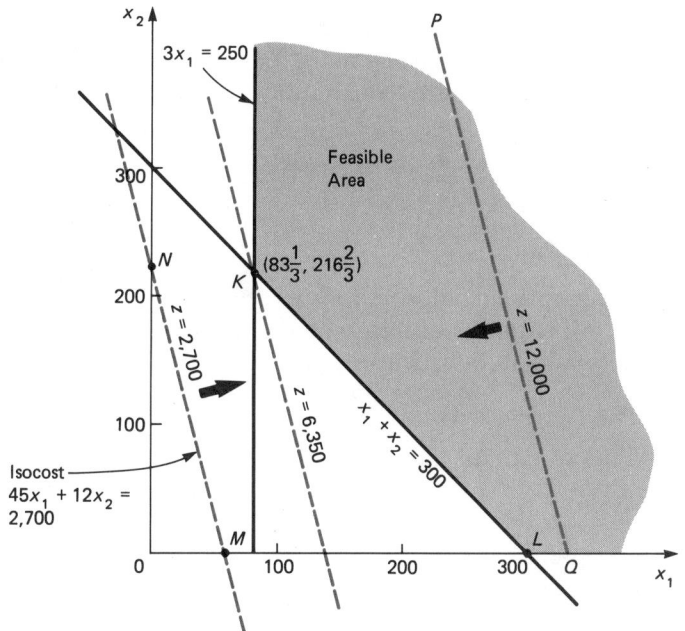

FIGURE 5.9
The blending problem

of the objective function is drawn (broken lines in Figure 5.9). These lines, in the minimization case, are called *isocost* lines.

Isocost lines

In the diagram, a value of $z = 2,700$ is arbitrarily selected. The isocost equation is:

$$45x_1 + 12x_2 = 2,700$$

This isocost line is shown as line *MN* in Figure 5.9; note that the line *does not* intersect the feasible solution space. Therefore, this isocost line must be moved *toward* the feasible area[20] until it first intersects a point(s) in this region (point *K*). The coordinates of point *K* can be read from the graph, or they can be computed as the intersection of the two linear equations. The solution for point *K* is:

$$x_1 = 83\frac{1}{3}$$
$$x_2 = 216\frac{2}{3}$$

$1 X_1 + 1 X_2 = 300$. $3X_1 + 0X_2 = 250$
$83.3 + 1 X_2 = 300$ $X_1 = 83.3$.
$1 X_2 = 300 - 83.3$
$= 216 \frac{2}{3}$.

---

[20] If the isocost line is constructed inside the feasible area, like line *PQ* in Figure 5.9, then the search moves in the direction of the arrow, toward the origin. Since the objective is cost minimization we search for the *lowest* level isocost which is still feasible.

This means that for every gallon of the finished paint, the following raw materials should be used: 83⅓ ounces of Alpha at a cost of 45 cents × 83⅓ = 3,750 cents and 216⅔ ounces of Beta at a cost of 12 cents × 216⅔ = 2,600 cents. The total cost is, therefore, 3,750 cents + 2,600 cents = 6,350 cents.

Graphing an equality   Thus far we have graphed only inequalities. If a constraint appears as an equality, then the feasible region of solutions is not an area any more, but a *line segment,* directly on the line describing the equality constraint.

5.5   UTILIZATION OF THE RESOURCES—SLACK AND SURPLUS VARIABLES

Slack variables

The optimal solution for the product-mix problem calls for $x_1 = 12$ and $x_2 = 11$. Let us examine now what will happen to the constraints if the optimal solution is used.

1.   The labor constraint

This constraint is expressed as:

$$\overbrace{2x_1 + 1x_2}^{\text{Demand for labor}} \leq \overbrace{40}^{\text{Supply of labor}}$$

Introducing the optimal values we get:

$$2(12) + 1(11) = 35 \text{ hours.}$$

That is, the demand for labor is 35 hours while the supply is 40. Therefore, there would be 40 − 35 = 5 hours of unused labor potential. This unused supply is called *slack.* The slack must take only nonnegative values; i.e., it can be either zero, or positive. Designating this slack by s_1 (where the 1 designates the first constraint), the labor constraint can be rewritten as:

$$2x_1 + 1x_2 + s_1 = 40$$

transforming the constraint into an equality.
The solution for s_1 is:

$$s_1 = 40 - (2x_1 + 1x_2) = 40 - 2(12) - 1(11) = 5$$

In general, in the optimal solution, any "smaller than or equal to" constraint will have a slack which can be either 0 or positive.

2.   The machine constraint

Similarly, the machine slack variable can be inserted into the constraint as:

$$x_1 + 3x_2 + s_2 = 45$$

Substituting the values of the optimal solution and solving for s_2:

$1 \times 1 - 3 \times 2$ when $X_1 = 12$ & $X_2 = 11$

$$s_2 = 45 - (1x_1 + 3x_2) = 45 - 12 - 33 = 0$$

In this case the machine time is *fully utilized* (no slack exists).   Full utilization: no slack

3. **The marketing constraint**
   Similarly:

$$1x_1 + s_3 = 12$$

   Solving:

$$s_3 = 12 - 1x_1 = 12 - 12 = 0$$

The implication again is that there is no slack; the constraint is met.

   Note: A glance at Figure 5.5 and 5.8 will show that a constraint with zero slack intersects the optimal solution point. A constraint with positive slack *does not* intersect the point of the optimal solution.

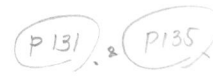 P 131 & P 135

Surplus variables

   Any "larger-than-or-equal-to" constraint has a surplus variable.

Example 1

Given:

$$2x_1 + 3x_2 \geq 50$$

Let the optimal solution be:

$$x_1 = 12; \; x_2 = 11$$

Introducing these values into the left side of the inequality, we get:

$$2(12) + 3(11) = 57 \qquad 24 + 33 = 57 \qquad 57 - 50 = 7 \cdots Surplus \; Variables$$

The value of the left side of the inequality is larger than the value of the right side. The difference, 7, in this case, is called a *surplus* variable. It indicates by how much the requirements of the right hand side are exceeded (overachievement). That is, a surplus variable shows by how much certain minimum specifications are exceeded.   Surplus variable s_4

   A surplus variable can either be positive or zero. It is written as:

$$2x_1 + 3x_2 - s_4 = 50$$

Notice again that the inequality has been changed to an equality. Introducing the values of the decision variables and solving for s_4:

$$s_4 = (2x_1 + 3x_2) - 50 = 2(12) + 3(11) - 50 = 7$$

Example 2

   Taking the first constraint of the blending problem:

$$1x_1 + 1x_2 - s_1 = 300$$
$$s_1 = 1x_1 + 1x_2 - 300 = 83\frac{1}{3} + 216\frac{2}{3} - 300 = 0$$

The value of the surplus is zero.

Note: A linear programming inequality constraint can be multiplied or divided by a constant without changing the optimal solution. For example, the inequality $3x_1 + 6x_2 \geq 15$ can be rewritten $x_1 + 2x_2 \geq 5$. However, if this is done the magnitude of the surplus (or slack) variable will be changed. Therefore, one should not change the original constraints. The slack and surplus variables also play an important role in the simplex method, as will be seen in Part B of this chapter.

Equality

Summary

Each "smaller-than-or-equal-to" constraint has a slack variable whose value is either positive or zero. Each "larger-than-or-equal-to" constraint has a surplus variable whose value is either positive or zero. Each equality constraint has neither slack nor surplus. Any constraints which intersect at the point of the optimal solution have neither slack nor surplus; i.e., have zero slack or surplus.

5.6   EXAMPLES OF APPLICATIONS

A production example

The ABC Corporation produces refrigerators and freezers. The metal framing department can make 90 frames for refrigerators each week if all department resources are allocated to refrigerators. On the other hand, the department can make 180 frames for freezers if all its resources are allocated entirely to freezers. The department can also make any linear combination[21] of frames for both.

The assembly department can put together 180 refrigerators or 150 freezers or any linear combination thereof, weekly. In addition, there are marketing constraints: The combined sales of freezers and refrigerators cannot be more than 160. In addition, no less than 30 refrigerators and 50 freezers must be produced each week.

The profit from selling a refrigerator is $72 and that of a freezer is $65. How many refrigerators and freezers should be produced each week in order to maximize profits?

Formulation

1.   The decision variables

y = number of refrigerators.
x = number of freezers.

---

[21] A linear combination means that since the capacity required for one refrigerator is the same as that for 2 freezers (90 to 180 ratio), then the department can make such combinations as 89 refrigerators plus 2 freezers or 88 refrigerators plus 4 freezers and so on.

2. *The objective function z, to be maximized*

$$\boxed{\text{maximize } z = 72y + 65x} \;\;✓$$

3. *The constraints*

The formulation of the constraints is more complicated. To show how they are derived, let us graph the situation of the framing department (Figure 5.10).

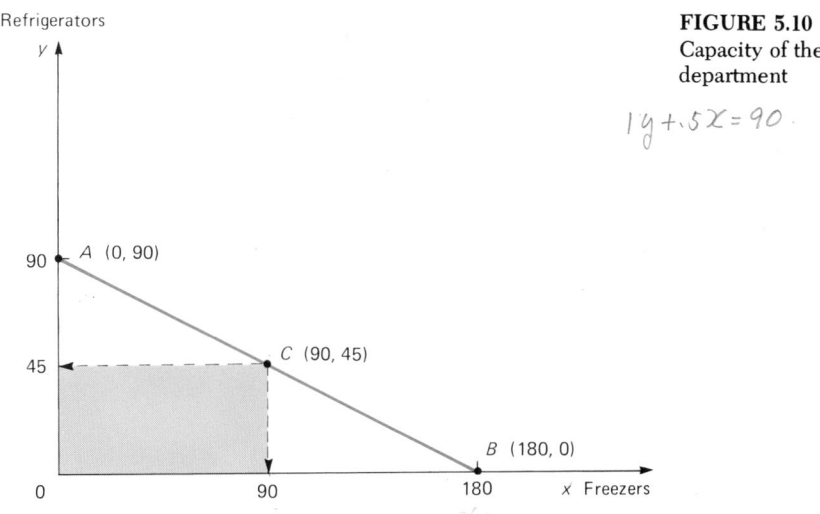

Refrigerators

$1y + .5x = 90.$

A (0, 90)

C (90, 45)

B (180, 0)

0   90   180   x Freezers

FIGURE 5.10
Capacity of the framing department

$x_2 = 180$

The department can produce 90 refrigerators at maximum capacity. This information is shown as point A; that is, zero freezers and 90 refrigerators. Similarly, point B (180, 0) designates that the department can make 180 freezers and zero refrigerators at maximum capacity. The straight line connecting points A and B indicates all other possible combinations of the department. For example, point C designates 90 freezers and 45 refrigerators. The problem is to find the equation of the straight line which designates the constraint. From geometry it is known that if the coordinates of two points are (x_1, y_1) and (x_2, y_2) then the equation of the straight line connecting these two points is:

$$y = \frac{y_2 x_1 - y_1 x_2}{x_1 - x_2} + \left(\frac{y_1 - y_2}{x_1 - x_2}\right) x \;\;✓$$

Thus, the equation of the straight line between (0, 90) and (180, 0) is:

$$y = 90 - \left(\frac{90}{180}\right) x = 90 - .5x$$

or

$$y + .5x = 90$$

and the inequality constraint is:

$$y + .5x \leq 90$$

Similarly, for the assembly department:

$$y + 1.2x \leq 180$$

The marketing constraints are expressed as:

$$y + x \leq 160$$
$$y \geq 30$$
$$x \geq 50$$

Summary of formulation

$$\text{maximize } 72y + 65x$$
subject to:
$$y + .5x \leq 90$$
$$y + 1.2x \leq 180$$
$$y + x \leq 160$$
$$y \geq 30$$
$$x \geq 50$$

The solution of this problem is $y = 30$, $x = 120$, and the maximum profit = \$9,960.

Crude oil refinery example

CAM Oil Company produces four products in its refinery: gasoline, heating oil, jet fuel, and lubricating oil. These products are made from four available crude oils. The process is schematically shown in Figure 5.11.

FIGURE 5.11
CAM Oil Company

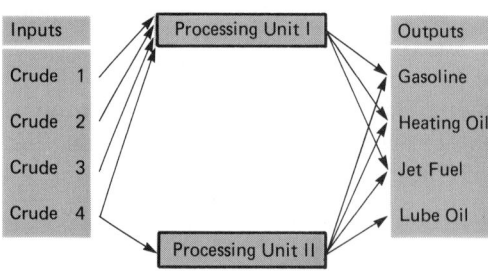

The first three crudes are processed in unit I; the fourth crude is processed in either unit I or unit II. Only unit II is capable of producing lube oil in addition to the other three products.

Resources (input) availability (in barrels per week)

Crude 1 and 3: up to 200,000 each
Crude 2: up to 150,000
Crude 4: up to 250,000

Input-output coefficients Table 5.2 shows the input-output relationship between crudes (inputs) and products (outputs). These are the yields. For example, a barrel of crude 1 yields .5 barrels of gasoline, .3 barrels of heating oil, and .1 barrels of jet fuel.

Marketability Each week, CAM can sell up to 250,000 barrels of gasoline; 120,000 barrels of heating oil; 30,000 barrels of lube oil; and 100,000 barrels of jet fuel.

TABLE 5.2
Input-output coefficients

	Gasoline	Heating oil	Lube oil	Jet fuel	Loss
Sales →	250,000	120,000	30,000	10,000	
Unit I					
Crude 1.............	.5	.3	0	.1	.1
2.............	.4	.2	0	.2	.2
3.............	.6	.2	0	.1	.1
4.............	.5	.1	0	.2	.2
Unit II					
Crude 4.............	.4	.1	.3	.1	.1

(handwritten margin notes: profit 15¢, 20, 11, 20, 30)

Profit For each barrel of crude 1 refined, CAM realizes 15 cents profit, No. 2 brings 20 cents per barrel, 3 brings 11 cents per barrel, and 4 brings 20 cents per barrel if processed in unit I and 30 cents per barrel if processed in unit II. The objective of CAM is to maximize profits. The problem is: how much crude oil of each available type should CAM refine each week to meet the profit maximization objective.

Formulation

1. **Define the decision variables**

   They are (all in barrels per week):

   x_1 = amount of crude 1 to be processed.
   x_2 = amount of crude 2 to be processed.
   x_3 = amount of crude 3 to be processed.
   x_4 = amount of crude 4 to be processed in unit I.
   x_5 = amount of crude 4 to be processed in unit II.
   ($x_4 + x_5$ = amount of crude 4 processed)

2. **The objective function to be maximized is the total profit**

   $$\text{maximize } z = 15x_1 + 20x_2 + 11x_3 + 20x_4 + 30x_5$$

3. **The constraints**

   Crude availability:

   a. $x_1 \le 200,000$
   b. $x_2 \le 150,000$
   c. $x_3 \le 200,000$
   d. $x_4 + x_5 \le 250,000$

Technology and marketability:

e. $.5x_1 + .4x_2 + .6x_3 + .5x_4 + .4x_5 \leq 250,000$ (for gasoline)
f. $.3x_1 + .2x_2 + .2x_3 + .1x_4 + .1x_5 \leq 120,000$ (heating oil)
g. $\qquad\qquad\qquad\qquad .3x_5 \leq 30,000$ (lube oil)
h. $.1x_1 + .2x_2 + .1x_3 + .2x_4 + .1x_5 \leq 100,000$ (jet fuel)

The problem has thus been formulated and can be solved as an LP problem.

The optimal (computerized) solution

$$x_1 = 150,000 \text{ barrels}$$
$$x_2 = 150,000 \text{ barrels}$$
$$x_3 = 0.$$
$$x_4 = 150,000 \text{ barrels}$$
$$x_5 = 100,000 \text{ barrels}$$

Total profit = 11,250,000 cents = \$112,500 (each week).

Moral: Even a few pennies per barrel can make you a millionaire if you use linear programming and happen to own an oil company.

Paper trimming problem

The Northwestern Paper Company produces rolls of paper, 12-inches wide × 1,000-feet long. These standard rolls are purchased by many of their clients. However, some clients prefer to receive special sizes, namely 2-inch, 3½-inch, or 5-inch rolls, all 1,000-feet long. The minimum amount of rolls required is 500 of 2-inch, 2,000 of 3½-inch, and 1,500 of 5-inch rolls. The special rolls can be cut out of the 12-inch standard rolls.

TABLE 5.3
Paper trimming alternatives

Alternatives	Size of rolls			Waste
	2-inch	*3½-inch*	*5-inch*	
1	6	0	0	0
2	1	0	2	0
3	2	2	0	1
4	0	2	1	0
5	3	0	1	1
6	4	1	0	½

The company is considering six cutting alternatives, each of which results in one inch of waste or less. These are shown in Table 5.3 which lists the number of rolls in each cutting alternative. Find the best cutting program to minimize the waste.

Formulation

1. *The decision variables*

    Let x_1 = number of 12-inch rolls to be cut according to alterna-
    tive 1, x_2 = number of rolls to be cut according to alternative 2,
    and so on.

2. *The objective function to be minimized is the "total waste":*

    $$\text{minimize } z = 0x_1 + 0x_2 + 1x_3 + 0x_4 + 1x_5 + \tfrac{1}{2}x_6$$

3. *The constraints*

    a. $6x_1 + 1x_2 + 2x_3 + 0x_4 + 3x_5 + 4x_6 \geq 500$ which reflects a
        minimum requirement for 2-inch rolls.
    b. $2x_3 + 2x_4 + 1x_6 \geq 2,000$ (for 3½-inch rolls)
    c. $2x_2 + 1x_4 + 1x_5 \geq 1,500$ (for 5-inch rolls)

    Solution (by computer)

    $$x_1 = 41.67, x_2 = 250, x_3 = 0, x_4 = 100, x_5 = 0, x_6 = 0$$

Total waste (objective function) is zero.

   This solution will result in exactly 500 rolls of 2-inch, 2,000 rolls
of 3½ inches and 1,500 rolls of 5 inches.

An agricultural application

   Sam Green just acquired a 5 acre orange grove in South Florida.
The U.S. Agriculture Department recommends that orange groves be
fertilized twice a year. The quantities of chemicals recommended by the
Agriculture Department, per acre, per application of fertilizer, are:

Nitrogen—at least 20 lbs.
Phosphoric acid—at least 25 lbs.
Potash—at least 30 lbs.
Chlorine—no more than 36 lbs.

   Fertilizers are sold on the market under various brands, in standard
bags of either 25 lbs. or 50 lbs. Each brand is designated by a system of 3
numbers. For example, 8–10–6 means that each bag contains 8 percent
(by weight) nitrogen, 10 percent phosphoric acid, and 6 percent potash.
   Sam is shopping for fertilizers, determined to pay as little as
possible; at the same time, he wants to follow the recommendations of
the Agriculture Department.

The fertilizers currently available on the market are:

Brand	Designation	Cost/bag	Chlorine content (%)	Weight
A	4–6–8	$5.50	8	50 lbs.
B	8–8–8	6.00	6	50 lbs.
C	6–6–20	5.00	5	25 lbs.

Find:

a. How many bags of each type should Sam buy each year?

b. Sam's yearly budget for fertilizer.

c. The excess amount of chemicals that the grove will receive each year.

d. The actual amount of chlorine, provided to the grove yearly, as compared to the recommended amount.

Formulation   This blending-type problem can be formulated in two different ways, depending on the definition of the decision variables. The problem is first solved for one application of the fertilizers per acre.

Formulation A

1.   The decision variables

These are the number of pounds of each of the fertilizers, i.e.:

x_1 = no. of pounds of brand A, per application, per acre

x_2 = no. of pounds of brand B, per application, per acre

x_3 = no. of pounds of brand C, per application, per acre

2.   The objective function

Each pound of brand A costs: 5.50/50 = .11

Each pound of brand B costs: 6.00/50 = .12

Each pound of brand C costs: 5.00/25 = .20

Therefore, the objective function, z, is:

$$z = .11x_1 + .12x_2 + .20x_3, \text{ and it is to be } minimized$$

3.   The constraints

a.   Provide at least 20 pounds of nitrogen. Nitrogen is provided by the three fertilizers according to the percentage designated, i.e.:

$$\underbrace{.04x_1}_{\substack{\text{provided by} \\ \text{brand A}}} + \underbrace{.08x_2}_{\substack{\text{provided by} \\ \text{brand B}}} + \underbrace{.06x_3}_{\substack{\text{provided by} \\ \text{brand C}}} \geq 20$$

b.   Provide at least 25 pounds of phosphoric acid. Similarly:

$$.06x_1 + .08x_2 + .06x_3 \geq 25$$

c. Provide at least 30 pounds of potash. Similarly:

$$.08x_1 + .08x_2 + .20x_3 \geq 30$$

d. Provide no more than 36 pounds of chlorine. Similarly:

$$.08x_1 + .06x_2 + .05x_3 \leq 36$$

The solution (by computer)

$$x_1 = 0$$
$$x_2 = 285.71$$
$$x_3 = 35.71$$
$$z = \$41.43$$

Note that this solution, even for five acres, results in a noninteger number of bags. Thus, the problem is really one of "integer programming," a topic we will address in Chapter 6.

Another formulation of this problem, aimed to get around the integer difficulty, is given below. Can you see why this formulation is no better than the one in A?

Formulation B

1. **The decision variables**

They are the number of *bags* of each brand:

y_1 = no. of bags of brand A, per acre, per application
y_2 = no. of bags of brand B, per acre, per application
y_3 = no. of bags of brand C, per acre, per application

2. **The objective function**

$$\text{minimize } z = 5.5y_1 + 6.0y_2 + 5.0y_3$$

3. **The constraints**

a. The nitrogen constraint:

$$.04(50)y_1 + .08(50)y_2 + .06(25)y_3 \geq 20$$

The student is encouraged to complete the formulation of this problem.

A finance (banking) application

Palmetto National Savings & Loan makes five kinds of loans. These loans, with the yearly interest rate charged to customers, are shown in the table below.

Type of loan	Interest charged (in percent)
Commercial loans	15
Home mortgage (first mortgage)	10
Home improvements	13.6
Home mortgage (second mortgage)	14
Short-term revolving loan	18

The bank has $53,000,000 in available funds. Its objective is to maximize yield on investment.

The demand for funds

The demand for short-term revolving loans never exceeds $5 million. All other demands are unlimited.

Policies and regulations

a. Home improvement loans cannot be higher than 20 percent of first mortgage loans.
b. Commercial loans must be smaller than or equal to the second mortgage loans.
c. The bank must invest at least 60 percent of the loans outstanding (total loans) in mortgages.
d. For safety reasons, there must be at least $2 invested in first mortgage loans for every dollar invested in second mortgage loans.
e. Short-term loans cannot exceed $5,000,000.

Find the best bank fund allocation plan.

Formulation

1. **The decision variables**

   x_1 = dollars invested in commercial loans.
   x_2 = dollars invested in first mortgages.
   x_3 = dollars invested in home improvements.
   x_4 = dollars invested in second mortgages.
   x_5 = dollars invested in short-term loans.

2. **The objective function**

   Total yearly yield, $z = .15x_1 + .10x_2 + .136x_3 + .14x_4 + .18x_5$ which is to be maximized.

3. **The constraints**

   Monthly availability: $x_1 + x_2 + x_3 + x_4 + x_5 \leq 53,000,000$
   policy a : $x_3 \leq .2x_2$
   b : $x_1 \leq x_4$
   c : $x_2 + x_4 \geq .6(x_1 + x_2 + x_3 + x_4 + x_5)$
   d : $x_2 \geq 2x_4$
   e : $x_5 \leq 5,000,000$

   ### The solution

   $$x_1 = 10,900,000$$
   $$x_2 = 21,800,000$$
   $$x_3 = 4,400,000$$
   $$x_4 = 10,900,000$$
   $$x_5 = 5,000,000$$
   $$z = 6,838,808$$

Paper manufacturing

A papermill produces two types of paper; for books and for magazines. Each ton of paper for books requires 2 tons of spruce and 3 tons of fir; each ton of paper for magazines requires 2 tons of spruce and 2 tons of fir. The company must supply at least 25,000 tons of paper for books and 100,000 tons of paper for magazines a year. The yearly availability of materials is 278,000 tons of spruce and 426,000 tons of fir. The marketing department requires that the amount of paper manufactured for magazines be at least 1.5 times that which is manufactured for books. Each ton of paper for books is sold for $750 while that for magazines is sold for $685 per ton. The cost of spruce is $100 per ton while a ton of fir cost $112.

Find:

a. The most profitable production plan.
b. The best use of the resources.
c. The annual profit.

Formulation

1. The decision variables

$$x_1 = \text{paper produced for books (in tons)}$$
$$x_2 = \text{paper produced for magazines (in tons)}$$

2. The objective function

Cost of making paper for books: $2(100) + 3(112) = 536$.
Revenue = 750. Thus, profit = $750 - 536 = \$214/\text{ton}$.

Cost of making paper for magazines: $2(100) + 2(112) = 424$.
Revenue = 685. Thus profit = $685 - 424 = \$261/\text{ton}$.

The objective function is:

$$\text{maximize } z = 214x_1 + 261x_2$$

3. The constraints

$$2x_1 + 2x_2 \leq 278,000 \text{ (spruce availability)}$$
$$3x_1 + 2x_2 \leq 426,000 \text{ (fir availability)}$$
$$x_1 \geq 25,000 \text{ (supply requirement)}$$
$$x_2 \geq 100,000 \text{ (supply requirement)}$$
$$x_2 \geq 1.5x_1 \ or: \ 1.5x_1 - x_2 \leq 0 \text{ (marketing requirement)}$$

The solution

a. The optimal solution is:

$$x_1 = 25,000$$
$$x_2 = 114,000$$

b. The spruce is used in full (slack = 0).
The fir is only partially utilized.
(There is a slack of 147,000 tons).

c. The annual profit is $z = \$35,104,000$.

A marketing application

The Everglade Shoe Company plans to allocate some or all of its monthly advertising budget of \$82,000 in the Miami Metropolitan area. It can purchase local radio spots at \$120 per spot, local TV spots at \$600 per spot, and local newspaper advertising at \$220 per insertion.

The company's policy requirements specify that the company must spend at least \$40,000 on TV but prohibits monthly newspaper expenditures in excess of \$60,000 or 50 percent of the TV expenditures, whichever is the larger.

The payoff from each advertising medium is a function of the size of its audience. The general experience of the firm is that the values of insertions and spots in terms of "audience points" (an arbitrary unit), are as given below:

Radio...........	40 audience points per spot
TV.............	180 audience points per spot
Newspapers	320 audience points per insertion

Find the optimal allocation of advertising expenditure among the three media.

Formulation

1. *The decision variables*

   x_1 = no. of spots allocated to radio.
   x_2 = no. of spots allocated to TV.
   x_3 = no. of insertions allocated to newspapers.

2. *The objective function*

   $$\text{maximize } z = 40x_1 + 180x_2 + 320x_3$$

3. *The constraints*

   $$120x_1 + 600x_2 + 220x_3 \leq 82,000$$
   $$600x_2 \geq 40,000$$

   and either

   $$220x_3 \leq 60,000$$

   or

   $$200x_3 \leq 300x_2$$

   and x_1, x_2, x_3 are integers.

The solution

The problem must be solved twice, once for each set of "either/or" constraints, and the better solution selected.

Either: $x_2 = 66\frac{2}{3}$, $x_3 = 190.9$, $z = 73,090.9$
Or: $x_2 = 91.1$, $x_3 = 124.24$, $z = 56,157.6$

The first solution is better. Rounding to integers:

$$x_2 = 66$$
$$x_3 = 191$$
$$z = \$73,000$$

5.7 CONCLUDING REMARKS

Linear programming is a powerful tool of management science, designed to solve allocation problems. Such problems appear in dozens of forms and complications. The major difficulty is that there are an infinite number of feasible solutions; therefore, finding the optimal or the *best of all* possible solutions is not usually possible by complete enumeration. Linear programming is a model that enables an efficient search for the optimal solution.

Linear programming models the allocation problem with two parts: a linear objective function which is to be maximized or minimized, and a set of linear constraints that describe the limitations and requirements subject to which the maximization or minimization is attempted.

The model is solved by an efficient algorithm called the simplex method. This method is presented in Part B of this chapter. The graphical method which was presented in Part A is very restricted in use. Part B of this chapter (as well as Chapters 6 and 7) deals with various topics and extensions that relax some of the limiting assumptions enabling linear programming to be applied to a wide range of situations.

5.8 PROBLEMS FOR PART A

1. The AA Corporation produces two products. Profit for product A is $60, and for product B $50. Each must pass through two machines, P and Q. Product A requires 10 minutes on machine P and 8 minutes on machine Q. Product B requires 20 minutes on machine P and 5 minutes on machine Q. Machine P is available 200 minutes a day while machine Q is available 80 minutes a day. The company must produce at least two units of product A and five of product B each day. Units which are not completed in a given day are finished the next day; that is, a portion of a product can be produced in the daily plan. What is the most profitable daily production plan?

    a. Formulate.

b. Solve graphically (specifically show all constraints and the objective function as well as the optimal solution).

c. How should the resources be allocated?

2. Given:

$$\text{maximize } z = 5x_1 + 5x_2$$
subject to:
1) $1x_1 + 2x_2 \leq 30$
2) $1x_1 + 1x_2 \leq 19$
3) $8x_1 + 3x_2 \leq 120$

a. Solve the problem graphically.

b. If the problem has more than one optimal solution explain why this is so and list all the optimal solutions.

c. Find the slacks or surpluses, or both, on all constraints.

3. Given a set of constraints:

1) $10x_1 + 8x_2 \leq 120$
2) $5x_1 + 5x_2 \geq 30$
3) $x_1 \geq 2$
4) $x_2 \leq 10$
5) $x_2 \geq x_1$

a. Graphically display the feasible area.

b. Compute the coordinates of all feasible corner (intersection) points.

c. If the objective function is:

$$\text{maximize } z = 5.5x_1 + 3x_2$$

find the value of the objective function at all corner points. Which corner point is the best one?

d. Graphically draw the slope of the objective function. Confirm the findings of part (c).

e. Find the slacks/surpluses on all constraints.

f. Suppose the objective function is:

$$\text{minimize } z = 5.5x_1 + 3x_2$$

What will the optimal solution be?

4. Given:

$$\text{maximize } z = 8x_1 + 6x_2$$
subject to:
1) $5x_1 + 2x_2 \leq 60$
2) $2x_1 + 4x_2 \leq 48$
3) $3x_1 \geq 15$
4) $5x_1 - 4x_2 \leq 40$

a. Graphically show the feasible solution area.

b. Compute the coordinates of all intersecting feasible corners.

c. Find the optimal solution.

d. Find the value of the objective function.

e. Find the slacks/surpluses on all constraints.

f. Suppose the last constraint is changed to a strict equality. What will the optimal solution be now?

5. A store sells men's and ladies' tennis shoes. It makes a profit of $1 a pair on the men's shoes and $1.20 a pair on the ladies'. It takes two minutes of a salesperson's time and two minutes of a cashier's time to sell a pair of men's shoes. It takes three minutes of a salesperson's time and one minute of a cashier's time per pair of women's shoes. The store is open eight hours per day, during which time there are two salespersons and one cashier on duty. How much of the salespersons' and the cashier's time should be allocated to the men's and ladies' shoes and how many shoes should the store sell in order to maximize profit each day? What is the profit?

a. Formulate as a linear programming problem.

b. Solve graphically.

6. A knitting machine can produce 1,000 pants or 3,000 shirts (or a combination of the two) each day. The finishing department can handle either 1,500 pants or 2,000 shirts (or a combination of the two) each day. The marketing department requires that at least 400 pants be produced each day. The company's stated objective is profit maximization.

a. If the profit from a pair of pants is $4 and that derived from a shirt is $1.50, how many of each type should be produced? Solve graphically.

Hint: This problem is similar to the production example in Section 5.6.

b. If the profit from a shirt is $2, what should be the *minimum* profit derived from selling a pair of pants that will justify production of pants only?

c. Examine the solutions to (a) and (b) and interpret the difference between them.

Can this interpretation be generalized to all LP graphical solutions?

7. The owner of Black Angus Ranch is trying to determine the correct mix of two types of beef feed, A and B, which cost 50 cents and 75 cents per pound respectively. Five essential ingredients are contained in the feed, as shown in the table below which also indicates the minimum daily requirements of each ingredient:

| | Percent per pound of feed | | Minimum daily requirement (pounds) |
Ingredient	Feed A	Feed B	
1	20	25	30
2	30	10	50
3	0	30	20
4	24	15	60
5	10	20	40

Find the least-cost daily blend for the ranch; that is, how many pounds of feed A and feed B will be included in the mix? (Solve graphically.)

8. The ABC Company produces valves. Two alternative production lines are available. The company just received an order for producing 1000 Mark I valves. Line 1 can produce the valves at a rate of 15 minutes for each valve. The production capacity on line 2 is 5 valves per hour. Line 1 is available, for this order, for not more than 200 hours at $8 an hour. Line 2 is available, for this order, for not more than 170 hours at $5 an hour.
   Find the best production plan.
   a. Formulate in two different ways. (*Hint:* In one of the ways, the decision variables are in terms of hours.)
   b. Solve graphically.
   c. Discuss the best allocation of resources.

Problems for formulation[22]

9. a. Given a constraint $3x_1 + 5x_2 - x_3 \le 80$
      The optimal solution is: $x_1 = 5$, $x_2 = 6$, $x_3 = 1$;

---

[22] The remaining problems in Part A of this chapter cannot be solved graphically. They are given for the purpose of formulation. A computer solution is suggested.

find the slack on this constraint.
   b. Given a constraint $5x_1 + 2x_2 + 8x_3 \ge 120$
      The optimal solution is: $x_1 = 20$, $x_2 = 10$, $x_3 = 0$;
      find the surplus on this constraint.

10. Carlo's International manufactures blue jeans. Three brands are considered: A, B, and C. The manufacture of brand A requires 2 minutes machine time, 30 minutes labor, and costs $7. Brand B requires 2.5 minutes machine time, 40 minutes labor, and costs $10 to produce. Finally, Brand C, the top of the line, requires 3 minutes machine time, 1 hour labor, and costs $13 to produce. Brand A sells for $12, Brand B for $14, and Brand C for $20.
   The company works on a weekly schedule of 5 days, with 2 shifts of 7.5 hours (net time) each. It has 4 machines available for production and 50 employees on each shift. Its weekly manufacturing budget is $10,000. Its declared objective is profit maximization.
   a. Formulate the problem as a linear program.
   b. Solve the problem (use the computer).

11. The H.E.E. Construction Company is building roads on the side of South Mountain. It is necessary to use explosives to blow up the underground boulders to make the surface level. There are three ingredients (A, B, C) in the explosive used. It is known that at least 10 ounces of the explosive must be used to get results. If more than 20 ounces is used, the explosion will be too damaging. Also, for an explosion, at least ¼ ounce of ingredient C must be used for every ounce of ingredient A, and at least 1 ounce of ingredient B must be used for every ounce of ingredient C. The costs of ingredients A, B, and C are $6, $18, and $20 per ounce, respectively. Find the least-cost explosive mix necessary to produce a safe explosion.

12. Westcan Corporation is considering producing five different types of small computers which yield the following per unit profits:

Type	A	B	C	D	E
Net profit ($000)	16	8	11	6	10

The company has $1,000,000 capital to invest in production and a capability of 10,000 working days.

The capital and labor requirements for each product are given below.

Type	Required capital per unit ($000)	Required per unit working days
A	20	200
B	15	120
C	16	150
D	10	80
E	14	100

Formulate as a linear program to find the best production plan:

a. If the company's objective is *profit maximization*.
b. If the company's objective is to produce the *maximum number of total units* (of all types together).

13. ABC Corporation can produce three products:

A which costs $6 per unit and sells for $9 per unit.
B which costs $5 per unit and sells for $6 per unit.
C which costs $8 per unit and sells for $9 per unit.

The company's declared objective is profit maximization. The company is planning a monthly production schedule. The marketing department requires the production of at least 100 units of product C and no more than 1,000 units of product A. The production department cannot produce more than 4,000 units of all products. Products are made on the grinding machine which can produce 20, 30, or 40 units of products A, B, or C respectively per hour. The machine is available for up to 100 hours each month. The marketing department also requires that there be at least twice as many units of B as of C in the monthly schedule. The finance department has set an upper budget of $15,000 for the schedule.

How many units of A, B, and C should the company produce?

14. Atlantic Chemical produces three products, A, B, and C, which can be extracted and blended from three ores: b_1, which costs $2 a ton and up to 1,000 tons of which is available a month; b_2, which costs $1.50 a ton and up to 800 tons a month are available; and b_3, which costs $3 a ton and is available in unlimited quantities. The company wishes to determine how much of each product to make from the available ores so as to maximize the profit from the overall operation. The requirements on the ores are as follows:

Product A requires
   5 tons b_1, 10 tons b_2, 10 tons b_3
Product B requires
   7 tons b_1,   8 tons b_2,   5 tons b_3
Product C requires
   10 tons b_1,   5 tons b_2, no tons b_3

Per ton of product

Sales price per ton: A = $130, B = $140, C = $100.

a. What important assumption, which is not usually implied in an LP problem, is necessary to formulate this problem in LP terms?
b. Formulate as a linear programming problem.

15. A market research firm wishes to conduct home visit interviews according to the quotas specified in the first column of the following table:

Type of household	Responding calls (quota)	Probability of response to calls		
		Morning	Afternoon	Evening
Single person	50	.1	.1	.5
Married, no children	100	.5	.4	.7
Married, children	150	.75	.6	.9

Since not all persons are at home at the time of the visit and not all persons cooperate, there is only a certain "probability of response" to the home visits (calls).

The following requirements are imposed:

1. The total number (responding and nonresponding) of morning calls must not exceed the total number of afternoon calls.

2. The total number of responding evening calls must be at least 20 percent and no more than 30 percent of the total number of all responding calls.

3. An evening call costs twice as much as a morning or an afternoon call.

Decide how the calls should be distributed among the three types of households (by the three times during the day) such that the *expected* quotas be fulfilled at a minimum cost. Formulate only.

16. Glades Discount Store is opening a new department with a storage area of 10,000 square feet. Management considers four products for display.

Product A: Costs $55, sells for $80, and requires 24 square feet per unit for storage.
Product B: Costs $100, sells for $130, and requires 20 square feet per unit for storage.
Product C: Costs $200, sells for $295, and requires 36 square feet per unit for storage.
Product D: Costs $300, sells for $399, and requires 50 square feet per unit for storage.

It is required that at least ten units of each product be on display. The company's objective is profit maximization.

Find out how many units of each product should be on display if the company has $600,000 available for purchasing the product. Formulate as a linear programming problem (assuming divisibility of the products; that is, ignore the fact that the answer should be in integer form).

17. Observe any business or economic process (except manufacturing) that involves allocation of scarce resources.

   a. Describe the process. Make up data if they are not available.
   b. Formulate the process as a linear program.
   c. Solve the problem (you may use the computer).
   d. Specify all assumptions made.
   e. Discuss the availability of data.
   f. Discuss anticipated problems in implementing the solution.

   Note: Try to be original, especially with regard to input data.

PART B: EXTENSIONS

5.9 THE SIMPLEX METHOD

LP in 1947

The simplex method is an iterative[23] algorithm for efficiently solving large linear programming problems. It was first developed in 1947 by G. B. Dantzig [3] and his associates in the U.S. Department of the Air Force. Some revisions in the method have since been made in order to increase computational efficiency, but the basic approach remains the same. The simplex method and its variations have now been programmed and coded for practically all makes and types of computers. Before launching into the simplex process, however, it will be worthwhile to spend some time visualizing, in graphic terms, what the simplex process does algebraically.

The simplex method

Graphical explanation of the simplex process

It was pointed out during the graphical solution procedure that the search for an optimal solution can be limited to only the corner points of the feasible solution space. This was easy enough to do by hand for a problem with only two variables and three constraints, but for larger problems a more efficient procedure for identifying and evaluating corner points is necessary. This is one of the main objectives of the simplex method.

Moving to adjacent corners

In the simplex method, the search usually starts at the origin and moves to that *adjacent corner* which increases (for maximization problems) the value of the objective function the most. Upon reaching such a corner the search moves to an even better corner adjacent to the new one. The process continues until no further improvement is possible. To illustrate this process in two dimensions, we reproduce Figure 5.5 as Figure 5.12. The search starts at the origin O and moves to corner C (corner C has a profit of $3,750 versus $3,600 at corner E, see Table 5.1) and then to the optimal point, corner G.

Optimality by iteration

The simplex process must always reach the optimum solution (if a solution exists) because in each iteration the objective function improves and there are only a finite number of corner points in the feasible solution space. Also, the optimum will be reached regardless of which direction the process starts. In Figure 5.12 for example, going first to point E would not have affected the ultimate solution, nor the number of iterations, though in other situations different routes will result in a different number of iterations.

---

[23] The iterative simplex procedure obtains an optimal solution by sequentially improving the previous solution. The improvement procedure follows the same steps each time; that is, it "iterates" through the same process in each pass.

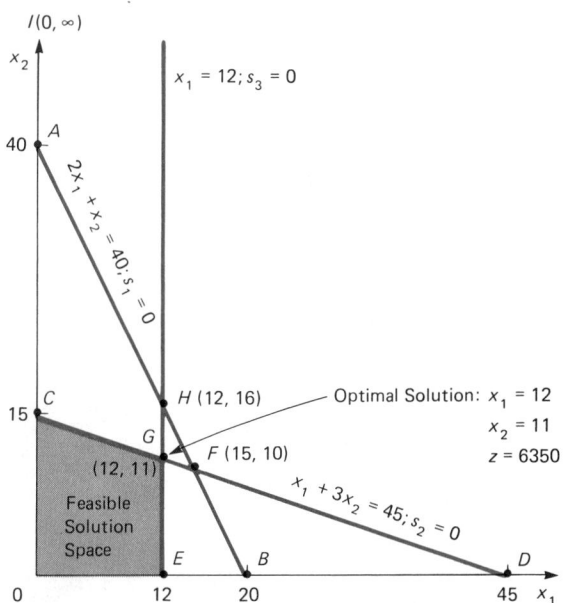

FIGURE 5.12
The product-mix
problem (basic solution
points)

The simplex process

The computational process of the simplex involves six steps as depicted in Figure 5.13. These steps are:

Step 1   Standardize the problem into a linear programming tableau.
Step 2   Generate an initial solution.
Step 3   Test the solution for optimality. If the solution is not optimal, improve (go to step 4); otherwise go to step 6.

The improvement of a nonoptimal solution is done in two steps: The steps

Step 4   Identify one variable that will leave the solution and one variable that will enter the solution.
Step 5   Generate an improved solution. The improved solution is checked for optimality. If it is not optimal, then steps 4 and 5 are repeated. If it is optimal, step 6 is undertaken.
Step 6   Find if more than one optimal solution exists.

This process guarantees that an optimal solution, if it exists, will be found in a finite number of iterations. The process will be illustrated through a product-mix example.

FIGURE 5.13
Schematic presentation
of the simplex method

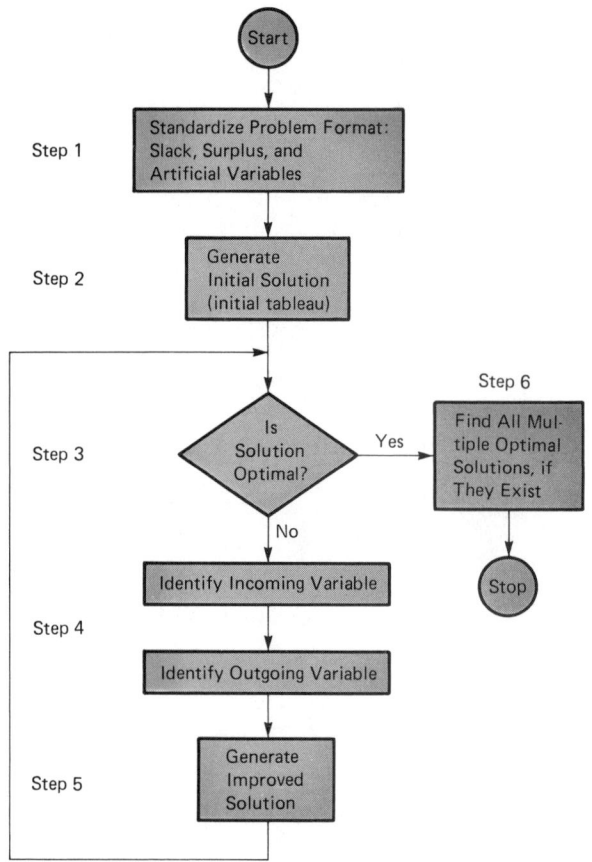

Example Let us reproduce the product-mix problem which was previously solved graphically.

$$\text{maximize } z = 300x_1 + 250x_2$$
$$\text{subject to:}$$
$$2x_1 + 1x_2 \leq 40$$
$$1x_1 + 3x_2 \leq 45$$
$$1x_1 + 0x_2 \leq 12$$

The graphical solution of the problem is shown in Figure 5.12.

Step 1: Standardize the problem

A standard form

Since only corner points of the feasible solution space are to be checked and since these points are defined by the intersection of equations, it is necessary to convert the inequalities in the problem statement into equations in order to find the coordinates of the intersecting points. Such a conversion depends on the type of constraints involved.

Constraints with inequalities of the "smaller-than-or-equal-to" type

A "slack" variable is added to each of these type constraints. For example, the labor constraint in the product-mix problem is: Slack variable

$$2x_1 + x_2 \leq 40$$

Adding a slack variable:

$$2x_1 + x_2 + s_1 = 40$$

where s_1 = slack of labor and $s_1 \geq 0$.

For example, if it was decided to produce 5 type-A sets and 15 type-B sets, then the total required labor hours would be

$$2 \times 5 + 1 \times 15 = 25.$$

However, 40 labor hours are available. Therefore, the unused portion of the labor hour supply, that is, the *slack*, s_1, is 15 hours. Note that a negative slack is not allowed. For instance, producing 20 type-A and 15 type-B sets results in a "slack" of -15 hours. That is, 15 more labor hours are required than are available. Lastly, note that if *no* sets, either A or B, were produced ($x_1 = x_2 = 0$ is a common starting point in the simplex procedure) then the slack s_1 would be 40:

$$2 \times 0 + 1 \times 0 + s_1 = 40.$$

Constraints with inequalities of the "larger-than-or-equal-to" type

Let us examine the blending constraint $x_1 + x_2 \geq 300$. Once a solution is found and the values of the variables are introduced into the constraint, then the left side can be either equal to *or* larger than 300. In the latter case there will be a *surplus*. Let us call it s_2. It is possible therefore to write the inequality $x_1 + x_2 \geq 300$ as: Surplus variable

$$1x_1 + 1x_2 - s_2 = 300$$

where $s_2 \geq 0$.

For example, if 160 ounces of Alpha and 150 ounces of Beta are used in the blend, then

$$160 + 150 - s_2 = 300$$

or the surplus, s_2, is 10. This solution would mean that it is more profitable to exceed the minimum specification than to meet it exactly.

Artificial variables

However, if no Alpha or Beta is produced ($x_1 = x_2 = 0$), then the equation $1x_1 + 1x_2 - 1s_2 = 300$ will result in the solution $s_2 = -300$ which is not allowable. Neither a slack nor a surplus can be negative.

Artificial variable

To overcome this difficulty an auxiliary variable, called an *artificial variable*, is introduced into the equation. The constraint is then written as:

$$1x_1 + 1x_2 - s_2 + a_2 = 300$$

where a_2 is the artificial variable for the constraint ($a_2 \geq 0$). When x_1, x_2, and s_2 are set to zero, then $a_2 = 300$.

Since the sole objective of the artificial variable is to avoid negative values of the variables in initial simplex solutions, it does not have any physical meaning and must be kept out of any final solution. In order to prevent such a variable from entering the optimal solution, a very large penalty (usually denoted by the symbol M) is assigned as a coefficient to the corresponding variable in the objective function.[24] (In computerized LP routines M is assigned the largest value the computer can hold.) This then keeps the artificial variable from ever being an attractive alternative solution. An example will be given later.

Penalty of M

Constraints with an equality

Consider a constraint given as an equality, say,

$$3x_1 + 1x_2 = 10$$

If, as an initial simplex solution, the two variables x_1 and x_2 are set to zero, a value of $0 = 10$ is obtained, which is unacceptable. This difficulty is again solved by adding an artificial variable:

$$3x_1 + 1x_2 + a_3 = 10$$

Then, when x_1 and x_2 are set to zero, $a_3 = 10$. Again, a penalty of M must be assigned to a_3 in the objective function to preclude using a_3 in the final solution because a_3 has no physical meaning.

We will return to this issue of artificial variables and how to handle them in the simplex in Section 5.10.

Once the constraints have been modified, the problem can then be written in a standard form.

Example a: The product-mix problem Since all the constraints in this example are of the type $\leq$, then it is necessary to add three slacks, one for each constraint ($s_1 =$ slack on labor, $s_2 =$ slack on machine time, and $s_3 =$ marketing slack). *The slack variables will have a coefficient of zero in the objective function* because "producing" slack (i.e., not using a resource) does not generate any profit, nor does it have any costs. The problem then can be written in a *standard form* as shown in Table 5.4.

---

[24] The magnitude of M should be large enough to *assure* that the artificial variable will be so undesirable that it will never enter a solution.

		TABLE 5.4
Objective function:	Maximize $z = 300x_1 + 250x_2 + 0s_1 + 0s_2 + 0s_3$	Standard form for the
subject to:	(1) $\qquad 2x_1 + 1x_2 + s_1 \qquad\qquad = 40$	product-mix problem
	(2) $\qquad 1x_1 + 3x_2 \qquad + s_2 \qquad = 45$	
	(3) $\qquad 1x_1 \qquad\qquad\qquad + s_3 = 12$	

Example b: The blending problem   The blending problem was formulated as:

$$\text{minimize } z = 45x_1 + 12x_2$$
$$\text{subject to:}$$
$$1x_1 + 1x_2 \geq 300$$
$$3x_1 + 0x_2 \geq 250$$

Since the constraints are of the "larger-than-or-equal-to" type, it is necessary to add both surplus and artificial variables. The resulting standard form is shown in Table 5.5. The surpluses have a coefficient of zero in the objective function because they incur no cost. However, to ensure that the artificial variables are kept out of the final solution, they are given a large cost penalty of $+M$ in the objective function (use $-M$ in a maximization problem).

		TABLE 5.5
Objective function:	Minimize $z = 45x_1 + 12x_2 + 0s_1 + 0s_2 + Ma_1 + Ma_2$	Standard form for the
subject to:	(1) $\qquad 1x_1 + 1x_2 - s_1 \qquad + a_1 \qquad = 300$	blending problem
	(2) $\qquad 3x_1 + 0x_2 \qquad - s_2 \qquad + a_2 = 250$	

Before proceeding to step 2 let us explain, again in graphical terms, what the simplex method does once the problem is written in standard form.

Basic variables and a basis

The product-mix maximization problem, as presented in Table 5.4 consists of a system of three linear equations describing the constraints and a family of isoprofit functions (the objective function). To determine corner points the intersection coordinates of the constraints must be calculated. In order to do so it is necessary to solve the three linear equations simultaneously.

Note that there exist five unknown variables: x_1, x_2, s_1, s_2, and s_3; on the other hand, there are only three equations. A solution to a system of linear equations requires that the number of equations equal the number of variables; otherwise there will be an infinite number of solutions. To overcome this problem, two of the five variables are set to zero. Then it is possible to solve the system of linear equations for the three remaining variables. In general, two cases are distinguished:

Basic solutions

The *basis*

1. Solutions with exactly m variables, where m is the number of constraints, are called *basic solutions*. The m variables in these solutions are called basic variables and they constitute the *basis* of the solution. The remaining variables have values of zero.
2. Solutions that include more than m nonzero variables are called *nonbasic* solutions.

Feasible—Infeasible

The *basic* solutions can be further divided into two groups: *feasible* and *infeasible*. The *feasible solutions* are those that satisfy *all* the constraints; that is, they are in the *feasible* area and the value of *all* their variables must be nonnegative.

Basic feasible

The simplex procedure searches for *basic feasible solutions* only (the corner points of the feasible area). In large linear programming problems, such solutions are a small part of all basic solutions. Thus, the amount of search is much less than that required by complete enumeration of all corner points.

Graphical illustration: The product-mix problem (from Figure 5.12) With three equations and five unknowns, there are ten possible ways of setting two of the variables to zero and solving for the remaining three variables. Thus, there are ten bases which are listed in Table 5.6.

TABLE 5.6
The ten possible bases for the product-mix problem

Basis no.	Variables in the solution					Corner points in Figure 5.12	Feasible?
	x_1	x_2	s_1	s_2	s_3		
1.....	0	0	40	45	12	O	Yes
2.....	0	40	0	−75	12	A	No
3.....	0	15	25	0	12	C	Yes
4.....	0	∞	−∞	−∞	0	I	No
5.....	20	0	0	25	−8	B	No
6.....	45	0	−50	0	−33	D	No
7.....	12	0	16	33	0	E	Yes
8.....	15	10	0	0	−3	F	No
9.....	12	16	0	−15	0	H	No
10.....	12	11	5	0	0	G	Yes

Each of these bases is a *basic solution*, as shown in Figure 5.12. But only the corner points $O, C, G,$ and E have nonnegative values for *all five* variables in Table 5.6.[25] Therefore, only *these* corner points (listed in Table 5.7) constitute the *feasible* basic solutions of Table 5.6. The search for an optimal solution is now narrowed from ten points to four.

---

[25] Slack variables cannot take negative values either and therefore points such as A and H correspond to infeasible solutions.

Notice in Table 5.7 that each succeeding corner includes all but one of the same basic variables though their *values* may differ. That is, C has two of the basic variables (s_1 and s_3) that O has and has x_2 replacing s_2, and G has the same basis as C except for x_1 replacing s_3. And in E, s_2 replaces x_2 of G. Returning to the origin O, s_3 replaces x_1 of E. Therefore, each pair of succeeding bases represent *adjacent* corners of the feasible solution space in Figure 5.12.

Corner	x_1	x_2	s_1	s_2	s_3
O......	0	0	40	45	12
C......	0	15	25	0	12
G......	12	11	5	0	0
E......	12	0	16	33	0

TABLE 5.7
The feasible corner points (basic feasible solutions)

This then will be the solution procedure of the simplex method. The search starts with a solution at the origin, O. Then it moves to an adjacent corner where the objective function achieves the largest initial improvement and continues on from corner to corner, improving the value of the objective function each time. At some point, no further improvement will be possible, signaling the attainment of the optimal solution. Note: In some cases the origin is not a feasible starting solution. This situation is handled in a special way as will be shown later.

Step 2: Generate an initial solution

The expression of the LP problem in the standard form of step 1 suggests an easy initial solution that is both basic and feasible. For example, the product-mix problem expressed in Table 5.4 has 3 constraint equations and 5 variables. Thus, there must be $5 - 3 = 2$ nonbasic variables with zero values and 3 basic variables to solve for. Reproducing these equations:

$$2x_1 + 1x_2 + 1s_1 = 40$$
$$1x_1 + 3x_2 + 1s_2 = 45$$
$$1x_1 + 0x_2 + 1s_3 = 12$$

A natural solution to this set of equations would be to set x_1 and x_2 as the nonbasic variables with s_1, s_2, and s_3 as the basic variables. This is because x_1 and x_2 appear in more than one equation, whereas s_1, s_2, and s_3 each appear only once and in different equations and can thus be solved easily. Setting $x_1 = x_2 = 0$ and solving for s_1, s_2, and s_3:

$$s_1 = 40, \ s_2 = 45, \ s_3 = 12.$$

The resulting profit is found from the objective function as:

$$z = 300x_1 + 250x_2 + 0s_1 + 0s_2 + 0s_3$$
$$= 300(0) + 250(0) + 0(40) + 0(45) + 0(12) = 0$$

Obtaining such a simple initial solution is, of course, the purpose of starting the simplex solultion process with a standard format. The simplex process then *continues to maintain* this simplified solution format through the *Gauss–Jordan method* of solving simultaneous equations (see Section A5 of Appendix A). That is, each iteration of the simplex involves again expressing the set of equations such that each basic variable appears in only one, a different one, of the equations. This is not as difficult as it may sound because the simplex begins from such a point (as in Table 5.4) and then switches only *one* of the basic variables for one of the nonbasic variables, as we saw in Table 5.7. Thus, reexpressing the equations in this special form only requires eliminating the new basic variable from all but one equation.

The Gauss–Jordan method

To facilitate the required manipulations of the equations the simplex process makes use of a specialized adaptation of the standard LP form shown in Table 5.4. This adaptation is called a "tableau" (*tabulated coefficients*).

The structure of a tableau

Figure 5.14 illustrates the initial tableau of the product-mix problem. Explanations of its major parts are included.

FIGURE 5.14
A tableau explanation

			Main body					
	List of basic variables	*Coefficients of objective function*	*Quantity in solution*	*Decision variables*		*Slack (surplus) variables*		
	Basis	*Unit profits*	*Quantity*	x_1	x_2	s_1	s_2	s_3
Basis Rows	s_1	0	40	2	1	1	0	0
	s_2	0	45	1	3	0	1	0
	s_3	0	12	1	0	0	0	1
c_j row (coefficients of objective function)				300	250	0	0	0
z_j row (new coefficient: per unit "losses")				0	0	0	0	0
$c_j - z_j$ row (the evaluator)				300	250	0	0	0

Discussion

Notice that the tableau includes three rows, one for each constraint. This correspondence will be maintained throughout the entire simplex manipulations.

The main body of the tableau corresponds to the standard format of the problem, as shown in Table 5.4. Notice however that the variables are not repeated in each row but are summarized on the top. Also notice that the right hand side quantities have been shifted to the left. The column "Basis" identifies the proposed initial solution variables ("boxed" in the table).

The z_j row   The row denoted z_j is labeled "unit loss". It shows the amount of profit the objective function will be *reduced* by when one unit of the variable, in each column, is *removed* from the basis. Initially, all z_j's have values of zero. The reason for this is that only slack variables are in the first tableau and their coefficients in the objective function are always initially zero.

Each value in this row is found as follows:

> *Rule:*   Multiply the elements in the "Unit Profits" column by the corresponding elements of the main body, on a variable by variable basis and total the results. For example, the z_j for column x_2 is: $0(1) + 0(3) + 0(0) = 0$.

The evaluator row: $c_j - z_j$ The bottom row, $c_j - z_j$, shows the *net* impact on the value of the objective function of bringing one unit of each of the column variables into the basis. The c_j's tell us how much will be gained while the z_j's tell us how much will simultaneously be lost. If the difference between the two is *positive* then the value of the objective function can be *increased* by introducing one unit of the variable into the solution. In maximization problems this is an indication of a possible *improvement*; i.e., if one (or more) of the $c_j - z_j$ values is positive then the solution is *not optimal*. This is the basis of the analysis to be conducted in step 3.

Economic interpretation   The value $c_j - z_j$ represents the *opportunity cost* of not having one unit of the corresponding variable in the solution. That is, it shows the marginal impact on the value of the objective function. (The value $c_j - z_j$ of the slack variables is related to the concept of the *dual variables* to be presented in Chapter 6.)

The value of the objective function z   Finally, the value of the objective function can be computed by multiplying each "Unit Profit" by its corresponding quantity, and then totaling the results. For example, the value of the objective function (total profit) in Figure 5.14 is:

$$0(40) + 0(45) + 0(12) = 0.$$

Step 3: Test for optimality

This test is made by examining the $c_j - z_j$ row in the tableau and using the following rule.

> **Rule for optimality**
>
> In an optimal solution of a maximization problem all the coefficients of the $c_j - z_j$ row must be nonpositive (either zero or negative).

That is, if bringing any other variable into the basis can only either decrease the profit or leave it unchanged, then the current solution must be optimal. Since both coefficients of x_1 and x_2 are positive in the $c_j - z_j$ row of Table 5.8, then introducing either x_1 or x_2 into the basis will *increase* the profit. Therefore, the current solution is *not* optimal.

Since the solution is not optimal it can be improved. The improvement is done by:

- Identifying the incoming variable.
- Identifying the outgoing variable.
- Building the improved tableau.

Step 4: Identify the incoming and outgoing variables

In order to illustrate this step the initial tableau of the product mix problem is presented in Table 5.8. The improvement is done by an exchange of variables: one incoming, one outgoing.

TABLE 5.8
The initial product-mix tableau (I)

	Basis	Unit profits	Quantity	Incoming x_1	x_2	s_1	s_2	s_3	Ratio
	s_1	0	40	2	1	[1]	0	0	$40/2 = 20$
	s_2	0	45	1	3	0	[1]	0	45
Outgoing	s_3	0	12	①	0	0	0	[1]	12
	c_j (unit profits)			300	250	0	0	0	
	z_j (unit losses)			0	0	0	0	0	
	$c_j - z_j$			300	250	0	0	0	

Incoming

The incoming variable An incoming variable (currently nonbasic, to be changed to a basic variable) is chosen by inspecting the $c_j - z_j$ row of the current solution for that variable with the *largest positive* coefficient. In this example, therefore, x_1 with a coefficient of 300, is chosen.

Rule for determining the incoming variable

Select the column with the largest positive coefficient in the $c_j - z_j$ row.

The outgoing variable   Once the incoming variable has been identified it is necessary to identify the outgoing variable.

Outgoing

The procedure for determining the *outgoing basic variable* (either s_1, s_2, or s_3 in the example) is somewhat more involved. In essence, the outgoing variable is that basic variable which is first reduced to zero as x_1 (the incoming variable) increases from zero. This is done as follows. For each basis row in the tableau, form the ratio of the "Quantity" to the coefficient of the incoming variable. In this case the incoming variable is x_1 so the three ratios are $40/2 = 20$, $45/1 = 45$, and $12/1 = 12$, which are listed in the rightmost column of the tableau. Select the row with the smallest ratio, ignoring any negative values; this row's basic variable will be the *outgoing* variable. In Table 5.8 the smallest ratio is 12 so the outgoing variable is s_3.

The coefficient of the incoming variable in the outgoing row is called the "pivot element" and is circled in Table 5.8 for later reference.

Pivot element

The above procedure is summarized in the following rule.

Rule for determining the outgoing variable

Look down the column of the incoming variable and consider only positive elements (coefficients). Then, divide the quantity of each constraint by the corresponding coefficient in the column of the incoming variable. The row with the smallest ratio is selected as the outgoing row.

Step 5: Generate an improved solution

The solution is improved by introducing the incoming variable into the basis and removing the outgoing variable.[26] This is done row by row on the old tableau, forming, in the process, a new one.

The procedure starts with transforming the row of the outgoing variable, then the other basis rows, and finally transforming the c_j, z_j, and $c_j - z_j$ rows.

---

[26] The mathematics executed in this step involve solving the new set of equations in the improved tableau. The Gauss–Jordan procedure (Appendix A) is applied through the special structure of the simplex method.

Transformation of the outgoing row

> *Rule:* Divide the main body elements and the "Quantity" of the outgoing row by the coefficient of the pivot element.

Since the coefficient is 1 in this case, the row is unchanged. Note that in the new row x_1 replaces s_3 in the "Basis" column and is thus boxed; as a result, the unit profit has been changed from 0 to 300. This information is now entered into the improved tableau (Table 5.9).

TABLE 5.9
First improved solution—Tableau II

Basis	Unit profits	Quantity	x_1	x_2	s_1	s_2	s_3	Ratio
s_1	0	16	0	1	1	0	−2	16
s_2	0	33	0	③	0	1	−1	11
x_1	300	12	1	0	0	0	1	∞
c_j			300	250	0	0	0	
z_j			300	0	0	0	300	
$c_j - z_j$			0	250	0	0	−300	

Transformation of the other rows

The transformation, again, deals only with the columns of the main body and the "Quantity". The process involves three activities:

First Identify the coefficient at the intersection of the row to be transformed and the incoming column. For example, the coefficient for the first row in Table 5.8 is 2; for the second one it is 1.

Second Multiply this number, in turn, by every element of the transformed outgoing row (the new third row here).

Third Subtract the result of the second activity from the old row (to be transformed) to derive the new transformed row.

Example: Transforming the first row

The coefficient for this row in the incoming column is 2.

	Quantity	x_1	x_2	s_1	s_2	s_3
The new third row (Table 5.9)	12	1	0	0	0	1
The row to be transformed (first row, Table 5.8)	40	2	1	1	0	0
Minus: 2 × new third row	−24	−2	0	0	0	−2
Result: New first row (Table 5.9)	16	0	1	1	0	−2

This is the first row in the improved tableau (Table 5.9). Notice that the "Basis" and the "Unit Profits" are transformed unchanged. The reason for this is that s_1 remains a basis variable.

Example: Transforming the second row

Here the coefficient is 1 and the mathematical manipulations are:

	Quantity	x_1	x_2	s_1	s_2	s_3
Second row	45	1	3	0	1	0
Minus: 1 × new third row	−12	−1	0	0	0	−1
Result: New second row (Table 5.9)	33	0	3	0	1	−1

Transformation of the c_j row

This row is transformed unchanged (always).

Computing the new z_j row

Multiply the "Unit Profits" in each row by the main body column coefficients and sum the results.

For the value in Table 5.9 under column:

$$
\begin{aligned}
x_1 \quad & 0(0) \; + 0(0) \;\; + 300(1) = 300 \\
x_2 \quad & 0(1) \; + 0(3) \;\; + 300(0) = 0 \\
s_1 \quad & 0(1) \; + 0(0) \;\; + 300(0) = 0 \\
s_2 \quad & 0(0) \; + 0(1) \;\; + 300(0) = 0 \\
s_3 \quad & 0(-2) + 0(-1) + 300(1) = 300
\end{aligned}
$$

Computing the new $c_j - z_j$ row

Simply subtract z_j from c_j.

Computing the new value of the objective function

The improved solution calls for $s_1 = 16$, $s_2 = 33$, and $x_1 = 12$ ($x_2 = 0$ and $s_3 = 0$ being nonbasic variables). The value of the objective function is thus:

$$z = 12(300) + 16(0) + 33(0) = \$3,600.$$

Step 3 (repeat): Test for optimality

The new solution must now be tested for optimality. It can be seen that the variable x_2 in the new $c_j - z_j$ row has a *positive coefficient*; therefore, the current solution is not optimal.

Step 4 (repeat): Identify incoming and outgoing variables

The incoming variable

In Tableau II (Table 5.9), x_2 has the largest positive coefficient in the $c_j - z_j$ row (250) and therefore it is the *incoming variable*.

The outgoing variable

Since the incoming variable is x_2, the ratios are:

For constraint 1: $\dfrac{16}{1} = 16$

For constraint 2: $\dfrac{33}{3} = 11 \leftarrow Smallest$

For constraint 3: $\dfrac{12}{0} = \infty$

The second row has the smallest ratio. This row contains the variable s_2 as a basic variable ("boxed" in Table 5.9). Hence, the variable s_2 is the outgoing variable. The exchange of x_2 for s_2 is equivalent to a move from corner E to corner G in Figure 5.12.

Step 5 (repeat): Generate an improved solution

The rows of the tableau of the *old solution* (Tableau II, Table 5.9) are transformed one at a time to a *new solution* (Tableau III, Table 5.10).

TABLE 5.10
Second improved
solution—Tableau III

Basis	Unit profits	Quantity	x_1	x_2	s_1	s_2	s_3	Ratio
s_1	0	5	0	0	1	$-\frac{1}{3}$	$-\frac{5}{3}$	
x_2	250	11	0	1	0	$\frac{1}{3}$	$-\frac{1}{3}$	
x_1	300	12	1	0	0	0	1	
c_j			300	250	0	0	0	
z_j			300	250	0	250/3	650/3	
$c_j - z_j$			0	0	0	$-250/3$	$-650/3$	

Step 3 (repeat): Test of optimality

Inspection of the new $c_j - z_j$ row in Table 5.10 reveals that there are no positive coefficients; hence, the second improved solution is optimal.

Interpretation of the results

The results of Table 5.10 can be read as follows:

The constraint rows

The solution values of the variables are:

row (3) $x_1 = 12$: Produce 12 model A sets.
row (2) $x_2 = 11$: Produce 11 model B sets.
row (1) $s_1 = 5$: Constraint 1 has a slack of 5; that is, only 35 hours of labor out of 40 hours will be utilized.

Note that all basic variables have a coefficient of 1. The other coefficients, for example, $-\frac{1}{3}$ in constraint 1 with s_2, are called the *ratios of substitution* between the row and column variables. They designate the trade-offs that occur when a nonbasic variable becomes a basic variable.

Ratios of substitution

The value of the objective function (profit)

The final profit can be calculated as:

$$0(5) + 250(11) + 300(12) = \$6350.$$

Step 6: Check for other optimal solutions

It is important to know if only one optimal solution exists (unique solution) or if there is more than one. Multiple optimal solutions allow management greater flexibility in implementing a solution.

The check for other optimal solutions is simple. If the coefficient of one of the *nonbasic* variables in the final $c_j - z_j$ row is zero, then multiple optimal solutions exist. A coefficient of zero means that this variable can enter the basis, creating another feasible solution, but with the *same* value of the objective function. If two solutions exist, then there must be an infinite number of optimal solutions that are linear combinations of these two solutions. In Table 5.10 there are no zero coefficients of nonbasic variables; hence, there is only one optimal solution to this problem.

5.10   SPECIAL SITUATIONS IN THE SIMPLEX METHOD

There are several special linear programming situations which require adjustments in the simplex procedure. These eight are described below.

A.   The simplex method: Minimization

The simplex method solves minimization problems in essentially the same manner as it solves maximization problems. There exist two alternative approaches for minimization problems.

Two ways to solve

The first approach is to solve the problem as a minimization problem directly, but this requires a slight change in the simplex procedure. The method of solving a minimization problem is basically the same as with a maximization problem except that all the coefficients in the $c_j - z_j$ row should be *positive* for the optimality test and the incoming variable is that variable in the $c_j - z_j$ row with the most *negative* coefficient. This method will not be pursued here.

Conversion   The second approach is to convert the problem into a maximization problem, to solve it as a maximization problem, and then translate the results in the light of the minimization objective.

Since minimizing a function is equivalent to maximizing the *negative* of that function, the only change required in order to convert a linear programming problem from minimization to maximization (or vice versa) is to multiply the objective function by -1. The constraints remain untouched.

Example 1. Given:

$$\text{minimize } z = 2x_1 - 5x_2$$

The problem is converted to:

$$\text{maximize } w = -2x_1 + 5x_2$$

When the solution is obtained (say $x_1 = 12$, $x_2 = 3$) the results should be substituted back into the *original* minimization objective function to obtain the minimized value of z; $z = 2(12) - 5(3) = 9$.

Example 2. Given:

$$\text{minimize } z = 5x_1 + 1x_2 - 2x_3$$

The problem is converted to:

$$\text{maximize } w = -5x_1 - 1x_2 + 2x_3$$

Example: Solving the blending problem   To illustrate this approach, as well as to demonstrate the procedure for handling artificial variables, the blending problem of Part A will be solved, starting from the standard form in Table 5.5. First, however, the objective function must be converted to maximization:

$$\text{max. } w = -45x_1 - 12x_2 - 0s_1 - 0s_2 - Ma_1 - Ma_2$$

where M is a very large number (e.g., 1000 or 10,000).

The equivalent tableau is given in Table 5.11. Note the inferiority of the initial "profit" solution (value of the objective function):

$$-M(300) - M(250) = -550M$$

The tableaus in Table 5.12 and 5.13 illustrate the solution process. It is suggested that the reader follow the calculations through on his or

TABLE 5.11
Tableau for the blending problem

Basis	Unit profits	Quantity	x_1	x_2	s_1	s_2	a_1	a_2	Ratio
a_1	$-M$	300	1	1	-1	0	1	0	300
a_2	$-M$	250	③	0	0	-1	0	1	250/3
c_j			-45	-12	0	0	$-M$	$-M$	
z_j			$-4M$	$-M$	M	M	$-M$	$-M$	
$c_j - z_j$			$-45 + 4M$	$-12 + M$	$-M$	$-M$	0	0	

TABLE 5.12
Second (improved) tableau (II)

Basis	Unit profits	Quantity x_1		x_2	s_1	s_2	a_1	a_2	Ratio
a_1	$-M$	216.67	0	①	-1	⅓	1	$-⅓$	216.67
x_1	-45	83.33	1	0	0	$-⅓$	0	⅓	∞
c_j			-45	-12	0	0	$-M$	$-M$	
z_j			-45	$-M$	M	$(15 - M/3)$	$-M$	$(-15 + M/3)$	
$c_j - z_j$			0	$-12 + M$	$-M$	$(M/3 - 15)$	0	$(15 - 4M/3)$	

TABLE 5.13
Third (optimal) tableau (III)

Basis	Unit profits	Quantity	x_1	x_2	s_1	s_2	a_1	a_2	Ratio
x_2	-12	216.67	0	1	-1	⅓	1	$-⅓$	
x_1	-45	83.33	1	0	0	$-⅓$	0	⅓	
c_j			-45	-12	0	0	$-M$	$-M$	
z_j			-45	-12	12	11	-12	-11	
$c_j - z_j$			0	0	-12	-11	$(12 - M)$	$(11 - M)$	

her own to ensure a complete understanding, not only of the minimization process and handling artificial variables, but of the simplex procedure itself.

Tableau III represents an optimal solution since all the coefficients in the $c_j - z_j$ row are negative or zero ($12 - M$ is a large negative number). The answer is thus:

$x_1 = 83.33$ ounces of Alpha
$x_2 = 216.67$ ounces of Beta
"Profit" $= -12(216.67) - 45(83.33) = -6350$ cents or
Cost $= -$"Profit" $= 6350$ cents.

Note that once an artificial variable leaves the basis it will never enter again because of the large penalty of M associated with it (1000 could have been used here instead of M).

B.   Two incoming variables

If two or more variables have the same largest coefficient in the $c_j - z_j$ row (see Table 5.14), then either may be arbitrarily chosen as the incoming variable. This will not affect the final solution.

174

TABLE 5.14
Tie for incoming variable

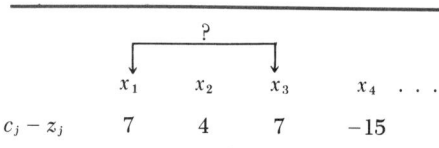

	x_1	x_2	x_3	x_4 ...
$c_j - z_j$	7	4	7	-15

C. Two outgoing basic variables (degeneracy)

The situations presented thus far had the property that the number of variables in the solution was the same as the number of constraints (not counting the nonnegativity constraints). If the number of positive variables in the solution is *less* than the number of constraints, the solution is "degenerate". An example of degeneracy occurs when three or more constraints intersect in the solution of a problem with two variables. This is shown in Figure 5.15.

FIGURE 5.15
Degeneracy in a two variable problem

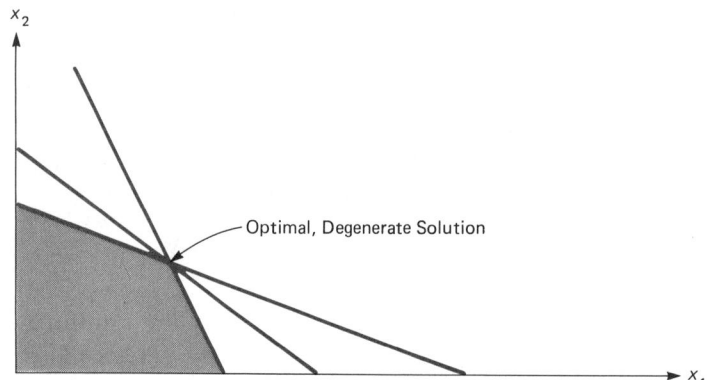

Optimal, Degenerate Solution

In the simplex procedure degeneracy occurs when two ratios tie for smallest (see Table 5.15). The problem is: Which of the two should go? Again, the choice for outgoing basic variable may be made arbitrarily without affecting the final solution. However, care must be exercised to recognize that the other basic variable (the one *not* selected as outgoing), even though having a new value of zero in the basis, is *still* a basic variable and is thus carried throughout the simplex calculation.

D. Unbounded solutions

Graphically, in this case, the feasible solution space extends indefinitely (Figure 5.16). The result in the simplex is that there is no

An infinite value

outgoing basic variable; the ratios are either infinite or negative (see Table 5.16). Therefore, the optimal solution is infinite. This result usually means that an error was made, the problem was misstated, or an incorrect assumption was made.

TABLE 5.15
Example of degeneracy in a tableau

Tie for outgoing variable:

Basis	Unit profits	Quantity	x_1	x_2	x_3	s_1	s_2	Ratio
s_1	—	50	0	0	①	1	2	$50/1 = 50$ ←┐
x_1	—	200	1	0	④	0	1	$200/4 = 50$ ←┘ Minimum?
x_2	—	250	0	1	2	0	5	$250/2 = 125$
$c_j - z_j$			0	0	3	0	1	

Improved tableau with s_1 arbitrarily selected as outgoing variable:

Basis	Unit profits	Quantity	x_1	x_2	x_3	s_1	s_2	Ratio
x_3	—	50	0	0	1	1	2	
x_1	—	0	1	0	0	−4	−7	
x_2	—	150	0	1	0	−2	0	
$c_j - z_j$			0	0	0	−3	−5	

Final solution: $x_3 = 50$, $x_1 = 0$ (just like nonbasic variables), $x_2 = 150$.

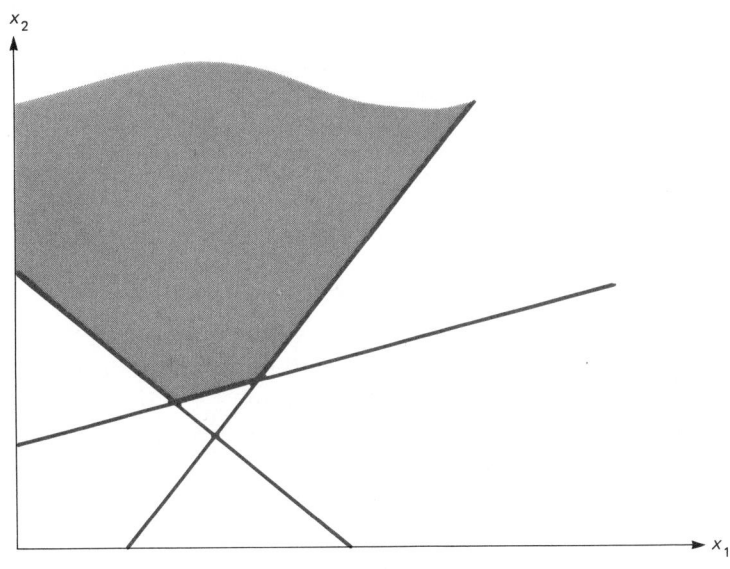

FIGURE 5.16
An unbounded
maximization problem

TABLE 5.16
No outgoing variable

Basis	Unit profits	Quantity	x_1	x_2	s_1	s_2	Ratio
s_1	—	180	1	−1	1	0	180/−1 (ignore)
s_2	—	55	5	0	0	1	55/0 = ∞
$c_j - z_j$			−2	3	0	0	

E. Unconstrained variables

Negative solutions

Occasionally a problem arises when some of the variables are *not* constrained to be nonnegative; that is, one or more of the decision variables may be allowed to be negative. In this case, the problem statement is modified slightly before employing the simplex (which *requires* that all variables be nonnegative). The modification is to replace the unconstrained variable, say, x_i, throughout the problem statement with the difference of two variables $(y_i - w_i)$, where both $y_i \geq 0$ and $w_i \geq 0$. The optimal simplex solution will then either have $y_i = 0$ in which case $x_i = -w_i$; or else $w_i = 0$ and $x_i = y_i$.

For example, suppose the following problem statement is given and x_2 is a temperature (°F) which may be either positive or negative.

$$\max. z = 40x_1 + 65x_2 - 8x_3$$
subject to:
$$x_1 + x_2 + x_3 \geq 1000$$
$$2x_1 \qquad -x_3 \leq 783$$
$$x_1, \qquad x_3 \geq 0$$

Then the problem would be recast as:

$$\max. z = 40x_1 + 65y - 65w - 8x_3$$
subject to:
$$x_1 + y - w + x_3 \geq 1000$$
$$2x_1 \qquad\qquad -x_3 \leq 783$$
$$x_1, \quad y, \quad w, \quad x_3 \geq 0$$

F. Negative right-hand quantity (b_i)

If one of the b_i quantities is negative then by multiplying the entire constraint by (-1) the constraint will be in proper form. Note that if the constraint was an inequality, multiplying by -1 will *reverse* the direction of the inequality ($\geq$ instead of $\leq$ and vice versa) which may thereby necessitate adding an artificial variable to obtain an initial basis.

For example, if one of the constraints in a problem is:

$$x_1 - 2x_2 + x_3 \leq -10$$

then multiplying by -1 yields:

$$-x_1 + 2x_2 - x_3 \geq 10$$

Adding slack and artificial variables further results in:

$$-x_1 + 2x_2 - x_3 - s_1 + a_1 = 10$$

G. No feasible solution

In some cases there will not be a feasible solution to the problem. Graphically, no solution space which simultaneously satisfies all constraints exists—See Figure 5.17. The clue to this situation, when using

No solutions

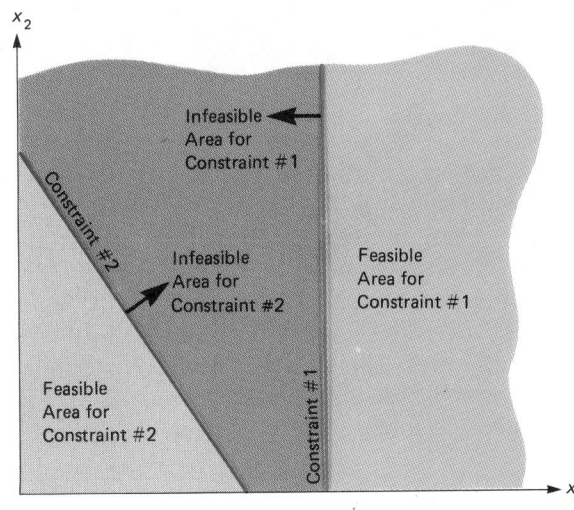

FIGURE 5.17
No feasible solution space (shaded regions are infeasible)

the simplex process, is that the optimal solution will still contain an *artificial* variable and the value of the $c_j - z_j$ row will still be on the order of $-M$ (see Table 5.17).

TABLE 5.17
No feasible solution

Basis	Unit profits	Quantity	x_1	x_2	s_1	s_2	a_1	a_2	Ratio
x_2	—	370	2	$\boxed{1}$	6	-1	0	0	
a_2	—	120	1	0	2	0	-3	$\boxed{1}$	
$c_j - z_j$			$(-M - 6)$	0	-17	$-2M$	-8	0	

H. Multiple optimal solutions

This situation is shown, for a maximization case, in Figure 5.18. The objective function, when moved as far as possible from the origin to the right, does not touch a corner point but rather a line segment between two

FIGURE 5.18
Multiple solutions case

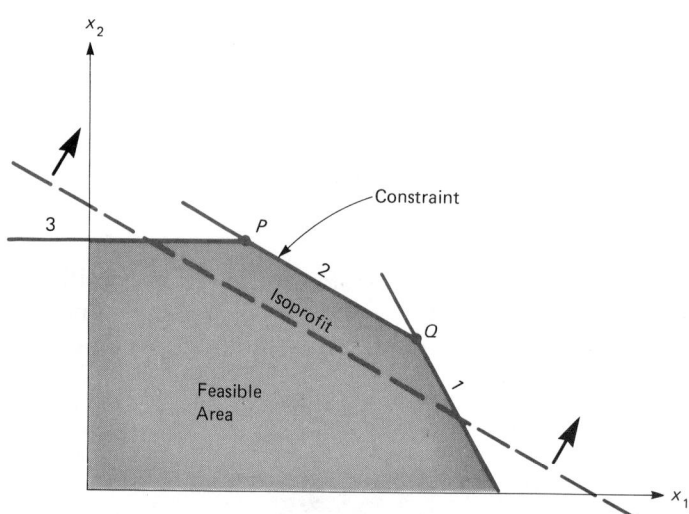

points (P and Q in Figure 5.18). This happens when the isoprofit line is parallel to an "active" (binding) constraint (#2 in Figure 5.18). In such a case there are optimal solutions both at corner P, at corner Q, and at an infinite number of points on the line segment PQ.

This situation can be recognized in the simplex procedure by the fact that one of the nonbasic variables in the $c_j - z_j$ row will have a value of 0 (see Table 5.18). Hence, a nonbasic variable may be brought into the solution basis, thereby creating a new solution with the same value of the objective function.

TABLE 5.18
The multiple solutions situation

Basis	Unit profits	Quantity	x_1	x_2	s_1	s_2	Ratio
x_2	—	6	2	1	2	0	$6/2 = 3$
s_2	—	18	6	0	3	1	$18/3 = 6$
$c_j - z_j$			-3	—	0	0	

5.11 PROBLEMS FOR PART B

18. Western National Bank is preparing to invest up to $5 million of its cash reserves. The bank is considering the following alternatives:

Alternative	Expected rate of return (percent)	Risk factor
U.S. Treasury securities	7.6	0
Corporate bonds	8.9	1
Loans to corporations	10.3	2
Stocks	14.0	5

The expected return is measured in percent over one year. The risk factor is a projection for next year, based on experience.

The bank investment policy requires that:

a. The amount loaned to corporations will not exceed the amount invested in U.S. Treasury securities.

b. The *weighted* risk factor will not exceed 1.9.

c. For every dollar invested in stocks there will be at least 0.5 dollars invested in U.S. Treasury securities.

d. The amount invested in stocks will not exceed 25 percent of the total amount invested.

Find the investment portfolio which will maximize the bank's return on investment.

(*Hint:* To find the weighted risk factor, multiply the amounts invested by the corresponding risk factor and divide by the total investment.)

19. Paint Fair Company advertises its weekly sales in newspapers, television, and radio. Each dollar spent in advertising in newspapers is estimated to reach an exposure of 12 buying customers; each dollar in TV reaches an exposure of 15 buying customers; and each dollar in radio reaches an exposure of 10 buying customers. The company has an agreement with all three media services according to which it will spend not less than 20 percent of its total money actually expended in each medium. Further, it is agreed that the combined newspaper and television budget will not be larger than three times the radio budget.

The company has just decided to spend no more than $17,000 on advertising. The problem is: How much should the company budget for each medium if it is interested in reaching as many buying customers as possible?

20. Given two LP graphical solutions. The optimal solution is marked by x.

In each case find:
1. Which constraints are redundant.
2. Which constraints will have a slack.
3. Which constraints will have a surplus.

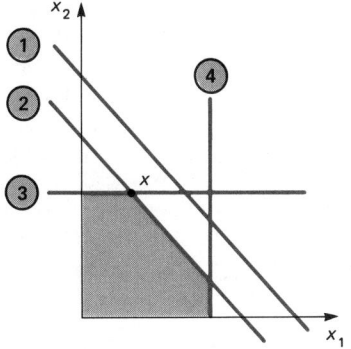

a. Maximization

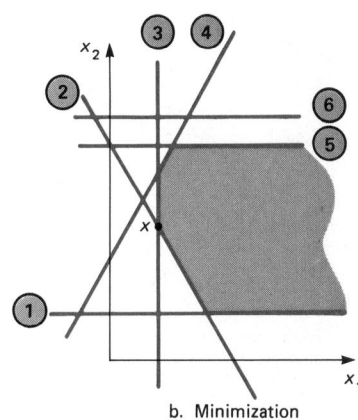

b. Minimization

21. Solve by the simplex method:

a. maximize $z = 8x_1 + 6x_2$
    subject to:
    $$4x_1 + 2x_2 \leq 60$$
    $$2x_1 + 4x_2 \leq 48$$
    $$x_1 \qquad\;\; \geq 5$$
    $$\qquad\; 3x_2 \geq 5$$

b. minimize $z = 2x_1 + 4x_2 + x_3$
    subject to:
    $$x_1 + 2x_2 - \;\; x_3 \geq 5$$
    $$2x_1 - \;\; x_2 + 2x_3 = 2$$
    $$-x_1 + 2x_2 + 2x_3 \geq 1$$
    $$\qquad\qquad\qquad x_3 \leq 2$$

22. COM Food Corporation specializes in menu preparation for restaurants, institutions, and individual families. The major idea of the program is to provide an adequate (and tasteful) diet at a minimal cost. Given below is a *simplified* diet problem.

The minimum daily nutrient requirements for an adult (of a certain age and in a given occupation) are:

Calories..........	2,860
Protein	80 grams
Iron	15 milligrams
Niacin	20 milligrams
Vitamin A........	20,000 units

A menu, when recommended by COM Food must supply *at least* these minimum daily requirements. In this simplified problem we shall assume that COM Food prepares one menu only. (In actual cases, a different menu would be prepared for every day of the week, or even every day of the month.)

Given below is a table of foods and prices (per pound) offered the customers.

Food	Price per pound ($)
Beef	1.00
Butter............	.79
Bread	.26
Carrots	.15
Halibut............	.80
Egg...............	.34
Cheese	1.10

The quantities of calories, protein, iron, and calcium included in each 100 grams of the above foods, are given below:

	Food	Calories	Protein	Iron (mg)	Niacin (mg)	Vitamin A (units)
A	Beef.....	309	26.0	3.1	4.1	0
B	Butter ...	716	.6	0	1	3,330
C	Bread....	276	8.5	.6	.9	—
D	Carrots ..	42	1.2	.6	.4	12,000
E	Halibut ..	182	26.2	.8	10.5	0
F	Egg	162	12.8	2.7	.3	1,140
G	Cheese ..	368	21.5	.5	.4	1,240

Find the least-cost food mix of the daily menu that satisfies minimum daily requirements.

a. Set up the problem as a linear program.
b. How many foods will be included in the optimal solution? Why? (Answer this *before* attempting to solve the problem.)
c. Review your answer to (b). Under what circumstance(s) will the answer to (b) be different?
d. Solve the problem: Give the quantities of the foods to be included and the total daily cost. (A computer is recommended.)
e. In what nutritional elements will you have a surplus? In what quantities?
f. The customer is unhappy with the proposed menu since it does not include beef and it includes too much bread and eggs, so the customer imposes the following requirements:

1. The menu must include at least 100 grams of beef.

2. The menu should not include more than 500 grams of bread and 200 grams of eggs.

Resolve the problem and find the optimal menu now. What is the additional cost and in what nutritional elements will there be a surplus? (How much?)

23. Western Valley Machine shop makes deluxe and regular skis on a weekly schedule for the area skiing enthusiasts. They have a contract with Apple Hill to supply 18 regular pairs of skis per week. They also sell both regular and deluxe skis to local sporting goods stores. A deluxe pair of skis requires 40 minutes for roughing and 20 minutes for finishing and a regular pair of skis requires 20 minutes for roughing and 26⅔ minutes for finishing. With only 1,000 minutes for roughing and 800 minutes of finishing time available per week and a profit realization of $4 and $3 for the deluxe and regular respectively, what weekly mix of the two types of skis should be produced to meet the contract's requirement and maximize profits?

a. Formulate as a linear program in two *different ways*.
b. Solve graphically (the formulation with the three constraints).
c. Solve by the simplex method.

24. Given:
minimize $z = 5x_1 + 4x_2$
subject to:

$$4x_1 + 2.5x_2 \geq 60$$
$$2x_1 + 5x_2 \geq 60$$
$$5x_1 + 4x_2 \geq 82$$

a. Solve the problem graphically.
b. Explain the uniqueness of the problem.
c. Solve the problem by the simplex method.
d. How is the uniqueness of this problem reflected in the simplex procedure?
e. Assume that the second constraint is changed to $2x_1 + 6x_2 \geq 60$. What will the impact of this change be? How will it be reflected in the simplex solution now?

25. The Deere Valve Company is developing an alloy to be used in the manufacture of valves. The research department has determined that

the alloy can be formed by mixing the alloying metals of iron, nickel, and chrome, provided that the proportions of the materials fall within certain limits. The chemists have set the following proportional limits on the quantities of iron, nickel, and chrome that may be used.

Limit	Iron	Nickel	Chrome
Upper..........	5	1*	—
Lower..........	3	1*	—
Upper..........	3	—	1*
Lower..........	2	—	1*
Upper..........	—	1*	3
Lower..........	—	1*	3

* Base.

The upper limit means that, for example, *no more* than 5 parts of iron should be used for each part of nickel; the lower limit means that at least 3 parts of iron should be used for each part of nickel, and so on.

If the unit costs of iron, nickel, and chrome are $1, $2, and $3, respectively, what is the lowest-cost mixture that will satisfy the quality requirements?

a. Formulate as a linear programming problem.

b. Solve (use a computer).

26. Given a problem:
maximize $z = 5x_1 + 3x_2$
subject to:
$$4x_1 + 2x_2 \leq 10$$
$$2x_1 + 2x_2 \leq 8$$
Solve the problem by the simplex method and/or graphically.

27. Solve Problem 26 adding a third constraint: $x_1 \geq 2$.

28. Solve Problem 26 if the $\leq$ sign in the first constraint is changed to an equality (=).

29. Solve Problem 26 if the constraint $4x_1 + 2x_2 \leq 10$ is replaced by $x_1 - x_2 \leq -1$.

30. Solve Problem 26 if both constraints are replaced by:
$$x_1 - x_2 \leq -1$$
$$x_1 \qquad \leq 1$$

31. Solve Problem 26 if the additional constraint $x_1 \geq 3$ is added.

5.12   CASE

THE DAPHNE JEWELRY COMPANY[27]

The Daphne Jewelry Company markets the bulk of its products through seven salespersons operating in seven separate sales territories (on a one-to-one basis). This is due to the fact that other area salespersons use Daphne's products only as a supplement to some other distributor's line. The seven leading salespersons follow just the opposite practice, using the products of other manufacturers to augment the Daphne line. For this reason the firm sets periodic sales quotas only for these persons.

The firm sells nine product lines. These are listed in Table 1, where each column shows how one dollar in sales in each of the seven territories is distributed among the various product lines. For example, the .07 coefficient for the first product, belts, indicates that on the average, 7 cents of every dollar's worth of merchandise sold in territory 1 is generated by belts. These distributions were found to be quite stable over time, regardless of the size of the account.

[27] Case developed by Dr. Malcolm Golden, University of Miami, and by Dr. Alan Parker, School of Business and Organizational Science, Florida International University. Reproduced with permission.

TABLE 1
Dollar distribution value of sales for nine products in seven territories

		Sales territory						
Product lines		No. 1	No. 2	No. 3	No. 4	No. 5	No. 6	No. 7
1.	Belts............	.07	.02	.01	.15	.18	.15	.00
2.	Buckles	.05	.00	.00	.10	.10	.07	.00
3.	Package goods......	.20	.35	.30	.25	.25	.25	.50
4.	Necklaces.........	.07	.07	.07	.10	.15	.10	.03
5.	Earrings..........	.15	.15	.15	.15	.15	.15	.15
6.	Bracelets	.10	.20	.10	.10	.10	.10	.05
7.	Gold stone........	.18	.10	.17	.10	.05	.05	.12
8.	Hemetite	.15	.08	.17	.02	.02	.10	.12
9.	Job turquoise.......	.03	.03	.03	.03	.00	.03	.03
	Total...........	1.00	1.00	1.00	1.00	1.00	1.00	1.00

TABLE 2
Daphne's market potential in
each of seven selling areas

Sales territory	Market potential (maximum)
No. 1	$ 225,000
No. 2	135,000
No. 3	150,000
No. 4	100,000
No. 5	210,000
No. 6	80,000
No. 7	250,000
Total	$1,150,000

The market potential of each sales territory for the next planning period is presented in Table 2. This is Daphne's estimate of "potential" demand for its products next year for each of the seven territories at the present level of advertising. These demand forecasts were based upon past sales records, information gathered from trade associations and governmental agencies, as well as independent forecasts made by consulting firms that specialize in economic analysis of trade areas.

The cost of a dollar's worth of merchandise required in the production of each product line, together with the corresponding sales commission paid on each dollar of sales, is depicted in Table 3. The production capacity of the nine product lines is given in Table 4.

During recent years the company's sales and profits have been growing very slowly. Last year the company netted about $200,000 on sales of about $650,000. Mr. Brown, the

TABLE 3
Material costs and sales commision for nine product lines

Product lines	Cost of $1 in merchandise	Sales commission on $1 in merchandise
1–6 inclusive........	$.50	$.15
7–9 inclusive........	.67	.10

TABLE 4
Product line capacity

Product line	Product line capacity
1...................	$ 70,000
2...................	20,000
3...................	210,000
4...................	70,000
5...................	150,000
6...................	100,000
7...................	150,000
8...................	150,000
9...................	30,000

president of Daphne Jewelry, was not pleased with the results. He felt there was a large quantity of unutilized production capacity as well as market potential. Mrs. Grant, the vice president of marketing, disagreed with Brown's assessment. She felt that the company was at or near optimal operating conditions, and that very little could be done within the framework of the existing conditions.

Last Monday, the president called the executive management team and requested proposals for improving the situation. The vice president for marketing suggested an increase in marketing efforts, especially in territories 2, 4, and 6, where current market potential is the lowest. The vice president for production suggested increasing production of those product lines that yield the highest return. The controller suggested dropping the least profitable products or territories, or both. The president was reluctant to accept any of these suggestions, since both the market potential and the production capacity were underutilized. Furthermore, the specific marketing plan proposed violated the production capabilities, while the proposed increase in certain product lines violated the marketing capabilities.

The president finally decided to call upon a management scientist who was asked to prepare a report to include the following items:

a. Evaluate the existing situation; determine if the company is indeed close to optimal operating conditions.
b. Analyze the marketing and production proposals brought forth by the vice presidents and the controller.
c. Submit other proposals; determine their feasibility and profitability.
d. Analyze the pricing and commission policies; submit recommendations.

5.13 GLOSSARY

Additivity assumption An assumption in LP that the returns are independent of each other and can be added together proportionally.

Allocation problem A problem involving the best allocation of scarce resources, commonly solved by LP.

Artificial variable A fictitious constraint parameter used in the simplex to obtain an initial solution.

Basic variable One of the variables currently in the basis.

Basis A solution in m variables of a system of m equations in n unknowns, where $n \geq m$. The other $n-m$ variables have the value zero.

Blending problem One of the two major types of LP problems.

Constraints Restrictions on the problem solution arising from limited resources, policy requirements, etc.

Degeneracy A situation in the simplex where a basic variable takes on the value zero, just like a nonbasic variable.

Divisibility assumption An assumption in LP that the resources are infinitely divisible, an unrealistic assumption when considering items such as automobiles or people.

Deterministic model A model where all parameters are assumed to be known with certainty, such as LP.

Feasible area The solution space or region which satisfies all the constraints simultaneously.

Inequality constraint A restriction on some combination of the variables such that they must be greater than or equal to a particular value.

Infeasible solution A solution which violates at least one constraint.

Integer programming A programming approach which recognizes the indivisibility of one or more of the decision variables.

Isocost (isoprofit) line Lines of constant cost (profit) on a graph, each line parallel to the others.

Iteration One pass through an algorithmic process, such as the simplex.

Marginal value   The additional return from having one more unit available.

Multiple solutions   When alternative optima exist.

Nonnegativity constraint   The restriction in LP that all decision variables must be positive or zero.

Normative   What *should* be.

Objective function   The statement of the goal of the program in mathematical form.

Product-mix problem   One of the two basic forms of LP problems.

Simplex method   A particular algorithm for solving programming problems stated as linear functions that only investigates feasible corner points of the solution space.

Slack variable   A variable representing the difference between the use of the resources and their availability.

Surplus variable   A variable representing the difference between the use of the resources and a minimum requirement.

Unbounded solution   A solution involving the infinite use of some resource.

Vertex   A corner point of the solution space corresponding to the intersection of two or more constraints.

5.14   REFERENCES AND BIBLIOGRAPHY

1.   Anderson, D. R., et al. *Linear Programming for Decision Making.* St. Paul, Minn.: West Publishing Co., (1974).

2.   Bazaraa, M. S. and Jarvis, J. J. *Linear Programming and Network Flows.* New York: John Wiley & Sons, Inc., 1977.

3.   Dantzig, G. F. *Linear Programming and Extensions.* Princeton, N.J.: Princeton University Press, 1963.

4.   Friendly, Jonathan.   "Shazam! A Shortcut for Computers." *New York Times.* November 11, 1979, p. E7.

5.   Gass, S. I. *An Illustrated Guide to Linear Programming.* New York: McGraw-Hill Book Co., 1970.

6.   Kolman, B. and Beck, R. E. *Elementary Linear Programming with Applications,* New York: Academic Press, 1980.

7.   Laidlaw, C. D. *Linear Programming for Urban Development and Plan Evaluation.* New York: Praeger Publishers, Inc., 1972.

8.   Lee, S. M. *Linear Optimization for Management.* New York: Petrocelli-Charter, 1976.

9.   Levin, R. L., and Lamone, R. P. *Linear Programming for Management Decisions,* Homewood, Ill.: Richard D. Irwin, 1969.

10.   Loomba, N. P. *Linear, Programming: A Managerial Perspective,* 2nd ed. New York: Macmillan, Inc., 1976.

11.   Loomba, N. P., and Turban, E. *Applied Programming in Management.* New York: Holt, Rinehart and Winston, Inc., 1974.

12.   Machol, R. E. *Elementary Systems Mathematics: Linear Programming for Business and Social Sciences.* New York: McGraw-Hill Book Co., 1976.

13.   Rothenberg, R. *Linear Programming,* New York: Elsevier North-Holland, 1980

6

no.

The linear programming problem addressed in Chapter 5 is a special case of the broad field of *mathematial programming*. This chapter focuses on other types of mathematical programming. Part A of this chapter is devoted to three interesting extensions of linear programming: duality, sensitivity analysis, and goal programming. These extensions deal mainly with the economic interpretation of the results of linear programming as used for managerial decision making.

Part B of the chapter discusses the concepts of *integer programming*, where the solution must be in integer units (14 persons, 3 airplanes, and so on). In addition a solution technique called *branch and bound* is presented. Finally, the technique of *nonlinear programming*, where the objective function and/or the constraints cannot be expressed in linear terms, is briefly discussed.

Topics in mathematical programming

PART A: BASICS

The Sekido Corporation—Part II

The optimal weekly production plan suggested by Suji Okita (12 units of type A TV sets and 11 of type B) was submitted to Sekido's executive committee for approval. During their weekly Monday morning meeting, the members of the committee raised the following questions:

1. Should additional resources (labor, machine time) be committed to the production of these TV sets? If so, how much?
2. If the available supply of Sekido's resources should happen to change, what effect will it have on the company's profit?
3. Would it be worthwhile to increase Sekido's marketing effort to increase potential sales from 12 to 13, 14, or even more? How much should the company be willing to invest in such a promotion?
4. What is the best production plan if some of the input variables (per unit profits, production technology) change?
5. What is the best production plan if objectives other than profit maximization are considered?

Upon returning home Suji found that Keiko was faced with similar questions at her office such as: What effect will certain changes in the paint specifications have on the total production cost? And what will happen to the optimal blending plan if other objectives are also considered?

Three very useful extensions of linear programming can be used to answer these and similar questions:

- Duality.
- Sensitivity analysis.
- Goal programming.

6.1 DUALITY

The primal—the dual

With every linear programming maximization problem there is an associated minimization problem and vice versa. Therefore, linear programming problems exist in pairs. The original problem is called the *primal*, while the complementary problem is termed the *dual*.

Duality plays an important role for these reasons:

1. *Several theories* which are used to develop methods for efficient computational shortcuts to the simplex method are based on the concept of duality.

An important economic interpretation

2. The dual problem has an *important economic interpretation*.
3. In some cases the use of the dual helps *overcome some computer capacity limitations*.

4. Some special procedures developed for *testing optimal solutions* are based on duality.

Theoretically, the dual problem is the same problem as the primal but mathematically transformed. Therefore, the solution of the primal (by the simplex method) gives the solution to the dual and vice versa.

Major properties

The following are some properties of duality:

1. If the primal is a maximization problem, the dual is a minimization problem, and vice versa.
2. An optimal solution to the dual exists only when the primal has an optimal solution (and vice versa.)
3. The value of the objective function of the *optimal solution* in both problems is the same.
4. The dual of the dual is the primal.
5. The solution of the dual problem can be obtained from the solution of the primal problem, and vice versa (if solved by a procedure such as the simplex method.)

Formulation of the dual to a maximization problem—an example

The product-mix problem discussed in Chapter 5 is reproduced below as the *primal:*

$$\text{maximize } z = 300x_1 + 250x_2$$
subject to:
$$\begin{array}{ll} 2x_1 + 1x_2 \le 40 & \text{(labor constraint)} \\ 1x_1 + 3x_2 \le 45 & \text{(machine time constraint)} \\ 1x_1 + 0x_2 \le 12 & \text{(marketing constraint)} \end{array}$$

Writing the Dual

The Objective Since the original problem calls for *maximization,* the dual will be a *minimization* problem. Recasting the primal

The decision variables For each constraint in the primal there is one decision variable in the dual. Thus, there will be, in this example, three variables to be denoted u_1, u_2, and u_3. The dual variables can be either positive, zero, or negative.

The objective function Remember that each dual variable corresponds to a constraint in the primal. The coefficient of each variable in the objective function of the dual is equal to the right-hand side (capacity, b_i) of the corresponding constraint in the primal. For example, the capacity of the labor (first) constraint in the primal is 40; thus the coefficient of u_1 in the dual's objective function is 40. The objective function for the dual is:

$$\text{minimize } w = 40u_1 + 45u_2 + 12u_3$$

The constraints[1] For each decision (unknown) variable in the primal there is a corresponding constraint in the dual. Since there are two primal variables, there will be two constraints in the dual. The right-hand side of the dual's constraints is the same as the corresponding coefficients of the objective function in the primal. For example, the coefficient of the *first* variable in the primal objective function is 300, and so will be the right-hand side of the dual's *first* constraint.

The coefficients of the constraints in the dual are formed from the coefficients of the primal's constraints by writing each column of these coefficients as a row. The coefficients of the primal's constraints are:

$$\begin{array}{cc} 2 & 1 \\ 1 & 3 \\ 1 & 0 \end{array}$$

With each column written as a row,[2] the result is:

Previous first column: 2   1   1
Previous second column: 1   3   0

Thus, the dual's constraints are:

$$2u_1 + 1u_2 + 1u_3 \geq 300$$
$$1u_1 + 3u_2 + 0u_3 \geq 250$$

Note that the signs of the inequalities are $\geq$ since all the constraints in the primal were of the $\leq$ standard format.

Standardization of the primal

The primal problem presented earlier contained only $\leq$ type constraints, and it was to be maximized. If a primal problem deviates from such a structure, it must then be transformed into the required standard format.

Example 1

Given a primal:

$$\text{minimize } y = 3x_1 + 4x_2 - 2x_3$$
$$\text{subject to:}$$
$$(1) \quad 1x_1 + 2x_2 - 3x_2 \geq 40$$

---

[1] Before structuring the dual constraints, all primal constraints should be transformed to $\leq$ in maximization; $\geq$ in minimization. The multiplication of an inequality by -1 changes its direction.

[2] If the coefficients of the primal are written in the form of a matrix, then the matrix of the coefficients in the dual is the *transpose* (see Appendix A) of the matrix in the primal.

$$(2) \quad 3x_1 + 5x_2 + 1x_3 \le 50$$
$$(3) \quad 0x_1 + 3x_2 + 2x_3 = 30$$

Step 1 If the objective function is to be minimized, convert it into maximization by multiplying it by -1.

We get: max $z = -3x_1 - 4x_2 + 2x_3$

Step 2 Multiply each $\ge$ constraint by -1 in order to convert it to a $\le$ type.
Constraint (1) thus becomes:

$$-1x_1 - 2x_2 + 3x_3 \le -40$$

Step 3 Split each equality constraint into two inequalities; one $\le$ and the other $\ge$. (Mathematically, an equation is equivalent to two inequalities, one $\le$ and one $\ge$.)

Thus, constraint (3) is expressed as:

(3a) $\quad 0x_1 + 3x_2 + 2x_3 \le 30$
(3b) $\quad 0x_1 + 3x_2 + 2x_3 \ge 30$

However, since constraint (3b) is of the $\ge$ type, it has to be multiplied by -1 in order to convert it to a $\le$ type.

Conclusion

The original problem can now be rewritten as:

Standardized primal	*Dual*

max. $z = -3x_1 - 4x_2 + 2x_3$ min. $w = -40u_1 + 50u_2 + 30u_3 - 30u_4$
subject to: subject to:

(1) $\quad -1x_1 - 2x_2 + 3x_3 \le -40$	$-1u_1 + 3u_2 \qquad\qquad\quad \ge -3$
(2) $\quad\;\; 3x_1 + 5x_2 + 1x_3 \le 50$	$-2u_1 + 5u_2 + 3u_3 - 3u_4 \ge -4$
(3/a) $\quad\; 0x_1 + 3x_2 + 2x_3 \le 30$	$\;\;3u_1 + 1u_2 + 2u_3 - 2u_4 \ge \;\; 2$
(3/b) $\quad -0x_1 - 3x_2 - 2x_3 \le -30$	

Example 2

In the previous example a primal minimization problem was converted to a standard maximization problem and then its dual was derived. Alternatively, the primal problem can be standardized as a minimization problem where all the constraints are of the $\ge$ type. Let us examine another example.

Given a primal:

min. $z = 2x_1 + 3x_2 - 1x_3$
subject to:
(1) $\quad 5x_1 + 1x_2 + 1x_3 \ge 20$
(2) $\quad 2x_1 + 1x_2 + 3x_3 = 24$
(3) $\quad 1x_1 + 2x_2 - 1x_3 \le 18$

Standardization   Constraints (2) and (3) are not in the standard form.

Step 1   Split constraint (2) into two constraints:

$$(2a) \quad 2x_1 + 1x_2 + 3x_3 \le 24$$
$$(2b) \quad 2x_1 + 1x_2 + 3x_3 \ge 24$$

Multiply (2a) by -1 to reverse the direction of the inequality:

$$(2a) \quad -2x_1 - 1x_2 - 3x_3 \ge -24$$

Step 2   Reverse the inequality of constraint (3) by multiplying it by -1:

$$(3) \quad -1x_1 - 2x_2 + 1x_3 \ge -18$$

Now the standardized primal and its dual can be written:

Standardized primal	*Dual*
min. $z = 2x_1 + 3x_2 - 1x_3$	max. $w = 20u_1 - 24u_2 + 24u_3 - 18u_4$
subject to:	subject to:
(1) $\quad 5x_1 + 1x_2 + 1x_3 \ge 20$	$5u_1 - 2u_2 + 2u_3 - 1u_4 \le 2$
(2a) $-2x_1 - 1x_2 - 3x_3 \ge -24$	$1u_1 - 1u_2 + 1u_3 - 2u_4 \le 3$
(2b) $\quad 2x_1 + 1x_2 + 3x_3 \ge 24$	$1u_1 - 3u_2 + 3u_3 + 1u_4 \le -1$
(3) $\quad -1x_1 - 2x_2 + 1x_3 \ge -18$	

Summary

The primal–dual relationship[3] is shown pictorially in Figure 6.1. The dual, once formulated, can be solved as any regular linear programming problem (e.g., using the simplex method). In addition, the use of the simplex method automatically gives the solution to the dual when the primal is being solved.

Solution to the Dual

The dual problem, once formulated, can be solved like any other linear programming problem. However, given a simplex solution to the

---

[3] The general form of the primal-dual relationship is:

Primal	*Dual*
maximize $z = \displaystyle\sum_{j=1}^{n} c_j x_j$	minimize $w = \displaystyle\sum_{i=1}^{m} b_i u_i$
subject to:	subject to:
$\displaystyle\sum_{j=1}^{n} a_{ij} x_j \le b_i$	$\displaystyle\sum_{i=1}^{m} a_{ij} u_i \ge c_j$

for $i = 1, 2, \ldots, m$ and $j = 1, 2, \ldots, n$

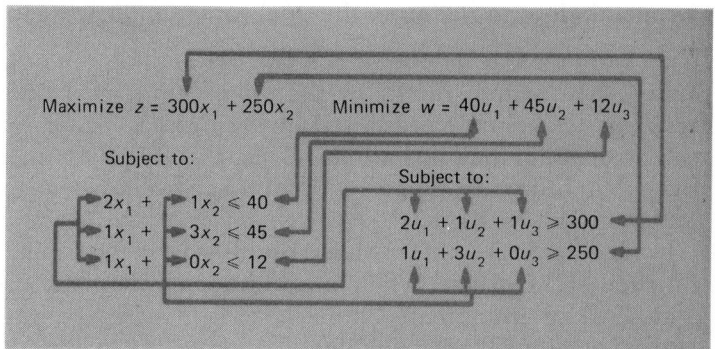

FIGURE 6.1
The primal–dual
relationship

primal, it is not necessary to solve the dual since the final tableau of the primal's solution provides *both* the optimal values of the primal and the dual problems.

Let us reproduce the final tableau of the product mix problem (Table 5.10) in Table 6.1.

Table 6.1
Reproduction of Table
5.10

Basis	Unit profit	Quantity	x_1	x_2	s_1	s_2	s_3
s_1	0	5	0	0	1	$-1/3$	$-5/3$
x_2	250	11	0	1	0	$1/3$	$-1/3$
x_1	300	12	1	0	0	0	1
c_j			300	250	0	0	0
z_j			300	250	0	250/3	650/3
$c_j - z_j$			0	0	0	$-250/3$	$-650/3$
Dual's solution:			t_1	t_2	$-u_1$	$-u_2$	$-u_3$

The optimal solution to the dual problem can be read directly in the $c_j - z_j$ row of the tableau since $u_j = -(c_j - z_j)$. The column s_1, which is related to the first constraint, has a $c_j - z_j$ value of zero; i.e., $u_1 = 0$. Similarly, $u_2 = 250/3$ (take the negative of the value shown) and $u_3 = 650/3$. Since the dual problem has two constraints, it has two surplus variables, t_1 and t_2, whose values can also be found in the primal's optimal tableau. Examining the $c_j - z_j$ row in the tableau we see that its value is zero under the x_1 column; i.e., the surplus t_1 of the first dual's constraint (which is associated with the primal x_1 varible) is zero. Similarly, the surplus t_2 of the second dual's constraint is zero.

Note: In solving dual problems irregularities may be encountered such as negative right hand "Quantity" values in the constraints. Special extensions of the simplex method, such as the dual-simplex algorithm can then be used. For details see [3, 6, or 8].

Economic interpretation of the dual (product-mix example)

The meaning of the dual's variables The dual variables, u_i, are called the *shadow prices* or the *opportunity costs* per unit of each resource (constraint) presented in the primal. These imaginary prices can be used for making various managerial decisions such as examining the profitability of purchasing additional resources and evaluating the trade-offs among them.

The dual variables measure the change in the value of the objective function of the primal, when one additional unit of a specific resource is added. If, for example, machine capacity is increased from 45 hours (the current machine time available) to 46 hours, the total profit will increase[4] by $u_2 = {}^{250}/_3 = \$83^1/_3$. Similarly, if the marketability of model A is increased from 12 sets to 13 sets, the total profit will increase by $u_3 = {}^{650}/_3 = \$216^2/_3$.

Thus, the $\$83^1/_3$ can be viewed as the value of one unit of machine time (*marginal value* of the resource). Therefore, the total value of the resource "machine time" is $83^1/_3 \times 45 = \$3,750$. Similarly, the value of one unit of "marketability" is $u_3 = {}^{650}/_3$; the total value of marketability is therefore $12 \times 216^2/_3 = \$2,600$. However, if labor availability is increased from 40 to 41 units, there will be *no gain* ($u_1 = 0$). The reason is that *labor is not utilized in full* at present; this is clearly shown by the fact that $s_1 = 5$ (i.e., slack in labor exists). A resource which is not fully utilized is considered a *free good* and obviously an increase in its supply will not increase profits.

The total value of all resources is therefore the value of machine time + marketability + labor time: $\$3,750 + \$2,600 + 0 = \$6,350$, which is exactly the value of the objective function in both the primal and the dual.

The interpretation of the objective function of the dual When the dual's unit value of the resources is multiplied by the available quantities (right-hand side of the constraints), a total value function is constructed as follows:

$$\text{Total value of labor} \quad = u_1 \left(\frac{\text{dollars}}{\text{hour}}\right) \times 40 \text{ hours} = \$40u_1$$

$$\text{Total value of machine} \quad = u_2 \left(\frac{\text{dollars}}{\text{hour}}\right) \times 45 \text{ hours} = \$45u_2$$

$$\text{Total value of marketing} = u_3 \left(\frac{\text{dollars}}{\text{unit}}\right) \times 12 \text{ units} = \$12 \, u_3$$

The total value of all resources is: $40u_1 + 45u_2 + 12u_3$.

---

[4] Provided that the structure of the optimal solution remains unchanged; that is, that the same variables participate in the optimal solution. See the next section (sensitivity analysis) for further discussion.

The objective of the manufacturer is to *minimize* the value of the resources used. Therefore, the dual's objective function is: min. $z = 40u_1 + 45u_2 + 12u_3$. This minimization is subject to two constraints.

The interpretation of the constraints   It is given that one unit of TV model A requires two hours of labor, one hour of machine time, and one unit of marketing effort. Investing *less than* these quantities will result in less than one unit of model A. Since the *profit* (or *contribution margin*) made from such a TV is $300, it can be said that the value of the invested resources *must* be at least $300, or $2u_1 + u_2 + u_3 \geq 300$.

Similarly, the constraint for model B is:

$$u_1 + 3u_2 \geq 250$$

Remember that these values are accounting or shadow price values that do not measure *cost* but measure potential contribution to profit.

The relationship between the dual's variables and the objective function   The dual variables by definition measure the change in the value of the objective function of the primal when the right-hand side of the primal's constraints are changed by one unit. The following relationship thus exists between the two:

Right-hand side	*If dual variable is*	*Then objective function value will*
add one unit	positive	increase
add one unit	negative	decrease
add one unit	zero	remain unchanged
delete one unit	positive	decrease
delete one unit	negative	increase
delete one unit	zero	remain unchanged

Notes:

- There is one dual variable for every constraint in the primal.
- If the change in the right-hand side is less than one unit, then the change in the objective function will be proportional. For example, if the right-hand side increased by .5, then the value of the objective function will increase by one half of the value of the dual variable.
- If the change in the right-hand side is more than one unit, then the change in the objective function will be proportionally greater. Such a change can be made only up to a certain limit, as will be discussed in the coming section on sensitivity analysis.

The relationship between the dual variables and the slack (surplus) variables   One dual variable exists for each constraint. It was shown earlier that each constraint will have either a slack or a surplus variable. The question is: What kind of relationship exists between the two types of variables? To understand this relationship one should review the economic interpretation of the dual variables. As stated, a dual whose value is zero signifies a "free good" for the constraint (or resource) it   A "free good" represents. Such a case occurs when the resource is *not* fully utilized; i.e., when it has a slack. In general,[5] the following relationship exists:

Dual	Slack or surplus
0	>0
Nonzero.	0

Note that when the dual is *nonzero* the resource is fully utilized (no slack or surplus). The reason for this is that if a constraint is fully utilized and one increases the supply of this constraint (right-hand side) it should increase the profit (in the case of maximization), while increasing the supply of a nonfully utilized resource (one with a slack), will not do any good; i.e., the value of the objective function will not be changed.

Managerial applications

Management can use the dual for decisions regarding addition, deletion, and tradeoffs of resources.

Example 1: Adding machine capacity   Suppose that management is considering the expansion of the available machine time. The estimated weekly cost is $50 per each hour increase. Should management expand? In order to answer this question one of two approaches may be used:

1. Resolve the problem, changing the machine constraint to $x_1 + 3x_2 \leq 46$; keep all other data unchanged and resolve the problem. The new solution calls for $x_1 = 12$, $x_2 = 11\frac{1}{3}$, and $z = 6{,}433\frac{1}{3}$. Since the addition to profit, $6{,}433\frac{1}{3} - 6{,}350 = \$83\frac{1}{3}$, is larger than the $50 required investment, it should be recommended.
2. Use the dual. Since the "worth" of machine time, $u_2 = \$83\frac{1}{3}$, is larger than the investment, the investment should be recommended.

Example 2: Cut back in resources   Suppose the advertising budget is cut so that only 11 rather than 12 units of model A can be sold each week. What is the impact on profit? The marketing people claim that it is $300 per week. The fact is that it is only $u_3 = \$216\frac{2}{3}$. The reason for this is that reducing x_1 to 11 releases one unit of machine time that enables the production of $\frac{1}{3}$ of model B (from 11 to $11\frac{1}{3}$). Such a change is worth $\$83\frac{1}{3}$ as seen before. Therefore, the net impact is $\$300 - \$83\frac{1}{3} = \$216\frac{2}{3}$.

Example 3: Should capacity be changed?   Given: The solution $x_1 = 5$, $x_2 = 1$, $z = \$50$ to a linear programming maximization problem. The problem includes a space constraint of $3x_1 + 5x_2 \leq 20$ (ft²) with a corresponding dual variable value of $1.80. Management is considering changing the space availability. An increase in availability costs $2.00

---

[5] Whenever there is a unique optimal solution.

per ft²; a decrease in availability reduces expenses by $1.60. What should management do and why?

If management increases the available space, the cost increase will be $2.00 per ft² while the contribution to profit will only be $1.80. Therefore, this is not advisable. If management decreases the available space, the contribution to profit will decrease by $1.80 while the expenses will be reduced by only $1.60. Therefore this is not advisable either. Thus, management should not change the space availability.

6.2 SENSITIVITY (OPTIMALITY) ANALYSIS

The optimal solution to a linear programming problem is based on a set of assumptions and on forecasting of future data such as prices. As a deterministic model, there is no provision for risk or uncertainty. Therefore, it is important for management to know *what* will happen to the optimal solution *if* changes occur in the input data upon which the LP model is based. The technique to address this issue is called *sensitivity analysis*.[6] Sensitivity analysis can be used as an aid for several other managerial decisions, such as product pricing policies.

The name "sensitivity analysis" derives from the fact that an analysis is made to find out how sensitive the optimal solution is to changes. There are two approaches for conducting sensitivity studies:

1. A trial-and-error approach According to this approach one may change the input data, hence forming a new problem. Then the problem is solved from the beginning and the results are compared with that of the old problem. This process is repeated for all desired changes. The deficiency of this approach is that it may become very lengthy, since there are large numbers of possible changes in the data. Another possible deficiency is that resolving a problem may be very expensive, especially for large scale problems.

2. Use of an analytical approach When an analytical approach is used there is no need to completely resolve the LP problem each time a change is made. Furthermore, information such as the "permissible range of change," which is directly provided by the analytical approach, can be provided by the trial-and-error approach only after an extremely lengthy experimentation period. The analytical approach finds the effects of:

- Changes in the coefficients in the objective function.
- Changes in the right-hand "quantity" side of the constraints.
- Changes in the input-output coefficients in the constraints.
- Adding or deleting a constraint.

---

[6] Other names are "optimality analysis," "postoptimality analysis," and "parametric programming."

It should be noted that the optimal solution may be changed in various ways: the value of the objective function (but not the basis) may be changed, its composition (the basic variables) may be changed, or the solution may become infeasible.

Changes in the coefficients of the objective function

Changes in the coefficients of the objective function are basically *product pricing* decisions. Two important managerial questions can be answered by the analysis:

- When does a price (or profit) *decrease* of a product, currently in the optimal solution (a basic variable), justify discontinuing its production?
- How much of a price (or profit) *increase* in a product, currently *not* in the optimal solution, justifies its production (inclusion in the optimal plan)?

Graphical explanation of the changes in the coefficients

Example 1: The product-mix problem Let us reproduce the product-mix problem:

$$\text{maximize } z = 300x_1 + 250x_2$$
$$\text{subject to:}$$
$$2x_1 + 1x_2 \leq 40$$
$$1x_1 + 3x_2 \leq 45$$
$$1x_1 \qquad \leq 12$$

The decision as to whether or not a product will be included in the optimal solution depends on its relative contribution to profit, as expressed in the objective function. In graphical terms, such a decision depends on the *slope* of the objective function. Let us examine the optimal graphical solution to the product-mix problem (Figure 6.2). The existing objective function (line *KL*) yields a solution at point *G* (12 units of x_1 and 11 of x_2). However, if we change the slope of the objective function so it is parallel to line *MN*, then the optimal solution will be at point *C* (produce 15 of x_2). The slope of the objective function can change if the coefficient of x_1 changes, the coefficient of x_2 changes, or the ratio between the coefficients of x_1 and x_2 is changed.

A change in solution from point *G* to point *C* will be achieved when the coefficient of x_2 is more than three times that of x_1. The reason for this is that with a ratio of exactly one to three the objective function will be parallel to the machine constraint, *CD*, with both points *C* and *G* being optimal. A smaller x_2/x_1 ratio means that *G* is the solution; a larger ratio means that *C* is the solution.

Limits on the coefficients

Consider Figure 6.2. The current solution involves both product A (i.e., x_1) and B (x_2). Assume that the profit contribution of x_1 remains 250

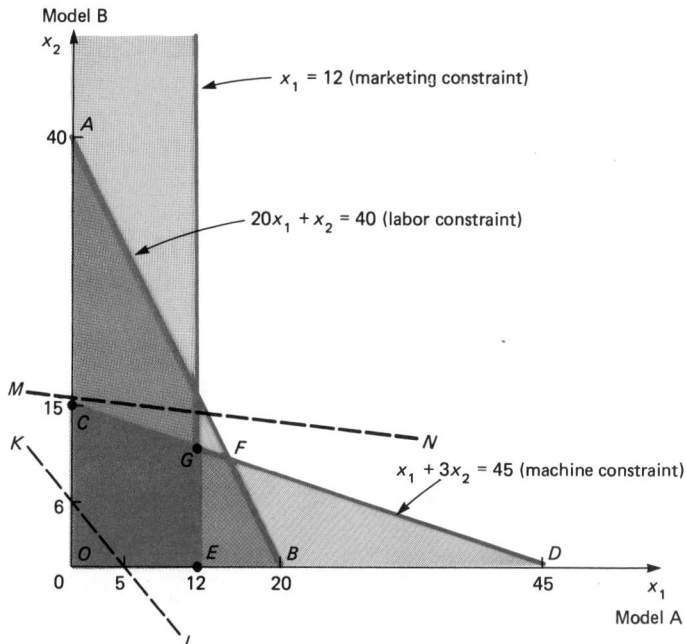

FIGURE 6.2
Solution to the
product-mix problem

while the profit contribution of x_2 increases. This increase will change the slope of line KL toward that of MN. When the profit contribution reaches 750 (exactly 3 times 250) the line will be parallel to CD and both points C and G will be in the optimal solution. Thus, 750 is the upper limit of the coefficient of x_2. Similarly, if the coefficient of x_2 remains 300, then the *lower* limit of the coefficient of x_1 is 100 (i.e., ⅓ of 300). If the profit contribution of x_1 becomes *less* than 100, then x_1 will not appear in the optimal solution (which will move to point C).

The example so far has dealt only with products that are in the solution. However, assume that the optimal solution was at point C to begin with (product x_2 only). Again, by figuring the appropriate slope it would have been possible to figure the necessary increase in the coefficient of x_1 which would result in the inclusion of x_1 in the optimal solution.

The graphical analysis is limited, of course, to two decision variables. A similar analysis is possible using the simplex method.

Use of the simplex method

The aim of the sensitivity analysis presented here is to find the *range* of no change in the composition of the basis. This range is composed of two limits; lower and upper. As long as a coefficient is within this range the current optimal solution will remain unchanged. Should the coefficient go above or below these limits, there will be a change in the basis and optimal solution. The limits of the range which were explained graphically above (as the ratio of the slopes) will now be computed with the help of the simplex tableau.

Example 2: Given a product-mix problem:

$$\text{max. } z = 5x_1 + 4.5x_2 + x_3$$

subject to:

$$15x_1 + 15.8x_2 + 0x_3 \leq 150$$
$$5x_1 + 6.4x_2 + 15x_3 \leq 77$$
$$0x_1 + 2.8x_2 + 11.8x_3 \leq 36$$

The optimal tableau of this problem is shown below.

Basis	Unit profits	Quantity	x_1	x_2	x_3	s_1	s_2	s_3
x_1	5	10	1	1.053	0	.067	0	0
x_3	1	1.8	0	.076	1	−0.22	.067	0
s_3	0	15.12	0	1.924	0	.258	−.773	1
c_j			5	4.5	1	0	0	0
z_j			5	5.342	1	.311	.067	0
$c_j - z_j$			0	−.842	0	−.311	−.067	0

The simplex approach distinguishes between an analysis of the coefficients of basic variables and nonbasic variables.

Analysis of basic variables The analysis will be conducted on products x_1 and x_3 which are in the basis.

Analysis for x_1

Step 1 Copy the $c_j - z_j$ row of the optimal solution.
Step 2 Copy the x_1 row; enter it just below the $c_j - z_j$ row.
Step 3 Divide each $c_j - z_j$ row entry, *for variables not in the solution* (x_2, s_1, and s_2) by the associated variable a_{ij} from the x_1 row.

	x_1	x_2	x_3	s_1	s_2	s_3
$c_j - z_j$ row	0	−.842	0	−.311	−.067	0
x_1 row	1	1.053	0	.067	0	0
$\dfrac{c_j - z_j \text{ row}}{x_1 \text{ row}}$	—	$\dfrac{-.842}{1.053} = -.8$	—	$\dfrac{-.311}{.067} = -4.64$	$\dfrac{-.067}{0} = -\infty$	—

Conclusion

The smallest positive number tells by how much the profit of x_1 can be increased before the solution is changed. Since there are no positive values the answer is ∞.

The *smallest (absolute value) negative number* ($-.8$ in this case), indicates by how much the coefficient of x_1 can be decreased without changing the solution.

The range   These two numbers constitute the range within which the price of x_1 can be changed from the current level of 5. The lower limit is $5 - 0.8 = 4.2$, and the upper limit is $5 + \infty = \infty$.

Analysis for variable x_3

	x_2	s_1	s_2
$c_j - z_j$ row	$-.842$	$-.311$	$-.067$
x_3 row	$.076$	$-.022$	$.067$
$\dfrac{c_j - z_j \text{ row}}{x_3 \text{ row}}$	$\dfrac{-.842}{.076} = -11.09$	$\dfrac{-.311}{-.022} = 14.13$	$\dfrac{-.067}{.067} = -1$

The least negative number is -1.
The least positive number is 14.13
  The range is:

$$\text{Lower limit} = 1 - 1 = 0$$
$$\text{Upper limit} = 1 + 14.13 = 15.13$$

Interpretation

a.   If the profit contribution of x_3 exceeds 15.13, then s_1 will enter into the solution; if this happens then x_1 (the only other product in the solution) will not be produced and the optimal solution will involve producing only x_3.

b.   For product x_3 to be removed from the solution (s_2 would enter), its price contribution will have to be less than zero (i.e., negative.) A similar interpretation would be made for variable x_1.

Summary

The analysis just performed can be summarized by Equations 6.1 and 6.2.

$$\text{Upper limit} = \min. \left[c_i + \frac{c_j - z_j}{a_{ij}} \right] \text{ for all } a_{ij} < 0 \qquad (6.1)$$

$$\text{Lower limit} = \max. \left[c_i + \frac{c_j - z_j}{a_{ij}} \right] \text{ for all } a_{ij} > 0 \qquad (6.2)$$

where:

c_i = Profit contribution of basic variable i

j = Index of nonbasic variable j

a_{ij} = Substitution ratio, in the optimal tableau, between basic variable i and nonbasic variable j.

Range for nonbasic variables

If there is a variable, j, not participating in the optimal basis, then, in order for this variable to be included in the optimal solution, its coefficient in the objective function will have to change from the existing c_j to a new level, c_j (new). This level is given by Inequality 6.3.

$$c_j \text{ (new)} \geq z_j \tag{6.3}$$

Computations

The only nonbasic decision variable is x_2 (with a coefficient c_2). By using Equation 6.3:

$$c_2 \text{ (new)} \geq z_2 = 5.342$$

That is, if the profit contribution of x_2 increases from 4.5 to over 5.342, then x_2 will be included in the solution.

This is the *upper limit* on the range of c_2. There is no *lower limit* on the range of c_2 because this is a maximization problem. Therefore, a coefficient of x_2 lower than the existing 4.5 will make it *even less desirable*.[7]

Capacity changes (changes in the righthand "quantity" side of the constraints)

The righthand side of the constraints expresses the capacities, or limitations, of the resources, or it makes explicit certain requirements. Management may be interested in finding out the effect of changes in these values (b_i's) on the optimal solution. Such a change may not affect the optimal solution, may change the composition of the basis, or may affect only the value of the objective function (same basis variables with different values). Of special interest is the impact on the dual's variables. Graphically, a change in any b_i is shown as a movement of the constraint, *parallel to itself.*

Example

Given: max. $z = 3x_1 + 4x_2$
          subject to:
          (1) $3x_1 + 5x_2 \leq 15$
          (2) $2x_1 + 1x_2 \leq 8$
          (3) $1x_2 \leq 2$

The graphical solution of this problem is shown in Figure 6.3 where point C is the optimal solution. Moving a binding constraint (such as 1 or 2) will change the location of the optimal solution. For example, if the capacity of constraint 2 is increased from 8 to 9 (line ST), then the optimal solution will move to point G. On the other hand, slightly moving constraint 3 will not affect the optimal solution at all (since the

---

[7] Essentially, the lower range for nonbasic variables, in maximization, is $-\infty$.

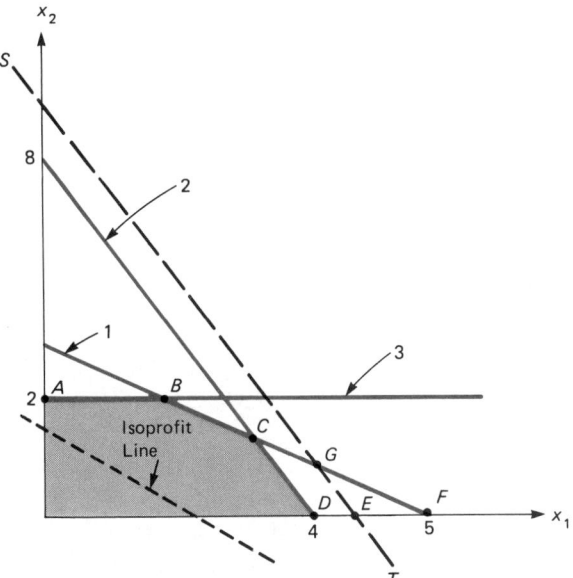

FIGURE 6.3
Changes in capacity

constraint is not binding). However, moving it further may change the location of the optimal solution. Management may be interested in finding the range of such changes. For example, moving constraint 2 more to the right will result in a situation where the solution is at point F (5 units of x_1, 0 of x_2). This will happen when the capacity of constraint 2 is 10; i.e., 10 is the upper limit on constraint 2.

Use of the simplex method to determine the range of b_i

The dual variable, as shown earlier, can tell management the impact on the objective function of a marginal (one unit) change in the righthand side values (b_i's). If a change in one unit is desirable, then management may want to find if a change of 2, 3, or more units is feasible with respect to the dual variable. Specifically, management would like to know the range of b_i over which the dual variable (shadow price) will remain valid.

The simplex method is going to be used in the following manner:

Step 1 List the "Quantity" column of the optimal table.
Step 2 List the subsitution ratios of the constraint whose range of b_i is analyzed.
Step 3 Divide the Quantity by the substitution ratio.
Step 4 Identify the least positive and the least negative results.

Example

Let us analyze the product mix problem which was solved graphically (Figure 6–3). The optimal simplex solution is given in Table 6.2.

TABLE 6.2
Optimal simplex solution of the product mix problem

Basis	Unit Profit	Quan-tity	x_1	x_2	s_1	s_2	s_3
x_1	3	3.57	1	0	−.143	.714	0
s_3	0	1.143	0	0	−.286	.428	1
x_2	4	0.857	0	1	.286	−.428	0
$c_j - z_j$			0	0	−.714	−.428	0

Analysis for the first constraint

Quantity	s_1	Q/s_1
3.57	−.143	−24.96
1.143	−.286	− 3.99
.857	.286	3.00

The least positive Q/s_1 (3.00 in our case) tells us how much the existing $b_1 = 15$ can be decreased.

The least negative Q/s_1 (3.99 in our case) tells us by how much the existing $b_1 = 15$ can be increased. Thus, the *range* over which b_1 can be changed is:

Lower limit = 15 − 3.00 = 12.00; Upper limit = 15 + 3.99 = 18.99

Analysis for the second constraint

Quantity	s_2	Q/s_2
3.57	.714	5
1.143	.428	2.67
.857	−.428	−2

Lower limit = 8 − 2.67 = 5.33
Upper limit = 8 + 2 = 10.00

Analysis for the third constraint

This is not a binding constraint, therefore the upper limit on b_3 is ∞. Since there is slack on this constraint, adding more capacity will not do us any good.

Quantity	s_3	Q/s_3
3.57............	0	∞
1.143...........	1	1.143
.857...........	0	∞

Upper limit = ∞
Lower limit = 2 − 1.143 = 0.857

As an alternative to a direct analysis of the b_i's, one can use the dual's c variables. Since the capacity values in linear programming are equivalent to the coefficients of the objective function of the dual, it is possible to conduct a sensitivity analysis of the primal's b_i's by writing the dual problem and conducting a sensitivity analysis on the coefficients of the objective function. Such a treatment would then establish upper and lower limits on the b_i's. These limits are very important since they tell management how much a capacity limit can be changed before the existing optimal basis changes, as will be shown next.

Changes in the input-output coefficients of the constraints

A change in the input-output coefficients (left-hand side) on the constraints is equivalent to changing the slope of the constraint (in the case of two decision variables). As a result of such a change the area of feasible solutions will be changed. The impact on the optimal solution depends on the magnitude of the change. An analytical treatment of this topic is beyond the scope of this text. (The interested reader should consult references [1,3,5, or 8].)

Adding or deleting constraints

The addition of a new constraint can lead to one of the following results. First, the constraint may be redundant in the sense that it does not further restrict the feasible solution set. In that case the optimal solution remains the same. Second, the constraint may decrease the feasible area but the optimal solution will remain the same. Third, the additional constraint may reduce the feasible area so as to make the current optimal solution infeasible, thereby creating the need for finding a new optimal solution.

To find the impact of an added constraint on the optimal solution all one has to do is to insert the value of the variables of the optimal solution into the new constraint. If the constraint is *not* violated, it belongs to the first or the second result above and there is no change in the optimal solution. If the constraint is violated, then the problem must be resolved.

When deleting a constraint one should check if the constraint is fully utilized (zero slack). If the answer is yes, the problem must be resolved; otherwise, there will be no change in the optimal solution.

A computer solution example

Real-life linear programming problems are too complex for a graphical or manual simplex solution. Therefore, they are solved with the aid of computers. Dozens of computer programs are available on the market: Control Data 3600 Ophelie LPS, GE 225 LPS, GE-LINPRO, IBM-LPS 1620-1311, and Univac 1107 LP.

Several of these were developed by users and contain not only a solution to the linear program and its dual but also some kind of sensitivity analysis. One such example follows.

Given: max $5000x_1 + 4000x_2$
subject to:
(1) $x_1 + x_2 \geq 5$
(2) $x_1 - 3x_2 \leq 0$
(3) $10x_1 + 15x_2 \leq 150$
(4) $20x_1 + 10x_2 \leq 160$
(5) $30x_1 + 10x_2 \geq 135$

The computer's optimal solution is:

Variable	Value
x_1	4.5
x_2	7.0

Value of the objective function = 50,500.
Slack and dual information:

Constraint number	Slack/surplus	Dual
1	6.5	0
2	16.5	0
3	0	150
4	0	175
5	70	0

Sensitivity analysis coefficients of the objective function

Variable	Upper allowable limit	Lower allowable limit
x_1	8,000.00	2,666.67
x_2	7,500.00	2,500.00

Right-hand side

Constraint	b_i	Upper allowable limit	Lower allowable limit
1	5	11.50	0
2	0	∞	−16.50
3	150	240.00	102.86
4	160	233.33	120.00
5	135	∞	65.00

6.3 GOAL PROGRAMMING

Mathematical programming is structured with a single objective function which is to be optimized. In the formulation discussed so far either one objective existed, or, if there were several objectives, only one objective was expressed in the objective function while the remaining objectives were expressed as constraints. For example, since it is impossible to maximize both the share of the market and the profit, they can be expressed as: maximize profit, subject to at least 10 percent share of the market. Since most organizations possess several contradictory goals, it is sometimes difficult to determine which goal to maximize and which goals should be expressed as constraints.

An alternative approach to the multiple goal situation was suggested in Chapter 4, in the form of consolidating all goals into a single goal using utility theory. However, this approach requires the use of a *subjective* valuation of utilities.

Goal programming (GP) is a method that offers a different approach to the solution of linear programming type problems that involve *multiple, conflicting goals.*

Multiple, conflicting goals

The basic idea of goal programming

Goal programming is based on the idea that goals can be *ranked* with respect to their importance in the organization. Ranking of goals enables the consideration of *low order* goals only after *higher order* goals are considered.

The general structure of GP

The objective function of GP expresses the attempt to minimize deviations from the goals. Deviations from the highest goal are driven to zero first. The process then continues for lower priority goals until all goals are satisfied, or until it becomes impossible to obtain a deviation of zero. If a deviational variable cannot be driven to zero, then the related goal cannot be fully achieved.

Formulation of a goal program

The objective function The objective function aims at minimizing the deviations from goals and is expressed as:

$$\text{minimize } z = P_1 U_1^+ d_1^+ + P_1 U_1^- d_1^- + P_2 U_2^+ d_2^+ + P_2 U_2^- d_2^-$$

where P_1, P_2, . . . designate the priorities, with P_1 being the highest priority, P_2 the second highest priority, and so on.[8]

d_1^+, d_2^+, . . . , are the deviations *above* the goals 1, 2, ... (over-achievement)

d_2^-, d_2^-, . . . , are the deviations *below* the goals 1, 2, ... (under-achievement)

U_i^+ is the weight or importance of a unit deviation in d_i^+ (for goal i); U_i^- is the weight of a unit of deviation in d_i^-.

---

[8] The relationship between the priorities is such that $P_j \geqslant P_{j+1}$, which implies that multiplication by a number, however large it may be, cannot make P_{j+1} more important, or even as important as P_j. The relationship between priorities remains *ordinal* (ranked).

The constraints   A constraint in the goal programming problem is written as:

$$a_1x_1 + a_2x_2 + \cdots - d_1^+ + d_1^- = b_1$$

where:

x_1, x_2 are the unknown variables.
a_1, a_2 are the coefficients of these variables.
b_1 is the *goal* or the target under consideration.

There will be one such constraint for each goal. In addition, there may be additional constraints as in a regular linear programming problem. Note that all deviations d_i^+ and d_i^- are nonnegative; that is, $d_i^+ \geq 0$, $d_i^- \geq 0$.

Example

Suppose that a marketing department considers the use of TV and magazines for advertising. The problem is how to budget advertising if the following goals are to be pursued:

Goal 1   The funds spent on advertising should not exceed the $200,000 budget. This goal is the most important and is labeled P_1.

Goal 2   The total exposure, measured by the number of people (audience) that see the advertising, should be at least 20 million. This is the second highest priority goal labeled P_2.

Goal 3   The effective exposures, that is, those audiences that will be influenced by the advertising, should be at least five million (labeled P_3).

Goal 4   There should be at least eight TV inserts, each of which costs $15,000 (labeled P_4).

Goal 5   There should be at least five magazine inserts, each of which costs $10,000 (labeled P_5).

A TV insert reaches two million people of which 800,000 are influenced. A magazine insert is read by one million people of which 300,000 are influenced.

The problem is to find out how many TV inserts (x_1) and how many magazine inserts (x_2) to place in order to attain the above goals.

Formulation

General notes about the deviations

The d^+ deviations are termed *overachievement* variables; the d^- variables are termed *underachievement* variables. In the formulation to come the following rules hold:

1. An overachievement variable will always have a minus sign (i.e., $-d_i^+$).
2. An underachievement variable will always have a plus sign (i.e., $+d_i^-$).

3. If *overachievement* is acceptable than the d_i^+ is eliminated from the constraint. For example, the requirement that we sell *at least* 23 of x_1 is written as:

$$x_1 + d_1^- = 23$$

(i.e., the interest is only with the underachievement).

4. If underachievement is acceptable then the d_i^- can be eliminated from the constraint. For example, the requirement that the budget for x_2 will be *no more than* \$1,000 can be written as:

$$x_2 - d_2^+ = 1000$$

5. If exact achievement is the goal, then both d^+, and d^- stay in the formulation. For example, the requirement to produce *exactly* 10 units of x_3 is expressed as:

$$x_3 - d_3^+ + d_3^- = 10$$

The deviations

Let:

d_1^+ = deviation over the budget
d_1^- = deviation below budget (unexpended funds).
d_2^+ = number of exposures above the required 20 million.
d_2^- = number of exposures below 20 million.
d_3^+ = number of effective exposures above five million.
d_3^- = number of effective exposures below five million.
d_4^+ = number of inserts above eight in TV.
d_4^- = number of inserts below eight in TV.
d_5^+ = number of inserts above five in magazines.
d_5^- = number of inserts below five in magazines.

The objective function

In goal programming an attempt is made to minimize the *relevant deviations* (that is, deviations which are acceptable are ignored). In the example, deviations d_1^-, d_2^+, d_3^+, d_4^+, and d_5^+ are all permissible and therefore they will not appear in the objective function. Assuming that all deviations have the same weight (coefficient of 1 in the priorities), then the objective function is written in the following manner:

$$\text{minimize } z = P_1 d_1^+ + P_2 d_2^- + P_3 d_3^- + P_4 d_4^- + P_5 d_5^-$$

Notice that the elements of the objective functions are *not* totaled. This is in contrast with linear programming.

The constraints

The budget constraint is:

    1. $15{,}000x_1 + 10{,}000x_2 - d_1^+ = 200{,}000.$

The exposure requirement is:

2. $2,000,000x_1 + 1,000,000x_2 + d_2^- = 20,000,000.$

The effective requirement is:

3. $800,000x_1 + 300,000x_2 + d_3^- = 5,000,000.$

The minimum TV inserts:

4. $x_1 + d_4^- = 8.$

The minimum magazine inserts:

5. $x_2 + d_5^- = 5.$

Solution

A special GP program was developed by Lee [7]. The solution gives the values of the x_j's as well as the deviations. It tells which goals are underachieved and which are overachieved. Due to the limited space in this text we will not execute such a computation.

Summary

Goal programming presents a novel approach to the solution of linear programming problems involving multiple, complicated goals. While there are many potential applications of the method, its use is still limited due to the need for modified simplex algorithms and the difficulties of assigning weights to the deviations.

6.4 PROBLEMS FOR PART A

1. Write the dual to the blending problem given in Section 5.2. Solve graphically.

2. Write the dual to Problem 5.21a. Solve by the simplex method. Compare to the simplex solution of the primal.

3. Given a linear programming problem:

    minimize $z = 6x_1 + 5x_2$
    subject to:
    (1) $4x_1 + 8x_2 \geq 80$
    (2) $6x_1 + 4x_2 \geq 100$
    (3) $5x_1 + 5x_2 \geq 95$
    (4) $6x_1 + 3x_2 \geq 110$

    a. Write the dual to the problem.
    b. Solve the dual by the simplex method (or by computer).

    c. What is the solution of the primal? (Answer *without* solving the primal.)
    d. What is the total value of each constraint?

4. Write the dual to the following problems:

    (a) max. $5x_1 + 3x_2 + x_3$
    subject to:
    $5x_1 + 3x_2 \leq 50$
    $2x_2 + x_3 \geq 20$
    $2x_1 + 3x_2 - x_3 = 26$

    (b) min. $6x_1 - 2x_2$
    subject to:
    $3x_1 + 4x_2 \geq 50$
    $x_1 + 2x_2 = 20$
    $2x_1 + 3x_2 \leq 45$

5. The solution to a linear programming minimization problem is $x_1 = 8$, $x_2 = 3$, $x_3 = 5$, $z = \$84.$

There is a raw material constraint that is expressed as:

$$7x_1 + 3x_2 - x_3 \leq 60$$

The dual variable of this constraint is −$2.6. Management is considering changing the availability of the raw material. Increasing the availability costs $2.50 per unit while decreasing raw material by one unit reduces expenses by $2.70. What would you advise management to do and why?

6. Given a LP problem:
$$\text{minimize } z = 300x_1 + 800x_2$$
subject to:
- (1) $\quad 2x_1 + 2x_2 \leq 1$
- (2) $\quad 4x_1 + 2x_2 \geq 1$
- (3) $\quad 10x_1 + 20x_2 \geq 6$
- (4) $\quad x_1 + x_2 = \frac{1}{2}$

a. Solve the problem graphically and by the simplex method.
b. Which of the constraints are fully utilized?
c. Use the shadow prices to find the impact on the objective function of the following changes:
1. Increase the right-hand side of constraint 1 by .5.
2. Decrease the right-hand side of constraint 1 by .1.
3. Increase the right-hand side of constraint 2 by .1.
4. Decrease the right-hand side of constraint 2 by .5.
5. Decrease the right-hand side of constraint 3 by .5.
6. Increase the right-hand side of constraint 4 by .1.
d. Verify the answer to (b) through observation of the graphical solution.

7. Write the dual to Problem 6. Solve by computer. Compare to the results of Problem 6.

8. Given the LP problem:
$$\text{maximize } z = 5000x_1 + 4000x_2$$
subject to:
$$x_1 + x_2 \geq 5$$
$$x_1 - 3x_2 \leq 0$$
$$10x_1 + 15x_2 \leq 150$$
$$20x_1 + 10x_2 \leq 160$$
$$30x_1 + 10x_2 \geq 135$$

Find:
a. The lower and upper limits on the coefficients of the basic variables.
b. The limit on the coefficients of the nonbasic variables.
c. The upper and lower limits on all five righthand side constraints.

9. Given:
$$\text{maximize } z = 2.5x_1 + 2.25x_2 + .5x_3$$
subject to:
$$7.5x_1 + 7.9x_2 \qquad \leq 75$$
$$2.5x_1 + 3.2x_2 + 7.5x_3 \leq 38.5$$
$$1.4x_2 + 5.8x_3 \leq 18$$

Find:
a. How much should the profit coefficient of x_2 be increased in order for it to be included in the optimal solution?
b. How much can the profit of x_1 be decreased without it dropping out of the optimal solution?
c. Change the right-hand side of the first constraint to 45; what impact will such a change have on the solution? Change it to 46 and check again. What can you conclude from the results?

10. Given a linear programming problem:
$$\text{maximize } z = 70x_1 + 30x_2$$
subject to:
$$2x_1 + x_2 \leq 1$$
$$x_1 + 8x_2 \leq 4$$

a. Solve graphically.
b. What price coefficient should the product, currently not in the optimal solution, have in order to be included in the optimal solution?
c. How much can the right-hand side of constraint 2 change before the optimal solution is changed? What will the impact of the change be?
d. How much can the coefficient of x_1 in constraint 1 change before the optimal solution is changed?
e. What will be the impact of the following additional constraint on the solution:
$$2x_1 + 5x_2 = 4$$

11. Refer to the blending problem in Chapter 5 (Figure 5.9).
a. What price will x_1 have to assume in order

for it to be eliminated from the optimal solution?

b. What change in the brightness requirement needs to occur in order to change the optimal solution?

c. What change in the coefficients of the hue constraint (a_{ij}) must occur in order to change the optimal solution?

12. Products A and B are considered for production. Each unit of A requires two hours of labor, three hours of machine time, and $20 capital. Each unit of B requires three hours of labor, two hours of machine time, and $25 in capital. There exist 2,000 hours of labor capacity and 2,200 hours of machine time. The profit on product A is $110; on product B it is $120.

Management objectives, in descending order, are:

1. No idle labor.
2. Produce at least 400 units of each product.
3. Total overtime should not exceed 250 hours.
4. A profit of at least $120,000.
5. Utilize machine time fully.

13. Formulate as a goal programming problem.

A production order of 300 units of product A must be executed within a week by AAA Manufacturing Company. Two production lines are available, each for 30 hours during the week. Production line 1 can produce five units per hour. Using production line 2 it takes 15 minutes to produce each unit. Overtime is available for line 1 at $15 per hour and for line 2 at $12 per hour.

Management goals, in decreasing order of importance, are:

1. Produce 300 units.
2. Maximum allowable overtime of four hours for line 1.
3. The cost of overtime must not be larger than $80.
4. Underutilization of either line during the regular working hours must be avoided. Assign weights to underutilization in direct proportion to their productivity (effectiveness).

Formulate as a goal program in order to find the best production plan.

PART B: EXTENSIONS

6.5 INTEGER PROGRAMMING

Jack Smith, the administrator of Southern General Hospital just returned from a meeting with the hospital board. He was in a gloomy mood since the board only approved funds for a minor expansion, $210,000, to be used for not more than ten hospital beds. He wanted to make the most of this authorization; that is, to get as much additional income as possible to improve the hospital's cash flow situation. So he called his assistant, Ruth, and asked her advice. There were two places where the additional beds could be added—in ward A and/or ward B. Each additional bed in ward A would generate $20 profit a day, versus $25 in ward B. For a moment he thought of placing all the additional beds in ward B; however, he remembered that the board insisted on at least two beds for ward A. Also, the expansion would cost $24,600 per bed in ward B and only $20,000 per bed in ward A. Thus, he could add more beds in ward A. The problem, therefore, was how many beds to add to each ward (say, x_1 to ward A and x_2 to ward B).

With all this information Jack instructed Ruth to go to work on the problem. Ruth, having just completed a course in management science, immediately realized that she was dealing with an allocation problem. As she formulated it she was very pleased to find out that it was linear, as follows:

maximize $z = 20x_1 + 25x_2$

subject to:

$$x_1 + x_2 \leq 10 \quad \text{(total bed limitation)}$$
$$\$20,000 \, x_1 + \$24,600 \, x_2 \leq 210,000 \text{ (budget constraint)}$$
$$x_1 \geq 2 \text{ (at least two beds in ward A)}$$

With only two variables and three constraints it seemed natural to try the graphical method (Figure 6.4). Ruth did so and found an optimal solution of two beds in ward A and 6.9 beds in ward B, with a total daily profit of $212.50 (point P in Figure 6.4). Examining the solution, Ruth immediately realized that she was dealing with an integer programming problem since 6.9 beds is obviously not feasible. Before she had a chance to reexamine the solution she was surprised by Jack.

"I don't know what they teach you there at school, but you have been working on the problem for more than half an hour; let me try it." At that stage Ruth had no choice but to look at Jack's attempt. Jack rationalized that in this case there are only a few alternatives; they are listed in Table 6.3. Obviously alternatives a_0 and a_1 should not be considered since there must be at least two beds in ward A. He also realized that alternatives a_2, a_3, a_4, a_5, a_6, and a_7, exceeded the available budget. Left with only alternatives a_8, a_9, and a_{10}, he computed their profits and declared: "It is best to build eight beds in ward A and two in

FIGURE 6.4
Graphical approach to
bed allocation.

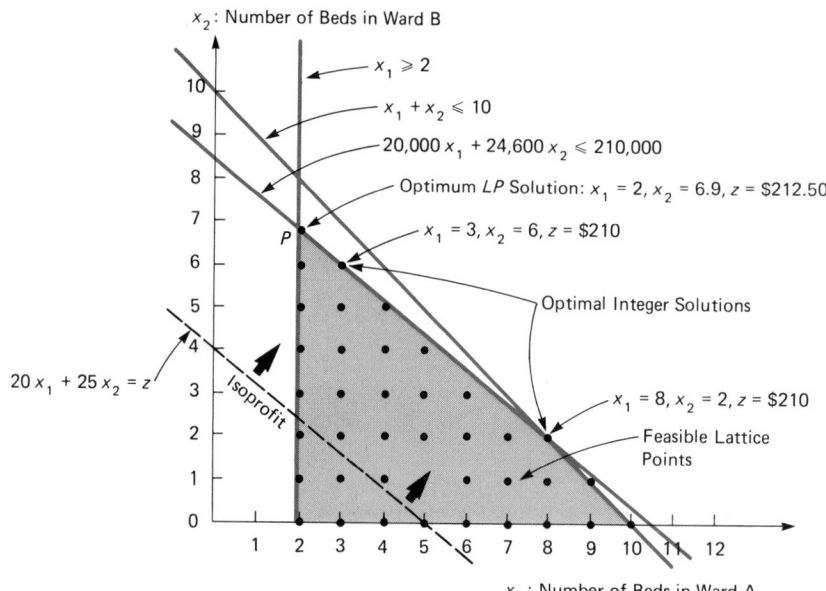

Note: • designates a feasible integer solution.

TABLE 6.3
Bed alternatives

Alternatives	Beds in ward A	Beds in ward B	Required expenses	Daily profit
a_0	0	10	246,000	(infeasible)
a_1	1	9	241,000	(infeasible)
a_2	2	8	236,800	(infeasible)
a_3	3	7	232,200	(infeasible)
a_4	4	6	227,600	(infeasible)
a_5	5	5	223,000	(infeasible)
a_6	6	4	218,400	(infeasible)
a_7	7	3	213,800	(infeasible)
a_8	8	2	209,200	$210
a_9	9	1	204,600	$205
a_{10}	10	0	200,000	$200

ward B; it will cost us $209,200, and it will generate a daily profit of $210.
As you see, we do not need your linear programming."

Ruth returned, disheartened, to her desk. After all, why spend time
on linear programming? Nevertheless, she decided to return to the
graphical solution. As she examined the points marked with a • in Figure
6.4 (feasible integer solution points), it took her only a moment to notice
that there was another solution. She called Jack and declared: "To get a
daily profit of $210 it is sufficient to build only six beds in ward B and

three in A⁹ at a total cost of $207,600, a savings of $1,600 in the required investment."[10] Jack was surprised; he checked and re-checked and finally admitted that the investment in "that linear programming course" was perhaps not so worthless.

Integer programming—The basics

The case just presented is an illustration of an *integer programming* problem. A mathematical programming problem which requires that some or all of the decision variables appearing in the optimal solution must be nonnegative whole numbers (such as 0, 1, 2, . . .), is classified as an integer programming problem. In other words, an *indivisibility* requirement is imposed either on all of the decision variables (an *all-integer* case) or on some of the decision variables (a *mixed-integer* case). Many practical problems involve integers. For example, it is impossible to have 2.7 elevators in a building, to admit 12.6 patients to a hospital, or to have 30.3 seats in a classroom.

An indivisibility

Mixed integers

Adding the indivisibility requirement results in additional constraints. This means that the optimal integer solution will be either inferior (the usual case) or at best as good as the optimal noninteger solution. In other words, there is a cost attached to imposing the indivisibility requirement. For example, in the optimal noninteger LP solution to the hospital expansion problem, a daily profit of $212.50 is expected, $2.50 more than in the all-integer solution. This difference is called the *cost of indivisibility.*

Cost of indivisibility

Integer programming is important not only because it allows us to solve practical problems with indivisibility requirements but also because it can be used as a computational tool in the solution of several complicated problems that cannot otherwise be solved (or cannot otherwise be solved effectively). For example, many nonlinear, as well as combinatorial problems[11] can be reduced to integer programming form. (For details see Loomba and Turban [8] or Salkin [10].)

When the indivisibility requirement is added to a regular linear programming problem, the result is an *integer* (linear) *programming* problem.[12]

---

[9] Notice that here there are two (and only two) optimal integer solutions. The reader may recall that in LP when more than one optimal solution exists there are an infinite number of optimal solutions.

[10] Ruth and Jack's solutions are both optimal from a mathematical point of view. However, Ruth's solution is superior since it requires less capital outlay. (The cost of capital outlay was disregarded in the formulation.) Multiple optimal solution situations give management greater flexibility of implementation since they can consider factors not expressed in the formal model.

[11] A combinatorial problem consists of finding, from among a finite set of feasible solutions (usually very large), a solution that optimizes the value of the objective function.

[12] When the indivisibility requirement is added to a *nonlinear* programming problem, the result is integer-nonlinear programming, a rather complex situation which will not be discussed in this text.

Methods of solution

Complete
enumeration

Complete enumeration   What Jack attempted to do in the hospital expansion case was to list all possible solutions, eliminate those which violate the constraints, and select the best solution by comparing the net profits. Such a process is called an *enumeration;* and if *all* feasible solutions are checked, it is termed a *complete enumeration.* What Jack did was to assume that he should enumerate only the alternatives involving ten beds (a partial enumeration), neglecting alternatives of nine or fewer beds.

Since most integer programming problems have a finite number of feasible solutions, these can be solved by complete enumeration. To do so it is necessary to assign all possible integer values to all variables and to check all possible feasible solution combinations to determine that combination which yields the best value of the objective function. In cases with a small number of variables and possible combinations, this method is efficient. However, in many practical problems there is a very large number of possible solution combinations and the enumeration method is therefore impractical.

There is one special case in which complete enumeration might be used to advantage. In several business and economic decision problems there are only two possible courses of action for every alternative under consideration, such as invest or not invest, accept or reject. For such cases, an implicit enumeration search, named the *zero-one algorithm,*

The zero-one
algorithm

has been developed (e.g., see Garfinkel and Nemhauser [6]). This method has, for example, been used in the problem of allocating funds to research and development projects and found to be very efficient with as many as 50 projects. Enumeration efforts, in general, may be reduced

Branch and bound

with the *branch and bound* approach (to be discussed later in this chapter).

Rounding the noninteger solution   A practical approach to an integer programming problem in some cases is to solve it as a regular linear programming problem and then round off the optimal results. The major advantage of such an approach is the saving of time and cost which would have been required for formulating and solving an integer programming model. The major disadvantage of the rounding approach is that the resultant solution may differ significantly from the optimal integer solution and, furthermore, may even be infeasible.

While the infeasibility problems can be avoided when rounding, by making sure that the constraints are not violated, it is impossible to tell offhand how close the rounded solution is to the optimal integer one. However, it is possible to tell how close the rounded integer solution is to the regular noninteger solution. If the difference between the two is not large, there is very little sense in investing time and money in an attempt to identify the optimal integer solution.[13]

---

[13] The logic for this approach is that the optimal integer solution must be inbetween the noninteger solution and the rounded solution. If the difference between these two is

A variant of the rounding method is the *trial-and-error* approach, in which one enumerates *selected* feasible integer solutions in the neighborhood of the optimal LP solution. For example, using this approach Ruth would have investigated the solutions: $(1,6(x_1 = 1, x_2 = 6))$, $(2,6)$, $(3,6)$, $(1,7)$, $(2,7)$, $(3,7)$, $(1,8)$, $(2,8)$, $(3,8)$.

The graphical method Integer programming problems with either two unknown variables or two constraints can be solved by the graphical method. Its major advantages are its simplicity and its applicability for solving both the all-integer and mixed-integer problems. Ruth used this method in the hospital expansion case.

The graphical approach for integer programming problems is similar to the graphical approach for solving regular linear programming problems; the difference lies in the nature of the *feasible solution spaces* for the two problems (see Figure 6.4). Whereas in the linear programming case the set of feasible solutions is a *space* bounded by the linear constraints, in integer programming the feasible area is a collection of *all-integer points*. Once such points are marked, the isoprofit line is moved away from the origin until it covers the last lattice points[14] in the feasible area (Points $(3,6)$ and $(8,2)$ in Figure 6.4).

Branch and bound This is a special type of enumeration procedure and is discussed in Section 6.6.

More complicated methods A host of more complicated methods are available for larger and more complex problems. All require computers. For a discussion see [6], [10], or [11]. Of special interest are the methods based on Gomory's "cutting plane" algorithm (see [5] and [11]). According to these methods, a feasible solution area is constructed by sequentially adding constraints which eliminate or "cut" infeasible areas from the original solution space. Thus, the solution region converges to the area circumscribed by the extreme lattice points. Dynamic programming (Chapter 9) can also be used to solve certain types of integer programming problems.

Trial and error (margin note)

The feasible solution space (margin note)

Cutting planes (margin note)

6.6 THE BRANCH AND BOUND METHOD

The branch and bound method is an intelligent search procedure for either an optimal or, with less computational effort, a close-to-optimal solution to certain managerial problems such as all-integer and mixed-integer problems.

The process in general

The process consists of dividing a problem into two or more *subproblems* for each of which two *bounds* on the objective function are

Dividing into subproblems (margin note)

---

small then the difference between the rounded and the true optimal integer solution is minimal.

[14] A lattice point here refers to a point with all-integer coordinates.

determined. The manner of determining bounds depends on the type of problem. A distinction is then made between *feasible bounding solutions* and *infeasible bounding solutions*. All subproblems whose objective functions are worse than the established feasible bound are eliminated from further consideration. The remaining subproblems are then subdivided and investigated. The process is repeated until no further subdivision is possible, at which point the optimal (or near optimal) solution has been reached.

   Example   Let us illustrate by solving a problem of finding the best assignment of three employees to three machines on a one-to-one basis. Table 6.4 shows the profits (determined from prior experience) derived from assigning each employee to each machine. For example, if Jim is assigned to a drilling machine, a profit of 2 is realized.

TABLE 6.4
An assignment problem

Machine Employee	Mill (x)	Lathe (y)	Drill (z)
Jim (a)	0	3	2
Bill (b)	2	4	1
Joe (c)	2	1	3

   Solution   First, the maximum possible profit is computed. To do so, the highest possible profit in the first row, which is 3, is selected; accordingly, Jim is assigned to the lathe (a to y, or ay). Next is the second row; 4 is the highest profit. Therefore an assignment of b to y is made. Similarly, c is assigned to z. The profit for this assignment (ay, by, cz) is: $3 + 4 + 3 = 10$. This solution is *infeasible* since two employees were assigned to machine y violating the one-to-one requirement. (If this solution had been feasible, it would also have been optimal and the problem would have been solved.) This solution, with the highest possible profit, is now used as the *upper bound*, an infeasible bound in this case.

Upper bound

First branching

   By changing *one assignment* in the *infeasible solution*, three new problems are formed. Suppose a change in the assignment to the milling machine (x) is chosen; then three subproblems will involve assigning a, b, and c consecutively to x. First, a is assigned to x. The original assignments of b and c (by, cz) are kept. This solution is feasible with a value of 7 (see Figure 6.5). Second, b is assigned to x. In this case the (feasible) solution is: ay, bx, and cz with a value of 8. Finally, c is assigned to x with the solution: cx, ay, and by (which is infeasible) with a value of 9.

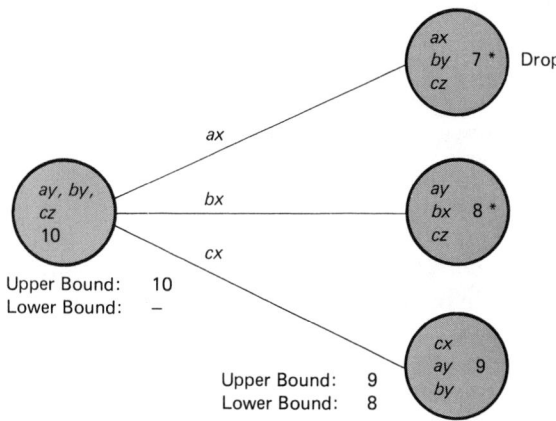

FIGURE 6.5
First branching
(*denotes feasible
solutions)

The original problem has now been partitioned into three new problems with a best (but infeasible) solution of 9 instead of 10. Therefore, 9 becomes the *new upper bound*.[15] It is still an infeasible solution but it has a value closer to the feasible area than the previous bound had. Of the proposed *feasible* solutions, the one with the *highest* value (of 8) is the best one. Therefore, it is set as the *lower* (feasible) *bound*. The optimal solution must now be between the *lower bound* of 8 and the *upper bound* of 9. Now the *ax* solution can be dropped from further consideration since it is *below* the lower bound.

Lower bound

Second branching

The next branching is from *cx* since this is the current best, but infeasible, solution. This time two branches are possible, *ay* and *by* (see Figure 6.6.

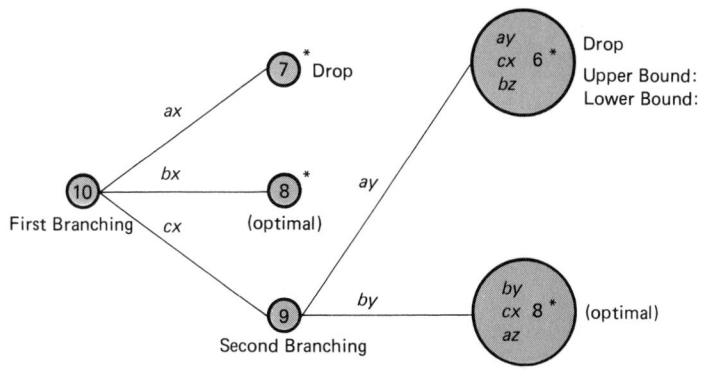

FIGURE 6.6
Second branching
(*denotes feasible
solutions)

---

[15] New bounds are generated at each branching because the partitioning of the problem *totally replaces* the previous problem.

Again, solutions whose value is less than the current lower bound are dropped; thus, *ay* with a profit of 6 is dropped. Since no further branching is possible (only feasible solutions remain and feasible solutions are not partitioned), the optimal solution has been reached. Here two optimal solutions with a profit of 8 have been identified:

1. *b* to *x*, *a* to *y*, *c* to *z*.
2. *c* to *x*, *b* to *y*, *a* to *z*.

Flexibility of branch and bound

The procedure for bounding is very flexible—in the example above for instance, the initial upper bound could have been found by selecting the largest value in each *column* rather than in each row.

Use in solving integer programming problems

The branch and bound technique can be used to solve integer programming problems. The first step is to solve the problem by linear programming without paying attention to the integer requirements. Then, if the solution is noninteger, a branching procedure is employed. This procedure splits the problem into two subproblems based on two integer values which are immediately above and below the noninteger value. Assume, for instance, that a variable x_2 in the LP solution equals 2.25; then the problem is divided into two subproblems by introducing two new constraints: $x_2 \geq 3$; and $x_2 \leq 2$, one constraint in each branch.

Example   The Worthy Company is a large manufacturer of household appliances. Recently its board of directors approved $25 million for constructing additional plants and/or warehouses. The construction of each warehouse will cost $2 million, and management does not want more than eight warehouses. The construction of each plant will cost $4 million, and management does not plan to construct more than five. It is estimated that each warehouse will contribute $31,000 per month to the company's profit, while each plant will contribute $60,000 per month. The problem is to determine the optimal number of plants and warehouses. Since fractions of plants or warehouses cannot be built, the problem is an integer programming one.

Formulation   The problem can be stated as follows (data are in thousands of dollars):

$$\text{maximize } z = 31x_1 + 60x_2$$
$$\text{subject to:}$$
$$2x_1 + 4x_2 \leq 25$$
$$x_1 \qquad \leq 8$$
$$x_2 \leq 5$$

and both x_1 and x_2 must be nonnegative integers, where:

x_1 = number of warehouses
x_2 = number of plants.

Solution   The optimal, noninteger solution (obtained graphically) is:

$x_1 = 8$ warehouses.
$x_2 = 2.25$ plants.
$z = 383$ (thousand dollars) profit.

The solution is not acceptable since x_2 is not an integer. The value of $z = 383$ is set as the initial *upper bound*. Now, the problem is divided into two subproblems, A and B.[16]

Subproblem A	*Subproblem B*
maximize $z = 31x_1 + 60x_2$	maximize $z = 31x_1 + 60x_2$
subject to:	subject to:
$2x_1 + 4x_2 \leq 25$	$2x_1 + 4x_2 \leq 25$
$x_1 \qquad \leq 8$	$x_1 \qquad \leq 8$
$x_2 \leq 5$	$x_2 \leq 5$
$x_2 \geq 3$	$x_2 \leq 2$
$x_1, \quad x_2$ are integers	$x_1, \quad x_2$ are integers

Optimal solution for subproblems A and B (obtained graphically):

For subproblem A: $x_1 = 6.5$, $x_2 = 3$, and $z = 381.5$.
For subproblem B: $x_1 = 8$, $x_2 = 2$, $z = 368$.

This information is shown in Figure 6.7 in "tree form." The search of subproblem B is stopped since it has the all-integer feasible solution $z = 368$ which is therefore considered as the *lower bound*. Subproblem A is searched further since it has a *noninteger solution* and the value of its objective function is greater than the current lower bound of 368. Thus, it is possible that the optimal integer solution to A will yield a value of z larger than 368. The second *upper bound* is set to 381.5, replacing the initial upper bound of 383.

Next, the solution of subproblem A is branched into two other subproblems: subproblem C, where an additional constraint of $x_1 \leq 6$ is added; and subproblem D, where an additional constraint of $x_1 \geq 7$ is added. The reason for adding these constraints is that since $x_1 = 6.5$ is not feasible (noninteger), then the feasible solution *must* be either $x_1 \leq 6$ or $x_1 \geq 7$.

Subproblem C	*Subproblem D*
maximize $z = 31x_1 + 60x_2$	maximize $z = 31x_1 + 60x_2$
subject to:	subject to:
$2x_1 + 4x_2 \leq 25$	$2x_1 + 4x_2 \leq 25$
$x_1 \qquad \leq 8$	$x_1 \qquad \leq 8$
$x_2 \leq 5$	$x_2 \leq 5$
$x_2 \geq 3$	$x_2 \geq 3$
$x_1 \qquad \leq 6$	$x_1 \qquad \geq 7$
x_1, x_2 are integers	x_1, x_2 are integers

---

[16] The logic for constructing the two subproblems is that since the optimal solution $x_2 = 2.25$ is not feasible, the integer feasible solution must be either in the region of $x_2 \leq 2$ or in the region of $x_2 \geq 3$.

FIGURE 6.7
· Branch and bound
solution

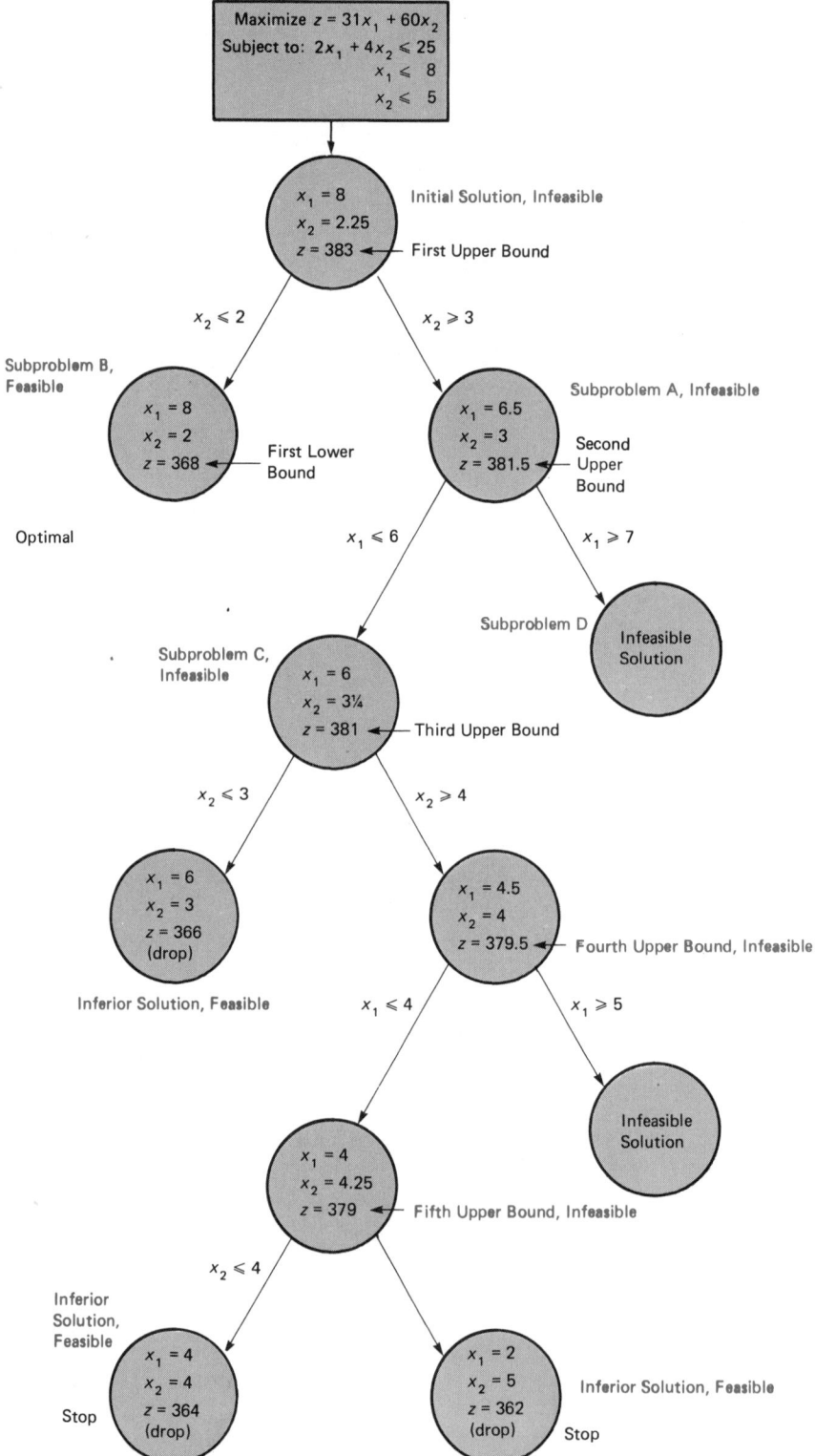

Solutions are circled. Additional constraints added at each branching are shown on the branch.

Subproblem D has no feasible solution since any value for x_1 (only ≥ 7 and ≤ 8 are considered) will violate the constraints $x_2 \geq 3$ and $2x_1 + 4x_2 \leq 25$ and, therefore, its solution is not considered. Subproblem C has a noninteger solution with a new third *upper bound* of $z = 381$ (see Figure 6.7). The process is continued until no further branching is possible, or until the new upper bound becomes equal to or smaller than the *lower bound*. In this case, the process stops with integer feasible solutions which are inferior to the lower bound $z = 368$; and, therefore, the optimal solution is:

$$x_1 = 8, \ x_2 = 2, \quad \text{and} \quad z = 368$$

Branch and bound can be efficiently coded into a computer routine; it works well in problems containing a few integer-valued variables. However, in problems with large numbers of integer-valued variables and in cases where the noninteger solution is far from optimal, then the number of required iterations may be too large for efficient application.

6.7 NONLINEAR PROGRAMMING

A nonlinear programming problem is a mathematical programming problem in which the objective function and/or one or more of the constraints are nonlinear.

Nonlinear functions

Functional relationships that contain such terms as $2x^3$, log $1/x$, $2e^x$, as well as discontinuous functions are termed *nonlinear functions*. In general, any functional relation that does not meet linearity conditions (see Appendix A) is considered nonlinear.

Nonlinear functions

Examples of nonlinear programming problems

1. minimize $z = 3x^2 - 2y$ (nonlinear objective function and linear constraints)

    subject to:
    $$3x + 4y \geq 12$$
    $$x - y \geq \ 3$$

2. minimize $z = 2xy - \dfrac{2}{x}$ (nonlinear objective function and nonlinear constraints)

    subject to:
    $$3x^2 + 2y \leq 100$$
    $$x \ + \ y^3 \leq \ \ 80$$

3. maximize $z = 5x + 7y$ (linear objective function and nonlinear constraints)

    subject to:
    $$x^2 + 2y^3 \leq 65$$
    $$2x^2 + \ y \ \leq 50$$

Solution methods   As opposed to the simplex method, which is a general method for solving linear programming problems, there is no general method for solving *all* nonlinear programming problems. Instead, various computational techniques, some of which are mathematically complicated, have been developed to solve different categories of nonlinear programs. These special computational methods are limiting factors in the use of nonlinear programming.

In this text we will not solve any nonlinear programming problems. For methods of solution, see Avriel [2], Loomba and Turban [8], or Zangwill [12].

Quadratic programming

Some of the less complicated types of nonlinear problems are those involving quadratic programming. These deal with the problem of minimizing a quadratic (second degree) objective function,[17] subject to linear constraints. Many practical problems can be formulated as quadratic programs. Fairly efficient solution techniques have been developed for quadratic programming problems but are beyond the scope of this text. (See Avriel [2] and Bradley [3].)

6.8   CONCLUDING REMARKS

Linear programming problems can be relatively easy to solve in comparison to the two other types of mathematical programming problems: integer programming and nonlinear programming. The use of integer and nonlinear programming is still very much an art based on experience and ingenuity and hence has not enjoyed the extended use that linear programming has seen.

6.9   PROBLEMS FOR PART B

14.   Given:

$$\text{maximize } z = x_1 + x_2$$

subject to:
$$2x_1 + x_2 \le 5$$
$$x_1 + 2x_2 \le 5$$
$$x_1, x_2 \text{ integer}$$

a.   Solve by complete enumeration.
b.   Solve graphically.

c.   Solve by rounding the noninteger LP solution.
d.   Find the cost of indivisibility.

15.   The Navy is considering three types of attack aircraft to equip its carriers: a supersonic type, a subsonic type, and a boost glide type. The effectiveness of any air vehicle to the fleet is determined by the expected military value of targets the aircraft can "kill" during military engagements of a certain length. These have

---

[17] Examples of quadratic functions are:

$$x_1^2; \ (x_1 - 2)^2; \ \text{and} \ x_1^2 + x_2^2 - 2x_1 + x_2$$

been estimated for the three types mentioned as follows:

Type	Expected value of target "killed"
Supersonic....................	30
Subsonic	24
Boost glide	25

The following numbers of aircraft could be accommodated if the entire deck is allocated to one specific type.

Type of aircraft	Number on full deck
Supersonic...............	60
Subsonic	120
Boost glide..............	160

In other words the deck can contain (if full) 60 supersonic or 120 subsonic, or 160 boost glide, or any linear combination of these types.

Personnel requirements and monthly maintenance costs are as follows:

Type	Personnel per aircraft	Maintenance cost per aircraft ($)
Supersonic.........	15	5,000
Subsonic	13	3,000
Boost glide	17	6,000

A carrier has facilities for 1,500 personnel, and the Navy's monthly maintenance budget for aircraft is $650,000 per carrier.

The problem is to find how many of each of the three types of aircraft should be purchased per carrier in order to maximize the value of the attack capability of a carrier. Formulate as an integer programming problem: Define the decision variables, establish the objective function, and determine the constraint relationships. (Formulate only.)

16. American Aviation Company organizes summer charter flights from New York to London. The company uses three types of aircraft whose operating cost and capacities are shown below.

Type of aircraft	Passenger capacity	Cost per flight	Maximum possible flights	Required crew
M-1........	100	$ 6,000	15	4
M-2........	180	8,000	12	12
M-3........	270	10,000	6	17

The company can spare a crew of only 140 for the entire mission. Thirty-two hundred students signed up for the summer, each paying $110.

All students *must* be flown. Find how many flights of each type should be used in order to maximize profit.

Formulate as a mathematical program. (Do not solve.)

17. Western Columbia Hospital has recently modernized one of its operating rooms so that it now contains the very latest in a variety of equipment. Only two types of operations are considered. The hospital desires to schedule as many operations as possible in this room which can handle up to 12 operations type A or 30 operations type B (or any linear combination) per day. Each A type operation requires 4 pints of blood, and each B type operation requires 5.5 pints of blood. The hospital has a blood inventory of 100 pints. At least 7 type A operations and no more than 20 type B operations should be performed. Find the best possible schedule.

   a. Set up the problem as an integer linear program.
   b. Solve the problem graphically and show the feasible area.
   c. Comment on the resource utilization in the optimal solution.
   d. Suppose that the value of each operation of type A is three times as important as that of type B. Reformulate, solve the problem, and comment on the result.

18. The W. V. Mower Blade Company wishes to market a deluxe and a regular model lawnmower blade. The deluxe requires five units of carbon steel and eight units of alloy steel per 150 blades, while the regular blade requires ten units of carbon steel and no alloy steel per 150 blades. Due to market conditions (recent boom), the company is left with only 300 units of carbon steel and 200 units of alloy steel. The deluxe blade also requires 2 hours of grinding time and 1.25 hours of finishing time per 150 blades while the regular needs 1 hour of grinding and .5 hours of finishing. The grinding department states that it has at most 50 hours available in the time period concerned, and

the finishing department can contribute 30 hours toward the production of the blades.

a. How can the firm maximize profit if $2 profit from a deluxe blade and $1.50 from a regular blade is realized? (Solve graphically.)

b. What is the best production plan if an *integer number of batches* must be produced? (Solve graphically.)

   Hint: Formulate the problem in batches of 150 blades.

19. Flamingo Computing Corporation manufactures two types of small computers, A and B. The company can produce up to seven computers a week. Of their ten available production teams, two are required for the production of each computer type A every week and three are required for the production of each computer type B.

   The company profit (in thousands of dollars) for each unit of type A sold is $8 - 2x_1$ (where x_1 is the amount sold of type A) and $5 - x_2$ for each unit of type B. All computers must be completed by the end of each week.

   The problem is to find the most profitable weekly production plan for the company. (Formulate only; do not solve.)

20. Solve Problem 14 by branch and bound.

21. Given an assignment problem: The cost of assigning jobs A, B, and C to machines M, N, O, and P is shown below.

   Find the best assignment. Solve by branch and bound.

Machine / Job	M	N	O	P
A	6	7	5	9
B	8	5	6	7
C	10	8	5	6

22. In branch and bound:

a. Discuss the role of the lower bound in minimization problems.

b. Discuss the role of the upper bound in minimization problems.

c. At what point can branches be dropped from consideration?

d. Discuss three ways of bounding the assignment example in Section 6.6. Which is best?

23. Explain why the value of the objective function in a product-mix integer programming problem can never exceed that of a similar linear programming problem where there is no integer requirement.

24. Give an example that will illustrate a case where:
There exists a linear programming problem that has a *noninteger* optimal solution valued z, and an integer requirement is imposed on the problem. The optimal integer solution also has a value of z, exactly the same as the noninteger solution. That is, the cost of indivisibility is zero. Use a graphical presentation.

6.10 CASE

HENSLEY VALVE CORP.

It was Monday morning and the weekly meeting of the Executive Committee was in full swing. There were two primary items on the agenda and both directly affected Hensley's profit margin.

Agenda Item A: The Proposed Tax Increase on Diesel Fuel.

Agenda Item B: Record Interest Rates.

"Gus, as Regional Manager in our largest selling region, what will be the result of our raising prices to offset this possible increase in our trucking costs?"

"Well J.B., it certainly won't help our

sales effort. Valve JBH-1 is only marginally profitable now but takes twice the time to sell as our more profitable JBH-2s. I'm afraid a price increase might wipe out the viability of our JBH-1 valves altogether."

"That's what I was afraid of too. Pat, how about the effect of that cancellation of the second NC machine we were hoping would help our productivity? I know you were counting on that to increase our output rate but with the latest two big jumps in the prime rate we simply can't afford it at this time."

"Yes, I realize that, J.B. I certainly hadn't expected the prime rate to go quite this high. Basically our output rates will remain limited, especially on old line 3 which produces the JBH-1 and 2 valves. Given the limited floor space and equipment and working three shifts on this line we can still produce at most 600 JBH-1s or 100 JBH-2s a week or any combination in between. I wondered if it would be worthwhile to have Tim Moran in our controller's office look at the interacting effect of all these changes? It seems that so many things are happening at once it may be best to totally change our product mix as well as our prices."

"I agree, Pat. It seems appropriate to undertake a complete contingency analysis of what we should do given any specific change in the market or combination of changes. I'll work up a memo to Tim this afternoon."

MEMO

TO: Tim Moran, Controller's Assistant
FROM: J. B. Hensley, President
SUBJECT: Reanalysis of Product Line

Please undertake a review of our JBH-1 and 2 valves for the next meeting of the Executive Committee on Monday morning. For this purpose you may assume their profitability to be $10 and $40 each, respectively. We have figured that a JBH-1 takes 4 manhours to sell and a 2 takes 2 manhours to sell. Sales has at most 1000 manhours a week available. Check with Pat Johnson for production figures on line 3. Items we would specifically like to know include:

- Given our limited capacities, how many of each valve should we currently be producing and selling to maximize our profits?
- What is an extra manhour of sales time worth?
- At what manhour sales effort is it not worth producing JBH-1s any longer?
- What is an increase in the capacity of line 3 worth?
- At what JBH-1 profitability will only JBH-1's be worth producing?
- What will be the effect on the solution of improving the JBH-1 marketing effort so it only takes 2.5 manhours to sell a unit? What per unit investment is this worth?

Please add any other information you find to be relevant. Thank you.

6.11 GLOSSARY

All-integer An integer programming problem where *all* the decision variables must be whole numbers.

Branch and bound An intelligent search procedure for optimal (sometimes close-to-optimal) solutions.

Branching Dividing a managerial problem into sub-problems.

Complete enumeration A comparison of *all* possible solution values.

Dual problem A linear programming complementary problem which is associated with an original linear programming (primal) problem.

Goal programming A mathematical programming extension where several goals can be treated in the model if they are ranked according to their importance. The objective is to minimize the deviations from the desired goals.

Indivisibility A requirement that the values of a variable be restricted to whole numbers.

Integer programming A mathematical programming problem which requires that some or all of the decision variables be whole numbers.

Mixed integer An integer programming problem where some but not all of the decision variables must be whole numbers.

Overachievement A variable that measures by how much a goal is exceeded.

Primal problem An original linear programming problem.

Quadratic programming A mathematic programming problem with a quadratic (second degree) objective function and linear constraints.

Sensitivity analysis An analysis of the impact of changes in the input data to a linear programming problem on its optimal solution.

Shadow price The value that is added to the value of the objective function when one unit is added to a linear programming constraint (right hand side). This value equals the *dual variable* of the resource.

Underachievement A variable that measures the difference between a given target and a performance which is lower (in absolute terms) than the standard.

6.12 REFERENCES AND BIBLIOGRAPHY

1. Anderson, D. R., et al. *Linear Programming for Decision Making.* St. Paul, Minn.: West Publishing Co., 1974.

2. Avriel, M. *Nonlinear Programming: Analysis and Methods,* Englewood Cliffs, N.J.: Prentice-Hall, Inc., 1976.

3. Bradley, S. P., et al. *Applied Mathematical Programming.* Reading, Mass.: Addison-Wesley Publishing Co., Inc., 1977.

4. Eppen, G. D. and Gould, F. J. *Quantitative Concepts for Management.* Englewood Cliffs, N.J.: Prentice-Hall, Inc., 1979.

5. Gal, T. *Postoptimal Analysis, Parametric Programming, and Related Topics.* New York: McGraw-Hill, 1979.

6. Garfinkel, R., and Nemhauser, G. L. *Integer Programming.* New York: John Wiley & Sons, Inc., 1972.

7. Lee, S. M. *Goal Programming for Decision Analysis.* Philadelphia: Auerbach Publishers, Inc., 1972.

8. Loomba, N. P., and Turban, E. *Applied Programming in Management.* New York: Holt, Rinehart and Winston, Inc., 1974.

9. Mitten, L. G. "Branch and Bound Methods: General Formulation and Properties." *Operations Research* 18 (1970): 24–34.

10. Salkin, H. *Integer Programming.* Reading Mass.: Addison-Wesley Publishing Co., Inc., 1975.

11. Taha, H. A. *Integer Programming: Theory, Applications and Computers.* New York: Academic Press, Inc., 1975.

12. Zangwill, W. I. *Nonlinear Programming: A Unified Approach.* Englewood Cliffs, N.J.: Prentice-Hall, Inc., 1969.

7

Distribution problems are a special type of linear programming problems. There are two main types of distribution problems: the transportation problem and the assignment problem.

The transportation problem deals with shipments from a number of sources to a number of destinations. Typically, each source is supply-limited, each destination has a known demand, and the shipping costs between sources and destinations are given. The object is to find the cheapest shipping schedule that satisfies demand without violating supply constraints.

The assignment problem deals with finding the best one-to-one match for each of a given number of "candidates" to a number of "positions." Typical situations include assigning workers to machines, teachers to classes, and so on. Different benefits or costs are involved in each match, and the goal is to maximize the total reward or minimize the total expense.

Due to their special structure, these problems can be solved by special computational procedures in an efficient manner.

Distribution models

PART A: BASICS

Bill Grout, Tuff's operations manager, knew he would have to face this problem sooner or later, and here it was, finally, on his desk. Tuff Cement Company had opened a new warehouse in New York to serve the fast-growing demand for cement in that region. Management now wondered which plants should supply it and to what extent. As manager of operations, Bill was responsible for making those decisions. Although the problem did not look complicated, he was having trouble matching demand to supply. The situation was as follows.

Tuff Cement Company has two processing plants, one in Bethlehem, Pennsylvania (A), with a supply capacity of 100 tons per day, and one in Baltimore, Maryland (B), with a supply capacity of 110 tons a day. Tuff also has three warehouses: R in Easton, Pennsylvania, S in Philadelphia, and the newly added T on Long Island in New York. The warehouses need, if possible, 80, 120, and 60 tons of cement each day, respectively, to meet their distribution demands.

The shipping costs from each plant to each warehouse are given below:

From	To	Cost per ton
A (Bethlehem)	R (Easton)	1
A (Bethlehem)	S (Philadelphia)	2
A (Bethlehem)	T (New York)	3
B (Baltimore)	R (Easton)	4
B (Baltimore)	S (Philadelphia)	1
B (Baltimore)	T (New York)	5

Tuff's distribution scheme is shown in Figure 7.1.

Bill's problem is to plan the shipments at the least possible cost. The managerial tool that will assure him of a least-cost solution is called the *transportation* model.

7.1 THE TRANSPORTATION PROBLEM—CHARACTERISTICS AND ASSUMPTIONS

Tuff's transportation situation is typical of a class of distribution problems that exhibit the following characteristics:

1. *The supply.* A *limited quantity* of one commodity such as cement, oil, or oranges is available at certain *sources* (or origins) such as factories, refineries, or groves.

2. *The demand.* There is a demand for the commodity at several *destinations* such as warehouses, distribution centers, or stores.

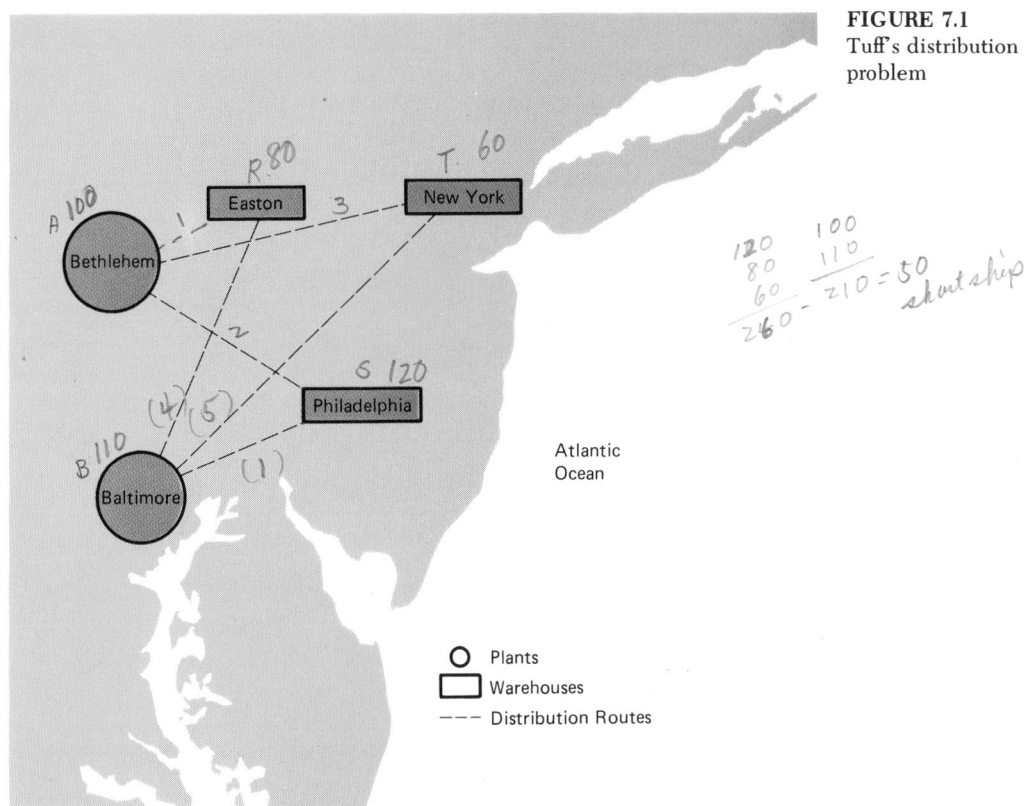

FIGURE 7.1
Tuff's distribution
problem

3. *The quantities.* The quantities of *supply* at each source and the demand or *requirements* at each destination are constant.

4. *The shipping cost.* The per unit costs of transporting the commodity from each source to each destination are assumed to be constant (e.g., $5 per ton). Usually they are based on the distance between the two points. Moving companies and the Post Office are examples of users of a similar cost system in their deliveries.

5. *It is assumed* that no shipments are allowed between sources or between destinations. Allowing such transshipments would require special adjustments in the model. (For details, see Loomba and Turban [7] or Wagner [8]).

6. *All supply and demand* quantities are given in whole numbers (integers).

7. *The problem* is to determine how many units should be shipped from each source to each destination (i.e., what routes to use and in what capacity) so that all demands are satisfied (if possible) at the minimum total shipping cost.

Transportation—a special type of distribution problem

Find the best shipment plan

Presentation in a tabular form

Transportation problems are presented in tabular form because it is a convenient form for applying special solution procedures. Table 7.1 shows Tuff's distribution problem.

TABLE 7.1
Tabular presentation of Tuff's problem

Source-supply (handwritten)

From plant \ To warehouse	*capacity* R	*capacity* S	*capacity* T	Supply
A	1 x_{AR}	$c_{AS} = 2$ x_{AS}	3 x_{AT}	$b_A = 100$
B	4 x_{BR}	1 x_{BS}	5 x_{BT}	$b_B = 110$
Demand	$d_R = 80$	$d_S = 120$	$d_T = 60$	210 / 260

Explanation of the table

Left side: The sources of supply (plants) are listed on the left. Each source is represented by a row.

Top: The destination points (warehouses) are listed at the top. Each destination is represented by a column.

Using a tabular form

Right side: This column designates the capacity (supply) at the sources.

Bottom: The requirements (demand) of each destination are listed here.

Center: The center of the table is composed of "cells." In this case there are six. Each is designated by the letter of its row and column; for example, cell AR is in row A and column R. The corresponding shipping costs (per ton) are in the upper right-hand corner of each cell. For example, the shipping cost from plant A to warehouse S is 2. In each cell there is also a decision variable. For example, in cell AR the variable is x_{AR}. This variable is the solution value for the quantity to be shipped from plant A to warehouse R.

Presentation as a linear program

Any transportation problem can be presented in the form of a linear programming problem. As such, it includes an objective function and constraints.

Formulation as an *LP*

The objective function The objective function calls for minimization of the total shipping cost, which is computed by multiplying the quantity shipped from each source i to each destination j (labeled x_{ij}), by its per unit shipping cost, c_{ij}, and totaling the results.

For example, using the data of Table 7.1, the objective function can be written as:

Cost · 1st Column of 1st row.

$$\text{minimize } z = (1x_{AR}) + 2x_{AS} + 3x_{AT} + 4x_{BR} + 1x_{BS} + 5x_{BT}$$

In general, the objective function can be written as:

$$\text{minimize } z = c_{11}x_{11} + c_{12}x_{12} + \cdots + c_{21}x_{21} + c_{22}x_{22} + \cdots + c_{mn}x_{mn} \quad (7.1) \quad \checkmark$$

where m = number of sources and n = number of destinations.

The supply and demand constraints   We consider three possible problem situations involving the supply and demand constraints. Either the supply is more than, the same as, or less than the demand.

a.   *Total supply > total demand:* In this case the total amount shipped from each supply point will be less than or equal to its upper limit, b_i. The total amount received at each demand point will be equal to its minimum requirement, d_j. This is expressed as:

$$x_{i1} + x_{i2} + \cdots + x_{in} \leq b_i \text{ for each supply point } i \quad (7.2)$$

$$x_{1j} + x_{2j} + \cdots + x_{nj} = d_j \text{ for each demand point } j \quad (7.3)$$

In our example this results in:

$$\left.\begin{array}{l} x_{AR} + x_{AS} + x_{AT} \leq 100 \\ x_{BR} + x_{BS} + x_{BT} \leq 110 \end{array}\right\} \text{supply constraints}$$

$$\left.\begin{array}{l} x_{AR} + x_{BR} \quad = \quad 80 \\ x_{AS} + x_{BS} \quad = 120 \\ x_{AT} + x_{BT} \quad = \quad 60 \end{array}\right\} \text{demand constraints}$$

b.   *Total supply = total demand:* In this situation all the constraints are equalities (=).

c.   *Total supply < total demand:* In this case the supply constraints are equalities and the demand constraints are of the ≤ form (cannot supply all demand).

Solving the transportation model

A transportation problem has a very large, sometimes infinite, number of feasible solutions. For example, consider the simple problem given in Table 7.2. Five feasible solutions are shown in Table 7.3. There are many others.

Many, many solutions

Supply
A = 100
B = 110
Demand
R = 80
S = 120
T = 60

TABLE 7.2
An example problem

Source \ Destination	1	2	Supply
A	6	8	60
B	10	7	70
Demand	80	50	130 / 130

$6 + 8 \leq 60$

$10 + 7 \leq 70$

TABLE 7.3
Feasible solutions to
Table 7.2

$4! = 12$

$9!$

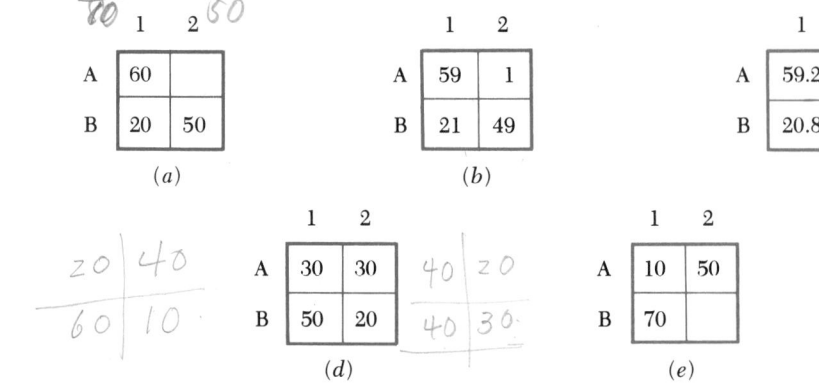

	1	2
A	60	
B	20	50

(a)

	1	2
A	59	1
B	21	49

(b)

	1	2
A	59.2	.8
B	20.8	49.2

(c)

	1	2
A	30	30
B	50	20

(d)

	1	2
A	10	50
B	70	

(e)

Solution method: Complete enumeration One approach is to generate solutions, as was done in Table 7.3. But even if only nonfractional ones are considered,[1] there may still exist a large number of solutions. Therefore, this could be a cumbersome and time-consuming job.

Some solution approaches

Solution method: Linear programming Since the transportation problem is indeed a linear programming problem, it can be solved as such. However, presentation of a large transportation problem in a linear programming format results in considerable computational effort.

Solution method: Transportation method The transportation method provides a computationally efficient procedure for solving large transportation problems. Section 7.2 that follows presents the method.

7.2   THE TRANSPORTATION METHOD

The transportation method is a search and evaluation algorithm, very similar to that of the simplex method in linear programming. The process involves the following five steps, as shown in Figure 7.2.

A five-step procedure

Step 1.   Arrange the data in tabular form

The transportation problem must first be arranged in tabular form. An example of such an arrangement for Tuff's problem was given in Table 7.1 with an explanation.

Step 2.   Balance the table

Balance—a must

The use of the transportation solution technique requires that the problem be *balanced*; that is, the total supply must equal the total

---

[1] In transportation problems, if the supply and demand are whole (integer) numbers, then the optimal solution *must* also be integer. Therefore only integer feasible solutions should be considered.

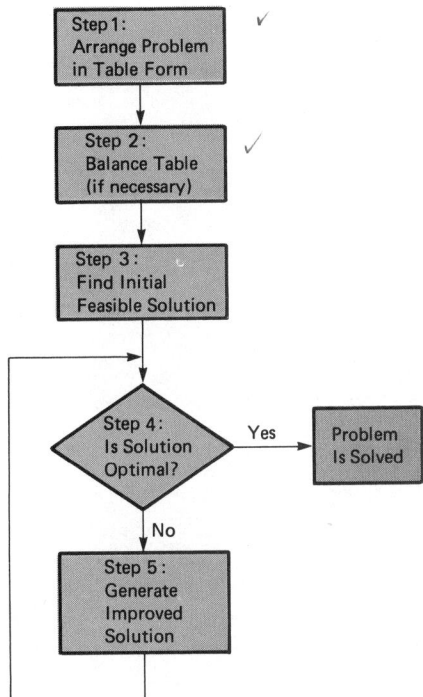

FIGURE 7.2
Steps in solving the
transportation problem

demand.[2] If the table is not balanced, this must first be done. Two causes of imbalance are excess supply and excess demand.

1. *Excess supply.* Table 7.4 shows an example of an unbalanced table where the total supply of 300 exceeds the total demand of 260. In this case there will be 40 unshipped units. Such a table is balanced by adding an artificial destination column for the excess supply (sometimes labeled a "dummy" destination). The amount in this column equals the excess supply, as shown in Table 7.5. The cost of "shipments" to the dummy is usually set at zero; this fixed cost does not favor any particular source or destination but simplifies the calculations.

Adding a dummy destination

2. *Excess demand.* When the total demand exceeds the total supply as in Tuff's problem (see Table 7.6), a dummy source row to supply the extra demand (50, in this case) is added. Again, the per unit shipping costs for the dummy row are set to zero. The results are shown in Table 7.7. Once the table is balanced, an initial feasible solution can be generated.

Adding a dummy source

---

[2] This requirement can be written as:

$$\sum_{i=1}^{m} b_i = \sum_{j=1}^{n} d_j$$

TABLE 7.4
Unbalanced table (excess supply)

Source \ Destination	R	S	T	Supply
A	1	2	3	200
B	4	1	5	100
Demand	80	120	60	300 / 260

= 40 unshipped

TABLE 7.5
Balanced table

Source \ Destination	R	S	T	D (dummy)	Supply
A	1	2	3	cost = 0 x_{AD}	200
B	4	1	5	0 x_{BD}	100
Demand	80	120	60	40 (excess supply)	300 / 300

TABLE 7.6
Unbalanced table (excess demand)

Source \ Destination	R	S	T	Supply
A	1	2	.3	100
B	4	1	5	110
Demand	80	120	60	210 / 260

= 50

③ **Step 3. The initial feasible solution**

An initial feasible solution[4] can be found by any of several available procedures. Two of these are demonstrated next.[5]

---

[4] An initial feasible solution is any feasible solution used to start the computations.
[5] A third method which gives an efficient initial solution is the Vogel approximation method (VAM). For details see any text in the references.

Source \ Destination	R	S	T	Supply
A	1	2	3	100
B	4	1	5	110
D (dummy)	0	0	0	50 (excess demand)
Demand	80	120	60	260 / 260 / 260

TABLE 7.7
Balanced table

1. Initial assignment by the Northwest Corner Rule

Northwest Corner Rule

a. Starting with the Northwest Corner (left, upmost in the table), allocate the *smaller amount* of either the row supply or the column demand.

b. Subtract from the row supply *and* from the column demand the amount allocated.

c. If the column demand is zero, move to the cell next on the right; if the row demand is zero, move down to the cell in the next row. If both are zero,[6] move first to the next cell on the right, then down one cell.

d. Once a cell is identified as per step *c* (above), it becomes a northwest cell. Allocate to it an amount as per step *a*.

e. Repeat the above steps *a-d* until all the remaining supply and demand is gone.

The advantage of this rule is that it is a simple mechanical process. The problem presented in Table 7.1 is balanced in Table 7.8 and serves as an example to illustrate an assignment by the Northwest Corner Rule.

Purely mechanical

Initially, an amount of 80 tons is allocated to cell AR, out of the 100 available in source A, meeting all the demand of destination R[7]. The remaining supply of 20 tons at source A is then allocated to cell AS, since that is the closest in the A row to AR. The capacity of row A has now been exhausted, but the demand of S has not yet been fully satisfied. Therefore, 100 tons of the 110-ton supply of source B is allocated to cell BS in order to meet the entire demand of destination S. Then, moving to the right in row B, the remaining supply of B (10 tons) is allocated to cell BT. This exhausts the supply in row B, but the destination T still needs

---

[6] Case of degeneracy, see discussion in Section 7.7.

[7] If the supply of source A were smaller than the demand of R, then the entire supply of A would have been allocated to cell AR.

TABLE 7.8
Initial solution by the
Northwest Corner Rule

✓

Source \ Destination	R	S	T	Supply	Remaining supply
A	1 80	2 20	3	100	~~20~~ 0
B	4	1 100	5 10	110	~~10~~ 0
D (dummy)	0	0	0 50	50	0
Demand	80	120	60	260	
Remaining demand	0	~~100~~ 0	~~50~~ 0		*shortage at T.*

50 units. Moving down column T the remainder (50 tons) is allocated to cell DT. In this fashion, the entire supply has been used and the entire demand has been satisfied. Cells which receive allocations are called *occupied* cells to distinguish them from the remaining empty or unoccupied ones.

Compute total cost

The initial solution shown in Table 7.8 calls for shipments of

80 tons from A to R at a cost of 80 × 1 = $ 80
20 tons from A to S at a cost of 20 × 2 =   40
100 tons from B to S at a cost of 100 × 1 =   100
10 tons from B to T at a cost of 10 × 5 =   50
50 tons from D to T at no cost   =   0

Total cost $270

Note that warehouse T supposedly obtains 50 tons from D (dummy); that is, there is a shortage (unsatisfied demand) of 50 tons at warehouse T.

Good initial solutions by least cost

2. **The Least-Cost (largest profit) Method** The least-cost method yields not only an initial feasible solution but also one which is close to optimal in small problems. The method is "heuristic" (see Chapter 14) in nature. To illustrate the method, another example, using cost data, is shown in Table 7.9.

Solution The least-cost method prescribes that the first allocation be made to the cell with the lowest cost (the highest profit in a maximization case). In this example, there is an additional consideration since cells AD and CE both have the lowest cost of $1. Cell AD is selected first because more units can be allocated to it (70) than to cell CE (50). Thus, an allocation of 70 is made to cell AD. As a result, the supply of A is reduced to 30 and the demand at D is completely satisfied.

Next, an allocation of 50 (maximum possible) is made to cell CE reducing the supply of C to 70. The process continues in this fashion

Source \ Destination	D		E		F		G		Supply
A	70	1		5		3	30	4	100
B		4		2	30	2	30	5	60
C		3	50	1	70	2		4	120
Demand	70		50		100		60	280	280

TABLE 7.9
Initial solution by the least-cost method

seeking the unoccupied cell with the lowest cost. The next search yields BF and CF, which each have a cost of $2. (BE is not considered because E is satisfied already.) Cell CF is filled in first since a larger quantity (120 − 50 = 70) can be placed there. Then the remaining requirement of 30 for column F is allocated to cell BF and source B's supply is reduced to 30.

Next, an allocation is made to cells with a cost of $4, since assignment to the cells with a cost of $3 is not possible under the supply and demand constraints. The only cell with a cost of $4 to which an assignment can be made is AG. The maximum possible quantity of 30 is assigned there. Finally, the remaining demand (30 in column G) is assigned to BG to complete the initial solution.

Once an initial solution is achieved (by any method) a test for optimality can be conducted.

Step 4.   Testing for optimality

The purpose of the optimality test is to test if the proposed solution, just generated, can be improved or not.

The procedure for testing optimality is analogous to that of the simplex method. A distinction is made between *basic* variables, those associated with the occupied cells, and *nonbasic* variables, those associated with the empty cells. For each empty cell, the effect of changing it to an occupied cell is examined. If any of these changes are favorable,[8] the solution is not optimal and a new solution must be designed.

"Basic" variables in the occupied cells

Two procedures for calculating the effect of such a change are:

1.   Stepping stone (discussed next).
2.   Modified distribution (MODI) (discussed in Part B).

___
   [8] A favorable change means an increase in the value of the objective function in maximization problems or a decrease in minimization problems.

Note: In both cases the solution to be checked for optimality must be nondegenerate; that is, the number of occupied cells must be $m + n - 1$ (where m = number of sources and n = number of destinations). The reason for this and a method to handle degeneracy are given in Section 7.7.

Degeneracy

The Stepping Stone Procedure

Example (**Tuff's problem**)   Table 7.8 (reproduced in Table 7.10) presents the initial solution to Tuff's problem.

TABLE 7.10
Table 7.8 reproduced

Source \ Destination	R	S	T	Supply
A	1 80	2 20	3	100
B	4	1 100	5 10	110
D (dummy)	0	0	0 50	50
Demand	80	120	60	260

The stepping stone procedure executes the final *two steps* of the transportation method.

Step 4: *Testing for optimality.* This is done by calculating the "cell evaluators" for all the empty cells.
Step 5: *Improving a nonoptimal solution.* This is done by:
1. Identifying the incoming cell.
2. Designing an improved solution

Finding the cell evaluator from a closed loop

Details of Step 4: Start with building a closed loop. A "cell evaluator" for an empty cell is a number designating the cost change that results from occupying that cell rather than one of the currently occupied cells. In order to fill an empty cell, a transfer has to be made from a currently occupied cell. Such a transfer, subject to the supply and demand constraints, will affect an even number of four or more cells. The evaluator is calculated by determining the overall effect on the total cost of shifting *one unit* to that empty cell. The signs of the cell evaluators enable us to test for optimality.

Shifting one unit

Gaining and losing cells

In Table 7.11 a demonstration is given of how to calculate the cell evaluator for the empty cell AT. One unit is moved from the occupied cell AS to AT (follow the top double arrow). Cell AT is called the *gaining cell* and a "+" sign is placed there; cell AS is labeled the *losing cell* and a

"−" sign is placed there. However, since one unit is moved to cell AT, column T will now have $1 + 10 + 50 = 61$, which is more than the 60 required. Therefore, in order to maintain the demand requirement, one unit is moved from the occupied cell, BT, to occupied cell BS (follow bottom double arrow). The new number of units in each cell is now circled.

TABLE 7.11
Evaluation of cell AT

Source \ Destination	R	S	T	Supply
A	1 80	2 ⑲ 20 −	3 ✓ ① + ● Start	100
B	4	⑩① 100 1	5 ⑨ 10	110
D (dummy)	0	0	0 50	50
Demand	80	120	60 ⟨ 61	260

gaining cell
−*Loosing cell*
$\quad$ S $\qquad$ I
A $\quad$ 20−1=19→ 0+1=1
B $\quad$ 100+1=101 10−1=9

As a result of this transaction, the row supply requirements are maintained:

$$\text{For row A:} \quad 80 + ⑲ + ① = 100 ✓$$
$$\text{For row B:} \quad ⑩① + ⑨ \quad = 110 ✓$$

and so are the column demands:

$$\text{For column S:} \quad ⑲ + ⑩① \quad = 120 ✓$$
$$\text{For column T:} \quad ① + ⑨ + 50 = 60 ✓$$

The entire movement process is indicated by a *closed loop* of arrows. Such a closed loop will involve at least four, and sometimes more, cells.

Rule for drawing each closed loop

When tracing a closed loop, start with the empty cell to be evaluated and, going clockwise, draw an arrow from it to an *occupied cell* in the same row (or column). Next, move vertically or horizontally (but never diagonally) to another *occupied* cell, "stepping over" unoccupied or occupied cells (if necessary) without changing them. Follow the same procedure to other occupied cells until returning to the original empty cell. At each turn of the loop (the loop may cross over itself at times), plus and minus signs are alternately placed in the cells, starting with a + sign in the empty

Stepping over cells

cell. One further important restriction is that there must be exactly one cell with a + sign and exactly one cell with a − sign in any row or column in which the loop turns. This restriction is imposed to ensure that the requirements of supply and demand will not be violated when the units are shifted. Note that an even number of at least four cells must participate in a loop and the occupied cells can be visited once and only once. Also, in a nondegenerate problem there is ony one possible way of drawing the loop for each empty cell.

Evaluation of Cell AT   Let us calculate the cost effect of the changes arising from the decision to ship one unit to the empty cell AT. In cells AT and BS, one unit is added so the additional cost is (3 + 1) = 4. In cells BT and AS, one unit is deleted and the cost is reduced by (5 + 2) = 7. Thus, by executing this exchange we simultaneously *increase* the total cost by 4 and *reduce* the total cost by 7; that is, alter the total cost by 4 − 7 = −3.

Cell evaluator

This value of −3 is then the *cell evaluator* of cell AT. The minus sign indicates a *possible cost reduction*; that is, the solution tested is improvable and therefore not optimal.

How to find the value of a cell evaluator

The value of a cell evaluator is the sum of the per unit shipping costs in the gaining cells less the sum of the per unit shipping costs in the losing cells of the closed loop.

This evaluation process must now be extended to *all* unoccupied cells.

Evaluation of Cell DR (involving six cells). In Table 7.12 the test is applied to cell DR. This time six cells participate in the evaluation.

TABLE 7.12
Evaluation of cell DR

Source \ Destination	R		S		T		Supply
A	80	1 ⑲ −	20 2 + ㉑		3		100
B		4	⑨ 1 − 100		⑪ 5 + 10		110
D (dummy)	① + Start	0		0	50 0 − ㊾		50
Demand	80		120		60		260

A move of one unit to DR will result in the addition of one unit to AS and BT and deletion of one unit each from AR, BS, and DT. The total cost impact of this closed loop is:

Gaining (+) cells	Cost	Losing (−) cells	Cost
DR.................	0	AR................	1
AS	2	BS	1
BT	5	DT................	0
Total.........	7	Total.........	2

Thus, such a move will add a cost of 7 (from the gaining cells) and subtract a cost of 2 (from the losing cells). The value of the cell evaluator DR is hence $7 - 2 = +5$. The plus sign indicates that a transfer to this cell increases cost and is *not* favorable.

Another way to interpret this situation is: A gaining cell (cell with a + sign) means an *increase* in the value of the objective function and a losing cell (− sign) means a *decrease*. Since the total increase (7) is larger than the total decrease (2), the value of the objective function will *increase* by $7 - 2 = 5$, an undesirable case in minimization.

Cost analysis By drawing these closed loops, *all* the empty cells of Table 7.12 can be evaluated. The results are:

Empty cell	Cell evaluator
AT..................	−3
BR	+4
DR	+5
DS	+4

Test of optimality Once the cell evaluators for *all* the empty cells have been computed, their signs are examined.

> *Test for a minimization (cost) problem*[9]
>
> *If one or more of the cell evaluators is negative,*[10] *the existing solution is not optimal.*

The logic for this test is that an empty cell (not presently part of the solution) with a negative cell evaluator will reduce the total cost if it becomes occupied. The present solution is thus *improvable* and therefore not optimal.

A minus evaluator means a possible cost reduction

In the example just presented, cell AT has a negative evaluator. Thus, the initial solution of Table 7.8 is *not optimal*.

---

[9] The test of optimality for a maximization (profit) case is reversed; that is, if any cell evaluator is positive, the solution is not optimal. A positive profit evaluator would mean an empty cell could thus increase the profit.

[10] A cell evaluator of 0 indicates the existence of another solution just as good as the current solution. Thus, in the final solution, if cell evaluators of 0 exist, this indicates the existence of multiple optimal solutions.

⑤ **Step 5. Improving a nonoptimal solution**

Having discovered that a solution is *not* optimal, the next step in the transportation method is to find a better solution. The operations in this step are:

1. Identify the "incoming" cell (empty cell to be occupied). In a minimization case the "incoming" cell is located by identifying the *most negative* cell evaluator.[11] In the example, the incoming cell is AT (since only one cell is negative).

Shifting units from cell to cell

2. *Design an improved solution.* Once the "incoming" cell has been identified, an improvement is made by shifting *as many units as possible,* along the "closed loop," into that empty cell. The quantity limit to this shifting process is reached when one of the "losing" cells becomes empty.[12] In our case, of the two "losing" cells in Table 7.11, AS and BT, cell BT becomes empty first, when ten units are shifted around the closed loop (ten from BT to BS, ten from AS to AT).

> **Rule for shifting units**
>
> In general, compare the number of units in all losing cells (−) in the loop of the most improvable empty cell (AT in our case). Select the *smallest* number (10 in this case). Add this number to all cells with a + sign and subtract it from all cells with a − sign. The result here is given in Table 7.13.

Once an improved solution is generated, the optimality test (step 4) is repeated.

TABLE 7.13
Improved solution

Source ╲ Destination	R		S		T		Supply
A		1		2		3	100
	80		20 − 10 = 10		0 + 10 = 10		
B		4		1		5	110
			100 + 10 = 110		10 − 10 = 0		
D (dummy)		0		0		0	50
						50	
Demand	80		120		60		260

---

[11] If two or more cells have the same value, then either may be selected.

[12] If two or more of the "losing" cells contain the same number of units, both will become empty simultaneously and a "degenerate" solution will result (see discussion in Part B of this chapter.)

Optimality test   The evaluators of all the empty cells are again computed for the improved solution of Table 7.13. The results are:

Empty cell	Cell evaluator
BR	+4
BT	+3
DR	+2
DS	+1

Since *all* the empty cells have nonnegative cell evaluators, an optimal solution has been obtained. This optimal solution calls for a shipment of:

80 units from A to R at a cost of $1/ton, total..........	$ 80
10 units from A to S at a cost of $2/ton, total..........	20
10 units from A to T at a cost of $3/ton, total..........	30
110 units from B to S at a cost of $1/ton, total..........	110
50 units from dummy to T at no cost	0
Total cost.....................................	$240

The total cost

This, compared with the original solution, represents a reduction in cost of $30. Notice that the demand requirements of destination T have, in reality, not been completely satisfied since 50 units are shipped out of the dummy source D.

The maximization case   If a transportation problem involves maximization, the same method can be used. The only difference is the test of optimality. A *positive* cell evaluator points to an improvement. An optimal solution will show no positive cell evaluators.

The stepping stone method is efficient for small sized transportation problems. For larger problems, however, the MODI method is recommended (see Part B).

MODI for large problems

Summary of the Stepping Stone Method

1. Compute the cell evaluators for all empty cells. This is done by subtracting the cost of the losing cells from that of the gaining cells.
2. If *all* cell evaluators are nonnegative (in a minimization case), then the solution is optimal. Otherwise an improvement (or alternate solution in the case of 0 evaluators) is possible.
3. Generating an improved solution involves identifying the incoming cell (that cell with the largest cost reduction potential for minimization problems) and transferring *as much as possible* to it. Once this has been done, a new solution is generated by adjusting the quantities in all losing and gaining cells along the loop.
4. The improved solution is then tested. If it is not optimal, another improvement is made. Eventually, an optimal solution (if one exists) will be reached.

The commonality of
transportation-type
problems

Transportation-type problems

Several production planning problems, routing problems, and scheduling problems can be formulated as transportation problems, thus increasing the applicability of the model.

Example: Production scheduling   Three garment plants are available for monthly production of four styles of men's shirts. The capacities of the three plants are 45,000, 93,000, and 60,000 shirts. The number of shirts required in styles *a* through *d* are 28,000, 65,000, 35,000, and 70,000, respectively. The profits, in dollars per shirt, at each plant for each style are shown in Table 7.14.

TABLE 7.14
The garment plants'
profits

Plant \ Style	a	b	c	d
1	8	12	−2	6
2	13	4	3	10
3	0	7	11	8

Find: How many shirts to produce in each plant, of each type so that profit is maximized.

Formulation as a transportation problem   Let the plants be considered as "sources" and the styles as "destinations." The capacities of the plants are the supply, and the required number of shirts of each style are the demand. The transportation table that describes the production scheduling problem is shown in Table 7.15. Notice that this is a *maximization* problem.

A maximization
problem

TABLE 7.15

Plant \ Style	a	b	c	d	Supply
1	8	12	−2	6	45,000
2	13	4	3	10	93,000
3	0	7	11	8	60,000
Requirements	28,000	65,000	35,000	70,000	198,000

Solution   Solving by the stepping stone method the results are:

Plant 1   manufactures 45,000 of style *b*
Plant 2   manufactures 28,000 of style *a* and 65,000
                of style *d*
Plant 3   manufactures 20,000 of style *b*, 35,000 of
                style *c* and 5,000 of style *d*
                        Total profit $2,119,000

7.3 THE ASSIGNMENT PROBLEM

A second type of distribution problem is the "assignment" problem. Let us illustrate with an example.

Example

The management of a utility company wants to assign three service teams to three geographical zones, one team to each zone. Because of each team's differing familiarity with each zone, there are differences in the efficiency of each team, a fact which is reflected in the different service costs which are shown in Table 7.16. For example, assigning team S_2 to zone Z_3 will result in a cost of $33,000. The problem is to find that assignment which minimizes the total cost.

Find the least-cost match

Service team \ Zone	Z_1	Z_2	Z_3
S_1	20	15	31
S_2	17	16	33
S_3	18	19	27

TABLE 7.16
Service costs (in $1,000s) of different team assignments

Characteristics of the assignment problem

The problem just presented is typical of a class of managerial problems with the following characteristics:

1. The objects under consideration, such as service teams, jobs, employees, or projects, are finite in number.
2. The objects have to be assigned on a one-to-one basis to other objects.
3. The result of each assignment can be expressed in terms of payoffs, such as costs or profits.
4. The aim is to assign all objects (if possible) in such a way that the total cost is minimized (or the total profit is maximized).

One-to-one basis

Several practical allocation problems can appear as assignment type problems. For example, a supervisor assigns subordinates to various jobs every morning, an employment agency matches employees and employers, a real estate agency matches houses to potential buyers, and teachers are assigned to classes.

Assignment—a common problem

Presentation of the assignment problem

1. *Table form.* The assignment problem is usually arranged in a tabular form. For example, Table 7.17 presents the utility company problem of Table 7.16. The assignment table is very similar to the transportation table. Indeed, the assignment problem is considered as a special transportation problem in which the supply at each source and the demand at each destination are always one unit.[13] As in the transportation problem, assignment problems can be balanced or not. In a balanced case, the number of objects to be assigned equals the number of objects to which they are assigned. Unbalanced problems can be balanced by adding a dummy with zero cost coefficients as in the transportation problem.

Assignment problem is a type of transportation problem

TABLE 7.17
The assignment table

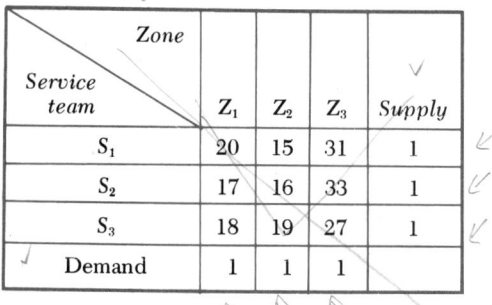

Service team \ Zone	Z_1	Z_2	Z_3	Supply
S_1	20	15	31	1
S_2	17	16	33	1
S_3	18	19	27	1
Demand	1	1	1	

2. *Presentation as a linear program.* The assignment problem is a special case of the transportation problem (and vice versa). It can also be presented as a linear programming problem.[14]

---

[13] Since the supply and demand are always equal to one unit in each row and column, there is no need to write them in the assignment table.

[14] The general presentation of the assignment problem is:
Let x_{ij} be the assignment of the ith source to the jth destination. If $x_{ij} = 0$, there will be no assignment of i to j; but if $x_{ij} = 1$, there is a match of i to j (x_{ij} *cannot* take any other value). Let c_{ij} be the *cost* associated with an assignment of i to j. The assignment problem can then be stated as follows:

$$\text{minimize } z = \sum_{i=1}^{m} \sum_{j=1}^{n} c_{ij} x_{ij}$$

subject to the linear constraints (in a balanced case):

$$\sum_{j=1}^{n} x_{ij} = 1 \qquad i = 1, 2, \ldots, m$$

$$\sum_{i=1}^{m} i_{ij} = 1 \qquad j = 1, 2, \ldots, n \tag{7.4}$$

and x_{ij} can take either the value of 1 or the value of zero.

Example   The utility company's problem is presented as a linear program.

$$\text{minimize } z = 20x_{11} + 15x_{12} + 31x_{13} + 17x_{21} + 16x_{22}$$
$$+ 33x_{23} + 18x_{31} + 19x_{32} + 27x_{33}$$

subject to:

$$\left.\begin{array}{l} x_{11} + x_{12} + x_{13} = 1 \\ x_{21} + x_{22} + x_{23} = 1 \\ x_{31} + x_{32} + x_{33} = 1 \end{array}\right\} \text{supply constraints}$$

and to:

$$\left.\begin{array}{l} x_{11} + x_{21} + x_{31} = 1 \\ x_{12} + x_{22} + x_{32} = 1 \\ x_{13} + x_{23} + x_{33} = 1 \end{array}\right\} \text{demand constraints}$$

and: x_{ij} either 0 or 1 for all i, j.

Notice that the constraints are given as equations. The reason this can be done is that the problem is balanced. In an unbalanced problem the number of items to be assigned differs from the number of objects to be assigned to and must be balanced before proceeding. The balancing is done by adding dummy supply and demand items. For example, if there are three jobs to be done on five machines, two dummy jobs must be added. A machine matched with a dummy job will, of course, in actuality be matched with nothing. Therefore, the cost (or profit) of such a match is considered to be zero.

Balancing an assignment problem

Methods for solving assignment problems

Complete enumeration   The assignment problem is usually a balanced problem with n items to be assigned to n objects. As such there are $n!$ (n factorial) different solutions to the problem. One way to find the optimal solution is to list and compare *all n!* solutions. This is called a complete enumeration approach. However, it is often impractical because the number of solutions, for even a relatively small problem, is unmanageably large.[15] For the problem presented in Table 7.17, there are only 3! or 6 solutions. These are listed in Table 7.18. Comparing all

$n!$ solutions

TABLE 7.18
Assignment alternative solutions (by enumeration)

Alternative	Combination			Total Cost
1..........	$S_1 Z_1$	$S_2 Z_2$	$S_3 Z_3$	20 + 16 + 27 = 63
2..........	$S_1 Z_1$	$S_3 Z_2$	$S_2 Z_3$	20 + 19 + 33 = 72
3..........	$S_2 Z_1$	$S_1 Z_2$	$S_3 Z_3$	17 + 15 + 27 = 59 ←*Minimum*
4..........	$S_2 Z_1$	$S_3 Z_2$	$S_1 Z_3$	17 + 19 + 31 = 67
5..........	$S_3 Z_1$	$S_2 Z_2$	$S_1 Z_3$	18 + 16 + 31 = 65
6..........	$S_3 Z_1$	$S_1 Z_2$	$S_2 Z_3$	18 + 15 + 33 = 66

[15] For example, for $n = 10$, $n! = 3{,}628{,}800$. These can be enumerated in seconds by a high-speed computer. However, for a larger n, say 20, even a computer is overwhelmed.

the possibilities indicates that alternative 3, which yields 59 (i.e., $59,000), is the optimal solution.

The simplex method   The simplex method can be used but it is rather inefficient[16] for solving the assignment problem.

The transportation model   Any assignment problem can be solved by the transportation method, since the assignment problem is a special case of the transportation problem. However, there are more efficient methods.

"Near-optimal" methods   Various computational methods are available for arriving at a "near-optimal" solution in a rapid way. These are mainly heuristic in nature (see Chapter 14).

Branch and bound   In Chapter 6 there is an illustration of how the branch and bound method can be used to solve the assignment problem.

The Hungarian method   The Hungarian method[17] is the most efficient way of solving large assignment problems.

The Hungarian method

The Hungarian method is an efficient solution procedure for solving large, balanced assignment problems. The procedure is based on the following theorem:

Konig's theorem

> If one subtracts (or adds) a constant number from all entries in any row or column of the assignment matrix, then the total cost of each of the *n!* possible assignments is reduced (or increased) by the constant number subtracted (or added).

Therefore, one can make these additions or subtractions to rows or columns without changing the ultimate optimal assignment. The total costs are changed but not the *relative* ones. The Hungarian method is next illustrated for the case of *cost* minimization.

The procedure   The solution procedure involves four major steps as shown in Figure 7.3.

Example   The method will be illustrated with the example in Table 7.17.

A total-opportunity-cost matrix

Step 1: Build the "total-opportunity-cost" matrix   This step involves the transformation of the cost matrix to what is termed a "total-opportunity-cost" matrix. It involves two operations.

First, the element with the lowest value (including zero and negative numbers) in each row is subtracted from all the other elements in that

---

[16] For example, an assignment problem of 10×10 will be transformed to a linear program with 100 variables, 20 constraints, and 20 slack (or artificial) variables resulting in a large matrix.

[17] Named after the Hungarian mathematician Konig, who first proved (1916) a theorem necessary to the development of the method.

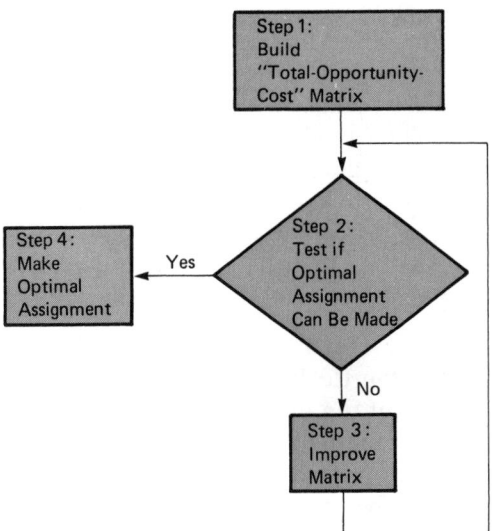

FIGURE 7.3
Solution steps for the
assignment problem

row. All negative numbers *disappear* in this step (they represent profit, in a cost table; or cost, in a profit table). For example, in the first row of Table 7.17 the lowest element is 15. The entire operation is shown in Table 7.19.

TABLE 7.19

20 − 15 = 5	15 − 15 = 0	31 − 15 = 16
17 − 16 = 1	16 − 16 = 0	33 − 16 = 17
18 − 18 = 0	19 − 18 = 1	27 − 18 = 9

→

5	0	16
1	0	17
0	1	9

New Matrix

Second, the smallest element (including zero) in each column of the new matrix is subtracted from all the elements of that column. The result is the "total-opportunity-cost" matrix as shown in Table 7.20.

TABLE 7.20
Total-opportunity-cost
matrix

5 − 0 = 5	0 − 0 = 0	16 − 9 = 7
1 − 0 = 1	0 − 0 = 0	17 − 9 = 8
0 − 0 = 0	1 − 0 = 1	9 − 9 = 0

→

5	0	7
1	0	8
0	1	0

Notice that this matrix now contains *at least* one zero in each row and column.

Step 2: The optimality test   Since all entries in the "total-opportunity-cost" matrix are nonnegative, the minimum value of the objective function (i.e., total cost) *cannot* be negative, no matter what assignments are made. Hence, the *minimum possible* cost is zero in the relative terms of the new table; the *real* cost with the *real* solution will, of course, be greater. Therefore, *if* a feasible assignment with a total opportunity cost of zero is found, this assignment must have the *lowest possible cost;* that is, it is optimal.

The "lowest possible cost" can be achieved if all the cell values, where assignments are made, are zeros. Thus, in testing for optimality one needs to know whether there are enough zeros in the table to permit a "zero" assignment for each row and each column.

Rather than using trial-and-error, we instead use a simple procedure that tests whether this can be done.

Draw the minimum
number of lines

1. Draw the *minimum* possible number of straight lines, horizontally and vertically, so that all zeros in the matrix are covered.
2. Count the number of these lines. If it equals *n* (the number of rows or columns), an optimal assignment can be made. If it is smaller than *n*, an improvement is possible.

Note: In some cases there are several alternative ways of drawing the minimum number of lines. Any of these may be chosen.

Let us find the minimum number of lines necessary to cover all the zeros in our case. The total-opportunity-cost matrix of Table 7.20 is reproduced in Table 7.21.

TABLE 7.21
The optimality test

Service team \ Zone	Z_1	Z_2	Z_3
S_1	5	0	7
S_2	1	0	8
S_3	0	1	0

2 lines to cover all the -0-

Note that the table has four "zero" cells. It is possible to cover all the zeros with two lines (shown as broken lines in Table 7.21); one through row S_3 and the other through column Z_2. According to the optimality test, since only two lines are needed to cover all the zeros, an optimal assignment cannot be made at this stage and an improved solution is possible.

Step 3: Improve the total-opportunity-cost matrix An improved total-opportunity-cost matrix is derived by the following three operations:

1. Find the *smallest* entry in the *uncovered* cells (cells with no lines through them) and subtract it from *all* entries in the uncovered cells. In our case, the lowest entry is 1 (cell $S_2 Z_1$).

An improved solution
2. Add the same *smallest* entry to those cells in which the lines intersect (cells with two lines through them). In our case there is only one such cell, $S_3 Z_2$.

3. Cells with one line through them, such as S_1Z_1, are transferred unchanged to the improved table.

The result is the *first improved total-opportunity-cost matrix*, Table 7.22. The *optimality test* is now applied to this matrix. Using the line-drawing procedure of step 2, a minimum of *three* lines is needed to cover all the zeros in Table 7.23. This means that an optimal assignment can now be made.

Zone / Service team	Z_1	Z_2	Z_3
S_1	5 – 1 = 4	0	7 – 1 = 6
S_2	1 – 1 = 0	0	8 – 1 = 7
S_3	0	1 + 1 = 2	0

TABLE 7.22
First operation for the improved matrix

Zone / Team	Z_1	Z_2	Z_3
S_1	4	0	6
S_2	0	0	7
S_3	0	2	0

TABLE 7.23
First improved total-opportunity-cost matrix

In those problems where the first improvement *does not yield* an optimal solution, we *keep on* improving the solution (by repeating step 3) until an optimal solution is achieved.

Step 4: Make an optimal assignment An optimal assignment should be made to cells with a zero entry, maintaining the one-to-one requirement. If only one solution exists, a fast procedure for finding it is to locate a row or column with only one 0 in it and make that assignment. Then drop that row and column from the matrix and repeat the procedure. If the solution is *not* unique there will be two or more zeros in a column or row to choose from. The choice is arbitrary.

The optimal assignment for our example is shown in Table 7.23 (squares around the zeros): S_1 to Z_2, S_2 to Z_1, and S_3 to Z_3. The total cost in this case is: 15 + 17 + 27 = 59 (thousand dollars). If more than one optimal solution exists, a trial-and-error approach can be used to find all possible combination assignments in the zero cells.

Multiple solutions are possible

The maximization case

The example just demonstrated was a minimization one. In maximization cases a convenient solution procedure involves transforming

Convert to
minimization the problem into a minimization problem (an opportunity loss table) by the following procedure (see example in Table 7.24):

1. Find the largest profit coefficient in the entire table (11 here).
2. Subtract each entry in the original table from the largest profit coefficient (see Table 7.24b).

TABLE 7.24

	R	S	T
A	8	6	10
B	11	9	6
C	4	7	5

a. Maximize
(before
transformation)

	R	S	T
A	11 − 8 = 3	11 − 6 = 5	11 − 10 = 1
B	11 − 11 = 0	11 − 9 = 2	11 − 6 = 5
C	11 − 4 = 7	11 − 7 = 4	11 − 5 = 6

b. Minimize (after transformation)

Once the transformed table is constructed, the Hungarian method can then be employed to solve the problem. Once a solution is obtained, the total profit can be computed using the original profit coefficients in the original table.

The process of the Hungarian method is summarized in Figure 7.4.

7.4 CONCLUDING REMARKS

The transportation and assignment models introduced in this chapter are special cases of linear programming. However, formulation and solution of such problems in the format of linear programming is too cumbersome. Due to their special structure, these problems are formulated as special algorithms which are extremely efficient when compared to the linear programming format. The larger the problem the greater is the advantage of the special algorithms.

In addition to actual transportation problems there are several production and scheduling problems that can be formulated as transportation type problems, thus increasing the applicability of the model.

7.5 PROBLEMS FOR PART A

1. Solve the transportation problem (with cost coefficients).

From \ To	1	2	3	Supply
A	67	42	51	250
B	61	24	39	400
C	29	47	60	300
D	43	31	42	200
Demand	400	150	600	

a. Find an initial solution using the least-cost method.

b. Find the optimal solution (use the stepping stone method).

2. Given a transportation problem (with cost coefficients):

Sources \ Destinations	1	2	3	4	Supply
A	1	5	3	4	100
B	4	2	2	4	60
C	3	1	2	4	120
Demand	70	50	100	60	

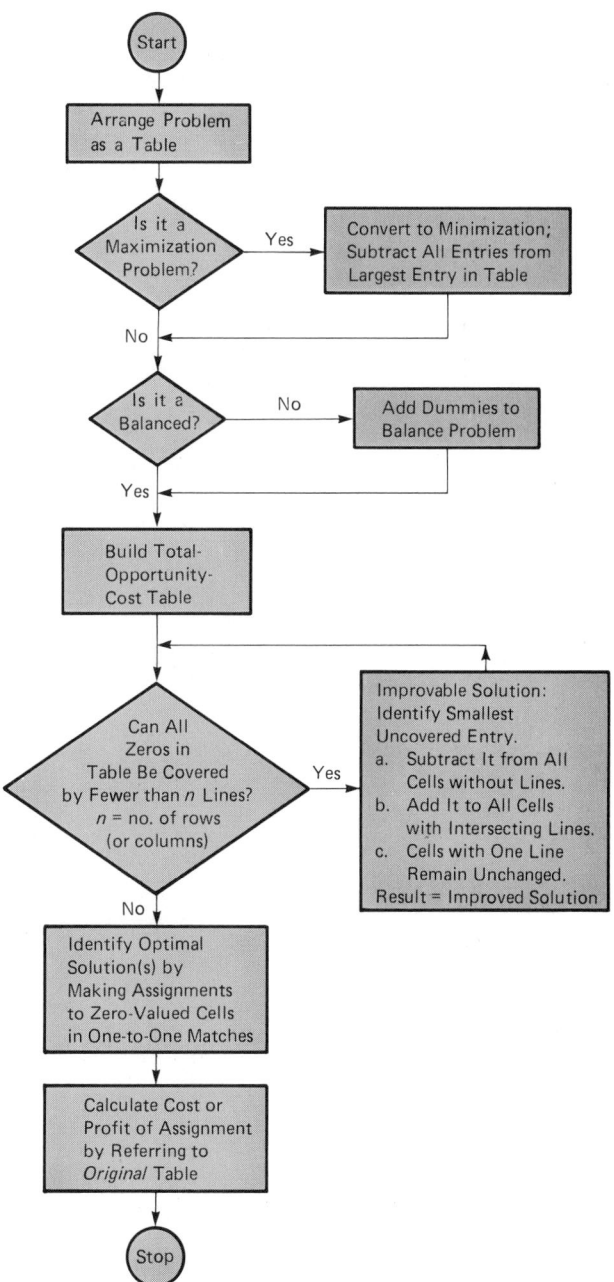

FIGURE 7.4
Flow chart of the
Hungarian method

a. Find an initial solution by the northwest corner rule.

b. Find an initial solution by the least-cost method.

c. Find an optimal solution by the stepping stone method: start with the results of part (*a*).

d. Are there any other optimal solutions?

e. Based on findings of part (*d*), comment on the number of occupied cells in an optimal solution.

3. The Fraser Silver Mine Company has two operating mines and three distributing warehouses located in different parts of the country. The company ships the ore by trucks. The capacity of mine 1 is 500 tons a week and that of mine 2 is 1,300 tons per week. The weekly sales potential of the three warehouses is 1,200 tons, 500 tons, and 700 tons. The shipping cost per ton from each mine to each warehouse is given below:

From mine number	To warehouse number	Shipping cost ($ per ton)
1.	1	8
1.	2	13
1.	3	9
2.	1	11
2.	2	14
2.	3	5

Find the best shipment schedule if the company's objective is to minimize the transportation cost.

a. Formulate as a transportation model.

b. Solve the problem (start with northwest corner).

4. Given below a transportation problem with *profit* coefficients,

a. Find the best solution (start with the northwest corner).

From \ To	1	2	Supply
A	6	4	50
B	3	5	80
C	8	7	60
D	5	9	40
Demand	80	100	

b. Present as a linear programming problem (do not solve).

5. Continental Electric Company buys fuel once a month for its five operational zones. Demand (in hundreds of thousands of drums) in each of the zones is given below:

Zone	Demand
A	28
B	60
C	36
D	45
E	16
Total	185

There are three bidders who wish to supply the demand: one in Texas, one in California, and one in Canada. The prices per drum (f.o.b.) and the maximum quantities available (in hundreds of thousands of drums) are given below:

	Price	Maximum supply
California	$10.00	80
Texas	11.50	60
Canada	9.50	120

Transportation costs between each bidder and each zone are given below (in $ per drum):

From \ To zone	A	B	C	D	E
California	1.8	1.6	1.3	.6	.3
Texas	1.6	1.2	.9	.2	.6
Canada	.8	1.0	1.1	1.2	1.6

Bids can be accepted for the entire quantity or for portions of it. Continental Electric's objective is to supply all demand in all zones at minimal total cost. Find the contract award policy that Continental Electric should follow.

6. The Pollution Control Board of Alligator County has 100 employees: 20 live in city A, 35 in city B, and 45 in city C. The employees have interchangeable skills and are to be assigned to various laboratories. The Water Laboratory requires 40 employees, the Air Lab requires 30 employees, the Solid Waste Lab

requires 20 employees, and the Central Lab requires 10 employees. The distance between the cities and the labs is shown on the map below (in miles along the available streets):

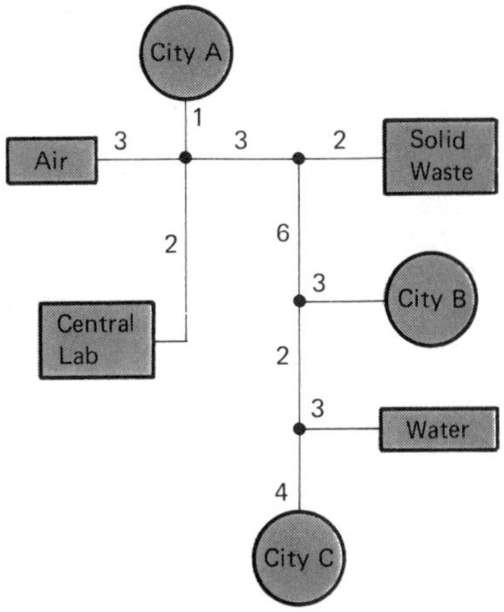

Workers travel by the shortest available route along the streets shown. What worker to lab arrangement minimizes the total distances traveled by all the employees?

a. Formulate as a transportation problem.
b. Solve.
c. What assumptions are necessary in this case?

7. A firm owns facilities at five geographically remote locations. It has manufacturing plants at points *A* and *B* with daily production capacities of 60 and 40 units, respectively. At points *C*, *D*, and *E* it has warehouses with daily demands of 20, 30, and 50 units, respectively. Shipping costs between these points are exactly proportional to the distances between them, which are indicated in miles below:

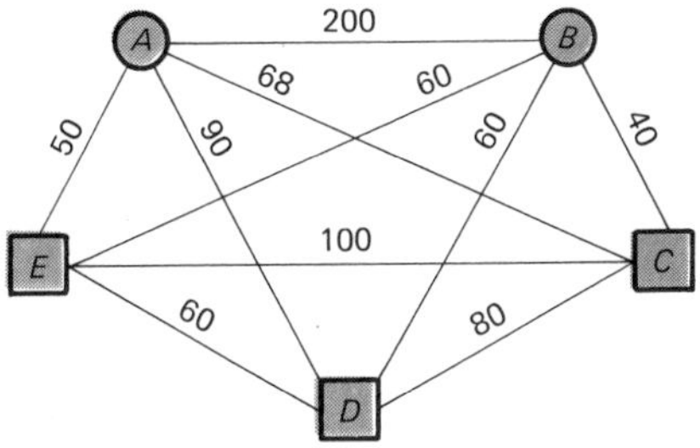

a. Given that the firm wishes to minimize its total transportation costs, formulate as a transportation problem.
b. Find the optimal solution; use the least-cost method to generate an initial solution.

Note: Shipments between plants, and also between warehouses, are prohibited.

8. The energy Czar is planning shipments of gasoline from two sources to three destinations. Per ton transportation costs are given in the following table:

From \ *To*	*C*	*D*	*E*
A	6	7	9
B	9	4	6

There are 1,000 tons available at A and 1,300 available at B. Since the destinations want as much as possible, the Czar has decided to ship out *all* available quantities. His object is to minimize total shipment cost.

a. Formulate as a transportation problem.
b. Solve.
c. Formulate in a linear programming format.

9. American Electronics produces three models of CB radios; A, B, and C. The estimated demand for the three models is 10,000, 12,000, and 7,000 units respectively. The radios can be produced on one of four available production lines; Q, R, S, and T, whose production capacities are: 6,000, 15,000, 20,000, and 5,000 units respectively. The manufacturing costs vary among the production lines and are shown in the table below (in $ per unit):

	Production line			
Model	*Q*	*R*	*S*	*T*
A	60	53	61	50
B	80	75	81	70
C	75	70	75	65

The company's objective is to meet all estimated demand at the lowest possible manufacturing cost. Use the transportation model to find the best production schedule.

10. The cost of assigning jobs A, B, and C on machines M, N, O, and P is shown below:

Job \ Machine	M	N	O	P
A	6	7	5	9
B	8	5	6	7
C	10	8	6	6

   a. Use the Hungarian method to find the least-cost assignment.
   b. Formulate as a linear program.

11. In a small job shop department there are three tasks to be assigned to three workers. The table below indicates the weekly profit achieved by assigning each worker to each job. (For example, assigning worker B to job III brings $3 profit.) Find the assignment that will maximize profit.

Worker \ Job	I	II	III
A	5	4	7
B	6	7	3
C	8	11	2

   a. Solve by complete enumeration.
   b. Solve by the Hungarian method.
   c. Formulate as a linear program.

12. Fraser City has a group of five social workers. The director of the group wishes to assign each of the workers to a residential area in the "best possible" manner. It was suggested that workers be rotated in the various areas for a few weeks and their efficiency measured by the number of complaints received. The table below gives the number of complaints in each

Worker \ Zone	I	II	III	IV	V
A	3	5	4	8	2
B	9	4	3	6	7
C	11	6	8	10	9
D	6	10	4	12	5
E	3	5	6	4	9

area against each worker in one month of service.

   a. Suggest the best assignment of workers to zones. Solve by the Hungarian method. (*Hint:* Attempt to minimize the total number of complaints.)
   b. Specify the necessary assumptions.

13. Given below is a table that shows the cost of the row personnel doing the column job. The cost figures in the matrix reflect the effectiveness of the person for the particular job weighted by his rate of pay.

Personnel \ Job	Bed making	Patient care	Patient examination
Physicians	—	20	11
Nurses	14	6	30
Nurse aids	5	11	—

Find the optimal assignment of personnel to jobs. Use the Hungarian method.

   Note: Some assignments are not feasible (e.g., physicians do not make beds). In such a case simply ignore the cell.

14. The Gem Electronics Corp. manufactures computers in two plants. The capacities of the plants are: plant A, 150 units/month; plant B, 120 units a month. The company has three buyers who distribute the product to a chain of stores. Demand is deterministic at the following constant rate:

Buyer I . . . . 60 units
Buyer II . . . . 120 units
Buyer III . . . . 80 units

   Transportation costs are given in the table below (in dollars per unit).

From plant	To buyer I	II	III
A	27	40	60
B	35	28	42

Find the quantities to be shipped from A and B to I, II, and III so as to minimize the total transportation costs.
   a. Solve by the transportation method.

b. Formulate as a linear program. Solve (use a computer).

15. AMA's maintenance shop has three groups of employees who have varying proficiencies in their skills. Group G-1, three skilled employees; group G-2, four semiskilled; and group G-3, with two specialists. Six jobs to be performed are relatively easy and three are complex (9 jobs total). Assigning one worker per job, find the best assignment schedule if the objective is to minimize total cost.

The table below gives the cost of the repairs:

If done by worker of group	Easy repair	Complex repair
G-1	10	24
G-2	9	28
G-3	12	20

a. Formulate as a transportation problem.
b. Solve.
c. Formulate (do not solve) as an assignment problem. (*Hint:* Nine variables are required.)

16. The Tilt Lumber Company has four lumberyards, with the following capacities:

A—3,000 tons.
B—2,000 tons.
C—1,800 tons.
D—6,000 tons.

The company has received a contract to supply lumber for three construction projects: Project 1, with a maximum demand of 5,200 tons and a selling price of $70 per ton; Project 2, with a maximum demand of 10,000 tons and a selling price of $50/ton; and Project 3, with a maximum demand of 10,000 tons and a selling price of $45/ton.

Transportation costs in dollars per ton are given in the table below:

	To		
Lumberyard	Project 1	Project 2	Project 3
A	10	15	30
B	18	12	20
C	25	10	25
D	35	20	12

Find the best schedule for the Tilt Lumber Company. Start with the least-cost method, proceed with the stepping stone method.

17. A firm which markets one product has four salespersons, A, B, C, and D, and three customers, I, II, and III. The firm's profit for selling one unit of its product to customer I is $100, to customer II is $120, and to customer III is $150. Sales of the firm's product to each customer depend upon the salesperson-customer rapport. The probability matrix for the sale of a unit of the product to each customer by each salesperson is as follows:

Customer / Salesperson	I	II	III
A	.7	.6	.6
B	.5	.7	.7
C	.4	.8	.5
D	.8	.6	.4

(For example, the probability that salesperson B can sell a unit of product to customer III is .7). If only one salesperson can be assigned to each customer, what is the optimal assignment?

PART B: EXTENSIONS

7.6 THE MODIFIED DISTRIBUTION PROCEDURE (MODI)

MODI as the LP dual

An efficient procedure for solving large transportation problems is the MODI (modified distribution) procedure which is based on the *dual* to the transportation problem. The reader will recall that every linear programming problem has a dual. The transportation problem, being a special case of linear programming, has its own dual.

When the dual is solved, its solution yields two types of variables:

Implicit costs

u_i = *implicit cost (or shadow price) of source i,*
(value of one more unit at source i).
v_j = *implicit cost of destination j,*
(value of one more unit at j).

The MODI procedure uses the values of u_i and v_j[18] to find the cell evaluators. Let us demonstrate.

The theoretical basis of MODI

In an *optimal solution* for a transportation problem, the forthcoming equations 7.5 and 7.6 must hold by definition:

$$c_{ij} - u_i - v_j \geq 0 \tag{7.5}$$

where c_{ij} is the per unit shipping cost between i and j, and

$$x_{ij}(c_{ij} - u_i - v_j) = 0 \tag{7.6}$$

where x_{ij} is the quantity to be shipped between i and j.

Two cases may occur

These two conditions imply that when optimality is reached, one of two things may occur:

Case a If $x_{ij} \neq 0$ (an occupied cell), then $c_{ij} - u_i - v_j = 0$ or $c_{ij} = u_i + v_j$, which means that an allocation i to j will be made if, and only if, the actual cost of transportation c_{ij} is equal to the sum of the implicit cost of source i plus the implicit cost of destination j. In such a case x_{ij} is called a basic variable;[19] that is, cell ij is occupied.

Case b If $x_{ij} = 0$, then one of two things may happen:

1. $c_{ij} > u_i + v_j$. In this case an allocation i to j is *not* made because the actual cost is larger than the sum of the implied costs of the source i and the destination j;

---

[18] u_i and v_j can be found by transforming the problem to a linear program and solving it by the simplex method. However, the MODI procedure *does not require*, as will be shown, the transformation to a linear program in order to find u_i and v_j.

[19] Or a nonbasic variable that has the potential of being in the basis as an alternative optimal solution; that is, when the cell evaluator equals zero.

2. $c_{ij} = u_i + v_j$, in which case the nonbasic variable has the potential of being in the basis as an alternative optimal solution.

    Note: c_{ij} *cannot* be smaller than $u_i + v_j$ without violating Equation 7.5.

    The conditions just presented are the foundation for the modified distribution procedure (MODI). The MODI procedure follows the same solution steps as the stepping stone procedure:

Step 1: Find an initial feasible solution.
Step 2: Calculate the cell evaluators and test for optimality. If the   The MODI steps
       solution is not optimal, improve it (next step).
Step 3: Identify the "incoming" cell and design an improved solution.
Step 4: Recycle until an optimal solution is obtained.

The major difference between MODI and the stepping stone procedure is in the optimality test, which involves a different approach for calculating the cell evaluators.

The concept of cell evaluators

    Let K_{ij} denote the cell evaluator, defined as:

$$K_{ij} = c_{ij} - (u_i + v_j) = c_{ij} - u_i - v_j \qquad (7.7)$$

The cell evaluator thus is the difference between the actual cost of   The cell evaluator
shipping one unit from i to j, c_{ij}, and the sum of the implicit costs of   from the implicit costs
source i and destination j.

    Let us investigate the concept of the cell evaluators by examining in Table 7.25 the initial solution of a previous example. In the initia¹ feasible solution there are five occupied cells. It can be shown that the evaluator of each of the *occupied* cells is zero.

    Now, if one assigns a complete set of row auxiliary numbers, u_i (to   Find implicit costs
be placed at the extreme right-hand side of the table), and a complete set   from occupied cells
of column auxiliary numbers, v_j (to be placed at the bottom of the table),

TABLE 7.25
Table 7.8 reproduced

Source \ Destination	R		S		T		Supply
A	80	1	20	2		3	100
B		4	100	1	10	5	110
D (dummy)		0		0	50	0	50
Demand	80		120		60		260

in such a way that the shipping cost per unit of *each* of the *occupied* cells equals the sum of its *row and column auxiliary numbers*, that is:

$$u_i + v_j = c_{ij} \tag{7.8}$$

then, the condition that the cell evaluator of each occupied cell be zero will be satisfied. Further, for the *empty* cells the sum of the row and column auxiliary numbers will normally be different from the actual cost of the cell, c_{ij}. This difference is the cell evaluator.

Assigning auxiliary row and column numbers

From each *occupied* cell, u_i and v_j are selected so that c_{ij} equals the sum of u_i and v_j. For the occupied cell AR, for example, u_1 and v_1 are chosen so $c_{11} = u_1 + v_1$. Similarly, for the occupied cell AS, u_1 and v_2 are selected so $c_{12} = c_1 + v_2$. This process must be carried out for *all* the occupied cells.

One arbitrary value

To determine all the row and column auxiliary numbers, one *arbitrary*[20] number, serving as either a row or a column number must first be chosen.[21] Then, the rest will be determined from the occupied cells by using the relationship $c_{ij} = u_i + v_j$. Insofar as *any* arbitrary number can be chosen to represent one of the u_i's or v_j's, we shall follow the practice of *making u_1 take the value zero*.[22]

An example of MODI

To illustrate the steps of MODI, the problem presented in Table 7.25 is used.

Step 1: *Find an initial solution.* The initial solution shown in Table 7.25 will be used.

Step 2: *Calculate the cell evaluators for all the empty cells and test for optimality.*

Arbitrarily a value of zero for u_1 is chosen. The next question is: What value must be given to v_1 so that for the first occupied cell AR, $c_{11} = u_1 + v_1$, or $1 = 0 + v_1$? Obviously, v_1 must take a value of 1. Again, what value must be given to v_2 so that $c_{12} = u_1 + v_2$, or $2 = 0 + v_2$? The value of v_2 must be 2. We can skip cell AT because it is unoccupied. Now, what value must be given to u_2 so that $c_{22} = u_2 + v_2$, or $1 = u_2 + 2$? Obviously, $u_2 = -1$. In a similar manner v_3 is found to be 6 and u_3 to be -6.

---

[20] The use of an arbitrary number means that the values of u_i and v_j are not the actual shadow prices as could have been generated if the simplex was employed. However, the *relative* relationship between all these shadow prices is being maintained.

[21] This is necessary because there is one less occupied cell $(m + n - 1)$ than the number of auxiliary variables $(m + n)$.

[22] It is even more efficient to let the u_i or v_j of the row or column with the most occupied cells take the value zero.

Source \ Destination	R	S	T	Supply	u_i
A	1 80	2 20	3	100	$u_1 = 0$
B	4	1 100	5 10	110	$u_2 = -1$
D (dummy)	0	0	0 50	50	$u_3 = -6$
Demand	80	120	60	260	
v_j	$v_1 = 1$	$v_2 = 2$	$v_3 = 6$		

TABLE 7.26
Finding the implicit costs

All the row and column numbers are entered in Table 7.26 in the new row v_j and the new column u_i.

Computing the cell evaluators Let us now calculate the cell evaluator for the empty cell BR. For cell BR the cell evaluator, according to Equation 7.7, is $K_{21} = c_{21} - u_2 - v_1 = 4 + 1 - 1 = 4$. Similarly, the cell evaluators of the other empty cells are calculated and summarized below:

Empty cell	Cell evaluator, K_{ij}
BR	$c_{21} - u_2 - v_1 = 4 + 1 - 1 = 4$
AT	$c_{13} - u_1 - v_3 = 3 - 0 - 6 = -3$
DR	$c_{31} - u_3 - v_1 = 0 + 6 - 1 = 5$
DS	$c_{32} - u_3 - v_2 = 0 + 6 - 2 = 4$

Test of optimality The optimality test is identical to that of the stepping stone method. Namely, an optimal solution requires that all cell evaluators be nonnegative.

Since the cell evaluator of AT is negative, the solution of Table 7.26 is *not optimal*. An improved solution is thus called for.

Step 3: Identify the "incoming" cell and design an improved solution The "incoming" cell for a minimization case is located by identifying, as in the stepping stone method, the most negative cell evaluator.[23] In this case, the "incoming" cell is AT. The improved solution is obtained by shifting as many units as possible into AT without violating the demand and supply requirements.[24] The improved solution is shown in Table 7.27.

Shifting units along the loop

Step 4: Recycle (until optimality is achieved) The next step is to test the solution of Table 7.27 for optimality. All cell evaluators for the empty cells are computed by first recalculating the u_i's and v_j's. This is accomplished by again using the equation $c_{ij} = u_i + v_j$ for the *occupied* cells.

---

[23] The largest positive evaluator in the case of maximization.

[24] A loop like the one in the stepping stone method is helpful in this operation.

TABLE 7.27
First improved solution

Source \ Destination	R	S	T	Supply	u_i
A	80 · 1	10 · 2	10 · 3	100	0
B	4	110 · 1	5	110	−1
D (dummy)	0	0	50 · 0	50	−3
Demand	80	120	60	260	
v_j	1	2	3		

The new u_i's and v_j's are entered in Table 7.27. The cell evaluators for the empty cells of Table 7.27 are calculated as:

Empty cell	Cell evaluator
BR	+4
BT	+3
DR	+2
DS	+1

Since *all* cell evaluators are positive, the solution in Table 7.27 is optimal.

Economic Interpretation of u_i *and* v_j The variables u_i and v_j used in the MODI procedure have an interesting economic interpretation. They are, in effect, the dual variables and, as such, represent implicit costs associated with the *i* sources and *j* destinations:

u_i is the value of one unit of the product at source *i*. In other words, u_i represents the *implicit cost of source i*.

v_j is the value of one unit of the product delivered at destination *j*. In other words, v_j is the *implicit cost of the destination j*.

u_i and v_j are *relative* costs

Since, in this procedure, one value of u_i (or v_j) is assigned arbitrarily, the values u_i and v_j are *relative* rather than absolute. Hence, u_i measures the *comparative locational disadvantage* of the various sources. Similarly, v_j measures the comparative disadvantage of the various destination locations.

For example, in the optimal solution:

$$v_1 = 1 \text{ for warehouse R}$$
$$v_3 = 3 \text{ for warehouse T}$$

This means that if the demand of warehouse T is increased by 1 ton and, at the same time, the requirement of warehouse R is decreased by 1 ton, then the total shipment cost will be *increased* by 2 ($v_3 - v_1 = 3 - 1 = 2$). In other words, warehouse T is less efficient. The policy implication is that if it is impossible to meet all the demand, warehouse T should be supplied only after all the demand at R is met.

Similarly, comparing v_2 and v_3, it can be seen that warehouse S is more efficient than warehouse T. This explains why, in the optimal solution (Table 7.27), the demand for warehouse T is not fully satisfied. It receives only 10 of the required demand of 60 tons.

Summary of MODI

Preparation: MODI requires a balanced transportation table.

Step 1: Derive an initial solution.

Step 2: Use equation $c_{ij} = u_i + v_j$ to compute all implicit costs of the occupied cells. Then compute the cell evaluators of all empty cells using equation $K_{ij} = c_{ij} - u_i - v_j$. Test for optimality as in the stepping stone method.

Step 3: Identify an incoming cell and design an improved solution as in the stepping stone method.

Step 4: Recycle the process until an optimal solution is found.

7.7 DEGENERACY

A transportation problem has m supply constraints and n demand constraints, or a total of $m + n$ constraints. Since transportation problems are either balanced to begin with or, if not, can be converted to a balanced problem, the total demand is assumed to equal the total supply. As a result of such equality it is possible to express one of the constraints in terms of the others: thus, one constraint is always redundant. Therefore, there are only $m + n - 1$ active constraints. This suggests that the transportation problem should have $m + n - 1$ active variables (occupied cells) in every *basic feasible solution* as well as in the *optimal solution*. $m + n - 1$ variables

Whenever the number of occupied cells is *less than* $(m + n - 1)$ the solution is called "degenerate." To handle degeneracy the previous solution technique must be slightly modified.

Degeneracy can develop in one of two ways. First, it can appear in the initial assignment if the supply equals demand[25] for any cell in which an assignment is to be made. Table 7.28 presents such a case (see cell AR). Note that the number of occupied cells in Table 7.28 is 3 instead of 4, i.e., $(m + n - 1 = 2 + 3 - 1 = 4)$.

Degeneracy can also develop during the improvement of solutions. If the quantities of two or more "losing" cells of a nondegenerate

---

[25] More generally the remaining supply (after some assignment) equals the remaining demand.

TABLE 7.28
Degenerate solution

Source \ Destination	R	S	T	Supply
A	100 [1]	[3]	[6]	100 / 100
B	[5]	30 [3]	40 [2]	70
Demand	100	30	40	170 / 170

solution are the same, they will become empty simultaneously when an incoming variable is introduced. The resultant solution will then be degenerate.

Degeneracy impedes the optimality test

A degenerate solution cannot be tested for optimality by the methods previously outlined. Therefore, a special treatment is called for.

How to resolve degeneracy

E is nil

Case 1: Degeneracy in the very first assignment In this case an extremely small amount, designated by E, (almost zero) of the commodity to be shipped is allocated to one (or more) of the empty cells of the first solution to bring the number of occupied cells to $m + n - 1$. In a minimization problem, E is allocated to the empty cell with the lowest cost and which still allows the optimality check[26] (in maximization

Two types of degeneracy

problems, to the cell with the highest profit coefficient). The problem is then solved as if it were nondegenerate.

Example Table 7.29a is a minimization example of a transportation problem (with cost data) in which degeneracy will develop when the initial solution is generated by the northwest corner rule (Table

TABLE 7.29a
A degenerate problem

From \ To	R	S	Supply
A	[3]	[3]	50
B	[4]	[6]	30
Demand	50	30	80

---

[26] The assignment of E should be made so the solution permits a check on optimality. If the configuration of occupied cells is such that after assigning E to the lowest cost cell and now having $m + n - 1$ occupied cells, a check on optimality is not possible, then E should be assigned to the second lowest cost cell instead, and so on.

7.29b). The solution of Table 7.29b is not optimal, and a better one must be designed. But this requires $m + n - 1$ occupied cells (i.e., $2 + 2 - 1 = 3$). The requirement can be met by adding the quantity E to the low-cost cell AS. It is then possible to arrive at the solution shown in Table 7.29c which is both optimal and nondegenerate.

From \ To	R	S	Supply
A	50 [3]	E [3]	50
B	[4]	30 [6]	30
Demand	50	30	80

TABLE 7.29b
Initial solution
(degenerate)

From \ To	R	S	Supply
A	20 [3]	30 [3]	50
B	30 [4]	[6]	30
Demand	50	30	80

TABLE 7.29c
Optimal solution
(nondegenerate)

Case 2: Degeneracy in intermediate solution stages   In this case E is assigned to one (or more) of the newly vacated cell(s). As mentioned earlier, the assignment must be made so that $m + n - 1$ cells will be "occupied" and an optimality check is possible.

Example   Table 7.30a contains an initial solution for a minimization problem (cost data). It is not optimal, and AT is the incoming cell.

From \ To	R	S	T	Supply
A	50 [5]	20 [4]	[2]	70
B	[6]	30 [3]	20 [2]	50
C	[1]	[5]	10 [1]	10
Demand	50	50	30	130

TABLE 7.30a
Initial solution

Where to place E

Table 7.30*b* shows the first improved solution. The solution is degenerate. In order to test optimality, *E* is added to cell BT (the newly vacated cell with the lowest cost coefficient). The solution of Table 7.30*b* is not optimal; and hence a second improved solution, Table 7.30*c*, is derived. The second improved solution is still degenerate but upon checking turns out to be optimal. To interpret the final solution the value *E* is ignored.

TABLE 7.30*b*
First improved solution
(degenerate)

From \ To	R		S		T		Supply
A	50	5		4	20	2	70
B		6	50	3	E	2	50
C		1		5	10	1	10
Demand	50		50		30		130

TABLE 7.30*c*
Second improved and
optimal solution
(degenerate)

From \ To	R		S		T		Supply
A	40	5		4	30	2	70
B		6	50	3	E	2	50
C	10	1		5		1	10
Demand	50		50		30		130

7.8 PROBLEMS FOR PART B

18. Solve Problem 2 by MODI. Start with the northwest corner rule.

19. In the transportation problem below, the data in the cells are profits per unit shipped.

The objective of the company is profit maximization. Find the best shipment schedule(s).

Note: Start with the northwest corner solution; use the stepping stone method. Watch for degeneracy.

From \ To	I	II	Capacity
A	6	4	60
B	3	5	100
C	7	2	80
Requirement	60	150	

20. Given the transportation cost table:

Ware-house \ Store	A	B	C	D	E	Capacity
1	4	7	3	9	6	200
2	3	2	4	6	5	400
3	5	6	2	5	3	600
4	8	4	5	7	3	700
Require-ment	600	400	500	100	300	

a. Find the initial solution by the northwest corner rule.
b. Find the transportation schedule that will minimize total shipping cost. Use MODI.

Hints: Watch for degeneracy and for more than one optimal solution.

21. Allied Bakeries make three types of bread: small, standard, and large. These are sold in each of their four distributing stores. The daily demand for the three types of bread and the selling prices are given below:

Type	Daily demand	Selling price (cents)
Small	500	24
Standard...........	1,200	29
Large	800	37

The bakery is capable of baking up to 1,000 loaves of each type daily. The cost per loaf, including transportation at each of the four distributing stores, is given below:

Store \ Bread	Small	Standard	Large
A	12	15	20
B	13	17	19
C	11	17	22
D	14	16	18

Find the best production-distribution system that will meet all demand.
a. Formulate as a transportation problem.
b. Solve by MODI. Start with the least cost method.

Note: Watch for degeneracy.

22. Eastern Railroad Company serves five cities, A-E. The distances between the cities are shown below:

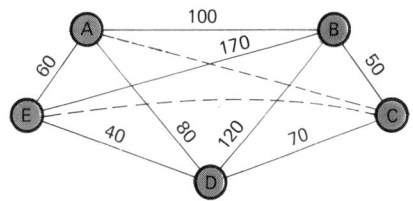

At the present time there is no connection between cities A and C, and E and C due to maintenance work on the rails.

On Sunday afternoon the company has 200 identical cars at the following cities: A—40, B—60, C—70, D—30.

By Monday empty cars are needed in the cities below as follows: B—40, D—50, and E—40.

The company wants to minimize the mileage traveled. All demands of Monday must be met. Find the best routing plan. Use MODI; start with the least cost method.

23. Westcan Machine Shop produces three products (A, B, and C) using its four automatic machines (1, 2, 3, and 4). Each is capable (unless otherwise specified) of making the product in one operation.

The table below shows the output, in units per hour, of each machine, for each product (X implies impossible combinations).

Product \ Machine	1	2	3	4
A	16	10	X	6
B	8	20	10	9
C	12	X	14	1

24. Formulate and solve Problem 10 as a transportation problem.

7.9 CASES

I—NORTHEASTERN BLOOD BANK

Northeastern General is the only hospital in a small mountain community. Dr. Alton, the chief surgeon, just completed the list of patients to be operated upon the next morning, specifying the blood which will be required during the operations.

Eight patients are on the list below with their blood type and quantity required.

Patient	Blood type	Quantity (pints)
Able	AB	3
Brook	B	2
Cock	A	6
Dean	O	3
Elm	B	4
Flint	AB	2
Gloss	A	2
Hope	O	2

The hospital's blood bank currently has the following blood inventory. (Blood comes in 1 pint containers.)

Blood type	Inventory (pints)
A	4
B	10
O	11
AB	7

A patient with blood type AB is considered a universal recipient; i.e., he can receive any type of blood. A blood type O is considered acceptable for transfusion to any type of patient.

Ann White, the director of the hospital's blood bank, has just received the list and computed the demand for blood as:

Type	Pints in demand	versus	Pints in stock
A	8		4
B	8		10
O	5		11
AB	5		7

Ann realizes that she is short by four pints of type A. However, this shortage can be covered by four pints of type O.

As she was ready to deliver the blood, she remembered the meeting she had with the hospital administrator last Friday. The meeting went as follows:

John Par (the administrator): Ann, the doctors are happy with your work. The patients always receive the required amount of the proper type of blood. There is only one problem.

Ann: What do you mean?

John: Well, the cost of acquiring blood is ever increasing, and the expenses of your department are increasing much faster than those of the other departments.

Ann: What can I do about the situation? I can't buy cheaper blood; we belong to a regional blood bank and can't negotiate prices.

John: That's true, but I understand that the cost of the different types of blood isn't the same, especially when the cost of transportation and special orders is added."

Ann: I just completed a study on this. Here are the figures:
type A = $30/pint, type B = $36/pint, type O = $35/pint, and type AB $40/pint.

John: This is interesting. It looks as though you might be able to save some money by substituting blood types.

Ann: That's possibly true but what will the physicians say if we increase the rate of blood substitutions?

John: I don't know. Let's check and find out.

a. Find the *least* total cost blood allocation plan. Use a transportation type model.

b. How much can Ann save by following the optimal solution as compared to her present policy of "matching blood to needs as close as possible?"

c. Even though substitutions may be safe from a clinical point of view, the physicians may not be too happy with the optimal solution. Why?

II—GREENHILL'S FEDERAL GRANT

The Greenhill's public hearing meeting turned stormy. Citizens from four suburbs were gathered at city hall to try to get the city's federal funds for their own suburbs.

The government recently awarded $750,000 to the city for road improvement. The city requested bids and five contractors submitted bids for work in the four suburbs. The bids are listed below (in thousands of dollars):

| Contractor | Suburb | | | |
	1	2	3	4
A	210	242	202	243
B	222	232	205	250
C	205	225	244	210
D	265	206	200	270
E	215	211	253	212

Since under the terms of the federal grant the work must be completed fairly soon, none of the contractors are large enough to perform more than one job. That is, it will be necessary to use a different contractor for each suburb's job.

From the bids it was clear to Greenhill's city council that the federal funds would not cover road improvements in all four suburbs. As they began to analyze the situation, they realized they needed some hard facts. Therefore, they called the finance director of Greenhills and requested the following information:

a. What is the *minimum* amount of money that the city must add to the government grant such that work may be done in all four suburbs?

b. What is the best contractor-to-suburb match?

c. Which of the contractors should not receive a job contract?

d. If the city cannot come up with any supplementary funds, only three suburbs will be repaired. Based on dollars and cents, which three suburbs should be selected such that the surplus from the government grant is maximized?

The director of finance asked you, a newly appointed assistant, to use some management science tools to answer these questions. What will your answers be?

7.10 GLOSSARY

Cell evaluator The opportunity cost involved in shipping one unit through a route that is not currently used. This route corresponds to a *cell* in the transportation table, since a cell is at the intersection of the source and destination of that route.

Closed loop A path showing the transfer of units in a revised transportation table.

Degeneracy (degenerate solution) A solution to a transportation problem in which there are fewer than m + n − 1 occupied cells in the transportation table.

Destination A place a shipment is directed to.

Dummy row(s), column(s) Row(s) or column(s) which are added to the transportation and assignment tables to equalize total supply and total demand (in the case of transportation) or to equalize the number of rows and columns (in the case of assignment).

Hungarian method An algorithm used to efficiently solve an assignment problem.

MODI (modified distribution method) An algorithm used to efficiently solve a transportation problem.

Northwest corner rule A procedure used to find an initial feasible solution to a transportation problem.

Source A place a shipment originates from.

Stepping stone procedure An algorithm used to test a transportation solution for optimality.

Transportation method An algorithm to efficiently solve transportation problems.

7.11 REFERENCES AND BIBLIOGRAPHY

1. Bierman, Harold, Jr.; Bonini, C. P.; and Hausman, W. H. *Quantitative Analysis for Business Decisions.* Homewood, Ill.: Richard D. Irwin, Inc., 1973.

2. Ford, L. R., and Fulkerson, D. R. *Flows in Networks.* Princeton, N.J.: Princeton University Press, 1962.

3. Frazer, J. R. *Applied Linear Programming.* Englewood Cliffs, N.J.: Prentice-Hall, Inc., 1968.

4. Gass, S. I. *Linear Programming: Methods and Applications.* New York: McGraw-Hill Book Co., 1969.

5. Harvey, C. *Operations Research, An Introduction to Linear Optimization and Decision Analysis.* New York: North-Holland, 1979.

6. Loomba, N. P. *Linear Programming.* 2d ed. Riverside, N.J.: Macmillan, Inc., 1976.

7. ———, and Turban, E. *Applied Programming for Management.* New York: Holt, Rinehart and Winston, Inc., 1974.

8. Wagner, H. M. *Principles of Operations Research with Applications to Managerial Decisions.* 2d ed. Englewood Cliffs, N.J.: Prentice-Hall, Inc., 1975.

8

Managerial situations involving a complex of interrelated activities can be modeled as "networks." Typical of these are: large construction projects (dams, bridges) consisting of a number of subtasks; transportation networks connecting a number of cities; utility and piping systems; and similar cases in which a complex of branches connects, either literally or figuratively, a set of locations. A systematic analysis of these situations enables the manager to plan, monitor, and reorganize resources so that objectives can be attained efficiently and on schedule.

Of special interest among the network models are the Program Evaluation and Review Technique (PERT) and the Critical Path Method (CPM).

Network models:
PERT and CPM

PART A: BASICS

The morning mail held exciting news for Judi Kosen, special projects manager for Restoration, Inc. As she anxiously opened the letter from the Proposal Review Committee, Environmental Projects Branch, Department of the Interior, her eyes spotted the words ". . . most cost-effective bid . . .," ". . . are pleased to award you. . . " With a whoop she yelled, "We won! We won!!" Then, to be sure there was no mistake, she reread the good news. After reading the letter four times, Judi settled back in her chair to contemplate the task before her.

Four month ago, Restoration, Inc., submitted a competitive bid to the Department of the Interior to revitalize Moose Lake in the northern part of the state. The company had developed a new technique to combat water pollution by increasing the basic amount of oxygen in a lake, called "oxygenation."

Oxygenation of a lake is a very complex project involving several of the company's departments as well as outside suppliers. It requires specialized equipment and supplies and specially trained personnel. The contract was for a period of more than a half a year, a long enough time for significant changes to occur in the economy, in prices and in the availability of resources. The Department of the Interior wanted the project to be completed on time. Therefore, the contract contained a $2,000 penalty clause for each week beyond the agreed-upon 30-week completion time. Judi realized that there were many factors that could cause a delay in such a complex project. She wondered if it were possible to plan the project so there would be as few delays as possible. Furthermore, she realized that discovery of any delay should be made as soon as possible, before it is too late to catch up or rectify the problem.

As she examined all of the various factors, operations, and activities involved in the project, she felt that planning, monitoring, and control-ling this job could be staggering. Just then she remembered a required course in operations management she had taken several years ago. The professor talked about the planning and control of large, complex projects. He explained some special managerial tool that had a long name and had to be abbreviated. It finally came back to her; yes—it was PERT.

8.1 INTRODUCTION TO PERT AND CPM

Characteristics of project management

Project versus production management

The Moose Lake situation is an example of *project management*. Project management is distinguished from production management primarily by the nonrepetitive nature of the work; a project is usually a one-time effort. Although similar work may have been done previously, or may be done in the future (Restoration, Inc., may receive a contract for the oxygenation of other lakes), it is not usually repeated in the identical manner of cars or TV sets being manufactured on a production line. The management of projects is more complicated than the management of a production line due to the following characteristics, generally typical of all projects to a greater or lesser degree.

1. The duration of a project lasts weeks, months, or even years. During such a long period many changes may occur, most of which are difficult to predict. Such changes may have a significant impact on project costs, technology, and resources.
2. The project is complex in nature, involving many interrelated activities. (Our example is highly simplified for the purpose of easier demonstration.)

   The complexity of projects
3. Delays in completion time may be very costly. Penalties for delays may amount to thousands of dollars per day. Completing projects late may result in lost opportunities and ill-will as well.
4. Projects are of a sequential nature. Some activities cannot start until others are completed.

Consequently, the planning, scheduling, and control of projects is rather complicated. Until just a few years ago, there were no generally accepted formal techniques to aid in project management. Each manager had his or her own management scheme. However, the need for formal tools soon become apparent. Two of the best known tools that fill this need are PERT[1] (Program Evaluation and Review Technique) which is used for managing the *time* (duration) of projects and CPM[2] (Critical Path Method) which is used for managing both *time* and the *cost* of projects.

PERT versus CPM

Definitions used in PERT and CPM

In order to explain the purpose, structure, and operation of PERT and CPM, it is helpful to define the following terms:

Activity An effort which requires resources and takes a certain amount of time for completion. Examples of activities are: studying for an examination, designing a part, connecting bridge girders, or preparing an order.

Activity: A time-consuming task

Event A specific accomplishment at a recognizable point in time; a milestone, a check point. For example: passing a course at a university, submission of engineering drafts, completion of a span on a bridge, or the arrival of a machine. Events *do not* have a time duration per se. To

Event: A milestone

---

[1] Developed by the U.S. Navy with Booz-Allen Hamilton and Lockheed Corporation to accelerate development of the Polaris in the late 1950s.

[2] Developed by Du Pont, Inc.

reach an event, all the activities that precede it *must* be completed. An event can be viewed as a goal attained while the activities leading to it can be viewed as the means of achieving it.

Project A collection of activities and events with a definable beginning and a definable end (the goal). For example: getting a college degree, patenting an invention, building a bridge, or installing new machinery.

Network A logical and chronological set of activities and events, graphically illustrating relationships among the various activities and events of the project.

Critical activity An activity which if delayed will hold up the scheduled completion date of the entire project.

A path A series of adjacent activities leading from one event to another.

Critical path The sequence of critical activities that forms a continuous path between the start of a project and its completion.

The differences and similarities between PERT and CPM

PERT is probabilistic

CPM includes costs

PERT and CPM are very similar in their approach; however, two distinctions are usually made. The first relates to the way in which activity durations are estimated. In PERT, three estimates are used to form a weighted average of the expected completion time, based on a probability distribution of completion times. Therefore, PERT is considered a probabilistic tool. In CPM, there is only one estimate of duration; that is, CPM is a deterministic tool. The second difference is that CPM allows an explicit estimate of costs in addition to time. Thus, while PERT is basically a tool for planning and control of time, CPM can be used to control both the time and the cost of the project.

PERT/CPM for scheduling and control

The basic objectives of PERT and CPM

PERT and CPM attempt to answer the following questions:

1. Which activities are critical? That is, which must be completed on time to keep the project on schedule?
2. Which activities are noncritical?
3. How much flexibility does management have in executing the noncritical activities?
4. What is the earliest expected completion date for the project?
5. What is the best way to handle delays that are detected during execution of the project?

In addition, PERT can be used to answer questions such as:

6. What is the chance of completing a project by a desired date?

7. For how long should a project be planned so that a given probability of completion is attained?

   Also, CPM can be used to answer such questions as:

8. What is the least-cost way to expedite the completion of a project?

9. What is the shortest possible time for a project to be completed?

The advantages of PERT and CPM

Detailed planning The use of PERT and CPM forces management to plan in detail and to define what must be done to accomplish the project's objectives on time.

Commitments and communications Management is forced to plan and make commitments regarding execution times and completion dates. The tools also provide for better communication among the various departments in an organization and between suppliers and the client.

Efficient monitoring The number of critical activities in a network (especially in a large one) is only a small portion of the total activities. Identification of the critical activities enables the use of an efficient monitoring system (mainly record keeping and reports) concentrating only on the critical activities.

Identifying potential problem areas The critical activities are also more likely to become problem areas. Once identified, contingency plans may be devised.

Proper use of resources Employing PERT or CPM enables management to use resources more wisely by examination of the overall plan. Resources can be transferred to bottleneck or trouble areas from other activities.

Control and rescheduling The tools enable management to follow up and correct deviations from schedule as soon as they are detected and thus minimize delays.

Governmental jobs Several government agencies (such as the U.S. Navy) require the submission of a PERT or CPM plan with bids.

Easily understood CPM and PERT can be easily understood because they provide a method for visualizing an entire project. Therefore, management can explain the tools to supervisors and employees in such a way that the chances of implementation are increased.

Adaptable to computers PERT and CPM are easily adaptable to computer use. Large projects can be planned by computers in seconds (user programs are available from most computer manufacturers). The computer is even capable of diagramming the networks.

Tools for decision making PERT and CPM allow management to check the effectiveness and efficiency of alternative ways of executing projects.

*Assess probability of completion (**in PERT only**)*   The probabilities of successfully meeting deadlines, finishing early, or finishing late can be assessed by the use of PERT.

*Cost-time tradeoffs (**in CPM only**)*   CPM enables management to evaluate tradeoffs between the cost of executing a job in the normal way or rushing activities (called "crashing") at a higher cost so as to finish earlier.

PERT and CPM analysis

Three stages

Recepts

The use of PERT or CPM involves three major stages: formulation, planning, and monitoring and control. These are illustrated in Figure 8.1.

FIGURE 8.1
PERT/CPM analysis steps

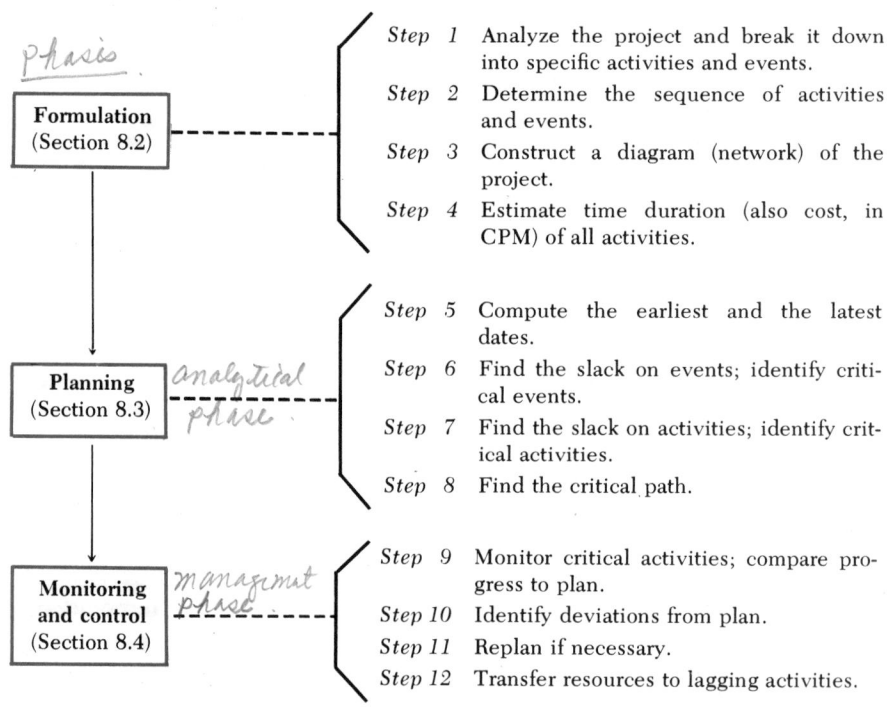

Phasis

Formulation (Section 8.2)	Step 1 Analyze the project and break it down into specific activities and events.
	Step 2 Determine the sequence of activities and events.
	Step 3 Construct a diagram (network) of the project.
	Step 4 Estimate time duration (also cost, in CPM) of all activities.

analytical phase

Planning (Section 8.3)	Step 5 Compute the earliest and the latest dates.
	Step 6 Find the slack on events; identify critical events.
	Step 7 Find the slack on activities; identify critical activities.
	Step 8 Find the critical path.

management phase

Monitoring and control (Section 8.4)	Step 9 Monitor critical activities; compare progress to plan.
	Step 10 Identify deviations from plan.
	Step 11 Replan if necessary.
	Step 12 Transfer resources to lagging activities.

8.2   CONSTRUCTION OF PERT AND CPM NETWORKS

Following the steps

In order to illustrate how to construct a PERT or a CPM network, let us return to the oxygenation problem and follow the general steps outlined in Section 8.1.

Step 1. Analysis of the project

After consultation with all department heads, a list of activities is agreed upon (see Table 8.1). Each activity is clearly defined and responsibility is assigned to the proper department heads.

Predecessor

Activity	Description	Required preceding activities
a............	Administrative setup	None
b............	Hire personnel	a
c............	Obtain materials	a
d...........	Transport materials to Moose Lake	c
e............	Gather measuring team	a
f............	Planning	c
g............	Assemble equipment	d, b
h............	Plan evaluation	e
i............	Oxygenation	f, g
j............	Measurement and evaluation	i, h

TABLE 8.1
Moose Lake project activities

Step 2. Sequence the activities

Once the content of each activity is defined, the sequence of execution is determined. For example, personnel cannot be hired before proper authorization is granted (administrative setup) and equipment cannot be assembled before all parts and materials are on site. This information is also shown in Table 8.1 (in the "Required Preceding Activities" column).

Step 3. Construct the network

The PERT (or CPM) network is a graphical representation of the information given in Table 8.1. It shows the interrelationship among the activities, the events, and the entire project.

To construct a network, start by viewing an activity as an arrow between two events (circles). For example, the first activity of the Moose Lake Project, the "administrative setup," is shown in Fig. 8.2.

An activity as an arrow

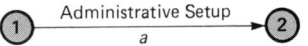

Administrative Setup
a

FIGURE 8.2
An Activity

The arrow points in the direction of the time flow, but its length is *not* related to the duration of the activity, rather it is arbitrarily set at a suitable length for drawing the diagram. The number circled in front of the arrow, 1, in Figure 8.2, is the event that *precedes* the activity. The number circled after the arrow, 2, in Figure 8.2 is the *succeeding* event. The numbering of the events is somewhat arbitrary—several methods are used in actual companies. The activity between events 1 and 2 is labeled "*a.*" It can also be labeled "1–2."

An event as a node

The construction of the network starts with event **1** (the beginning of the project) which precedes the first activity (*a*). This will always be the activity (or activities) that *does not* require any preceding activity. It is placed at the left side of the diagram (similar to the start of a decision tree); the event before this activity is marked **1**, and the one after it is marked **2.** Next, the data show that activities b, c, and e must all be preceded by activity a, whose conclusion is event **2.** Therefore, all of these activities can start only after **2** has been declared. This is shown in Figure 8.3.

FIGURE 8.3
Precedence
requirements

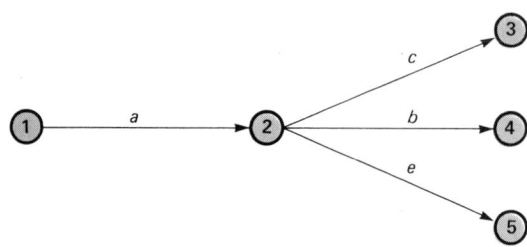

At the end of each activity, a number is assigned to designate the forthcoming event. The assignment of the numbers **3, 4,** and **5** is made as the network progresses, from left to right. The representation in Figure 8.3 shows that activities b, c, and e can be conducted simultaneously but none can start until activity a has been completed. Note that activity c was placed above activity b in the diagram; this was done merely as a matter of convenience for drawing the remaining diagram.

Project grows to the right

    The construction of the entire network continues in the same manner. Out of event **3,** succeeding activities d and f are extended (Figure 8.4). Out of event **4** the succeeding activity g is drawn, and out of event **5** the succeeding activity h is drawn. The diagram grows to the right until all activities and events are depicted.

FIGURE 8.4
PERT network for
Moose Lake project

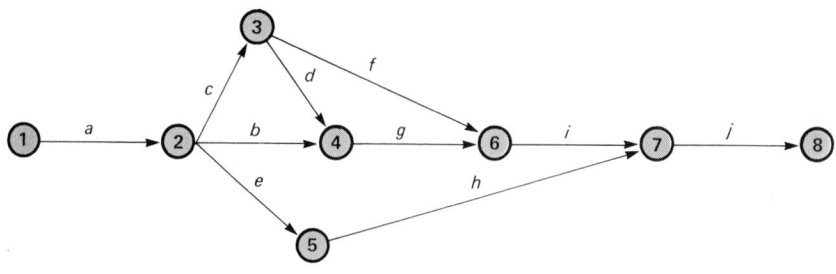

Dummy activities for proper sequencing

    Dummy activities In the construction of a network, care must be taken to assure that the activities and events are in proper sequence. One device that helps proper sequencing is dummy activities.

    Dummy activities are characterized by their use of zero time and zero resources; their function in this text is to designate a precedence relationship. Graphically such activities are shown as broken lines.

Example. Given a network with:

Activity	Required preceding activities
a	None
b	None
c	b
d	a, c
e	a
f	d, e

In order to diagram this network it is necessary to use a dummy activity, as shown in Figure 8.5.

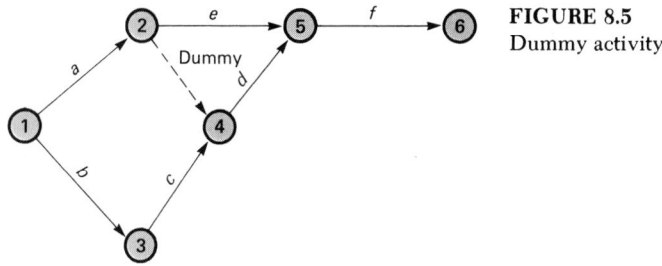

FIGURE 8.5
Dummy activity

Step 4. Estimate the duration of all activities

Once the network is completely drawn, the activity durations,[3] designated as t_e's, are entered on the diagram (in parentheses, above the arcs), as shown in Figure 8.6. Now the first stage is complete and the planning stage begins, as will be shown in the next section.

$T_E = duration$

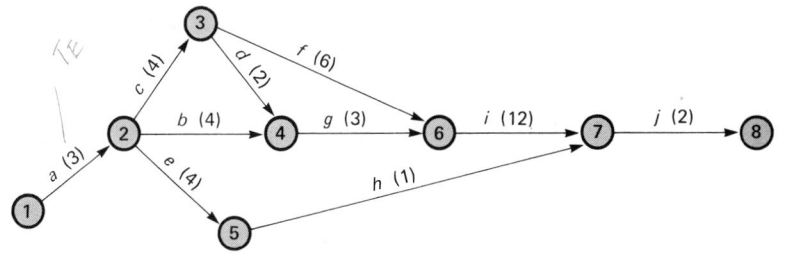

FIGURE 8.6
Time estimates for the project

_____
[3] Activity durations for PERT are estimated by a procedure discussed in Section 8.6. Activity durations for CPM are considered to be known with certainty from past experience.

8.3 PLANNING

Several methods exist for the computations required in the planning stage in PERT or CPM analysis. In this text, two methods are presented: an analytical method and complete enumeration.

Step 5. An analytical solution: Computing the earliest and latest dates

An analytical solution is available which makes the search process for the critical path, even for complex problems, relatively simple. Also, valuable additional information is secured. This solution is based on two important concepts:

- The earliest possible event date—T_E.
- The latest allowable event date—T_L.

The earliest date: T_E By definition the earliest date, T_E, for an event to occur, is immediately after *all* the preceding activities have been completed. For example, if a certain event is preceded by two activities, and the earliest date that activity 1 can be completed is 15 weeks, and the earliest date that activity 2 can be completed is 17 weeks, then the earliest time that the event can occur is at the conclusion of 17 weeks. Since this rule is true for every event including the last one, then *the earliest possible date for completing the entire project is the earliest date of the last event.*

The latest allowable date: T_L The latest allowable date for each event, T_L, is the latest date that an event can occur *without causing a delay* in the already determined project's completion date. The completion date for the project can be either the earliest possible completion date, or any other agreed upon date. Unless otherwise stated, we will use the earliest possible completion date for our calculations. The computation is done as follows.

Find T_E for each event In order to compute T_E for an event, the duration for each path leading to the event is computed. If several paths lead to an event, then the path with the *largest elapsed* time is considered.

Example. We will now find T_E for all events. To begin with, Figure 8.6 is reproduced as Figure 8.7.

Event 1: This is the event at the beginning of the project. The T_E for this event is set to zero. This information is written above the event (Figure 8.7). *For event* 2: there is only one activity from event 1 to 2; its duration is three weeks. The T_E for event 2 is thus 3. Similarly, T_E for event 3 is seven weeks and for event 5 is seven weeks.

For event 4: Note that T_E is to be determined by the longest path leading to an event. However, it is not necessary to compute all paths

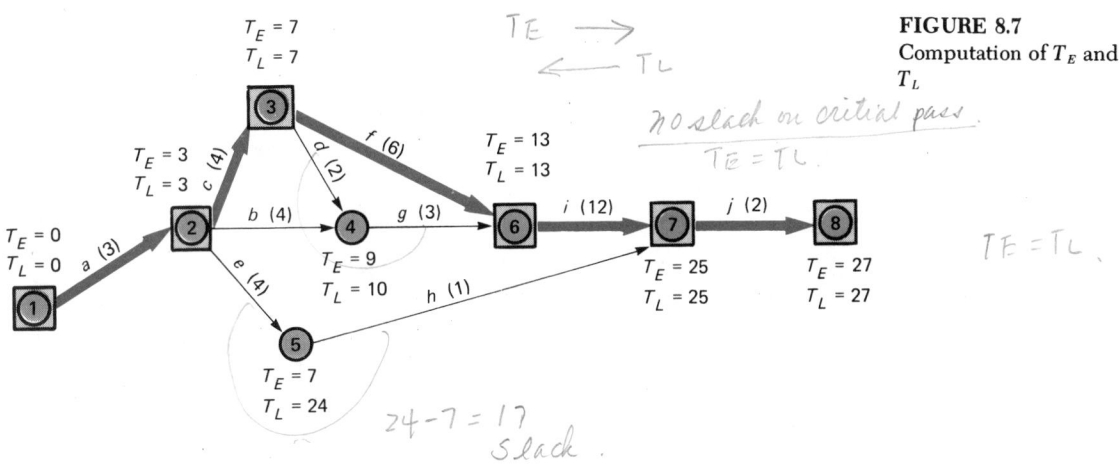

FIGURE 8.7
Computation of T_E and T_L

leading to an event to figure the longest one; use can be made of existing information, using the following formula:

> Length of a Path = Duration of the Last Activity on the Path + T_E of the Preceding Event

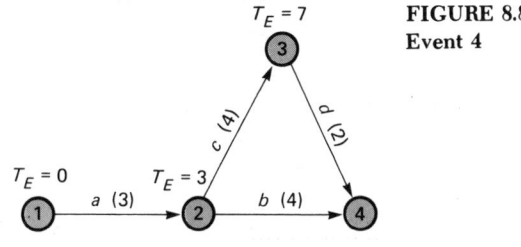

FIGURE 8.8
Event 4

Figure 8.8 shows the portion of the network leading to event **4**. For event **4** to be declared, both activity d and activity b must be completed. Now, the length of the path **1 – 2 – 3 – 4** is determined as:

$$\begin{aligned} T_E \text{ for event 3} = & \quad 7 \\ + \text{ duration of activity } d = & \quad \underline{2} \\ \text{Total} \ldots \ldots \ldots \ldots & \quad 9 \end{aligned}$$

The length of path **1 – 2 – 4** is determined as:

Length of a path

$$\begin{aligned} T_E \text{ for event 2} = & \quad 3 \\ + \text{ duration of activity } b = & \quad \underline{4} \\ \text{Total} \ldots \ldots \ldots \ldots & \quad 7 \end{aligned}$$

Now, all T_E's leading to the event are compared. Since 9 is the larger number, T_E for event **4** will be 9.

Event **6**: Two paths are considered:

path 1 – 2 – 3 – 6

whose length is: $T_E = 7$ (for event **3**) $+ 6 = 13$, and

path 1 − 2 − 3 − 4 − 6

whose length is $9 + 3 = 12$. Thus, the larger is 13 weeks.

The rest of the earliest start values are obtained in the same manner (shown in Figure 8.7). Event **8** designates the *end* of the project, since no activities emerge from it. Therefore, the earliest date for this event, 27 weeks, is the earliest date that the entire project can be completed. (This is good news for Judi as project director since the agreed upon completion time was 30 weeks.)

Working backwards to find T_L

Find T_L for each event   (Refer to Figure 8.7.) To compute each T_L start from the last event (**8**) and work backwards all the way to event **1**.

For event **8**: T_L for the last event is set equal to the computed earliest completion time of the project (27 weeks).

For event **7**: Since the latest that event **8** can occur is 27 weeks, and since it takes 2 weeks to complete activity *j*, then the latest allowable date that event **7** can occur is $27 − 2 = 25$ weeks.

For event **6**: Since the latest that event **7** can occur is 25 and since activity *i* lasts 12 weeks, then the latest time for event **6** is $25 − 12 = 13$.

For event **5**: In a similar manner T_L is found to be 24 (T_L for **7** is 25 minus 1 week for activity *h* = 24).

For event **4**: In a similar manner T_L is computed as 10.

For event **3**: Here two activities, *d* and *f* must be considered. Since activity *d* lasts 2 weeks, and since it must be completed no later than the 10th week (the latest allowable time for event **4**), then activity *d* must start not later than $10 − 2 = 8$. Activity *f* takes 6 weeks; it must be completed, at the latest, by week 13 (which is T_L for event **6**). Therefore, activity *f* must be started *not later* than $13 − 6 = 7$.

Now, to enable both activities to start on time so that there will be no delay in the entire project, event **3** must occur, *at the latest*, by week 7, which is the *smaller* of the two T_L's. Computation is continued in the same manner, event by event, until event **1** is reached. Of special interest is event **2**. Here three T_L's and activities must be considered. For *c*, $7 − 4 = 3$; for *b*, $10 − 4 = 6$; and for *e*, $24 − 4 = 20$. The *smallest one*, three weeks, is selected as T_L for event **2**. For event **1** T_L is zero.[4]

Step 6.   Find the slack on the events; identify critical events

The difference between the T_L and the T_E, for each event, is defined as *slack* (S).

$$S = T_L − T_E \qquad (8.1)$$

---

[4] For the first event, T_L must be zero. Otherwise, there is a mistake in the computation.

Two cases are distinguished:

1.) *When $T_L = T_E$ for the last event (the end of the project).* In this case
   slacks in the network can either be zero, whereupon the events are
   called *critical events,* or larger than zero, whereupon the events are
   considered to have positive slack.

   In our example (Figure 8.7) $T_L = T_E$ for the final event and all
critical events have zero slack. These are shown with a box around them
to aid in quick recognition. Note that only events **4** and **5** are not critical
here.

2. *When $T_L \neq T_E$ for the last event.* In this case the *critical* events are
    defined as those events with the *minimum slack,* which *can* be
    negative (when $T_L < T_E$).

   What is the meaning of slack? Since T_E is the earliest that an event
can be reached and T_L is the latest that the event can occur without
delaying the entire project, then the difference, the slack, tells how long
the event can "linger" *without* delaying the entire project. Any delay in
a critical event will cause a delay in the entire project.

   Let us examine event **5**. For this event the slack is: $T_L - T_E = 24 - 7$
$= 17$ weeks. The meaning of this is that although event **5** can be reached
in 7 weeks, management has the flexibility to reach this event at any time
during the next 17 weeks (up to the 24th week) without causing a delay
in the entire project.

Step 7.   Find the slack on the activities; identify critical activities

   Similar to the slack on an event, there is also slack on activities.
This slack tells us how long the activity can "linger" without delaying
the entire project. Equation 8.2 can be used to find the amount of slack:

Activity slack =	T_L	—	T_E	—	t_e	
	at the end		at the		duration	(8.2)
	of the		beginning		of the	
	activity		of the		activity	
			activity			

In our example we get the following results:

Activity	T_L	minus	T_E	minus	t_e	= *Slack*
a............	3		0		3	0
b............	10		3		4	3
c............	7		3		4	0
d............	10		7		2	1
e............	24		3		4	17
f............	13		7		6	0
g............	13		9		3	1
h............	25		7		1	17
i............	25		13		12	0
j............	27		25		2	0

Again, two cases are distinguished:

1. *When* $T_L = T_E$ *for the last event.* In this case an activity with zero slack is defined as a *critical activity.*
2. *When* $T_L \neq T_E$ *for the last event.* In this case the activities with the *minimum slack* are the critical ones.

Step 8. Find the critical path

The critical activities and events constitute the critical path

The critical path is that path in the network, leading from the beginning of the project to its end, *all* of whose activities and events are critical.

This definition implies that if $T_L = T_E$ for the last event, then there is *zero slack* on the critical path. Otherwise, the critical path is that path with the minimum slack on it.

The critical path has certain additional characteristics:

1. *There can be more than one critical path in the network.*
2. *The critical path is the longest path in the network.*

In our example, the critical path is:

$$1 - 2 - 3 - 6 - 7 - 8$$

Monitoring the critical path

The importance of identifying the critical path is that it points out those activities and events which are critical and, as such, must be carefully monitored and controlled. Before getting into these topics, however, let us note some additional characteristics of the PERT/CPM network.

Some Additional Characteristics

A. *Regular slack*

Such a case did not occur in our example but is shown in Figure 8.9. Activity $1 - 3$ has a duration of 6 weeks, while the path $1 - 2 - 3$ has a duration of 13 weeks. Therefore, activity $1 - 3$ can linger $13 - 6 = 7$ weeks; that is, there is a seven-week slack on the activity.

FIGURE 8.9
Regular slack

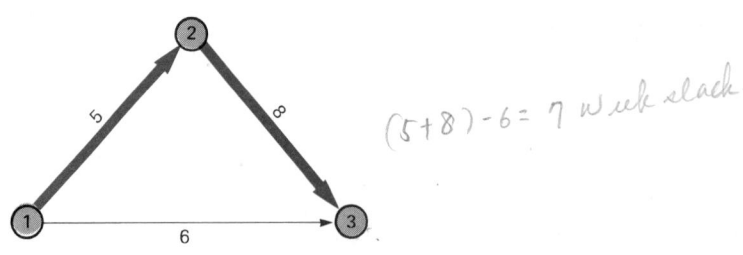

$(5 + 8) - 6 = 7$ week slack.

B. *Floating slack (slack on a path)*

Whenever there are two or more noncritical activities, or noncritical events, connected in a series, the slack is called *floating*. An example of floating slack is shown in Figure 8.10 where activities *e* and *h* are connected in series. The critical portion of the path between events **2** and **7** requires 22 weeks.

Floating = shared

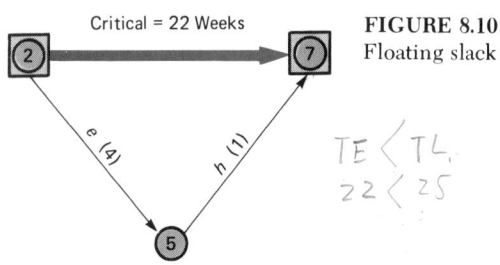

Critical = 22 Weeks

FIGURE 8.10
Floating slack

$TE < TL.$
$22 < 25$

Activity *e* requires four weeks and activity *h* requires one week, a total of five weeks. Therefore, there is a slack of $22 - 5 = 17$ weeks which can be used on both *e* and *h*. For example, a slack of 17 on *e* and zero on *h*, 16 on *e* and 1 on *h*, and so on.

Another example of floating slack   Figure 8.11 shows a situation with two noncritical events, **2** and **3**, and three noncritical activities *a*, *b*, and *c*. Activities *a*, *b*, and *c* together require $3 + 4 + 5 = 12$ weeks. Therefore, there is a slack of $30 - 12 = 18$ on both events **2** and **3** (e.g., 18 on **2**, zero on **3**; 17 on **2** and 1 on **3**, and so on). That is, there is a floating slack of 18 on events **2** and **3**.

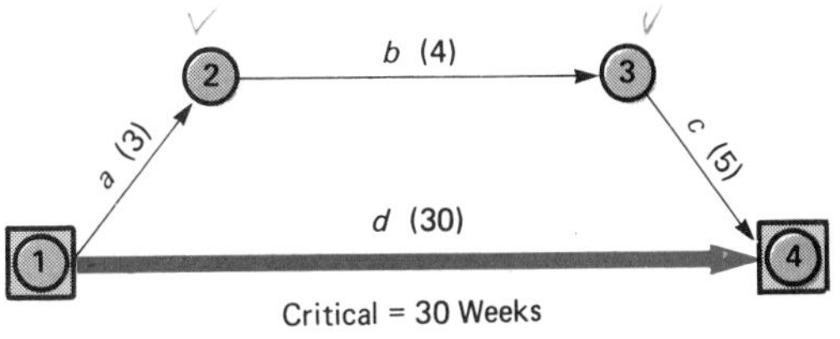

$30-12=18$ weeks slack.

FIGURE 8.11

There is also a slack of $30 - 12 = 18$ on *activities a*, *b*, and *c* combined. Again, one may use the 18 on activity *a* alone, or six weeks on each activity, and so on. (There are as many possibilities as there are ways of allocating 18 among three recipients.)

In a situation of floating slack, it can be viewed as being on a path, rather than on an individual activity. For example, in Figure 8.11 there is a slack of 18 on path $1 - 2 - 3 - 4$.

C. *Total slack in the network*

Management may also be interested in the total slack in the network. To find this, go through all activities and add slack times, making sure to count a floating slack only once. The total maximum slack in the case of Moose Lake is 21 weeks, computed as:

Activities	Slack
b	3
e (or h)	17
d (or g)	1
Total	21 weeks

(activity h is floating with e, and g is floating with d).

Completion of the slack calculations now allows management to establish a complete project plan taking critical activities and slack into account in labor and resource planning and budgeting.

D. The case when $T_L \neq T_E$ for the project

In the previous computations we assumed that $T_L = T_E$ for the last event. However, this may not always be the case.

If T_L is larger than T_E for the last event, then the slack for the last event will be positive.

Example In the Moose Lake project, Judi can consider T_L as 30 (the agreed upon completion time). Thus the slack on event **8** will be 30 − 27 = 3 and so will the slacks on all critical events. Further, the slack on all noncritical events will be 3 weeks larger too. For example, for event **5** the new $T_L = 27$; since $T_E = 7$ (unchanged) then the slack for event **5** = 27 − 7 = 20 weeks.

If T_L is smaller than T_E for the last event a *negative slack* will result, indicating that the desired date cannot be achieved and a delay of the magnitude of the negative value is expected.

E. A critical path leading to an event

The critical path procedure outlined previously can also be used to find the critical path leading to any desired event. For example, the critical path to event **4** is: **1 − 2 − 3 − 4.**

F. Use of complete enumeration

In small problems, like the one in the example, the critical path may be identified by listing all possible paths leading from the beginning of the project to its end. The path with the *largest* duration is the

critical path (composed of all critical activities and events). The reason for this is that in order to complete the project, all activities *must* be accomplished. Since the longest path is longer than any other, its completion gives enough elapsed time to complete *all other paths*. This guarantees that every single activity in the network will be accomplished. In the Moose Lake example, the following four paths are identified:

		Total duration (weeks)	
Path 1	$1 - 2 - 3 - 4 - 6 - 7 - 8$	26	
Path 2	$1 - 2 - 3 - 6 - 7 - 8$	27	← *Maximum*
Path 3	$1 - 2 - 4 - 6 - 7 - 8$	24	
Path 4	$1 - 2 - 5 - 7 - 8$	10	

When *all* paths are compared (complete enumeration approach), the longest path is found to be Path 2 with a duration of 27 weeks.

In large, complex networks with hundreds of activities, especially when continuous updating is required, the complete enumeration approach may take a long time. In such cases the analytical approach is used.

G. Multiple critical paths

In this example there is a single critical path for the project. However, in other problems, multiple paths may occur. For example, if activity *d* were three weeks, there would have been *two* critical paths. The one already identified:

$$1 - 2 - 3 - 6 - 7 - 8$$

and another one:

$$1 - 2 - 3 - 4 - 6 - 7 - 8$$

H. Several starting events

The examples given so far exhibit a single starting event. However, this is not necessary and real projects often do have multiple starting events (e.g., see Problem 9.)

8.4   PERT AND CPM AS CONTROL TOOLS

The previous section showed how to construct a network, how to find the critical events and activities, how to find the critical path, and how to compute slack time. This information is crucial to the development of the *plan* of the project. Having done that, a complete planning document results and detailed work orders can be issued. From this point on, PERT and CPM can be used as tools for monitoring and control.

The project plan

Steps 9–12.   Replanning and adjusting projects

Suppose the Moose Lake project started on schedule. However, the very first activity, the administrative setup, is delayed. Although the duration of this critical activity had been estimated as three weeks, it is now clear that it will take four weeks to handle all the administrative details. Thus, when the time comes for event **2**, its T_E will be 4, rather than 3. The slack in event **2**, according to Equation 8.1, will be:

$$S = T_L - T_E = 3 - 4 = -1$$

That is, the slack has a negative value and is labeled as *negative slack*. A negative slack value means that the project is behind. If T_E's are now computed for all the remaining critical events, including the ending event, there will be a negative slack of 1. This implies that the *entire project* will be delayed by one week. What can management do about this?

Dealing with a delay

Look for a moment at event **5**, which is not critical. The previous slack for this event was computed as $24 - 7 = 17$; now it will be $24 - 8 = 16$, still a positive slack.

Activities b, d, e, and h likewise possess positive slack. This means that these activities can still be delayed without delaying the entire project. Slowing down noncritical activities may release resources (such as labor, tools, and equipment) which may then be transferred to one (or more) of the critical activities. If such a transfer could reduce the completion time of any critical activity by one week, the delay could be eliminated and the project still be completed on schedule.

Transferring resources

A similar situation may develop if a noncritical activity such as g requires six rather than three weeks for completion. The T_E for event **6** would then be 15 weeks, and a negative slack of 2 would be formed at event **6**. Notice that the critical path will be changed to **1–2–3–4–6–7–8** and activities d and g will become critical. In general, any deviation of the actual time from the computed duration should be reported to the project director, who in turn will recompute the critical path. Previously noncritical events and activities may become critical and vice versa.

In addition to transferring resources to critical activities, management may correct delays by some other actions such as:

- Relaxing the technical specifications or the required quality.
- Changing the scope of the project by reducing the desired goals and consequently the amount of work.
- Changing the sequencing of activities.
- Pouring additional resources into the project.
- Expediting activities by various incentives.
- Starting activities while preceding ones are still being completed.

Other ways to correct delays

8.5 PROBLEMS FOR PART A

1. The events of the project below are designated as 1, 2, and so on.

   a. Draw the network.
   b. Find the critical path by complete enumeration.

   c. Find, for all events, the earliest and latest dates.
   d. Find the slacks on all the events and activities.
   e. Find the critical path using the T_E's and T_L's.

Activity	Preceding event	Succeeding event	t_e (weeks)	Preceding activities
a	1	2	3	none
b	1	3	6	none
c	1	4	8	none
d	2	5	7	a
e	3	5	5	b
f	4	5	10	c
g	4	6	4	c
h	5	7	5	d, e, f
i	6	7	6	g

2. Given the following PERT network (times are in weeks):

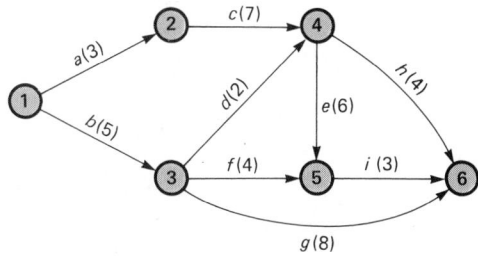

Determine:

a. The T_E and T_L for each event.
b. The slacks on all events and activities.
c. The critical activities and path.
d. The floating slacks.
e. The total slack in the network.

3. Suppose that management has a contract to finish the project in Problem 2 in 22 weeks.

Determine:

a. The slack on event **3**.
b. The slack on activity **g**.

4. Given the following schedule for a liability work package done as part of an accounting audit in a corporation:

Activity	Duration (days)	Preceding activities
a. Obtain schedule of liabilities	3	None
b. Mail confirmation	15	a
c. Test pension plan	5	a
d. Vouch selected liabilities	60	a
e. Test accruals and amortization	6	d
f. Process confirmations	40	b
g. Reconcile interest expense to debt	10	c, e

Activity	Duration (days)	Preceding activities
h. Verify debt restriction compliance	7	f
i. Investigate debit balances	6	g
j. Review subsequent payments	12	h, i

Find:

a. The critical path.
b. The slack time on "process confirmations."
c. The slack time on "test pension plan."
d. The slack time on "verify debt restriction compliance."

5. In the project network shown in the figure below, the number alongside each activity designates the activity duration (t_e) in weeks.

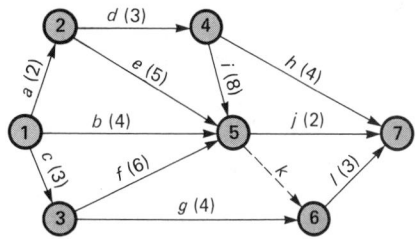

Determine:

a. The T_E and T_L for each event.
b. The earliest time that the project can be completed.
c. The slack on all events and activities.
d. The critical events and activities.
e. The critical path.
f. The floating slacks and the total slack in the network.

6. Given the following information regarding a project:

Activity	t_e (weeks)	Preceding activities
a	3	none
b	1	none
c	3	a
d	4	a
e	4	b
f	5	b
g	2	c, e
h	3	f

a. Draw the network.
b. What is the critical path?
c. What will the scheduled (earliest completion) time for the entire project be?
d. What is the critical path to event **4** (end of activities *c* and *e*)? What is the earliest time that this event can be reached?
e. What is the effect on the project if activity *e* takes an extra week? Two extra weeks? Three extra weeks?

7. Construct a network for the project below and find its critical path. (Use a complete enumeration approach.)

Activity	t_e (weeks)	Preceding activities
a...........	3	None
b...........	5	a
c...........	3	a
d...........	1	c
e...........	3	b
f...........	4	b, d
g...........	2	c
h...........	3	g, f
i...........	1	e, h

8. Construct a network for the project:

Activity	t_e (weeks)	Preceding activities
a...........	3	None
b...........	5	None
c...........	14	a
d...........	5	a
e...........	4	b
f...........	7	b
g...........	8	d, e
h...........	5	g, f

a. Draw the network.
b. Find the critical path by complete enumeration.
c. Assume activity *a* took 5 weeks. Replan the project.
d. From where would you suggest transferring resources, and to what activities, such that the original target date may be maintained?

9. Given a PERT network:

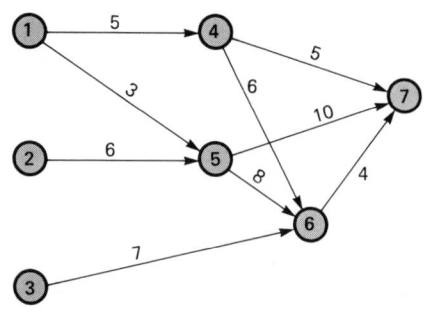

Note that three activities can start immediately.

Find:

a. The critical path.
b. The earliest time to complete the project.
c. The slack on activities 4-6, 5-6, and 4-7.

PART B: EXTENSIONS

8.6 ESTIMATE OF ACTIVITY TIME IN PERT

Since the Moose Lake Project was an experimental project, it is suitable for a PERT analysis. Judi asked each department to submit three estimates of duration time[5] for each activity the department was responsible for, using the following guidelines:

Three time estimates

Optimistic estimate (t_o): An estimate of the *shortest possible time* (duration) in which the activity can be accomplished. This estimate, by definition, has a chance of one in a hundred (.01) of occurring.

Most likely estimate (t_m): The duration which would occur most often if the activity were repeated under exactly the same conditions many times. Equivalently, it is the time that would be estimated most often by experts.

Pessimistic estimate (t_p): The longest time that the activity could take. It should be a time that is exceeded no more than once in a hundred occasions.

All three estimates are entered in Table 8.2. Notice that in some cases $t_o = t_p = t_m$; that is, the exact time duration is known.

TABLE 8.2
Moose Lake Project activities (weeks)

Activity	Description	t_o (opti- mistic)	t_m (most likely)	t_p (pessi- mistic)	t_e (weighted average)
a..............	Administrative setup	1	3	5	3
b..............	Hire personnel	1	3	11	4
c..............	Obtain materials	3	4	5	4
d..............	Transport materials to Moose Lake	1	2	3	2
e..............	Gather measuring team	3	3	9	4
f..............	Planning	2	5	14	6
g..............	Assemble equipment	2	3	4	3
h..............	Plan evaluation	1	1	1	1
i..............	Oxygenation	12	12	12	12
j..............	Measurement and evaluation	1	2	3	2

---

[5] Projects are usually measured with a week as the logical unit of time. However, PERT analyses also use days, especially in short-term projects.

Computing the weighted average

Once the three time estimates are obtained, their weighted average is computed. This average, which is called the mean time of an activity, t_e, is a *weighted average* of the three time estimates and it is computed using Equation 8.3:

$$t_e = \frac{t_o + 4t_m + t_p}{6}$$
(8.3)

where t_e is the weighted average duration of the activity.[6]

Note: In CPM, t_e designates the duration time which is considered to be known with certainty.

The formula gives four times more weight to the most likely estimate than to the pessimistic or optimistic estimates. The division by 6 is to obtain a weighted average of $1 + 4 + 1 = 6$ weights.

A weighted average

For example, in Table 8.2, for activity a the weighted average is:

$$t_e = \frac{1 + 4\,(3) + 5}{6} = 3 \text{ weeks}$$

and for activity b the weighted duration is:

$$t_e = \frac{1 + 4\,(3) + 11}{6} = 4 \text{ weeks}$$

This information is then added to the original data in the t_e column (Table 8.2) which is the source for the information entered in Figure 8.6.

8.7 FINDING THE PROBABILITIES OF COMPLETION IN PERT

PERT has more capabilities than just as a planning and control tool. It can also be used to give management an indication of risk in terms of project delay. This is a crucial analysis which considers the chance of completing the project on, before, or after scheduled dates.

The consideration of risk

The three estimates of activity duration in PERT, t_o, t_m, and t_p are assumed to follow a frequency distribution called the Beta distribution, shown in Figure 8.12 for activity b as an example ($t_o = 1$, $t_m = 3$, $t_p = 11$, and their average $t_e = 4$).

Approaching the normal distribution

Even though estimates of each activity duration follow the Beta distribution, the estimate of the combined duration of several activities (such as those on the critical path) approaches the *normal* distribution and is centered around the "early completion time" of the project. Therefore, there is a 50 percent chance that the *entire* project will be completed by its earliest projected time (27 weeks in our example from

---

[6] This is based on the assumption that the Beta distribution is the probability distribution of duration times.

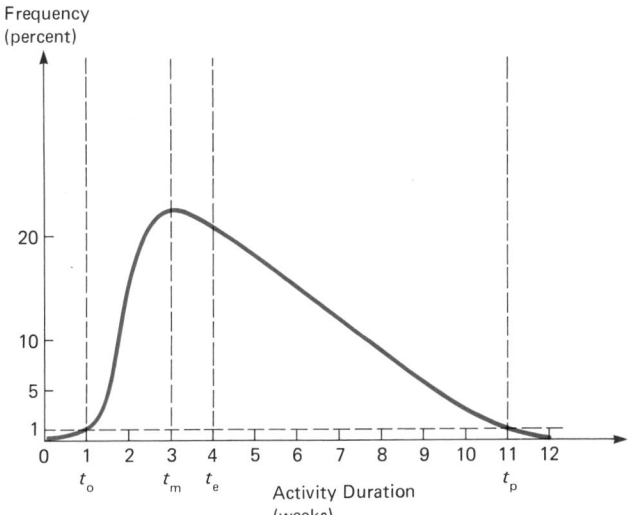

FIGURE 8.12
Activity time distribution
for activity b

Part A). However, a "50 percent chance" may not be sufficient informa- Only 50% chance
tion for management. Management may want to know the period that has of completion by
a larger chance of completion (say, 70 percent). Similarly, management earliest time
may want to know the chances of completing the project in a given
amount of time, say 25 or 30 weeks. To answer such questions, an
analysis involving the probability associated with the duration times is
conducted.

Since each activity's duration involves three estimates, it is possible to calculate a *standard deviation* for the activity. The standard
deviation of the Beta distribution of activity durations is given by
Equation 8.4.

$$\text{Standard Deviation of an Activity} = \sigma = \frac{t_p - t_o}{6} \qquad (8.4)$$

The variance of the activity's distribution is given by Equation 8.5.

$$\text{Variance of Activity} = \sigma^2 = \left(\frac{t_p - t_o}{6}\right)^2 \qquad (8.5)$$

For example, for activity b, the standard deviation is:

$$\sigma_b = \frac{11 - 1}{6} = 1.67 \text{ weeks}$$

and the variance is:

$$\sigma_b^2 = 1.67^2 = 2.78 \text{ weeks}$$

For activities h and i the variance is zero since $t_p = t_o$ for these activities. This means that no uncertainty is involved in their estimates. The larger the variance, the greater the degree of uncertainty involved in estimating the duration of the activity.

Assuming the durations of the activities are independent of each other, the variance of a *group* of activities (designated by V) can be computed by adding the variances of the activities in that group. The value of V is then expressed by Equation 8.6.

$$V = \sigma_1^2 + \sigma_2^2 + \cdots \sigma_n^2 \qquad (8.6)$$

where n is the number of activities in the group.

Of special interest are the activities that comprise the *critical path*. For example, in the Moose Lake project, the variance for the critical path[7] is given as:

The variance along the critical path

$$V = \sigma_a^2 + \sigma_c^2 + \sigma_f^2 + \sigma_i^2 + \sigma_j^2$$
$$= .44 + .11 + 4.00 + 0 + .11 = 4.66$$

A critical path to each event

Note: The value of V can be computed, in a similar manner, for *any event* in the network by considering the group of activities along the critical path leading to that event.

Managerial applications

The managerial questions raised at the beginning of this section—the chance of completing the project in a certain desired time and the duration necessary for obtaining any desired probability of completion—can now be answered. Let:

S = scheduled project completion time. The earliest time (T_E) computed for the last event, 27 weeks in the example.

D = the desired completion time, 30 weeks in the example.

Z = the number of standard deviations of a normal distribution (see Appendix C, Table C1) corresponding to the probability of completing the project by the desired completion time.

$$Z = \frac{D - S}{\sqrt{V}} \qquad (8.7)$$

Example 1: Finding the probability of completion in a desired time, D Management wishes to know the probability of completing the

---

[7] If more than one critical path exists, then V should be computed for *all* such paths. Use the path with the largest V to compute probabilities of completion for dates *after* the expected completion time; use the smallest V for probabilities of completion for dates *before* the expected completion time.

Moose Lake project, *on or before* the 30th week, as specified in the contract.

Thus: $D = 30$, $S = 27$ (as computed), $V = 4.66$ (as computed).

Therefore:

$$Z = \frac{30 - 27}{\sqrt{4.66}} = \frac{3}{2.16} = 1.39$$

The probability equivalent to $Z = 1.39$ can be found in Table C1 as .91774. Therefore, there is a 91.77 percent chance of completing the Moose Lake project in 30 weeks. (Remember that there is a 50 percent chance of completing the project in 27 weeks.) Figure 8.13 depicts the situation.

Using the normal distribution

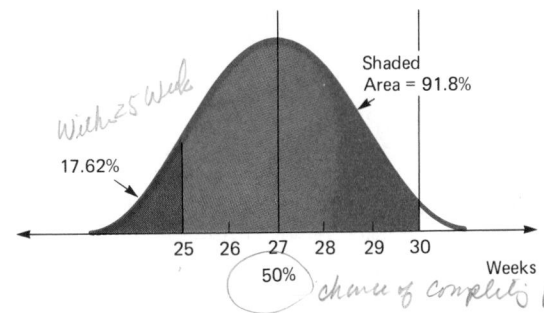

FIGURE 8.13
Chance of completing the project in 25, 27, and 30 weeks

In a similar manner, the Z for completing the project in 25 weeks is:

$$Z = \frac{25 - 27}{2.16} = -.93$$

If the normal distribution tables included negative numbers, the probability could be read directly from them. Since this is usually not the case, the probability for $Z = +.93$ is read first (which is .8238). This value is then subtracted from 1.0 (the total area under the curve); that is, $1 - .8238 = .1762$. Thus, there is only a 17.62 percent chance of completing the project in 25 weeks (see Figure 8.13).

Note: If Z is negative, the corresponding probability is always less than 50 percent. If Z is positive, the corresponding probability is always more than 50 percent; and if Z is 0, the corresponding probability is exactly 50 percent.

Example 2: Finding the duration associated with a desired probability In the previous example a chance of 91.77 percent of completing the project in 30 weeks was computed. Suppose that management would like to know for what duration they can be 80 percent sure of completion. To do so Table C1 is consulted. The value of Z associated with 80 percent is searched for. The answer is $Z = .845$. Using Equation 8.7 with D as the unknown we obtain:

Working backwards to find the completion date

$$D = Z \sqrt{V} + S \quad \text{or} \quad D = .845 \times 2.16 + 27 = 28.83 \text{ weeks}$$

That is, there is an 80 percent chance of completing the project in 28.83 weeks. The computation of D enables management to make delivery commitments knowing the degree of risk assumed.

The variance of a noncritical path

The danger of noncritical paths

The probability of completing a project was found to be related to the variance of the critical path (Equation 8.7). Suppose, however, that there is a noncritical path whose variance V is *larger* than the variance of the critical path. What might its effect be on the probability of completion? If Equation 8.7 is used for the new path, then the probability of completion by the desired time might very well be *lower* than that computed using the critical path. Therefore, in PERT analysis, it is wise to also consider noncritical paths with large variances.

8.8 THE CRITICAL PATH METHOD (CPM): COST-TIME RELATIONSHIPS

Expediting projects

CPM analysis is used to evaluate various alternatives of executing projects in those cases where it is possible to *expedite* the execution of some or all of the project's activities. Expediting activities requires additional resources which means increasing the cost of the project. However, considerable savings may be realized in projects finished ahead of schedule. An example of such a case was observed in Palm Beach, Florida, where two builders constructed two large condominium projects. With the economic slump of 1975 the demand for condominiums dropped considerably. One of the builders decided to expedite construction, at a considerable cost, in order to finish first. He sold 240 units in a short time, exhausting the demand. When the second builder completed his project he could not sell the units and was forced to file for bankruptcy.

Thus, the decision of how much to expedite may be of great importance to management. The tool for performing such an analysis is called CPM.

The basic idea

Normal or crash?

Figure 8.14 presents the relationship in CPM between cost and time. An activity can be performed in a *normal manner* (normal point in Figure 8.14 requiring T_n units of time and C_n units of money (where n designates "normal"). In an extreme case, the activity can be performed on a "crash" basis (e.g., using overtime, special services, extra tools) at a time T_c and a cost C_c (where c designates "crash"). No activity can be executed in less time than T_c or more than T_n, but can take any value between.

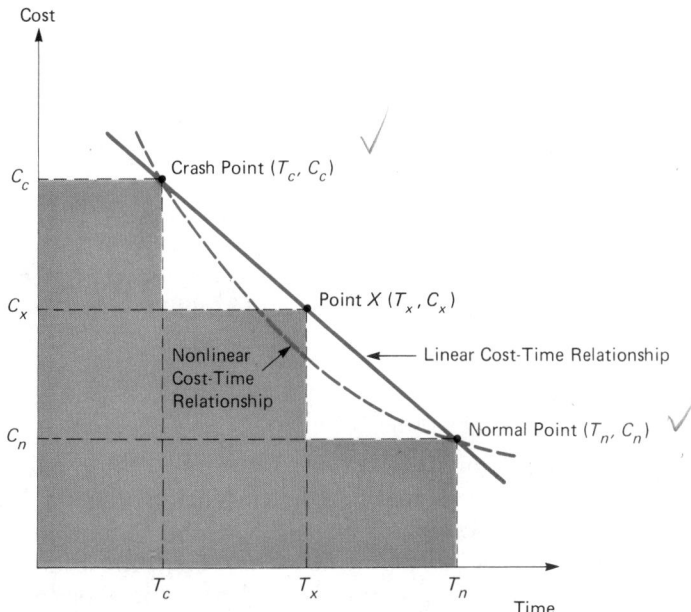

FIGURE 8.14
CPM cost-time tradeoffs
for an activity

The crash point and the normal point can be connected by a *straight line.* Any intermediate point X, on the straight line, will involve T_x time and C_x cost. The relationship between time and cost is given by the slope of the straight line (Equation 8.8).

$$\text{“Slope”} = \frac{C_c - C_n}{T_n - T_c} \tag{8.8}$$

The "slope"[8] gives us the *cost increase* associated with a reduction of one unit of the activity duration. The assumption of a linear relationship between cost and time is not valid in all cases. In some cases the relationships are described by a nonlinear function (the broken curve in Figure 8.14) and the solid line only approximates the broken line. In other cases a step-wise curve is applicable (see Problem 14). It is customary to write the normal and crash data for each activity directly on the diagram as shown in Figure 8.15 (time above the line, cost underneath). For example, for activity **1–3** the normal time is five weeks at a cost of $4,000; the crash time is three weeks at a cost of $5,200.

The slope as a tradeoff

The "slope" of activity **1–3** is:

$$\frac{\$5,200 - \$4,000}{5 - 3} = \$600 \text{ per week}$$

Cost of Crash Time − Cost of Normal time
normal time − Crash time

---

[8] The true slope will actually be a negative number since the direction of the line is from northwest to southeast; however, Equation 8.8 yields a *positive* number which we use as a cost *increase*.

FIGURE 8.15
CPM labeling

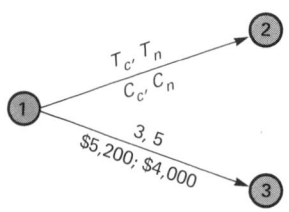

This is the cost required to expedite the activity by one week. The linear relationship means that it will cost $1,200 to expedite the activity by two weeks and so on, up to the crash point.

The CPM analysis

The CPM analysis examines the total cost involved in executing the project at various scheduled times starting with the lowest cost–longest duration alternative and ending with the higher cost–shortest duration alternative. The additional cost of expediting the project can then be compared with the possible savings from the expedited completion (e.g., a client may pay a bonus for completion ahead of schedule).

Solve the problem twice

The CPM analysis starts by solving the problem twice. First, attention is paid only to *normal times.* Using the procedure outlined in Part A of this chapter and assuming that the normal times are the t_e's, a solution is derived. Then the total cost is computed using the normal cost figures. Second, by considering only the *crash times* as t_e's, another solution is derived, and its cost is also computed.

Once the two solutions are computed, the cost-time tradeoffs are used to find the least-cost plan for any number of weeks (days) between the *all crash* and *all normal* plans. This cost can then be compared with the anticipated benefits.

Example A network of activities for a maintenance project is shown in Figure 8.16.[9] The problem is to find the least-cost plan for various project durations.

FIGURE 8.16
A maintenance project

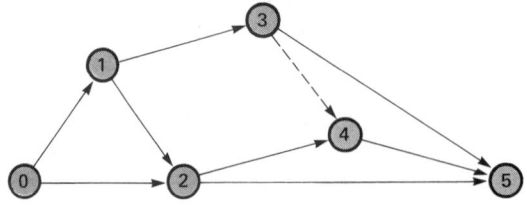

---

[9] The broken line from event 3 to event 4 designates a requirement that event 4 cannot occur before event 3. The activity 3–4 is a "dummy" activity. Note that the activities here are designated by the number of the preceding and succeeding events.

The normal time (in days) and cost as well as the crash time and cost are shown in Table 8.3. The column "cost slope" indicates the incremental *increase* in cost when the duration of the project is decreased by one day, computed from Equation 8.7. For example, for activity **1–3**:

$$\text{Slope} = \frac{340 - 280}{9 - 7} = \frac{60}{2} = \$30 \text{ per day}$$

Solution   The first observation that can be made from Table 8.3 is that if all activities are performed in the normal duration, the total cost will be $1,860. Second, if all activities are performed on a crash basis, the total cost will be $2,860. The *times* required to complete the project on an *all-normal* basis and on an *all-crash* basis should be determined next.

| | Normal | | Crash | | Cost |
Activity	Time	Cost	Time	Cost	slope
0–1	5	$ 100	4	$ 140	40
0–2	9	200	7	300	50
1–2	7	250	4	340	30
1–3	9	280	7	340	30
2–4	5	250	2	460	70
2–5	11	400	7	720	80
3–5	6	300	4	420	60
4–5	8	80	6	140	30
Total		$1,860		$2,860	

TABLE 8.3
Time and cost information

All-normal basis   Considering first *all-normal* times (disregard the normal costs, the crash time and the crash cost) the critical path can be computed using the procedures shown in Part A of this chapter. The results are shown in Figure 8.17. The critical path is **0–1–2–4–5** for a duration of 25 days and a cost of $1,860.

All normal—least cost—longest time

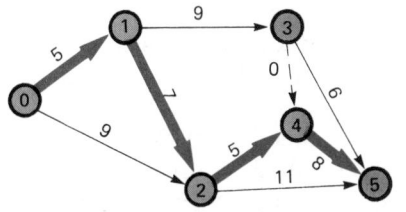

FIGURE 8.17
All-normal solution, 25 days

All-crash solution   In a similar manner, the critical path of *all-crash* duration is computed (Figure 8.18).

All crash—most expensive—shortest time

The critical path is **0–1–3–4–5** for a duration of 17 days and a cost of $2,860.

FIGURE 8.18
All-crash solution, 17 days

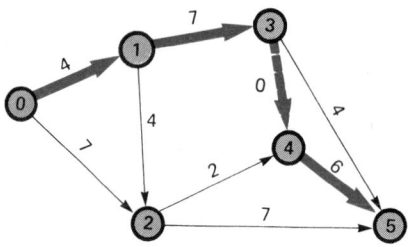

At this stage the following analysis is performed:

a. Determine the *minimum* cost for the crash time of 17 days.
b. Determine the least-cost plan for any desired number of days, between all-normal to all-crash.

Find the minimum cost for the crash time

So far it was found that it is possible to perform the project in 17 days at a cost of $2,860. The question is whether it is possible to perform the project in 17 days but at a lower cost.

Expanding

To achieve a cost reduction, the noncritical activities could be performed at a slower pace. (This is called *expanding* the activities.) There is a simple procedure for this.

Step 1 All *noncritical* activities found in Figure 8.18 are listed with their appropriate cost slope:

Noncritical activities	Cost slope
0–2.............	50
1–2.............	30
2–4.............	70
3–5.............	60
2–5.............	80

Step 2 The activity with the *largest* slope is selected (activity **2–5**) first. The largest savings can be made if this activity is expanded first. It would be desirable to expand it *as much as possible* to achieve as large a cost reduction as possible. Since activity **2–5** is on two noncritical paths **0–1–2–5** and **0–2–5**, it can be expanded until one of these becomes critical.

Since path **0–2–5** now takes 14 days, it can be expanded by 3 days to make it critical, up to 17 days. However, path **0–1–2–5** now takes 15 days and therefore only 2 days can be added to it to make it critical. Therefore, the maximum number of days that can be added to activity **2–5** is 2 (the smaller of the two). There is another point that should be checked in expanding an activity. The crash time of activity **2–5** is seven days. The normal time is given as 11 days. Therefore, expansion by two days is feasible. In other cases it *may not be feasible* to expand up to the maximum length allowed by the length of the noncritical path because of the normal time limitations that are imposed on an individual activity.

(In other words, it is assumed that the normal time is the *slowest* execution time of an activity.)

The expansion of activity **2–5** now yields an additional critical path **0–1–2–5** that will take 17 days at a cost reduction of $160.

Step 3   Activity **2–4** which has the *second largest* cost reduction potential is expanded next. Here an expansion of only one day is possible at a $70 saving. In a similar manner the expansion of activity **3–5** by two days will yield an additional $120, and finally activity **0–2** can be expanded by one day resulting in a $50 saving. Notice that since activity **2–5** has been expanded to nine days, the maximum that activity **0–2** can be expanded is to eight days (17 − 9 = 8). It is impossible to expand activity **1–2** since it became *critical* as a result of the expansion of activity **2–5**.

The total cost savings are: 160 + 70 + 120 + 50 = 400. Thus, the revised plan calls for a 17-day project, at a total cost of $2,860 − $400 = $2,460.

This new schedule is shown in Figure 8.19. Notice that all activities are now *critical*; that is, no further expansion is possible.

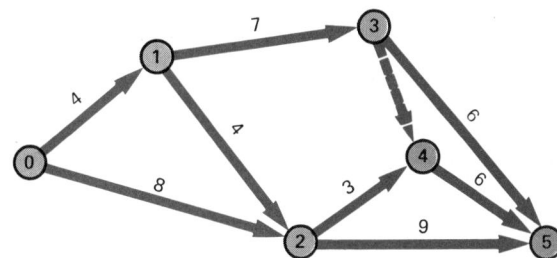

FIGURE 8.19
Least-cost, crash schedule of 17 days ($2,460)

The information is then entered into a cost-time diagram (Figure 8.20) as point *A*.

The cost-time diagram

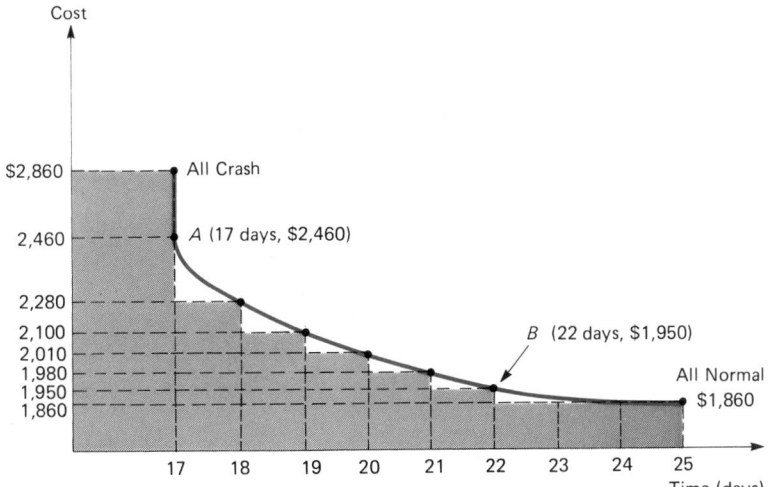

FIGURE 8.20
Cost-time trade-offs

Determine the least-cost plan for any desired number of days

The normal schedule is the *longest* (slowest) schedule for carrying out the project, and costs the *least*. On the other hand, the all-crash schedule is the *fastest* but is almost the most expensive. In certain cases management needs to know the cost of carrying out the project at some point between the fastest and the slowest. Such a situation may develop, for example, when a customer offers to pay a certain amount as a bonus for finishing ahead of schedule.

Example: Least-cost plan for 22 days   Let us assume that management would like to find the least-cost plan for 22 days. Two approaches are available: either *compressing* the project from 25 days (all normal) to 22 days, or *expanding* the project from 17 days (all crash) up to 22. The former approach will be illustrated here.

Compress or expand?

The first step is to list all critical activities of the all-normal schedule (Figure 8.17). The list of these activities and their slopes follows:

Critical activity	Slope
0–1	40
1–2	30
2–4	70
4–5	30

The activity with the *least* slope will be compressed first, since decreasing the project time by one day will result in the smallest increase in cost. In the example, either activity **1–2** or activity **4–5** can be selected since both have the smallest slope (lowest cost). Arbitrarily, activity **1–2** is selected.

How much can activity **1–2** be compressed? The most an activity can be compressed is up to its *crash time* (four days here). However, such a reduction may create one (or more) additional critical paths. The minute an additional critical path is created, the compression should be stopped and a cost reevaluation made. In the example, two additional critical paths are formed after activity **1–2** is reduced from seven to four days. Thus, the maximum project compression is to 22 days (see Figure 8.21) at a cost of $1,860 + 90 = $1,950 (point *B* in Figure 8.20).

Multiple critical paths

FIGURE 8.21
A 22-day least-cost schedule

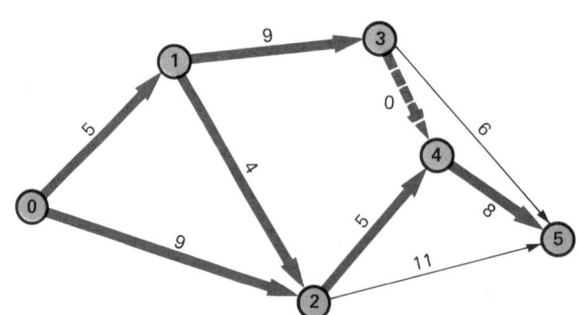

Notice that the compression to 22 days also tells us that the best plan for achieving 24 days is to cut 1 day from activity **1–2** and the best plan for 23 days is cutting 2 days from activity **1–2**.

Compression to 20 days   In a similar manner, the best plan for 21 days can be found. Starting with 22 days, the *critical* activity **4–5** (Figure 8.21) is expedited since its cost increase is now the smallest. Compressing by one day yields a 21 day schedule with a cost of $1,980. This activity could be compressed by two days to its crash time of six days. After compressing it by two days, we get a 20 day schedule at a cost of $2,010 (see Figure 8.22). This information is now entered in Figure 8.20. Note that the entire network is now critical.

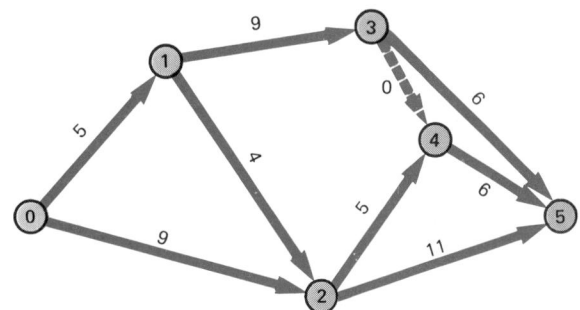

FIGURE 8.22
A 20-day least-cost schedule

Additional compression   At this stage, a single activity can no longer be considered by itself since there are several critical paths involved. For example, if activity **1–3** is reduced by 1 day, the critical path **0–1–3–5** will be reduced to 19 days but other critical paths will also have to be reduced by 1 day. In this case activities **2–4** and **2–5** have to be compressed by one day each and the cost effect will be felt in two places. Therefore, it is necessary to check all combinations of possible   Check all possibilities
reductions to make sure that the smallest total cost is added. This is done by taking the smallest slope on a path (rather than an activity) first and adding the resultant cost impact to the other paths.

Then a computation is made for the least slope on the next path taking into consideration the impact on the resultant cost, and so on. Finally, all alternatives are compared and the one with the least-cost increase is selected. In the example, a compression of activities **0–1** and **0–2** by 1 day results in a 19-day schedule at a cost of $2,010 + 40 + 50 = $2,100 (see Figure 8.23).

Further compression is done in the same manner. An 18-day schedule can be obtained with a cost of $2,280, and a 17-day schedule has a cost of $2,460.

All these results are entered in Figure 8.20 for the purpose of evaluation of the anticipated benefits.

FIGURE 8.23
A 19-day, least-cost
schedule

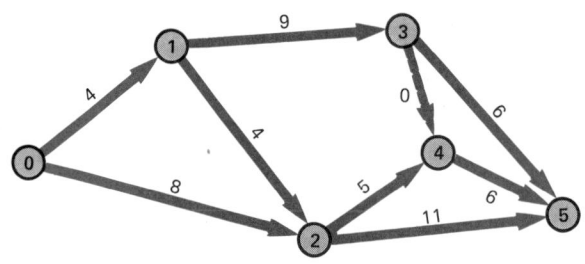

8.9   OTHER NETWORK METHODS

Over the years, several other network techniques have been developed. Some of these are modifications and extensions of PERT and CPM. Various techniques can be classified as either project or nonproject oriented.

Nonproject networks, too

Project-oriented techniques

PERT/Cost   The PERT technique is a time-oriented method that helps plan and control activity times. PERT/Cost is an extension that permits the planning and control of both time and cost. The basic concept of PERT/Cost is that costs are to be measured and controlled primarily on a project basis rather than, say, a departmental basis. Thus, individual activities (or groups of activities) form cost centers for both accounting purposes and managerial control. This is in contrast to conventional cost methods where organizational units, such as departments, are the cost centers. There are several variations of PERT/Cost. For further details see Wiest and Levy [11].

Line of balance (LOB)   This tool is used for monitoring critical activities (which have previously been identified by techniques such as PERT) by graphically investigating deviations from the schedule. See [10] for details.

Other techniques   Several other planning techniques such as: PERT II, PERT III, PERT IV, LESS, TOPS, COMET, PROPT, and the like (all extensions or modifications of PERT or CPM), are available (see [4]).

Graphical evaluation and review technique (GERT)   The application of PERT assumes that all activities must be completed before an event can be realized, that events can not be repeated, that all activities in the network must be completed, that estimates follow the Beta distribution, and that the critical path is the one with the longest elapsed time (sum of mean activity times), even though variances from those mean times exist. GERT is an extension of PERT where all of the above assumptions are relaxed; that is, they are not imposed any longer. (For details see [2] and [13].)

Nonproject-oriented network techniques

Several nonproject-oriented network techniques are similar in their structure to PERT and CPM, but employ different approaches for their solution. Nonproject-oriented network problems include, for example, designing transportation networks in the best manner, designing oil and water piping systems, and routing commodities to destinations. Of these problems, prototypes of maximal flow, shortest route, and the minimal spanning tree are of special interest (see [12]).

8.10   CONCLUSION

PERT and CPM are tools for planning, monitoring, and controlling large, complex projects.

Formulation

The project under consideration is presented graphically as network. Such a presentation is based on the following assumptions:

The assumptions

1. The project can be subdivided into a set of predictable, independent activities, each of which has a clear beginning and end.
2. Each activity can be sequenced as to its predecessors or successors. An activity cannot start until all its predecessors are completed.
3. The network is not cyclical; that is, each activity is executed once and only once during the life of the project. Any repeating activity is considered a different activity.
4. Activity times may be estimated, either as a single-point estimate (CPM) or as a three-point estimate (PERT).
5. The durations of the activities are independent of each other.

In addition, special assumptions are made with respect to:

PERT

a.   Activity duration is assumed to follow the Beta distribution.
b.   The variance of the length of the project is assumed to be equal to the sum of the variances of the activities on the critical path.

CPM

a.   Duration of an activity has a negative linear relation to its execution cost.
b.   The normal time for an activity is the slowest. Executing an activity in a normal time costs the least.

As with any other models, here too, not all the assumptions hold in all cases. However, most of these assumptions hold, at least for the short run, for many complex projects. (For further discussion, see Wiest and Levy [11].) The relaxation of some of these assumptions leads to more complicated network models such as GERT. (See [2] and [13].)

Methodology and solution approaches

The major objective of PERT and CPM analyses is to identify the *critical activities* of a project. The search for these activities can be done through a comparison of all paths in the network (complete enumeration), looking for the longest path (which is labeled the critical path), or through a special algorithm which computes the slack times in the network. In the algorithm case, all events with no slack are situated on the critical path. Finally, PERT and CPM can also be presented as linear programming models (a presentation which makes the computations rather cumbersome). The interested reader is referred to Wiest and Levy [11].

PERT versus CPM

The distinction between PERT and CPM centers around two areas. In PERT, a three-point estimate of time is used which introduces a probabilistic element into the results. In CPM, a cost-time relationship is exhibited and the cost of shortening the project's completion time is evaluated.

Application

PERT and CPM are powerful and flexible tools for decision making. Specifically, they can be used in planning, monitoring, and controlling large projects. Due to their graphical presentation and simple conceptual basis they are relatively easy to explain and therefore easy to implement. Further assistance in implementation is achieved through adaptability to computers. A wide range of computer preprogrammed routines is available from most computer manufacturers.

Identification of critical events and activities enables management to exercise better control of the project, using a management-by-exception philosophy. In addition, control becomes even more effective since the corrective actions and replanning can take effect as soon as deviations in critical activities are reported.

In summary, PERT and CPM can be most effective amplifiers of managers' skills.

8.11 PROBLEMS FOR PART B

10. Given the following project:

   a. Find all "earliest dates," including project completion (T_E's for all events).
   b. Find all "latest dates" (T_L's for all events).
   c. Determine the critical path and the event slack values.
   d. What is the critical path leading to event 5?
   e. What will happen if activity 4–5's actual time slips to 9?
   f. What will be the slack on activity 3–5 if activity 4–5 slips to 9 weeks and activity 5–7 takes 6 weeks.

Activity	Times (weeks)		
	Opti- mistic	Most likely	Pessi- mistic
1–2	5	11	11
1–3	10	10	10
1–4	2	5	8
2–6	1	7	13
3–6	4	4	10
3–7	4	7	10
3–5	2	2	2
4–5	0	6	6
5–7	2	8	14
6–7	1	4	7

11. *a.* Find the probability of finishing the pro-
    ject in Problem 10 in 19 weeks. In 17
    weeks. In 24 weeks.
  b. What is the probability of completing
    event **5** in Problem 10 by 9 weeks?
  c. If management wants to be 80 percent sure
    that the project will be completed by a
    "guaranteed" date, what date should be
    quoted?

12. The following event completion times have
been estimated by a contracting firm:

Activity	Times		
	Opti- mistic	Likely	Pessi- mistic
1–2.	3	6	9
1–3.	1	4	7
3–2.	0	3	6
3–4.	3	3	3
3–5.	2	2	8
2–4.	0	0	6
2–5.	2	5	8
4–6.	4	4	10
4–5.	1	1	1
5–6.	1	4	7

If the firm can complete the project within 14
days, it will be given a $20,000 bonus. If not, it
must pay a penalty of $3,500. Should the firm
accept the contract? What other factors are
probably relevant? Are there any noncritical
paths whose variance might become important?

13. Given a PERT network:

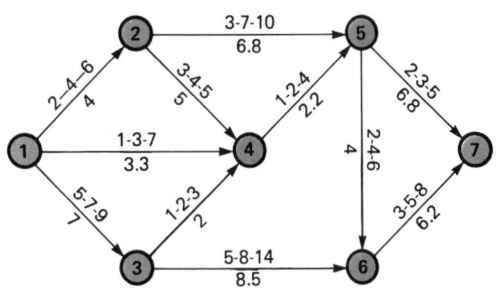

Find:
a. The estimated project completion time.
b. The critical path.
c. The slack on events **2** and **3.**
d. The slack on activities **1–4, 2–5.**
e. The probability the project will be com-
    pleted in 20 weeks.
f. The probability the project will be com-
    pleted in 30 weeks.
g. The number of weeks required to com-
    plete the project with 95 percent certainty.

14. The following data were obtained from a study
of the times required to overhaul a chemical
plant:

Activity	Crash schedule		Normal schedule	
	Time	Cost	Time	Cost
1–2.	3	6	5	4
1–3.	1	5	5	3
2–4.	5	7	10	4
3–4.	2	6	7	4
2–6.	2	5	6	3
4–6.	5	9	11	6
4–5.	4	6	6	3
6–7.	1	4	5	2
5–7.	1	5	4	2

Note: Costs are given in thousands of dollars;
time in weeks.
a. Find the all-normal schedule and cost.
b. Find the all-crash schedule and cost.
c. Find the total cost required to expedite all
    activities from all normal (case *a*) to all
    crash (case *b*).
d. Find the *least-cost* plan for the all-crash
    time schedule. Start from the all-crash pro-
    gram (*b*).

e. Find the least cost for an intermediate time schedule of 17 weeks.

15. Reconsider Problem 1 under the constraint that the project *must* be completed in 16 weeks. This time, however, activities *c, f, h,* and *i* may be crashed as follows:

Activity	Crash time (weeks)	Additional cost per week
c	7	40
f	6	20
h	2	10
i	3	30

Find the best schedule and its cost.

16. The CPM network below has a normal time and a fixed cost of $90/day.

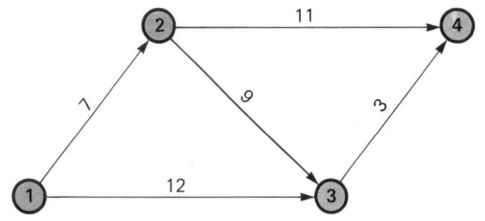

The various activities can be reduced up to their crash time with the additional costs shown:

Activity	Crash time	Cost increase, per day reduction
1–2	4	30 first day, 50 second, 70 third
2–3	6	40 first day, 45 second, 65 third
1–3	10	60 each
2–4	9	35 first, 60 second
3–4	3	——

Find the least cost schedule.

Hint: Start with the normal time of 19 days **1–2–3–4**). The total cost there is 19 × 90 = $1,710. Then start cutting to 18. You save $90 fixed cost but have a cost increase of $30 when you cut activity 1–2 by 1 day. Continue until no further reductions are possible or the cost climbs.

8.12 CASE

THE SHARON CONSTRUCTION CORPORATION

The Sharon Construction Corporation has been awarded a contract for the construction of a 20,000-seat stadium. The construction must start by February 15 and be completed within one year. A penalty clause of $15,000 per week of delay beyond February 15 of next year is written into the contract.

Jim Brown, the president of the company, called for a planning meeting. In the meeting he expressed great satisfaction at obtaining the contract, revealing that the company could net as much as $300,000 on the project. He was confident that the project could be completed on time with an allowance made for the usual delays anticipated in such a large project.

Bonnie Green, the director of personnel, agreed that in a normal year only slight delays might develop due to a shortage of labor.

However, she reminded the president that for such a large project, the company would have to use unionized employees and that the construction industry labor agreements were to expire on November 30. Past experience indicated a fifty-fifty chance for a strike.

Jim Brown agreed that a strike might cause a problem. Unfortunately, there was no way to change the contract. He inquired about the prospective length of a strike. Bonnie figured that such a strike would last at least 8 weeks (70 percent chance) and possibly 12 weeks (30 percent chance).

Jim was not too pleased with these prospects. However, before he had a chance to discuss contingency plans he was interrupted by Jack White, the vice president for engineering. Jack commented that an extremely cold December had been predicted. This factor had not been taken into consideration during earlier estimates since previous forecasts called for milder weather. Concrete pouring in a cold December would require in one out of every three cases (depending on the temperature) special heating that cost $500 per week.

This additional information did not please Jim at all. The chances for delay were mounting. And an overhead expense of $500 per week would be incurred in case of any delay.

The technical details of the project are given in the appendix to this case.

The management team was asked to consider alternatives for coping with the situation. At the end of the week five proposals were submitted.

1. Expedite the pouring of seat gallery supports. This would cost $20,000 and cut the duration of the activity to six weeks.
2. The same as proposal 1, but in addition, put a double shift on the filling of the field. A cost of $10,000 would result in a five-week time reduction.
3. The roof is very important since it precedes several activities. The use of three shifts and some overtime could cut six weeks off the roofing at an additional cost of only $9,000.
4. Do nothing until December 1. Then, if December is indeed cold, defer the pouring until the cold wave breaks, schedule permitting, and heat whenever necessary. If a strike occurs, wait until it is over (no other choice) and then expedite *all* remaining activities. In that case, the duration of any activity could be cut to no more than one third of its normal duration. The additional cost per activity for any week which is cut would be $3,000.
5. Do not take any special action; that is, hope and pray that no strike and no cold December occur (no cost).

Analyze the five proposals and make recommendations.

Appendix: Technical details of the stadium

The stadium is an indoor structure with a seating capacity of 20,000. The project begins with clearing the site, an activity that lasts eight weeks. Once the site is clear, the work can start simultaneously on the structure itself and on the field.

The work in the field involves subsurface drainage which lasts eight weeks, followed by filling for the playing field and track. Only with the completion of the filling (14 weeks), can the installation of the artificial playing turf take place, an activity that consumes 12 weeks.

The work on the structure itself starts with excavation followed by the pouring of concrete footings. Each of these activities takes four weeks. Next comes the pouring of supports for seat galleries (12 weeks), followed by erecting pre-cast galleries (13 weeks). The seats can then be poured (four weeks), and are ready for painting. However, the painting (three weeks) cannot begin until the dressing rooms are completed (four weeks). The dressing rooms can be completed only after the roof is erected (eight weeks). The roof must be erected on a steel structure which takes four weeks to install. This activity can start only after the concrete footings are poured.

Once the roof is erected, work can start simultaneously on the lights (five weeks) and on the scoreboard and other facilities (four weeks). Assume there are 28 days in February and that February 15 falls on a Monday.

8.13 GLOSSARY

Activity A specific job or task which is part of a project and requires time and resources for completion.

CPM (critical path method) A tool which plans and monitors both time and cost where expediting of activities (crashing) is possible.

Crashing Expediting an activity so that it will be completed in less than its normal time up to the minimum possible duration.

Critical activity Any activity on the critical path. All of these activities have either zero slack or the same amount of minimum slack in the network.

Critical path The longest path(s) in the network. This path has the least slack in the network. It is wholly composed of critical activities and critical events.

Dummy activity A fictitious activity which requires no time for completion. Its main purpose is to establish the precedence relationship in a network.

Duration time The time required to complete an activity.

Earliest date (T_E) The earliest time (counted from the beginning of the project) at which an event, or activity, may be finished.

Event A specific accomplishment at a recognizable point in time; a milestone, a check point. An event occurs when *all* preceding activities have been completed. Events use neither time nor resources.

Expected time (t_e) Average duration time for an activity.

Floating slack A slack shared by two or more activities.

Graphical evaluation and review technique (GERT) An extension of PERT that relaxes several of PERT's assumptions making it more realistic (and more complex).

Latest allowable date (T_L) The latest date (counted from the beginning of the project) at which an event can occur without holding up the project's earliest completion date.

Most likely time estimate (t_m) An estimate of an activity duration time which is considered to be the most likely (modal value).

Network A graphical presentation of a project showing the sequential relationship of activities. It consists of nodes representing events and arcs representing activities.

Normal time The lowest-cost activity times in a CPM network.

Optimistic time estimate (t_o) An estimate of an activity's duration under ideal conditions; the shortest possible time to complete the activity. Such conditions occur only one out of 100 times.

Path (in the network) A sequence of activities (described by arcs) leading from the beginning of the project to its end.

PERT (program evaluation and review technique) A planning and monitoring technique for projects based on three time estimates for each activity's duration.

PERT/Cost An extension of PERT that allows the planning and control of both time and cost in a project.

Pessimistic time estimate (t_p) An estimate of the activity's duration under the worst possible conditions which may occur in only one out of 100 cases.

Project A collection of activities with a definable beginning and a definable end (the goal).

Slack The extra time that an activity (or an event) can be held up without delaying the project's completion.

8.14 REFERENCES AND BIBLIOGRAPHY

1. Battersby, A. *Network Analysis for Planning and Scheduling.* 3d ed. New York: John Wiley & Sons, Inc., 1970.

2. Clayton, E. R., and Moore, L. J. "PERT vs. GERT." *Journal of Systems Management* 23 (1972):11–19.

3. Davis, E. W. *Project Management: Techniques, Applications, and Managerial Issues.* Norcross, Ga.: American Institute of Industrial Engineers, Inc., # AIIE-PP&C-76-1, 1976.

4. Elmaghraby, S. B. *Activity Networks: Project Planning and Control by Network Models,* New York: John Wiley & Sons, Inc., 1977.

5. Ford, L. R., and Fulkerson, D. R. *Flows in Networks.* Princeton, N.J.: Princeton University Press, 1962.

6. Harris, R. B. *Precedence and Arrow Networking Techniques for Construction.* New York: John Wiley & Sons, Inc., 1978.

7. Hoare, H. R. *Project Management Using Network Analysis.* Maidenhead, England: McGraw-Hill Book Co., Ltd., 1973.

8. I.B.M. *PERT: A Dynamic Project Planning and Control Tool.* White Plains, N.Y.: IBM, Technical Publication Department, #E20-8067-1, 1964.

9. Moder, J. J., and Phillips, C. R. *Project Management with CPM and PERT.* New York: Van Nostrand-Reinhold Co., 1970.

10. Turban, E. "The Line of Balance—A Management by Exception Tool." *The Journal of Industrial Engineering* 19 (1968):440–448.

11. Wiest, J., and Levy, F. *Management Guide to PERT-CPM.* 2d ed. Englewood Cliffs, N.J.: Prentice Hall, Inc., 1977.

12. Wagner, H. M. *Principles of Operations Research.* 2d ed. Englewood Cliffs, N.J.: Prentice Hall, Inc., 1975.

13. Whitehouse, G. E. *Systems Analysis and Design Using Network Techniques.* Englewood Cliffs, N.J.: Prentice-Hall, Inc., 1973.

9

The managerial problems presented in the previous chapters dealt with situations involving a single decision. Management, however, must frequently consider a *sequence* of decisions where each decision affects future decisions. The tool used for solving certain types of such *sequential decision problems* is called *dynamic programming*.

No single model for solving dynamic programming problems exists. Therefore, these problems are classified into groups, each with its own formulation and method of solution. However, the basic approach and logic for solving all dynamic programming problems is the same. In Part A of the chapter, the basic structure and terminology of dynamic programming are discussed. Some examples are also given to illustrate the prototype problems and their solution approaches.

In Part B of the chapter the mathematics of the dynamic programming method are formulated and additional examples are given.

Dynamic
programming

PART A: BASICS

Jeff knew that he was in trouble. It had been only three days since he received the job he had waited so long for, a dinner cook at the prestigious Queen's Hotel. The recipe for dinner that evening called for 7 ounces of wine; but Jeff, new on the job, could only find a 5-ounce cup and an 8 ounce cup. The problem[1] was that dinner time was quickly approaching, and no time remained to search for other measuring cups or to buy or borrow one. Jeff was tempted to use the 8-ounce cup, filling it not quite to capacity; but as a good cook he knew that accuracy in the use of wine was very important.

Jeff did some quick thinking. Clearly, if 7 ounces of wine were to be contained in one of the cups, it must be the 8-ounce cup. The problem then became one of getting 7 ounces into the 8-ounce cup. Proceeding in the same manner, he realized that if 2 ounces of wine were already in the 8-ounce cup, his problem would have been solved. He could then use a full 5-ounce cup of wine to add to the 2 ounces. How then could he pour 2 ounces of wine into the 8-ounce cup? Presumably by filling one of the cups and then pouring some out. Using the 8-ounce cup meant filling it up and pouring out 6 ounces. Using the 5-ounce cup it would be necessary to pour out 3 ounces. In either case, he needed a 6-ounce or a 3-ounce cup, but he had neither. Which alternative should he explore further? Jeff felt that he was getting nowhere, and dinner time was almost at hand. The problem however intrigued him, and he considered it a bit longer.

After a moment of reflection he was sure that his problem could be solved. If 5 ounces of wine were in the 8-ounce cup (which could be accomplished by filling the 5-ounce cup and pouring it into the 8-ounce cup) and he then refilled the 5-ounce cup and poured it into the 8-ounce cup until the latter was full, then there would be *exactly 2 ounces* left in the 5-ounce cup! All that was left to do then was to empty the 8-ounce cup, pour the 2 ounces from the 5- to the 8-ounce cup, refill the 5-ounce cup and add it to the 2 ounces in the 8-ounce cup to get exactly the required 7 ounces.

"Eureka!" cried Jeff. Only a minute or so was required to pour *exactly* 7 ounces of wine over the dinner beef. Jeff did not realize that his thinking followed the general thought process of perhaps the most fascinating tool of management science—*dynamic programming* (DP).

---

[1] This problem is adapted from a similar one given in Nemhauser [7].

9.1   THE NATURE OF DYNAMIC PROGRAMMING

Jeff's approach to the solution of his problem is typical of dynamic programming (developed by Bellman [2]), which has the following characteristics:

Segmentation

Jeff approached the problem as follows: Since he could not solve the problem in one shot, he asked himself if there was any intermediate position which, if achieved, could take him to his target of 7 ounces. He soon realized that if 2 ounces were already in the 8-ounce cup, then he could solve his original problem. At this point two things actually happened:

1. Jeff *created* and *solved* a second problem, namely, *if* there were 2 ounces of wine in the 8-ounce cup, then, in order to get 7 ounces, all that remained was to add 5 ounces from the second cup to the 2 ounces.
2. Jeff *created* a third problem, namely, how to place 2 ounces of wine in the 8-ounce cup.

Two problems from one

Overall, the original problem was *segmented* into two smaller ones. Once the two smaller problems were solved, the solution to the original problem was achieved.

Sequence of decisions

The segmentation of the complex problem into smaller problems resulted in a *sequence of decisions*. Jeff actually made two decisions. **Each problem a stage**   Each of the smaller problems created is labeled a *stage*.

In a multistage decision problem a sequence of decisions either exists already or must be constructed. For example, the decision about how much preventive maintenance to give to an automobile this year is interrelated with the maintenance (or replacement) decision to be made next year. If the intent is to sell or replace the car next year, less maintenance will probably be prescribed this year. However, if the intent is to keep the car for several years, more extensive maintenance may be recommended.

Rollback approach

Start from the end first   Jeff started the analysis by first solving the last of the newly created problems. Namely, how to achieve the goal of 7 ounces, once 2 ounces were in the cup. Only then did he proceed to solve the next to last problem, namely, how to get 2 ounces in the cup. Such an approach is called the rollback or backward approach, since the problem closest to the target is solved first. Most dynamic programming (DP) problems are solved in this manner. There are, however, certain DP problems which are solved "forward"; that is, start with the problem farthest from the goal first. The approach to be selected depends on the convenience and speed of computation.

Problems solved by dynamic programming

Dynamic programming can solve problems which can either be segmented into a sequence of decisions (such as Jeff's problem) *or* are composed of a series of small problems to begin with.

DP for segmented problems

Before considering the general structure and terminology of dynamic programming, the sequential decision process is illustrated in more detail with another example.

9.2   THE STAGECOACH PROBLEM

In the good old days, stagecoaches were the only means of public transportation. A traveling salesperson, living in San Francisco, decided to cross the country to New York. Figure 9.1 depicts the available stagecoach routes. Each circle on the map represents an exchange point. At an exchange point the traveler moved to another stagecoach since the horses needed to rest. The exchange points are numbered from 1 to 11 as a matter of convenience. The distance in "travel days" is marked above the routes. The problem is to find the route from San Francisco to New York that requires the fewest days of travel.

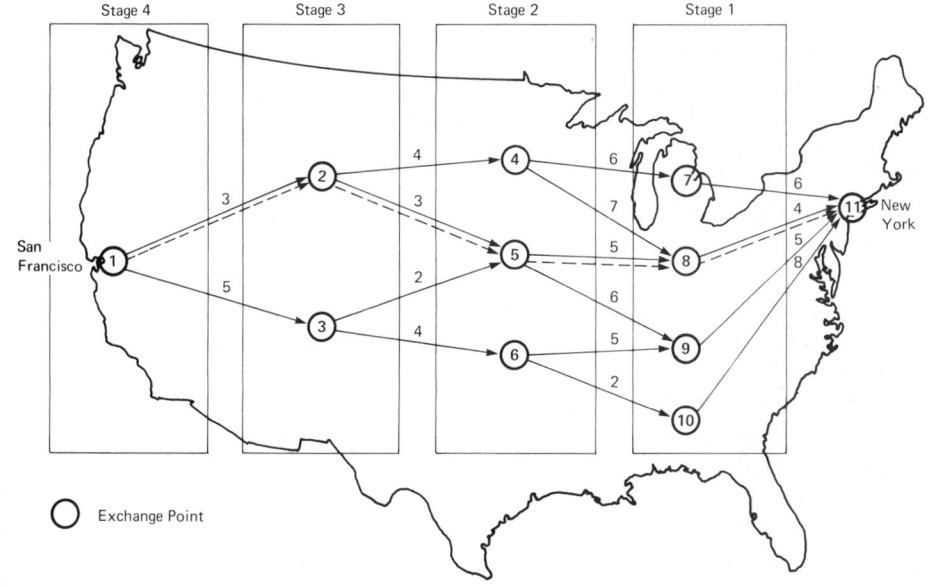

FIGURE 9.1
The stagecoach problem

Solution by complete enumeration

There are only eight possible routes as shown in Table 9.1. Thus, by complete enumeration, route **1—2—5—8—11** (doubled in Figure 9.1 by a broken line) is found to be the fastest, requiring only 15 days.

TABLE 9.1
Possible routes and days of travel—complete enumeration

Route	Days of travel	
①→②→④→⑦→⑪	19	
①→②→④→⑧→⑪	18	
①→②→⑤→⑧→⑪	15	←Minimum
①→②→⑤→⑨→⑪	17	
①→③→⑤→⑧→⑪	16	
①→③→⑤→⑨→⑪	18	
①→③→⑥→⑨→⑪	19	
①→③→⑥→⑩→⑪	19	

The problem with enumeration

In large travel networks, a complete listing and computation of all possible routes may be cumbersome, especially when constraints on travel (e.g., fares and probability of delays) are taken into consideration. Also, the problem may be more complicated when additional objectives (such as safety and fun) are taken into consideration. For those cases, dynamic programming is prescribed.

Solution by dynamic programming (DP)

The first step of dynamic programming is the segmentation of the given problem into smaller problems or *stages*. A stage, in this example, is a decision point where the traveler must decide which stagecoach to take next. This segmentation is done as follows: In San Francisco the traveler must decide on going to either **2** or to **3**. Once the traveler gets to either **2** or to **3**, he (or she) must make another decision which will get him to either **4, 5,** or **6**. A decision at **4, 5,** or **6** will take him to **7, 8, 9,** or **10** from which he may then travel directly to New York, **11.** Thus, no matter

Four stagecoaches, eleven states

which route the traveler selects, he will travel in *four stagecoaches.* Therefore, the problem can be broken into four smaller problems, each made at a zone (stage) regarding what stagecoach to take next. The stages are marked backward, from 4 to 1, for convenience in employing the rollback concept.

In each *stage* the decision maker can be at one and only one exchange point. The exchange points in these examples correspond to what are called *states* in DP. A state is the condition which a system, or the problem, can occupy in a particular stage.

DP eliminates some routes

The use of dynamic programming eliminates the need to investigate *all* possible routes as is done in complete enumeration. In this example the computational work involved in DP is larger than that involved in complete enumeration. However, the larger the DP problem the larger are the savings over complete enumeration.

Details of the solution

The solution procedure uses a rollback analysis; that is, the end of the problem is analyzed first. The salesperson thus first assumes that he (or she) is in New York. The salesperson then repeatedly considers the question of how to proceed from any given exchange point (state) to New York so as to minimize the travel time. The computation is done by stages, starting from the *last* stage which is labeled 1. *Starting from the end*

Stage 1 Once the traveler is in New York he (or she) has reached his goal. Immediately before that he must be in one of the exchange points **7, 8, 9,** or **10.** These points are the states of stage 1. Note that there is *only one* possible way of getting from each of these points to New York. That is, if the traveler is, for example, in exchange point 7, then the *best* and only choice for him is to travel by route $7 \rightarrow 11$ in order to reach New York. In other words, it does not matter how the traveler reached exchange point 7; once he is there he should travel by route $7 \rightarrow 11$ to New York. A similar analysis is made for all other exchange points at stage 1. The results are shown in Table 9.2, and should be treated on an "if-then" basis (e.g., *if* the traveler is in exchange point **7,** *then* the *best* way to continue traveling is $7 \rightarrow 11$, for six days of travel).

TABLE 9.2
The first stage

State	Alternative route	Days of travel to New York	Best route (days)
7	⑦→⑪	6	6
8	⑧→⑪	4	4
9	⑨→⑪	5	5
10	⑩→⑪	8	8

The computation of this stage can be summarized as:

The evaluation of the effectiveness in this case is based on "days of travel." The smaller the number of days, the better. The number of days of travel is the payoff or the *reward*. *The reward*

Stage 2 In order to reach any of the exchange points in stage 1: **7, 8, 9,** or **10,** the traveler must be in one of the stagecoaches that started at exchange points **4, 5,** or **6.** Hence these exchange points are the states of *stage 2*.

From each of these states, the best possibility of getting to New York is examined. However, instead of enumerating all routes to New York, only the routes to the states of stage 1 are examined. This is done because it is *already known* how to get from each state in stage 1 to New York in the best way.

Considering state **4** first, there are two alternative ways of reaching stage 1: $4 \rightarrow 7$ or $4 \rightarrow 8$. The former requires six days plus optimal time to New York, computed in stage 1 as 6, for a total of 12. The latter requires 7 days + 4 days = 11 days. Of the two, the better is $4 \rightarrow 8$ with 11 days. Similar computations are executed for states **5** and **6**. The results are shown in Table 9.3. Notice that the best solution is computed for each state independently.

TABLE 9.3
The second stage

State	Alternative route	Distance to stage 1	Best distance from stage 1 to New York (from Table 9.2)	Total distance	Best route
4	④→ ⑦	6	6	12	
	④→ ⑧	7	4	11	←
5	⑤→ ⑧	5	4	9	←
	⑤→ ⑨	6	5	11	
6	⑥→ ⑨	5	5	10	←
	⑥→ ⑩	2	8	10	←

Stage 3 In order to get to either exchange point **4**, **5**, or **6**, in the previous stage, it is necessary to exchange stagecoaches at points **2** or **3**. These points are the states of stage 3.

Table 9.4 summarizes the computations for the third stage. Note that the best results found in stage 2 above are used as an input for computing stage 3.

TABLE 9.4
The third stage

State	Alternative route	Distance to stage 2	Best distance from stage 2 to New York (from Table 9.3)	Total distance	Best route
2	②→④	4	11	15	
	②→⑤	3	9	12	←
3	③→⑤	2	9	11	←
	③→⑥	4	10	14	

Stage 4 Finally, the traveler is at the initial point. There are two alternatives here: either go to exchange point **2** or to exchange point **3**.

There is only one state to be examined, state **1**. The computations are shown in Table 9.5.

State	Alternative route	Distance to stage 3 (immediate reward)	Best distance from stage 3 to New York (from Table 9.4)	Total distance (reward)	Best route
1	①→②	3	12	15	←
	①→③	5	11	16	

TABLE 9.5
The fourth stage

Now it is possible to reconstruct the optimal solution for the entire problem, this time going forward. In stage 4 the solution is to go **1 → 2**. In stage 3 we know that *if* one is at state **2** it is best to go to state **5** (Table 9.4). In stage 2 we know that if one is at state **5** it is best to go to state **8** (Table 9.3). Finally Table 9.2 tells us that from state **8** the best way to get to New York is **8 → 11**. The optimal travel route is:

$$1 \rightarrow 2 \rightarrow 5 \rightarrow 8 \rightarrow 11$$

for a total of 15 travel days (Table 9.5 gives this total).

Note that in each of the stages and for each state the following computations were executed (see Table 9.5):

a. Total Distance (reward) = Distance to Previous Stage (immediate reward) + Best Distance from Previous Stage to New York (optimal reward in previous stage)

b. Best Route (optimal reward) = Smallest Total Distance (reward).

These two computational procedures are the backbone of dynamic programming.

9.3 TERMINOLOGY AND STRUCTURE

The stagecoach example will be used to help define the six major terms and concepts of dynamic programming.

Stages The stagecoach problem was solved by breaking it into four subproblems, each of which is considered a *stage*. Thus, the first step in any dynamic programming solution is to divide the problem into stages, if it is not originally so divided.

Definition: A stage refers to a particular decision point on the solution route. For example, each time a decision about the next stagecoach has to be made a stage is encountered.

A stage as a decision point

States At each stage the traveling salesperson could have been in one (and only one) of several possible exchange points, each of which is considered a *state*. As the salesperson traveled along the route, he moved from state to state.

A state as an exchange point

The decision process A DP solution is viewed as a process of moving from stage to stage making a decision at each. The direction of the move can be either forwards, from the *initial* to the *final* stage, or backwards, which is termed "rollback", from the *final* to the *initial* stage. At each stage a decision about what state to be in, is made. However, in some DP problems the system does not change its state even though it goes through several stages. For example, a machine may remain in good condition for several weeks in the case where each stage is considered to be one week and the possible conditions of the machine are the states.

Reward The dependent variable in the stagecoach example was the "days of travel." In dynamic programming the dependent variable is called the *reward*. Three types of reward are distinguished:

Three types of rewards

1. Immediate reward This is the reward associated with a move between two adjacent stages. For example, in Table 9.5 the column "Distance to stage 3" designates the reward. This reward is an *immediate reward* for each alternative route (state to state) between two adjacent stages.

2. The total reward An examination of Tables 9.3, 9.4, and 9.5 indicates that at each stage, and *for each state in that stage,* the total reward (i.e., the total distance from each state to New York) was derived as the sum of the *immediate reward* (distance to previous stage), plus the *optimal reward* obtained in the previous stage.

3. Optimal total reward In each stage and for each state there are usually several alternatives to reach the next stage and eventually the goal. For each alternative the total reward is computed (according to 2). The best of all total rewards in each state is the *optimal total reward*.

In terms of the stagecoach example, the optimal total reward for each exchange point (state) is the shortest route from that exchange point to New York.

Notice that the optimal total reward from the last state (San Francisco) gives the optimal solution for the original unsegmented problem.

The recursive relation

The recursive relation The function that ties together the immediate reward, the total reward, and the optimal total reward is called the *recursive relation*. This function will be discussed in more detail in Part B. This relationship is derived from the principle of optimality.

A policy as a contingency plan

Policy A policy in DP refers to a complete, predetermined plan for selecting a course of action under every possible circumstance. In addition to solving the original problem, DP solves several subproblems. The solution to these is in a form of a *policy*. For example, in the stagecoach problem the solution in Table 9.4 says: *if* you are at state **2** it is best to go to **5**; *if* you are at state **3** go also to **5**. Overall, dynamic programming dictates an *optimal policy* to follow, which is the *best* of all possible policies for the entire problem, derived from the collection of policies for the subproblems.

The basic idea—the principle of optimality   In dynamic programming, the analysis is based on Bellman's *principle of optimality* [2] which states:

> An optimal policy has the property that whatever the initial state and initial decision are, the remaining decisions must constitute an optimal policy with regard to the state resulting from the first decision.

In the stagecoach example this principle implies that:

> If an exchange point is on the optimal route, then the shortest path from that exchange point to New York is also on the optimal route.

The implication of the principle of optimality is that, starting at a current stage, the optimal policy (decision) for the remaining stages depends only upon the state at the current stage and not upon the means that the system used in arriving at that state. (That is, the optimal policy is independent of the policies [decisions] adopted at prior stages.)   The basic principle of DP

The structure of dynamic programming

To illustrate the general structure of a DP problem, let us visualize what happened in an *intermediate stage* (3) of the stagecoach problem (Table 9.4) by viewing it as an input-output system.

Assume that we arrived at stage 3 somehow; then, a question may be asked: What is the best route to arrive at stage 2? (Remember, this is exactly how Jeff approached his problem: "Assume that 2 ounces are in the large cup, what is the best way to get 7 ounces in that cup?")

The answer to such a question depends on what state we are in at stage 3. If we are in state **2**, then route **2 → 5** will be selected. If we are in state **3**, then route **3 → 5** will be selected.

The actual location (state **2** or state **3**) can be determined only after stage 4 is analyzed (see Table 9.5). Therefore, the *input* to stage 3 is the *output* of stage 4. In a similar manner, the *output* of stage 3 is the *input* to stage 2. In graphical terms this is shown as follows: Input-decision-reward-output

Let: s_3 = input into stage 3 (state **2** or **3**).
d_3 = decision at state **3**.
r_3 = reward at stage 3.
s_2 = output to stage 2 (state **4, 5,** or **6**).

Then, the input-output relationship can be viewed as a diagram as shown in Figure 9.2.

Diagrams like that of Figure 9.2 can be drawn for every stage in the problem. Since the stages are connected, the entire DP process can be shown as a chain of input-output relationships. In Figure 9.3 the stagecoach problem is displayed in this manner.

Diagramming the DP problem in this manner helps its formulation in mathematical terms, as will be shown in Part B.

FIGURE 9.2
Stage 3 input and output

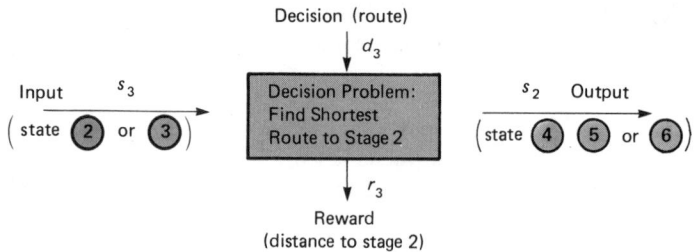

FIGURE 9.3
The stagecoach problem

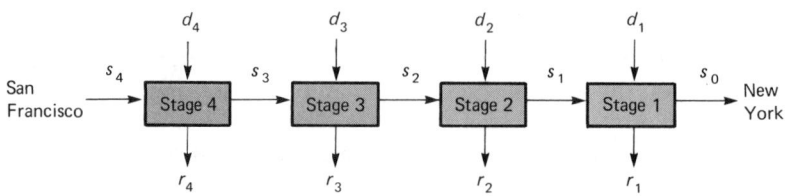

Prototype dynamic programming problems

Unlike most other mathematical models, no *standard* recursive relation exists. Therefore, it is impossible to use a general computational tool (such as the simplex method in linear programming). However, it is possible to classify DP problems into "families" (or prototypes) and build a special computational procedure for each. While these prototypes differ in their structures and computational procedures, they share the general approach of DP. These prototypes are:

Families of DP problems

1. *Allocation processes.* These processes (to be discussed in the next section) are segmented into smaller allocation problems.
2. *Multiperiod processes.* These processes are originally segmented, having two or more time periods. These are also known as smoothing or scheduling processes.
3. *Network processes.* PERT and other networks can often be viewed as DP problems and solved as such. The stagecoach problem is one example of a network process.
4. *Multistage production processes.* These problems arise in industrial production situations.
5. *Feedback control processes.* Feedback problems occur in electronics, aerospace, and automated production.
6. *Markovian decisions.* Markovian situations are discussed in Chapter 10.

The remainder of this chapter is primarily devoted to illustrating some of these prototype problems; other examples can be found in Bellman and Dreyfus [3].

9.4   ALLOCATION PROCESSES

The allocation of resources among potential recipients is a major problem of organizations. In cases with a linear objective function and constraints, the problem may be presented as a linear programming problem. However, in many cases the mathematical programming formulation leads to integer or nonlinear models which require difficult or costly solution procedures. Dynamic programming offers a better way to handle some of these complicated cases.

An investment example

The management of the Southern Corporation is considering the allocation of $4 million among its three plants. It has already been decided that the allocation per plant is to be either 0, 1, 2, 3, or 4 million dollars. (An investment is made in whole units of $1 million.)

Each plant has submitted its forecast of yearly returns corresponding to different levels of money invested. The forecast returns are given in Table 9.6. For example, an initial investment of $2 million in plant A will yield a return of $.5 million. The problem is to determine the optimal allocation of money to each plant in order to maximize the overall expected return. This problem cannot be solved as a linear program, first because it is an integer programming problem and, moreover, because the returns are nonlinear.

DP for investment decisions

Amount allocated (in million $)	Return (reward) ($ million)		
	Plant A	*Plant B*	*Plant C*
0	0	0	0
1	.2	.3	.4
2	.5	.6	.9
3	1.5	1.2	1.1
4	1.4	1.5	1.6

TABLE 9.6
Southern Corporation investment alternatives

Formulation   In order to solve this problem it will be segmented into three stages; each stage represents an allocation to one plant. The relationship between the stages is shown in Figure 9.4. Again, a rollback

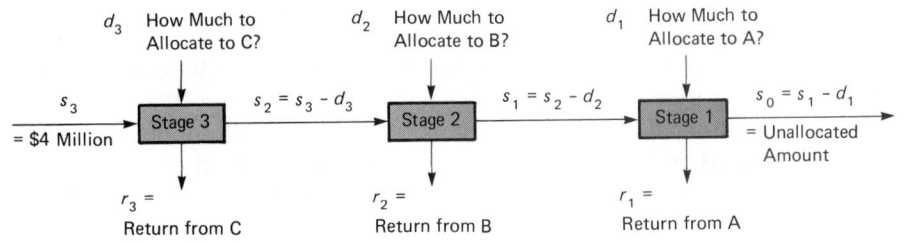

FIGURE 9.4
An allocation problem

approach will be followed. First an allocation will be made to plant A (arbitrarily considered the "last" plant), then to B, and then to C.

States In each stage there are five possible states; allocate either 0, 1, 2, 3, or 4.

Solution

Stage 1 In this stage either $0, $1, $2, $3, or $4 million will be available for allocation to plant A. The computed returns from the investment in plant A are given in Table 9.7. The amount available (0, 1, 2, 3, or 4) is designated s_1. The optimal policy is: If 0, 1, 2, or 3 are available, the best solution is to allocate all the money. But if $4 million are available, then it is best to allocate only $3 million since the optimal return from $3 million is larger than the return from $4 million (a situation which is unusual but possible). This information is shown in Table 9.7; the last column is composed of the highest reward (optimal) in each row. The numbers that are shaded are the highest, and they point to the optimal policy (decision).

TABLE 9.7
Stage 1: Allocation to plant A

Amount s_1, to be allocated	Decision d_1: How much to give to Plant A, by state					Optimal Reward
	0	1	2	3	4	
0	0					0
1	0	.2				.2
2	0	.2	.5			.5
3	0	.2	.5	1.5		1.5
4	0	.2	.5	1.5	1.4	1.5

Stage 2 At this stage it is necessary to determine how to split the available dollars between A and B. Let us designate the allocation to both A and B as s_2.

Thus, of the allocated amount s_2, plant B gets d_2 while the remaining $s_2 - d_2$ is allocated to plant A in the best possible way, as computed in stage 1.

For each value of s_2 (0, 1, 2, 3, or 4) there are several alternatives for allocation; they must all be considered. This is done by examining all five possible states.

For state $s_2 = 0$: No allocation, no return.

For state $s_2 = 1$: Either 1 to B and 0 to A (total return of .3 + 0 = .3) or 0 to B and 1 to A (total return of 0 + .2 = .2). It is clear that 1 to B is a better allocation. That is, *if* $1 million is ever left to be allocated between A and B, B should get it. This information is then entered in Table 9.8. Table 9.8 includes the computations for all the remaining states. In each state the optimal total reward is computed.

TABLE 9.8
Stage 2: Allocation to plant B

Amount s_2, to be allocated	Decision d_2: How much to allocate to B; the remainder goes to A in an optimal manner					Optimal reward
	0	*1*	*2*	*3*	*4*	
0	0					0
1	0 + .2 = .2	.3 + 0 = .3				.3
2	0 + .5 = .5	.3 + .2 = .5	.6 + 0 = .6			.6
3	0 + 1.5 = 1.5	.3 + .5 = .8	.6 + .2 = .8	1.2 + 0 = 1.2		1.5
4	0 + 1.5 = 1.5	.3 + 1.5 = 1.8	.6 + .5 = 1.1	1.2 + .2 = 1.4	1.5 + 0 = 1.5	1.8

In general, the computations in the body of the table are those of the *total reward*, which is the sum of the immediate reward plus the optimal reward from stage 1.

Example for state $s_2 = 3$. The row 3 in Table 9.8 was computed as shown in Table 9.9. Once all total rewards are computed for each row, then the *highest* one is selected and designated as the "optimal total reward."

TABLE 9.9
Detailed computation of $s_2 = 3$

d_2 Allocation to B	Remainder to allocate to A	Immediate reward	Optimal from stage 1	Total reward	Optimal total reward
0...............	3	0	1.5	1.5	←
1...............	2	.3	.5	.8	
2...............	1	.6	.2	.8	
3...............	0	1.2	0	1.2	

Stage 3 In this stage an allocation decision is made to C and the remaining amount is then *best allocated* between A and B, according to the policy described in stage 2. At this final stage only one state will be shown:[2] $s_3 = 4$. The computations are shown in Table 9.10 in the standard manner used before, and in a somewhat more detailed manner in Table 9.11. Thus, the best allocation is: $d_3 = 1$, $d_2 = 0$, $d_1 = 3$; that is, 1 to C and 3 to A with a return of $1.9 million.

Some observations

Several valuable observations can be made from the example shown here.

---
[2] The other states are inferior and therefore are omitted.

TABLE 9.10
Stage 3: Allocation to plant C, state $s_3 = 4$

s_3	Amount allocated to C, d_3					Optimal total reward
	0	*1*	*2*	*3*	*4*	
4	$0 + 1.8 = 1.8$	$.4 + 1.5 = \boxed{1.9}$	$.9 + .6 = 1.5$	$1.1 + .3 = 1.4$	$1.6 + 0 = 1.6$	$\boxed{1.9}$

TABLE 9.11
Stage 3, state $s_3 = 4$

Alternatives	Reward to C	Reward from best allocation among A and B (as computed in stage 2)	Optimal total reward	
$d_3 = 4$ to C, 0 to A & B	1.6	0	1.6	
$d_3 = 3$ to C, 1 to A & B*	1.1	.3 (1 to B)	1.4	
$d_3 = 2$ to C, 2 to A & B	.9	.6 (2 to B)	1.5	
$d_3 = 1$ to C, 3 to A & B	.4	1.5 (3 to A)	1.9	←Maximum
$d_3 = 0$ to C, 4 to A & B	0	1.8 (1 to B, 3 to A)	1.8	(best)

* Allocated between A and B in an optimal manner as computed in stage 2.

1. For every value of s, at every stage, the optimal return is computed in the analysis.
2. The marginal return for a given allocation policy, as s is increased (decreased) in units of $1 million, can easily be observed from previously computed tables.
3. A sensitivity analysis can easily be performed. For example, if management decides to consider only two plants, then the optimal solution can be found in the intermediate computations. (For example, if only A and B are considered, the best solution is read from Table 9.8 as: $d_2 = 1$ and $d_1 = 3$ for a total return of $1.8 million.)

DP advantages and characteristics

4. The dynamic programming procedure also identifies the *second* best alternative. In this case it is (Table 9.10): $d_3 = 0$; that is, allocate nothing to C, 1 to B and 3 to A with an expected profit of $1.8 million. Similarly, the third best solution, and so on, can be found. These solutions are frequently important when qualitative factors have to be considered.
5. Adding a new plant to the problem merely adds an additional stage to the computations.
6. The dynamic programming process required 18 calculations for this problem. A solution by complete enumeration would have required only 15 calculations. Again, there is no saving of computational effort in such small problems. However, the savings would have been large had the problem been larger.

9.5 CONCLUDING REMARKS

Dynamic programming is an approach for finding an optimal solution to a problem by breaking it into smaller subproblems, each labeled a *stage.* In each stage, that is, for each subproblem, there exist several *states,* or positions, that the system under study can occupy.

The dynamic programming procedure considers one subproblem (stage) at a time, usually beginning from the *ending* stage. For each stage, a set of optimal solutions is derived for each state in that stage with the aid of complete enumeration or using an algorithm, such as linear programming. This set is then used for the stage next in line. The process continues until all the subproblems are solved. The solution to the subproblems then leads to an optimal solution for the original problem.

The application of dynamic programming is limited by two factors. First, the approach has to be tailored for each different type of problem. Every time a problem differs slightly, then a new formulation must be designed. Second, while DP can be used to solve complex problems where other tools fail, it suffers from the "curse of dimensionality." The primary effect of this "curse" is an exponential growth in the amount of computation with problem size; that is, if the problem doubles in size, the amount of computation quadruples. Despite the meager number of applications of DP it has tremendous potential due to its ability to attack difficult problems that other optimization tools fail to solve.

Some limitations of DP

The curse of dimensionality

9.6 PROBLEMS FOR PART A

1. Given the following network:

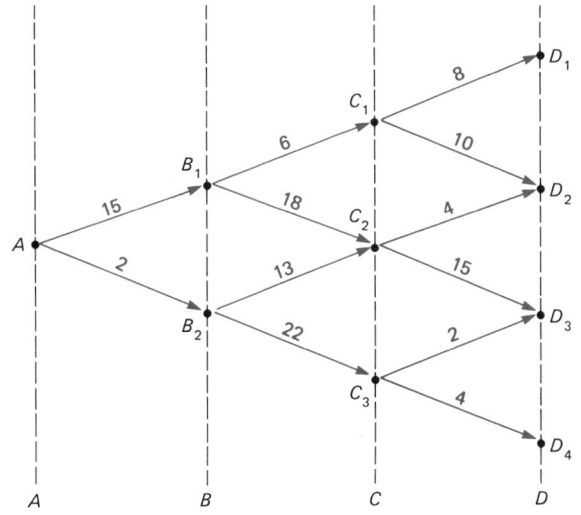

Determine the shortest path in the network going from point A to *any* point on the line D. Use dynamic programming.

2. XYZ Publishing Company divides the country into two zones: eastern with headquarters in Philadelphia and western with headquarters in Los Angeles. Regional sales centers in the eastern zone are in Atlanta, Boston, and Chicago. Regional sales centers in the western zone are in Seattle, Denver, Houston, and Reno.

The president wants to fly from Philadelphia to Los Angeles and stop in one eastern and one western sales center. The estimated travel expenses from Philadelphia to the eastern centers (assuming that the eastern center is visited first), are: Boston, $100; Atlanta, $130;

Chicago, $110. The estimated travel expenses between the eastern centers and the western centers are:

	Denver	Reno	Houston	Seattle
Boston.......	160	150	180	180
Atlanta	80	130	110	200
Chicago......	130	100	140	150

The travel expenses from each of the western centers to Los Angeles are: Seattle, $230; Denver, $190; Houston, $140; Reno, $180.

Find which cities the president should visit in order to minimize travel expenses (use dynamic programming).

3. BB Auto Repair Shop, Inc., has three departments: metal, painting, and testing. Cars are repaired through all three departments. The metal department has three parallel work stations: M, N, and O. The painting department has two parallel work stations: P and Q. And the testing department has three parallel work stations: T, U, and V.

Whenever a car is towed in, its repair costs are estimated. This morning a car was brought in, and management would like to know through which stations the car should be processed to minimize the cost.

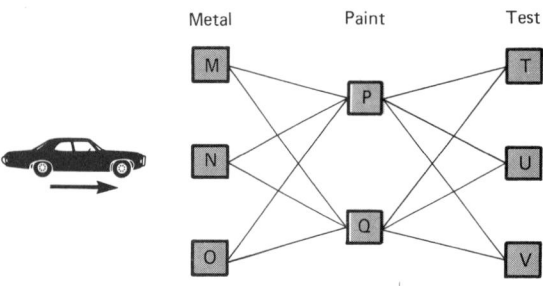

Metal   Paint   Test

The costs at stations M, N, and O are 200, 220, and 230, respectively. The cost at painting and testing depends on what happened in the previous stations. For example, if the metal work is not perfect, as is frequently the case in station M, the painting cost is slightly higher. The conditional cost relationships are:

Cost in the painting department

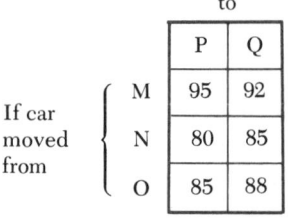

		to	
		P	Q
If car moved from	M	95	92
	N	80	85
	O	85	88

Cost in the testing department

		to		
		T	U	V
If car moved from	P	25	30	32
	Q	32	30	26

Find the sequence of stations that will minimize the repair cost (use dynamic programming).

4. Atlantic Electric Corporation produces and sells CB radios. A new model has just been developed with an estimated life of four years. The company must decide on an initial price which, in order to be competitive, must be either $90, $100, or $110. The company's policy is to change prices, if necessary, only once a year. When a change is made (up *or* down), it is a $10 change.

The anticipated yearly profit from making and selling the CB radios, for each price/year combination, is given in the following table (in thousands of dollars):

Price \ Year	1	2	3	4
90	20	18	30	24
100	24	18	35	28
110	25	15	32	31

For example, if the price in the third year is $90, then the company will make $30,000.

Find the optimal prices the company should set each year. Use dynamic programming. *Hint:* Stages are years; states are price levels. Assume the price levels are either $90, $100, or $110 all the time.

5. ABC Development Corporation plans to use one or more of three subcontractors to build six cooling units. The corporation would like to determine the best allocation of cooling units to subcontractors.

The table below shows the bids submitted by each subcontractor. The data are in thousands of dollars.

Units (number)	Subcon- tractor A	Subcon- tractor B	Subcon- tractor C
1	5	4	5
2	10	8	9
3	14	11	12
4	17	18	18
5	20	25	24
6	27	30	30

For example, subcontractor A would build two units for $10,000 and three units for $14,000. Differences in the bids result from locational considerations and other such variations.

Use dynamic programming to determine the best allocation of six cooling units among the subcontractors.

6. A sales manager must decide how to allocate her four available salespersons among three districts in her territory. The sales results (in thousands of dollars per month) are shown below as a function of the number of salespersons assigned to a district.

   a. Use dynamic programming to find that assignment of salespersons to districts which will maximize sales.

District \ Salespersons assigned	0	1	2	3	4
A	5	10	13	15	17
B	6	10	14	17	15
C	4	9	11	15	18

   b. Without resolving the problem, find the second best assignment.
   c. Without resolving the problem, find the best solution if only three salespersons are available.

7. A fancy restaurant operates a fleet of vans for deliveries. A new van costs $10,000. It is estimated that in the future the vans will continue to cost $10,000. The operating cost and the resale value as related to the age of the van are given below:

Age of van	Operating cost ($)	Resale value ($)
1	2,000	7,000
2	2,500	5,000
3	3,000	3,500
4	3,700	2,200
5	4,500	1,000
6	5,500	600

All the data, including the cost of new vans, are given in present values and are assumed to remain constant in the future.

Replacement decisions are made once a year. The restaurant buys only new vans. Find the replacement policy (i.e., at what age a van should be replaced) that minimizes the total cost.

PART B: EXTENSIONS

9.7 PROBABILISTIC PROBLEMS

DP can deal with risk

The previous two examples of DP dealt with deterministic situations. DP, however, can deal effectively with probabilistic problems as well.

Example: The purchasing agent's problem

A purchasing agent must buy, for his company, a special beryllium alloy in a market that trades only once a week. Each week there is a 20 percent chance that the alloy will cost $10,000; 50 percent that it will cost $11,000, and 30 percent that it will cost $12,000. At the present time, the agent knows that in order to meet the company's production schedule, the alloy must be bought within the next month (four trading weeks). The agent worries that if he waits too long, price rises may force him to buy the alloy at a premium. On the other hand, if he buys early, future prices may be lower and he may miss an opportunity to economize. Thus, the timing of the purchase poses a delicate managerial problem.

Formulation The agent's decision of "when to buy" can be viewed as a sequence of decisions. In each of the four trading weeks, a decision must be made between two alternatives: either to buy or to wait. The analysis starts from the final week and proceeds *backwards* in time.

Stages: Each week is considered a stage; therefore, there will be four stages.

States: There are two states in each week, to buy or to wait.

Reward: The expected (average) price is used as the criterion. It is labeled r_i where i designates the stage.

Solution

Stage 1 Rolling back, the first stage occurs at week 4. At that time there is no choice; if the alloy has not already been bought, it *must* be bought then. The expected price of the alloy is computed as the expected value, designated by $E(r_1)$.

$$E(r_1) = .2 \times \$10,000 + .5 \times \$11,000 + .3 \times \$12,000 = \$11,100$$

This situation is shown in a decision tree presentation in Figure 9.5.

Stage 2 (third week) The agent can either *buy* at the price prevailing that week (either $10,000, $11,000, or $12,000) or he can *wait* until the fourth week. The decision is based on the following criterion:

If the prevailing price at the third week is *more* than the expected price in the last week (already calculated as $11,100), the agent should

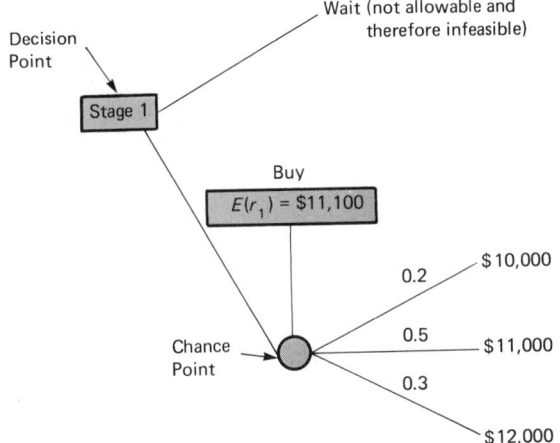

FIGURE 9.5
Decision at stage 1

wait until the final week. If the prevailing price is *less* than the expected price in the final week, the agent should buy. If the two prices are the same, he is indifferent between the two alternatives. The agent may now extend the decision tree (Figure 9.6) for the analysis.

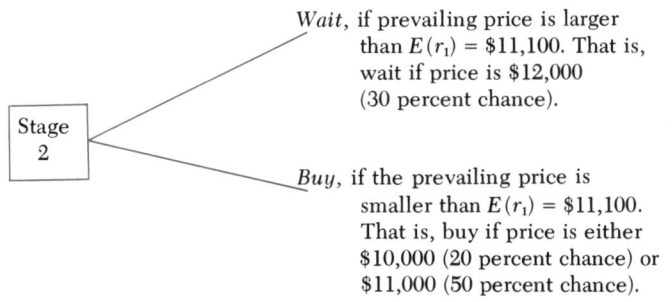

FIGURE 9.6
Decision at stage 2

Since the price at any week can take only three possible values, it is possible to compute the expected reward in much the same way as was done for stage 1:

- There is a 30 percent chance of waiting, in which case the reward will be $11,100, realized in week 4.
- There is a 20 percent chance of buying at $10,000.
- There is a 50 percent chance of buying at $11,000.

The expected reward at stage 2 is therefore:

$$E(r_2) = \underbrace{.2(\$10,000) + .5(\$11,000)}_{\text{Immediate reward}} + \underbrace{.3(\$11,100)}_{\substack{\text{Best reward from} \\ \text{previous stage}}} = \$10,830$$

332

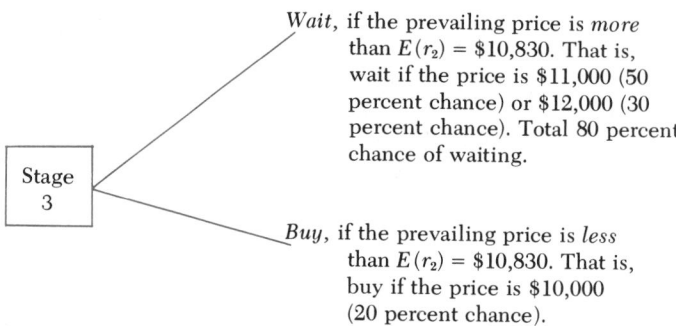

FIGURE 9.7
Decision at stage 3

Stage 3 (second week)   The agent will buy if the price is less than $E(r_2)$ and wait if it is more. The situation is shown in Figure 9.7. The expected reward is:

If *wait* (80 percent):   the expected price will be $10,830.
If *buy* (20 percent):   the price will be $10,000.

$$E(r_3) = .2(\$10,000) + .8(\$10,830) = \$10,664$$

Stage 4 (initial week)   The agent will buy if the price at the first week is smaller than $E(r_3)$, otherwise wait. Figure 9.8 shows this situation.

FIGURE 9.8
Decision at stage 4

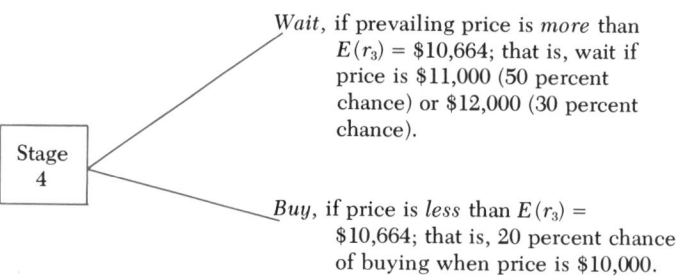

The expected reward is:

$$E(r_4) = .2(\$10,000) + (.5 + .3)(\$10,664) = \$10,531$$

FIGURE 9.9
Decision rules for the purchasing agent

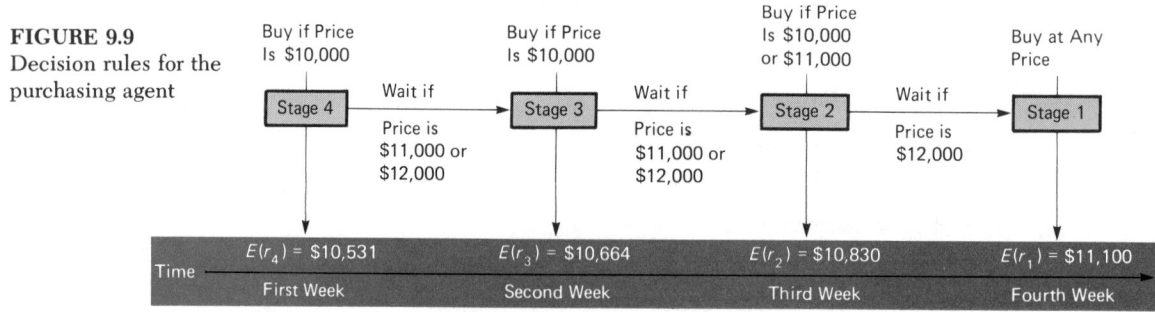

Summary

If the purchasing agent pursues the *optimal policy*, then the expected price he will pay is $10,531. The decision rules for each week are shown in Figure 9.9.

9.8 MATHEMATICAL PRESENTATION AND OPTIMIZATION TECHNIQUES

In all previous examples we avoided mathematical symbols whenever possible. However, we stated over and over again that the relationship between the reward at each stage and the optimal reward is the key to the DP process. This reward relationship is called the *recursive relationship*. In dynamic programming it is possible to write a recursive relationship for each problem. Once such an equation has been written it is much easier to execute the DP computations. The recursive relationship expresses the notion that an optimal reward at any given stage, for any given state, is given as the value of the best alternative, when each alternative includes the total of the immediate reward and the optimal reward computed in the previous stage.

The recursive relationship

General formulation

Let:

n = index for current stage. This index tells how many stages exist from the current stage to the end of the process (problem).

$n - 1$ = previous stage.

s_n = state of the system in the current stage for which the recursive relations hold.

s_{n-1} = state in the previous stage.

$f_n(s_n)$ = total reward realized for each alternative, starting from state s in stage n to the end of the process.

$f_n^*(s_n)$ = optimal total reward; that is, the best $f_n(s_n)$ from state s in stage n.

$f_{n-1}^*(s_{n-1})$ = optimal total reward obtained in the previous stage.

$r_n(s_n,d_n)$ = immediate reward realized in stage n, when decision d_n is made for a specific value s_n of the state variable.

d_n = decision among alternatives made at stage n in the state under consideration.

The recursive relationship (minimization) for state s, at stage n, is then:

$$f_n^*(s_n) = \min_{d_n} \left[r_n(s_n,d_n) + f_{n-1}^*(s_{n-1}) \right] \qquad (9.1)$$

We will fit this formulation to a DP problem in Section 9.9.

Optimization techniques

The basic approach of dynamic programming is to reduce a complex problem into a series of simpler subproblems. However, once such a reduction has been performed, it is still necessary to solve the subproblems. The following methods can be used in solving these subproblems:

Enumeration In many cases complete enumeration is very efficient since the number of possible solutions in the subproblems is usually finite and small. In some cases it is possible to approximate an infinite number of possible solutions by using a finite number (e.g., replace a continuous function by a discrete one) and then employ enumeration.

Classical calculus The classical calculus methods can be used for certain nonconstrained optimization problems, as well as for simple cases of constrained optimization.

Lagrange multipliers and the Kuhn-Tucker conditions Equality constraints can be handled with the aid of the Lagrangian function. Inequality constraints are treated with the help of the Kuhn-Tucker conditions. (Refer to [6] or [8].)

Mathematical programming In certain cases the subproblems are actually linear, integer, or nonlinear programming problems and can be solved as such.

Sequential search In some cases iterative procedures may be used where the solution is improved step by step (e.g., see Nemhauser [7]).

Other techniques Several other optimization techniques can be used. See Nemhauser [7] and Gluss [5] for details.

9.9 THE KNAPSACK PROBLEM

Consider the following problem. A knapsack or a container has a limited weight and/or volume capacity. It is to be loaded with different items, each with a given weight (or volume). Each item has a certain value. The problem is to find what items to include in the knapsack to maximize the total value.

What should go in the knapsack?

An example of a knapsack problem is a spaceship where weight is limited. The problem is: What instruments to include so that the scientific utility of the mission is maximized.

Another example involves production scheduling. Suppose that it is necessary to determine how many units to produce, among several possible products, on one machine. The value of the products is known and so is their use of machine time, which is limited. The problem is: What products to produce and in what quantities (integer) so that the value is maximized. The knapsack problem appears in various forms and can often be formulated as an integer programming problem. Integer programming problems are, however, often difficult to solve, especially if they are nonlinear. Therefore, dynamic programming is used.

Example

Four types of items are considered for loading on an airplane. The weights and values of the types of items are given in Table 9.12. Find which items should be loaded on the plane, and in what quantities if the maximum capacity of the plane is 11 tons and the objective is to maximize the value of the shipment.

Item	Weight (tons)	Value
A	2	18
B	4	25
C	5	30
D	3	20

TABLE 9.12
Knapsack items

Mathematical presentation

Let:
  n = the stage (item) under consideration.
  x_n = number of items of type n to load.
  v_n = value of one type n item.
  w_n = weight of one type n item.
  K = maximum available capacity.
  s_n = state (remaining weight available) at stage n.
      Integer programming formulation The problem can be presented as:

$$\text{maximize } z = \sum_{n=1}^{4} v_n x_n \qquad (9.2)$$

$$\text{subject to:}$$

$$\sum_{n=1}^{4} w_n x_n \le K$$

and x_n is a nonnegative integer.
    For our example:

$$\text{maximize } z = 18x_1 + 25x_2 + 30x_3 + 20x_4$$
$$\text{subject to:}$$
$$2x_1 + 4x_2 + 5x_3 + 3x_4 \le 11$$

and x_1, x_2, x_3, x_4 are nonnegative integers.
    Dynamic programming formulation This problem is an extension of the allocation problem discussed in Section 9.4.

Stages: Each type of item is considered a stage.

States: The remaining capacity (in integer tons) available for allocation; that is, the states are 0, 1, 2, . . . , 11

The decision at each stage: How many units of each item to include in the optimal mix.

The recursive relationship: The recursive relationship for this problem is:

$$f_n^*(s_n) = \max_{x_n} \left[v_n x_n + f_{n-1}^*(s_n - w_n x_n) \right] \qquad (9.3)$$

where:

s_n designates the amount of the remaining weight available for allocation.

$v_n x_n$ = immediate reward.

$f_n^*(s_n)$ = optimal total reward starting at stage n, for state s_n.

$f_{n-1}^*(s_n - w_n x_n)$ = optimal reward at the previous stage.

Solution Since there are four items, there will be four stages.

Stage 1 (item D) Table 9.13 shows the states on the left side. On the top the possible number of units of D that can be loaded are shown.

TABLE 9.13
Stage 1: Item D

State, s_1	$x_1 = 0$	$x_1 = 1$	$x_1 = 2$	$x_1 = 3$	$f_1^*(s_1)$
		$f_1(s_1) = v_1 x_1 = 20x_1$			
0	0				0
1	0				0
2	0				0
3	0	20			20
4	0	20			20
5	0	20			20
6	0	20	40		40
7	0	20	40		40
8	0	20	40		40
9	0	20	40	60	60
10	0	20	40	60	60
11	0	20	40	60	60

Since the weight of D is 3 tons, then either 0, 1, 2, or 3 units can be loaded. The body of the table gives the reward computed by the formula given at the top of the table.

Mathematical statement of stage 1 The reward function is given by $v_1 x_1 = 20x_1$, where x_1 designates the number of units of D.

The optimal solution column is designated by $f_1^*(s_1)$ = maximum

$[v_1x_1]$, where $f_1^*(s_1)$ is the optimal reward starting from state s_1 and using an optimal policy from stage 1 to the end.

Stage 2 (item C) At this stage an allocation is made to item C, with the remaining weight utilized according to the best policy recommended in stage 1. Table 9.14 shows the rewards for the various states. The total rewards are $f_2(s_2) = 30x_2 + f_1^*(s_2 - 5x_2)$; and the optimal reward is the maximum of $f_2(s_2)$. For example, in state 10, if 10 tons are available, then the following alternatives are available:

TABLE 9.14
Stage 2: Item C

	$f_2(s_2) = 30x_2 + f_1^*(s_2 - 5x_2)$			
State, s_2	$x_2 = 0$	$x_2 = 1$	$x_2 = 2$	$f_2^*(s_2)$
0	0			0
1	0			0
2	0			0
3	20			20
4	20			20
5	20	30		30
6	40	30		40
7	40	30		40
8	40	50		50
9	60	50		60
10	60	50	60	60
11	60	70	60	70

a. Zero to C, then 10 goes to D. From Table 9.13 we know that the optimal allocation of 10 to D yields 60.
b. One to C, then there are 5 tons remaining. The best allocation of 5 (from stage 1) yields 20 plus the 30 achieved from the allocation of one to C for a total yield of 50.
c. Two to C, this takes 10 tons; that is, nothing remains. Therefore, the reward is $2 \times 30 = 60$.

The computations are similar to the allocation problem of Section 9.4.

Stage 3 (item B) The results are shown in Table 9.15. The total reward function is:

$$f_3(s_3) = 25x_3 + f_2^*(s_3 - 4x_3) \quad \text{and} \quad f_3^*(s_3) = \max f_3(s_3)$$

Stage 4 (item A) The results for stage 4 are shown in Table 9.16. The optimal policy i given by $f_4^*(s_4) = \max [18x_4 + f_3^*(s_4 - 2x_4)]$.

Optimal solution The starting state is $s_4 = 11$, and its solution is the solution to the entire problem. The optimal solution is read as: $x_4 = 4$; that is, four units of A (weighing 8 tons). The remaining $11 - 8 = 3$ tons are allocated in the optimal manner according to stage 3 (Table

TABLE 9.15
Stage 3: Item B

State, s_3	$x_3 = 0$	$x_3 = 1$	$x_3 = 2$	$f_3^*(s_3)$
		$f_3(s_3) = 25x_3 + f_2^*(s_3 - 4x_3)$		
0	0			0
1	0			0
2	0			0
3	20			20
4	20	25		25
5	30	25		30
6	40	25		40
7	40	45		45
8	50	45	50	50
9	60	55	50	55
10	60	65	50	65
11	70	65	70	70

TABLE 9.16
Stage 4: Item A

State, s_4	$x_4 = 0$	$x_4 = 1$	$x_4 = 2$	$x_4 = 3$	$x_4 = 4$	$x_4 = 5$	$f_4^*(s_4)$
			$f_4(s_4) = 18x_4 + f_3^*(s_4 - 2x_4)$				
11	70	78	81	84	92	90	92

9.15). Thus $x_3 = 0$ and no units of B are included. The check then continues to stage 2 (Table 9.14). According to this table, $x_2 = 0$. Moving finally to stage 1 (Table 9.13), the optimal solution for 3 tons is $x_4 = 1$. Therefore, the best solution is:

$$x_1 = 4 \text{ units of A}$$
$$x_4 = 1 \text{ unit of D}$$

The total reward is:

$$18 \times 4 + 20 \times 1 = 92$$

The knapsack problem has several variations. For example, it may be required that at least one unit of each item be included. Another variation is that no more than one unit of each item is to be included. Cost minimization can be the objective. Additional constraints may also be added such as volume limits. Some of these variations are given in the problem section.

9.10 PROBLEMS FOR PART B

8. You own 1,000 shares of a certain company which you *must* sell, for tax reasons, on or before the end of the fifth forthcoming trading day.

The price of a share fluctuates between $20 and $22. At any given day there is a chance of 25 percent of selling the shares at $20, 45 percent of selling them at $21, and 30 percent of selling them at $22.

a. Suggest an optimal policy. Assume that all

shares are sold in one trade (use dynamic programming).

b. How much money will you receive for your shares if the commission is 25 cents per share?

9. Reconsider Problem 1. Suppose that the result of the choice made at each node is probabilistic. Namely, when one selects a route there is only a 60 percent chance of pursuing that route. For example, if a decision made at node A was to go to B_1, the actual result would be 60 percent at B_1 and 40 percent at B_2. Use DP to find the path with the lowest expected value of the sum of the numbers along the arcs.

10. Suppose you own an option to buy 100 shares of the ABC Corporation at a certain price. Such options are traded on Mondays through Fridays on the American and Chicago exchanges. Today is Monday, and your option will expire on Friday; at that time you will be able to sell it for $175. From your experience you know that the price movement of this type of option during the last week of expiration will behave in the following manner:

Monday: 60 percent chance for $300, 40 percent chance for $200.

Tuesday: 40 percent chance for $350, 40 percent chance for $250, 20 percent chance for $150.

Wednesday: 20 percent chance for $400, 60 percent chance for $200, 20 percent chance for $150.

Thursday: 50 percent chance for $300, 50 percent chance for $200.

Friday: 100 percent chance for $175.

The reason for such sharp movements is that in the last days before the expiration date some traders who sold the option short must buy it back. Also the stock itself moves up and down quickly.

The commission for selling an option is $25 regardless of its price. Use dynamic programming to find the best trading policy for options of this type.

11. A truck can carry a total of 10 tons. Three types of boxes are available for shipment. The boxes weigh 2, 1, and 3 tons respectively and their value is $50, $30, and $70 respectively. The truck delivers ten times a day. It is required that at least one unit of each type of box be delivered in each shipment.

a. Use dynamic programming to determine the loading policy which will maximize the value of the shipments.

b. Find the daily dollar value of the shipment.

c. Formulate as an integer programming problem.

12. DEF Trucking Company delivers four types of containers between two cities. The company wants to load *at least* 14 tons on each truck. The weight and the handling cost which is paid to porters for each type of container is given as:

Container	Weight (tons)	Handling cost
A	4	$20
B	2	15
C	5	23
D	3	18

Find how many containers of each type should be loaded on each truck in order to minimize the total handling cost.

a. Formulate as an integer program.

b. Formulate and solve by dynamic programming.

13. Formulate the recursive relations for (a) the allocation example of Section 9.4, (b) the stagecoach problem of Section 9.2, and (c) the purchasing agent problem of Section 9.7.

9.11 CASE

THE PERSONNEL DIRECTOR

Bud Friendly, personnel director for Glades Corporation, was on the phone explaining his problem to the Manager of Marketing Research:

"Mrs. Rich, with only three days to hire that customer rep we won't be able to interview many applicants. It takes a full day to screen each one, including interviews, reference checks, and appraisals so the most we can consider is three applicants. Obviously, if the first or second candidate is excellent we will hire that candidate but what if they're not?"

"Look, Bud. In the past we have found that of every ten candidates you screen, three are 'excellent', five are 'good', and two are 'poor'. Surely in three days you can come up with a superior candidate."

"But Mrs. Rich, if I delay an early decision on a 'good' candidate, hoping to find an 'excellent' one, he or she might take another job instead and then we might have to settle on a 'poor' candidate on the last day."

"Well, I don't know what to advise you. I can say this though. A 'good' candidate is worth twice as much as a 'poor' one and an 'excellent' candidate is worth twice that again. Good luck Bud."

Questions:
1. Use dynamic programming to advise Bud on a hiring policy.
2. What will be the candidate's expected worth if an optimal policy is followed?

9.12   GLOSSARY

Immediate reward   The reward resulting from a move between two adjacent stages. It is the value added to the objective function when moving from stage to stage.

Knapsack problem   A classical allocation problem which determines the optimal mix of items to be put in a limited space (knapsack, bag, container) such that the total value of the items is maximized.

Optimization techniques   Mathematical techniques that can be used to optimally solve the subproblem.

Policy   A complete predetermined choice plan under every possible circumstance.

Principle of optimality   Bellman's principle which is the basis for solving dynamic programming problems.

Recursive relation   The function used in dynamic programming to compute the value of the objective function.

Reward   The payoff or the value of the objective function.

Rollback   A solution approach in which the subproblems which are closest to the end point are solved first.

Segmentation   Breaking up a complex problem into a sequence of smaller subproblems.

Sequential decision making   A decision-making process involving two or more interrelated decisions which are made one after the other.

Stage   A decision point in a sequence of decisions. A subproblem.

State   A condition or a possible alternative for each subdecision or stage. The possible condition for the system (or process) at each stage.

9.13   REFERENCES AND BIBLIOGRAPHY

1.   Beckmann, Martin J. *Dynamic Programming of Economic Decisions.* New York: Springer-Verlag New York Inc., 1968.

2.   Bellman, R. *Dynamic Programming.* Princeton, N.J.: Princeton University Press, 1957.

3.   Bellman, R., and Dreyfus, S. E.   *Applied Dynamic Programming.* Princeton, N.J.: Princeton University Press, 1962.

4.   Bertsekas, D. P.   *Dynamic Programming and Stochastic Control.* New York: Academic Press, 1976.

5.   Gluss, Brian.   *An Elementary Introduction to Dy-*

namic Programming: A State Equation Approach. Rockleigh, N.J.: Allyn & Bacon, Inc., 1972.

6. Hastings, N. A. J. *Dynamic Programming with Managerial Applications.* New York: Crane, Russak & Co., 1973.

7. Nemhauser, G. L. *Introduction to Dynamic Pro-*

gramming. New York: John Wiley & Sons, Inc., 1966.

8. Norman, J. M. *Elementary Dynamic Programming.* New York: Crane, Russak & Co., 1975.

9. White, D. J. *Dynamic Programming.* San Francisco: Holden-Day, Inc., 1969.

10

A Markov analysis is a procedure that can be used to describe the behavior of a system in a dynamic situation. Specifically, it describes and predicts the movement of a system, among different system states, as time passes.

Movements of people, inventories, monetary accounts, and even taxi cabs are a few examples of situations that can be described by Markov processes. To be able to predict the future movements and condition of such a system would clearly be of value to management. This is basically the goal of a Markov analysis.

Markov analysis makes predictions such as:

1. The probability of finding a system in any particular state at any given time.
2. The long-run probabilities of being in each state.

The use of such predictions as a basis for managerial decision making is illustrated throughout the chapter.

Markov analysis

PART A: BASICS

John Byer, director of Product Planning for P&C Chemical Corporation, felt somewhat satisfied as he scanned the latest marketing research results of last year's big gamble. The argument, as he recalled the meeting of the Executive Committee, centered around the question of competing with one's own product. P&C's original entry, known inside the company by the code "Brand A," in the already well-established household detergents market had been well accepted by the market until two years ago when a competitor moved in with a flashy promotional campaign and began luring P&C's customers away. John's suggestion to the Executive Committee was to bring out an improved detergent (Brand B) with a countering advertising campaign stressing the quality of the new brand based on P&C's experience in the area with the successful Brand A.

But the executive vice president, Bill Harmon, was deeply worried that Brand B might compete more with P&C's own Brand A than with the competitor's brand. Other members of the committee pointed out that these would probably be customers P&C would have lost to the competition anyway, but this did not seem to appease Bill. Finally, John pointed out how common it was in the detergent market for companies to offer multiple brands, in stark contrast to their chemicals market. He argued that detergents, being in the consumer market, were totally unlike industrial chemicals.

The Executive Committee finally decided to go along with John's idea, but they were not completely convinced. Thus, the first year's report took on special importance for John. At the time of the introduction of Brand B a year ago P&C held 40 percent of the market and the competitor had 60 percent. The twelve month report summary now indicated that Brand A's share had dropped somewhat to 27.5 percent but that the competitor's share had almost been halved, now standing at 35 percent, the losses in each case going to the new Brand B, currently holding 37.5 percent of the market.

The detailed report showed month-to-month "brand loyalty" (brand switching) figures from the date of introduction of Brand B until this last month. Initially the rate of shifting between brands changed every month, but it has now settled down to the general situation illustrated in Figure 10.1 Customers were still being drawn from Brand A to the competitor (Brand C) to the extent of 60 percent of them each month (the remainder divided evenly at 20 percent each between switching to B and staying with A). However, half of the competitor's market (Brand C) would return to A in any particular month, with another 20 percent switching from C to B, resulting in the competition maintaining only 30 percent of their customers. Of particular interest

FIGURE 10.1
Month-to-month brand
switching

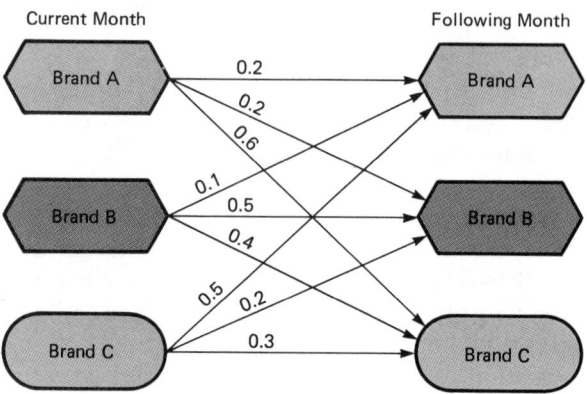

Current Month

Following Month

Brand A — 0.2 — Brand A
0.2
0.6
Brand B — 0.1
0.5
0.4
Brand C — 0.5
0.2
0.3 — Brand C

was the response to Brand B, with half of B's purchasers remaining loyal to B and only 40 percent switching to C.

John felt that these figures substantiated his words from a year earlier and saved P&C from failing in this new market venture. Although John realized that the competition might upset this delicate balance at any moment with a new production introduction or a new marketing campaign, he wondered how the market shares would shift in the coming months, given the brand switching results above. In particular, he wondered what the ultimate market shares would be if conditions ever settled down.

10.1. MARKOV SYSTEMS

The situation presented in the preceding incident is concerned with the prediction of market shares in a dynamic market. Such predictions are based on what is termed a *Markov*[1] *analysis* and can be used as a basis for determining market strategies and product planning. Notice that John Byer is not asking about how to determine the *best* marketing strategy, but rather he wishes to determine the *behavior* of the "system" (the household detergent purchasers in this case). Thus, for the first time in this book we deal with a *descriptive* rather than with a *normative* analysis. Other features of the incident are:

Markov analysis is descriptive—not normative

1. The situation occurs in a chance environment consisting of two or more possible outcomes (three here) at fixed intervals of time. Such a process is referred to as a *stochastic* (or probabilistic) process.
2. The situation involves a multiperiod (monthly here) case. The

---

[1] In honor of the Russian mathematician A. Markov, who developed the technique in 1907.

aiming

customer's brand switching propensities are followed for many months. The probabilities of switching (shown in Figure 10.1) are termed the *transition probabilities* of the stochastic process.

Transition probabilities

3. The situation is dynamic in nature[2] since the customer's brand choices may change from month to month.

movement .

Markov processes

As stated before, the customer's brand switching is a *stochastic process*. If a customer's brand choice in any given month depends *only* on his (or her) choice the month before (i.e., not on the choice 2, 3, or more months previously), the stochastic process is called a *Markov process*. In addition, if the transition probabilities of the customer's switching from one brand (*state*) to another remain constant over time, then the Markov process is called a homogeneous *Markov chain*.[3]

Stochastic process, Markov process, Markov chain

The characteristics of a Markov analysis

A Markov analysis is conducted on a system which can usually be interpreted in two different ways: either as *the fraction of a group* (e.g., percentage of detergent purchasers) or *the probability of an individual* (e.g., chance of a customer purchasing Brand X). To familiarize the reader with both of these (equivalent) interpretations, we will use both quite frequently in this chapter.

Two interpretations

As a *descriptive tool* the major objective of Markov chain analysis is the prediction of the future behavior of managerial systems.[4] A prediction can be achieved, in some cases, by other tools such as decision trees (coupled with complete enumeration) or simulation. The advantage of Markov chain analysis is that the computational work is relatively uncomplicated and can be carried out very rapidly. Small problems can be solved manually; for larger problems a standard computer package can be used.

Advantage of simple manipulations.

Necessary assumptions

In the Markov chains discussed in Part A of this chapter, the following assumptions are made:

1. The system has a finite number of states, none of which is "absorbing" (a state which, once entered, cannot be left).

---

[2] Markov analysis is related to dynamic programming. However, dynamic programming is a normative tool and therefore has an optimization objective, while Markov analysis is a descriptive tool. Markov analysis can also be used to solve certain types of dynamic programming problems (e.g., see Howard [4]).

[3] This chapter deals only with homogeneous Markov chains.

[4] A "system" in this chapter can be a person, an organization, the demand for a product, a machine, or other such entity.

2. The system's condition in any given period depends only on its condition in the preceding period and on the transition probabilities.
3. The transition probabilities are constant over time.
4. Changes in the system may occur once and only once each period (once a month in the example).
5. All time periods are equal in length.

The assumptions as reflected in the detergent incident

Finite number of states, none of which is absorbing In this example the *condition* of the system was limited to three *states* (brands). If there was a brand from which a customer *never* switched, then this would be termed an *absorbing* state. It is assumed here that none of the states is absorbing.

Present brand choice is dependent on the previous month's choice It was assumed that the brand choice in any given month was influenced *only* by the choice in the previous month. This may or may not be a realistic assumption, depending on the circumstances.

One more point should be made concerning the information necessary for a prediction of the future. The reader may wonder if other considerations such as the customer's tastes or income might be more relevant to a prediction than his previous brand choice. Quite possibly! And if data on these variables were available, it could be used in improving the prediction based on the Markov analysis.

Constant transition probabilities It may well be that the probabilities between months may begin changing again. If so, a more complicated analysis is required (consult reference [4]).

One change per period This requirement is usually satisfied by choosing a natural time period for the system. Detergents usually last about a month for many customers.

Equal time periods This assumption is satisfied since the brand purchases are monitored on a monthly basis. If purchases change faster, the time period can be shortened (e.g., a week rather than a month).

What the Markov analysis predicts

Based on historical information concerning the system, predictions can be made for the following:

1. The probability of finding the system in any particular state, at any given time (Section 10.3).
2. The long-run (steady state) probabilities of being in each state (Section 10.4).

10.2   TRANSITION PROBABILITIES

The Markov process describes the movement of a system from a certain condition (or state) in the current stage (time period)[5] to one of n possible states in the next stage. The system moves in an uncertain environment. All that is known is the probability associated with any possible move (transition). This probability, termed the *transition probability*, p_{ij}, is the likelihood that the system, currently in state i, will move to state j in the next period. The transition probability concept is the key to Markov analysis.

Transition probabilities—the key ✓

Transition diagram

Let us return to the detergent example. Figure 10.2 illustrates the three possible brand choices of the customers. The arrows show the

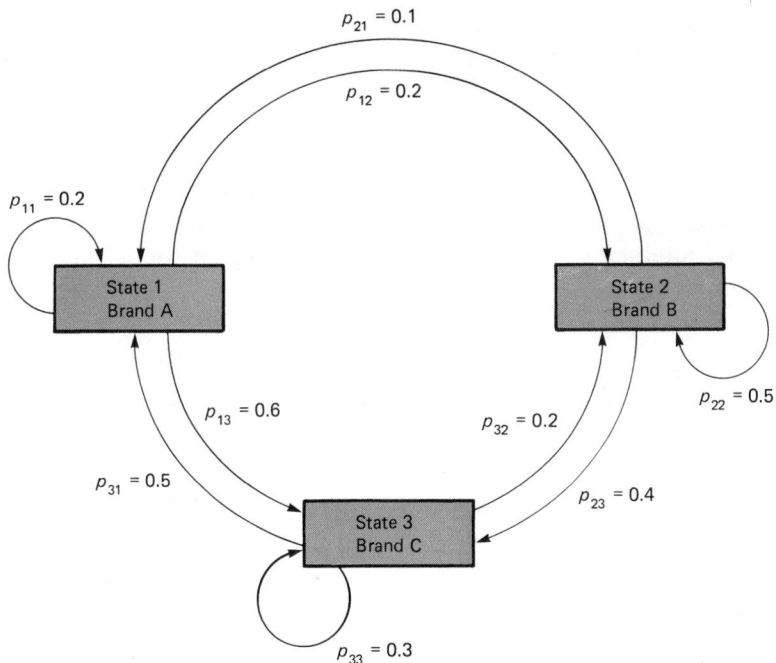

FIGURE 10.2
Transition diagram of the Markov process

probabilities of a customer (or the fraction of detergent purchasers) moving from state to state (brand to brand), as computed by the available historical data.

---

[5] As in dynamic programming, here too, stages do not have to be time periods.

The transition matrix

Another way of expressing the system's movement is in tabular or matrix form, as shown in Table 10.1. Such a table is called a *transition matrix* (denoted by P).[6]

TABLE 10.1
The transition matrix

Current month's brand choice		Next month's brand choice		
		P&C's brand A	P&C's brand B	Competitor's brand C
P&C's brand A	(A)	.2	.2	.6
P&C's brand B	(B)	.1	.5	.4
Competitor's Brand	(C)	.5	.2	.3

Note that the sum of the probabilities in every row is 1.0. That is, the customers must choose one of the three brands the next month since these are the only brands available. Formally, for any row i:

$$p_{i1} + p_{i2} + \cdots + p_{in} = 1 \qquad (10.1)[7]$$

The transition matrix as a set of probability vectors

The set of transition probabilities across any row (current state) is called a *probability vector* and represents all possibilities of moving from one state in the current period to one of the n states in the next period.

---

[6] The general structure of a transition matrix is:

To
State at the next period

From

State in the current period

$$
\begin{array}{c}
\\
\\
\\
\\
\end{array}
\begin{array}{c}
s_1 \\
s_i \\
s_n
\end{array}
\begin{array}{c}
\begin{array}{ccccc}
s_1 & s_2 & \cdots & s_j & \cdots & s_n
\end{array} \\
\left[
\begin{array}{cccccc}
p_{11} & p_{12} & \cdots & p_{1j} & \cdots & p_{1n} \\
& & & & & \\
p_{i1} & p_{i2} & & p_{ij} & & p_{in} \\
& & & & & \\
p_{n1} & p_{n2} & \cdots & p_{nj} & \cdots & p_{nn}
\end{array}
\right] = P
\end{array}
$$

[7] In abbreviated form:

$$\sum_{j=1}^{n} p_{ij} = 1$$

In addition to the transition probabilities which are usually *given* in Markov analysis, there is another set of probabilities which is predicted by the analysis. These will be discussed next.

10.3   TRANSIENT BEHAVIOR AND STATE PROBABILITIES

Independent state probabilities

Let us denote the probability that the system will occupy a particular state i, at period k by $q_i(k)$. For example, $q_3(5)$ means: "the probability that the system will be in state 3 at the fifth period." Note here that the *initial condition* is unspecified; only the final state (in period k) is mentioned. This probability is called the *state probability*. Since the system must occupy one and only one of the possible states at any given period, including period k, then the sum of all q_i values must equal 1. Formally:

Unspecified initial conditions

State probability

state i
period K.
probability $= q_i(K)$.

$$q_1(k) + q_2(k) + \cdots + q_n(k) = 1 \qquad \text{for every } k \qquad (10.2)^8$$

where:

n = number of states.
k = number of transitions (periods ahead) = 0, 1, 2, ...

Example   Let us consider the detergent example to illustrate the determination of these $q_i(k)$ probabilities. The states of the system—Brand A, B, and C—are designated as 1, 2, and 3, respectively. The probability $q_1(0)$ represents the probability of a customer choosing Brand A this month (time zero); $q_1(1)$ represents the probability of choosing Brand A after "one transition"; that is, after one month, and so on.

State probabilities   The probability distribution of the customer choosing any given brand (1, 2, 3) in any given month (k), can be written as a row vector:[9]

$$Q(k) = [q_1(k), q_2(k), q_3(k)] \qquad (10.3)$$

In general, for n states we can write:

$$Q(k) = [q_1(k), q_2(k), \ldots, q_n(k)] \qquad (10.4)$$

---

[8] Equation 10.2 can be expressed as:

$$\sum_{i=1}^{n} q_i(k) = 1$$

[9] For a review of matrix algebra, see Appendix A.

Initial state probabilities in the detergent example   Let us denote the month in the example as the initial state, labeled $k = 0$. The initial state probabilities were given in the case as:

Initial state $q_1(0) = .275$ current share of the market for Brand A
$q_2(0) = .375$ current share of the market for Brand B
$q_3(0) = .350$ current share of the market for Brand C

These values can be summarized as:

$$Q(0) = [q_1(0), q_2(0), q_3(0)] = [.275, .375, .350]$$

The state probabilities the next month $(k = 1)$ To compute the state probabilities we will use the transition matrix of Table 10.1 (reproduced as Table 10.2). The states are labeled Brand A = 1, B = 2, and C = 3.

TABLE 10.2
Transition matrix for the
detergent example
(Table 10.1 reproduced)

From \ To	A 1	B 2	C 3
A 1	.2	.2	.6
B 2	.1	.5	.4
C 3	.5	.2	.3

Three ways to choose Brand A

The value of $q_1(1)$ is first computed. This is the probability that the customer will choose Brand 1 (A) after one month. There are three ways for this to occur:

1. A customer who last purchased Brand A could continue to purchase Brand A (probability of .2).
2. A customer could switch to Brand A from Brand B (probability of .1).
3. A customer could switch to Brand A from Brand C (chance of .5).

Conditional probabilities

Note: all the above probabilities are *conditional* probabilities. That is, each depends on the customer's last purchase. Therefore, the chance of choosing Brand A in the next month, $q_1(1)$, is the sum of the following probabilities:

1. The probability of continuing to choose Brand A *given that* the customer last purchased Brand A. This probability is computed as $q_1(0)p_{11} = .275 (.2)$. $q_1(0) = .275$ & $P_{11} = .2$.
2. The probability of choosing Brand A given that the customer last purchased Brand B. It is computed as: $q_2(0)p_{21} = .375 (.1)$.
3. The probability of choosing A given that the customer last purchased C. It is given by $q_3(0)p_{31} = .350 (.5)$.

Formally:

$$q_1(1) = .275(.2) + .375(.1) + .350(.5) = .2675$$

This is the sum of the chance of being in each state times the chance of switching from there to Brand A. In vector notation this can be written as:

$$q_1(1) = [Q(0)] \begin{bmatrix} .2 \\ .1 \\ .5 \end{bmatrix} = .2675 \quad \checkmark$$

That is: Multiply the $Q(0)$ vector times the first column vector (Brand A) in the transition matrix P.

Similarly, the values of $q_2(1)$ and $q_3(1)$ are:

$$q_2(1) = [Q(0)] \begin{bmatrix} .2 \\ .5 \\ .2 \end{bmatrix} = .275(.2) + .375(.5) + .350(.2) = .3625$$

$$q_3(1) = [Q(0)] \begin{bmatrix} .6 \\ .4 \\ .3 \end{bmatrix} = .4200$$

Tree presentation   The relationship between the transition and state probabilities can be seen in a probability tree presentation (Figure 10.3).

FIGURE 10.3   Tree presentation of transition and state probabilities

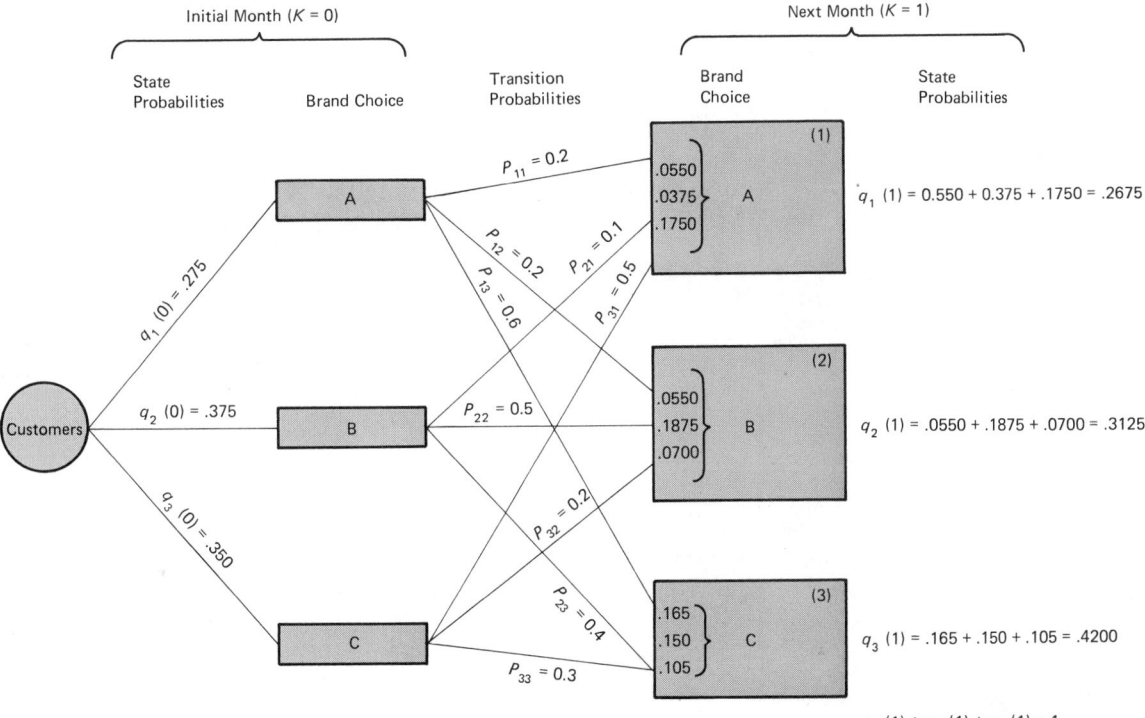

Generalization It is the probability of $q_1(1)$ together with $q_2(1)$ and $q_3(1)$ that are the components of $Q(1)$. In matrix notation $Q(1)$ is computed as the product of $Q(0)$ and P:

$$Q(1) = [q_1(1), q_2(1), q_3(1)] = Q(0)P \tag{10.5}$$

where P is the transition probability matrix of the system. Thus:

$$Q(1) = Q(0)P \tag{10.6}$$

and by similar reasoning it can be shown that:

$$Q(2) = Q(1)P \tag{10.7}$$

Introducing the value of $Q(1)$ from Equation 10.6 into Equation 10.7 results in:

$$Q(2) = Q(1)P = Q(0)PP = Q(0)P^2 \tag{10.8}$$

Similar computations can be performed for $Q(3), Q(4), \ldots$ In general:

$$Q(k) = Q(k-1)P = Q(k-2)P^2 = \cdots = Q(k-k)P^k = Q(0)P^k \tag{10.9}$$

John Byer's first question

Using Equation 10.9, John Byer could address his first question; namely, what the market shares will be the first, second, third month from now and so on. For example, for the first two months:

$q_3(1) = $ the probability of choosing Brand C (state #3) one month from now. This was already computed as .42 (or 42 percent).

$q_3(2) = $ the probability of choosing Brand C two months from now.

In order to find $q_3(2)$, Equation 10.9 is used with $k = 2$: $Q(2) = Q(0)P^2$. Thus, P^2 must first be calculated:

$$P^2 = P \times P = \begin{bmatrix} .2 & .2 & .6 \\ .1 & .5 & .4 \\ .5 & .2 & .3 \end{bmatrix}^2 = \begin{bmatrix} .36 & .26 & .38 \\ .27 & .35 & .38 \\ .27 & .26 & .47 \end{bmatrix}$$

Since $q_3(2)$ is the third entry in the row vector $Q(2) = [q_1(2), q_2(2), q_3(2)]$, it can be found by multiplying the third column of P^2 by $Q(0)$; that is:

$q_3(2) = Q(0) \times$ [the Brand C (third) column vector of P^2]
$= .275 \times .38 + .375 \times .38 + .35 \times .47 = .4115$ or 41.15 percent.

In a similar manner it is possible to find $q_1(k)$, $q_2(k)$, and $q_3(k)$ for any desired k.

State probabilities given initial condition

In the previous discussion the state probabilities (i.e., market shares) were interpreted in terms of the fraction of the group of detergent purchasers. However, in some instances management may be interested in finding out the state probabilities in terms of the chances of a particular purchaser buying a particular brand, *given* that he or she previously purchased Brand X.

Example   A customer last purchased Brand B (state 2). Find the probability that she will purchase Brand C (state 3) in two months $(k = 2)$.

Solution   Let us use a tree diagram (Figure 10.4) to follow the customer's possible purchases. The tree first shows the chances of switching from Brand B to either A, B, or C after one month. Then it

FIGURE 10.4
Tree diagram for Brand B purchaser

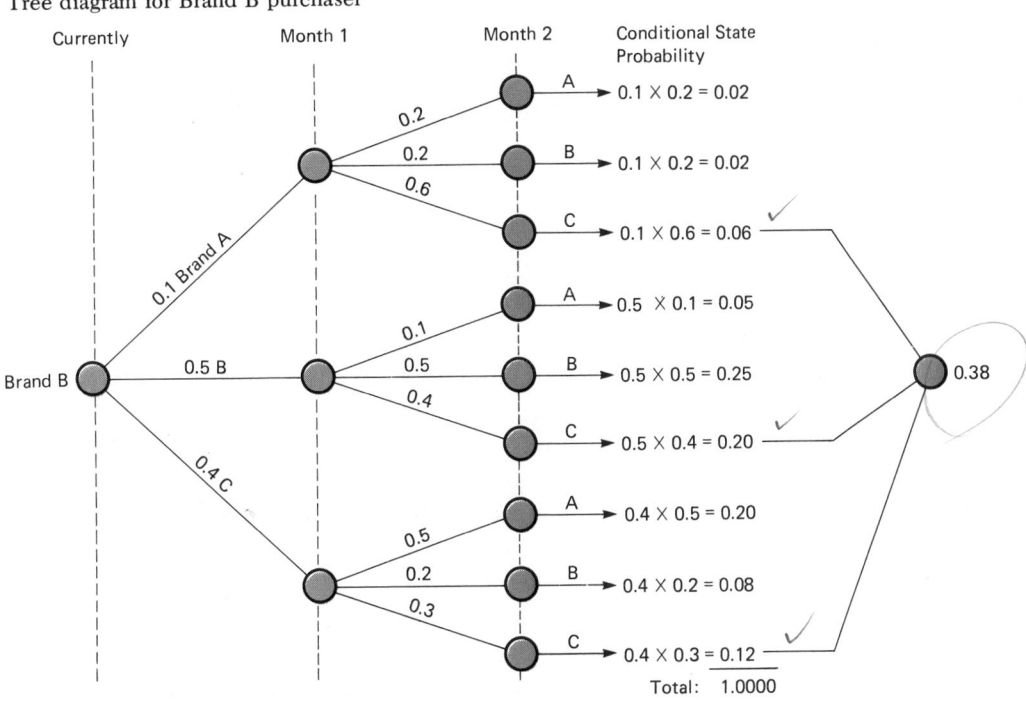

shows the probabilities of switching among these brands in month 2. For example, the probability that the customer will purchase Brand C in month 2 is the sum of the following three probabilities:

$$
\begin{array}{rl}
.06 & \text{(switch from A to C at month 2)} \\
.20 & \text{(switch from B to C at month 2)} \\
+ \ .12 & \text{(stay with C at month 2)} \\
\hline
\text{Total} \quad .38 &
\end{array}
$$

Similarly, the chance for the Brand B customer to purchase Brand A after two months is:

$$.02 + .05 + .20 = .27$$

Her chance of purchasing Brand B again is:

$$.02 + .25 + .08 = .35$$

Note also that the total probabilities of the purchases sum to 1.0 (.38 + .27 + .35 = 1).

Conditional state probabilities

Generalization Conditional state probabilities can be expressed[10] as $q_{ij}(k)$, that is, the probability of being in state i, *given* initial condition j, after k transitions. Thus, $q_{32}(2)$, means: the probability of buying Brand C given that Brand B was initially purchased, after two transitions.

Mathematical presentation The computation of the decision tree can be done with matrix algebra as follows:

1. Multiply the transition matrix by itself k times. For example, in the detergent case; for $k = 2$:

$$P^2 = \begin{bmatrix} .2 & .2 & .6 \\ .1 & .5 & .4 \\ .5 & .3 & .3 \end{bmatrix}^2 = \begin{bmatrix} .36 & .26 & .38 \\ .27 & .35 & .38 \\ .27 & .26 & .47 \end{bmatrix}$$

2. Each initial condition (j) is equivalent to a row, each final state (i) to a column. Note that this is the *reverse* of the usual interpretation of i and j. For example:

$$q_{32}(2) = .38$$
$$q_{13}(2) = .27$$

The computation of the state probabilities provides management with valuable descriptive information about the system's behavior. Additional valuable information is provided by analyzing the system in a "stabilized" (steady state) condition which is discussed next.

10.4 STEADY STATE (EQUILIBRIUM)

One of the major properties of Markov chains is that, in the long run, the process usually stabilizes. A stabilized system is said to be in a *steady state* or in *equilibrium*.

Steady state—long run stability

The phenomenon of equilibrium probabilities is expressed as:

$$Q(k) = Q(k - 1) \tag{10.10}$$

---

[10] Note that

$$\sum_i q_{ij}(k) = 1, \text{ for } j = 1, 2, \ldots$$

That is, the state probabilities in period k are the same as in the previous period. Introducing expression 10.10 into Equation 10.9, the following formulation for the steady state is obtained:

$$Q(k) = Q(k)P \quad \text{or} \quad Q = QP \quad (10.11)$$

where the deletion of the index k denotes *equilibrium* probabilities. Equation 10.11 can also be presented as:

Equilibrium probability

$$Q = [q_1, q_2, \ldots, q_n] \begin{bmatrix} p_{11} & p_{12} & \cdots & p_{1n} \\ p_{21} & p_{22} & \cdots & p_{2n} \\ \cdot & \cdot & & \cdot \\ \cdot & \cdot & & \cdot \\ \cdot & \cdot & & \cdot \\ p_{n1} & p_{n2} & \cdots & p_{nn} \end{bmatrix} \quad (10.12)$$

The matrix multiplication shown in Equation 10.12 results in a system of n simultaneous linear equations[11], as per Equation 10.13.

$$\begin{aligned} q_1 &= p_{11}q_1 + p_{21}q_2 + \cdots p_{n1}q_n \\ q_2 &= p_{12}q_1 + p_{22}q_2 + \cdots p_{n2}q_n \\ &\cdots\cdots\cdots\cdots\cdots\cdots\cdots\cdots \\ q_n &= p_{1n}q_1 + p_{2n}q_2 + \cdots p_{nn}q_n \end{aligned} \quad (10.13)$$

In Equation 10.13 it so happens that one equation is redundant[12] and cannot be used to obtain a solution; therefore a replacement equation *must* be added. Using Equation 10.2 $\left(\sum_{i=1}^{n} q_i = 1 \right)$ as a replacement, it is possible to derive a solution for the steady state vector Q.

Replacing a redundant equation

Before returning to the problem of finding Q in the detergent example, let us consider some additional examples:

The case of two states

The simplest case is that of a 2×2 transition matrix. In this case Equation 10.12 is expressed as:

$$[q_1 \quad q_2] = [q_1 \quad q_2]\begin{bmatrix} p_{11} & p_{12} \\ p_{21} & p_{22} \end{bmatrix} = [q_1p_{11} + q_2p_{21}; \, q_1p_{12} + q_2p_{22}] \quad (10.14)$$

---

[11] Equation 10.13 can also be expressed as:

$$q_j = \sum_{i=1}^{n} p_{ij}q_i, \text{ for } j = 1, 2, \ldots, n$$

[12] A redundant equation presents the same information as that given by another equation in a different form. For example: $x_1 + 2x_2 = 50$ and $2x_1 + 4x_2 = 100$ are redundant.

Example 1 Given a transition matrix:

$$
\begin{array}{cc}
& A \quad B \\
\begin{array}{c} A \\ B \end{array} & \begin{bmatrix} .2 & .8 \\ .3 & .7 \end{bmatrix}
\end{array}
$$

Find the steady state probabilities utilizing Equation 10.14:

1. $q_1 = p_{11}q_1 + p_{21}q_2 = .2q_1 + .3q_2$
2. $q_2 = p_{12}q_1 + p_{22}q_2 = .8q_1 + .7q_2$
3. Also, it is known that $q_1 + q_2 = 1$

This system can be solved by considering either Equations 1 and 3 or Equations 2 and 3 (since one of the first two equations is redundant and can be dropped).

Solution[13], *Using Equations 1 and 3* Equation 3 can be rewritten as $q_1 = 1 - q_2$. Introducing this value into Equation 1: $1 - q_2 = .2(1 - q_2) + .3 q_2$. Solving for q_2 the solution $q_2 = 8/11$ is obtained. Introducing this value into Equation 3 yields the solution for q_1: $q_1 = 3/11$. Thus, *in equilibrium* there is a chance of 3/11 that the system will be in state A, and a chance of 8/11 that it will be in state B.

Example 2 Given a transition matrix:

$$
\begin{bmatrix}
.3 & 0 & .7 \\
0 & .2 & .8 \\
.5 & .4 & .1
\end{bmatrix}
$$

Find the steady state probabilities.

Equation 10.12 is utilized to find the steady state vector:

$$
Q = [q_1 \quad q_2 \quad q_3] = [q_1 \quad q_2 \quad q_3] \times \begin{bmatrix} .3 & 0 & .7 \\ 0 & .2 & .8 \\ .5 & .4 & .1 \end{bmatrix}
$$

Executing the multiplication, a system of three simultaneous linear equations is obtained:

1. $q_1 = .3q_1 + 0q_2 + .5q_3$
2. $q_2 = 0q_1 + .2q_2 + .4q_3$
3. $q_3 = .7q_1 + .8q_2 + .1q_3$

In addition, Equation 10.2 for three states contributes:

4. $q_1 + q_2 + q_3 = 1$.

To solve this system any two of the first three equations, plus the fourth one, may be considered. The following solution then is obtained:

$$
q_1 = \frac{10}{31}, \quad q_2 = \frac{7}{31}, \quad q_3 = \frac{14}{31}
$$

---

[13] For methods of solving simultaneous linear equations, see Appendix A.

A simple test can be employed to assure that an equilibrium solution has been obtained. Check if Equation 10.11 holds; that is, if $Q = QP$. In the above example:

$$\begin{bmatrix} \dfrac{10}{31} & \dfrac{7}{31} & \dfrac{14}{31} \end{bmatrix} \times \begin{Bmatrix} .3 & 0 & .7 \\ 0 & .2 & .8 \\ .5 & .4 & .1 \end{Bmatrix} = \begin{bmatrix} \dfrac{10}{31} & \dfrac{7}{31} & \dfrac{14}{31} \end{bmatrix}$$

$$Q \qquad \times \qquad P \qquad = \qquad Q$$

Thus, it does check.

The following example will help clarify the process through which steady state is achieved.

Example 3   One half of Glade County's population lives in the city and one half in the suburbs. The initial condition of this system can therefore be described as:

$$Q(0) = [.5 \quad .5]$$

There is an 80 percent chance that a suburban resident will remain in the suburbs and a 20 percent chance that he or she will move to the city within the next year. A city dweller has a fifty-fifty chance of staying in the city or moving to the suburbs. The transition matrix describing this process is:

Exodus to the suburbs

$$\text{Today:} \begin{array}{l} \\ \text{Suburb} \\ \text{City} \end{array} \overset{\displaystyle \begin{array}{l} \text{Next Year:} \\ \text{Suburb} \quad \text{City} \end{array}}{\begin{bmatrix} .8 & .2 \\ .5 & .5 \end{bmatrix}} = P$$

Using Equation 10.9 the population distribution after any desired number of years can be found. Results[14] are shown in Table 10.3.

TABLE 10.3
The approach to steady state

(k) Year	$q_1(k)$* Percentage in suburbs	$q_2(k)$ Percentage in city	Formula used
0	50	50	$Q(0)$ Given
1	65	35	$Q(1) = Q(0)P$
2	69.5	30.5	$Q(2) = Q(1)P$
3	70.85	29.15	$Q(3) = Q(2)P$
4	71.255	28.745	.
....	.	.	.
....	.	.	.
....	.	.	.
n (large).......	71.4286	28.5714	$Q = QP$

* q_1 and q_2, the probabilities of an individual being in the suburbs or in the city, respectively, also correspond to the percentage of the population in the suburbs and in the city. For example, after one year, 35 percent of the total population will be in the city.

[14] The reader is encouraged to derive this table for him- or herself.

The probability distributions $q_1(k)$ and $q_2(k)$ of Table 10.3 show that as equilibrium is approached, the changes in the probability distribution become smaller. In the long run (steady state) about 71.43 percent of the population will reside in the suburbs and 28.57 percent in the city.

Let us return now to the detergent example. With the equilibrium Equation 10.11 John Byer's second question concerning the ultimate market shares can be addressed. The equilibrium conditions are computed as:[15]

Market shares in equilibrium

$$Q = [.297 \quad .286 \quad .417]$$

This means that once steady state has been achieved, the market shares of A, B, and C in any given month in the future are 29.7 percent, 28.6 percent, and 41.7 percent, respectively.

Summary: How is a steady state situation recognized:

As seen earlier, the state probabilities changed over time. In the detergent example we found that:

Initially	$Q(0) = [.2750 \quad .3750 \quad .3500]$
After a month	$Q(1) = [.2675 \quad .3125 \quad .4200]$

That is, $Q(0) \neq Q(1)$.

A steady state condition is recognized when the state probabilities remain *unchanged* from period to period.

Formally, such a condition is expressed by Equation 10.10, namely: $Q(k) = Q(k - 1)$.

Characteristics of the steady state situation

From Equation 10.11 it can be seen that the steady state conditions can be expressed by a set of probabilities Q, which are called the steady state (or equilibrium) probabilities. These probabilities are constant state probabilities, and they depend only on the transition matrix. In contrast, state probabilities are *not* in equilibrium and *do* depend on the initial conditions and the number of transitions.

10.5   MANAGERIAL APPLICATIONS

Markov analysis to test "what-if" questions

Markov analysis is used to predict a system's behavior. Therefore, it is considered a descriptive tool that provides information which can be used as a basis for making decisions by either complete enumeration of

---

[15] The reader is encouraged to derive these probabilities for him- or herself, using Table 10.1 and Equation 10.12.

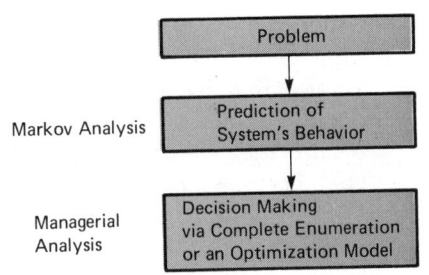

FIGURE 10.5
Managerial analysis
using Markov chains

all alternatives *or* through additional optimization models. The relationship between the Markov analysis and the managerial analysis is shown in Figure 10.5.

In this section an extension of the detergent example is given. Other examples are given in the problem sections of 10.7 and 10.9.

Promotional policy planning

P&C is considering two alternative policies for promoting its products.

1. Promote brand A only. This will cost $150,000 invested in a lump sum and is expected to change the transition matrix to:

	To		
From	A	B	C
A	.6	.2	.2
B	.4	.4	.2
C	.6	.1	.3

2. Promote brand B only. This will cost $280,000 (lump sum, one shot) and is expected to change the transition matrix to:

	To		
From	A	B	C
A	.1	.5	.4
B	.2	.8	.0
C	.3	.5	.2

Find:

1. Which policy will bring larger increases in P&C's total share of the market in the long run?

2. Which policy will be more efficient (gain per dollar invested) in the long run?
3. Assume that each percentage of increased share in the total market is worth $10,000 to P&C; which policy (if any) should P&C take?
4. What is the "break-even point" for each of the two possible policies? That is, at what dollar value of worth, for each percentage gain, will the policies start to be profitable, disregarding interest rates?

Solution:

1. If only brand A is promoted, the following market equilibrium (using the new transition matrix) is obtained:

$$A = .555, B = .223, C = .223 \qquad \text{(rounded)}$$

The total of brands A + B increases from .297 + .286 = .583 to .778 (or 77.8 percent of the market). If only brand B is promoted, the equilibrium (using the third transition matrix) is: A = .190, B = .715, C = .095, for a total of .905 to A + B. Thus, promoting B only is preferable, since it will result in a larger share of the market.
2. Promoting A only is more efficient since:

Promoting A: 19.5 percent increase[16] for $150,000 investment = .13 percent per $1,000 investment.
Promoting B: 32.2 percent increase for $280,000 investment = .115 percent per $1,000 investment.

3. For promoting A: $10,000 × 19.5 = $195,000; less $150,000 (cost) = $45,000. For promoting B: $10,000 × 32.2 = $322,000, less $280,000 (cost) = $42,200. Thus, promoting A is better. This solution was expected since the same answer was obtained earlier in part 2, but here it is in absolute terms.
4. In promoting A only, let x be dollars per 1 percent gain. To break even the total gain must equal the expenses; that is, 19.5 (x) = $150,000.

Solving: x = $7,678, for each 1 percent gain.
If only B is promoted: 32.2 (x) = $280,000.
Solving: x = $8,685 for each one percent gain.

10.6 SUMMARY AND CONCLUDING REMARKS

Markov analysis is a descriptive tool designed to predict the behavior of a system over time. The analysis applies in a dynamic, probabilistic environment where most other management science tools fail.

---

[16] .778 − .297 − .286 = .195.

What information is provided?

The analysis can provide information about the chances of a system occupying any state at any future time. Such information can be used by management to determine the *effectiveness* of a system under various operating conditions. This enables management to compare various policies and projects by considering each relevant transition matrix.

Determining system effectiveness

Difficulties in application

A key difficulty in the application of Markov chain analysis is that of obtaining the transition matrix. Historical data can serve this purpose in some cases. In other cases, the subjective beliefs of management may be used.

Using historical or subjective data

Markov chain analysis can be applied as an auxiliary tool to a host of managerial problems which are dynamic in nature such as replacement, maintenance, brand loyalty, investment evaluation, and management of ecology. In addition, it is used in dynamic programming [4] and in organization theory. Ultimately, the extent of the applications of Markov chains will depend on the ability to relax the restrictive assumptions and to solve the modified models efficiently.

10.7   PROBLEMS FOR PART A

1. A survey of textile machines in the ABC Corporation indicated the following condition of the machines:

   January 1: Two hundred in excellent condition, 80 in good condition, 20 in fair condition.

   February 1: Of those found in excellent condition on January 1, 180 are still in excellent condition, 20 in good. Of those found in good condition in January, 60 are still in good condition, 16 are in excellent condition (maintenance is given routinely), and 4 are in fair condition. Of those found in fair shape in January, 2 are in good condition and 18 are in fair condition.

   Construct the transition matrix.

2. Given the following transition matrix:

$$P = \begin{array}{c} \\ s_1 \\ s_2 \end{array} \begin{array}{cc} s_1 & s_2 \\ \left[\begin{array}{cc} .2 & .8 \\ .6 & .4 \end{array}\right] \end{array}$$

   The system is now in state s_2 (i.e., $q_2(0) = 1$). Find the probability vector $Q(3)$ after three periods.

3. A survey of a two-brand market indicates that 80 percent of brand A's customers remain loyal to their brand (state 1) and 20 percent switch to brand B (state 2) each period (say, a week). It is also known that 40 percent of B's customers are loyal and that 60 percent switch to A. This information is presented as a *brand switching* (transition) matrix:

$$\begin{array}{c} \text{Next week} \\ \begin{array}{c} \text{This A} \\ \text{week B} \end{array} \begin{array}{cc} A & B \\ \left[\begin{array}{cc} .8 & .2 \\ .6 & .4 \end{array}\right] \end{array} = P \end{array}$$

   Assume that a consumer is currently buying product B. Find:
   a. The probabilities that the consumer will buy products A and B after one week.
   b. The probabilities that the consumer will buy products A and B after two weeks.
   c. The equilibrium (steady state) probabilities.

4. Continental Corporation operates a large fleet of cars for which an extensive preventive main-

tenance program is utilized. The cars can be classified in one of three states: good (G), fair (F), and poor (P). The transition matrix of these cars is given below:

$$\begin{array}{c} & & \text{To} \\ & & \begin{array}{ccc} G & F & P \end{array} \\ \text{From} \begin{array}{c} G \\ F \\ P \end{array} & \begin{bmatrix} .6 & .3 & .1 \\ .2 & .6 & .2 \\ .1 & .4 & .5 \end{bmatrix} \end{array}$$

a. Assume that currently there are 100 cars in good shape, 60 in fair shape, and 20 in poor shape. How many cars will be found in each condition next week?

b. How many cars will be found in each condition once the process stabilizes (steady state)?

5. Buckaday Rent-A-Car has a fleet of 1,000 cars. The company has three rental offices, A, B, and C. Cars can be picked up at and returned to any office. Customers return cars to each of the offices according to the following probabilities:

Picked up at \ Returned to	A	B	C
A	.7	.1	.2
B	.3	.5	.2
C	0	.2	.8

a. How many cars should the company keep in each office and why? What special assumption must be made in order to answer this question?

b. Near which office should the maintenance facilities be located and why?

6. A university's service department is considering leasing one of two possible computers. A computer can be found in operating condition "O" or nonoperating condition "NO." The daily transition matrix of the two computers under identical maintenance is given below:

	O	NO
O	.95	.05
NO	.90	.10

Computer A

	O	NO
O	.98	.02
NO	.85	.15

Computer B

a. Which computer should the university lease if the leasing charges are the same?

b. If charges are not the same, what additional information is necessary to determine which computer to lease? Under what conditions should the university lease computer A and under what conditions computer B?

7. Given below are two transition matrices.

	A	B	C
A	.8	.1	.1
B	0	.4	.6
C	0	.6	.4

Matrix 1

	A	B	C
A	.2	.1	.7
B	0	1.0	0
C	0	.6	.4

Matrix 2

a. Analyze these matrices and explain their uniqueness.

b. Find the steady state probabilities. Do not set up any equations, use logic!

8. A company's job rotation program shows the following rotations among its employees between March and April, 1976.

			Gains		
Dept.	March	From checking	From loans	From savings	April
Checking	18	0	3	2	20
Loans	12	2	0	1	10
Savings	10	1	2	0	10

a. What would you expect the June results to be?

b. What assumptions were necessary in a) above?

9. A yearly follow-up of a certain metropolitan area residents' mobility showed that 6 percent of the residents in the city move to the suburbs. At the same time, 3 percent of the suburbs' residents move to the city. Assume that the moving percentages remain unchanged and the total number of people in the combined area remains constant (500,000). The average yearly taxes paid by a city dweller is $100 per capita, and by a suburb dweller is $200 per capita.

a. How much tax will the metro government collect (assume 100 percent collection) two years from now if 40 percent of the population currently live in the suburbs.

b. The metro government proposed to induce people to stay in the city by reducing yearly taxes for city dwellers (only) to $50 per capita. As a *result* of this change population movement from the city to the suburbs will be reduced from 6 percent to 5 percent while population movement from the suburbs to the city will be changed from 3 percent to 5 percent. How much tax would be collected each year in the long run (steady state) if the proposal is rejected; that is, if the existing tax structure remains unchanged?

c. How much tax will the metro government lose, each year, in the long run, if the proposal is accepted.

d. If the total number of people in the metropolitan area is changing due to additions from other metropolitan areas, what pattern of change should be assumed in order to employ the Markov chain approach?

10. Three major oil companies compete in a certain marketing zone. Company A runs a promotion campaign 50 percent of the time, and Company B runs one 30 percent of the time. Company C does no advertising. All campaigns are run on a weekly basis. The average buyer shows the following purchasing habit:

a. If only one company advertises, a buyer will buy from that company.

b. If no one advertises, a buyer will buy from C.

c. If *both* A and B advertise, the buyer will review the previous week's decision. If in the previous week the buyer bought from A, he or she will do so again. If in the previous week the buyer bought from B, he or she will buy from B again. However, if in the previous week the buyer bought from C, the product will be selected at random from either A, B, or C (each with one-third chance of being selected).

Find the long-run market distribution among the three oil companies.

11. Carefully read the following statement.

"*Why Worry?*"
"There are only two things to worry about—either you are well or you are sick. If you are well, then there is nothing to worry about. But if you are sick, there are two things to worry about. Either you will get well or you will die. If you get well, there is nothing to worry about. If you die, there are only two things to worry about—either you will go to Heaven or to Hell. If you go to Heaven, there is nothing to worry about. But if you go to Hell, you'll be so damn busy shaking hands with friends, you won't have time to worry!"

a. Assume that the chances of moving among the events described are known and constant. Would it be possible to describe this process as a Markov process? Why or why not?

b. If the answer to part (*a*) is no, would it be possible to make certain assumptions which will turn the answer to (*a*) into yes? Name these assumptions.

c. Is it possible to describe the process as a decision tree (assuming that the probabilities of the events are known)? If the answer is no, explain why. If the answer is yes, draw the decision tree and comment on the relationship between Markov chains and decision trees.

12. Explain why a transition probability is a conditional probability.

13. Explain why steady state conditions are always independent of the initial conditions of the system.

14. The air in Metro City is classified as being in one of nine levels of pollution. Observations show that the following transition probability matrix exists. (Consider one day as a period.)

From \ To	1	2	3	4	5	6	7	8	9
1	.22	.28	.20	.15	.10	.05	0	0	0
2	.10	.20	.30	.20	.10	.10	0	0	0
3	.10	.10	.20	.40	.10	.05	.05	0	0
4	.05	.10	.10	.20	.40	.10	.05	0	0
5	0	0	.10	.10	.20	.30	.20	.10	0
6	0	0	0	.07	.08	.15	.40	.20	.10
7	0	0	0	.05	.10	.15	.36	.20	.14
8	0	0	.05	.07	.08	.10	.15	.30	.25
9	0	0	.06	.06	.08	.10	.15	.25	.30

← state = 9.

9 state

For how many days during the year (365 days) is the air polluted at each level? (Use of a computer is recommended.)

15. Hopeful Hospital is using volunteer help in three departments. On May 1, there were 20 volunteers in departments A, 16 in B, and 14 in C. Volunteers are free to move between departments once a month.

   The table below shows the *gains* in volunteers, in each department, on June 1.

| Depart-ment | Gains | | | |
	From A	From B	From C	Volunteers on June 1
A........	16	0	1	17
B........	3	12	1	16
C........	1	4	12	17

   a. Write the formulas that will show the long-run probability distribution of volunteers among the 3 departments.
   b. Solve the equations to find the probabilities.

16. Taxi-cab of Miami has 100 cabs; currently, 70 are located at the airport and 30 are at the beach. The probability that a car located at the beach will be called for a trip to the airport is 80 percent. The net profit of such a trip is $5. Otherwise, the cab will be called for a local trip where a profit of $2 is realized.

   The probability that a cab located at the airport will be called to the beach is 90 percent. The net profit is $5 for such a trip. There is a 10 percent chance that the cab will be called for a trip to the airport. In this case, the cab will return to the airport parking, netting $3.

   Note: Once a trip is completed, the cabs return to the port nearest to their unloading point.
   Find:

   a. What assumption should be made so that a Markov chain approach can be used for this problem.
   b. How many cabs will be at each location after three periods.
   c. The per-period profit for the company in a steady state situation.
   d. Cab #135 (nicknamed Fair Lady) is currently parked at the airport. What is the chance of this cab being located at the beach after two trips?

PART B: EXTENSIONS

10.8 ABSORBING STATES

A system is said to be in an "absorbing" state if, once there, it cannot exit to some other state. There are numerous practical examples of absorbing states. A bankrupt business, a river or lake irreversibly destroyed by pollution and sediment, and a building destroyed by fire are examples of "absorbing state" situations.

Examples of absorbing states

Analysis of absorbing Markov chains can provide management with answers to at least three important questions:

1. What is the average number of periods that the system will be in *each* nonabsorbing state before it is absorbed?
2. How long is the system expected to stay in nonabsorbing states before it is absorbed?
3. What is the probability of moving into each absorbing state starting from each nonabsorbing state?

Answers to three questions

Such information has an important practical value for managerial decisions in areas such as replacement of equipment, marketing, and maintenance as will be demonstrated in the following personnel management example.

A labor training program

Participants in a certain labor training program can be found in one of four given states: s_1, no service (not in the training program); s_2, discharged; s_3, in training; and s_4, employed. Table 10.4 shows the

TABLE 10.4
A training problem

Status on January 1, 1980	Status on February 1, 1980									
	s_1 No service		s_2 Discharged		s_3 In training		s_4 Employed		Total	
	No.	Percent	No.	Percent	No.	Percent	No.	Percent	No.	Percent
s_1 No service......	10	10.0	60	60.0	30	30.0	0	.0	100	100.0
s_2 Discharged	0	.0	100	100.0	0	.0	0	.0	100	100.0
s_3 In training......	60	20.0	60	20.0	150	50.0	30	10.0	300	100.0
s_4 Employed	0	.0	0	.0	0	.0	500	100.0	500	100.0

proportion of the program population which has changed categories (states) in the most recent month.

The first step is to construct the *transition matrix* (assuming that the transition probabilities are constant over time). The numbers in the matrix below (derived from Table 10.4) represent the fraction of people who have transferred from one category to another during the month. States s_2 and s_4 are defined as *absorbing states* since all the entries in rows s_2 and s_4 are zero except the one corresponding to the *same* state which has the value of one. *If a system is in an absorbing state, there is a zero probability of moving from that state to any other state.*

To From	s_1	s_2	s_3	s_4
s_1	.1	.6	.3	0
s_2	0	1.0	0	0
s_3	.2	.2	.5	.1
s_4	0	0	0	1.0

The fundamental matrix

Step 1 Cross off the rows with the absorbing states (s_2 and s_4 in our case).

Step 2 Arrange the remaining rows and columns in two groups: absorbing and nonabsorbing. In our example:

	Absorbing (A)		Nonabsorbing (N)	
	s_2	s_4	s_1	s_3
s_1	.6	0	.1	.3
s_3	.2	.1	.2	.5

The left matrix (absorbing) will be called A; the right one, N.

In this case:

$$A = \begin{bmatrix} .6 & 0 \\ .2 & .1 \end{bmatrix}, \text{ and } N = \begin{bmatrix} .1 & .3 \\ .2 & .5 \end{bmatrix}$$

Fundamental matrix

Step 3 Define a new matrix, termed the *fundamental matrix* (F), according to Equation 10.15:

$$F = (I - N)^{-1} \qquad (10.15)$$

where I is a *unit (identity) matrix*[17] and the -1 stands for the *inverse* (see Appendix A). In our case:

$$F = \left(\begin{bmatrix} 1 & 0 \\ 0 & 1 \end{bmatrix} - \begin{bmatrix} .1 & .3 \\ .2 & .5 \end{bmatrix} \right)^{-1} = \begin{bmatrix} .9 & -.3 \\ -.2 & .5 \end{bmatrix}^{-1} = \begin{array}{c} \\ s_1 \\ \\ s_3 \end{array} \begin{array}{cc} s_1 & s_3 \\ \begin{bmatrix} \dfrac{50}{39} & \dfrac{30}{39} \\ \dfrac{20}{39} & \dfrac{90}{39} \end{bmatrix} \end{array}$$

The entries in the fundamental matrix give the *average number of periods* (months in our case) *the system will be in each nonabsorbing state until it gets absorbed.* If an employee started in state s_1, then he or she will spend $^{50}/_{39} = 1.28$ months (on the average) in state s_1 and $^{30}/_{39} = .77$ months in state s_3 before being "absorbed"; that is, either employed (state s_4) or discharged (state s_2). If the employee was in s_3, then he or she will spend $^{20}/_{39} = .51$ months in state s_1 and $^{90}/_{39} = 2.31$ in state s_3 before being "absorbed" into either s_4 or s_2.

The meaning of the entries in the fundamental matrix

Step 4 To find the average number of periods to absorption, add the entries in the rows of matrix F:

If an employee starts in state s_1 it will take:

$$\frac{50}{39} + \frac{30}{39} = \frac{80}{39} = 2.05$$

months until he or she is "absorbed" into either s_2 or s_4. If the employee starts in state s_3, it will take $^{110}/_{39}$ or 2.82 months until he or she is "absorbed" somewhere.

Step 5 Finally, it is of interest to know the probabilities of moving from any nonabsorbing state to each absorbing state. These probabilities are given by a matrix B whose formula is:

$$B = FA \qquad\qquad (10.16)$$

In our case:

$$B = \begin{bmatrix} \dfrac{50}{39} & \dfrac{30}{39} \\ \dfrac{20}{39} & \dfrac{90}{39} \end{bmatrix} \begin{bmatrix} .6 & 0 \\ .2 & .1 \end{bmatrix} = \begin{array}{c} \\ s_1 \\ \\ s_3 \end{array} \begin{array}{cc} s_2 & s_4 \\ \begin{bmatrix} \dfrac{36}{39} & \dfrac{3}{39} \\ \dfrac{30}{39} & \dfrac{9}{39} \end{bmatrix} \end{array}$$

These results may be interpreted as follows: If an employee is in state s_1, there is a probability of $^{36}/_{39}$ or .92 that he or she will be "absorbed" by state s_2 (i.e., discharged) and $^3/_{39}$ or .08 by state s_4 (i.e.,

Interpreting the results

---

[17] A unit or identity matrix contains zeros in all elements except the diagonal from upper left to lower right which is filled in with ones (see Appendix A).

employed). Similarly, if an employee starts from s_3, there is a $30/39 = .77$ chance that he or she will be absorbed by state s_2, and $9/39 = .23$ chance of being absorbed by state s_4. Note again that the sum of the probabilities in each row is 1.

The results obtained in the above analysis can be compared to desired standards, or to results obtained from alternative training programs. Different programs will result in different movements of employees from category to category. In other words, each program will result in a different transition matrix. Given the monthly costs of each program, the administration can determine the cost-benefit relationship of different labor training programs.

10.9 PROBLEMS FOR PART B

17. Given the transition matrix below, find the appropriate *fundamental* matrix.

$$\begin{bmatrix} 1.0 & 0 & 0 & 0 \\ .3 & .2 & .5 & 0 \\ .1 & .6 & .1 & .2 \\ 0 & 1.0 & 0 & 0 \end{bmatrix}$$

18. Assume a machine is currently maintained in either good (G), fair (F), or poor (P) condition. Suppose that management decides to stop all preventive maintenance and let the machine fail. If preventive maintenance stops, the machine will have a new state, complete failure (D). The transition matrix under these conditions is given below:

$$\begin{array}{c} \\ \\ \text{From} \end{array} \begin{array}{c} \\ G \\ F \\ P \\ D \end{array} \begin{array}{c} \quad\ \text{To} \\ \begin{array}{cccc} G & F & P & D \end{array} \\ \begin{bmatrix} .4 & .3 & .2 & .1 \\ 0 & .5 & .3 & .2 \\ 0 & 0 & .1 & .9 \\ 0 & 0 & 0 & 1 \end{bmatrix} \end{array}$$

Assuming the machine is presently in good condition, management wants to know:

a. How many weeks the machine is expected to go before it fails.

b. How many weeks (on the average) it will operate in good, fair, and poor condition before it fails.

c. What its probability of failing is. What would this probability be, given that the machine was in fair condition to start? In poor condition?

19. Suppose a new labor training program became available. What information would you need to determine if it were better or worse than the program described in Section 10.8? If you wished to determine the cost-benefit of both programs, what information would you need and how would you conduct the analysis?

10.10 CASE

SPRINGFIELD GENERAL HOSPITAL

Dr. Bill Parker, medical director of Springfield General Hospital, has just been informed that an ambulance is rushing in an accident victim who may require surgery using the heart-lung machine. This hospital has only one such expensive machine which is not in use now but is heavily scheduled for sur-

geries in the next few days. Dr. Parker has called the management science unit to provide him with estimates of the following:

a. The likelihood that the victim will require service on the heart-lung machine during each of the next few days.

b. The prognosis for such cases.

After quickly reviewing their records, the management science analysts compiled the following information:

1. In the past, 112 such victims entered the hospital. At admittance, 72 were found to be in satisfactory condition, 24 were diagnosed as fair, and 16 were considered to be in critical condition, requiring the heart-lung machine.
2. Of the 72 in satisfactory condition, 63 (87.5 percent) were still in satisfactory condition the following day while the condition of 9 (12.5 percent) had deteriorated due to complications and these persons were considered to be in fair condition. None had deteriorated to the point of being in critical condition.
3. Of the 24 in fair condition, 12 (50 percent) were still in the same condition the following day, while 8 (33.3 percent) had improved to satisfactory condition; but 4 (16.7 percent) had deteriorated so much they were classified as critical.
4. Of the 16 in critical condition, 10 (62.5 percent) had improved to fair by the fol-

lowing day, 4 (25 percent) were still in critical condition, and 2 (12.5 percent) had improved significantly to the level of satisfactory.

With this information on hand, the management analysts can answer Dr. Parker's questions.

Questions:
1. What is the likelihood of the patient requiring the heart-lung machine today or in the next two days?
2. What are the steady-state transition probabilities?
3. Assume now that in addition to the 112 victims listed in the records there were another eight found who were discharged. Six of these were discharged alive from "satisfactory" status and two had expired from "critical" status.
4. Starting from each nonabsorbing state, what is the average number of days in each state and to discharged?
5. From each nonabsorbing state what is the probability of expiring as opposed to being discharged alive?

10.11 GLOSSARY

Absorbing state   A state which, once entered, cannot be left.

Descriptive   Illustrating a system and how it reacts.

Equilibrium   (see Steady state).

Markov chain   A Markov process with constant transition probabilities.

Markov process   A stochastic process whose probability of being in any state depends only on its previous state and the transition matrix.

Normative   Prescriptive; that is, what *should* be done.

State   A condition that a system may be in.

Steady state   A point where the chances of finding a system in any particular condition are unchanged from period to period.

Stochastic   Probabilistic; that is, with an exhaustive set of probabilities or chances of outcomes.

Transition probability   The chance of a system moving from one state to another.

10.12 REFERENCES AND BIBLIOGRAPHY

1. Derman, C. *Finite State Markov Decision Processes.* New York: Academic Press, 1970.

2. Ehrenbeg, A. S. C. "An Appraisal of Markov Brand-Switching Models." *Journal of Marketing Re-*

search 2 (1965) 347–62. (This article contains an extensive reference list of Markov chains.)

3. Freedman, D. *Markov Chains*. San Francisco: Holden-Day, Inc., 1971.

4. Howard, R. A. *Dynamic Probabilistic Systems*. Vol. 1 and 2. New York: John Wiley & Sons, Inc., 1971.

5. Kemeny, J. G., et al. *Finite Mathematics with Business Applications*. 2d ed. Englewood Cliffs, N.J.: Prentice-Hall, Inc., 1972.

6. Martin, J. J. *Baysian Decision Problems and Markov Chains*. New York: John Wiley & Sons, Inc., 1967.

7. Mine, H., and Osaki, S. *Markovian Decision Processes*. New York: American Elsevier Publishing Co., Inc., 1970.

11

Game theory provides an analytical framework for the study of decision making in a competitive or conflicting situation. Developed initially by Von Neuman and Morgenstern [12], the concept of a "game" is used to develop rational criteria for making decisions in such situations. Game theory has aroused much interest because of its novel mathematical properties and its potential applications to the managerial, social, and behavioral sciences.

In this text, emphasis is placed on the most developed aspect of the subject, the two-person, zero-sum game. This topic, along with an introductory discussion of nonzero-sum games and games with more than two players, is presented in Part A of the chapter. Part B contains some additional solution techniques.

Game theory

PART A: BASICS

In 1943, General Kenney, commander of the Allied Air Forces in the Southwest Pacific, was faced with a problem. The Japanese were about to reinforce their army in New Guinea from their base in New Britain. Kenney's mission was to bomb and destroy the convoy of reinforcements. The Japanese had a choice of alternative sailing routes. They could either sail north of New Britain, where the weather was rainy and visibility poor for reconnaissance, or southward, where the weather was generally fair (see Figure 11.1). In either case, the journey would take three days. Kenney's problem was to decide where to concentrate the bulk of his reconnaissance aircraft to search for the convoy. The Japanese wanted their ships to have minimal exposure to enemy bombers and, of course, Kenney wanted as many days of bombing exposure as possible.

FIGURE 11.1
The convoy's
alternatives

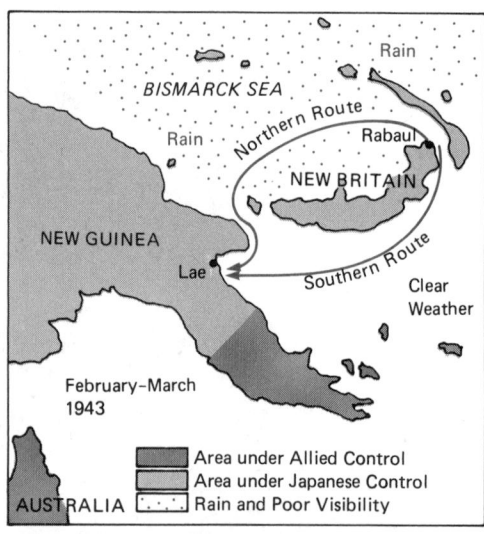

Source: O. G. Haywood, Jr., "Military Decisions and Game Theory." *Journal of the Operations Research Society of America*, vol. 2, no. 4 (November 1954), p. 366.

The following were the possible "days of bombing exposure":

1. If Kenney concentrated his aircraft on the northern route and the Japanese sailed north, the Japanese would not be found until the second day. There would thus be two days of exposure.
2. If Kenney concentrated on the northern route and the Japanese sailed south, they might easily be missed on the first day. There would again be two days of exposure.

3. If Kenney concentrated on the southern route and the Japanese sailed north, they would not be discovered until the third day, resulting in only one day of exposure.
4. If Kenney concentrated on the southern route and the Japanese sailed south, they would be sighted immediately for three full days of exposure.

The problem faced by both sides was what course of action to take.

11.1 INTRODUCTION

The nature of game theory problems

The military situation just presented illustrates decision making *under conflict* or *competition*. Its main characteristic is that two or more decision makers are involved and the consequences (payoff) to each depends on the courses of action taken by all. Further, objectives do not coincide and may, as illustrated in the military example, be completely opposed. As a matter of fact, each party is usually trying to maximize his or her overall welfare at the expense of the others.

Decision under conflict

Such situations are similar to parlor and other types of games. For this reason the name "game theory" was adopted. Yet, situations analyzed with the aid of this tool are a far cry from "games." Marketing strategies, international military conflicts, labor-management negotiations, and potential mergers are just a few examples of real life game theory problems.

"Game" presentation

The complexity of game theory problems

The presence of two or more decision makers with conflicting objectives makes this type of problem complex for mathematical analysis. The tools discussed in the previous chapters cannot handle such situations.

Since no standard tool applies, there was a need to develop a special one. Game theory thus evolved as a mathematical process for formally developing optimal solutions for problems under competition or conflict.

Methodology of game theory

The managerial situation, problem, or conflict is presented in game format. The decision makers are viewed as players. Game theory aims at prescribing optimal playing strategies for the participants. A *strategy* is

Optimal strategies

Payoffs for strategies

defined as a complete, predetermined plan for selecting a course of action, under every possible circumstance.[1] An *optimal strategy* is the best among all possible strategies. In addition, the model computes the payoffs or consequences of the decisions to all parties involved.

The format of the game, the special terminology involved, the assumptions upon which the model is constructed, and the solution procedure for the model are discussed in the remaining sections. Specifically, Section 11.2 is devoted to a discussion of the format, assumptions, and classification of games. In Sections 11.3 and 11.4, a solution procedure for a simple category of game problems is presented. In Section 11.5, a summary of the theory as applied so far is given. Section 11.6 deals with more complicated categories of games, and Section 11.7 concludes Part A of the chapter.

In Part B, the Extensions, three topics are presented. Two additional solution techniques for more complicated games are given in Sections 11.9 and 11.10. Some of the theoretical aspects are then discussed in 11.11.

11.2 FORMAT, ASSUMPTIONS, AND CLASSIFICATION OF GAMES

The military conflict example will illustrate the presentation of the basic format of games and the related terminology. In this section the assumptions of games and their classifications will be discussed.

The format of games and major assumptions

Games are arranged in a prescribed format. Certain rules and regulations which express the assumptions apply, and a specially developed terminology is used. The major aspects of the format concern:

The game situation

1. *The number of participants (termed "players").* The military example involved two players. In other situations three, four, or more players may participate. A player can be a single individual or a group of individuals with the same objective.
2. *Timing.* It would have been easier for Kenney if he could have waited in his decision until the Japanese made their move (and vice versa). However, both had to decide simultaneously. *Simultaneous decisions are assumed in all game situations.*
3. *Conflicting goals.* Each party is interested in maximizing his or her welfare at the expense of the other.
4. *Repetition.* The military conflict is an example of a one-shot decision, which is termed *a play.* A series of repetitive decisions

---

[1] This differs from the typical military or business definition which outlines only the main aspects of a plan, leaving a certain amount of freedom for improvisation. In contrast, this definition contains all details as well as the overall plan.

(plays) is called *a game*. It is generally assumed that most instances involve repetitive situations.

5. *Payoff*.   The consequence of the decisions of the opponents in the military conflict was measured in terms of "days of bombing exposure." Such results are called *payoffs*. The *average payoff per play* is termed the *value of the game*. A game whose value is zero is called a *fair game*.

6. *Information availability*.   Both Kenney and the Japanese were aware of all pertinent information. In general, it is assumed that each player knows *all* possible courses of action (finite number) open to the opponent as well as *all* anticipated payoffs. The cost of collecting this information is not considered relevant to the formal analysis.

Games composed of plays

Zero value = fair game

Presentation of games

Games are presented either in tabular (termed "normal") or tree[2] (termed "extensive") form, depending on preference and the type of analysis or experimentation to be performed.

Normal form (a tabular presentation)   A game is said to be in *normal form* when the entire sequence of decisions which must be made throughout the game is lumped together in a single strategy. This is the common form of games and the one used in this text. This form is limited to the case of two players.

An example of normal form presentation using the military conflict.   In this situation, there were two decision makers: Kenney, with two possible courses of action: a_1, concentrate on northern route, or a_2, concentrate on southern route; and the Japanese who had to decide either to sail north, (b_1), or south (b_2). The above situation is presented in normal form as a payoff table in Table 11.1.

Tree or normal form

Allies \ Japan	North, b_1	South, b_2
Northern, a_1	2	2
Southern, a_2	1	3

TABLE 11.1
The military conflict as a game payoff table

A game payoff table is similar to a decision payoff table (see Chapter 3). The difference between the two is that in a decision table there is only one decision maker, situated at the left of the table, who makes decisions in uncertain environments, expressed as "states of nature." In the game table on the other hand, there are two decision makers, one on the left and the other at the top (replacing the "states of

The payoff table

nature" in a decision table). For this reason, a decision table is sometimes viewed as a "one-player game against nature." The information in the cells is the payoff (number of days exposure, in this case). A *positive* number means a *gain* to the player situated at the *left* side of the table ("Allies" in Table 11.1). This gain is the loss of the player situated at the top of the table (Japan). A negative number means a *loss* to the player situated at the left and a gain to the player at the top of the table.

Classification of games

Games may be classified according to the number of players (e.g., two-person games, three-person games) and whether the game is *zero-sum* or *nonzero-sum*. These latter terms are defined next.

Your loss is my gain!

1. *Zero-sum games.* In zero-sum games the winner(s) receives the entire amount of the payoff which is contributed by the loser(s). Such a game is always strictly competitive. The players' objective is to win as much as they can at the expense of the rival. That is, the players have diametrically opposed interests with regard to the outcome of the game. Zero-sum games with two decision makers are labeled "two-person, zero-sum games" and are the major subject of this chapter. Two assumptions are necessary for the analysis of these games:

    a. All two-person, zero-sum games are solvable.
    b. The utility functions of the players, with respect to the outcome of the game, are identical.[3] In other words, the payoffs are transferable to either player with the same value to each.

2. *Nonzero-sum games.* In a nonzero-sum game the gains of one player differ from the losses of the other (they can be either smaller or larger, but not equal). This means that some other parties in the environment may share in the gains or the losses. Therefore, nonzero-sum games, as will be illustrated later, are not strictly competitive, and there is a possibility of cooperation.

Solving games

The solution tells us the best strategy and resulting payoff

A solution to game problems provides us with answers to these two questions:

1. What strategy should each player follow to maximize his or her welfare?
2. What will the payoff to each player be if the recommended strategy is followed?

---

[3] This assumption is imperative for defining zero-sum games because if the utility functions of the competitors were not identical, the game would be of nonzero-sum type (see Section 11.6).

Unfortunately, clear answers can be given only in a few instances of conflicts, namely for two-person, zero-sum games. The following sections deal with such solutions. Two-person, zero-sum games are divided into two groups: those with a pure strategy solution (Section 11.3) and those with a mixed strategy solution (Section 11.4).

11.3 TWO-PERSON, ZERO-SUM GAMES—PURE STRATEGY

The Allies-Japanese conflict presented earlier is an example of such a game. The term *pure strategy* refers to a prescribed solution in which one alternative is repeatedly recommended to each player, regardless of what the other player does. This is to be contrasted from a mixed strategy, where players change from alternative to alternative when the game is repeated.

A pure strategy

Analysis of the Allies-Japanese conflict

The Allies-Japanese conflict is reproduced in Table 11.2. As the reader may recall, it was assumed that each player knew the alternatives available to the opponent and the conditional number of "days of exposure" for each decision. Furthermore, since game theory assumes that the decision makers are rational, it is evident that the Allies will try to *maximize* the days of exposure while the Japanese will try to *minimize* them.

Japan / Allies	North (b_1)	South (b_2)
North (a_1)	2	2
South (a_2)	1	3

TABLE 11.2
Allies–Japanese conflict
(Table 11.1 reproduced)

The Allies can get the maximum "days of exposure" (three) if they select a_2 and the Japanese select b_2. However, the Allies realize that the Japanese, being rational players, will not select b_2. The reason for this is that *no matter what the Allies do*, the Japanese will be at least as well off, or better off, selecting b_1 rather than b_2! If the Allies select a_1, the Japanese will be subjected to two days of bombing exposure regardless of whether they had taken b_1 or b_2. But if the Allies follow a_2, the Japanese choice of b_2 would subject them to only one day of exposure, as compared to three from b_2. Therefore, knowing that the Japanese will select b_1, the Allies will select a_1.

Another way to look at this situation is to assume that both players are extremely cautious in their decisions and instead of gambling will take a conservative, or pessimistic, approach.

A pessimistic, or
"minimax" approach

This approach, which is also called the *minimax* approach since it is based on the Minimax Theorem (see Part B of this chapter), implies that:

1. Both players determine the *worst possible payoff* associated with each of their alternatives.
2. Then, they each select that alternative which yields *the best* of these worst payoffs.

TABLE 11.3
Pessimistic selection

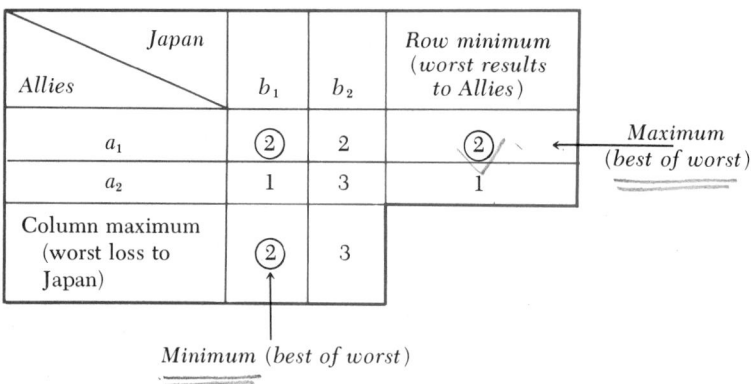

The choices of both players are illustrated in Table 11.3 The steps involved in solving the game of Table 11.3 using this approach are:

Solving the game

For the Allies

Step 1: Find the *minimum* value in each row. That is, find the worst payoff for each course of action. In this example the minimum is 2 in row a_1 and 1 in row a_2. Write it in a new column, at the right-hand side of the table.

Step 2: Select the row with the maximum of the minimums computed in step 1, as the best strategy. In this example the highest value in the newly added third column is 2. Hence, the Allies should select a_1 (the northern route).

For the Japanese

Step 1: Find the maximum in each column. In this case the maximum is 2 in column b_1 and 3 in column b_2. Write it in a new, bottom row.

Step 2: Select the column with the minimum of the maximums of step 1 as the best strategy. In this case select the lower value in the third (bottom) row, which is 2. Hence, the Japanese should sail the northern route (alternative b_1).

Maximin and minimax

Another way of looking at this is to say that player A attempts to maximize his minimum gains ("maximin"), while player B attempts to minimize his maximum losses ("minimax"). In a pure strategy game, the maximin value *must* equal the minimax value.[4] (Notice that both solutions yield 2 which is circled in Table 11.3.)

Solution to the Allies–Japanese conflict

The solution to a game answers two questions:

1. What strategy *should* each player follow? In the example:

    The Allies should follow a_1.
    The Japanese should follow b_1.

2. What will the ultimate outcome of the game (*value of the game*) be if the players follow the prescribed strategy? In the example: There will be two days of exposure. *Note:* This solution was actually adopted by both sides during the war with a resultant two days of bombing exposure.

Some notes on a pure strategy game

Change in strategy   In pure strategy games there is no incentive to change the prescribed strategy. Any player deviating from the prescribed strategy will find either no improvement or (usually) a worsening of his payoffs.

Multiple solutions   It is possible for games to have several solutions. For example, the game presented in Table 11.4 has two solutions for player A (play a_2 and/or a_4).

Multiple solutions

TABLE 11.4
Multiple solution case

Player B

		b_1	b_2	b_3	Minimum	
	a_1	7	-1	2	-1	
	a_2	4	4	6	④	← *Maximum*
Player A	a_3	6	3	0	0	
	a_4	7	4	5	④	← *Maximum*

Maximum 7   ④   6
             ↑
         Mini-
         mum

Dominance   An alternative course of action is said to "dominate" another when all the payoffs in the row (or the column) of that alternative

A dominating alternative

---

[4] Pure strategies exist only when the solution has reached a point of equilibrium or steady state, referred to as a saddle point. Therefore pure strategy games are also called "saddle point" or "strictly determined" games. For a detailed discussion of saddle points see Luce and Raiffa [8].

are as good as *and at least one is better than* the corresponding payoffs of the other. For example, in Table 11.4, alternative a_4 is better than alternative a_3, for player A, no matter what player B does. Thus, alternative a_4 is said to *dominate a_3.*

Row dominance does not seem to exist, at first sight, in Table 11.3; but column b_1 dominates column b_2 for the Japanese. Thus, the table can be reduced to that shown in Table 11.5. *Now,* however, row a_1 dominates row a_2, resulting in the final solution of (a_1, b_1). Thus, it should be noted that row (column) dominance should always be *rechecked* if a column (row) has just been deleted by dominance.

TABLE 11.5
Reduced table

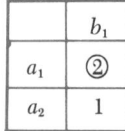

Another example of dominance is given in Table 11.6. Alternative a_2 dominates a_3, but a_1 dominates both a_2 and a_3. Likewise, b_1 dominates b_2 but not b_3 or b_4 (b_3 also dominates b_2).

TABLE 11.6
Dominance illustration

Player B

		b_1	b_2	b_3	b_4
	a_1	3	3	3	4
Player A	a_2	2	3	2	1
	a_3	2	2	2	0

Delete dominated alternatives

Summary Row dominance requires the dominating row to have entries which are larger than and/or equal to the entries in the dominated row (since A is receiving the payoff). For column dominance the entries must be smaller than and/or equal to the dominated column (since B is *losing* the payoff). Dominated rows and columns can be deleted from the matrix since they play no further role in the solution. This makes the table smaller and easier for further computations.

As can be seen in the examples, dominance will result in *a solution* in case of pure strategy games. Therefore, it could be used instead of minimax as a tool for solving pure strategy games. However, a major objective of dominance is to reduce the size of the matrix when mixed strategy games (discussed below) are encountered. Mixed strategy games are much easier to solve if they can be reduced in size first.

11.4   TWO-PERSON, ZERO-SUM GAMES—MIXED STRATEGY

Some two-person, zero-sum games are not pure strategy games. The way to judge if a game is one of pure strategy or not is to try to solve it by the pessimistic approach. If the "best of the worst" values is the same for both players (as was shown to be the case in Table 11.3), the game is a pure strategy game. Otherwise it is necessary to use a solution method called *mixed strategy*.

A mixed strategy

A marketing example

Two competing companies are to make a decision regarding an investment in a new promotional campaign. Company A considers two alternative courses of action:

a_1 = advertise in all media.
a_2 = advertise in newspapers only.

Company B considers two alternatives:

b_1 = run a sweepstake.
b_2 = run a big sale.

If company A advertises in all media and company B runs a sweepstake, then company A will increase its share of the market, at the expense of B, by 4 percent. If A advertises in all media and B runs a big sale, A will lose 1 percent of the market. If A advertises in newspapers only and B runs a sweepstake, A will lose 2 percent; and if A advertises in newspapers only and B runs a big sale, then A will gain 1 percent.

A \ B	b_1 Run a sweep-stake	b_2 Run a big sale
a_1 Advertise, all media	4	−1
a_2 Advertise, newspaper only	−2	1

TABLE 11.7
A marketing problem

√

It is assumed that the above information is known to both companies. Furthermore, it is assumed that the objective of the companies is to maintain as large a share of the market as possible. The information is summarized in the payoff matrix of Table 11.7.

Note again that positive numbers mean a gain to A (and consequently a loss to B) and negative numbers imply a loss to A and a gain to B.

Analysis of the marketing example game

Suppose a pessimistic approach is attempted (see Table 11.8) for this problem. The solution recommends that player A use a_1 and that player B use b_2. Note that the maximum value for player A of -1 (circled) is *not* equal to the minimum value for player B of 1. Assume that on the first play player A selects alternative a_1 (his proposed maximin) and player B selects alternative b_2 (his proposed minimax). As soon as A finds out that B is playing b_2, player A's second move will be a shift to a_2, since he will receive a larger payoff than playing a_1. When B finds out that A has shifted to a_2, he will shift to b_1. Then, as A finds out about this shift, he will change back to a_1, and so on.

TABLE 11.8
Minimax approach to the marketing problem

Minimax ≠ maximin

A \ B	b_1	b_2	Row minimum	
a_1	4	-1	$\boxed{-1}$	← Maximum (of minimums)
a_2	-2	1	-2	
Column maximum	4	①		

↑
Minimum (of maximums)

Both players will soon find out that:

1. It is better to shift from alternative to alternative (*mix* the alternatives) rather than play the same one all the time as with a pure strategy approach.

Maintain secrecy
2. They should practice maximum secrecy with their plans so that the opponent will not be able to guess the next move.

3. The average payoff is determined by the fraction of time (proportion) that each of the alternatives is played, and there is a certain fraction that is best for each player.

Randomly mix choices
The above points elaborate the basic idea of *mixed strategy* games. The best strategy in such a game is a *random selection* of alternatives which conform, in the long run,[5] to predetermined proportions. These proportions are designated by a frequency distribution. For example, the prescribed solution for player A may be to select alternative a_1 20 percent of the time and alternative a_2 80 percent of the time. Then, out of a series of, say, ten decisions, player A should select a_1 twice and a_2 eight

---

[5] The mixed strategy approach is based on expected value. (See Chapter 3 for discussion.)

times. The sequence of the decisions must be randomly determined,[6] however, to maintain secrecy.

Summary

A solution to a mixed strategy problem includes:
1. *Computation of the best proportion mix of the alternatives.*
2. *Computation of the value of the game,* which is the expected (average) gain or loss, per play, to player A.

Analytical solution to a mixed strategy game with two choices open to each player (2×2 game)

Let us consider the data in Table 11.7 for illustrating a mixed strategy game. This information is reproduced in Table 11.9 with corresponding generalized symbols.[7]

TABLE 11.9
Solving a mixed strategy game (c_{ij} = payoff)

	Player B			
	Proportions		(q)	$(1-q)$
		Choices	b_1	b_2
Player A	(p)	a_1	$c_{11}=4$	$c_{12}=-1$
	$(1-p)$	a_2	$c_{21}=-2$	$c_{22}=1$

Solution   Let us assume that player B plays alternative b_1 consistently and player A plays a_1 in p of the cases and a_2 in $(1-p)$ of the cases. The *expected payoff* (V_1) to player A is then (using an expected value formula and treating the proportion as probabilities):

Calculating the expected payoff

$$V_1 = p(4) + (1-p)(-2)$$

Similarly, when B plays b_2 consistently, the expected payoff to A is:

$$V_2 = p(-1) + (1-p)(1)$$

---

[6] One way to assure random choice is to take ten pieces of paper and write a_1 on two of them and a_2 on eight of them. Then mix them up in a container and, without looking, draw one piece of paper for the first play. Return the paper and draw a second piece for the next play, and so on. For other ways of random selection, see Chapter 14.

[7] With two choices, the proportions for A could be denoted as p_1 and p_2; however, since $p_1 + p_2 = 1$ or $p_2 = 1 - p_1$, there is only one unknown, which is designated as p in this case. A similar designation is made for B, using q instead of p.

Player A desires to mix his strategies so that player B cannot reduce A's gain by shifting strategies. To do so, the expected payoff to A when B plays either strategy b_1 or strategy b_2 should be the same. That is, the two expected payoffs V_1 and V_2 must be equal:

$$\overbrace{p(4) + (1 - p)(-2)}^{V_1, \text{ when B plays } b_1} = \overbrace{p(-1) + (1 - p)(1)}^{V_2, \text{ when B plays } b_2}$$

or

$$4p - 2 + 2p = -p + 1 - p$$

This equation is then solved for p, yielding a solution of $8p = 3$ or $p = \frac{3}{8}$. That is, the proportion for a_1 is $\frac{3}{8}$ and for a_2 is $1 - \frac{3}{8} = \frac{5}{8}$.

The general case The requirement that $V_1 = V_2$ yields the following equation:

$$pc_{11} + (1 - p)c_{21} = pc_{12} + (1 - p)c_{22}$$

Rearrangement of this equation yields the following:

$$p = \frac{c_{22} - c_{21}}{c_{11} - c_{12} - c_{21} + c_{22}} \tag{11.1}$$

In our example, the proportion p, for playing a_1, is prescribed for player A:

$$p = \frac{1 - (-2)}{4 - (-1) - (-2) + 1} = \frac{3}{8}$$

and the proportion for playing a_2 is:

$$1 - p = 1 - \frac{3}{8} = \frac{5}{8}$$

Thus, player A should choose alternative a_1 in $\frac{3}{8}$ of the plays and alternative a_2 for the remaining $\frac{5}{8}$ of the plays. Of course, alternatives should be "mixed" randomly. Similarly, for player B, the proportion q of playing b_1 is derived by equating $V_1 = V_2$ for the columns, which, in this case, yields the following equation:

$$qc_{11} + (1 - q)c_{12} = qc_{21} + (1 - q)c_{22}$$

or

$$q = \frac{c_{22} - c_{12}}{c_{11} - c_{12} - c_{21} + c_{22}} \tag{11.2}$$

In our example

$$q = \frac{1 - (-1)}{4 - (-1) - (-2) + 1} = \frac{2}{8} = .25$$

and the proportion for playing b_2 is $1 - q = .75$. Thus player B should randomly mix his strategies so that in the long run b_1 is chosen 25 percent and b_2 is chosen 75 percent of the time the game is played.

The value of the game   Once p and q are established, the *value of the game*, V, can be determined. Assuming that player A plays with the prescribed probability p, his or her payoff (expected average reward per play) can be found by using *one* of the following four[8] equations:

Calculating the value of the game

$$
\begin{aligned}
\text{either} \quad & V = pc_{11} + (1 - p)c_{21} \\
\text{or} \quad & V = pc_{12} + (1 - p)c_{22} \\
\text{or} \quad & V = qc_{11} + (1 - q)c_{12} \\
\text{or} \quad & V = qc_{21} + (1 - q)c_{22}
\end{aligned}
\tag{11.3}
$$

In our example:

$$V = \frac{3}{8} \times 4 + \frac{5}{8} \times (-2) = \frac{1}{4}$$

$$V = \frac{3}{8} \times (-1) + \frac{5}{8} \times 1 = \frac{1}{4}$$

$$V = \frac{1}{4} \times 4 + \frac{3}{4} \times (-1) = \frac{1}{4}$$

$$V = \frac{1}{4} \times (-2) + \frac{3}{4} \times 1 = \frac{1}{4}$$

Thus, the value of the game is $\frac{1}{4}$. Since a game matrix is in terms of the payoff to A, then there is an expected gain of $\frac{1}{4}$ to A and an expected loss (per play) of $\frac{1}{4}$ to B. To summarize the solution for our example:

Player A: Play a_1 $\frac{3}{8}$ of the time and a_2 $\frac{5}{8}$ of the time.
Player B: Play b_1 $\frac{1}{4}$ of the time and b_2 $\frac{3}{4}$ of the time.

The value of the game is $\frac{1}{4}$; that is, A's expected gain is $\frac{1}{4}$ and B's expected loss is $\frac{1}{4}$.

11.5   SUMMARY OF TWO-PERSON, ZERO-SUM GAMES

The material and examples presented so far in this chapter can be summarized as follows:

Formulation

Competitive and conflicting decision situations can be presented in the form of a game. So far the discussion was limited to cases involving

---

[8] A good check is to compute V in alternate ways. In a correct solution, the results must be the same.

two competitors. The situation is presented in the form of a game payoff matrix which includes the following information:

1. All courses of action open to both decision makers.
2. All the conditional payoffs resulting from any combination of decisions made by both players.

Assumptions

It is assumed that the decision makers know the information presented in the decision matrix and that they decide on choices simultaneously. It is also assumed that they employ a rational approach in trying to resolve the conflict in their favor.

The conceptual basis for the solution is the assumption that the value of the gain to the winner is exactly the same as that of the loss to the loser. Furthermore, it is assumed that a player will try to make conservative decisions by using the pessimistic approach; that is, a player will attempt to maximize minimum gains or minimize maximum losses. (A discussion of these assumptions is given in Part B of this chapter.)

Solution approach

The solution approach depends on the category of the game. If it is a pure strategy game, the solution can be derived using the pessimistic approach. If it is a mixed strategy game, then its solution method depends on its size. Although all games can be solved by the use of linear programming (see Part B of this chapter), it is much easier to solve small games of 2×2 size by Equations 11.1, 11.2, and 11.3. Furthermore, games of the size $2 \times M$[9] can be graphically reduced to 2×2 games (see Williams [13]).

The major idea of a mixed strategy game is that the decision maker must switch among the available alternatives as the situation is repeated. This contrasts with the pure strategy games in which he (or she) must stick to one and only one choice. A solution to the mixed strategy game involves computation of a proportion mix, a ratio indicating the percent of time that each alternative is to be used.

Since a game is viewed as composed of a series of repetitive plays, the result is computed as an average or expected payoff per play, labeled the value of the game.

The solution procedure is schematically shown in Figure 11.2.

---

[9] A game in which player A has two alternatives and player B has many (M) alternatives.

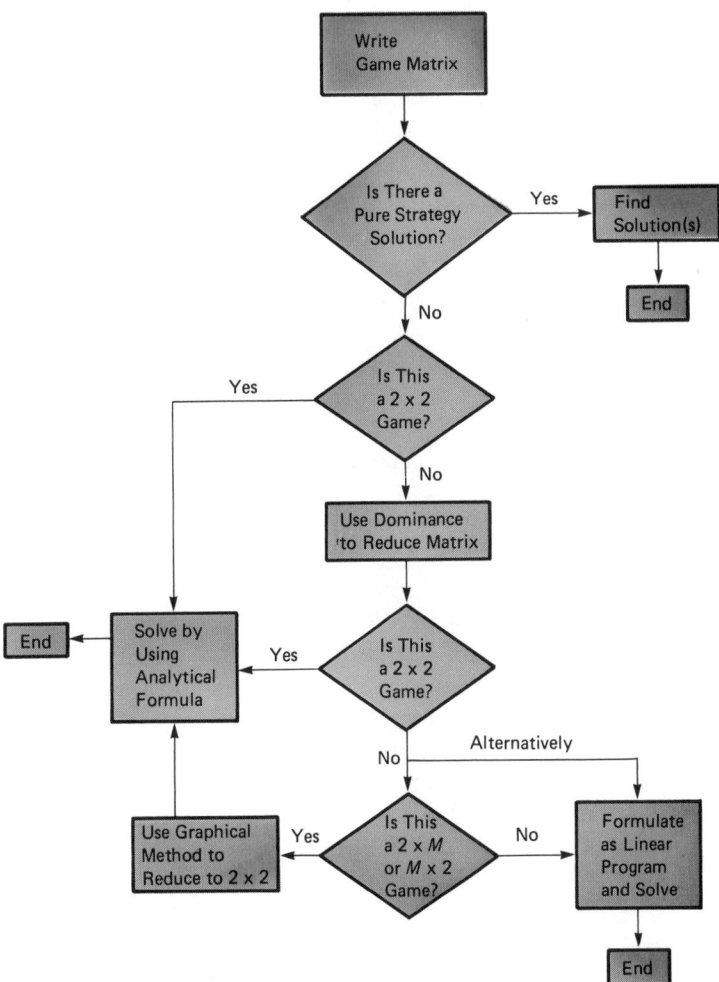

FIGURE 11.2
Schematic procedure for solving two-person, zero-sum games

11.6   NONZERO-SUM GAMES AND N-PERSON GAMES

Nonzero sum games

In zero-sum games, the sum of the payoffs to all players at any given play is zero. In the case of two players, whatever one loses the other wins. Now suppose that the sum of the payoffs is not zero. For example, suppose the winer must pay taxes on the gain. In such a case, that gain is *smaller* than the opponent's loss. Or suppose that a poor person plays a rich person. The *value* (utility) of the money to the poor person is probably much higher than to the rich one and, therefore, although the gain in terms of dollars equals the loss, the utility gained by a poor winner is probably much larger than the utility lost by a rich loser. These and similar situations are treated as nonzero-sum games.

When your loss is *not* my gain

Example: The prisoners' dilemma

Two suspected bank robbers have been apprehended and questioned separately. The district attorney offers each (separately) a chance of confessing. Each robber knows that if he confesses, he will get only one year in jail if his confession is used to convict his accomplice, who will then be sentenced to ten years. However, if his accomplice also confesses, each will receive five years. On the other hand, if neither confesses, each will only get three years. (The district attorney has enough evidence to ensure conviction on a lesser charge.) The prisoners cannot communicate with each other, but they know all the above information (arranged in Table 11.10).

TABLE 11.10
The prisoner's dilemma

Prisoner A \ Prisoner B	Confess	Not confess
Confess	(5, 5)	(1, 10)
Not confess	(10, 1)	(3,3)

The data in the cells represent "years in jail." In each cell there are two numbers. The left one designates A's "payoff," the right, B's. The prisoners are facing a dilemma—*to confess or not to confess!*

The prisoners' dilemma is a classical example of a *nonzero-sum game*. The approach to the solution of the two-person, zero-sum game was obtained via minimax, which is based on the assumption that player B's losses are player A's gains. This is justified by viewing the goals of the two players as *diametrically opposed.*

Let us analyze the prisoners' dilemma by the pessimistic approach. To do so, the data in Table 11.10 is divided into two tables, one for prisoner A and one for prisoner B (Table 11.11).

TABLE 11.11

A's table

A \ B	Confess	Not confess
Confess	5	1
Not confess	10	3

confess < not confess
                choice

B's table

A \ B	Confess	Not confess
Confess	5	10
Not confess	1	3

Analysis   If prisoner A used minimax, he would confess since the worst outcome following confession would be five years in jail. (Notice that the "confess" row dominates the "not confess" row; thus the latter will not be considered by A.) Similarly, using the minimax approach, prisoner B will confess, too.

The above approach seems to suggest that the solution of games such as this is not really very different from that of zero-sum games. The problem is that the minimax approach is not always the best. In this case, two prisoners not acquainted with the theory of games might both refuse to confess and thereby serve only three years each, while two sophisticated prisoners, following game theory logic, would end up serving five years each.

The role of communication

Now, let us examine the same situation assuming communication between the prisoners were possible. In this case, the prisoners would decide (if they trusted each other) *not to confess* and thus get three years each. This illustrates the importance of *communication* and *cooperation*[10] in nonzero-sum games. The solution achieved with cooperation in the above example is superior to the minimax solution.

The role of communication and cooperation

Furthermore, the prisoners' dilemma is an example of a "one-shot" decision. When repetitive decisions are involved, it is logical to assume that the robbers will arrive at a decision "not to confess," even without communicating.

General discussion

In the case of two players, a nonzero-sum situation may occur when their goals are not diametrically opposed. In such a case, one cannot conclude that just because player B has the power to limit player A's gains, he will necessarily do so. Such situations are rather common in reality. For example:

- When the amount gained by the winner is not the same as that lost by the loser (due, for instance, to taxes or special expenses).
- When the quantity of the commodity that changes hands remains the same but the value attached to it by the opponents differs.
- When both sides can gain from an agreement as in the case of some labor-management disputes.

The solution process of nonzero-sum games is much more complicated than the one prescribed by minimax, since the problem is more complex and may include additional features such as communication

---

[10] For a discussion of cooperative games, see Luce and Raiffa [8].

and bargaining.[11] The possibility of bargaining arises especially in repetitive games. If bargaining occurs, then considerations such as the psychological status and the relative bargaining strength of the competitors enter the picture. The possibility of bargaining opens the door to other factors—threats, bluffs, and conspiracy—all of which complicate the analysis even further.

The role of personality

Another complication, as Rapoport [9] points out, is that the concept of rationality itself becomes ambiguous. In zero-sum games, the minimax criterion is sufficient to obtain a solution to the game. In the case of nonzero-sum games, however, behavioral considerations arise (such as "Should I respond to his bid to cooperate, or should I exploit his vulnerability?") which may hamper obtaining a simple, rational solution through strictly mathematical means. Nonzero-sum games can be solved only with reference to the personalities and the needs of the particular participants and, therefore, are quite useful in experimental gaming (see Buchler and Nutini [5]).

N-person games (N > 2)

The complexity of coalitions

Example Three companies—A, B, and C—are competing in one market, presently equally divided among them. Assume that A offers B the opportunity to form a *coalition* against C, which will mean the elimination of C. A offers B 55 percent of the future market. When C finds this out, he could offer to join with B against A, offering B 60 percent of the future market. When A discovers the latest offer, he or she may offer 65 percent to B or to C. This process could go on and on.

The example illustrates one of the major features of games involving three or more decision makers—coalitions. In many cases, their formation stabilizes after a certain period, resulting in only two groups. At that point, the approach of two-person games can be used. However, there are 2^{N-1} possible ways of forming two coalitions when N decision makers are involved.

Several studies (see [5], [9], and [11]) have investigated the formation of coalitions. Two general rules have been observed to operate:

1. An individual joins a coalition if he or she remains at least as well off as before.
2. Each coalition usually gives rise to another competing one (counter-coalition).

With respect to the above rules, there are some unanswered questions. For example:

How are coalitions formed?
Will people join for maximum payoff?

---

[11] See Rapoport [9].

Why do countercoalitions exist, though they sometimes promise less payoff than not forming the countercoalition?

Other studies in this area have investigated what produces conditions of stability. In most of these situations a normative approach which prescribes "what the decision makers *should* do" is meaningless. Scientists, therefore, carry out *experiments* to find out what people actually do in such situations.

11.7 CONCLUSION

The reader, now familiar with the major concepts and rules of game theory, can appreciate some of the roadblocks in applying it to real situations of conflict. Concepts such as moves, strategies, complete information, payoff matrix, and simultaneous decisions are theoretical idealizations with intuitive meaning but very little practicability. It seems that even the two-person, zero-sum game, the only game model currently completely solved mathematically, is oversimplified. Moreover, even if the assumptions of a given conflict are more or less reasonable and the model replicates reality, behavioral problems such as convincing the players to use the proportion-mix strategy approach may interfere with any analytical solution.

Game theory only provides a starting point for the study and analysis of conflicts; but because in real life these are so complex, the current stage of the theory is not capable of actually solving most cases. Realizing this, one may ask: "Why study game theory if its application is so obscure?" The answer is:

1. Game theory stimulates us to think about conflicts in a novel way. It helps form a framework for working on complex problems. Concepts such as strategy and payoff give valuable orientation to those who must think about complicated conflict situations. *(Novel way to analyze conflict)*
2. It leads us to see why the existing theory is inadequate. It stimulates us to think and to look around for better solutions, thereby initiating further research.
3. The theory is applicable to almost any type of conflict (military, economic, political, and social, to name a few).
4. The game formulation often helps explain much of the phenomena being observed.
5. Game theory formulations and solutions may give the reader a better understanding of the intricacies of life and help explain social behavior.

Although many of the accomplishments of game theory are of a rather conceptual or of a general nature, its ideas, methodology, and vocabulary have become part of the daily thinking and language of many decision makers in a broad spectrum of activities ranging from corporation board meetings to top-level political conferences. Perhaps the best evidence that game theory has come of age is the recent publication (1972) of the periodical *International Journal of Game Theory*, the first journal wholly devoted to game theory. Another encouraging bit of evidence is RAND Corporation's bibliography [1] listing over 400 papers and books, many of which are related to applications of game theory.

11.8 PROBLEMS FOR PART A

1. Find the best strategy (strategies) for each player in the following two-person, zero-sum games. Also find the value of the game to both players. Circle the points of maximin and minimax.

a.

	b_1	b_2
a_1	1	3
a_2	7	4

b.

	b_1	b_2
a_1	−1	0
a_2	1	3

c.

	b_1	b_2	b_3
a_1	1	−2	3
a_2	−2	−5	−3
a_3	−1	−6	−5

d.

	b_1	b_2	b_3	b_4	b_5
a_1	3	3	1	6	0
a_2	−1	1	2	0	8
a_3	6	−3	2	1	4
a_4	5	3	3	6	4

2. Two companies are competing in a duopolistic market.[12] Both attempt to increase their share of the market which is now equally divided. Company A plans to have a weekly advertising campaign which can increase its share of the

[12] A market with only two competitors.

market by 3 percent (of the total market) if company B does nothing. Company B, however, plans a weekly price cut which will result in a 4 percent gain to B if A does nothing and 1 percent gain to B if A uses the advertising campaign. No change in the market is foreseen if both companies do nothing.

a. Arrange the problem in a payoff table.

b. Suggest the best strategy for each company to follow.

3. Solve the following game:

	b_1	b_2
a_1	3	−2
a_2	1	5

4. Given below is a payoff table for two manufacturers, A and B, competing in one market. Each has to make a decision between two alternatives.

	B b_1	b_2
A a_1	−2	3
a_2	1	0

a. Assuming that this is a repetitive decision, what is the best policy for the manufacturers?

b. Let the figures in the payoff table be percentage of change in market share; what will the average gain (loss) to each manufacturer be?

c. As a manager of company B, would you follow the prescribed strategy? Why or why not?

5. A and B play a game in which each has three coins, A has a 2 cent coin, a nickel, and a dime. B has a penny, a nickel, and a dime. Each selects one of his or her coins without knowledge of the other's choice. If the sum of the two coins adds to an odd number, A wins B's coin. If the sum is an even number, B wins A's coin.

a. Arrange the payoff table.

Solve the games. What can you conclude about the relationship among the three games in this case?

8. Two companies plan a TV advertising campaign for a competitive product. TV ads run during four basic periods: morning (M), afternoon (A), evening (E), and night (N). Advertising time is available in units; company A can afford one unit only, and company B can afford two units. Thus, company A has four choices, advertise in M, A, E, or N, while company B has ten alternatives as shown below:

		B									
		$M(2)$	$A(2)$	$E(2)$	$N(2)$	$M(1)$ $A(1)$	$M(1)$ $E(1)$	$M(1)$ $N(1)$	$A(1)$ $E(1)$	$A(1)$ $N(1)$	$E(1)$ $N(1)$
A	M	.30	.25	.20	.30	.25	.20	.30	.20	.25	.25
	A	.35	.25	.20	.40	.30	.25	.30	.20	.25	.30
	E	.40	.30	.25	.50	.30	.35	.35	.25	.30	.35
	N	.25	.20	.10	.25	.20	.15	.20	.15	.20	.20

b. Find the best strategy for both players.
c. If you had to play the game, would you rather be A or B? Why?

6. Check the following payoff table for dominance:

	b_1	b_2	b_3	b_4	b_5
a_1	-3	4	3	2	0
a_2	2	1	4	6	3
a_3	2	1	3	5	1
a_4	1	6	-4	3	1
a_5	2	1	3	4	1

Show the reduced matrix.

7. Given three game tables:

TABLE 1

	b_1	b_2
a_1	3	-2
a_2	-3	0

TABLE 2

	b_1	b_2
a_1	5	0
a_2	-1	2

TABLE 3

	b_1	b_2
a_1	6	-4
a_2	-6	0

The payoff table shows the conditional share of the market captured by company A. For example, if A uses one unit in the morning and B uses two units in the morning, then A gets 30 percent of the market and B gets the remaining 70 percent.

It is assumed that the objective of each company is to maximize its share of the market and that the cost of advertising is the same per unit.

View this situation as a zero-sum game.

a. What action should each company take?
b. How will the market then be divided?

9. Two companies compete in a market and consider promotional campaigns. If both advertise simultaneously, the market share will remain unchanged and both will lose the expenses of the campaign which are estimated by company A to equal 9 units of utility and by B to equal 11 units. If neither advertises, there will be no change in the market (i.e., no change in utility). If A advertises and B does not, A will gain 6 units, B will lose 14 units. If B advertises and A does not, B will gain 8 units and A will lose 14 units. What strategy should the two companies follow?

a. Present the problem in game form. Write two payoff tables: one for company A and one for company B.

b. Solve by minimax. Assume that the companies do not communicate with each other. Comment on the results.

c. Assume that the companies communicate and cooperate prior to the decision. What will they do then?

d. What could be the difference between a one-shot decision and a repetitive decision in the noncooperative case (part [*b*])?

10. Any farmer's dilemma is how much to plant each season. Several factors contribute to the dilemma. In the first place, nature is merciless and he (or she) who plants does not know how much he will be able to reap. Secondly, there are many farmers competing in the market and there is little cooperation between them with regard to the amount planted. Thirdly, the market is also merciless. There is an upper limit to quantities that can be sold, and prices drop very rapidly as quantities increase. If a farmer plants large quantities (which means large expenses), he may suffer a huge loss if prices drop. On the other hand, if he plants small quantities, he may lose the opportunity for making large profits. A farmer's dilemma can be presented as a two-person game if we envision all other farmers as one competitor. Let us assume that nature's influence is negligible and that the farmer's problem is whether to plant on a small scale (100 acres) or on a large scale (250 acres). We assume for simplicity that the other farmers will plant either on a small scale (2,000 acres) or on a large scale (5,000 acres).

There are four possible consequences in this situation:

1. All farmers including ours, plant on a small scale. In that case, there will be 2,100 acres planted, and the profit per acre will be $100.

2. All farmers plant on a large scale. The total planted acreage will be 5,250, and the profit per acre will be $10.

3. Our farmer plants 100 acres; the others plant 5,000 acres. The profit per acre will be $12.

4. Our farmer plants 250 acres, and the rest plant 2,000 acres. The expected profit is $90 per acre.

a. Present the problem in matrix form (two matrices, one for our farmer and one for the "other" farmers).

b. Solve using the minimax approach. Assume no communication.

c. Solve assuming communication and cooperation.

11. Two competing companies consider the advertising alternatives below. The table shows the alternatives and the percent increase in market share for company A. One percent of the share of the market is considered equal to $10,000.

			B		
	B_1	B_2	B_3	B_4	B_5
A_1	1	0	−1	−8	−9
A_2	5	3	5	−7	−3
A_3	7	−1	1	7	9

(A labels the rows A_1, A_2, A_3.)

Find:

1. The optimal strategy of each company.
2. The average, per period, monetary gain (loss) to company B.

PART B: EXTENSIONS

11.9   GRAPHICAL SOLUTION

Consider the game shown in Table 11.12, which is the marketing game solved previously by the analytical method. Assume that player B plays b_1 all the time. What will the value of such a game be

TABLE 11.12
(Table 11.7 reproduced)

			b_1	b_2
	(p)	a_1	4	-1
Player A	$(1-p)$	a_2	-2	1

Player B

to player A? The value will depend on what A does. If A plays a_1 all the time, the value of the game will be 4. If A plays a_2 all the time, the value will be -2; and if A mixes his or her choices with a proportion p, then the *expected value* of the game will be $V_1 = 4p - 2(1 - p)$, or $6p - 2$. Similarly, if B plays b_2 all the time, the value of the game to A will be $-p + (1 - p)$, or $-2p + 1$.

The values $V_1 = 6p - 2$ and $V_2 = -2p + 1$ can be represented graphically by straight lines. These lines are shown in Figure 11.3.

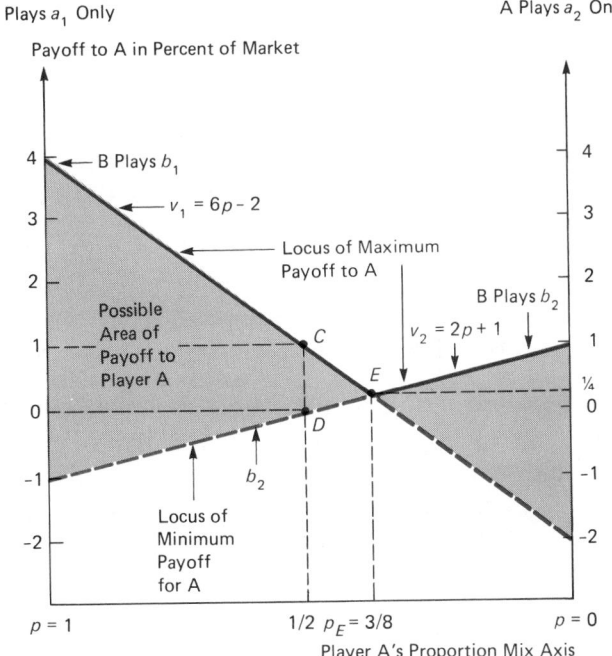

A Plays a_1 Only

A Plays a_2 Only

FIGURE 11.3
Player A's strategy mix

Payoff to A in Percent of Market

B Plays b_1

$v_1 = 6p - 2$

Locus of Maximum Payoff to A

B Plays b_2

Possible Area of Payoff to Player A

$v_2 = 2p + 1$

C

E

D

b_2

Locus of Minimum Payoff for A

$p = 1$

$1/2$ $p_E = 3/8$

$p = 0$

Player A's Proportion Mix Axis

Value of p

Construction of the lines

The horizontal axis, which represents the proportion of time that A will play a_1, is constructed first, starting with $p = 0$ on the right side up to $p = 1$ on the left side. Every point on the horizontal axis represents the proportion mix between a_1 and a_2. At the far left ($p = 1$) player A will choose a_1 all the time, while at the other end ($p = 0$) alternative a_2 is played all the time. At any other point there is a mix of the two alternatives. For example, at $p = \frac{1}{3}$, the mix consists of choosing a_1 $\frac{1}{3}$ of the time and a_2 $\frac{2}{3}$ of the time.

Plotting the strategies

The vertical axis represents the payoff to player A. The scaling of this axis is set arbitrarily (e.g., $1'' = 3$ percent of the market). Now, two straight lines are plotted, each corresponding to one of B's alternatives, in the following way: For the payoff resulting from B playing b_1 all the time, a *straight line* is drawn from 4 percent on the left side to -2 percent on the right side. This is the line[13] $V_1 = 6p - 2$. Note that 4 percent is in cell c_{11} and that -2 is in cell c_{21} of Table 11.12. Next, a straight line is drawn for the situation in which B plays b_2 all the time: from -1 percent on the left to 1 percent on the right (these figures are in the b_2 column), describing the line $V_2 = -2p + 1$.

Let us now examine the case in which A mixes his alternatives, say .5 of a_1 and .5 of a_2 (i.e., at a point $p = \frac{1}{2}$). The value of the game may be either 1 percent (.5 times 4 percent plus .5 times -2 percent) if B sticks to b_1; or 0 (.5 times -1 percent plus .5 times 1 percent) if B plays b_2. These values are shown as points C and D, respectively, in Figure 11.3. If B mixes his choices, the payoff will be between 1 and 0 (graphically shown as the line CD).

The boundaries as payoffs

The shaded area represents the entire feasible area of payoffs when p varies between 0 and 1. Player A will try to look for a payoff on the *upper boundary* of this feasible area (bold line) which is the locus of maximum payoffs to A. Player B will try to establish the payoff at the *lower boundary* (broken line) of the feasible area (locus of minimum payoffs to A). For example, if player A tries to get 4 percent by playing a_1 all the time, then B will find out and play b_2 all the time; thus A will lose 1 percent instead of gaining 4 percent. The same situation holds true for every point on the boundary except E. At that point, *no matter what B does*, the payoff to A is the maximum possible for that value of p_E. However, it is also equal to the minimum payoff; that is, point E is the lowest on the upper boundary and the highest on the lower boundary at the same time.

The proportion p_E can be read off the horizontal axis as $\frac{3}{8}$; that is, A should play a_1 $\frac{3}{8}$ of the time (and therefore a_2 $\frac{5}{8}$ of the time). The value of

---

[13] The line has the following meaning: If we set $p = 0$, then player A plays a_2 all the time with a payoff of -2. If $p = 1$, then the payoff is $(6 \times 1) - 2 = 4$, which is achieved when A plays a_1 all the time.

the game is found at point E and can be read off the vertical axis as $V = \frac{1}{4}$ percent.

In a similar manner, it is possible to present B's situation on an additional chart. It will reveal that B's best strategy is to mix b_1 $\frac{1}{4}$ of the time and b_2 $\frac{3}{4}$ of the time. To sum up, the solution of this game is:

$$p = \frac{3}{8} \text{ (play } a_1\text{)};$$
$$1 - p = \frac{5}{8} \text{ (play } a_2\text{)};$$
$$q = \frac{1}{4} \text{ (play } b_1\text{) and}$$
$$1 - q = \frac{3}{4} \text{ (play } b_2\text{)}.$$

The average gain to player A is $\frac{1}{4}$ (B loses $\frac{1}{4}$).

The graphical method can be used to solve games where one of the players has two alternatives and the other has three or more alternatives. (For details, see Williams [13].) A more general method that can handle games of any size is transformation to linear programming.

11.10 LINEAR PROGRAMMING AS A METHOD OF SOLUTION

In order to demonstrate the use of linear programming in solving games, the earlier example of a 2 × 2 game will be used. Linear programming, however, can be used with a game of any size, within practical limits. The example is reproduced as Table 11.13.

TABLE 11.13

B A	b_1	b_2
a_1	4	−1
a_2	−2	1

The solution involves two stages:

1. If negative values exist, it becomes necessary to "scale-up" all entries by adding a fixed number to them. (The scaling does not affect the optimal solution except to increase its value by the scaled-up figure.) Scaling will make all entries either zero[14] or positive. In our case, 3 is added to all cells as shown in Table 11.14.

TABLE 11.14

B A	b_1	b_2
a_1	7	2
a_2	1	4

---

[14] In scaling for a linear programming computer solution, it is generally wise to scale in such a way as to produce as many zeros as possible to reduce computer calculation and to save storage space. But, here we deliberately scaled up so that zeros are avoided in order to illustrate a more general example.

2. Transformation into linear programming form. Each game can be transformed to either a maximization or a minimization form.

Example: Transformation to a minimization problem

Let us look at the problem from the point of view of player A. Player A wants to design his game in such a manner that *at least* a payoff u is guaranteed. Assume that he mixes a_1 and a_2 with proportions p_1 and p_2. Then, the above requirement can be written as two inequalities:

Step 1. *Write the inequalities (constraints).*

$7p_1 + 1p_2 \geq u$ (The expected gain, when player B plays b_1 all the time, is at least as large as u.)

$2p_1 + 4p_2 \geq u$ (The expected gain, when player B plays b_2 all the time, is at least as large as u.)

The coefficients of each of the two inequalities are determined by reading each column of the game matrix, starting with the first.

Step 2. *Divide the inequalities by u.* The result is:

$$\frac{7p_1}{u} + \frac{1p_2}{u} \geq 1$$

$$\frac{2p_1}{u} + \frac{4p_2}{u} \geq 1 \tag{11.4}$$

Step 3. *Introduce auxiliary variables.* Now, let us introduce two new variables, x_1 and x_2, whose value, by definition, is given as:

$$x_1 = \frac{p_1}{u} \quad \text{and} \quad x_2 = \frac{p_2}{u} \tag{11.5}$$

Having introduced the new variables into Equation 11.4, the constraints can now be rewritten as:

$$7x_1 + 1x_2 \geq 1$$
$$2x_1 + 4x_2 \geq 1$$

Step 4. *Construct the objective function.* Because player A has only two courses of action to choose from, there are only two proportions to consider (p_1 and p_2) whose sum equals one ($p_1 + p_2 = 1$).

Now, divide the equation $p_1 + p_2 = 1$ by u. The result is:

$$\frac{p_1}{u} + \frac{p_2}{u} = \frac{1}{u}$$

Introducing the auxiliary variables x_1 and x_2 we obtain:

$$x_1 + x_2 = \frac{1}{u} \qquad (11.6)$$

Player A would like to have no less than u, but he would also like u to be as high as possible, or to maximize u. This is equivalent to minimizing $1/u$ or to minimizing $x_1 + x_2$. Hence, player A can now formulate the problem.

Step 5. *Formulate the linear programming problem.* The result of the previous step is the objective function.

$$\text{minimize } w = x_1 + x_2$$

The objective function is subject to the constraints derived in step 3.

$$7x_1 + 1x_2 \geq 1$$
$$2x_1 + 4x_2 \geq 1$$

Step 6. *Solve the linear programming problem.* The optimal solution is:

$$x_1 = \frac{3}{26} \quad \text{and} \quad x_2 = \frac{5}{26}$$

A linear programming presentation for player B can be generated similarly. (This time the objective function is to be *maximized.*)

$$\text{maximize } z = y_1 + y_2$$
$$\text{subject to: } 7y_1 + 2y_2 \leq 1$$
$$1y_1 + 4y_2 \leq 1$$

where y_1 and y_2 are auxiliary variables:

$$y_1 = \frac{q_1}{u}; \ y_2 = \frac{q_2}{u}.$$

The optimal solution for this problem is:

$$y_1 = \frac{1}{13}$$

$$y_2 = \frac{3}{13}$$

Step 7. *Find the proportion mix.* In order to find the proportions (p for player A, q for B) of the mixed strategy, a *transformation ratio*, **Transformation ratio** t, is defined as:

$$t = \sum y_i = \sum x_j \qquad (11.7)$$

In our case, we get:

$$t = \sum y_i = \frac{1}{13} + \frac{3}{13} = \frac{4}{13}$$

or

$$t = \sum x_j = \frac{3}{26} + \frac{5}{26} = \frac{8}{26} = \frac{4}{13}$$

Now, all y_i's and x_j's are divided by the transformation ratio to get the proportion mix for both players.

For player A:

$$p_j = \frac{x_j}{t} \tag{11.8}$$

In the example:

$$p_1 = \frac{3/26}{4/13} = \frac{3}{8}$$

$$p_2 = \frac{5/26}{4/13} = \frac{5}{8}$$

For player B:

$$q_i = \frac{y_i}{t} \tag{11.9}$$

In the example:

$$q_1 = \frac{1/13}{4/13} = \frac{1}{4}$$

$$q_2 = \frac{3/13}{4/13} = \frac{3}{4}$$

Step 8. Finally, the value of the game is computed. Using Equation 11.10:

$$V = \frac{1}{t} - k \tag{11.10}$$

where k is the number added while scaling up.

In our case, $k = 3$ and $t = 4/13$, thus $1/t = 13/4$ and V is:

$$V = \frac{13}{4} - 3 = \frac{1}{4}$$

Summary of the solution:

Player A: Play a_1 ⅜ of the time, a_2 ⅝ of the time.

Player B: Play b_1 ¼ of the time, b_2 ¾ of the time.
A gains in each play, on the average, ¼ from B.

11.11   PAYOFFS, VALUES, AND THE MINIMAX THEOREM

Game theory is a branch of mathematics which can be studied without relating it to behavioral problems, to applications, or to actual games. However, these factors are important to us. Therefore, some are discussed below.

Outcome of the game and actual payoff to the players

In Section 11.1 payoff was defined as the "consequence of the decisions." An outcome of a specific game can be "a win," "a loss," or "a draw." Furthermore, the payoff can be quantitative in nature, measured in units such as dollars or market share, or it can be expressed in qualitative terms, such as "prices will probably hold, but there is a good chance that company A will lose the Los Angeles market." It is reasonable to assume that the players' behavior is determined not by the outcome but by the *importance* or the *value* attached to the outcome. In two-person, zero-sum games, we are faced not only with the problem of translating outcomes to values but sometimes with the additional problem of dealing with probabilistic or risky decisions. The analytical treatment of such problems is the key contribution of Von Neuman and Morgenstern [12]. They used the idea of *cardinal utility theory* in the following way:

Cardinal utility theory

First, they assumed that the outcome of a game can be expressed by utilities whenever necessary. Then they introduced the idea that utility functions can be so arranged that the *expected utility of the outcome of a risky decision is always equal to the weighted average of its prizes.*[15]

As an example, consider the game presented in Table 11.15. According to Von Neuman and Morgenstern, if player A plays a_1 40

	b_1	b_2
a_1	4	-1
a_2	-2	1

TABLE 11.15

percent of the time and a_2 60 percent of the time, then the expected utility, if player B plays b_1 constantly (assuming that the figures in the cells represent utilities to A) is:

$$.4 \times 4 + .6 \times (-2) = .4$$

---

[15] These assumptions are also used in the application of the expected value principle in decision making under risk (see Chapter 3).

The minimax theorem

The solution of two-person, zero-sum games is based on the minimax theorem, which states that *each player should play in such a way as to maximize his or her minimum gains.* Players are expected to follow this theory because:

1. If player A maximizes the minimum payoff, he or she can get *at least* a value of $\underline{V}$ ($\underline{V}$ means V or more).
2. If player B follows the minimax approach, he or she can limit A's gain to no more than $\bar{V}$; that is, limit losses to $\bar{V}$ ($\bar{V}$ means V or less).

The minimax idea

The minimax theorem of game theory states that if mixed strategies are allowed, then there always exists a value of the game, V, such that:

$$\bar{V} = \underline{V} = V \qquad (11.11)$$

The minimax criterion defines a solution to two-person, zero-sum games when several simplifying assumptions are made. However, as experiments indicate, the players often do not follow the minimax approach, especially in mixed strategy cases.

11.12   PROBLEMS FOR PART B

12. Examine Figure 11.3 and graphically find the best strategy and payoff to player B if player A plays:
    a. a_2 80 percent of the time.
    b. a_2 20 percent of the time.
13. Show a graphical solution for the pure strategy case (the Allies-Japan case) of Table 11.2 and explain the difference between it and mixed strategy.
14. Given the two-person, zero-sum games:

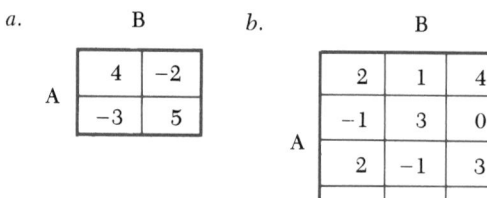

Write the equivalent linear programming problems for both (a) and (b). Find the optimal strategies and the value of the game.

15. Change the following linear programming problems into game form.
    a. maximize $z = 3x_1 + 3.5x_2$
       subject to:
       $$x_1 + 2x_2 \le 4,000$$
       $$4x_1 + 3x_2 \le 12,000$$
    b. minimize $w = 2x_1 + x_2$
       subject to:
       $$3x_1 + 2x_2 \ge 20$$
       $$x_1 + 3x_2 \ge 16$$

11.13   CASE

THE VIDEOTAPE STRATEGY

The Soonie Company is a manufacturer of videotapes. Being a leader in its field, the company runs national ads comparing its products to those of Pany, its major competitor.

Soonie uses three advertising strategies: a_1—a direct attack on their competitor; a_2—an indirect attack; and a_3—no attack at all.

Pany is a more conservative company. It uses these advertising strategies: b_1—"our products are of the highest quality"; b_2—"our products give you more for your money"; and b_3—"sure, you can buy other products, but. . . ."

Soonie's advertising budget amounts to hundreds of thousands of dollars annually. Basic ad strategy decisions are made monthly. Recent sales results indicate that the company's market share actually fluctuates too much and has periodic sharp declines. In its last meeting the board of directors asked Soonie's president to study the situation.

Amy White, the newly appointed Director of Marketing Research, was authorized to investigate the problem. Using computerized time series and regression analyses, she attempted to find the relationship between advertising policies and sales levels. After analyzing historical data for the past few years (videotapes are relatively new products) she decided there was no correlation between the two. Then she realized that Soonie's market share also depended on Pany's strategy. However, it was impossible to know exactly what the competition had in mind in the past.

"We should record what level of ads Pany uses," Amy thought to herself. For a moment she felt hopeless. Then she called a meeting of all key sales representatives, asking them to indicate how Soonie's ads pulled in relation to various strategies used by Pany. Ad effectiveness was based on the following four-point scale: 4 = excellent; 3 = good; 2 = fair; 1 = poor.

Although the sales reps disagreed on several of the possible results, she constructed an average response that looked like this:

If Soonie employs strategy a_1 and Pany employs b_1 the response to Soonie's strategy is *good*. Similarly, for the other possibilities the results were:

If Soonie employs	If Pany employs	The results for Soonie
a_1	b_2	Excellent
a_1	b_3	Fair
a_2	b_1	Poor
a_2	b_2	Good
a_2	b_3	Fair
a_3	b_1	Fair
a_3	b_2	Good
a_3	b_3	Excellent

A quick review of these results indicated that there was no one superior strategy. Poor to fair results were possible for each of Soonie's alternatives. "I can see now why my computerized programs failed to show any conclusive results. I wish we had a better information system."

At this point, the company's president called Amy and requested "specific recommendations for future ad strategies." For a moment Amy thought that she should tell him that she had found no relationship between strategy and sales level. Then she figured that this was probably not true.

What should Amy do? Consider such factors as the lack of collusion between the competitors, possible cooperation between the competitors, and overall market size.

11.14. GLOSSARY

Dominance A case where one decision alternative is superior to another alternative under all circumstances.

A fair game A game whose value is zero.

A game A series of repetitive decisions (plays).

Minimax theorem The theorem which is the basis for the solution to the two-person, zero-sum game. This theorem maintains that each player acts to maximize his minimum possible gain (or minimize his maximum loss.)

Mixed strategy A case where the decision maker should change his alternative courses of action at random, according to a predetermined proportion.

Nonzero-sum game A game where the winner(s) receives either less or more than what the loser(s) contributed.

N-person game A conflict involving more than two decision makers.

A play One move (one decision) in a game.

Pure strategy A case where the best strategy is to repeatedly stick to one decision alternative no matter what the opposition does.

Strategy A complete, predetermined plan for selecting the appropriate course of action for every possible circumstance.

Two-person game A conflict with two parties.

Value of the game The average payoff per play.

Zero-sum game A game where the winner(s) receives, and the loser(s) contributes, the entire amount at stake.

11.15 REFERENCES AND BIBLIOGRAPHY

1. *A Bibliography of Selected RAND Publications: Game Theory.* Santa Monica, Calif: The Rand Corp., SB-1039, October 1971.

2. Bacharach, M. *Economics and the Theory of Games.* Boulder, Colo.: Westview Press, 1977.

3. Bell, R. I. *Having It Your Way: The Strategy of Settling Everyday Conflicts.* New York: W. W. Norton & Co., Inc., 1977.

4. Bowen, K. C. *Research Games: An Approach to the Study of Decision Processes.* New York: Halsted Press, 1978.

5. Buchler, I. R., and Nutini, H. G. *Game Theory in the Behavioral Sciences.* Pittsburgh, Pa.: University of Pittsburgh Press, 1969.

6. Davis, M. D. *Game Theory: A Nontechnical Introduction.* New York: Basic Books, Inc., Publishers, 1970.

7. Harsanyi, J. C. *Rational Behavior and Bargaining Equilibrium in Games and Social Situations.* New York: Cambridge University Press, 1977.

8. Luce, R. D., and Raiffa, H. *Games and Decisions.* New York: John Wiley & Sons, Inc., 1957.

9. Rapoport, A. *Two-Person Game Theory.* Ann Arbor: The University of Michigan Press, 1966.

10. Shakun, M. G., ed. "Game Theory and Gaming," a special issue of *Management Science*, vol. 18, no. 5 (January 1972).

11. Shubik, M. *The Uses and Methods of Game Theory.* New York: Elsevier, 1975.

12. Von Neumann, J., and Morgenstern, O. *Theory of Games and Economic Behavior.* 3d ed. Princeton, N.J.: Princeton University Press, 1953.

13. Williams, J. D. *The Complete Strategyst.* Rev. ed. New York: McGraw-Hill Book Co., 1966.

12

The use of mathematical models to determine the best inventory level to maintain and the best time to reorder merchandise is one of the oldest techniques of management science.

Part A of this chapter is directed toward determining a proper balance between the cost of holding an inventory and the cost of placing an order. The result is the classical "economic order quantity" (EOQ) model. Part A also covers the applicability and limitations of this model and closes with a discussion of some practical inventory systems.

The most common extension of the EOQ model is the "economic lot size" (ELS) production model, presented in Part B. Also presented there are the quantity discount model, the establishment of safety stock, and the treatment of shortages.

Inventory models

PART A: BASICS

As Jed Stowe, the director of the company's administrative services, walked out of the vice-president's office, it was clear that Jed was disgusted. Just last month, Jed recalled, the vice-president had complained about the secretaries "wasting time filling out requisition (order) forms for supplies." Almost in the same breath he mentioned the possibility of an inventory shortage due to an impending strike against their major supplier. In the face of those comments Jed thought that a simple solution for both of the vice-president's concerns was to order supplies in larger amounts, but less frequently. Thus, the number of orders would be reduced (less work for the secretaries) and protection would exist in the event of a strike against the supplier. This strategy carried the additional advantage of allowing the company to obtain discounts given by the supplier on large orders.

Yesterday, however, the previous month's operating cost report came out and the cost of keeping the inventory had jumped to a record high. Jed was summoned to the vice-president's office where he learned that the additional inventory cost due to his larger orders caused a cash-flow problem to the company. Jed concluded that there was simply no way to win.

12.1 INVENTORY SYSTEMS

Characteristics of the situation

Jed Stowe's plight illustrates a typical inventory dilemma. An inventory is any stock of economic resources that is stored for future use. Jed's case called attention to the following dilemma: If a commodity is ordered frequently, then the costs of ordering (paperwork, secretarial time) are high. On the other hand, ordering more units less frequently saves on ordering costs but increases the expense of keeping a larger inventory. Thus, the proper ordering policy is a dilemma indeed. The management problem in this case is: *How frequently should supplies be ordered?*

This is a problem for management because the dilemma exists for many of the items in stock, sometimes tens of thousands of items. Further, due to continuous changes in prices the solution should be updated periodically. What makes the situation even more complicated is that there are many (theoretically infinite) possible solutions to the problem. An item may be ordered on a daily basis to once every ten years or so.

For all these reasons a trial-and-error solution is not practical. Management science provides models that execute the search for an *optimal* solution rather quickly.

Two conflicting costs

How frequently to order supplies?

Types and examples of inventories

Several types of inventories are maintained by organizations. Some of the major inventories are:

1. Raw materials.
2. Finished goods.
3. Semifinished products. *– Work in process.*
4. Spare parts and supplies

Some specific examples of inventories are:

- Items on the shelves of department and food stores.
- Unused telephone numbers the phone company is holding.
- Cash on hand at the bank (reserves).
- Blood in blood banks.
- Standby pilots and stewardesses employed by airlines.
- Empty space in a warehouse for incoming shipments.

Blood, cash, spaces

Inventory problems

Several inventory problems will be discussed in this chapter. Specialized tools were developed to treat certain of these; others can be solved by standard tools such as linear programming, dynamic programming, decision tables, and simulation. Examples are given in the appropriate chapters. This chapter deals only with specialized inventory models. Before such models are introduced, however, the purpose that inventories serve should be examined.

Inventory functions

The following is a list of the major reasons for maintaining an inventory:

Protection against fluctuating demand Inventories are kept to meet peak demand. For example, blood is stored in hospitals in quantities sufficient to meet the needs of a major accident.

Protection against limited supply A strike by the supplier's employees is one reason why deliveries may not arrive on time. Lack of material at the supplier level, strikes in the transportation network, or a snow storm are other possible causes for shortages. Inventories are kept as a buffer that can be used until late deliveries arrive.

Many reasons for inventory

Protection against inflation Inventories are often kept as a hedge against inflation. In this case inventories are built up in anticipation of a price increase. This speculative practice is especially common in the commodity markets (such as wheat or gold).

Benefits of large quantities Purchasing large quantities of an item often entitles the buyer to a *discount* (lower per unit price). Similarly, in the case of manufacturing of large production lots, the utilization of more efficient automated equipment can be justified by the reduction in the per unit manufacturing cost.

Savings on ordering cost   Ordering in large quantities reduces the number of times that an order must be placed and processed. Since a fixed cost is associated with placing each order, the fewer times one places an order, the lower the total cost of ordering will be.

Other reasons   Inventories are kept for several other reasons: An inventory may improve the bargaining power of a firm with a supplier (or with its own employees) by making the company less dependent on them. Inventories also are kept so that machines can be shut down for overhauls. An inventory of labor is maintained to meet fluctuating production demands in order to reduce hiring, firing, and training costs.

12.2   THE STRUCTURE OF THE INVENTORY SYSTEM

The inventory models described in the remainder of this chapter pertain to an individual item in stock. This means, for example, that with an inventory system for three different items the model must be employed three times.

Inventory ordering—a cyclical process

An inventory system involves *a cyclical process*, which is assumed to run over several periods, whose major characteristics are:

Inventory level

An item is stocked in a warehouse, store, or any other storage area. This stock constitutes an *inventory*. The size of the inventory is called the *inventory level* (or the inventory *on hand*).

Demand and depletion

The inventory is *depleted* as *demand* occurs. Assume that one starts with an inventory of 100 units, as shown in Figure 12.1. As time passes,

FIGURE 12.1
An inventory system

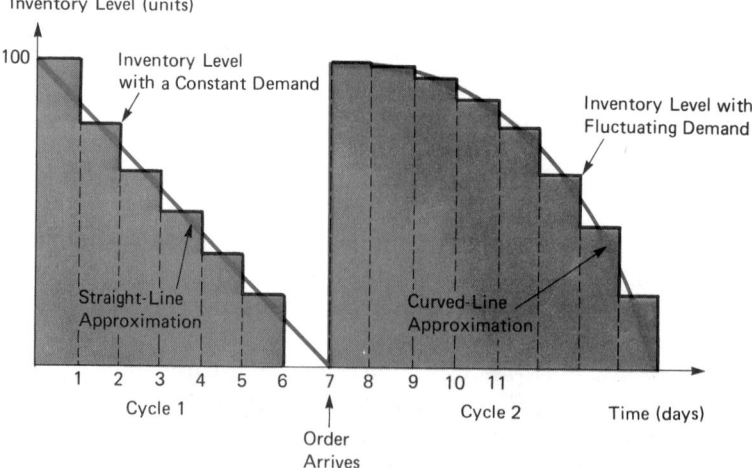

the inventory level declines due to the demand for the item in stock. The *rate of demand* determines the depletion rate and the inventory level. The higher the rate of demand, the quicker the inventory is reduced. The rate of demand can be constant, (e.g., five units per day), or may fluctuate (e.g., three units on the first day and seven on the second). A *constant demand* reduces the inventory level in equal steps. Graphically, it is shown as a stairway (see cycle 1 in Figure 12.1). The steps of the constant demand can be approximated by a straight line. A *fluctuating* (variable) *demand* is shown by unequal steps, as in cycle 2 of Figure 12.1, and can be approximated by a curve.

Constant or fluctuating demand

Reordering

To rebuild an inventory, the item is replenished periodically. When the inventory level is reduced to a certain level called the *reorder point*, a *replenishment* order is placed (see Figure 12.2). The time between reordering and receiving the order is called the *lead time*.

Reorder points and lead times

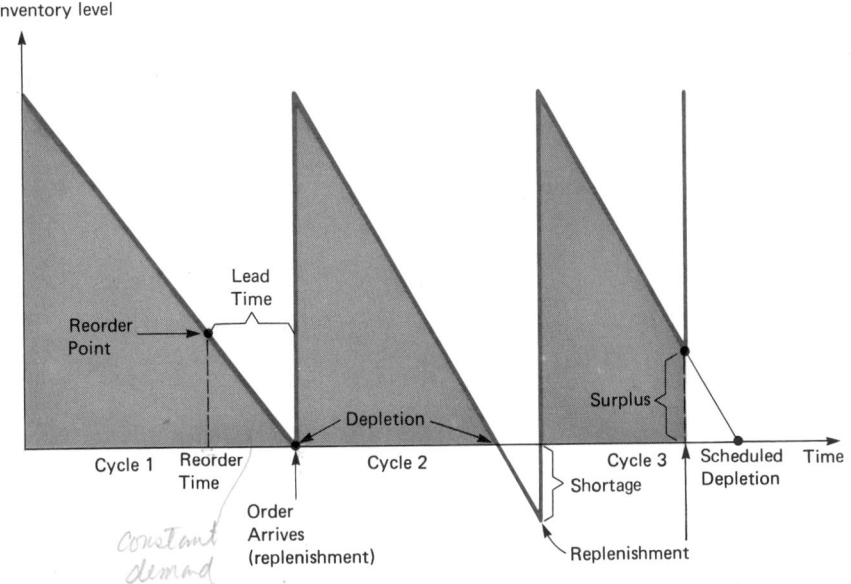

FIGURE 12.2
Reordering, replenishment, and a shortage

Replenishment, shortages, and surpluses

In some basic inventory models, it is assumed that the reordering is scheduled so that the replenishment will arrive exactly when the inventory level reaches zero. Such an assumption holds if the demand is constant (as shown in cycle 1 of Figure 12.2). However, if the demand fluctuates and/or the lead time varies, the shipment may arrive either before or after the stock is completely depleted; that is, the depletion and replenishment do not coincide. In such a case a surplus or a shortage will occur. If the shipment arrives *after* depletion, then the demand

Shortage from demand
fluctuation or lead
time variation
cannot be met and a *shortage* (or *stockout*) will occur. This is shown by the second cycle of Figure 12.2. When the shipment arrives *prior* to depletion, an inventory level larger than zero, or a *surplus*, exists, as demonstrated by the third cycle of Figure 12.2.

Safety stock

Shortages can be eliminated or reduced by deliberately building up a *safety stock*. This topic is discussed in detail in Section 12.15.

The average inventory

For purposes of inventory decision making, as well as for other managerial uses, such as insurance and taxation, the concept of an *average inventory* is used. To illustrate, let us assume that during a five-day period the inventory levels are as follows:

Monday	Tuesday	Wednesday	Thursday	Friday
16	12	8	4	0

The average inventory is then:

$$\frac{16 + 12 + 8 + 4 + 0}{5} = \frac{40}{5} = 8 \text{ units}$$

This is shown in Figure 12.3.

FIGURE 12.3
Average inventory

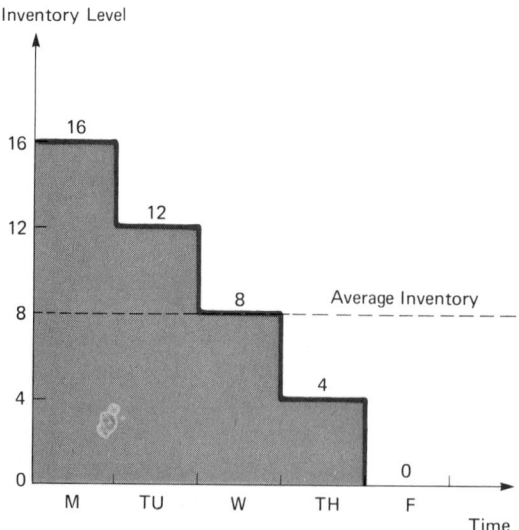

If the demand is *constant*, the average inventory can be computed by adding the inventory at the beginning of a cycle (16 in this example) to the inventory at the end of the cycle (0 in this case) and dividing it by 2. If the inventory at the end of the cycle is 0 (as in this example), the *average inventory equals exactly one half of the initial inventory.*

Average inventory as one-half the maximum

Basic inventory decisions

The major decisions that management makes in the inventory area and which will be discussed in this chapter are:

1. How much to order at one time. (What the order quantity should be.)
2. When to order this quantity. (What the reorder point should be.)
3. Should a safety stock be built up? How large should it be?

Other inventory decisions are often made by management but they will not be discussed in this text.[1] Some of these decisions are:

- Where to stock.
- How the inventory system should be staffed.
- Whether the inventory system should be computerized.

Other inventory decisions

The most common criteria considered in inventory analysis are inventory-related costs. Inventory models compute these costs, total them, and then search for a policy or an alternative solution which *minimizes* the total cost. Before presenting the models, it is necessary therefore to discuss these costs.

12.3   INVENTORY COSTS

Inventory problems are usually examined from a cost rather than from a profit standpoint. The major types of inventory costs are:

Ordering cost

Ordering cost includes all the necessary expenses of placing orders. It is assumed to be a fixed cost per order; that is, each time an order is placed the same expenses occur. Included in the ordering cost are the clerical and paperwork expenses of purchasing, inspection, receiving, bookkeeping, and data processing that are directly related to ordering, as well as the expenses of delivery, postage, and the related overhead (such as fixed telephone charges). The cost of ordering can be computed by dividing the total annual cost related to ordering by the number of orders processed that year.

---

[1] Such decisions are discussed in texts specializing in inventory management. (See Green [3], Lewis [7], Peterson [11], and Tersine [12].

Example A typical ordering cost calculation is:

Category	Expense ($)
Department head	25,000
Clerk(s)	26,000
Secretary	12,000
Receiving clerk	14,000
Accounting expense	16,000
Data processing	3,000
Supplies	1,200
Phone, postage	800
Overhead	20,000
Total	108,000

If the department processed 2,000 orders during the year then the ordering cost is:

$$\frac{108,000}{2,000} = \$54 \text{ per order.}$$

Holding (carrying) cost

The expenses of holding or carrying the inventory include such components as:

- *Cost of capital:* The interest paid on the capital invested in inventories.
- *Storage:* Cost of maintaining the storage space. This includes rental fees, lights, heat, security, and janitorial services.
- *Storekeeping operations:* Expenses such as record keeping and taking of physical inventory.
- *Insurance* and *taxes.*
- *Obsolescence* and *deterioration* of the items stored.

Two holding cost expressions

All holding costs are totaled and expressed either in terms of "dollars per item per year," or in "percentage of the value of the inventory."

Shortage (or stockout) cost

Shortage costs occur when an item is out of stock and demand is unsatisfied. Depending on the item under consideration, shortage costs may include the following:

In the case of raw materials: costs of idled production, spoilage of products or materials, and the cost of placing and fulfilling special expediting orders.

In the case of finished goods: costs of "ill will"[2] to the seller (the loss of customers) due to inability to deliver or due to late deliveries.

In the case of replacement parts: costs of idle machines, idle labor, spoilage of materials, and delays in shipment.

In other cases: the shortage of blood or ambulances may cost a life; and a shortage of fire engines may result in excessive damage caused by a fire.

Shortages may be temporary ("back orders"), in which case they are eliminated when the supply arrives, or permanent in the sense that sales are lost.

Back orders versus lost sales

Item cost

Item (or unit) cost is the price paid for one unit of the commodity under consideration. It is not a direct inventory cost, as the items must be eventually procured anyway, but it may be influenced by inventory decisions. For example, ordering large quantities may result in a lower per unit price due to *quantity discounts.*

Quantity discounts

12.4   THE ECONOMIC ORDER QUANTITY MODEL

The economic order quantity (EOQ) model, which was developed prior to World War I, is the most elementary of all inventory models. Its objective is to determine the *optimal quantity to order.* It answers the following questions:

How much to order

1. How much should be ordered each time?
2. What will the total cost be?

Assumptions

The EOQ model assumes the following:

- The demand for the item is constant over time (e.g., two units per day).

- The per unit holding cost and ordering cost are independent of the quantity ordered.

- The replenishment is scheduled in such a way that shipments arrive exactly when the inventory level reaches zero. Therefore, there will never be a shortage.

- Since only one item is being considered, orders for different items are independent of each other.

---

[2] The cost of ill will or the loss of goodwill reflects the anticipated loss of future profits due to customers' dissatisfaction.

FIGURE 12.4
The inventory process

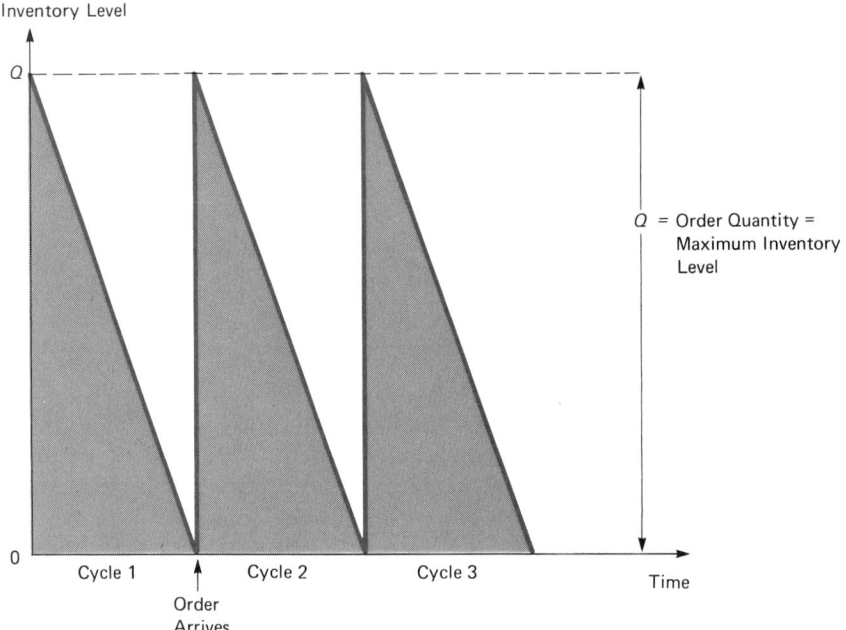

The behavior of the inventory level under the above assumptions is shown in Figure 12.4.

An examination of Figure 12.4 indicates that all cycles are equal, that orders arrive exactly when the inventory level reaches zero, that the order quantity Q is equal in all cycles, and that the maximum inventory level is also Q.

Example

Everglades University uses 1,200 boxes of typing paper each year. The university is trying to determine how many boxes to order at one time. The information it considers is:

Annual demand, D = 1,200 boxes.
Ordering cost, K = \$5 per order.
Holding cost, H = \$1.20 per box, per year.

The problem is to find the quantity to be ordered, Q. (As we shall see, finding this quantity will also tell us how often to order.)

Figure 12.5 demonstrates three possible ordering policies: annually, quarterly, and monthly. Let us examine these:

1. Annual policy: Order once a year, therefore Q = 1,200 boxes.
2. Quarterly: Order once a quarter, four times a year. Q = 1,200/4 = 300 boxes at a time.

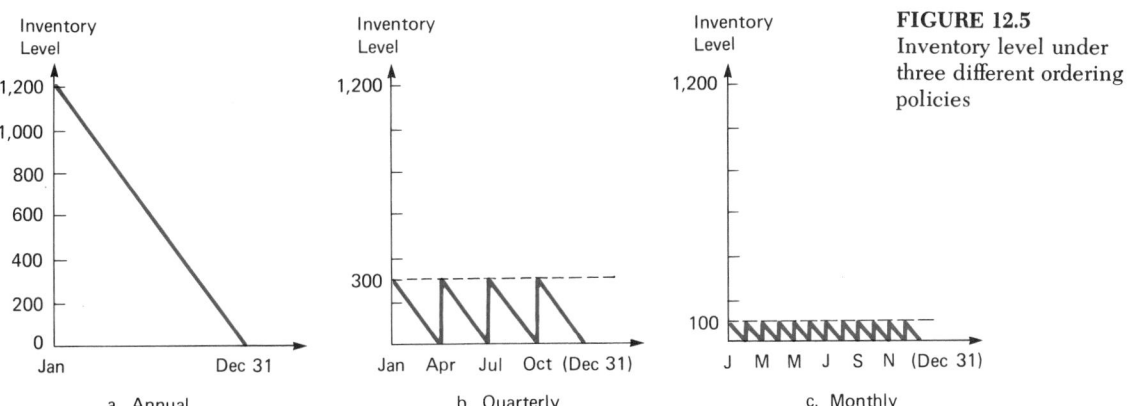

FIGURE 12.5
Inventory level under three different ordering policies

3. Monthly: Order once a month, 12 times a year. $Q = 1,200/12 = 100$ boxes at a time.

Other ordering policies could also be considered; for example, once a week, semiannually, or once every two years. The problem faced by management is: *Which ordering policy is the best?*

Which policy costs less?

Solution using a trial-and-error approach

One way of solving this problem would be to compute the total annual inventory cost for each of the suggested policies. The policy with the lowest total cost is the best one. The total cost[3] is given by Equation 12.1.

$$TC = T_O + T_H$$
$$\begin{Bmatrix} \text{Total annual} \\ \text{inventory cost} \end{Bmatrix} = \begin{Bmatrix} \text{Total annual} \\ \text{ordering cost} \end{Bmatrix} + \begin{Bmatrix} \text{Total annual} \\ \text{holding cost} \end{Bmatrix} \quad (12.1)$$

Let us execute the calculation step by step:

Step 1. Find total annual ordering cost, T_O The total annual ordering cost is given as the number of times an order is placed, N, multiplied by the ordering cost, K. This is expressed in Equation 12.2.

$$T_O = NK \quad (12.2)$$

---

[3] The total annual inventory cost includes only the relevant costs. Therefore, such factors as the cost of the units and the cost of the analysis (which are the same for all alternative policies) are not included in the model.

(handwritten margin notes)
T_0 = Total annual ordering cost

n = number of times an order is placed

K = ordering cost

But, the number of times an order is placed during a year is given by the total yearly demand, D, divided by the order quantity, Q:

(handwritten) D = total annual demand
Q = order quantity

$$N = \frac{D}{Q}$$

(handwritten) $Q = \frac{1,200}{1.4} = 1,200$ (12.3)

$N = \frac{1,200}{1,200} = 1.$

Thus, the equation for T_0 is:

$$T_0 = NK = \frac{D}{Q} K$$

(handwritten) $= \frac{1,200}{1,200} \times 5$ (12.4)

T_0 in the three proposed policies is:

Annual: $N = 1,$ $K = 5,$ $T_0 = 1(5) = \$5$
Quarterly: $N = 4,$ $K = 5,$ $T_0 = 4(5) = \$20$
Monthly: $N = 12,$ $K = 5,$ $T_0 = 12(5) = \$60$

The above values are entered in Figure 12.6, as points a (for the annual policy), b (for quarterly), and c (for monthly). Points a, b, and c are then connected, resulting in a *total annual ordering cost* curve. The curve indicates that as the order quantity, Q, increases, the total annual cost of ordering decreases. The reason for this is that the larger the order size, the fewer the number of orders per year.

FIGURE 12.6
The total annual
ordering cost curve

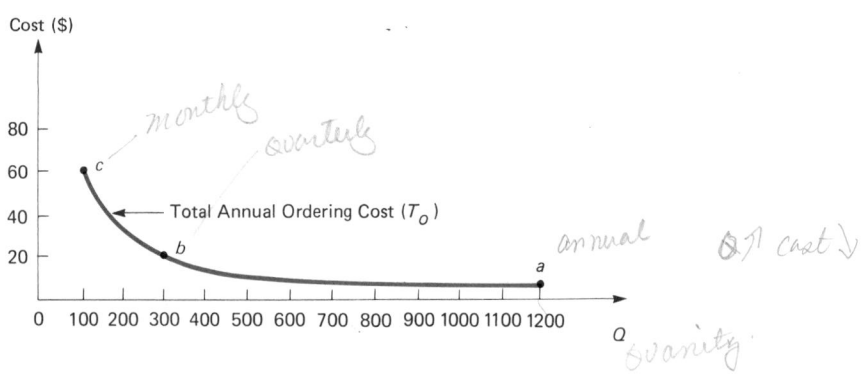

Total Annual Ordering Cost (T_0)

Step 2. Find total annual holding cost, T_H The total annual holding cost is computed by multiplying the holding cost (measured in dollars per item per year), H, by the *number of units kept in inventory*. The problem is that the inventory level is changing from day to day; therefore, the number of units kept in inventory fluctuates over time. To solve this problem, the *average inventory* on hand is used. When the demand is constant, the average inventory is the midway point between the highest and the lowest inventory level. Since the assumptions require that the lowest inventory level be zero, the average inventory equals exactly one half of the maximum inventory. However, in the EOQ

model the maximum inventory equals the order quantity, Q. Consequently, the average inventory equals one half of Q (Equation 12.5).

— Q of each order

$$\text{Average inventory} = \frac{Q}{2} \qquad (12.5)$$

H = Holding cost per year @ unit

Therefore, the total annual inventory holding cost, T_H, will be:

$$T_H = H\frac{Q}{2} \qquad (12.6)$$

The total annual inventory holding cost for the three proposed ordering
policies is:

Holding cost @ unit

Total Holding cost

Annual: $Q = 1{,}200$, $T_H = 1.20\left(\dfrac{1{,}200}{2}\right) = \$720$

Quarterly: $Q = 300$, $T_H = 1.20\left(\dfrac{300}{2}\right) = \$180$

Monthly: $Q = 100$, $T_H = 1.20\left(\dfrac{100}{2}\right) = \$60$

It is evident that the value of Q will be in direct proportion to the
value of T_H. This information is shown graphically in Figure 12.7.

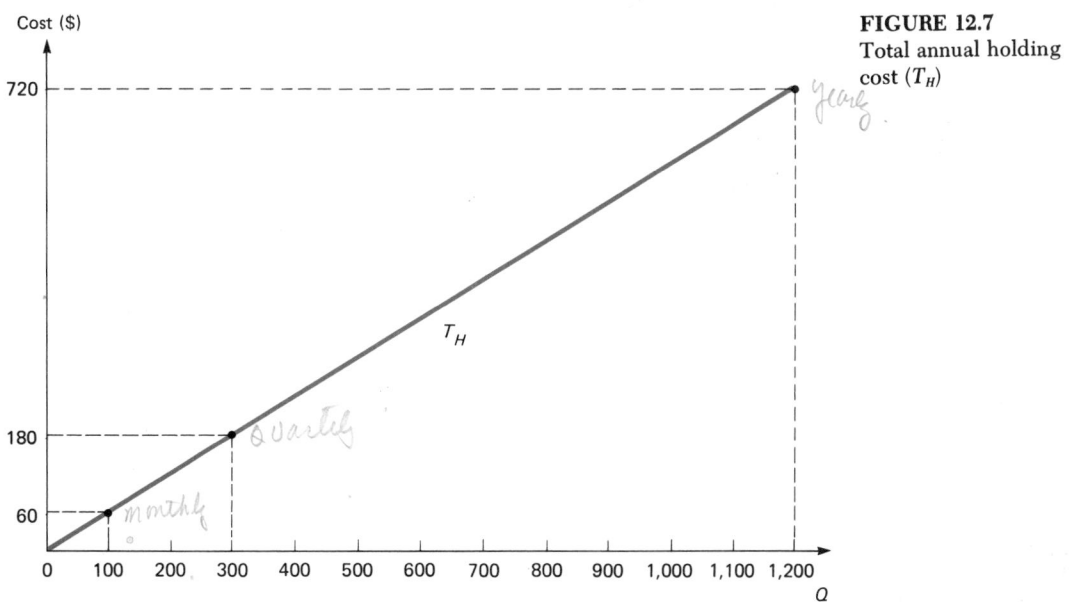

FIGURE 12.7
Total annual holding
cost (T_H)

Step 3. Compute total annual inventory cost, TC Using Equation 12.1 the total annual cost for the proposed policies is: •

Policy	$T_0 + T_H = TC$	
Annual	5 + 720 = 725	
Quarterly	20 + 180 = 200	
Monthly	60 + 60 = 120	← *Minimum*

Checking other possible policies, too

Comparing the three alternatives, the best ordering policy is "monthly" since it has the lowest total cost of $120. However, since other possible ordering policies (e.g., semi-annually, weekly) were not checked, no assurance exists that monthly ordering is indeed the *optimal* policy. To check *all* possible policies may involve much computational work, especially since these calculations must be made and continuously updated for every item in the stock. Therefore, a more efficient method is provided through the economic order quantity (EOQ) formula.

The EOQ formula

It was shown previously that the total cost, TC, can be expressed as:

$$TC = T_0 + T_H = \frac{DK}{Q} + \frac{HQ}{2} \qquad (12.7)$$

where D is the annual demand, K is the ordering cost, H is the holding cost, and Q is the quantity to be ordered. The problem is to find that Q for which TC is the minimum.

Graphical solution One way to find TC is to combine T_0 and T_H graphically and then to find a minimum point on the combined curve. Figure 12.8 shows TC as the summation of T_0 and T_H.[4] The minimum value of TC occurs at the intersection[5] of T_H and T_0, that is, where T_H equals T_0.

Analytical solution Equation 12.8 equates the ordering cost and the holding cost which characterize the minimum.

$$\frac{HQ}{2} = \frac{KD}{Q} \qquad (12.8)$$

---

[4] Summation of two curves is done as shown in Figure 12.8 for $Q = 200$ (point A). Take the distance A to B and add it to the distance A to C. The result is the distance A to D.

[5] With other forms of cost curves, the minimum point on the total cost curve may occur at a point other than the intersection.

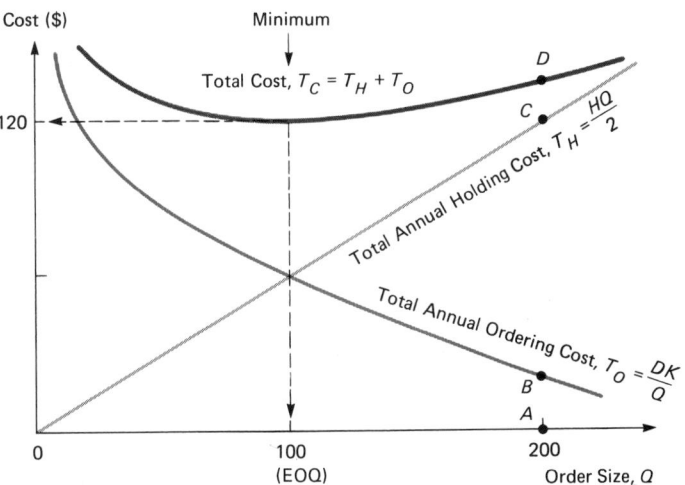

FIGURE 12.8
Ordering, holding, and
total cost variation with
order size

By manipulation of Equation 12.8[6] it is possible to compute the
optimal value of Q, labeled Q^*; that is, the EOQ.[7]

EOQ: The *optimal*
Q^*

$$(Q^*)^2 = \frac{2KD}{H} \quad \text{or} \quad Q^* = \sqrt{\frac{2KD}{H}} \qquad (12.9)$$

where K is the ordering cost (in dollars), D is the annual demand (in
units), and H is the holding cost (in dollars per unit per time period).

Solution to the example

$$Q^* = \sqrt{\frac{2(5)(1,200)}{1.20}} = 100 \text{ boxes}$$

The optimal solution calls for an order size of 100 boxes at a time.
For a yearly demand of 1,200 this means 12 orders per year, or once a
month. Thus, the monthly order policy is indeed optimal.

---

[6] Multiply each side by Q; then divide each side by $H/2$.

[7] The EOQ can also be obtained through calculus: $TC = HQ/2 + KD/Q$. Setting the
first derivative to 0:

$$\frac{dTC}{dQ} = \frac{H}{2} - \frac{KD}{Q^2} = 0 \quad \text{or} \quad Q^* = \sqrt{\frac{2KD}{H}}$$

To verify that this is a minimum point we check for a positive second derivative:

$$\frac{d^2TC}{dQ^2} = \frac{2KD}{Q^3} < 0$$

Since the second derivative is positive (K, D, and Q can take only positive values) the point
is a minimum point indeed.

Additional information provided by EOQ

In addition to the size of the order to be placed, the EOQ can be used to provide the following information:

a. *The best number of orders* to be placed in a year. Using Equation 12.3 we find:

$$N = \frac{D}{Q^*} = \frac{1,200}{100} = 12 \text{ times}$$

b. *The maximum inventory on hand,* and *the average inventory level.* The maximum inventory is equal to Q^* or 100 in the example. The average inventory is one half of Q^*, which is 50 in the example.

Other information from The EOQ

c. *The number of days' supply.* The computation of the EOQ also helps provide the number of "days' supply," d. This information tells management the length of each inventory cycle. This is given in Equation 12.10.

$$d = \frac{365}{N} \tag{12.10}$$

In the example:

$$d = \frac{365}{N} = \frac{365}{12} = 30.4 \text{ days}$$

d. *The dollar value of an optimal order and of the average inventory.*[8] Sometimes it is useful to know the dollar value of the EOQ; this is obtained by multiplying Q by the unit cost. Assume in the example that the cost of one box of paper is $10. Thus, Q in dollars is 100(10) or $1,000. That is, the university orders $1,000 worth of supplies at a time. Similarly, the dollar value of the average inventory is:

$$\frac{100}{2}(10) = \$500.$$

e. *The total cost.* Using Equation 12.7 the total cost can now be computed.

$$TC = \frac{DK}{Q^*} + \frac{HQ^*}{2} = \frac{(1,200)5}{100} + \frac{1.2(100)}{2} = 60 + 60 = \$120$$

---

[8] This information is important since the dollar value of the average inventory is useful for such purposes as cash-flow determination, tax assessment, and calculation of depreciation.

Notice that the two components of the total cost, the ordering cost and the holding cost, *must equal* each other whenever the optimal Q is used[9] ($60 each in the example).

$T_H = T_o$ in the optimal solution

12.5   APPLICATION OF THE EOQ MODEL

In applying the EOQ formula the following points may be helpful:

Holding cost given as a percentage of value

It is sometimes common to express the holding cost as a percentage of the value in inventory. For example, it may be stated that the inventory holding costs are 30 percent per year. This means that if the item is worth $20 then H = .3 × $20 = $6 per item, per year.

With a 10-15 percent cost of capital (interest per year) it is not unusual to find that the cost of holding inventory is 30 percent or even higher.

When demand is given in dollars

In some cases the demand for an item is given in terms of dollars rather than in units. Two cases are then distinguished:

Demand in dollars

1. *The unit cost is given.* In this case simply convert the demand to units by dividing the dollar value into the unit cost.
2. *The unit cost is not given.* In such a case the holding cost *must* be expressed as a percentage.

Example   A recreation department's annual budget for supplies is $200,000. The ordering cost is $50, and the holding cost is 20 percent of the value of the item. Find the EOQ, the optimal number of orders, and the total inventory costs.

Given:

D: Annual *dollar value* of demand = $200,000.
K: Ordering cost, in dollars = $50.
H: Holding cost, .2 (i.e., 20%).

Solution:

---

[9] If for some reason Q is known, *the input variables* can then be found as:

The ordering cost:	$K = \dfrac{Q^2 H}{2D}$	(12.11)
The annual demand:	$D = \dfrac{Q^2 H}{2K}$	(12.12)
The holding cost, per unit per year:	$H = \dfrac{2KD}{Q^2}$	(12.13)

Using EOQ formula (Equation 12.9):

$$Q^* = \sqrt{\frac{2KD}{H}} = \sqrt{\frac{2(50)(200,000)}{.2}} = \$10,000$$

Thus, the optimal policy is to order $10,000 worth of supplies at a time. Because the yearly demand is $200,000, there will be $N = 20$ orders per year (Equation 12.3). $N = 260,000 / 10,000$
The total annual inventory costs are: $= 20$

$$\checkmark \quad TC = \frac{KD}{Q^*} + \frac{Q^*H}{2} = \frac{50(200,000)}{10,000} + \frac{10,000(.2)}{2} = \$2,000$$

The cost impact of deviations from the EOQ (sensitivity analysis)

Sensitivity analysis

In some situations it is not convenient to actually order the EOQ. Using the university's supply situation in Section 12.4 as an example, the EOQ calls for 100 boxes, but suppose that they are packed 40 to a case. In such an event, it is possible to buy either 80 or 120 boxes, but not 100. Let us examine the effect of overordering, (120), versus underordering (80).

For 80 boxes The total annual cost for an order of 80 will be (use Equation 12.7 with $Q = 80$):

$$TC = \frac{DK}{Q} + \frac{HQ}{2} = \frac{(1,200)5}{80} + \frac{(1.2)80}{2} = \$123$$

Compared with the cost of $120 for the EOQ of 100 (as previously computed), there is an increase of only $3 which is about 2.5 percent, even though the order quantity was decreased by 20 percent.

For 120 boxes

$$TC = \frac{5(1,200)}{120} + \frac{120(1.2)}{2} = \$122$$

Thus, overordering by 20 percent caused the total annual inventory cost to rise by less than 2 percent.

In a similar manner, it can be shown that a change of 10 percent in the order quantity increases the total inventory cost by only about ½ percent. In other words, the EOQ formula is *relatively insensitive to changes in the quantity ordered.* This property gives management greater flexibility in implementing the EOQ since the theoretical order quantity can be changed by as much as 20 percent or more with only a slight impact on the total inventory cost.

Cost insensitive to
order quantity

Note that the sensitivity for decreasing the EOQ is *larger* than the sensitivity of increasing it (cost increase of $3 on the down side versus cost increase of $2 on the up side for a change of 20 units from EOQ). Another example is that changing EOQ from 100 to 50 (deviation of 50), will increase the total cost from $120 to $150 (an increase of 25 percent). A look at Figure 12.8 shows us why this is so. The curve of total cost increases faster when Q decreases, especially when Q is very small.

The sensitivity of the EOQ to changes in input data

Let us examine the EOQ formula:

$$Q^* = \sqrt{\frac{2KD}{H}}$$

One can see that the quantity Q, is proportional to the square root of the input data (K, D, and H). This means that if K or D quadruples, for example, then Q^* will be doubled, and if H quadruples, then Q^* will be halved. Table 12.1 compares the original university purchasing problem with three changes: change 1, quadruple D; change 2, quadruple K; change 3, quadruple H.

Table 12.1

	Original problem	Change ①	Change ②	Change ③
Given	D = 1,200 K = 5 H = 1.20	D = 4,800 K = 5 H = 1.20	D = 1,200 K = 20 H = 1.20	D = 1,200 K = 5 H = 4.80
Computed	Q^* = 100	Q^* = 200	Q^* = 200	Q^* = 50
Total cost	TC = $120	TC = $240	TC = $240	TC = $240

The managerial implication of the sensitivity of the EOQ is that the order quantity should *not* be increased or decreased in direct proportion to the changes in the input data. Some managers make the mistake of doubling their EOQ when the demand doubles. Instead, they should increase it only by $\sqrt{2} = 1.41$, since the EOQ is directly proportional to the *square root* of the demand.

Nonproportional changes

When to order (the reorder point)

The decision *when* to order does not depend on the optimal value of Q. Rather, it is a function of the demand and the lead time to resupply. For example, if the demand is 50 per week and the lead time is two weeks, then the order should be placed when the inventory level is 100 units (two weeks' supply).

Rounding the result

The computed EOQ may be noninteger; e.g., 6.3 units. In such a situation the result may be rounded to 6 or 7. The total cost for 6 should be calculated and compared to that for 7 to decide whether to round down or up. Rounding is often done to comply with required bulk quantities, such as six cartons per case.

12.6   DISCUSSION OF THE EOQ ASSUMPTIONS

In order to derive the EOQ, a list of assumptions was outlined in Section 12.4. These assumptions enabled us to develop a rather simple inventory formula. These assumptions were:

Constant demand   In the EOQ model, a constant demand was assumed (e.g., five units per day). In reality, demand may be three units one day and seven the next. If this demand is known in advance, constant average demand may be used as an approximation. However, if the demand is not known in advance (i.e., when it is not deterministic), it is necessary to modify the EOQ formulation (e.g., by using safety stock as shown in Section 12.15 or by using special stochastic models (see Lewis [7]).

Constant unit price   The EOQ analysis that assumes constant unit price, can be extended to include variable prices due to discounts as larger quantities are ordered. This procedure is discussed in Section 12.12.

Constant holding cost   It is assumed that the holding cost is constant. However, as the level of inventory increases, the holding cost may decrease (e.g., due to storage efficiency) or increase (e.g., due to higher capital costs). Such a situation can be handled by a procedure similar to the one used for quantity discounts.

Constant ordering cost   This assumption is usually valid. For exceptional cases, the EOQ model can be modified by computing different values for different ordering costs. Again, this situation resembles the quantity discount case.

No shortages   The assumption is made that all demand is immediately supplied and therefore there will never be a shortage. As long as the demand is constant and delivery time is either constant or zero the assumption will hold. Otherwise, a safety stock should be added or a modified model with a shortage (Section 12.14) can be used.

Instantaneous (or fixed) delivery time   It is assumed that deliveries are received on a desired date. This can be assured by instantaneous delivery; for example, if the supplier happens to be in the same area and can deliver quickly on short notice. Alternatively, if the lead time and the demand are both constant, an order can be placed so that the delivery will arrive exactly on a desired date. But in the case of variations in the lead time or the demand, the EOQ must be modified as shown in Part B.

Independent orders   Quite often several items are purchased from the same supplier and the ordering cost can be reduced by ordering several items in one order. This saves paperwork, transportation costs, and may also result in discounts. Special models have been developed to deal with situations where several items are ordered together, a practice known as *joint ordering.* (See Tersine [12].)

Joint ordering

Single goal of cost minimization   This assumption is not always true. Sometimes, for example, the service level is more important (e.g., in blood inventory).

Summary

The EOQ model is summarized in Figure 12.9.

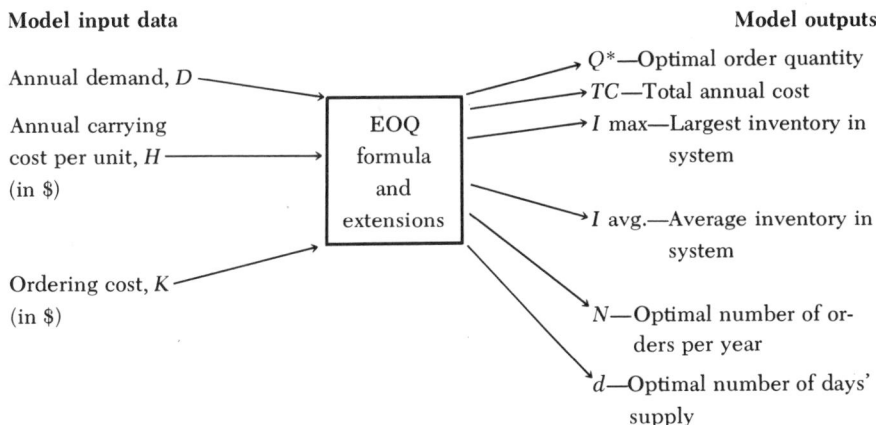

Model input data

Annual demand, D

Annual carrying cost per unit, H (in \$)

Ordering cost, K (in \$)

EOQ formula and extensions

Model outputs

Q^*—Optimal order quantity

TC—Total annual cost

I max—Largest inventory in system

I avg.—Average inventory in system

N—Optimal number of orders per year

d—Optimal number of days' supply

FIGURE 12.9
Summary of the EOQ model

Formulation

Objective function: minimize TC
Constraints: no constraints in the regular model.

12.7   INVENTORY SYSTEMS

The A-B-C classification system

Some organizations carry such a large number (thousands) of items in inventory that it would be impractical to try to exercise control over every single item, using the EOQ analysis. Remember that each time any input data (such as demand or ordering cost) is changed, the EOQ has to be recomputed.

One method frequently used to identify the items that deserve tight

ABC, value-volume,
80–20

control is called the *A-B-C classification* system or the *value-volume analysis*.[10]

The A-B-C classification system segregates all items in stock into three groups, A, B, and C, based on the annual dollar inventory value of the items.[11]

The A group Group A usually includes 10 percent of the items which account for 70 percent[12] of the total annual inventory cost for the company (see Figure 12.10). Special attention should be paid to every item in this group, and application of the EOQ formula is recommended for every one of the items.

FIGURE 12.10
A-B-C inventory categories

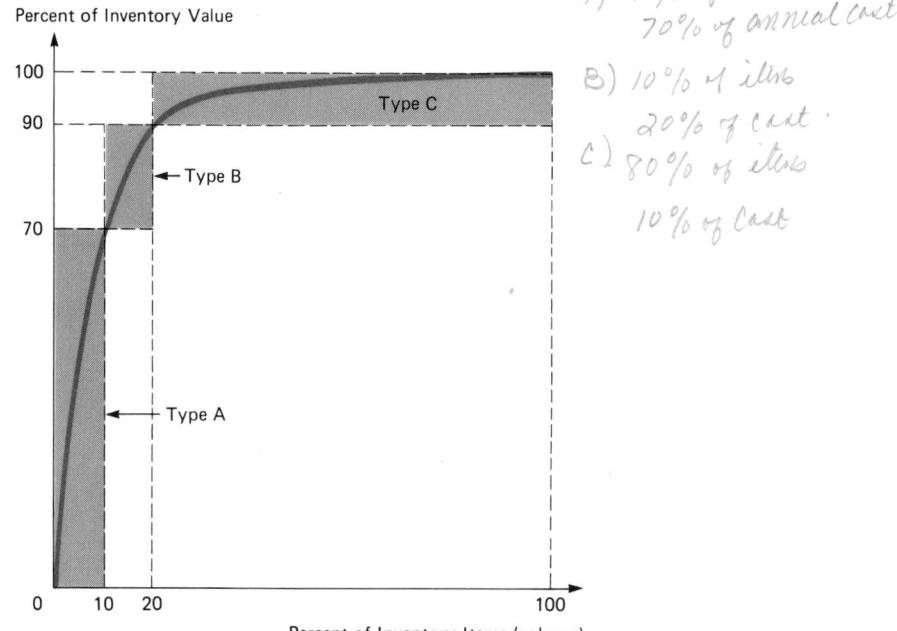

Percent of Inventory Value

Percent of Inventory Items (volume)

Handwritten notes:
A) 10% of items
   70% of annual cost
B) 10% of items
   20% of cost
C) 80% of items
   10% of cost

The B group Items in this group constitute another 10 percent in inventory volume but are worth only 20 percent of the total value. Accordingly, items in this group merit somewhat less control than those in group A. For example, an EOQ may still be used, but updating due to changes in input data may be done only once a year.

---

[10] Other names are the *Pareto* analysis and the "80–20" method. The idea is based on the economic phenomenon observed by Pareto, an Italian economist (1848–1923), that a few items usually account for the majority of the value.

[11] Other criteria for classifying items are the cost, amount of use, or importance of the items.

[12] The percentages in the A, B, and C categories may vary according to the situation.

Adding the groups A and B together shows that 20 percent of the items account for 90 percent of the dollar value of the inventory.

The C group   The remaining 80 percent of the items account for only 10 percent of the inventory dollar value. These are small usage items such as nuts, bolts, and nails. Control over such items should be minimal since the potential savings rarely justifies the expense of the control exercised.

Classification into three categories is traditional but not mandatory. Classification into two, four, or even more categories can be found in some companies. What is important to remember is that some items in inventory deserve detailed and continuous planning and control, whereas others do not merit such consideration. Thus, different classes of items should be subjected to different inventory systems as discussed next.

The fixed-quantity (perpetual) system

This system dictates that a fixed-quantity order be placed each time the inventory level reaches the reorder point. The fixed quantity could be determined by the EOQ formula. A "safety stock" is usually added (at a level determined by experience or by computation as shown in Section 12.12). This system is used mainly for type A items.

Safety stock

A special, less expensive to administer version of the fixed-quantity system, called the *two-bin* system, is frequently used for type B and C items. The inventory is stored in a large bin with the exception of a safety stock kept in a smaller bin. Demand depletion of the large bin acts as a signal to reorder. While awaiting replenishment of the large bin, demand is supplied from the small bin. When the shipment arrives, the smaller bin is refilled first and the remainder then goes into the larger bin. The amount to be ordered can be based on the EOQ but is usually based on experience. This system is practical if the stock can be conveniently separated into two bins; if not, a perpetual auditing (counting) of the amount on hand (balance) is required, increasing the cost substantially.

The two-bin system

The fixed-time (periodic, or *s, S*) system

This inventory involves a periodic auditing (e.g., once a month) of the inventory. If at that time the stock of an item is below the predesignated level, s, an order is placed, to return the inventory level to another predetermined, maximum level S.[13] Although amounts ordered each cycle will vary, as shown in Figure 12.11, this system allows *joint reordering* of items in the same period at a substantial savings. The major disadvantages of the s, S system are:

s, S system

Joint reordering possible

---

[13] The levels of s and S can be determined by a mathematical model or by experience.

FIGURE 12.11
Periodic (s, S) inventory system

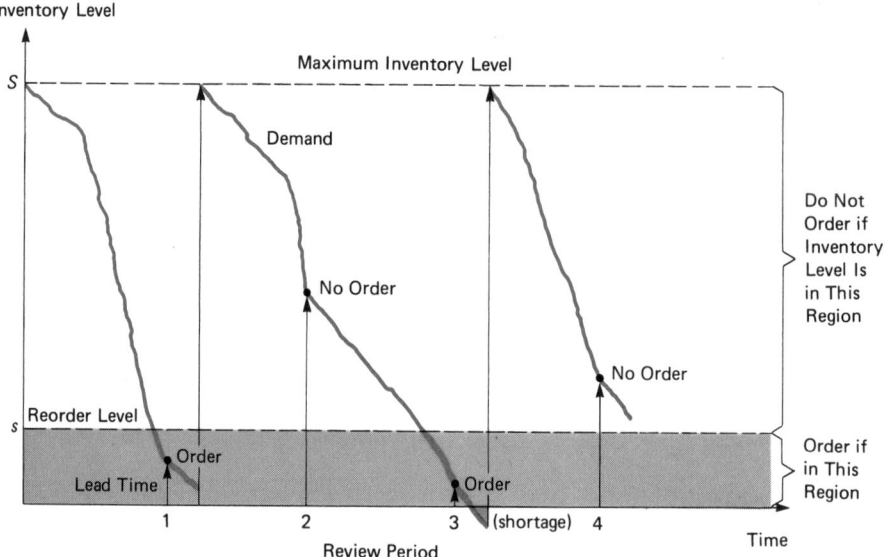

1. A large safety stock may be needed to reduce the possibility of shortages.
2. The nonuniform order sizes may be inconvenient to fill. The method is used mainly for group A items and sometimes for group B items.

The base-stock system

A version of this method is the so-called *base-stock* system in which orders are placed as soon as demand occurs, *regardless of the inventory level*, to bring the inventory back to its maximum level, S. This method is practical where the number of units in inventory is very small (e.g., 1–5).

Rule of thumb systems

Type C items are typically of such low value that the effort required either to determine the EOQ or audit frequently cannot be economically justified. Thus, these items are typically ordered on the basis of experience or when stock is depleted. The control imposed on such items is minimal.

Computerized systems

Computer use is common

Inventory systems in medium and large sized organizations are usually computerized. The computer system follows the inventory level in a manner similar to that of a computerized banking system following a cash balance. All transactions are recorded, and the balance is computed immediately. Whenever the inventory level is at or below the reorder point, the computer signals to place a new order. The same computer issues and prints the purchasing orders. The reorder point and the order quantity can be computed with the aid of one of the models presented in this chapter, by the aid of more complicated models such as MRP (see

Part B), with the use of simulation (see example in Chapter 14), or by using a trial-and-error approach. In addition, computers are used to prepare management reports concerning the overall inventory system.

12.8 CONCLUSION

The models presented in this chapter deal with the simplest inventory situations. Yet, they are widely applied in inventory control systems and give satisfactory results even in places where real-life conditions do not conform exactly to the model's format and the underlying assumptions. The insensitivity of the models provides management with more flexibility enabling deviation from optimal solutions at a small cost.

Inventory models are one of the most common applications of management science. This is partly due to their insensitivity but mainly attributable to the possibility of realizing quick and significant savings. Further, since the application of such models only affects people minimally, human resistance to implementation is not such a problem.

The models are basically cost models attempting to minimize the total inventory expense. This inventory expense may be extremely high in some instances and thus, so are the potential savings.

12.9 PROBLEMS FOR PART A

1. The ABC Company needs 10,000 lamps annually. It costs $45 to place one order and 10 cents to store each lamp for a year.
   Find:
   a. The economic order quantity.
   b. The total inventory cost per year.
   c. How many orders will be placed each year.

2. Sunshine Corporation uses 840,000 bags of fertilizer each year for its orange groves. It costs the company $100 to place an order and 50 cents to store a bag for a year. How many month's supply should the company purchase at one time using the economic order quantity formula?

3. Columbia City buys office supplies for $500,000 each year. It costs $80 to place one order. Annual per item holding costs are 20 percent.
   a. What is the dollar value of the EOQ?
   b. How many times should orders be placed each year?
   c. What is the total annual ordering cost?
   d. What is the total annual carrying cost?

4. Eastwood State Park uses 1,000 bags of food each month. It costs $30 to place a purchase order, and the carrying cost is $1.125 per bag per year.
   a. Find the economic order quanity.
   b. How many "months supply of food" are contained in one order?

5. Assume an inventory system where a demand of 2,500 units per year must be supplied and where orders are shipped immediately.
   a. Find how often orders should be placed (how many times a year) if the ordering cost is $40 per order, and the cost of the product is $1 per unit. The annual per unit carrying cost is 20 percent of the value of the product.
   b. Find the total carrying and ordering cost.
   c. What will happen to the EOQ if demand increases to 10,000 units? What will happen to the total inventory cost?

6. American Department Store sells 4,050 vacuum cleaners a year. One cleaner occupies 6 square feet of storage space. Each cleaner costs $50, and the annual per unit holding cost is 16 percent of each cleaner. Placing an order costs $32. There is presently an area of 900 square

feet for storage. Using the EOQ, would it be profitable for the store to increase the storage area if it costs 50¢ a square foot per year?

7. The Costly Company buys its raw materials ten times a year, 100 units each time. It is known that this purchasing policy is an optimal one (most economic). The company pays $50 per unit. Annual carrying cost is 20 percent of the value stored.

Find:

a. The cost of placing one order (ordering cost).

b. The total cost (ordering, carrying, and parts) for one year.

c. Assume that the yearly demand has increased from X to $4X$, all other conditions remain the same; what will the new economic lot size be? What general conclusions may you arrive at?

8. Producers Company is using $200,000 of a certain material per year. The inventory holding cost is 20 percent. The cost of placing an order is $50.

a. How often should an order for the material be placed?

b. What is the total inventory cost involved?

c. The company wants to place four orders a year; how much more than the optimal solution found in parts (a) and (b) will it cost the company?

d. After establishing the optimal policy, it was found that there is a price increase of 10 percent in the material. What ordering policy would you suggest now?

e. What will the effect on the total inventory cost be if the company orders once a month? (Compare to part (a) of this problem.)

9. Find the reorder point (number of units still remaining in stock) for the following three situations:

	Annual demand	Lead time
Case A.	5,200	2 weeks
Case B.	60	1 month
Case C.	600	17 days

Assume 50 working weeks and 300 working days/year.

10. The following data give expenditures for carrying light bulbs in a department store.

Annual sales (units)	10,000
Annual cost of capital.	$1200.00
Insurance (per unit)	.05
Taxes and licenses (per unit)	.03
Rent, maintenance (per unit)	.12
Annual paperwork	800.00

Find H, the annual carrying cost per unit.

11. Northwest Hospital buys surgical gloves in lots of 1,200 dozen which represents a four-month supply. The carrying cost per dozen is $12.50 and the ordering cost is $100 per order.

Find:

a. The economic order quantity.

b. The annual inventory cost.

12. CORDON Industries produces 7,200 energy conserving devices each year. The company sells these units at $10 apiece. CORDON's objective is to produce these units at the least possible cost. One option is to produce all the units once a year. Alternatively, the company may produce several times during the year. Each such production period is called a "run" and these runs are equal in size. Assume that the startup cost for each production run is $300 and the holding cost is computed at 30 percent.

Find:

a. The annual cost of one run per year.

b. The optimal size and cost of the production run.

c. The optimal number of production runs per year.

13. For what household items do you use: (a) a perpetual, (b) a periodic, or (c) a rule of thumb inventory system?

14. Which items in a typical household would be classified as type A items? Which as type C items (in an A-B-C classification system)?

15. What would the modification be to the EOQ formula if the carrying charge is a function of the *maximum* inventory level rather than the average?

PART B: EXTENSIONS

12.10   PRODUCTION RUNS: ECONOMIC LOT SIZE (ELS)

The EOQ model has an interesting extension in the production area where items are often produced in large lots rather than in small lots that exactly meet demand. When more is produced than demanded, an inventory is accumulated. When the accumulated inventory is large enough, a period of no production occurs. The demand then is met from stocks as long as they last. When these are depleted, another large lot is produced, and so on.

ELS a modification of EOQ

Advantages

The major advantage of producing large lots ("batches") is that savings of the *setup cost* can be realized. Setup cost includes the expense required to "tear down" the machines from a previous production run as well as that of preparing the machines for the upcoming run. It also includes the cost of processing the necessary paperwork. The larger the production run, the fewer times it will be repeated each year, and therefore fewer setups will be required. Another advantage is the reduction in the *unit production cost*[14] due to the possibility of buying expensive but efficient tools and machines for producing large quantities. Also, better control over quality can be expected.

Disadvantages

The major disadvantage of producing large lots is that the accumulated inventory has a holding cost. Thus, the production of lots which are too large may result in additional inventory costs larger than the setup costs saved.

Management is interested in finding the production quantity for a lot that minimizes the sum of the holding inventory and setup costs. Such a problem is called the economic lot size (ELS) problem.

Example

Energy Sol produces a certain energy saving device. The demand for the device, D, is 1,800 units per year (or six units each day, assuming 300 working days in a year). The company can produce at an annual rate, P, of 7,200 units (or 24 per day). Setup cost, K, is \$300. There is an inventory holding cost, H, of \$36 per unit, per year. The problem is to find the economic lot size, which is designated by L.

---

[14] A reduction in unit production cost is equivalent to a *quantity discount* and can be treated as such (see next section).

FIGURE 12.12
Inventory level for ELS
model

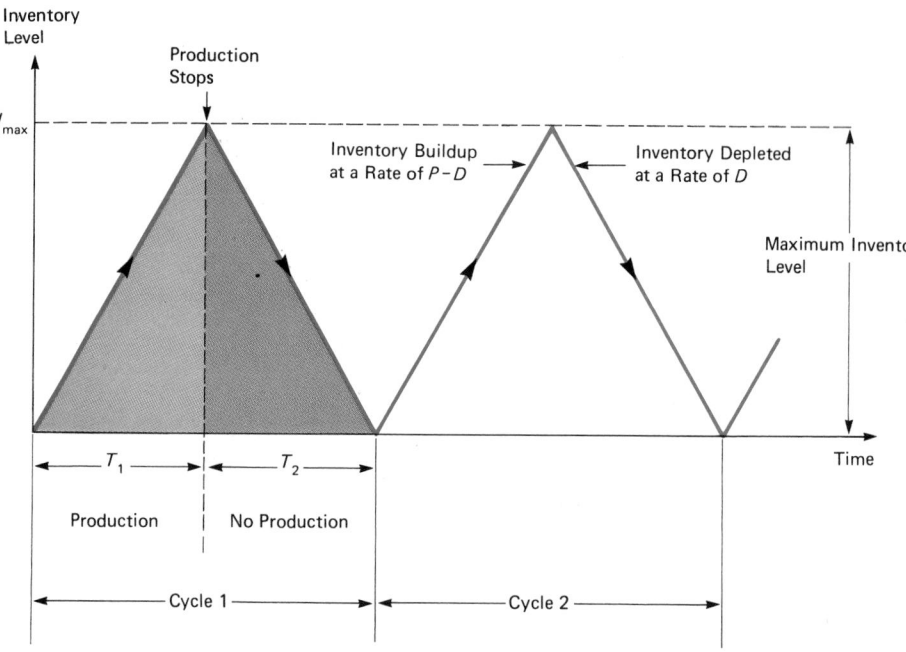

Schematic illustration   The process is shown in Figure 12.12. As in the regular EOQ illustration, the time axis is divided into cycles, each with the following elements:

The production period, T_1   During this period a lot of size L is made. Since the company produces at the rate P and delivers at a rate D, an inventory is accumulated at the rate of $P - D$. The length of the production period is given by Equation 12.14:

$$T_1 = \frac{L}{P} \tag{12.14}$$

where L is the lot size to be produced.

The maximum inventory   The inventory is accumulated at a rate of $P - D$ during period T_1 and will reach a peak at the end of T_1. The maximum inventory is given by Equation 12.15:

$$I_{max} = (P - D)T_1 = (P - D)\frac{L}{P} \tag{12.15}$$

The average inventory   As in the EOQ case the average inventory equals half the maximum inventory:

$$I_{avg} = (1/2)I_{max} = \frac{(P - D)L}{2P} \tag{12.16}$$

The annual holding cost   The annual holding cost is given, as in the regular EOQ, by the product of the average inventory and the annual holding cost per unit (H):

$$\text{Annual Holding Cost} = \frac{H(P - D)L}{2P} \qquad (12.17)$$

The depletion period, T_2   During this period the production stops and the inventory is depleted. Since demand is at a rate of D, the length of the period is given by:

$$T_2 = \frac{I_{max}}{D} = \frac{(P - D)L}{PD} \qquad (12.18)$$

A cycle   A cycle is composed of:

$$\text{Cycle} = T_1 + T_2 \qquad (12.19)$$

Number of cycles per year   The number of cycles per year, N, is determined by the annual demand divided by L.

$$N = \frac{D}{L} \qquad (12.20)$$

The annual setup cost   The setup cost per cycle is given as K. Therefore, the total annual setup cost is the product of K times the number of cycles. That is:

$$\text{Annual Setup Cost} = \frac{KD}{L} \qquad (12.21)$$

Total annual cost = total holding cost + total setup cost

$$TC = \frac{H(P - D)L}{2P} + \frac{KD}{L} \qquad (12.22)$$

Finding the ELS   The optimal lot size, L, is found by equating the annual holding cost to the annual setup cost:

$$H(P - D) \frac{L}{2P} = \frac{KD}{L}$$

After proper manipulation[15] the result is:

$$L^* = \sqrt{\frac{2PKD}{H(P - D)}} \qquad (12.23)$$

---

[15] Equation 12.23 can also be found by taking the first derivative of Equation 12.22, setting it to zero, and solving for L^*.

Solution to Energy Sol's problem Given:

Annual demand, $D = 1,800$.
Annual production capability, $P = 7,200$.
Setup cost, $K = \$300$.
Holding cost per unit per year, $H = \$36$.

Inserting the data given into Equation 12.23:

$$L^* = \sqrt{\frac{2PKD}{H(P-D)}} = \sqrt{\frac{2(7,200)(300)(1,800)}{36(7,200 - 1,800)}}$$

$$= 200 \text{ units per production run}$$

Using Equations 12.14 through 12.21:

$$T_1 = \frac{L^*}{P} = \frac{200}{7,200}$$

$$= .0278 \text{ years; assuming 300 working days this will be } 8\tfrac{1}{3} \text{ days.}$$

$$I_{max} = (P - D)T_1 = 5,400 \times .0278 = 150 \text{ units.}$$

$$I_{avg} = \frac{I_{max}}{2} = 75 \text{ units.}$$

$$T_2 = \frac{I_{max}}{D} = \frac{150}{1,800} = .0833 \text{ years, or 25 working days.}$$

A cycle $= T_1 + T_2 = .0278 + .0833 = .111$ years, or $33\tfrac{1}{3}$ working days.

The above information is entered on Figure 12.13. Additional information that can be derived is:

$$N = \frac{D}{L^*} = \frac{1,800}{200} = 9 \text{ cycles per year}$$

$$\text{Annual holding cost} = \frac{36 \times (7,200 - 1,800)200}{2 \times 7,200} = \$2,700$$

$$\text{Annual setup cost} = \frac{300(1,800)}{200} = \$2,700$$

FIGURE 12.13
The Energy Sol
production process

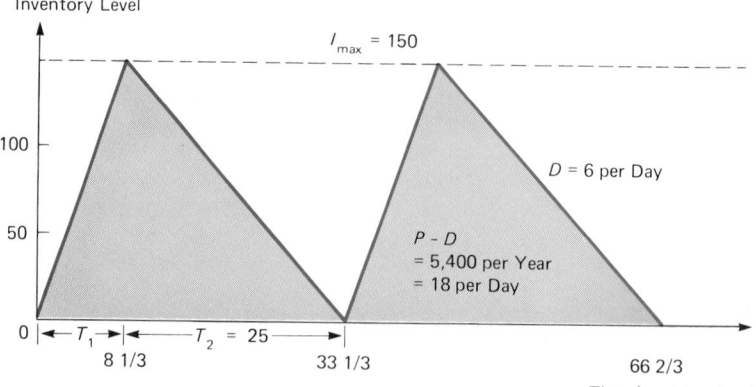

Note: These two costs *must* be equal in an optimal solution.

Total Annual Cost = Annual Setup + Annual Holding Cost = $5,400

12.11   SINGLE PERIOD INVENTORIES

There exist some situations where the inventory question is simply a one-period problem due to the product's high degree of perishability or obsolescence. This problem is classically known as "the newsboy problem" since day-old newspapers are considered worthless. Similar one-period situations are: church bake sales, Christmas tree sales, and Easter bunnies at the pet store. Seasonal products such as holiday greeting cards, spring dresses, and certain holiday foods and flowers are other examples of the one-period problem.[16]

The "Newsboy" problem

The common element in all these situations is that the product is only ordered once and there is a penalty associated with underordering as well as a penalty associated with overordering. The underordering penalty is the loss of potential profit (opportunity cost) plus a possible loss of customer goodwill. The "overordering" penalty is primarily the cost of the leftover product. There may additionally be disposal costs which add to the penalty or a salvage value which decreases the penalty.

Underorder or overorder?

A discrete demand distribution example

THE GROCERY buys its tomatoes once a week. A crate of tomatoes costs $6 and sells for $11 (i.e., a profit of $5 per crate sold). Any crates remaining unsold at the end of the week are sold as animal food for $2 a crate. Observations show that past sales ranged from 16 to 20 crates a week. Since demand is relatively constant, it is assumed that sales will continue at the same rate.

Suppose that a study, taken over the sales of the last 50 weeks, showed the following results:

Number of crates demanded	Number of weeks
16	4
17	10
18	12
19	15
20	9
	Total 50

The problem is to find how many crates THE GROCERY should order each week so that the profit will be maximized.

---

[16] The same problem with a modified structure is the situation of those firms and people who must accept reservations or appointments for their services. This category consists of such services as: motels and hotels, restaurants, airlines, doctors, and hairdressers.

Solution using a decision table   Since demand ranges between 16 and 20 there is no sense in ordering less than 16, nor more than 20. Therefore, there are only five alternatives of ordering: 16, 17, 18, 19, and 20 crates. There are 5 possible states of nature (demand); they are given with their respective probabilities below.

16 crates with a chance of 4 out of 50 = 8 percent = .08,
17 crates with a chance of 10/50 = .20,
18 crates with a chance of 12/50 = .24,
19 crates with a chance of 15/50 = .30,
and 20 crates with a chance of 9/50 = .18.

The information can be arranged in a decision table form (Table 12.2).

TABLE 12.2
THE GROCERY
decision table

Probabili-ties	Demand					Expected value of profit ($)
	→.08	.20	.24	.30	.18	
Alternatives	16	17	18	19	20	
16	80	80	80	80	80	80.00
17	76	85	85	85	85	84.28
18	72	81	90	90	90	86.76
19	68	77	86	95	95	87.08 ← *Maximum*
20	64	73	82	91	100	84.70

To demonstrate the calculation of the numbers in the table, if 16 crates are ordered and the demand is 16 or more, a profit of $5 × 16 = $80 will be realized. It is assumed here that there is no cost for unsatisfied customers (cost of "ill-will"). If 17 crates are ordered and there is only a demand for 16, 16 crates will be sold for $80 profit, and the 17th crate will be sold at a 6 − 2 = $4 loss; i.e., the total profit is: 80 − 4 = $76. For every crate overordered, a loss of $4 is recorded. Thus, if 20 crates are ordered and the demand is 16, the profit will be $64: 80 − (4 × 4) = $64.

Solution   Using expected value as a criterion, the best strategy is: order 19 crates each week at an expected profit of

.08($68) + .20($77) + .24($86) + .30($95) + .18($95) = $87.08

Other criteria may, of course, also be employed. For example, the maximin criterion would order 16 crates for a sure profit of $80.00 (the largest among the set (80, 76, 72, 68, 64) and the maximax criterion would indicate an order for 20 crates for a profit of $100.

Solution by marginal analysis

Small inventory problems can be solved using the decision table approach rather quickly. However, the solution of problems with dozens or hundreds of possible alternatives requires excessive computations. To overcome this difficulty, marginal analysis can be used. Marginal analysis can also be used for the solution of more complicated problems involving continuous demand distributions and costs due to "ill-will."

Excessive number of alternatives

The basic idea of marginal analysis is to compare two opposing costs, the cost of overordering and the cost of underordering, on an "additional-unit" basis. Let us demonstrate. Let:

p = probability of selling *at least* one more unit.
$1 - p$ = probability of *not* selling one more unit.
MP = profit realized from selling that additional unit (marginal profit).
ML = loss realized if the additional unit is not sold (marginal loss).

General formulation

The expected profit is equal to the probability of selling the unit times its marginal profit:

$$\text{Expected profit} = p \, (\text{MP})$$

Similarly, the expected loss is given as:

$$\text{Expected loss} = (1 - p) \, \text{ML}$$

To find out whether or not an additional unit should be ordered (at a given level of ordering), it is necessary to compare the expected profit versus the expected loss of the next unit. As long as the expected profit is *larger* than the expected loss, a unit should be added. Units will be added, one at a time, until the point where the *expected profit* equals the *expected loss*. This condition is expressed mathematically as:

Keep ordering more until . . .

$$p \, (\text{MP}) = (1 - p) \, \text{ML}$$

Solving for p:

$$p = \frac{\text{ML}}{\text{ML} + \text{MP}} \qquad (12.24)$$

In other words, in order to justify ordering (or stocking) a unit, the probability of selling that unit must be *at least* equal to p. The problem now is how to find that last (optimal) unit.

Application to the example

$$\text{MP} = 11 - 6 = \$5$$
$$\text{ML} = \; 6 - 2 = \$4, \text{ therefore: } p = \frac{4}{4 + 5} = .444$$

It is necessary now to relate p to the *cumulative probability of demand;* i.e., the probability that one *or more* crates will be sold. For example, the probability of selling 19 or more crates (that is, 19 or 20) is .18 + .30 = .48 (see Table 12.3).

TABLE 12.3
Cumulative probability of demand

Number of crates, N	Probability of demand	Cumulative probability (of selling N or more)
16	.08	1.00
17	.20	.92
18	.24	.72
19	.30	.48
20	.18	.18

Note that the cumulative probability for 19 crates is .48, more than $p = .444$, and, hence, 19 should be stocked; but at 20 crates .18 is less than .444 and, hence, 20 cannot be justified. Therefore, the optimal order policy is 19 crates.

12.12   QUANTITY DISCOUNTS

Sellers frequently offer buyers a price discount for purchasing large quantities ("cheaper by the dozen"). There may be several price intervals (or price breaks) such as $10 each unit for quantities up to 99, $9 each unit for 100 to 499, $8 each unit for 500 up to 999, and $7 each unit for 1,000 and over.

The practice of quantity discounts is widely spread since it offers advantages to both buyer and seller. These are listed, together with some possible disadvantages, in Table 12.4.

We distinguish two cases of discounting:

a.   A discount is offered at one price level.

b.   A discount is offered at several levels (price breaks).

TABLE 12.4
Quantity buying considerations

	Advantages	Disadvantages
Buyer	Lower unit price Less paperwork Cheaper transportation Fewer stockouts Uniform goods (coming from same shipment) Security (against such factors as strikes, price increases)	Larger inventories Higher holding cost Risk of deterioration and obsolescence Higher capital requirements Older stock on hand
Seller	Cheaper transportation Less paperwork Larger production runs (thus, lower production costs per unit)	Lower unit prices Less bargaining power with buyers

Example 1—Discount offered at one level

The city of Northstar uses 100 replacement lamps a month for its street lights. Each lamp costs the city $8. Ordering costs are estimated at $27 per order and the holding costs (primarily the cost of capital) are 25 percent. The city currently orders according to the EOQ. The supplier has now offered the city a 2 percent discount if the city will buy 600 lamps at a time. Should the city accept the offer?

Solution

Given:

D = 100 units per month × 12 months = 1,200 units/year
H = .25 × 8.00 = $2.00 per lamp per year
K = 27

$$\text{EOQ} = \sqrt{\frac{2 \times 27 \times 1200}{2}} = 180 \text{ lamps}$$

The current total annual inventory cost is:

$$\text{TC} = \frac{27 \times 1200}{180} + \frac{180 \times 2}{2} = \$360 \text{ per year}$$

To this cost should be added the item cost, which is relevant when discounts on the item cost are considered.

Annual cost of items = $8.00 × 1200 lamps = $9,600

Thus, the total *system* cost is $360 + $9600 = $9960.

Review of the discount offer   The analysis is conducted on an annual basis. The offer to buy 600 units at a 2 percent discount will reduce the item cost, the holding cost will be higher since the city will buy 600 units instead of 180, and the ordering cost will decrease with fewer orders. The analysis is shown in Table 12.5.

TABLE 12.5
Cost comparison on an annual basis

No discount	Discount
Q* = 180 K = 27 D = 1200 H = 2.00	Q* = 600 (given) K = 27 D = 1200 H = 1.96, (2 percent less than previous H*)
Total annual ordering cost = $ 180	$\frac{KD}{Q} = \frac{27 \times 1200}{600} = \$\ 54$
Total annual holding cost = 180	$\frac{QH}{2} = \frac{600 \times 1.96}{2} = 588$
Total annual unit cost = 9,600	2 percent off 9,408
Total cost 9,960	10,050

* H has been changed in the proportion of the discount. The reason for this is that the major portion of H is the cost of capital. Since the unit cost decreases, the cost of capital will decrease also.

Conclusion The discount offer should be rejected. The city will be at a disadvantage to accept it. A higher discount rate should be negotiated instead (e.g., a 5 percent discount is favorable).

Example 2—Discounts at price breaks

General Hospital buys a certain antibiotic from a large supplier. The drug can be bought at the following prices:

For quantities of 1 up to 4,999—$2.75 a unit.
For quantities from 5,000 to 9,999—$2.60 a unit.
For quantities over 10,000 units—$2.50 a unit.

The demand (D) for the drug in the hospital is 50,000 units a year. There is an ordering charge (K) of $50 per order and a holding cost (H) of 20 percent of the cost of the item, per unit, per year. The problem is to find the optimal purchasing policy for the hospital.

Solution

Step 1 Find the EOQ (labeled Q_1^*) for the *lowest price level* ($2.50 in our case). Using the EOQ formula we get:

$$Q_1^* = \sqrt{\frac{2KD}{H}} = \sqrt{\frac{2 \times 50 \times 50,000}{.5}} = \sqrt{10,000,000} = 3,163 \text{ units}$$

(Note that $H = 20$ percent of $2.50 = .2(2.5) = \$.5$)

Step 2 Compare Q_1^* to the quantity required for the price break (10,000 in our case). If Q_1^* is *larger* than this quantity, the problem is solved. If it is *smaller,* the solution is *not feasible* and the search for the lowest cost ordering quantity continues (in this example 3,163 is smaller than 10,000).

Step 3 Select the next higher item cost ($2.60 in this example) and calculate Q_2^*, using the EOQ formula:

$$Q_2^* = \sqrt{\frac{2 \times 50 \times 50,000}{.52}} = \sqrt{9,615,385} = 3,101 \text{ units}$$

(Notice that H has been changed to $.2(2.60) = \$.52$.)

Step 4 Repeat step 2. Compare Q_2^* to the range which is required for the equivalent price. In this example the price of $2.60 is in the range of 5,000–9,999. Since Q_2^* is not within this range, the solution is *not feasible* and the search continues.

Step 5 Compute the EOQ for the next higher price ($2.75 in the example):

$$Q_3^* = \sqrt{\frac{2 \times 50 \times 50,000}{.2 \times 2.75}} = \sqrt{9,090,910} = 3,015$$

Step 6 Repeat step 2. This time Q_3^* is within the appropriate range for the price of $2.75. Therefore, it is a *feasible* solution.
Step 7. Cost comparison (on an annual basis) Now a cost comparison is executed. The total annual cost is computed for the feasible EOQ.

Then, it is compared with the total annual cost of each of the minimum quantities required for each price break. (These are 10,000 units and 5,000 units.) The total annual cost is computed according to Equation 12.25:

$$TC = \text{Ordering Cost} + \text{Holding Cost} + \text{Units Cost}$$

$$TC = \frac{DK}{Q} + \frac{HQ}{2} + pD \qquad (12.25)$$

where p is the price of one unit.

Computing the total cost, TC, we get:

$$TC_1 \text{ (for 10,000)} = \frac{50,000}{10,000}(50) + \frac{.2(2.5)10,000}{2} + 50,000(2.5)$$

$$\text{Ordering Cost} + \text{Holding Cost} + \text{Units Cost}$$

$$= \underline{\underline{\$127,750}}$$

$$TC_2 \text{ (for 5,000)} = \frac{50,000}{5,000}(50) + \frac{.2(2.6)5,000}{2} + 50,000(2.6)$$

$$= \underline{\underline{\$131,800}}$$

$$TC_3 \text{ (for } Q_3 = 3,015) = \frac{50,000}{3,015}(50) + \frac{.2(2.75)3,015}{2} + 50,000(2.75)$$

$$= \underline{\underline{\$139,158}}$$

Therefore, an order for 10,000 units at a time should be placed since it exhibits the lowest total cost of $127,750 per year.

The process of solving for the EOQ with quantity discounts is shown in Figure 12.14.

12.13. MATERIAL REQUIREMENTS PLANNING (MRP)

The EOQ inventory control system assumes that demand is essentially constant. This is often the case for items which are *independently* demanded, such as finished goods, supplies, and spare parts. However, many inventoried items consist of subassemblies whose demand, being *dependent* upon the demand for finished goods, is "lumpy" rather than constant. For example, in producing a batch of tables, the demand for table legs occurs at a high rate (4 per table) for a very short time—immediately prior to assembling the top and apron to the legs. To constantly hold all these legs in inventory to meet a peak demand that rarely occurs would cost a lot of money. Therefore, the EOQ is not useful in this case. It would be much better to have the legs arrive in inventory *just prior* to the time when they are needed. This is the major purpose of MRP.

Independent versus dependent demand

Lumpy dependent demand

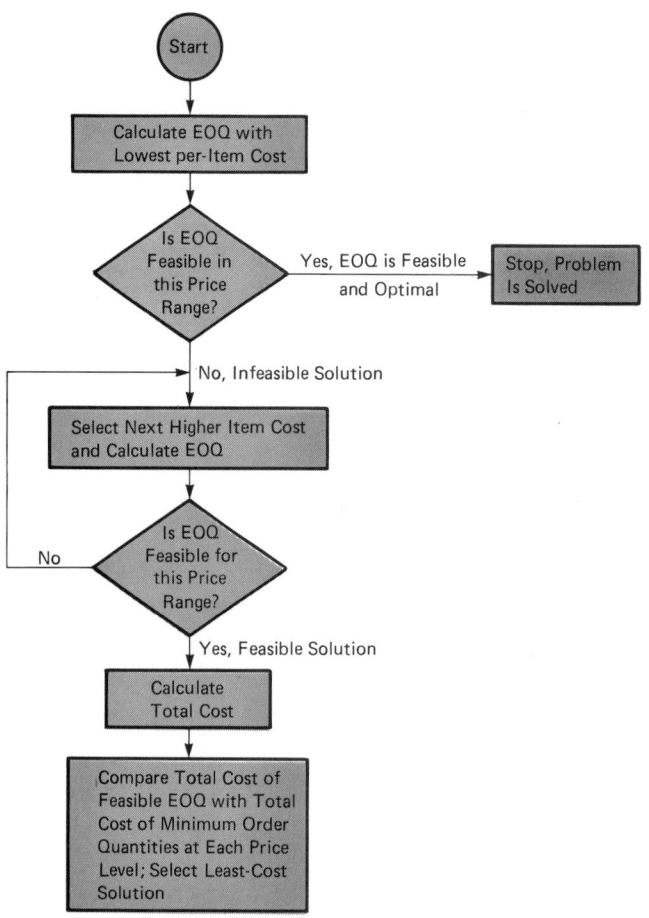

FIGURE 12.14
Flow diagram for quantity discounts of EOQ

Each product typically consists of several subcomponents—for a company with many products the number of subcomponents and parts may reach tens of thousands. To keep track of all these parts on a *finished product* basis clearly requires a computer. Therefore, until the advent of economical computer power in the 1960s, MRP was not feasible for many situations. In actuality, MRP is only one component in a production planning and control system that includes other computer components to schedule production jobs, purchase materials, check capacity requirements, forecast product demands, and so on.

MRP requires computer power

MRP as one part of a larger system

The Elements of MRP

Three sets of data requirements

The MRP system is composed of three data elements:

1. A master production schedule.
2. A bill of materials file.
3. An inventory master file.

The master production schedule (MPS) The MPS is a schedule listing how many of each item will be required and when; this is called a "time-phased" schedule. The items may be finished goods, spares, or subcomponents. The demand is based upon both forecasts and actual customer orders to date.

It is the MPS that drives the MRP system. To assemble the end items (called "parent" or "level 0" items) the subcomponents must be ready on time. To have the subcomponents ready for final assembly on time, *their* subcomponents (parts) must be produced, or purchased, by the necessary date. And so on. The time it takes to get these subcomponents is called their *lead time*. The MRP system takes these lead and assembly times into account in determining when to release work orders and purchase requisitions. An example of an MPS will be given soon.

"Parent" or "Level 0" items in the MPS

The bill of materials (B/M) The MRP system knows what items constitute each end product, and each subassembly, from the B/M. The B/M includes all of the raw materials, components, and subassemblies, and the quantities, required to produce the item. A typical bill of materials, and a "product tree" formed from the B/M, are given in Figures 12.15 and 12.16.

Building the product tree from the B/M

Top		(one)	manufactured
Walnut veneer	15 ft²	(one)	purchased
Particle board	½″ × 15 ft²	(one)	manufactured
Veneer strip	½″ × 17 feet	(one)	purchased
Apron		(one)	manufactured
Veneer strip	3″ × 15 feet	(one)	purchased
Particle board	3″ × 5½ feet	(two)	manufactured
Particle board	3″ × 2 feet	(two)	manufactured
Wood screws	1½″ flathead	(eight)	purchased
Legs		(four)	manufactured
Walnut	1½″ × 1½″ × 2′	(one)	manufactured
Anchors		(one)	manufactured
¹⁄₁₆″ Steel ribbon		(one)	purchased
6–32 Screws		(two)	purchased
6–32 Nuts		(two)	purchased

FIGURE 12.15
Bill of materials for walnut table

The inventory master file (IMF) This file contains detailed information on the number of items on hand in inventory, on order with suppliers, and previously committed to production items. If sufficient items are available, the system commits them to use; if not, purchase or work orders are scheduled for release at the proper time so that items will be available when needed with the least possible inventory.

Inspecting the IMF for material availability

The MRP computation process

As an order is added to the MPS, the MRP system "explodes" the B/M to determine what subcomponents will be required in what quantities in what time periods. The "explosion" simply consists of

Exploding the B/M to determine time-phased material requirements

FIGURE 12.16
Walnut table product
tree

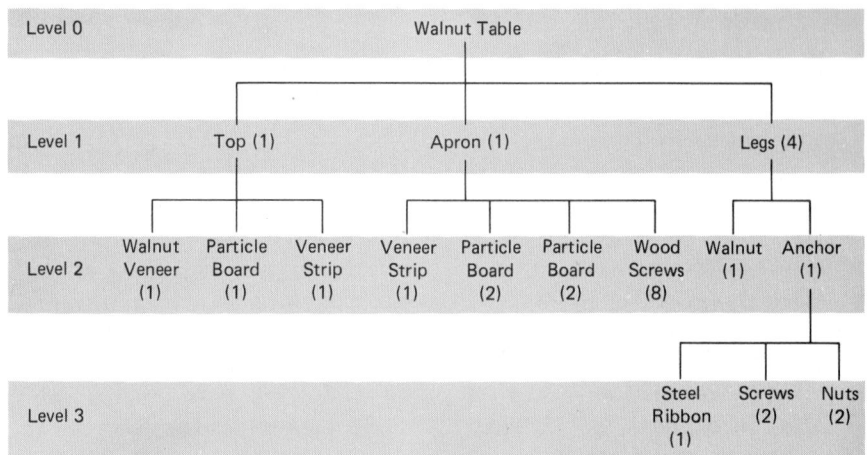

stepping down through the B/M levels and determining the quantity and lead times of subcomponents to support the purchase, manufacture, or assembly at each level. The result is a "time-phased" set of production requirements to support the parent order.

An example is given in Table 12.6 for a demand of 100 tables in week 15 and 70 tables in week 18. Note that because of an on-hand inventory of 90 tables and planned receipts of 30, only $(100 + 70) - 90 - 30 = 50$ are exploded through the B/M.

TABLE 12.6
Level 0 MPS for walnut table (2-week lead time)

	Week							
	12	*13*	*14*	*15*	*16*	*17*	*18*	*19*
Gross requirements				100			70	
On hand	90	90	120	120	20	20	20	0
Net requirements.							50	
Planned receipts		30						
Planned releases					50			

The levels 1, 2, and 3 exploded schedules for a portion of the B/M are shown in Table 12.7. The gross requirements at any level are based on the planned releases at the previous level. Notice, however, that gross requirements can be accumulated for several products; for example, the anchors and screws have externally generated demands upon them as well. (They are also used in oak tables whose schedule is not illustrated here.)

Externally generated demands also

Work and purchase order releases

The planned release of work orders for 50 tables in week 16 (Table 12.6) generates a gross requirement of $4 \times 50 = 200$ legs in week 16. Since 130 are already in stock (Table 12.7a), only 70 need be released in

TABLE 12.7
B/M explosion for subcomponent requirements

a. Level 1: Legs (one-week lead time)

	Week							
	11	12	13	14	15	16	17	18
Gross requirements......						200		
On hand...............	130	130	130	130	130	130	0	0
Net requirements						70		
Planned receipts........								
Planned releases........					(70)			

$\angle\!\!-\times 1 = \rceil$

b. Level 2: Anchors (one-week lead time)

	Week							
	11	12	13	14	15	16	17	18
Gross requirements......			10		(70)		40	
On hand...............	35	35	60	50	50	0	0	0
Net requirements					20		40	
Planned receipts........		25						
Planned releases........				(20)		(40)		

$\angle\!\!-\times 2 = \rceil \quad \angle\!\!-\times 2 = \rceil$

c. Level 3: Screws (three-week lead time)

	Week							
	11	12	13	14	15	16	17	18
Gross requirements......		50		(40)		(80)		40
On hand...............	80	80	30	30	0	0	0	0
Net requirements				10		80		40
Planned receipts........								
Planned releases........	10		80		40			

week 15. This generates a gross requirement for 70 anchors in week 15 (Table 12.7b). Considering other external requirements for anchors (e.g., 10 in week 13), inventory on hand, and planned receipts, two work orders are released in weeks 14 and 16 for more anchors. These work orders generate, in turn, requirements for twice as many screws, and purchase orders are thus placed for screws in weeks 11, 13, and 15 (Table 12.7c).

The lot-sizing problem

Note in Table 12.7b that work orders were released for anchors in weeks 14 and 16 (and purchase orders for screws in weeks 11, 13, and 15). Clearly, it may well be worthwhile to consider combining these orders and avoiding an extra setup or ordering charge. But, how many orders ahead should be included? This is known as the "lot-sizing problem."

One systematic solution procedure to this problem, called the *part-period balancing method*, attempts to balance the cost of holding inventory with the cost of ordering. (The EOQ occurred where these costs were equal, you may remember.)

As an example, suppose the cost of placing one order for screws in Table 12.7c (in any amount) is $5 and the cost of holding them one week in inventory is $.01 each. The three possible purchase quantities in week 11 are thus: 10, 10 + 80 for week 13 = 90, or 10 + 80 + 40 for week 15 = 130. The part-period method says to select that order size whose holding cost will be closest to $5 (the ordering cost). The three holding costs are:

$$c_{10} = (10) \ (0 \text{ weeks}) \ \$.01 = \$0$$
$$c_{90} = \$.01 \ [10(0) + 80(2)] = \$1.60$$
$$c_{130} = \$.01 \ [10(0) + 80(2) + 40(4)] = \$3.20$$

Therefore, 130 should be ordered in week 11.

Summary

MRP has emerged as the best inventory control system for job lot production with a dependent demand. It allows a *near zero* inventory level since the inventory is closely coordinated with the production schedule. In contrast to the EOQ that controls one item at a time, MRP can control several products simultaneously when they share common components or parts. Therefore, most MRP systems are large in size and require a computer for processing. A number of software firms offer industrial MRP packages, such as IBM, Arista, Burroughs, Cincom, and the like.

12.14   PLANNED SHORTAGES

In the previous section the use of safety stock as a protection against shortages was suggested. However, safety stock increases the inventory level and may result in excessive holding cost. Therefore, it may be better to allow shortages to occur rather than to build up a safety stock. The penalty may be temporary (backlogged) or permanent (lost). In either case there is a penalty. The problem to be addressed now is to find the economic order quantity in a case in which a shortage is allowed and safety stock is not considered. A situation of this type is shown in Figure 12.17.

The symbols to be used in this section, some of which are shown in the figure, are:

Q = order quantity.
D = annual demand.
K = order cost.

S = maximum inventory level.
H = holding cost per unit per year.
S/D = time during which inventory is positive (no stockout).
Q/D = time of one cycle.
G = shortage cost per unit per year.

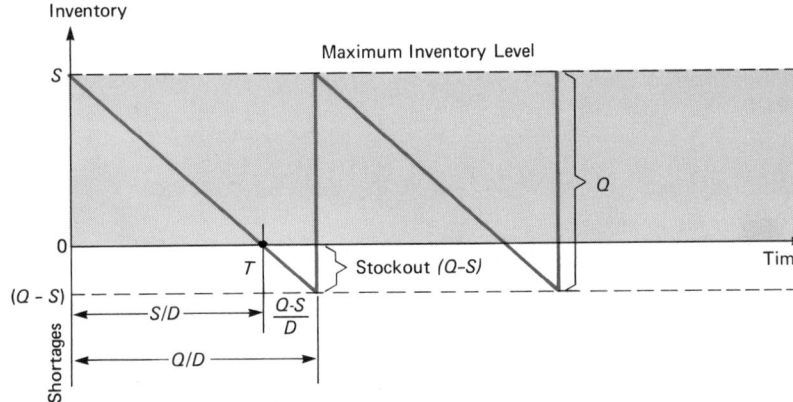

FIGURE 12.17
An inventory situation with planned shortages

Computation of costs

In this situation there are three relevant costs: an *ordering cost*, a *holding cost*, and a *shortage cost*.

Total annual ordering cost   As in the regular EOQ: KD/Q.

Total annual holding cost   The annual holding cost, however, is not $HQ/2$ or even $HS/2$, corresponding to the regular EOQ, since during the time duration of the shortage period there is *no inventory at all*. The average inventory level is calculated from the total "unit years" of inventory in a cycle, divided by the total length of a cycle (Q/D). The number of unit years is given[18] by Equation 12.26:

$$\text{Unit Years of Inventory (per cycle)} = \frac{1}{2}\left(\frac{S}{D}\right)S = \frac{S^2}{2D} \quad (12.26)$$

Thus, the average inventory is:

$$\text{Average Inventory} = \frac{S^2/2D}{Q/D} = \frac{S^2}{2Q} \quad (12.27)$$

and the holding cost is:

$$\text{Annual Holding Cost} = \frac{HS^2}{2Q} \quad (12.28)$$

---

[18] Equation 12.26 is derived from the area of the triangle *OST* (Figure 12.17).

The shortage cost Applying the same type of analysis for the calculation of the annual shortage cost, where G is the annual cost per unit of being out of stock, the total shortage cost is expressed by Equation 12.29:

$$\text{Annual Shortage Cost} = \frac{G(Q - S)^2}{2Q} \tag{12.29}$$

The total relevant cost, TC The total cost is the sum of all three costs:

$$TC = \frac{KD}{Q} + \frac{HS^2}{2Q} + \frac{G(Q - S)^2}{2Q} \tag{12.30}$$

The optimal ordering quantity is:[19]

$$Q^* = \sqrt{\frac{2KD}{H}\left(\frac{G + H}{G}\right)} \tag{12.31}$$

with a maximum inventory level:

$$S = \sqrt{\frac{2KD}{H}\left(\frac{G}{G + H}\right)} \tag{12.32}$$

Example (using the data of the problem from Section 12.4)

$K = \$5.$
$H = \$1.20$ per unit per year.
$D = 1{,}200$ units.

Also given:

$G = \$2.40$ per unit per year.

Solution: according to Equations 12.31 and 12.32:

$$Q^* = \sqrt{\frac{2(5)1{,}200}{1.20} \times \left(\frac{2.4 + 1.2}{2.4}\right)} = 122 \text{ units}$$

$$S = \sqrt{\frac{2(5)1{,}200}{1.20} \times \left(\frac{2.4}{2.4 + 1.2}\right)} = 81.5 \text{ units}$$

---

[19] In order to find the minimum TC, partial derivatives with respect to both Q and S are taken and are set to 0:

$$\frac{\partial TC}{\partial Q} = -\frac{KD}{Q^2} - \frac{HS^2}{2Q^2} + \frac{G(Q - S)}{Q} - \frac{G(Q - S)^2}{2Q^2} = 0$$

$$\frac{\partial TC}{\partial S} = \frac{HS}{Q} - \frac{G(Q - S)}{Q} = 0$$

When these are solved simultaneously, Equations 12.31 and 12.32 result.

The previous no-shortage solution was $Q^* = 100$, and the maximum inventory was the same, namely 100. Now the quantity ordered has increased by about $1/5$, but the maximum inventory level is only about $4/5$ the previous level.

In conducting this type of analysis it is important to compute the total cost after Q^* is established and compare it to the cost of using safety stock instead.

12.15   SAFETY STOCKS AND SERVICE LEVELS

So far it has been assumed that the demand and the lead time are constant. As a result, it was possible to adopt an inventory policy whereby an item would *never be out of stock.* Running out of stock (a *stockout* or a *shortage*) implies that demand cannot be filled on time. Stockouts result from either delays in deliveries and/or from unexpected rises in demand during the lead time. These situations are depicted in Figure 12.18.

Stockout

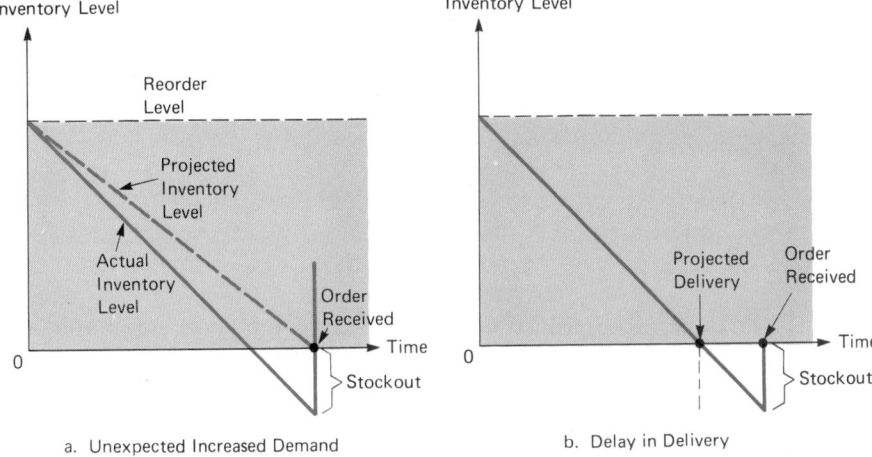

a. Unexpected Increased Demand   b. Delay in Delivery

FIGURE 12.18
Factors contributing to an inventory stockout

For protection against a stockout, an order can be computed and placed so that the delivery will arrive when a certain level of inventory is still remaining, rather than at the scheduled depletion of the stock. The managerial problem is *determining the proper level of this "safety stock."*

What level of safety stock?

Example

Assume an average demand of ten units per day and a lead time of six days. In such a case, there is an average demand during the lead time of $10(6) = 60$ units. Now assume that protection against a stockout (safety stock) of up to 50 units is desired. The reorder point will be: $60 + 50 =$

110 units. In general, the following relationship exists between the reorder point and the safety stock:

$$\text{Reorder Point} = \text{Demand during Lead Time} + \text{Safety Stock} \qquad (12.33)$$

The concept of service level

To build up a safety stock which would prevent shortages in *all* cases could be very expensive. The cost of incurring a once-a-year shortage may be much smaller than the cost of maintaining the safety stock. Therefore, management may wish to maintain a safety stock that will protect against a shortage not in all cases but, say, 80 percent of the time. The percentage of time that all demand is met (in this example, the 80 percent) is called the *service level*. The service level is defined as the probability of *not* running out of stock, that is:

$$\text{Service Level} = 1 - \text{Probability of Running Out of Stock} \qquad (12.34)$$

The higher the service level, the higher the required safety stock with its associated inventory cost, and the lower the chance of a shortage and its consequences. Service levels are usually determined by management policies but may also be determined mathematically in such a way that the total cost of keeping the safety stock and incurring expenses during shortages is minimized. Let us show how.

Example   The average demand for product G is ten units a day. The lead time is known to be six days. Therefore, the *average* demand during the lead time is 6×10, or 60. The lead time demand follows a
normal distribution (see Appendix B) with a *standard deviation* of 8.59 units.

With a normal distribution there is exactly a 50 percent chance that the demand during the lead time will be more than the average of 60 units.

Using the tables for the area under the normal curve (see Table C1 in Appendix C), the relationship between a desired *service level* (which is equivalent to the area under the normal curve) and the number of standard deviations, Z, can be found. For example, for a 50 percent (.50) service level, $Z = 0$; for a 67 percent (.67) service level, $Z = .44$; for a 90 percent service level, $Z = 1.28$.

Suppose that management is interested in providing a 90 percent service level. To find the safety stock required for such a level, Equation 12.35 can be used:

$$\text{Safety Stock} = Z \times \sigma \qquad (12.35)$$

where Z is the number of standard deviations equivalent to the desired service level and σ is the standard deviation of the demand during the reorder period (8.59 in this case). For this example:

Safety stock = $1.28 \times 8.59 = 11$ units

This information is shown in Figure 12.19.

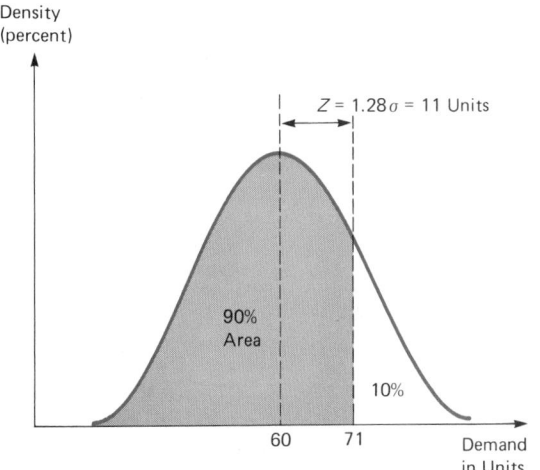

FIGURE 12.19
Service level of 90
percent

Note that in addition to the average demand of 60 units needed during the reorder period, there is a need for a safety stock of 11 to assure a service level of 90 percent. In a similar manner it can be found that in order to assure a 95 percent service level, a safety stock of 14 units is required; and to assure a 99.9 percent service level, 26.5 units of safety stock are needed.

Finding the best level of safety stock

Equation 12.35 tells management what amount of safety stock is required in order to maintain a desired service level. However, management may also be interested in knowing the cost of maintaining a desired service level. The establishment of a safety stock involves two costs:

1. The cost of a shortage, which declines as the safety stock increases.
2. The cost of keeping the safety stock, which increases as the safety stock increases.

The total cost that management is interested in is the sum of the two (see Figure 12.20). Management may be interested in finding the relationship between this total cost and the service level. Management may also be interested in determining the service level for which the total cost is the lowest. The following computations illustrate such an analysis.

FIGURE 12.20
Safety stock costs

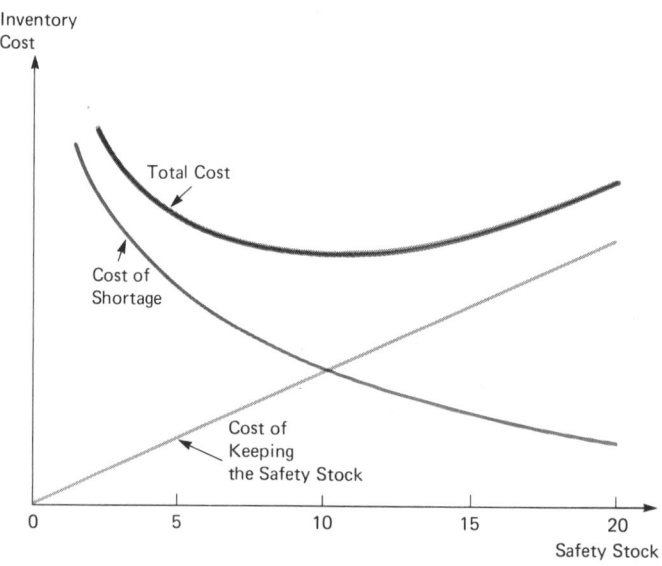

The cost of shortage

The cost of the shortage is given by Equation 12.36:

$$\text{Annual Cost of Shortage} = \frac{\pi BD}{Q}$$ (12.36)

where:

π = the probability of shortage (which equals 1 − the service level).
B = average cost of one shortage.[17]
D = annual demand.
Q = order quantity.
$\dfrac{D}{Q}$ = the number of cycles per year.

The cost of holding safety stock

The cost of holding safety stock is given by Equation 12.37:

$$\text{Annual Holding Cost} = H(\text{safety stock}) = HZ\sigma$$ (12.37)

---

[17] We have used the *average* cost per shortage here for the sake of simplicity. In Problem 12.24 we show a case with a *variable* cost per shortage.

where:

H = holding cost, per unit per year.
Z = number of standard deviations required to maintain a desired service level.
σ = the standard deviation of demand during the lead time.

The sum of the cost in Equations 12.36 and 12.37 is the total relevant cost for each service level:

$$TC = \frac{\pi BD}{Q} + HZ\sigma \qquad (12.38)$$

To find the best level of safety stock, the total relevant cost, TC, is computed for several desired service levels (e.g., 80 percent, 90 percent, 95 percent, 99 percent, etc.) and the lowst one is chosen.

Example   In the example of product G the following data are given:

Lead time = 6 days.
Demand = 10 units per day or 2,500 per year (with 250 working days).
Standard deviation = 8.59 units during the lead time.
K = order cost = $160 per order.
H = holding cost = $20 per unit per year.
B = shortage cost = $100 per shortage.

Management insists that a service level of at least 90 percent be maintained.

The problem is to find the cost of maintaining this 90 percent service level and whether there is one above it which would cost less.

Solution   First, the EOQ is computed disregarding shortages and safety stock.

$$\text{EOQ} = \sqrt{\frac{2KD}{H}} = \sqrt{\frac{2(160)2,500}{20}} = 200 \text{ units per order}$$

Computation for 90 percent service level   It was shown earlier that a safety stock of 11 units will guarantee a 90 percent service level. The total annual holding cost of a safety stock of 11 units is:

$$H(\text{safety stock}) = 20(11) = \$220$$

The total annual shortage cost (according to Equation 12.36) is:

$$\text{Shortage Cost} = \frac{\pi BD}{Q^*} = \frac{.1(100)(2,500)}{200} = \$125$$

Therefore, the *total relevant costs* are 220 + 125 = $345. Using a trial-and-error approach the analyst now searches for a possible lower cost service level above 90 percent.

Try a service level of 95 percent It was mentioned earlier that the necessary safety stock for a 95 percent service level is 14. Thus, the total annual holding cost of safety stock is (14)(20) or $280, and the total annual shortage cost = .05 × 100 × 2,500/200 = $62.50. Therefore, the *total relevant costs* are 280 + 62.50 = $342.50

Try a service level of 99.9 percent The necessary safety stock for 99.9 percent was stated to be 26.5. Rounding to 27 units, the total annual holding cost of safety stock is 27(20) or $540 and the total annual shortage cost is:

$$.001 \times 100 \times \frac{2,500}{200} = \$1.25$$

The *total relevant costs* are:

$$540 + 1.25 = \$541.25$$

Comparing the three service levels, 95 percent is the best. However, this process could have been continued in the same manner for any other desired service (level (e.g., 91 percent, etc.) until an even lower total cost level might have been found.

12.16 PROBLEMS FOR PART B

16. Canographic Corporation produces computer plotters for the West Coast. The monthly demand for the plotters is 20 units. The company has a production capacity of 80 units per month. There is a setup cost of $750 per production run. Each plotter kept in stock for one month costs $25 in holding cost. Management's policy is to supply *all* demand; thus, no shortage is allowed.
    a. Show the inventory cycle graphically (without any data).
    b. Find the best production plan (i.e., how many units to produce each production run). A whole number of units must be produced in each run. A production run may involve a fraction of a day.
    c. How many days of production will there be in each cycle (assume 20 manufacturing and demand days per month)?
    d. In part (*a*), find the length of the total cycle and the maximum inventory level.
    e. Assuming the company produces 60 units in each production run, what will the effect

on the total monthly cost be? (Compare to the minimum cost.)

17. Union Machine Corporation operates a punch press that produces 20 units of product M each hour. The press is in operation five hours a day. In order to set up the press for product M, it is necessary to shut it down for two hours. Setup time costs the company $15 per hour.

    The demand for product M is 40 units a day, during 250 operating days in a year. The inventory carrying cost, for each unit of product M, is $1 per year.

    Determine:

    a. The optimal production lot.
    b. The production and no-production periods.
    c. The total annual inventory cost.

18. Amerland Corporation produces industrial air cleaners in the *most economical way*, in lot sizes of 600 units. Each unit costs $300. The company operates 360 days a year and is capable of producing 30 units daily. The demand

rate is 300 units per month. Inventory carrying cost is 25 percent of the value stored.

Find:

a. The length of a production run.
b. The maximum inventory, in units.
c. The length of the "no-production" periods.
d. The total yearly inventory cost.

19. Central Airlines buys special valves at $10 apiece. The company uses 24,500 valves each year. It costs $20 to place an order, and the unit carrying cost per year is considered to be 20 percent of the value stored.

   a. Find how many valves should be purchased at a time (using EOQ).
   b. Should the company accept an offer of 2 percent discount on the valves if they are purchased quarterly?

20. Given an inventory system with the following data:

   Yearly demand = 120 units.
   Ordering cost = $45.
   Price of unit = $200.
   Annual carrying cost = 24 percent of value stored.

   Determine:

   a. The economic order quantity.
   b. The supplier offered a 1 percent discount on the unit price if the items are purchased in lots of 100 at a time. Should management accept the offer?
   c. The minimum percentage discount that will make the offer attractive.

21. XYZ department store sells 25,000 type A shirts a year. The supplier offers a generous quantity discount. His price list is given below:

Quantity	Price ($) per shirt for entire quantity
0–999	2.50
1,000–1,749	2.00
1,750–2,499	1.50
2,500 and over	1.00

   Given: Order cost, $20. Inventory carrying cost, 20 percent of the value of the item.

Find the EOQ for each price level and check its feasibility. In the infeasible cases compute cost data for the closest possible limit. Compare total cost at all quantity levels and suggest the best inventory policy for XYZ.

22. Formulate an algorithm (set of decision rules) to solve the quantity discount problem when only one price break exists.

23. A company uses a certain product which is demanded at an average rate of ten units a working day. The company operates on a five-day a week schedule.

   Replenishment occurs once every six weeks. Storage cost per unit is $6 (paid only if the unit is stored for the entire six-week period). Shortage cost is $30 per unit per week. The table below gives the probability of demand during the six weeks.

Quantity demanded	Probability
60	.05
150	.10
240	.15
300	.40
360	.15
450	.10
540	.05

   Find the best safety level. Use the trial-and-error approach to check safety levels of 0, 60, 150, and 240.

24. Westcan Electric Corporation distributes large industrial transformers in the West Coast. Demand is known to be 60 units per month. The company can order transformers any time and delivery from the plant is instantaneous. There is a fixed cost of $800 associated with each order. The company can store the product in its warehouse in an attempt to reduce the fixed cost per order by increasing the order size; however, this creates a holding cost per unit of $150 per month. If demand is not satisfied, the company loses $250 (loss of good will) per unit demanded each month (assume 30 days per month).

   a. Find the quantity the company should order each time in order to minimize its total relevant inventory cost.
   b. Find the minimum cost per cycle if the optimal ordering policy is used.

c. How many units of demand will be supplied late each period?
d. How often should an order be placed?
e. What are the possible consequences of this policy in the long run?

25. The lead time for a product is ten days. The demand for the product is 20 units per day. It is known that the standard deviation of the demand during the lead time is 15 units. Assume a normal distribution for the demand.

Management would like to provide a service level of 85 percent or 90 percent, whichever is less expensive.

The company orders ten times a year, and the holding and shortage costs are:

H = $20 per unit per year.
G = $80 per unit short per year.

Should the company use the 85 percent or the 90 percent service level?

26. Tampa Electric Corp. wishes to determine the number of special batteries it should maintain. Each time the company runs out of batteries it costs the company $700. The holding cost of a battery is $80 per year. The company now orders four times a year. The following historical data on inventory levels and stockouts is available.

Inventory level	Probability of stockout
20	.60
30	.30
40	.20
50	.10

Find:

a. The total annual inventory and stockout cost for an inventory level of 20 batteries.
b. Which of the given inventory levels will be the most desirable?

27. A company can produce ten units of product M per day, during 250 working days per year. The cost of producing one unit is $10. The cost of setting up one production run amounts to $100. The inventory carrying cost, per year, is 30 percent of the value stored. The company sells 1,500 units of product M each year. The company's objective is profit maximization.

Find:

a. The economic lot size.
b. The annual number of production runs.
c. The total annual cost of carrying inventory.
d. The production time (T_1).
e. The maximum inventory level.
f. The depletion period (T_2).
g. The company is considering producing a two-year supply in one production run. If they do so they will be able to cut production cost by 10 percent. Show whether such an alternative will be profitable.

28. I produce parts for $5 each. If I run out of spares I must make a special run and they will cost $15 each. If my probability of demand for spares is constant (discrete) between 1 and 10, how many spares should I produce?

29. Ambulances cost $10,000 each. Goodwill loss due to a death is X. The chance of needing two ambulances is 1 in a 100 and three is 1 in a 1,000. If the hospital buys three ambulances, what is the minimum value of X?

30. You run a restaurant with 100 tables which are available on a reservations-only basis. If you accept N reservations you will actually get N-19, N-18, ... N customers with a probability of .05 each. For each unavailable table you lose a profit of $9. Rent, etc., is $10 per table. Each customer who must be turned away because of over-reserving costs you $6 in damages and $5 in bad publicity. How many reservations should you accept? (Hint: $Q^* = 100$).

31. Given the following MPS, IMF, and product tree, determine the planned releases for item 1342.

Item	Lead time	On hand	Demand in week (number)				
			11	12	13	14	15
19.	1 week	100	100	0	100	200	0
1342. . . .	2 weeks	200	0	500	0	0	0
102.	1 week	0	50	0	0	0	0
312.	2 weeks	0	5	0	0	10	0

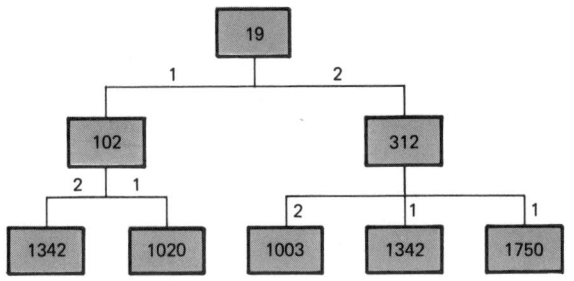

32. Conduct a part-period lot sizing for table legs given the following demand schedule. Hold-ing a leg in inventory costs $1/week. Ordering/shipping costs $100 for any size order. Lead time is virtually instantaneous.

Week	Demand for table legs
10.	85
11.	40
12.	25
13.	40
14.	105
15.	75
16.	80

12.17   CASE

Visutech

Visutech is a manufacturer of industrial cameras which are currently selling for $4,200 a unit. The demand for the product is stable in the quantity of 6000 units per year.

The company had little competition up to last year. At that time two Japanese companies entered the market. Visutech sales started to drop. In order to boost sales the company decided not to increase prices even though inflation pushed the production cost by 11 percent. As a result, the company gained back its share of the market. However, earnings decreased significantly.

At present the company produces at a rate that exactly meets the demand. In this manner the unit cost is estimated to be $4,000. There is a $6,000 setup cost for each production start up and monthly production is 500 units per lot.

The company's cost containment committee met last Monday. Two proposals were submitted to the committee:

a.   Change the frequency of production to produce the most economic lot sizes. The company's production capacity is estimated at 2,000 units/month.

b.   Buy sub-assemblies in Japan and assemble them at the plant. The Japanese can ship the parts in lots of 1,000 once every two months. The cost of each sub-assembled unit is $3,000. The assembly work requires no setup cost; it is done continuously at a cost of $1,010 per unit. The Japanese supplier will offer a 3 percent discount if Visutech is willing to receive shipments twice a year.

Being a management scientist working for the cost containment committee, what would you advise them to do? (*Hint:* Consider the alternative of no change.)

General information

The company computes its inventory carrying cost at an annual rate of 25 percent. Ordering cost for vendor's work is considered to be $60 per order. An order must be prepared for every shipment.

CASE II—EMCO CORPORATION[20]

The Emco Corporation, a midwestern manufacturer of desk calculators, has the public image of a well managed corporation in a growth industry. If the company is able to maintain its present rate of growth, it will be number one in its field within a few years. Emco has sales offices in approximately 100 cities in the United States. Emco calculators are sold or rented to both large and small customers in a number of different industries. Exhibit 1 shows the firm's income statement for the past five years.

had been used as floor demonstrators in the sales offices. Thus, today, the two major sources of used equipment are trade-ins and former demonstrators.

Some of the machines are sold while others are directed into a used rental program. Those sold to wholesalers or dealers are in either an as-is or reconditioned state. The as-is units are sold from any one of ten regional headquarters when a large quantity is accumulated. All non-Emco trade-ins are sold as-is. The reconditioned units are sold from the

EXHIBIT 1

EMCO CORPORATION
Income Statement
For the Past Five Years
($000s)

	1967	1966	1965	1964	1963
Gross income........	$599,000	$450,000	$330,000	$315,000	$290,000
Cost of goods sold....	200,000	150,000	120,000	115,000	140,000
Gross profit	339,000	300,000	210,000	200,000	150,000
Net income	55,000	45,000	33,000	27,000	15,000

The company has always followed a policy of giving liberal trade-ins on Emco and non-Emco equipment to increase sales in this competitive industry. About ten years ago, Mr. E. Miller, a former salesman showed management that there was a market for these trade-ins. He was then put in charge of the used equipment department. His job was to maintain an orderly market in used equipment—maintaining high prices on the used units sold so as not to cut into the sales of new calculators. The department staff, which was composed mostly of former salesmen, grew from 10 to 45 over a ten year period. It was discovered that there was a market for machines that

factory, where they have been collected by company vans from the sales offices on a quarterly basis.

The machines in the used rental program have all been reconditioned. Once they have been reconditioned, they are shipped to regional headquarters to await renting for periods ranging from two weeks to one year.

All Emco products have a seven digit serial number which is used for inventory classification purposes. The inventory of used equipment is broken down into Emco trade-ins, non-Emco trade-ins, former demonstrators, and reconditioned calculators in the used rental program. Machines are classified as Emco trade-ins and non-Emco trade-ins at the time the customer receives his new Emco unit. When the sales offices receive new calculators for demonstration purposes, the old demonstrators are then considered former

[20] This case was prepared by Dean Harold Lazarus, School of Business Administration, Hofstra University, and John D. McGarr of the Graduate School of Business Administration of New York University for class discussion.

EXHIBIT 2

Income Statements
Used Equipment
($000s)

	1967	1966	1965	1964	1963
Gross income	$25,600	$19,020	$14,150	$9,100	$5,000
Net earnings before taxes	(2,504)	500	(1,700)	(1,800)	(1,000)

EXHIBIT 3

Income Statements
Used Equipment by Source
($000s)

	1967	1966	1965	1964	1963
Sales					
Gross income	$19,000	$14,000	$11,100	$7,000	n.a.
Net earnings before taxes........	(4,514)	(1,630)	(2,900)	(2,900)	n.a.
Rental					
Gross income	6,600	5,020	3,050	2,100	n.a.
Net earnings before taxes........	2,010	2,130	1,200	1,100	n.a.

demonstrators. The demonstrators are replaced on a yearly cycle. Machines are transferred to the used rental program at the discretion of the used equipment department.

Mr. S. Carlson, the controller of Emco, recently set up a profit analysis area within the finance department. The objective of this new area is to evaluate the profitability of the firm's various operations.

The profit analysis area was called upon by the controller to make an analysis of a proposal put forth by Mr. Miller. He proposed that the firm put new machines into the high profit used rental program for six months and then sell them in the used market. Mr. Miller reasoned that the demand for machines in the used market was greater than the present inventory or the forecasted additions to inventory, for the remainder of the year.

Mr. A. Ernst, a financial analyst, received this proposal. In order to get some background, Mr. Ernst first computed income statements for the past five years. Exhibit 2 shows these statements, while Exhibit 3 gives a breakdown of Exhibit 2 into the sales and rental programs of used equipment.

These statements puzzled Mr. Ernst since everyone was under the impression that the used equipment department was a profitable operation.

The factory inventory classification report for June 1968 is shown in Exhibit 4.

The used equipment department had made a forecast of trade-ins and former demonstrators which they expected to be added to the inventory for the rest of the year. They also forecasted their sales for the remainder of the year. This data is shown in Exhibit 5.

At first Mr. Ernst thought it obvious that there were enough machines in inventory and

EXHIBIT 4

Inventory classification report—June 1968

	Units
Emco trade-ins	17,586
Non-Emco trade-ins	9,987
Former demonstrators	29,543
Total	57,116
Used rental program	20,437*

* 4,543 machines in district office warehouses awaiting rental.

EXHIBIT 5
Used equipment department forecast—June 1968

	Units
July–Dec. 1968 additions to inventory	
Emco trade-ins.........................	19,642
Non-Emco trade-ins	7,679
Former demonstrators....................	23,113
Total.............................	50,434
Sales forecast............................	70,445
Forecast addition to used rental program.......	2,000

incoming flows to cover the forecasted demand. Mr. Ernst then checked the factory on the physical inventory. He called the factory and, after speaking with several managers in the inventory area who didn't know where this information was or even if the factory had it, he finally received the June 1968 report on physical inventory. The report is shown in Exhibit 6.

EXHIBIT 6
Used equipment physical inventory report—June 1968

	Units		
	At sales office	At plant	Total
Emco trade-ins	5,843	2,894	8,737
Non-Emco trade-ins	3,435	1,015	4,450
Former demonstrators	7,364	6,775	14,139
Total			27,326

When Mr. Ernst called Mr. Miller to ask about the discrepancies in the inventory figures, he found that Mr. Miller was on a trip to Los Angeles. Mr. Ernst spoke, instead, to a former salesman who had recently joined the used equipment department. The former salesman, when asked about the inventory figures, told Mr. Ernst, in a laughing manner, that some salesmen would "misplace" demonstrators and others would forget that customers had machines to trade in when the new calculators were installed. The former salesman related that he had just received a letter from the New York sales office manager asking what he should do about 150 demonstrators, still in factory packaging, that had been accumulating in the office warehouse. The average age of these demonstrators was three years.

After this conversation, Mr. Ernst collected his figures (Exhibits 2–6), went to the used equipment department to pick up a copy of the letter from the manager of the New York sales office and went to Mr. Carlson's office. After hearing Mr. Ernst's presentation, Mr. Carlson agreed to permit Mr. Ernst to make a full study of this department. The two men then began to formulate a strategy for the investigation of this operation.

Analyze this case and ascertain the nature of Emco's problem. Where are the missing calculators?

12.18 GLOSSARY

The A-B-C classification system Inventory items are classified into three groups: A (high value, small quantity), B (medium value, larger quantity), C (small value, many items—the nuts and bolts). Classification is made for control purposes.

Average inventory The average amount of inventory, usually on a one-year period. It is equal to one half of the maximum inventory of the EOQ model.

Backorder A temporary shortage. Items that will be delivered (or produced) later.

The base stock system An inventory system in which an order is placed as soon as a unit is taken from stock.

Bill of materials (B/M) The list of raw materials, components, and subassemblies, and the quantities, needed to produce an item.

Carrying cost   Same as holding cost.

Days' supply   The length of time (days) that an inventory will last without renewal (replenishment or stockout).

Dependent demand   Demand for items that are parts of items whose production is already planned.

Depletion   Reduction of the inventory to a zero point of no inventory.

Economic lot size (ELS)   A manufacturing lot or batch size which will minimize the total annual costs of setup and holding inventory.

Economic order quantity (EOQ)   A quantity of an item which, if purchased at one time, will minimize the total annual inventory ordering and holding costs.

Explode   Stepping down through the bill of materials levels to determine what parts will be required, in what quantities, and when.

The fixed quantity (perpetual) system   An inventory system where orders for fixed amounts are placed whenever an agreed upon reorder point is reached (i.e., order whenever stock is down to ten units).

The fixed time (periodic or s,S) system   An inventory system where varying sized orders are placed periodically (e.g., once a month).

Holding cost   Costs associated with storing inventory, such as: cost of capital, insurance, renting storage space, and taxes.

Inventory master file (IMF)   The computer file that contains a listing of on-hand, on-order, and committed inventory.

Joint ordering   Placing orders for different items (usually with one supplier) as one combined order.

Lead time   The time between placing an order and its delivery.

Level   The stage of subcomponent assemblies in the bill of materials, the finished product being designated as level 0.

Lot sizing   Determining the best amount of items to produce or purchase at a given time.

Lumpy demand   Demand which comes in groups, with little or no demand occurring between the groups.

Master production schedule (MPS)   The time-phased list of products, and the quantities, that are to be produced.

Material requirements planning (MRP)   An inventory control system for dependent demand items.

Ordering cost   The costs of placing one order for an item, including paperwork, inspection of the incoming order, and telephone calls.

Parent item   The finish product (level 0).

Part-period balancing   A lot-sizing approach for dependent demand items that attempts to equate holding with setup costs.

Planned shortage   Allowing shortages to occur from time to time rather than keeping a large inventory.

Quantity discount   A discount on the unit cost offered by the supplier to a buyer willing to buy in large lots.

Reorder point   The inventory level at which an order for an item is placed.

Replenishment   Describes the arrival of a shipment or renewal of the inventory.

Safety stock   Inventory maintained specifically to reduce shortages when demand is high or when the lead time is too long.

Service level   The percent of time that all demand is met on request. The probability of *not* running out of stock.

Setup costs   Expenses incurred to start up a production run (paperwork, tool preparation, and clean up).

Shortage   Inability to provide the item from stock. Available inventory is insufficient to meet demand.

Stockout   Same as shortage.

The two-bin system   An inventory system where items are stored in two bins: large and small. Demand is satisfied from the large bin first. Depletion of the large bin signifies the need to reorder.

12.19   REFERENCES AND BIBLIOGRAPHY

1.   Brown, R. G. *Decision Rules for Inventory Management.* New York: Holt, Rinehart and Winston, Inc., 1967.

2.   Fuchs, Jerome H. *Computerized Inventory Control Systems.* Englewood Cliffs, N.J.: Prentice-Hall, Inc., 1978.

3. Green, J. H. *Production and Inventory Control Handbook.* New York: McGraw-Hill Book Co., 1970.

4. International Business Machines. *Wholesale IMPACT, Inventory Management and Program Activity Control Technique.* White Plains, N.Y., 1962.

5. Johnson, L. A., and Montgomery, D. C. *Operations Research in Production Planning, Scheduling and Inventory Control.* New York: John Wiley & Sons, Inc., 1974.

6. Larson, S. *Inventory Systems and Controls Handbook.* Englewood Cliffs, N.J.: Prentice-Hall, Inc., 1976.

7. Lewis, C. D. *Demand Analysis and Inventory Control.* Lexington, Mass.: Lexington Books, 1975.

8. ————. *Scientific Inventory Control.* New York: American Elsevier Publishing Co., Inc., 1970.

9. Lipman, B. E. *How to Control and Reduce Inventory.* Englewood Cliffs, N.J.: Prentice-Hall, Inc., 1975.

10. Orlicky, J. *Material Requirements Planning.* New York: McGraw-Hill Book Co., 1975.

11. Peterson, R. and Silver, E. A. *Decision Systems for Inventory Management and Production Planning.* New York: John Wiley & Sons, Inc., 1979.

12. Tersine, R. J. *Material Management and Inventory Control.* New York: Elsevier–North Holland, 1976.

13. Thomas, A. B. *Inventory Control in Production and Management.* Boston: Cahners Publishing Co., Inc., 1970.

13

The more society becomes interdependent, psychologically, economically, and technically, the more individuals encounter waiting lines, or queues, in their daily lives. People queue at doctors' offices, supermarkets, gasoline stations, and tool booths. Waiting lines may also involve non-humans as customers: airplanes circling airports and machines waiting for repairs. The problem of managing waiting lines is complex, since the cost of providing services of all kinds is rapidly increasing.

The objective is to determine the appropriate level of service. The method of analyzing waiting line problems illustrated in this chapter is called queuing theory.

In Part A of this chapter the queuing problem is formulated and a solution using equations for simple problems is derived. In Part B, more complex queuing systems are addressed and graphs substituting for formulas are presented to facilitate the analysis of these systems. For even more complex queuing systems, the technique of simulation, presented in Chapter 14, is necessary.

Waiting lines

PART A: BASICS

All American Aviation Company has a specialized machine shop that serves the airlines in Plain City. At the present time the shop employs about 400 mechanics. Willie Davis, the material manager, just returned, troubled, from the regular Monday executive committee meeting. It was only a week ago that he placed his best employee, John, in the "tool crib," the machine shop's center for distributing specialized tools. He took this action after continuous complaints from the production manager about long waiting lines there. It appeared to Willie that the tool crib was the scapegoat for everything that went wrong with production.

This week Willie was sure that the problem of the waiting lines had been solved because John seemed to be handling the situation well. However, in this morning's meeting Willie was again under the gun. He therefore started wondering if it might be necessary to add a second clerk. He reasoned that with two clerks, the waiting time at the tool crib would be reduced by one half. However, he was not sure that such a reduction would justify the additional clerical cost.

Willie's reasoning that doubling the capacity of the tool crib would decrease the waiting time by one half seemed so logical and obvious that it didn't occur to him that it might be incorrect. His error will be analyzed later in this chapter.

13.1   THE QUEUING SITUATION

Characteristics of waiting line situations

The incident at the All American Aviation Company is typical of a situation that arises in the delivery of services, when the relationship between the demand and supply varies over time.

Varying demand— varying service

On the one hand, the demand for services is unstable. There are foreseeable fluctuations during certain time periods (e.g., rush hours as at the beginning and the end of shifts at the tool crib). In addition, there are unforeseeable changes in the pattern of demand. On the other hand, the length of service may vary, due to particular requirements of those requesting the service. The result is difficulty in meeting demand immediately upon request, especially during rush hours.

Expensive to meet peak demand

The only way that demand can be immediately supplied, all the time, is to build a high service capacity that can always meet peak demand. Such a situation can be observed in an electric utility company. However, the balancing of demand and supply at an electric company is relatively easy since demand, although fluctuating, is predictable, and capacity can be added or deleted as needed, at relatively low cost once the generators have been constructed. In other areas, it is *very expensive* to build, operate, and maintain a service facility so that all demands will be met, all the time, upon request. It may also be expensive to constantly change the capacity in an existing service facility to fit the demand. Instead, service facilities are usually designed so that their capacity is less than the maximum demand. As a result, whenever demand exceeds capacity, a *waiting line,* or a *queue* is formed; that is, the customers do not get service immediately upon request but must wait.

Formation of a queue

The management of services is indeed complicated. While management would like to satisfy the customer ("the customer is always right"), it is very expensive, sometimes even impossible, to satisfy everyone immediately, all the time. Therefore, management is interested in finding the *appropriate level of services.* The theory applied to this problem is called *queuing* or *waiting line* theory.

Pioneered by A. K. Erlang, A Danish engineer in the telephone industry in the early '20s, queuing theory extended in application, especially after World War II, to a large number of situations. For example:

Erlang pioneers queuing theory

- Determining the capacity of an emergency room in a hospital.
- Determining the number of runways at an airport.
- Determining the number of elevators in a building.
- Determining the number of traffic lights and their frequency of operation.
- Determining the number of flights between two cities.
- Determining the number of first-class seats in an airplane.
- Determining the size of a restaurant.
- Determining the number of employees in a store room, in a typing pool, or in a nursing team.

The structure of a queuing system

A queuing system (Figure 13.1) is composed of the following parts:

The customers and their source (Section 13.4) Customers are defined as those in need of service. Customers can be people, airplanes, machines, or raw materials. The customers are generated from a *population* or a *source.* For example, a hospital's "population" would be the sick requiring hospitalization.

The source

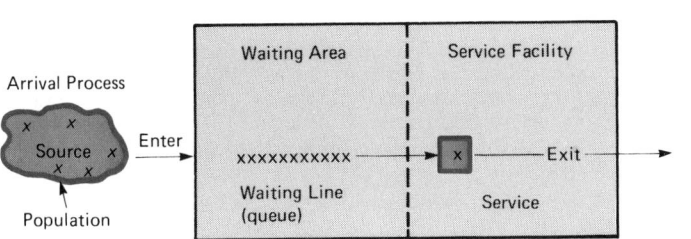

FIGURE 13.1
The major components of a queuing system

The arrival process (Section 13.4) The manner in which customers show up at the service facility is called the arrival process.

The service facility and the service process (Section 13.5) The service is provided by a *service facility* (or facilities). This may be a person (a bank teller, a barber), a machine (elevator, gasoline pump), or a space (airport runway, parking lot, hospital bed), to mention just a few. A service facility may include one person or several people operating as a team.

The queue (Section 13.6) Whenever an arriving customer finds that the service facility is busy, a *queue*, or waiting line, is formed.

13.2 THE MANAGERIAL PROBLEM

Looking at Willie Davis's situation, it is now possible to understand the managerial problem of waiting lines. As a responsible manager, Willie realizes that he must satisfy his customers. On the other hand, there is a cost attached to the provision of this service. In general, the basic problem of the management of waiting lines is: What is an "appropriate" level of service?[1]

The basic queuing problem: What level of service?

Decisions about an "appropriate" level of service are:

a. If only one service station exists, then the decision involves the *speed* of service, which can be increased by adding more personnel and/or equipment.
b. If additional service stations can be added, then the decision is: How many more is best?

Cost considerations

In making such decisions, the object is typically to minimize total cost. Management must consider both the cost of providing the service and the cost of customers waiting (lost time, loss of good will, lost sales, and so on). Unfortunately, these costs are in direct opposition to each other, as shown in Figure 13.2.[2]

Opposing costs

That is, the cost of providing the service increases with the service level,[3] while the waiting time (and its cost) declines with the service level. Unfortunately, the cost of waiting, in many cases, cannot be expressed in terms of dollars. This issue is discussed below.

---

[1] In addition to this basic decision, management will have to make several related decisions regarding such factors as the priorities of service and the operating hours. These decisions will not be discussed in this text. The interested reader is referred to texts on queuing theory such as Cooper [3], Newell [8], and White [11].

[2] Observe the resemblance of Figure 13.2 to the one associated with the EOQ model (Figure 12.8).

[3] The service level may be measured by the capacity (number of facilities or speed) of the service.

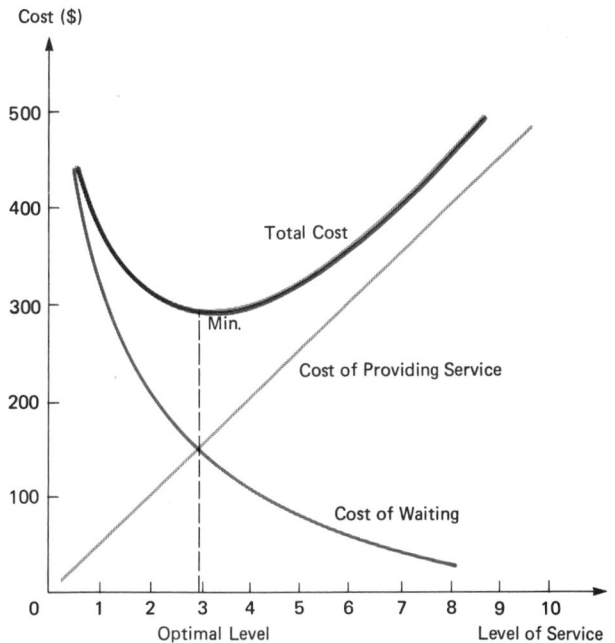

FIGURE 13.2
The queuing system costs

The costs involved in a queuing situation

The facility cost   The cost of providing a service includes:

1. Cost of construction (capital investment) as expressed by interest and amortization.
2. Cost of operation: labor and materials required for operations.
3. Cost of maintenance and repair.
4. Other costs: insurance, taxes, rental of space, and other fixed costs.

The cost of waiting customers   The cost of waiting time is more difficult to assess. It involves several components. For example a waiting customer may get impatient and leave, thus resulting in a loss of revenue and possible loss of repeat business due to his or her dissatisfaction. There may also be an "ill-will" cost incurred. That is, when talk is spread about the poor service given at a facility, other customers may not come. A more extreme situation would be that of a patient waiting for surgery. If the patient waits too long, he or she may die. In addition to the loss of revenue to the hospital and the cost of ill will, there is an additional cost to the customer; in this case the loss of his or her life.

Ill-will costs

The difficulties in expressing the cost of waiting are especially severe in cases where the customers are *external* to the organization providing the service and the provider of the service is a nonprofit organization. In such a case, one may raise such questions as: "Cost to whom (e.g., to the patient, to the doctor, or to society)?" Or, "Is the cost

Internal versus external customers

directly proportional to the waiting time?" The answer to such a question is not simple since it involves personal values, social priorities and other qualitative factors. For this reason, instead of attempting to minimize the total cost of the system, management will attempt instead to achieve some goal(s) related to the level of the service (such as a maximum waiting time of ten minutes). Such goals(s) are derived from the "measures of performance" which are discussed later in this chapter.

Level of service or minimize costs?

When the customers are internal to the organization providing the service, it is usually easier to place a dollar value on the waiting time, since waiting usually involves lost wages or production. In cases where a dollar value can be placed on waiting time, a cost analysis of queuing systems can be performed as will be shown in Section 13.8.

13.3. THE METHODOLOGY OF QUEUING ANALYSIS

Queuing is a descriptive tool

The queuing methodology is basically a *descriptive* tool of analysis. As such it is similar to a Markov analysis. As the reader may recall, the major objective of the Markov analysis was *prediction* of a system's behavior. Here too, the major objective of waiting line theory is *prediction* of the behavior of a system as reflected in its *operating characteristics* or *measures of performance*. Although queuing theory is basically descriptive it can also be used at times to determine the optimal number of service facilities or the optimal speed of a facility. Such normative applications are, however, limited.

Predicting operating characteristics

The managerial application of waiting line theory involves the use of computed measures of performance for selecting an alternative solution to a queuing problem, usually among small numbers of alternatives. The entire process involves three steps:

a. Establish the measures of performance (or the operating characteristics) of the queuing system.
b. Compute the measures of performance.
c. Conduct a comparative analysis.

a. Establish the measures of performance of the system

In this step a model of the problem is formulated and the *measures of performance* are decided upon. Examples of such measures are:

- The average waiting time per customer.
- The average number of customers in the waiting line.
- The utilization (busy period) of the service facility, or else its idle time.

b. Compute the measures of performance

The queuing problem is modeled by a system composed of three components:

1. The arrival process (Section 13.4).
2. The service facility (Section 13.5).
3. The waiting line (Section 13.6).

Model composed of three components

Once the problem has been formulated in this manner, one of two solution methods is employed to find the measures of performance:

1. For problems in which certain theoretical statistical distributions can describe the actual data, formulas (Section 13.7) or equivalent graphs (Sections 13.12–13.15) can be used.
2. For other problems, simulation (see Chapter 14) is used.

The measures of performance are then computed for every course of action under consideration as explained next.

c. Comparative analysis

In queuing analysis, there are usually only a small number of alternatives to be evaluated. For example, in a decision about the number of elevators to be constructed in a new building, ten possibilities would be a realistic consideration, but not 5,000. The number of feasible alternatives in a service system is usually small because of human, technical, financial, and legal constraints. Alternatives may differ in the size of the facility, the number of facilities, the speed of service, the priorities given to customers or in the operating procedures. For each alternative, the measures of effectiveness must be computed.

Limited alternatives

The alternative solutions are then compared on the basis of their overall effectiveness. One approach here is the use of the total cost curve as shown in Figure 13.2. The major problem in this step may be the cost assessment. A queuing system usually involves several measures of performance, and it is necessary to establish a common one (such as a total cost or a total utility) to quantitatively compare the alternatives.[4] In some cases a qualitative comparison of the multiple measures of effectiveness is performed and no attempt is made to consolidate the multiple measures.

Comparing the alternatives

In a limited number of cases the comparative analysis leads to an optimal solution—for example, a decision regarding the choice of the proper number of identical service facilities (see Example 2 in Section 13.12).

---

[4] Methods discussed in Chapter 4 can be utilized here.

13.4 THE ARRIVAL PROCESS

Description of arrivals

Arriving customers are classified according to the following:

Source: Finite versus infinite Two cases are of primary interest: when the source (population) is basically *infinite*[5] (or unlimited), such as the number of people visiting Niagara Falls, or when it is *finite*, as when a repair crew in a factory is responsible for maintaining a dozen machines. Unless otherwise specified, *queuing theory assumes an infinite population.*

Batch versus individual arrivals Customers may arrive in *batches* (such as the arrival of a family to a restaurant) or *individually* (such as the arrival of an airplane at an airport). In this text, *individual arrivals are assumed* in all cases.

Scheduled versus nonscheduled arrivals Customers arrive at a service facility either on a scheduled basis (by appointment) or without prior notification. If they come without prior notification, their arrival time is not exactly known but historical data enables us to describe arrivals by some *frequency distribution* (see Appendix B).

Quantitative measures of arrivals

As indicated earlier, arrivals may be either scheduled or unexpected. In both cases, the arrival process can be described by either the *arrival rate* (the number of arrivals per unit of time) or by the *interarrival times* (the time between two consecutive arrivals). The difference is that in scheduled arrivals the arrival rates are fixed, while in unscheduled arrivals the times are *random variables* and we must therefore talk about *averages and frequency distributions* of the times.

The arrival rate and the interarrival times (unscheduled arrivals)

The arrival process can be described by either the *mean arrival rate* or by the *mean interarrival time*. As an example, consider the situation at a tool crib (an area for storage and dispersal of tools) between 7:00 and 8:00 A.M. Figure 13.3 shows that seven employees arrived during the hour. Therefore, the *mean arrival rate* is seven per hour. The times between two consecutive arrivals vary. For example, there are eight minutes between the first arrival and the second, while there are two minutes between the second and third arrivals. These times between arrivals are called the *interarrival times*. The *average* (or *mean*) interarrival time during the first hour is

---

[5] No population is really infinite. What is meant is that the population is large enough that the probability of a second arrival is not significantly changed by the first arrival.

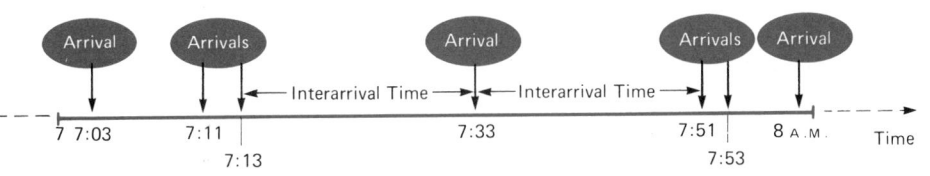

FIGURE 13.3
Arrivals at the tool crib

60/7 = 8.6 minutes = 1/7 of an hour. The average interarrival time is exactly the *inverse* of the mean arrival rate. Let us examine these times through examples.

The arrival rate (unscheduled arrivals)

Assume that the arrival times of employees to the tool crib were recorded over a period of 100 hours. Of these 100 hours there were 5 hours within which there were 0 arrivals (5 percent of all cases), 6 hours where there was only 1 arrival, and so on. Such results can be described in the form of a frequency distribution or histogram, as shown in Figure 13.4. The shape of Figure 13.4 is very similar to the theoreti-

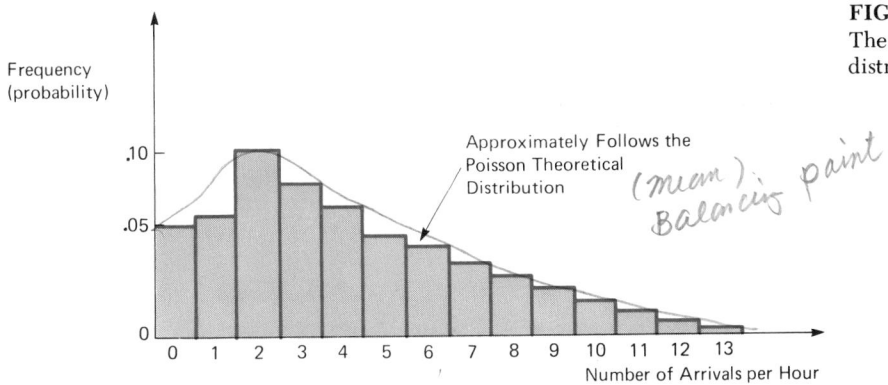

FIGURE 13.4
The frequency distribution of arrivals

cal *Poisson distribution* (see Appendix B). Such a distribution is very common in queuing systems.

The Poisson distribution occurs when customers, in a given period of time, arrive *at random*. Random arrival means that even if the mean number of arrivals in a time period is known, the exact moment of arrival cannot be predicted. Thus, each moment in the time span has the same chance of having an arrival. Such behavior is observed when arrivals are independent of each other; namely, when the arrival time is unaffected by preceding or future arrivals. Examples of such arrivals are customers to gasoline stations and failures of machines.

Poisson arrivals

Poisson is also random

FIGURE 13.5
The interarrival times

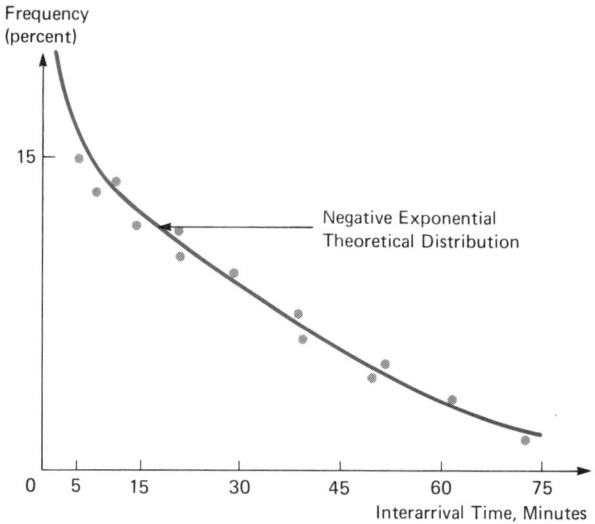

The interarrival time (unscheduled arrivals)

As an alternative to the arrival rate, the interarrival time can also be used. In Figure 13.5 the interarrival frequency distribution is shown. After continuous observation of these times, it is possible to say that in perhaps 15 percent of the cases the time between two consecutive arrivals was 3 minutes, in 12 percent of the cases it was 5 minutes, in 10 percent of the cases it was 13 minutes, and so on. This information is recorded by the dots in Figure 13.5.

If the arrival rate of Figure 13.4 follows the Poisson distribution, then the interarrival times of Figure 13.5 are distributed according to the *negative exponential* distribution (see Appendix B).[6]

Exponential interarrival times

13.5 THE SERVICE PROCESS

Several basic arrangements of service facilities exist:

1. Single facility (such as a dentist's chair).
2. Multiple, parallel, identical facilities (such as five pumps in a gasoline station).
3. Multiple, parallel, but not identical facilities (such as express and regular check-out counters in a supermarket).
4. Service facilities that are arranged in a series. The customer enters the first facility and gets a portion of the service, then moves

---

[6] Notice that in Figure 13.5 the distribution is a curve, "connecting" the points. Such a distribution is a continuous distribution. The distribution of Figure 13.4 on the other hand is composed of intervals and is called a discrete distribution.

on to the second facility, and so on, as though he or she is on an assembly line. An example of such an arrangement is the registration process at a university, or a restaurant where you may wait first for a table, then for the food, and finally at the cashier.

5. Combinations of the above.

Figure 13.6 illustrates some of these possible service arrangements. The arrows into the boxes represent arriving and waiting customers, the boxes represent the service facilities, and the arrows out represent served customers.

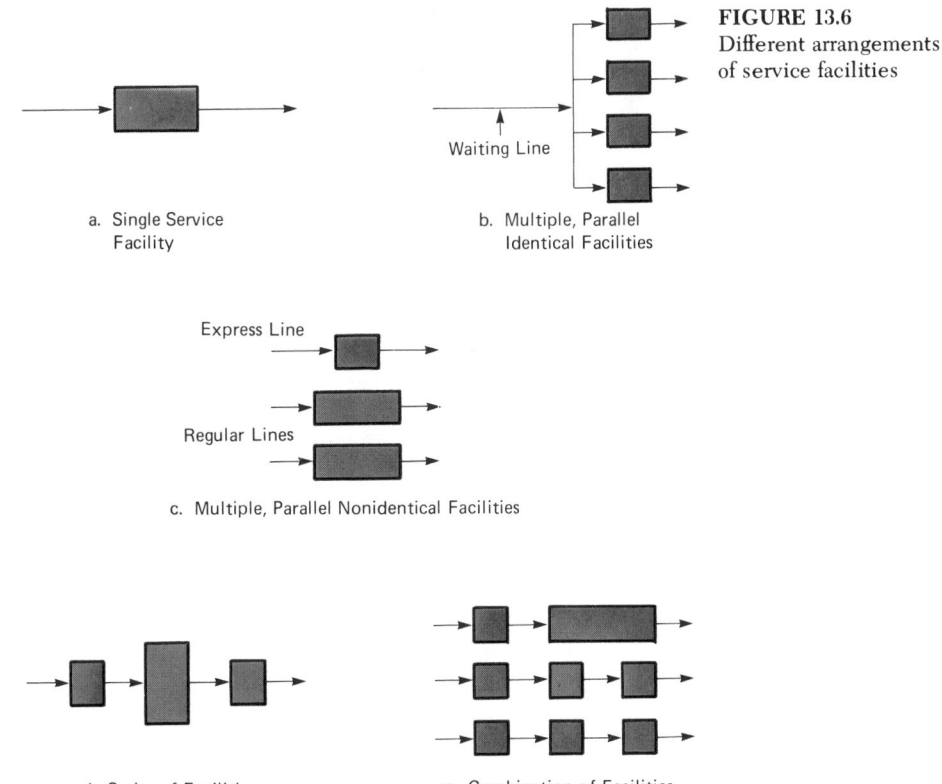

FIGURE 13.6
Different arrangements of service facilities

a. Single Service Facility

b. Multiple, Parallel Identical Facilities

Waiting Line

Express Line

Regular Lines

c. Multiple, Parallel Nonidentical Facilities

d. Series of Facilities

e. Combination of Facilities

Description of the service time

The service given in a facility consumes time. The length of time of the service may be *constant* (e.g., exactly ten minutes for each service) or it may *fluctuate*.[7] A fluctuating service time may be described by a frequency distribution.

Constant versus fluctuating service

---

[7] Service times may, in actuality, be affected by the length of the waiting line. If the line is long, the servers may work faster because of psychological and social pressures. In this text, the length of the line is assumed *not* to affect the service rate.

There are two ways of describing fluctuating service times. One is to describe the *average length of the service* (e.g., 15 minutes, on the average); the other is the average *service rate* or how many customers can be served, on the average, each hour (e.g., four per hour).

The length of service (service time)

Exponential service time

A fluctuating service time may follow one of several statistical distributions. Most common is the *negative exponential* (as in Figure 13.5). For example, the length of telephone calls is distributed in this fashion. A less common distribution is the *normal distribution* (Appendix B), such as might be used in describing the time required for repairing a car.

The service rate

Inverse relationship

The service rate measures the service capacity of the facility in terms of customers per unit of time. The mean service rate is the *inverse* of the mean service time. For example, if the average service time is one half of an hour, then the mean service rate is $1 \div \frac{1}{2} = 2$ customers per hour. If the service time is exponentially distributed, then the service rate can be proven to be random and is thus Poisson distributed.

13.6 THE WAITING LINE

The queue discipline

A queue is formed whenever customers arrive and the facility is busy. The characteristics of the queue depend on rules and regulations that are termed the *queue discipline*.

Queue discipline

The queue discipline describes the policies that determine the manner in which customers are selected for service. Examples of some common disciplines are:

Some priority systems

A priority system Priority is given to selected customers. For example, those with five items or less in a supermarket can go to the express lane. The handicapped and passengers with reservations board airplanes first.

Emergency (preemptive priority) systems This is a system in which an important customer not only has priority in entrance but can even interrupt a less important customer in the middle of his or her service. For example, in an emergency case in a hospital, the doctor may leave the regular patient in the middle of the treatment. That is, the regular patient is *preempted* by the emergency one.

Last-in, first-served (*LIFS*)   Last arrivals are served first. This system is commonly used with parts and materials in a warehouse since it reduces handling and transportation.

First-in, first-served (*FIFS*)   Customers that arrive first are served first.

In this text the FIFS queue discipline is assumed.   *assumption* ①

The organization of the queue

Queues may be organized in various ways. For example, customers may be screened at a main gate and then referred to one of several lines (such as in some theaters or banks) depending on the service and the queue discipline. In some cases there is one line for several parallel service facilities. Arrangements may also depend on the physical area available for the queue.

The behavior in a queue

Some interesting observations of human behavior in queues are:

1. *Balking*—Customers refusing to join the queue, usually because of its length.
2. *Reneging*—Customers tiring and leaving the queue before they are served.
3. *Jockeying*—Customers switching between waiting lines (a common scene in a bank).   Human behavior
4. *Combining, dividing*—Combining or dividing queues at certain queue lengths (e.g., in a supermarket when a counter is closed or opened).
5. *Cycling*—Returning to the queue immediately after obtaining service. (Children taking turns at a playground or cars at a mine.)

In this text we assume that a customer enters the system, stays in the line (if necessary), receives the service, and leaves. If a customer   *assumption* ②
behaves otherwise (according to any of the above observations), the queuing system becomes very complex, requiring simulation for its analysis.

13.7   SOLUTION APPROACHES: SINGLE FACILITY

There are two basic approaches to the solution of queuing problems: analytical and simulation.

The analytic approach   The measures of performance are deter-   Simulation versus
mined through the use of formulas. Unfortunately, many queuing   analytical approach
situations are so complex that the analytic approach is completely
impractical or even impossible.

Simulation   For those situations in which the analytic approach is unsuitable, the procedure of simulation can be used. The process of solving queues by simulation will be deferred to Chapter 14 where the necessary theory is presented first.

The single service facility—An analytic approach

Deterministic system: Constant times   The simplest and the rarest of all waiting line situations involves constant arrival rates and constant service times. Three cases can be distinguished:

1. *Arrival rate equals service rate.* Assume that people arrive every ten minutes, to a single server, where the service takes exactly ten minutes. Then the server will be utilized continuously (100 percent utilization), and there will be no waiting line.

2. *Arrival rate larger than service rate.* Assume that there are six arrivals per hour (one every 10 minutes) and the service rate is only five per hour (12 minutes each). Therefore, one arrival cannot be served each hour, and a waiting line will build up (at a rate of one per hour). Such a waiting line will grow and grow as time passes and is termed *explosive.*

3. *Arrival rate smaller than service rate.* Assume that there are again six arrivals per hour but the service capacity is eight per hour. In this case the facility will be utilized only $6/8 = 75$ percent of the time. There will never be a waiting line (if the arrivals are scheduled properly).

Note that in case 1 there is no waiting line and no idle facility. In the second case the facility is fully utilized but a waiting line is formed. In the third case there is no waiting line but the facility is not fully utilized. *In all these cases there cannot be a waiting line and underutilization in the same situation.* However, when nonconstant (fluctuating) times are involved, it is common to have *both* idle facilities at times and waiting lines at other times in the same service system as will be shown later.

Poisson-exponential system   A Poisson-exponential system exhibits the following characteristics:

Arrival rate. The arrival rate is assumed to be random and is described by the *Poisson* distribution. The *average* arrival rate is designated by the Greek letter "lambda," λ.

Service time. The service time is assumed to follow the *negative exponential* distribution. The *average* service rate is designated by the Greek letter "mu," μ, and the *average* service time by $1/\mu$. (In some texts the letters A and S are used in place of λ and μ.)

The *major assumptions* for the operation of such a single-server system are:

1. Infinite source of population.
2. First-come, first-served treatment.
3. The ratio λ/μ is smaller than 1. This ratio is designated by the Greek letter "rho," ρ. The ratio is a measure of the *utilization* of the system. If the utilization factor is equal to or larger than 1, the waiting line will increase without bound (will be *explosive*), a situation which is unacceptable to management.
4. Steady state (equilibrium) exists[8]. A system is in a "transient state" when its behavior is still dependent on the initial conditions. However, our interest is in the "long-run" behavior of the system, commonly known as "steady state." A steady state condition occurs when the system becomes *independent of time*.

Some assumptions

[handwritten: $\lambda/\mu < 1 = \rho$
if $\lambda > \mu > 1 = $ explosive]

Measurements of performance (operating characteristics)

A queuing system is usually evaluated by one or more of the following measures of performance (given with their respective formulas). These measures are all functions of only two given variables, λ and μ, which must be stated in the same time dimensions.

The average waiting time, W. The average time a customer spends in the system—waiting for the service *and* being served.

$$W = \frac{1}{\mu - \lambda} \tag{13.1}$$

The average waiting time in the queue, W_q This is the average time a customer will wait, in the queue, before the service starts.

$$W_q = \frac{\lambda}{\mu(\mu - \lambda)} = \left(\frac{\lambda}{\mu}\right)\frac{1}{\mu - \lambda} \tag{13.2}$$

The average number of customers in the system, L The average number of customers in the system; that is, counting those in the queue and those being served, is:

$$L = \frac{\lambda}{\mu - \lambda} = (\lambda)\frac{1}{\mu - \lambda} \tag{13.3}$$

The average number of customers in the queue, L_q The average number of customers in the queue measures the average length of the waiting line.

---

[8] For a discussion refer to the chapter on Markov chains. Notice the resemblance between the two techniques.

$$L_q = \frac{\lambda^2}{\mu(\mu - \lambda)} \qquad (13.4)$$

The probability of an empty facility, P_o The probability that there are no customers in the system (that the facility is idle) is:

$$P_o = 1 - \frac{\lambda}{\mu} \qquad (13.5)$$

The probability of the system being busy, P_w The probability of the system being busy, P_w is the same as the probability of *not* finding an empty system, i.e.:

$$P_w = 1 - P_o = \frac{\lambda}{\mu} \qquad (13.6)$$

The probability of being in the system (waiting and being served) longer than time t. The probability is:

$$P(T > t) = e^{(\lambda - \mu)t} \qquad (13.7)$$

where:

$e = 2.718$ (the base of the natural logarithms).
$t =$ specified time.
$T =$ time in the system.

The probability of finding exactly n customers in the system, P_n

$$P_n = \left(\frac{\lambda}{\mu}\right)^n \left(1 - \frac{\lambda}{\mu}\right) \qquad (13.8)$$

The probability that the number of customers in the system, n, will be larger than a desired number of customers, N.

$$P(n > N) = \left(\frac{\lambda}{\mu}\right)^{N+1} \qquad (13.9)$$

Note: The following relationships are extremely important.

$$L = \lambda W$$
$$L_q = \lambda W_q \qquad (13.10)$$
$$W = W_q + \frac{1}{\mu}$$

They enable us to find, L, L_q, W and W_q as soon as one of these is found analytically. These relationships hold for other queuing systems as well.

Some or all of these measures of performance are computed for the alternative systems under consideration. Then, an evaluation of the overall performance is conducted as will be shown next.

Managerial use of the measures of performance

Some of these measures can be used in a cost analysis, such as shown in the next section. Others are used to aid in determining service level policies. For example:

a. A fast food restaurant wants to design its service facility such that a customer will not wait, on the average, more than two minutes (i.e., $W_q \le 2$ min.) before being served.

b. A telephone company desires that the probability of any customer being without telephone service more than two days is 3 percent (i.e., $P(T > 2 \text{ days}) = .03$).

c. A bank's policy that the number of customers at its drive-in facility will exceed ten only 5 percent of the time (i.e., $P(n > 10) = .05$).

d. A city information service should be busy at least 60 percent of the day (i.e., $P_w > .6$).

The use of the various measures of performance is further demonstrated in the examples throughout this chapter, in the problems at the end of the chapter, and in Section 13.9, Managerial Applications.

13.8   COST ANALYSIS OF QUEUING SYSTEMS

In certain situations it is possible to express the waiting costs in terms of dollars and cents. Queuing systems can then be compared on the basis of their total cost (TC) which is composed of two components: the facility cost (C_F) and the total cost of waiting customers (C_W).

$$TC = C_F + C_W \qquad (13.11)$$

Costs are computed on one of two bases: either as "cost per unit of time (hourly, daily)," or as "cost per customer served." In this text, the cost per unit of time basis is used.

Computing the cost of waiting

If the waiting cost can be directly linked to the waiting time prior to service, then C_W will be determined by W_q. Similarly, if the waiting cost is related to the length of the period the customer is in the system (waiting and being served), then the cost is a function of W. Here we will assume that the waiting cost (regardless if it is linked to W or W_q) is *proportional* to the waiting time; i.e., if the cost of waiting for an hour is $12, then the cost of waiting two hours is $2 \times 12 = \$24$.

Let C be the cost of one customer waiting one unit of time. Then the *waiting cost* per unit time for the queuing system as a whole is given by:

$$C_W = W\lambda C = LC \qquad (13.12)$$

where W is the average time in the system *per customer* (use W_q if the cost is directly proportional to the time in the queue) and λ is the average arrival rate per unit of time under consideration.

The cost incurred by providing the service, C_F, is typically composed of both fixed and variable costs. The annual fixed cost (amortization, insurance, taxes) and the variable (hourly) cost must both be converted into the same time units as used in Equation 13.12 so the cost components can be added together.

The cost of service

The cost of service can be given in the following ways:

a. Per hour (or other time unit) of service (e.g., $20/hour).
b. Per customer served (e.g., $5/customer). If four customers are served during the hour, then the hourly cost is 4 × $5 = $20.
c. Per unit capacity of service. For example, $2 for each customer that can be served. If the facility is capable of serving ten customers per hour, then the hourly cost will be $2 × 10 = $20.

13.9 MANAGERIAL APPLICATIONS OF POISSON-EXPONENTIAL QUEUING SYSTEMS

Example 1. The tool crib problem

The All American Aviation Company tool crib[9] is staffed by one clerk who can serve 12 production employees, on the average, each hour. The production employees arrive at the tool crib every six minutes, on the average. Find the measures of performance expressed in Formulas 13.1–13.10.

Solution It is necessary first to change the time dimensions of λ and μ to a common denominator. λ is now given in minutes. μ in hours. We will use hours as the common denominator.

The problem states that $\mu = 12$ per hour. For λ, the arrival of one customer every six minutes means one customer every $1/10$ of an hour. Therefore, the arrival rate, λ, is ten customers per hour.

Thus, in all the following formulas we shall use: $\lambda = 10$, $\mu = 12$.

---

[9] A tool crib is a storeroom where large and special tools (sometimes also parts and materials) are stored. The tools are borrowed by employees who need them.

1. Average waiting time in the system.

$$W = \frac{1}{\mu - \lambda} = \frac{1}{12 - 10} = .5 \text{ hours, per employee}$$

2. The average waiting time in the line.

$$W_q = \frac{\lambda}{\mu(\mu - \lambda)} = \frac{10}{12(12 - 10)} = .417 \text{ hours, per employee}$$

3. The average number of employees in the tool crib area.

$$L = \frac{\lambda}{\mu - \lambda} = \frac{10}{12 - 10} = 5 \text{ employees}$$

4. The average number of employees in the line.

$$L_q = \frac{\lambda^2}{\mu(\mu - \lambda)} = \frac{100}{12(12 - 10)} = 4.17 \text{ employees}$$

5. The probability that the tool crib clerk will be idle.

$$P_o = 1 - \frac{\lambda}{\mu} = 1 - \frac{10}{12} = .167$$

6. The probability of finding the system busy:

$$P_w = \left(\frac{\lambda}{\mu}\right) = \frac{10}{12} = .833$$

7. The chance of waiting longer than ½ hour in the system. That is, $t = \frac{1}{2}$.

(13.7)

$$P(T > t) = e^{(10-12)1/2} = \frac{1}{e} = .368 \checkmark$$

8. The probability of finding four employees in the system, $n = 4$.

$$P_4 = \left(\frac{\lambda}{\mu}\right)^n \left(1 - \frac{\lambda}{\mu}\right) = \left(\frac{10}{12}\right)^4 \left(1 - \frac{10}{12}\right) = .0814 \checkmark \qquad (13.8)$$

9. The probability of finding more than three employees in the system.

$$P(n > 3 = \left(\frac{\lambda}{\mu}\right)^{N+1} = \left(\frac{10}{12}\right)^4 = .488 \checkmark \qquad (13.9).$$

In the following example it will be shown how to use such measures of effectiveness in a comparative analysis.

Example 2. The duplicating machine

The XYZ Corporation is considering leasing one of two possible self-service duplicating machines. The Mark I is capable of duplicating 20 jobs each hour at a cost of $50 per day. Alternatively, the Mark II can duplicate 24 jobs per hour at a cost of $80 per day. The duplicating center is open ten hours a day with an average arrival of 18 jobs per hour. The duplication is performed by employees arriving from various departments, whose average hourly wage is $5. Should the company lease Mark I or Mark II?

Solution   To assess the alternatives, it is necessary to compute[10] the same measures of performance in both systems; we will compute the measures shown in Table 13.1. *job @ hour*   20   24

machine cost @ day   50   80

TABLE 13.1
Comparing measures of performance

	Mark I	Mark II
λ, given per hour	18	18
μ, given per hour	20	24
ρ, utilization $= \dfrac{\lambda}{\mu}$	$\dfrac{18}{20} = .9$ *Too many waiting*	$\dfrac{18}{24} = .75$ *reasonable*
W (Equation 13.1) hours per customer	$\dfrac{1}{20-18} = \dfrac{1}{2}$	$\dfrac{1}{24-18} = \dfrac{1}{6}$
L (Equation 13.3) customers *(every hour, 9 people are waiting)*	$\dfrac{18}{20-18} = 9$ *people*	$\dfrac{18}{24-18} = 3$ *people*
P_o (Equation 13.5)	$1 - .9 = .1$	$1 - .75 = .25$

cost ... @ day   *450 @ day*   *80 / day*
people   *$5 / hour*   *$5 / hour*

Cost comparison on a daily basis

Mark I   Since each employee will spend $W = \frac{1}{2}$ hour in the duplicating center and since 180 persons arrive at the center each day (18 per hour times 10 hours), there will be a total waiting time of $\frac{1}{2}(180)$ = 90 employee-hours, each day. At $5 an hour this waiting time will cost the company 5(90) = $450 a day. The total cost is thus $450 + $50 daily machine cost = $500 per day.

Mark II   With $W = \frac{1}{6}$ hour per employee, there will be a total wait of $\frac{1}{6}(180)$ = 30 employee-hours each day. The cost now is only 5(30) = $150. Add to this the $80 cost of renting Mark II for a total cost of $150 + $80 = $230, or $270 per day lower than the Mark I.

Note that even though Mark II is only utilized 75 percent of the time, it is still the better machine to lease.

These computations are summarized in Table 13.2.

Note: In comparing Mark I and Mark II, notice that Mark II is only 20 percent faster (i.e., its service capacity is 1.2 times that of Mark I). Yet, the waiting time was cut down by almost 67 percent (from $\frac{1}{2}$ hour to $\frac{1}{6}$ of an hour). This is one indication that a "commonsense" approach (such as, double the service rate so the waiting time will be cut in half) is incorrect in queuing situations.

---

[10] We will assume that the service rate for the duplicating jobs is random. In essence this implies that the number of copies is random. However, if exactly one (or n) copies were needed per job, then the service time would be constant, a case discussed in Part B of this chapter.

TABLE 13.2
Cost comparison for the duplicating machine

System	Facility cost, C_F	λ	W	C	$C_W = \lambda W C$	TC ($/hour)	TC ($/day)
					Cost of waiting		
Mark I	$50/day = $5/hour	18	1/2	5	1/2 × 18 × 5 = 45	5 + 45 = 50	500
Mark II	$80/day = $8/hour	18	1/6	5	1/6 × 18 × 5 = 15	8 + 15 = 23	230

Margin notes: 9 × 10 × 5 = 450 ; 50 + 450 = 500 day ; 80 / 150 / 230 @ day

Example 3. Truck loading

A plant distributes its products by trucks. The average loading time is 20 minutes per truck. Trucks arrive at a rate of two each hour. Management feels that the existing loading facility is more than adequate. However, the drivers complain that they have to wait "more than half of the time." Analyze the situation and find how much money the company can save by speeding up loading if the waiting time of a truck is figured at $10 per hour and the plant is in operation eight hours each day.

Margin note: 8 Hrs × 2 = 16. load a Day

Solution Given λ = 2 and μ = 3 (20 minutes service means 3 per hour). Using Equation 13.6, the chance of having to wait in line is equal to 2/3 or 66.7 percent, so the drivers' complaints are legitimate. Using Equation 13.2, the average waiting time for a driver in the line is:[11]

Margin note: 60/20 = 3. $P_W = 1 - P_0 = \frac{\lambda}{\mu} = \frac{2}{3} = 66.7$

$$W_q = \frac{2}{3(3-2)} = \frac{2}{3} \text{ hours} = 40 \text{ minutes}$$

Margin notes: $W_q = \frac{\lambda}{\mu(\mu-\lambda)}$; $60 \times \frac{2}{3} = 40$.

Since there are 2 × 8 = 16 loads a day, there is a waiting time of 2(16)/3 = 10⅔ hours, each day, which costs the company, at $10 an hour, a total of $106.67. Therefore, the company should consider alternatives which could reduce this cost.

Automatic device The reader is encouraged to examine the following situation: An automatic device that can load ten trucks an hour is available at a cost of $90 per day over the cost of the existing facility. Should management replace the existing facility? (Solution: Yes, W_q is reduced to .025 hours and the daily cost of waiting to $4. Total daily savings: $106.67 − (90 + 4) = $12.67.)

The results are summarized in Table 13.3.

TABLE 13.3
Cost comparison for the truck loading problem

System	Facility cost, C_F	λ	W	C	C_W	TC ($/hour)	TC ($/day)
					Cost of waiting		
Existing system	Irrelevant	2	2/3	$10	13.33	$13.33	106.67
Proposed (automatic)	$90/day = $11.25/hour	2	.025	$10	0.50	11.25 + .50 = $11.75	94.00

[11] The problem can also be solved using W rather than W_q yielding the same conclusion. The reason for using W_q is that this is basically a wasted time.

13.10   CONCLUDING REMARKS

Waiting line (queuing) theory is a tool used mainly for computing measures of performance of systems providing services. This information is used by management to design service systems and to improve their operations.

Recognition of the distributions

The models discussed so far, as well as some of those to be discussed in the extensions of this chapter, assume Poisson arrival rates and exponential service times. The question now is how to find out if a certain arrival rate or a certain service time indeed follows these distributions.

Data is required

To begin with one must collect data. This can be done through continuous observation, through a sample observation, or through an analysis of historical data (e.g., arrival times to emergency rooms are usually recorded). The first step is to determine how much data to collect. This question can be answered with the aid of statistical theory. Next, one should check if λ and μ remained unchanged throughout the period of data collection (again statistical methods are available). It is

Stable conditions

necessary that these measures be stable, otherwise the formulas cannot be applied.

Once λ and μ are found to be stable, frequency distributions (Appendix B) can be constructed. The general shape and the amount of spread around the mean of the distributions should suggest certain standard probability distributions.

Check mean and standard deviation

A quick way to check a distribution is to compute its mean and standard deviation. In the exponential distribution, the mean and the standard deviation must be equal, and in the Poisson the mean must equal the variance. Such a test can rule out distributions which are not Poisson or exponential. However, in order to be sure, the chi-square goodness of fit test should be applied. (For the application of such a test see the texts listed in Appendix B.) Graphical examination of the histograms and comparison with probabilities in statistical tables can be used as an approximation.

Solution approaches

"Common sense" solutions are least desirable in waiting line situations. For example, most managers are likely to assume that to obtain the most efficient operations, they must make the average service rate approximate the average arrival rate; i.e., have a utilization close to 1.0. Such a design will ordinarily be far from efficient when arrivals and service times are subject to chance variations. "Doubling the speed will cut waiting time in half" is another common-sense fallacy. Therefore, the use of models is very important.

In the event that the arrival rate and the service time follow certain theoretical distributions, formulas and/or charts can be used to compute the operating characteristics of queuing systems. However, if the theoretical distributions are not close to reality, or if the system is complex, then the technique of simulation must be used.

13.11 PROBLEMS FOR PART A[12]

1. The number of customers arriving at the loan department of the Everglades National Bank was recorded over a period of 100 hours. The following table indicates the number of customers that arrived each hour:

Customers per hour	Number of times recorded
0	10
1	20
2	30
3	15
4	15
5	10
Total	100

Compute:
   a. The average arrival rate per hour.
   b. The average interarrival time in minutes.
   Graph the distribution of arrivals.

2. Given below is the distribution of repair times, as recorded for 550 repairs:

Hours, per repair	Number of times recorded
1	110
2	165
3	165
4	85
5	25
Total	550

Determine:
   a. The average repair time in hours.
   b. The average number of repairs per day (24 hours).
   Graph the distribution of service times.

3. A physician scheduled checkup patients at the rate of one every 15 minutes. Assume that the patients arrive exactly on schedule. Assume a constant checkup rate of four patients per hour.
   a. Calculate the waiting line which is likely to be generated after four hours.
   b. Assume the physician can see five patients in an hour. What will be the waiting line after four hours, and what will be the physician's rate of utilization?
   c. What will happen if the physician can see only three patients an hour. How long will the line be after four hours?

4. Identify the customers and the servers in the following systems:
   a. Telephone booth.
   b. Airport runways.
   c. Parking lot.
   d. A secretarial pool.
   e. Maintenance center.
   f. Hospital.
   g. Automobile assembly line.
   h. Elevators in a building.
   i. Traffic lights.

5. ABC Vending Corporation operates vending machines in one town. The machines break down at an average rate of 2 per hour. An hour of down-time of a machine is considered as a loss of $13. Currently the machines are surveyed by the company maintenance crew which is capable of repairing each machine in 24 minutes. The hourly cost of the maintenance team is $20. A maintenance contractor offered to take over the maintenance work. The contractor can repair three machines each hour, and his hourly charge is $40. Should management accept the contractor's offer?

6. A service system has an average interarrival time of two minutes and an average service rate of 60 per hour.
   Find:
   a. The probability that a customer will have to wait.

---

[12] In Problems 5–16 assume random arrivals (Poisson) and a negative exponential service time.

b. The probability that four persons are in the system.

c. The probability of finding more than three in the system.

d. The probability of finding exactly four customers in the waiting line.

e. The probability that fewer than four are in the system.

7. A tool crib clerk is serving a maintenance department with a large number of employees who earn $8 per hour. The clerk earns $5.00 per hour. The workers arrive at the tool crib at an average rate of 6.2 per hour. The average service time is eight minutes.

a. What is the probability of finding no workers at the tool crib (either waiting or being served)?

b. What is the average waiting time (before being served) per worker?

c. What is the average number of workers waiting in line (excluding the one being served)?

d. Would you recommend installing an incentive plan which will reduce the average service time to 6.4 minutes and will cost the company $2 per hour?

e. Another clerk can be hired at $5.00 per hour. The two clerks will operate as a single team serving one line with an average service time of four minutes. Would you recommend hiring the additional clerk? (Assume no incentives.)

f. If you had the alternative of installing the incentive plan with the existing system or hiring a second clerk, which one would you recommend?

g. Two more clerks can be hired (at $5, each) per hour to help the single clerk, reducing the average service time to two minutes. Would you recommend this over hiring one more clerk? Why (not)?

8. Given an arrival rate $\lambda = 3$, find values of L_q and W_q for the following values of μ: 3.1, 3.5, 4, and 6. When does serving efficiency become important?

9. Given a waiting line system with:
1. Average interarrival times of six minutes.
2. Space necessary for accommodating a waiting customer = 5 square feet.

3. Cost per hour of waiting time per customer = $2.

4. It was also observed that the facility is idle 20 percent of the time.

Find:

a. The area necessary to accommodate the average waiting line.

b. Is it profitable to invest $5 an hour in the facility if the service rate can be doubled (twice as fast)?

10. Sunny Engineering Corporation is designing a special machine for processing chickens. The chickens arrive from the farms on trucks, in cages, at a rate of ten trucks per hour. If the chickens are kept in the cage in the waiting area more than three hours, they will start to die causing damage to the processor. Determine the minimum average processing rate (in truckloads per hour) that must be designed for the machine, in order to assure that the cages will be processed on the average, in three hours or less. That is, waiting and processing time is three hours or less.

11. N.B.G. Airport currently operates with one runway for landings. The average landing time is 3 minutes. Airplanes arrive at the airport at the rate of 17 per hour. The estimated average fuel consumption for an airplane waiting for a landing is 10 gallons per minute. A gallon of fuel costs $2.

Find:

a. The average number of airplanes circling the airport in a "holding pattern;" i.e., waiting for permission to land. Do not include the landing airplane.

b. The average cost of fuel "burned" by an airplane waiting to land.

c. The chance of finding less than three airplanes in the airport vicinity (in the waiting line and landing).

d. The utilization of the runway.

12. Five cars arrive at an emissions testing garage each hour. The average service time is six minutes. The garage can accommodate only three cars (waiting and being served). Any car which cannot be accommodated in the garage is parked in a No-Parking area on the street, where there is a 40 percent chance of being fined $10.

The owner of the garage pays the fines. The garage is in operation 48 hours per week. Cars completed are picked up immediately by the customers.

Find the weekly fines collected (in $).

13. The Nasty Pelican is a one-man shop where people arrive at the average rate of 20 per hour. Joe, the proprietor, services a customer, on the average, in two minutes. During the noontime rush the arrival rate increases to one arriving customer every two minutes.

    Find:

    a. How fast must Joe work to insure that a noontime customer will not wait for service, on the average, more than ten minutes?

    b. What is the probability that six or more people are in the shop during the nonrush period?

    c. What is the average waiting time during the regular hours?

14. Customers arrive at a service facility every 12 minutes, on the average. The average service time is ten minutes. The operation of the existing system costs $5 an hour. The facility is in operation eight hours a day.

    Find:

    a. If the waiting (prior to service) area, that can accommodate three customers, is sufficient 90 percent of the time.

    b. It is proposed to speed up the service so ten customers can be served in an hour. The additional cost of this higher speed is $24 per day. If an hour waiting time (prior to service), per customer, is worth $1, is the investment justified?

15. Customers arrive at a one-person barbershop with an average interarrival time of 20 minutes. The average time for a haircut is 12 minutes.

    a. The owner wishes to have enough seats in the waiting area so that no more than 5 percent of the arriving customers will have to stand. How many seats should be provided?

    b. Suppose there is only sufficient space in the waiting area for five seats. What is the probability that an arriving customer will not find a seat?

16. The Industrial Engineering department of First National Bank conducted a study to determine the effectiveness of its two drive-in stations. These stations operate independently of each other and each has its own waiting line. The study involved random observations of the number of cars in a line (including the one being served). The results of the first day of study are given below:

Time	Cars in station 1	Cars in station 2
9:12	3	2
9:37	5	3
10:04	2	2
11:30	0	4
11:58	4	2
12:20	3	3
12:39	2	2
1:23	5	1
1:37	4	5
2:06	2	3
2:19	1	0
2:46	3	4

In addition, it was noted that line 1 served 84 customers and was open six hours while line 2 served 79 customers and was open six hours and 15 minutes. Find the utilization of each line and which is better utilized.

PART B: EXTENSIONS

13.12. MULTI-FACILITY QUEUING SYSTEMS

A multi-facility (multi-server, multi-channel) queuing system is composed of several identical and parallel service facilities. Such a situation is depicted in Figure 13.7. Note that only one waiting line exists which feeds the multiple service facilities. Whenever a server is free, the first customer in the queue goes to that service facility. An

FIGURE 13.7.
The multi-facility
waiting line system

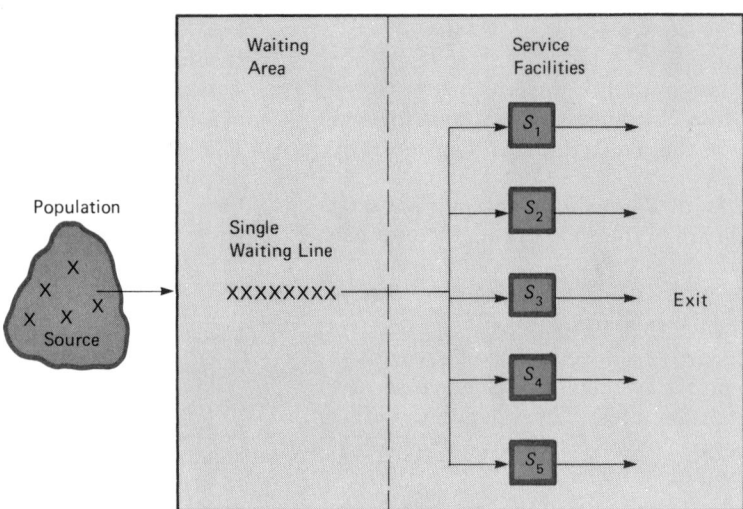

example of such a situation is an IRS (Internal Revenue Service) office where arrivals get a number as they arrive and then the numbers are called sequentially as the examiners become free. Another example is airplanes circling a large airport with two runways; whenever a runway becomes free, an airplane is directed to that runway. Thus, this is *not* like the supermarket situation, where several waiting lines exist, one for each server.

"Take a number
please"

There are several managerial problems in a multi-facility system. For example, management is concerned with determining the proper number of servers, whether to use identical or nonidentical servers (e.g., whether or not to open an "express lane" in the supermarket), and the organization of the waiting line (one line for all servers, one line per server). Such decisions are based on the computation of the *measures of effectiveness.*

An "express lane?"

In this section the simplest multiserver system is analyzed. In such a system the following assumptions are made:

Assumptions

1. Poisson-exponential systems, as described in Part A of this chapter.
2. Identical service facilities.

3. One waiting line exists.
4. The arrival rate λ is smaller than the combined service rate $(K\mu)$ of all K service facilities. $\lambda < (K\mu)$

Formulas for computing the measures of effectiveness

Let:

λ = arrival rate

μ = service rate of *each* facility

K = number of servers (service facilities)

ρ = utilization factor of one server. $\rho = \lambda/\mu$ as in the single facility system.

$\bar{\rho}$ = utilization factor of the entire system:

$$\bar{\rho} = \frac{\rho}{K} = \frac{\lambda}{K\mu} \tag{13.13}$$

Assuming that $\lambda < K\mu$, then some of the most common measures of effectiveness are:

1. The probability of finding no customers in the system (an "idle" system):

$$P_o = \frac{1}{\dfrac{\rho^K}{K!(1-\bar{\rho})} + \displaystyle\sum_{i=0}^{K-1}\dfrac{\rho^i}{i!}} \tag{13.14}$$

where i = index of summation.

2. The probability of finding exactly n customers in the system:

and

$$P_n = P_o\frac{\rho^n}{n!} \qquad \text{when } n \leq K$$

$$P_n = \frac{P_o\bar{\rho}^n K^K}{K!} \qquad \text{when } n \geq K$$

$$\tag{13.15}$$

3. The average number of customers in the waiting line:

$$L_q = \frac{P_o\rho^K\bar{\rho}}{K!(1-\bar{\rho})^2} \tag{13.16}[13]$$

---

[13] Given L_q, this equation yields the following for P_o:

$$P_o = \frac{L_q K!(1-\bar{\rho})^2}{\rho^k\bar{\rho}}$$

4. The average number of customers in the system:

$$L = L_q + \rho \qquad (13.17)$$

5. The average waiting time per customer, before service:

$$W_q = \frac{L_q}{\lambda} \qquad (13.18)$$

6. The average time a customer spends in the system (waiting and service):

$$W = \frac{L}{\lambda} = W_q + \frac{1}{\mu} \qquad (13.19)$$

Use of Graphs for Solving Queuing Problems

In order to save computational time in applying Equations 13.14–13.19, a graphical equivalent can be used. Figure 13.8 is a graph of Equation 13.16 in terms of various values of K, λ, and μ.

Using a graph

The process The graphical solution process is a simple, five step procedure, as demonstrated below.

Given: $\lambda = 36$/hour; $\mu = 10$/hour, and $K = 5$.

Step 1 Compute the ratio λ/μ; use the μ of one server. In our example $\lambda/\mu = 36/10 = 3.6$.

Easier—but less accurate

Step 2 Go to Figure 13.8; mark the ratio computed on the λ/μ axis (point U).

Step 3 Go vertically up until the curve that designates the number of servers is intersected. In our example, it is the curve $K = 5$, and the point is Y.

Step 4 Make a left turn, 90°; go left until the L_q axis is reached (point V in Figure 13.8). Read the result (slightly above 1).

Step 5 Using Equations 13.17, 13.18 and 13.19, the values of L, W, or W_q may now be computed.

This process can be depicted as:

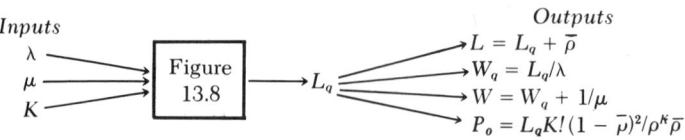

Inputs
λ
μ
K

Figure 13.8

$\rightarrow L_q$

Outputs
$L = L_q + \bar{\rho}$
$W_q = L_q/\lambda$
$W = W_q + 1/\mu$
$P_o = L_q K! (1 - \bar{\rho})^2/\rho^K \bar{\rho}$

Example 1 Parishioners arrive randomly to church for confession, at an average rate of 5.8 per hour. Father Bailey estimates that an average confession lasts ten minutes. However, he is worried about the possi-

FIGURE 13.8
The multi-facility queue

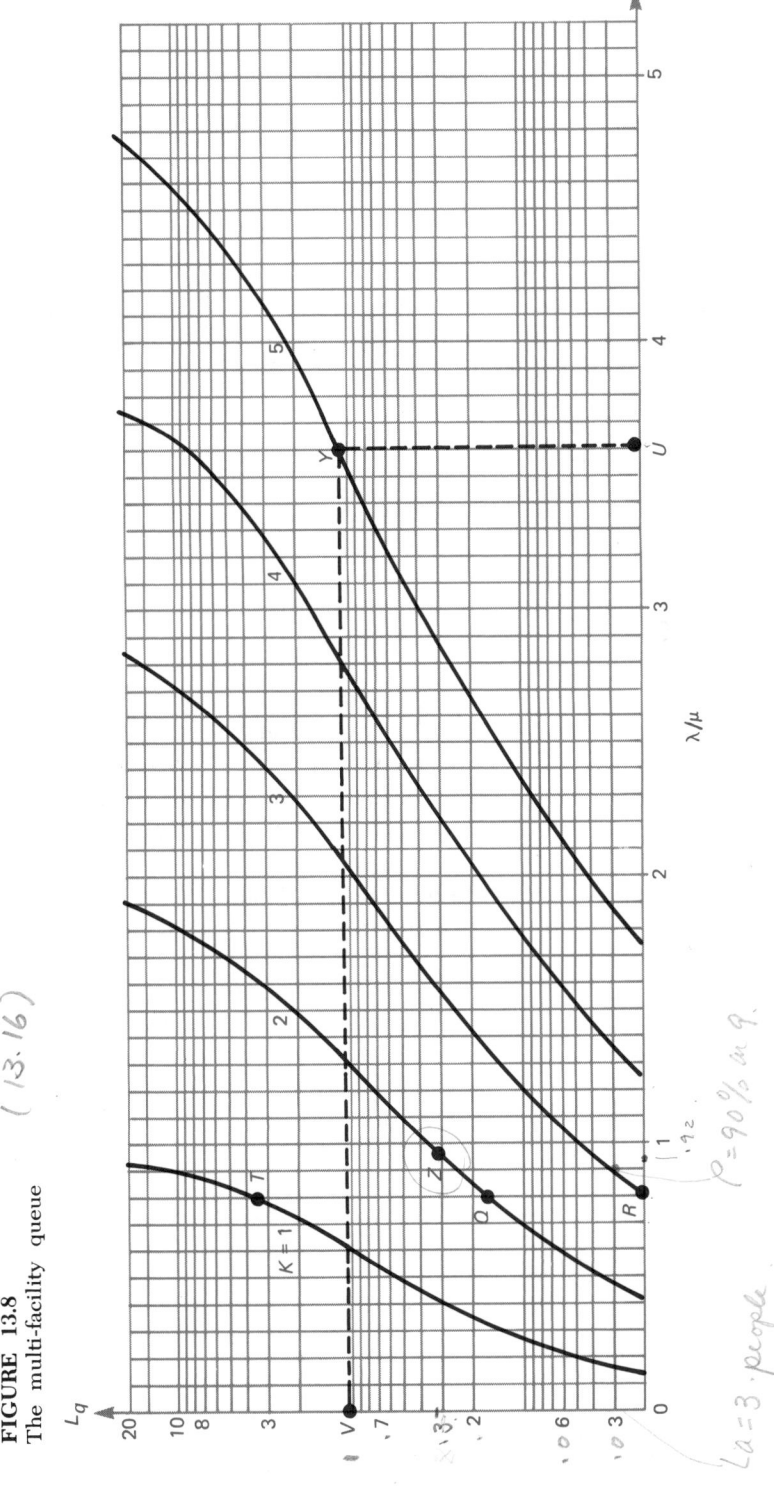

Formula
(13.16)

$\rho = 90\%$ in 9.

$Lq = 3$ people

bility of a long queue and wonders if he should ask more priests to hear confessions.

Solution   In this problem it is given that:

$$\lambda = 5.8 \text{ per hour}$$

$$\frac{1}{\mu} = 10 \text{ minutes} = \frac{1}{6} \text{ hour}$$

$$\mu = 6 \text{ per hour}$$

If only one priest hears confession, then it is a system with a single server and therefore the equations in Section 13.7 can be used[14] to generate the following information:

$$L = \frac{\lambda}{\mu - \lambda} = \frac{5.8}{.2} = 29 \text{ parishioners in the church.}$$

$$L_q = \frac{\lambda^2}{\mu(\mu - \lambda)} = \frac{5.8(5.8)}{6(.2)} = 28.03 \text{ parishioners in the waiting line.}$$

$$W = \frac{1}{\mu - \lambda} = \frac{1}{.2} = 5 \text{ hours average time in the church (waiting and service) per parishioner.}$$

$$W_q = \frac{\lambda}{\mu(\mu - \lambda)} = \frac{5.8}{6(.2)} = 4.83 \text{ hours average wait in the queue, per parishioner.}$$

The results above certainly corroborate Father Bailey's anxieties: an expected line length of 28 parishioners and a total time of five hours before they may leave for home. Let us now examine the result of having a second priest to hear confessions.

Solution with two priests   For this situation Figure 13.8 will be used.

Using the values of λ and μ, we find, at the intersection of $\lambda/\mu = .967$ and $K = 2$, a value of $L_q = .3$ (point Z on Figure 13.8). Then, applying Equations 13.18, 13.19, and 13.17 we get:

$$W_q = \frac{L_q}{\lambda} = \frac{.3}{5.8} = .0517 \text{ hours}$$
$$= 3.1 \text{ minutes}$$

$$W = W_q + \frac{1}{\mu} = .0517 + \frac{1}{6} = .2183 \text{ hours}$$
$$= 13.1 \text{ minutes}$$

$$L = L_q + \frac{\lambda}{\mu} = .3 + \frac{5.8}{6} = 1.267 \text{ parishioners in the church}$$

---

[14] Of course, Figure 13.8 could also have been used with $K = 1$. It is suggested that the student check the analytical solution by using the graph.

Notice that adding just one more priest to hear confessions did not cut the queue length and waiting time just in half—(that would have resulted in a line of 14 parishioners and a total time of 2.5 hours); instead, the results indicate an average waiting line of only .3 persons and an average waiting time prior to the confession of only 3.1 minutes. This amazing result is due to the *randomness* of the arrivals, and the fact that idle service time between arrivals cannot be stored, resulting in an excessive queue in the case of one priest.

Not a commonsense result at all

Example 2   Star Oil service station is considering how many of its eight identical gasoline pumps to staff during the night. Past experience indicates that there are an average of 16 random arrivals per hour during the 9:00 P.M.—7:00 A.M. period. Each customer brings the station an average profit of $1.50. The service time takes three minutes on the average, and follows a negative exponential distribution.

μ 3 min ar 20.
λ . 16.
10 Hubs.

Long waiting lines create ill will. In addition, customers may not enter the station if they see long lines. Therefore, the management of Star Oil estimates that each total customer-hour of waiting time in the service station effectively costs $3. The operating cost of manning each pump is $5 per hour. Find how many pumps should be manned so that total profit is maximized.

Solution   In this system $\lambda = 16$, $\mu = 60/3 = 20$.

For One Pump

How many pumps are best?

$$W_q = \frac{\lambda}{\mu(\mu - \lambda)} = \frac{16}{20(20 - 16)} = \frac{16}{20(4)} = \frac{16}{80} = .2 \text{ hours per customer}$$

This value can also be obtained from Figure 13.8 and Equation 13.18: At $\lambda/\mu = .8$ and $K = 1$ the value of L_q in Figure 13.8 (point T) is 3.2; thus $W_q = 3.2/16 = .2$.

Since there are 16 customers each hour, the cost of ill will is $16(.2)($3) = 9.60 per hour.

The total profit per hour is:

Gross profit: 16 customers × 1.5 = $24.
Less operating expenses = $5.
Less ill-will expense = $9.60.
Net profit: 24 − (5 + 9.6) = $9.40 per hour.

Two Pumps

To compute W_q for two pumps, Figure 13.8 is used with $\lambda/\mu = .8$ and $K = 2$. The result is (point Q) $L_q = .14$. Thus $W_q = .14/16 = .00875$, and the cost of ill will is $16(.00875)($3) = $.42$. The total net profit per hour is now: $24 − 5(2) − .42 = 13.58, which is considerably better than the case of one pump.

Three Pumps

From Figure 13.8, $L_q = .022$ (point R). Thus, $W_q = .022/16 =$

.00138, and the cost of ill will is 16(.00138)($3) = $.066. The total profit is: $24–5(3) − .066 = $8.93, which is less than with one pump.

Four Pumps or More

There is no need to check; since the cost of ill will is minimal, then adding more pumps (attendants) will increase costs.

Comparison These computations are summarized in Table 13.4. The best number of pumps is 2 with an hourly net profit of $13.58.

TABLE 13.4
Optimal number of service facilities

Number of pumps	Facility cost	W_q	Cost of waiting ($W_q \lambda \times \$3$)	Total cost	Net profit = $24 − total cost$	
1...............	5	.2	$9.60	$14.60	$ 9.40	
2...............	10	.00875	.42	10.42	13.58	← Maximum
3...............	15	.00138	.066	15.07	8.93	
4...............	20	negligible	negligible	20.00	4.00	

13.13   FINITE SOURCE QUEUING SYSTEMS

If the number of customers is limited

All waiting line situations discussed thus far assumed an infinite population source. However, in some real-life situations the number of customers is small and cannot be considered infinite. For example, there may be only nine production employees coming to the tool crib, or the number of airplanes arriving at a small airport each day may be limited to 12. Another very common situation is the so-called machine repair problem:

Companies often have maintenance teams whose primary function is to repair certain machines used for production when these break down. For instance, there may be one service person and five bottling machines. Another example is a production employee who supervises 15 textile machines. In such cases the machines are viewed as the "customers" which require service.

Finite (limited) source with a single server

Let M denote the finite number of customers in the source and λ denote each (identical) customer's individual arrival rate (*not* the group of all M customers). The basic formulas, assuming a Poisson-exponential system are:

$$P_o = 1/\sum_{i=0}^{M} \left[\frac{M!}{(M-i)!} \left(\frac{\lambda}{\mu}\right)^i \right]$$

(13.20)

where i = summation index.

$$P_n = P_o \left(\frac{\lambda}{\mu}\right)^n \frac{M!}{(M-n)!} \qquad (13.21)$$

$$L_q = M - \frac{\lambda + \mu}{\lambda}(1 - P_o) \qquad (13.22)[15]$$

$$L = L_q + (1 - P_o) \qquad (13.23)$$

$$W_q = \frac{L_q}{\mu(1 - P_o)} \qquad (13.24)$$

$$W = W_q + \frac{1}{\mu} \qquad (13.25)$$

As previously, a graphical equivalent (Figure 13.9) can be used here, too.

Example   The ABC Bottling Corporation has five machines. Each breaks down once every 2½ weeks, on the average. Thus, $\lambda = 1/2.5 = .4$ per week. The repair capacity is one machine per week: $\mu = 1$. Find the operating characteristics of the system.

Solution: Given: $\lambda = .4$, $\mu = 1$, $M = 5$.

Instead of using the equations, the graph of Figure 13.9 will be used.

First we compute $\lambda/\mu = .4$. This information is necessary for reading the horizontal axis. Then, for $M = 5$, the appropriate curve is selected and point T, at the intersection of the curve $M = 5$ and an λ/μ value of .4, is identified. The coordinate of point T on the vertical axis gives the value of L_q, which is 1.7 in this case. Note that even though the machines are failing at a rate of $.4 \times 5 = 2$ machines per week, a rate which is faster than the repair capacity of one machine per week, the service person is capable of fixing the machines without causing an explosive waiting line. The reason for this is the finiteness of the source of the arrivals. That is, when two machines are in queue waiting for service and one is being serviced, only two remain available to join the queue, and the rate at which *they* fail is $.4 \times 2 = .8$ or less than one per week (which is the repair capacity of the service person).

Once L_q is computed, other operating characteristics of the system, such as P_o, L, W_q, and W can be computed using Equations 13.22–13.25.

---

[15] This equation yields the following formula for P_o:

$$P_o = \frac{\lambda(L_q - M) + \lambda + \mu}{\lambda + \mu}$$

FIGURE 13.9
The single-server
limited-source queue

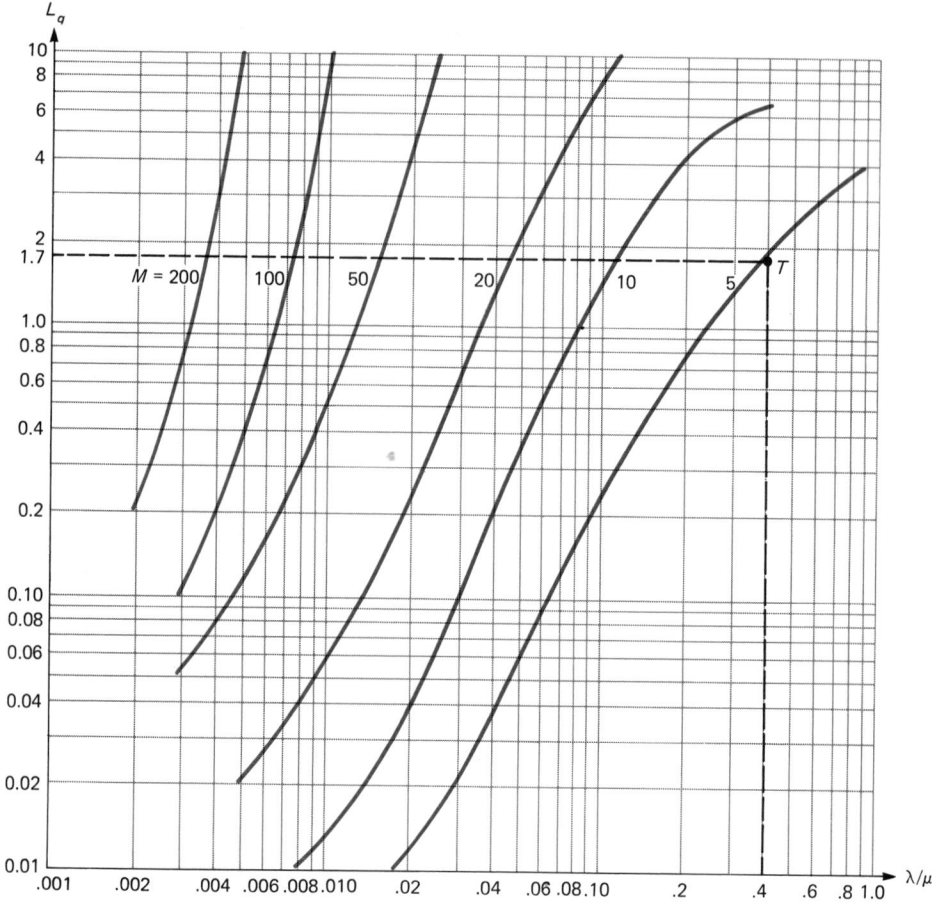

For example, from Equation 13.22 it is possible to compute P_o.

$$P_o = \frac{\lambda(L_q - M) + \lambda + \mu}{(\lambda + \mu)} = \frac{.4(1.7 - 5) + .4 + 1}{.4 + 1} = .057$$

Finite source with multiple servers

In this case only a graphical presentation is given. Figure 13.10 gives the results for five servers, $K = 5$. Formulas 13.23–13.25 are applicable here too.

13.14 QUEUING SYSTEMS WITH A MAXIMUM QUEUE LENGTH

In all the previous situations, no limits were set on the size of the waiting line. In the real world, however, there are many situations where the storage capacity of the waiting line is limited. For example, at gas stations there is only so much room for cars to wait. Another example

Limited queue

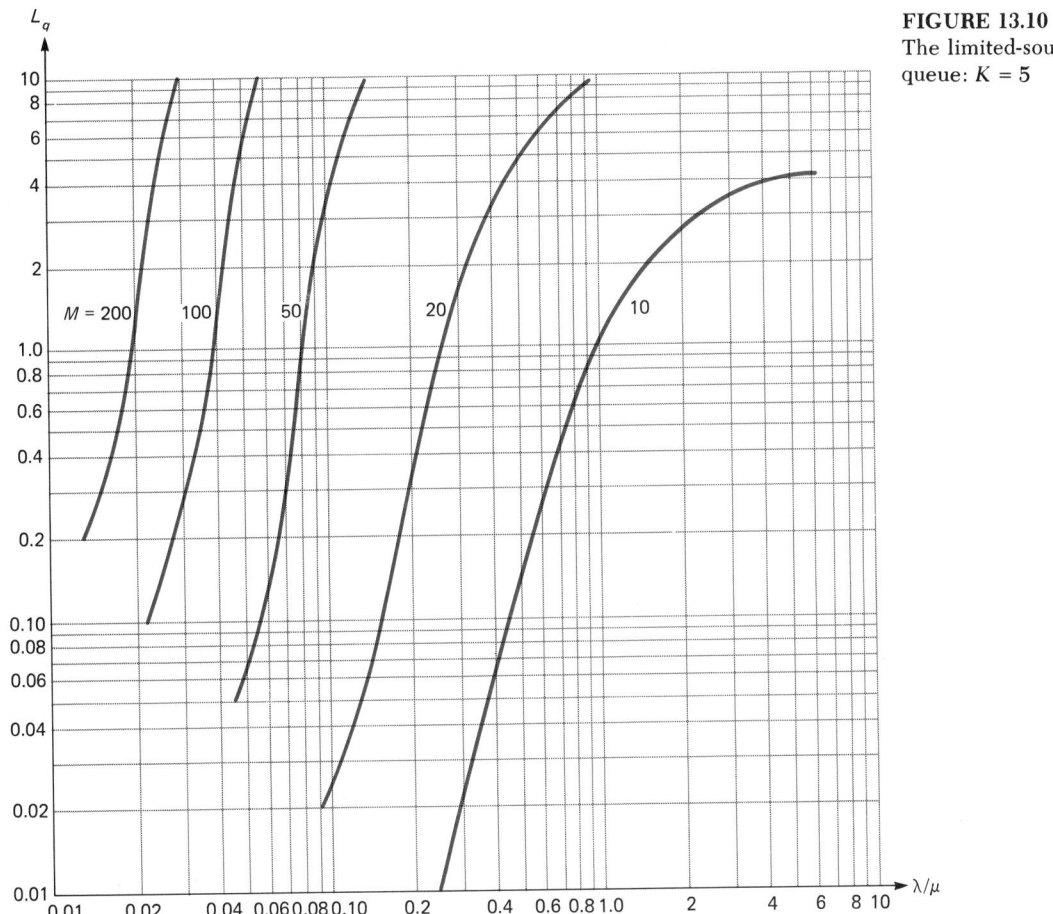

FIGURE 13.10
The limited-source
queue: $K = 5$

is a parking lot. Any customers that arrive while the waiting area is full must leave the system permanently without being served.

Let the maximum capacity of the system (including both the waiting line and the customers that are being served) be designated by T. Again, a Poisson-exponential system is assumed.

The single-server and the multiple-server cases

The relevant equations for the single-server ($K = 1$) case are:

$$P_o = \frac{1 - \rho}{1 - \rho^{T+1}}$$

(13.26)

$$P_n = P_o \rho^n$$

(13.27)

$$L_q = \frac{\rho}{1 - \rho} - \frac{T\rho^{T+1} + \rho}{1 - \rho^{T+1}}$$

(13.28)

The values of L, W_q, and W are the same as those given by Equations 13.23 to 13.25. Figure 13.11 is the graph of Equation 13.28, for various values of T. The figure can be used also to find L_q for multiple servers (5 and 10).

13.15 QUEUING SYSTEMS WITH A CONSTANT SERVICE TIME AND POISSON ARRIVALS

Human-machine systems

In some situations the service time can be considered as constant. For example, automated servers such as vending machines perform service at essentially a constant rate. Also, humans servicing nonhuman customers (an "oil change" on a car) frequently perform at an approximately constant rate.

The measures of performance for a single-server system with Poisson (random) arrivals and a constant service time, assuming all the other assumptions of a Poisson-exponential system, are given in Equations 13.29–13.33.

The single-server case

$$L_q = \frac{\lambda^2}{2\mu(\mu - \lambda)} \tag{13.29}$$

Note that this value is exactly one half of the value of L_q for a negative exponential service time, as expressed in Equation 13.4. The equations for P_o, L, W_q, and W are given below:

$$P_o = 1 - \frac{\lambda}{\mu} \tag{13.30}$$

$$L = L_q + \rho = \frac{2\lambda\mu - \lambda^2}{2\mu(\mu - \lambda)} \tag{13.31}$$

$$W_q = L_q/\lambda = \frac{\lambda}{2\mu(\mu - \lambda)} \tag{13.32}$$

$$W = L/\lambda = \frac{2\mu - \lambda}{2\mu(\mu - \lambda)} \tag{13.33}$$

Figure 13.12 presents the values of L_q corresponding to Equation 13.29 (use the value of $K = 1$).

Multiple servers

This situation is considerably more complex than the negative exponential case; therefore, formulas are not given here. Figure 13.12

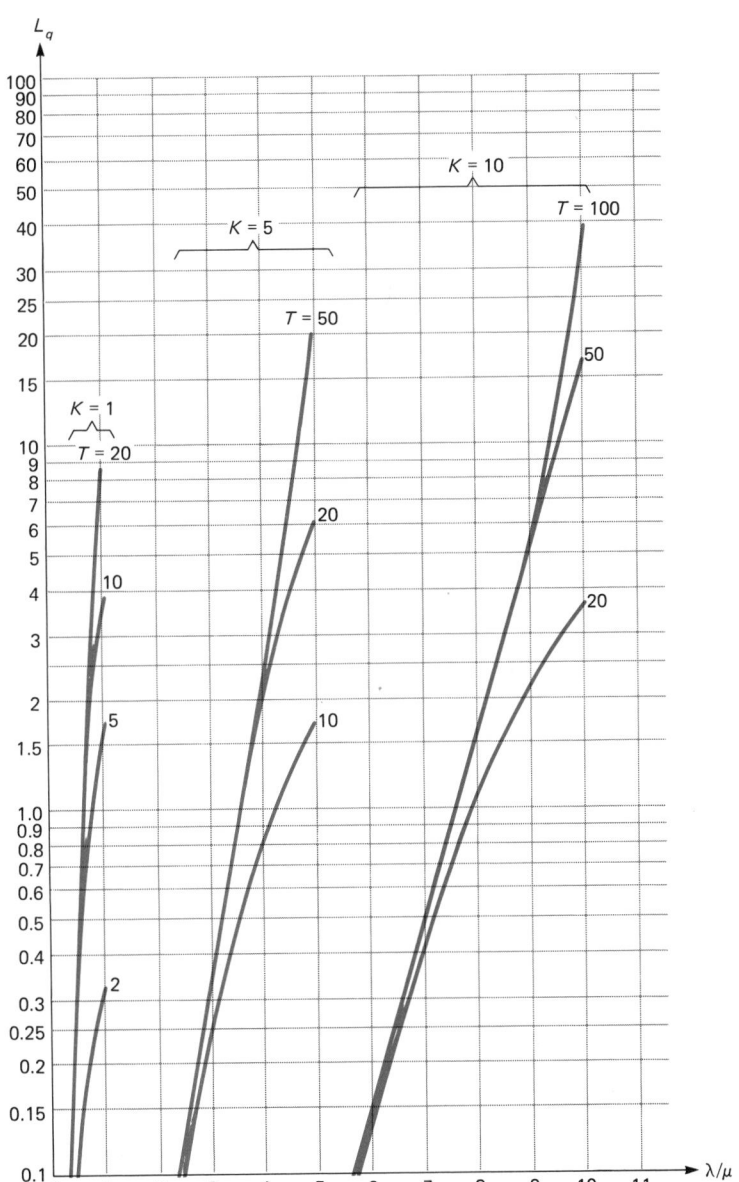

FIGURE 13.11
The maximal-length
queue

FIGURE 13.12
The constant-service-time queue

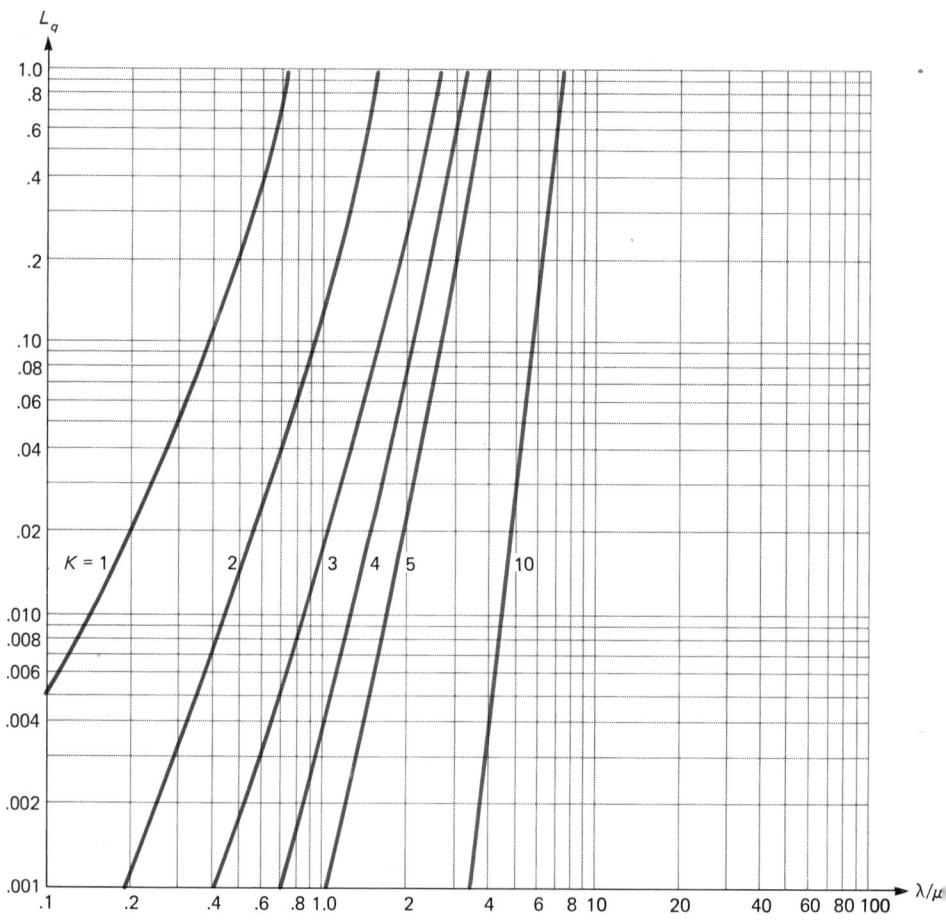

depicts the values of L_q for both single and multiple servers (K = number of servers), in a fashion similar to Figure 13.8, and read in exactly the same manner.

13.16 SERIAL QUEUES

Service in stages

In certain service situations a customer or a product receives service at a number of stations. The customer (product) moves from station to station and possibly from queue to queue. Under certain assumptions such a process may be analyzed rather easily. Multiple servers may even be included in the process.

The first two necessary assumptions are that the source is infinite and the queues in each station are not limited in length. Secondly, in the case of multiple servers, within each station, all servers must have the same exponential service time distribution. Thirdly, the customers at the first station arrive randomly (Poisson). Finally, $\lambda < K\mu$ at every station, where K = number of servers, so that an explosive queue is not formed somewhere in the system. Under the above assumptions, the output from each station will also be Poisson, with the average rate λ. Since each station has Poisson arrivals it may be treated independently of the others and Figure 13.8 can be used for computing the measures of performance throughout the entire process.

Poisson in . . .
Poisson out

Example

Consider a three-station process, where the arrival rate $\lambda = 5$ per hour. The number of servers are:

$K_1 = 1$ (for station 1)
$K_2 = 3$ (for station 2)
$K_3 = 2$ (for station 3)

The service rates per hour per server are:

$$\mu_1 = 6 \text{ (for station 1)}$$
$$\mu_2 = 2 \text{ (for station 2)}$$
$$\mu_3 = 4 \text{ (for station 3)}$$

The problem is shown schematically in Figure 13.13. Find the queue waiting times within the process.

FIGURE 13.13 A serial queue situation (combined with parallel servers)

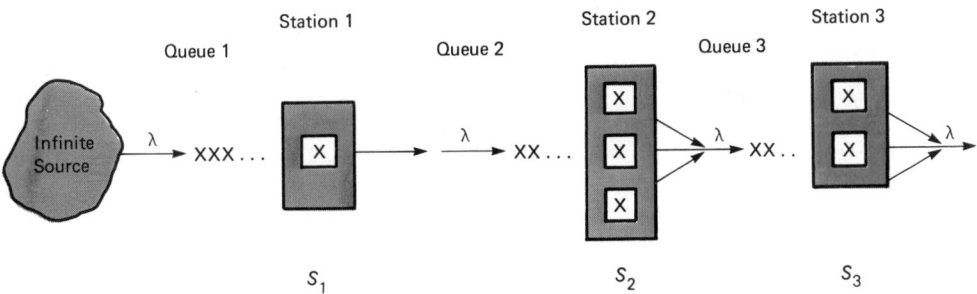

Solution *(all times in hours)*

Station 1   (Single server, use formulas of Section 13.7 or Figure 13.8.)

$$\frac{\lambda}{\mu_1} = .833, L_{q_1} = 4.5; W_{q_1} = \frac{4.5}{5} = .90; W_1 = .90 + \frac{1}{6} = 1.07$$

Station 2   (Multiple server, use Figure 13.8.)

$$\frac{\lambda}{\mu_2} = 2.5, L_{q_2} = 3.6; W_{q_2} = \frac{3.6}{5} = .72; W_2 = .72 + \frac{1}{2} = 1.22$$

Station 3   (Multiple server, use Figure 13.8.)

$$\frac{\lambda}{\mu_3} = 1.25; L_{q_3} = .8; W_{q_3} = \frac{.8}{5} = .16; W_3 = .16 + \frac{1}{4} = .41$$

The total queue waiting time in the system is thus

$$W_{q_1} + W_{q_2} + W_{q_3} = .90 + .72 + .16 = 1.78 \text{ hours}$$

13.17   PROBLEMS FOR PART B

Note: Assume a Poisson-exponential system unless otherwise specified.

17. The post office of Northwood City would like to know how many windows to staff so the average number of customers waiting for service does not exceed eight. The average service time is three minutes and the post office uses a single queue system, as illustrated below. How many windows should the post office staff on Monday mornings when the average arrival rate is 60 customers per hour?

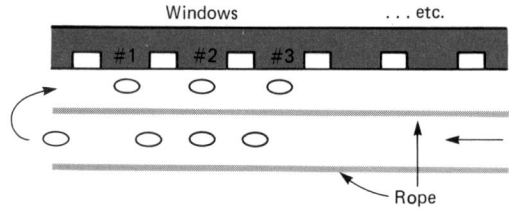

18. Mrs. Grouch and Mr. Mean each have a private secretary who can type letters at the average rate of four per hour. They generate letters at the average rate of three per hour each and have been wondering if they would benefit by pooling the two secretaries. What would you suggest? (Show calculations.)

19. The supervisor of the maintenance department of Everglade City is faced with a decision regarding maintenance on the city's heavy equipment. He is considering three alternatives:

a. Hire a first-class mechanic, which will cost the city $14.20 per hour (including fringe benefits). Such a mechanic can repair five units per eight-hour day.

b. Hire two second class mechanics, each of whom will cost the city $11.50 per hour. If the two serve one waiting line, they can each fix four units a day (they will work separately).

c. Subcontract the maintenance to ABC Engineering at a cost of $50 per unit repaired. The average repair time is one hour.

   The quality of repairs in all three alternatives is considered the same. Currently there is an average of four units of heavy equipment requiring daily repair (assume random arrivals). A unit of heavy equipment not in operation costs the city $25 per hour since the city must lease alternative equipment. Find the total daily cost of the three alternatives.

20. Trucks are loaded by forklifts at a rate of four per hour. An hour of forklift operation costs $10. The trucks arrive at an average rate of one every 20 minutes. An idle hour (waiting for loading) for a truck is estimated to cost $16. Find how many forklifts should be used. Assumption: Only one forklift can be used per truck.

21. The keen competition in the successful fast-food industry has forced the management of Burger Corporation to study the operation of their various restaurants. At their Northwest-

ern restaurant, where they receive the most complaints, an analysis revealed the following:

During rush hours customers arrive at an average rate of one each minute. The attendants can serve, on the average, 66 customers per hour. Burger's president cannot understand why there are so many complaints about the Northwestern restaurant. As the president states: "Why do they complain? We can serve even 10 percent more without any problems."

a. Explain to the president why you think there are so many complaints.

b. What will happen if the average number of customers grows by 10 percent?

c. It was proposed that two teams, each with an hourly serving capacity of 33 customers, replace the existing team that can serve 66 customers per hour. If there is no cost involved in such a change, would you recommend it? Show why. (Assume that the two teams serve a single waiting line.)

Hint: Assume that the number of complaints is a function of waiting time per customer.

22. Eastern Machine Company has a tool crib with two clerks. Both clerks issue spare parts and tools to maintenance workers. Maintenance workers arrive at a rate of 20 per hour, each wanting either a part (40 percent) or a tool (60 percent), but not both. The average issuing time is five minutes per order (service by one clerk). Each clerk currently issues both parts and tools. A maintenance worker not at his or her bench costs the company $5 per hour. It was proposed that the two clerks be specialized. Namely: One will issue spare parts only, and the other will issue tools only.

a. Would you advise specialization of the clerks if the service time does not change?

b. Would you advise specialization if the service time is reduced to four minutes per order?

Hint: Treat the current situation as a multiple station system with two servers. Treat the specialization as two single stations.

23. Western Bakeries serves 480 customers during eight hours of operation. The average service time per customer is four minutes. Currently there are five servers at the bakery serving one line.

Find:

a. The utilization of the bakery.

b. The average number of customers at the bakery.

c. The average waiting time (prior to service) in the bakery (per customer), in minutes.

d. The average number of customers being served.

e. The probability of finding no customers in the bakery.

f. The probability of finding exactly three customers in the bakery.

24. A mechanic-operator services five machines. When a machine needs an adjustment, it is shut down. An adjustment takes 15 minutes. Each machine needs an adjustment, on the average, once every two hours.

Compute:

a. The average number of operating machines.

b. The average number of inoperative machines.

c. The utilization rate of the machines.

d. The probability that all five machines are working.

e. The weekly cost of inoperative machines if one hour of downtime costs $10 and the machines are in operation eight hours each day five days a week.

25. Five factory service persons maintain 20 old machines which break down at an average rate of 15 per week. If the machines are repaired, one by each service person, at an average rate of two per week, what is the expected line length of inoperative machines?

26. A gasoline station is served by one employee who is capable of serving 30 customers per hour. There is a maximum space for five cars in the station (served and in line). Cars arrive at the station at an average rate of one every three minutes. Cars that do not have parking space leave and do not return.

Find:

a. The average number of cars *waiting* for service.

b. The average waiting time in line per car.

c. The probability of finding the station without any cars.

d. The probability of finding three cars in the station.

e. It was proposed to increase the space so that ten cars could be accommodated. The investment in such a case is $.50 per car space per hour. A car that leaves the station means a loss of $1 profit. Shoud the space be enlarged or not?

27. A restaurant with an 85-seat capacity has a bar that can accommodate 15 additional waiting customers. Customers who cannot be seated in the bar leave the restaurant. There are ten waitresses at the restaurant, each capable of serving three customers each hour. Customers arrive at the restaurant at a rate of 29 per hour.

   Find the average number of customers waiting for service in the restaurant and bar. Assume that all customers go into the restaurant upon arrival if room is available.

28. A five-stage manufacturing process receives raw materials (in units) randomly and must process an average of 12 units each day (eight hours). The data of the system are as follows:

Stage	No. of parallel servers in stage (K)	Service capabilities (per eight-hour day) (per server)
1	2	7
2	1	15
3	5	3
4	3	4.5
5	1	30

a. Find the *expected time* for a unit in the entire processing system (from arrival until finished in stage 5).

b. Find the average waiting time prior to entering the processing system.

c. The cost of a server in the system is $6 per hour. Unit waiting time costs $1/hour. Would it be profitable to add more servers to the system? If yes, in what stage(s) should they be placed?

d. As an alternative to adding more servers would a transfer of servers among stages be profitable?

Assume:

1. The arrival rate cannot be changed.
2. Servers are paid on an hourly basis, and if they work a portion of an hour they are paid proportionally.

13.18 CASE

Newtown Maintenance Division

The city of Newtown is, like many other cities today, caught in a severe financial squeeze. Up to now, previous city managers have taken a short-term approach to Newtown's maintenance and repair services in the expectation that future tax receipts would improve. However, Newtown's voters have just rejected the fourth proposed tax increase on the ballot for city services in as many years and the expected relief of future tax revenues now looks hopeless.

The new city manager has decided that a long-term policy must finally be established that recognizes the reality of continued low funding for city services. One portion of this problem is the manner of making the daily repairs to the city's streets. Calls for repairs arrive randomly at the average rate of two per day. It is the mayor's declared policy that the city will respond to all calls for street repairs within one week (five eight-hour working days) of the call.

The city manager has two alternatives for servicing street repairs:

1. He can use any number of standard city crews which cost $79 per hour and can each repair a street, on the average, in ten hours.

2. He can lease special heavy duty street repairing equipment and use smaller crews, resulting in an hourly cost of $90 per crew. These special crews can repair the average street in only seven hours.

Make a recommendation to the city manager concerning these two alternatives. How soon can the mayor claim the city will respond to calls under the cheapest of the above two policies? What would the effect be of the mayor insisting that the response time be reduced to *two* working days?

13.19 GLOSSARY

Arrival rate   The number of units arriving at the service facility for service.

Balking   Refusing to join a waiting line.

Cycling   Returning to the queue following service.

Explosive queue   A situation where the customers arrive faster than the service and the queue builds up without a decrease.

FIFS   The first in, first served service discipline.

Interarrival time   The time between customer arrivals at the service facility.

Jockeying   Shifting back and forth between queues.

LIFS   Last in, first served, a priority system used in warehouses and stores.

Multi-facility   A service facility with multiple service stations in parallel, each providing the same service.

Negative exponential   A type of statistical distribution.

Parallel   At the same time; simultaneous.

Poisson   A type of statistical distribution.

Poisson-exponential system   The elementary queue with random arrivals and services.

Preemptive priority   When one can interrupt a preceding service.

Queue   A waiting line.

Queue discipline   The policy of selecting customers for service.

Random   Based completely on chance.

Reneging   Leaving the system before service; backing out.

Serial   One following the other.

Service rate   The number of units that can be served in a unit of time.

Service facility   The station where recipients are served.

Source   The population of customers for a queue.

Utilization ratio   The fraction of time the server is busy.

13.20 REFERENCES AND BIBLIOGRAPHY

1. Bhat, U. N. "Sixty Years of Queuing Theory." *Management Science* 15 (1969):B–280.

2. Cohen, J. W. *The Single-Server Queue.* Amsterdam: North-Holland, 1969.

3. Cooper, R. B. *Introduction to Queueing Theory.* New York: Macmillan, Inc., 1972.

4. Gross, D., and Harris, C. N. *Fundamentals of Queuing Theory.* New York: John Wiley & Sons, Inc., 1974.

5. Hillier, F. S., and Lieberman, G. J. *Introduction to Operations Research.* 3d ed. San Francisco: Holden-Day, Inc., 1979.

6. Hillier, F. S. and Yu, O. S. *Queuing Tables and Graphs.* Amsterdam: Elsevier-North Holland, 1979.

7. Jaiswal, N. K. *Priority Queues.* New York: Academic Press, 1968.

8. Newell, G. F. *Application of Queueing Theory.* London: Chapman and Hall, Ltd., 1971.

9. Panico, J. A. *Queuing Theory.* Englewood Cliffs, N.J.: Prentice-Hall, Inc., 1969.

10. Peck, L. G., and Hazelwood, R. N. *Finite Queuing Tables.* New York: John Wiley & Sons, Inc., 1958.

11. White, J. A., et al. *Analysis of Queuing Systems.* New York: Academic Press, 1975.

14

The application of the management science tools described in the earlier chapters is frequently limited to relatively simple managerial problems. When managerial problems become complex they often no longer fit the standard problem classifications that are solved by the standard tools. Development of special optimization models to handle such problems may be too costly in terms of dollars and time or the task may even be impossible. For such cases simulation models are useful. A simulation model involves trial-and-error experimentation with a mathematical model in order to describe and evaluate the system's behavior. Five types of simulation models will be discussed in this chapter:

1. Artificial intelligence.
2. Heuristic programming.
3. Operational games.
4. System simulation.
5. Monte Carlo simulation.

Simulation

PART A: BASICS

". . . and a left, another left! Clay is still dancing and back-pedaling but he's slowed a lot. Rocky lands a right—and another jab! Rocky's nose is bleeding again, but he's looking spryer, refreshed. Another jab by Rocky. AND HE'S DOWN!! Clay is on the mat!! Rocky connected a powerhouse, folks!! Four, five!! The referee is over him! Seven!! He's on his knees. Nine! Ten!! He's out!!! Rocky Marciano has won!! In 57 seconds of this 13th round. . . ."

Sixteen million people around the world watched this exciting match between two of the world's most celebrated heavyweight champions. In the United States one million fans paid $5 apiece to see this action at their local movie houses—and none of it was real! But that didn't bother the fans; they loved it anyway. What the fans saw was a computerized *simulation* of a fight. The simulation was necessary because Rocky Marciano was at that time 45 years old and hadn't fought in 14 years. What was described was a match between Muhammad Ali (then known as Cassius Clay) and the Marciano champion of 14 years earlier.

The process used by Miami producer-promoter Murray Woroner to build the simulated fight was as follows. First, he had about 100 boxers and boxing writers draw up 129 ring variables such as vulnerability to cuts, ability to take a punch, having a killer instinct, and so on. Then 400 sportswriters, fighters, and managers rated the two champs, Rocky Marciano and Muhammad Ali, on each of the 129 factors.

Simultaneously, Woroner had Marciano and Ali stage 75 rounds of "Hollywood style" boxing (somewhat "pulled punches") in a movie studio before five color cameras. For this fight, Marciano trimmed off 50 pounds and wore a toupee. Because of Rocky's age it was necessary to film the 225 total minutes in 1-minute segments. Five possible endings were shot: a knockout for each, technical knockout decision for each, and a draw.

Then an NCR 315 computer simulated a fight between the two heavyweights using the expert's ratings on the 129 ring variables, and, based on the results, selected the appropriate film segments. It took four months to edit the 100,000 feet of film into the final 6,300 feet needed to match the computer printout. Crowd noises, punch sounds, and a sportscaster were then dubbed in to add realism. The final ending was held top secret so only Woroner and the film editor knew the outcome.[1]

Ali looked like the winner from the start, dancing, jabbing, and eluding Marciano's heavy punches. Ali's jabs were cutting Rocky to

---

[1] For his efforts, Woroner grossed about $6 million. Rocky had contracted for a fixed sum of $35,000 while Ali took a negligible fixed amount but 10 percent of the profits, thus netting about $200,000. Sadly, Rocky died in a plane crash three weeks after the camera-staged fight; the final match was one of the greatest, and the most unusual, of his career.

ribbons and had bloodied his nose by the fourth round. At one point Ali had Marciano on the mat but Rocky rallied late in the match and knocked his opponent down for the first time in the tenth round. As Ali slowed up, Rocky's punches had more effect until that final exciting blow in the 13th round.

14.1   THE GENERAL NATURE OF SIMULATION

To achieve an impossible setting

The Ali-Marciano simulated fight enabled the promoter to achieve a desired physical setting otherwise impossible to achieve (at 45, Marciano could certainly not perform as well as when he was 31). This arrangement enabled the promoter to "experiment" in order to find out what would have been the result of a 10- or 15-round fight.

The fight was an example of a type of simulation called "system simulation" where every possible action sets another event in action and all elements may influence the action of all other elements. The nature of the outcome of the system is not, however, foreordained once an initial act occurs. The simulation allows for chance events, errors, acts of nature, lag times, and even indecision to occur. In the case of the fight, the movements and countermovements of the opponents, their reaction times, and even the extent of damage from each punch were selected by the computer based on probabilities given by the boxers, writers, and managers.

War games and monopoly

Other familiar simulations are the mock war games that national armies regularly schedule, primarily for their reservists, and Monopoly, the real estate game. Other, not so familiar, simulations are:

- Simulation models of urban systems.
- Corporate organizational (policy) models.
- Business games used for training.
- Flights to the planets and moon.
- Plant and warehouse location models.
- Determination of the proper size of repair crews.
- Econometric models of national economies.
- Network models of traffic intersections to determine the best sequencing of traffic lights.
- Queuing models of airport runway takeoffs and landings.
- Air basin models to determine pollution sources, concentrations, and dynamics.
- Dam and river basin models to determine the effect of weather and operating policies on the hydroelectric output and water supply.

A flexible tool

From the above list, it can be seen that simulation is one of the most flexible models in the tool kit of management scientists. It can be applied to many different types of problems and yields a great deal of information concerning the effectiveness of different operating policies under various conditions and assumptions.

What is simulation?

Simulation has many meanings, depending upon the area where it is being used. To *simulate,* according to the dictionary, means to assume the appearance or characteristics of reality. In management science it generally refers to *the use of a digital computer to perform experiments on a model of a management system.*

Major characteristics

To begin, simulation is not strictly a type of model; models in general *represent* reality while simulation *imitates* it. In practical terms this means that there are fewer simplifications of reality in simulation models than in other models.

Second, simulation is a technique for *conducting experiments.* Therefore, simulation involves the testing of specific values of the decision variables in the model and observing the impact on the output variables.

Simulation is a *descriptive* rather than a normative tool; that is, there is no search for an optimal solution. Instead, a simulation describes and/or predicts the characteristics of a given system under different circumstances. Once these characteristics are known, the best among several policies can be selected. The simulation process often consists of repetition of an experiment many, many times to obtain an estimate of the overall effect of certain actions. It can be executed manually in some cases, but a computer is usually needed.

Finally, simulation is usually called for only when the problem under investigation is too complex to be treated by analytical models (such as EOQ) or by numerical optimization techniques (such as linear programming). Complexity here means that the problem either cannot be formulated mathematically or the formulation is too involved for a solution.

Imitation—not representation

Conducting experiments

Descriptive rather than normative

Advantages and disadvantages of simulation

The increased acceptance of simulation at the higher managerial levels is probably due to a number of factors:

1. Simulation theory is relatively straightforward.
2. The simulation model is simply the aggregate of many elementary relationships and interdependencies, much of which is introduced slowly by request of the manager and in a patchwork manner.
3. Simulation is descriptive rather than normative. This allows the manager to ask "what if" type questions (especially when used

"What if" questions

with an on-line computer). Thus, managers who employ a trial-and-error approach to problem solving can do it faster and cheaper with the aid of simulation and computers.

4. An accurate simulation model requires an *intimate* knowledge of the problem, thus forcing the management scientist to constantly interface with the manager.

5. The model is built from the manager's perspective and in his or her decision structure rather than the management scientist's.

6. The simulation model is built for one particular problem and, typically, will not solve any other problem. Thus, no generalized understanding is required of the manager; every component in the model corresponds one to one with a part of the real-life model.

7. Simulation can handle an extremely wide variation in problem types such as inventory and staffing as well as higher managerial level functions like planning. Thus, it is "always there" when the manager needs it.

Always there

8. The manager can experiment with different variables to determine which are important and with different policies and alternatives to determine which are the best. The experimentation is done with a model rather than by interfering with the system.

9. Simulation, in general, allows for inclusion of the real-life complexities of problems; simplifications are not necessary. For example: Simulation utilizes the real-life probability distributions rather than approximate theoretical distributions.

Time compression

10. Due to the nature of simulation a great amount of *time compression* can be attained, giving the manager some feel as to the long-term (one to ten years) effects of various policies, in a matter of minutes.

11. The great amount of time compression enables experimentation with a very large sample (especially when computers are used). Therefore, as much accuracy can be achieved as desired at a relatively low cost.

The primary disadvantages of simulation are:

No guarantee of optimality

1. An optimal solution cannot be guaranteed.
2. Constructing a simulation model is frequently a slow and costly process.
3. Solutions and inferences from a simulation study are usually not transferable to other problems. This is due to the incorporation in the model of the unique factors of the problem.
4. Simulation is so easy to apply that analytical solutions which can yield better results are often overlooked.

Five types of simulation are presented in this text:

Five types of simulation

1. Artificial intelligence.
2. Heuristic programming.
3. Operational games.

4. System simulation.
5. Monte Carlo simulation.

Of these, only Monte Carlo will be discussed in detail.

14.2 ARTIFICIAL INTELLIGENCE

The use of computers in management science, as discussed so far in this text, has been mainly as a fast and accurate tool for making the computations required for "well-defined" problems. However, computers can also be used to help solve the more difficult "ill-defined" problems. The basic question in using a computer to solve an ill-defined problem is: "Can a computer be programmed to exhibit intelligence?" Specifically, can it make observations, consider hypotheses, recognize analogies, and learn from its own experience?

Attempts to "tame" the computer and teach it to "think" were made   Do computers think?
as early as the early 1940s. Substantial progress has been made since that time; but the entire subject, which is called *artificial intelligence,* is still in the formative stage of its development. It falls under the heading of simulation because the task is to imitate (i.e., simulate) human thought.

Artificial intelligence is oriented toward *search, pattern recognition, inductive inference,* and *learning*—all of which are basic activities in human problem solving.[2] At this stage of development, these basic activities are taken as components rather than as overall artificial intelligence when used in the actual process of problem solving. An exception has been the use of artificial intelligence in the solution of some combinatorial type problems[3] that have been solved by *heuristic programming* (to be discussed in the next section). In such cases an improvement of the decision rules (heuristics) through learning was achieved.

14.3 HEURISTIC PROGRAMMING

The determination of optimal solutions to some complex decision problems could involve a prohibitive amount of time and cost or it may even be an impossible task. In such situations, it is sometimes possible to arrive at *satisfactory* solutions more quickly and less expensively by using *heuristics.*

Heuristics (from the Greek word for "discovery") are step-by-step   Satisfactory rather
procedures which, in a finite number of steps, arrive at a *satisfactory*   than optimal
solution. (Note that an algorithm also progresses step-by-step towards a solution, but an *optimal* one.) It is important to note the difference

---

[2] To obtain more information about these basic activities and the foundations of artificial intelligence, the reader is encouraged to read Minsky's article [6] or consult the journal *Artificial Intelligence.*

[3] Combinatorial type problems were discussed in Chapter 6.

between heuristics and "rules of thumb." A rule of thumb is usually developed as a result of a trial-and-error experience. It does not possess any analytical foundation. Heuristics, on the other hand, are rules which are developed on the basis of a solid and rigorous analysis of the problem, possibly with designed experimentation.

While heuristics are used primarily for solving ill-structured problems, they can also be used to provide satisfactory solutions to certain complex, well-structured problems, much more quickly and cheaply than algorithms. The main difficulty in using heuristics is that they are not as general as algorithms. Therefore, they can normally be used only for the specific situation for which they were intended.

Heuristic programming

Heuristic programming is the approach of employing heuristics to arrive at feasible and "good enough" solutions to such complex problems. Heuristic programs are usually executed by a computer, although a manual execution is possible in simple cases.

For example, in evaluating investments in the stock market the investor may have rules such as this: "Only companies whose assets are at least three times larger than their liabilities should be considered." The employment of several similar rules may reduce the number of feasible investment alternatives from thousands to a dozen.

In studying examples of applied heuristic programming, one can observe that the computer attempts to reduce the amount of search for a satisfactory solution. In such a search the computer is taught how to explore only relatively fertile paths and ignore relatively sterile ones. The computer choices are made by using heuristics which can be improved in the course of the search (through learning).

Heuristic programming has been used for helping solve problems such as:

- Sales forecasting.
- Investment decisions (portfolios of stock).
- Facilities location.
- Job shop scheduling.
- Work force and production level determination.
- Plant layout.
- Large project scheduling.
- Inventory control.
- Balancing assembly lines.

Part B of this chapter presents an example concerning the sequencing of different jobs through a machine.

14.4 OPERATIONAL GAMING (BUSINESS GAMES)

Profiting in an oligopoly

Operational games are simulation models involving several participants who are engaged in playing a game that simulates a realistic competitive situation. Typically, a number of teams are organized as an oligopoly,[4] each team trying to maximize its own profit by making periodic decisions in areas such as production, inventory, marketing, investment, maintenance, research, and financing. (An example is given in Part B of this chapter.) Similar games exist for the services and nonprofit sectors. For example, hospital games [12] allow the examination of decisions concerning staffing, room rates, expansion, and fund drives.

The two primary purposes of games are for *training* and *research.*

Training

Management games have been very popular for training—both in industry and in the academic setting. The advantages claimed are: (1) that learning is much faster and more permanent when the participant is active in the training process than when he is passive, and (2) the game introduces interfunctional dependencies (such as the relationship between production and marketing) in the organization, in a congenial manner.

A great advantage of games, as in any other simulation, is the time compression factor—many years of operating experience can be obtained over the duration of a short period. This gives the participants an opportunity to test unusual tactics which they would not be able to try in real organizations.

Research

Games are used for research purposes to provide insight into the behavior of organizations, the decision-making process, and the interactions within a team. When used to study managerial decision making, the manager's rate of learning as he or she continues to play the game, is also analzyed. Observing the dynamics of team decision making sheds light on important research areas, such as: the roles assumed by individuals, the effect of personality types and managerial styles, the emergence of "politics," and team conflict and cooperation.

14.5 SYSTEM SIMULATION

System simulation is typically concerned with modeling the dynamics of very large systems, such as the national monetary system, the production process of an automobile, or the dynamics of a rocket launching. Included in this definition is the concept of *industrial dynamics* as espoused by J. Forrester [14]. **Industrial dynamics**

Equations simulating the flows of materials, products, and people, as well as time lags and feedbacks of the system, are programmed into a

---

[4] An oligopoly is a market where only a small number of sellers operate.

computer. These equations represent the relevant characteristics of the real-life system in its operating environment. Then different managerial policies are tested on the simulation model to see their effect. On the basis of the results, some understanding of the system is gained and the best of all tested policies is identified. The variables describing the environment can then be changed to test the sensitivity of the best policy. To help in simulating systems, numerous special computer programming languages such as DYNAMO, GPSS, and SIMSCRIPT exist.

Example

Simulation of a paper manufacturer The simulation starts with the raw materials: the existing forest timber and used paper available for recycling (see Figure 14.1). A set of equations effectively "translates"

FIGURE 14.1
Paper manufacturer system dynamics

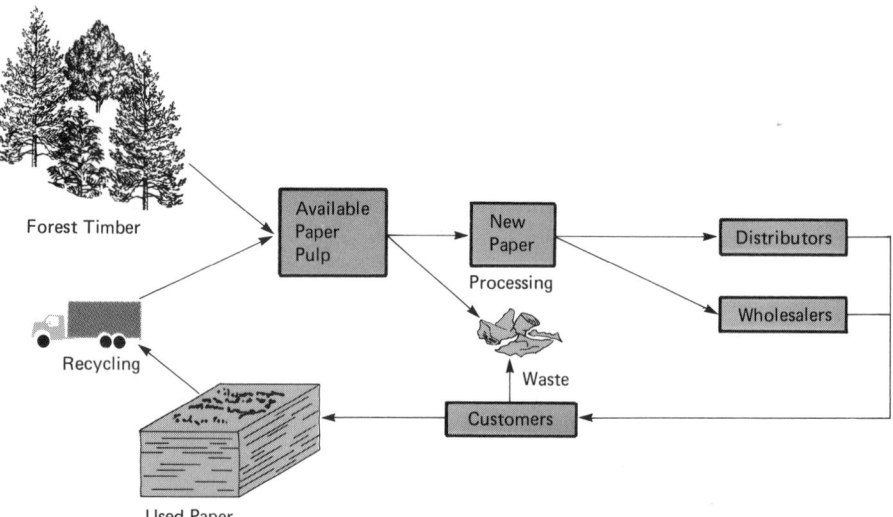

the timber into available pulp. Another set of equations does the same thing for the used paper. The plant itself is then simulated by equations which "translate" the conversion of pulp into paper and waste. Lag times between pulp input and paper output are included, as well as the lag time for shipping of distributors and wholesalers, from there to customers, and from customers to waste or back into the plant as used paper.

Under this system simulation, management can test the effect of varying environmental conditions, such as:

- Fire destruction of timberland.
- Decreased customer demand.
- Increased land values.
- Transportation strikes.

on such dependent variables as: annual costs, profits, revenues, reserve timberland, and total assets. In addition, the impact of various managerial (controllable) policies on the dependent variables can be tested. These include:

- Alternative uses of the timberland.
- Increased prices.
- Decreased production.
- Faster transportation.
- Earlier knowledge of customer demand.

The result is a significantly improved basis for managerial decision making. Risk can be evaluated against potential profits. Frequently the system simulation also gives the manager greater insight into the dynamic workings of the system itself, thus further improving his or her managerial decision-making ability.

14.6 SIMULATION OF DECISIONS UNDER RISK–MONTE CARLO

Managerial systems of decisions under risk exhibit chance elements in their behavior. As such, they can be simulated with the aid of a technique called Monte Carlo (named after the famous gambling kingdom). The technique involves random *sampling* from the probability distributions which represent the real-life processes.

Sampling from the probability distribution

Let us illustrate the basic idea of Monte Carlo simulation by comparing it to other techniques.

Example: A dice game

People love to play with dice—as evidenced by the popularity of various games of chance. Suppose that a player would like to know the chance of getting a total of 7 in one roll of two dice. There are six different ways to get 7 in a roll of two dice, as shown in Figure 14.2.

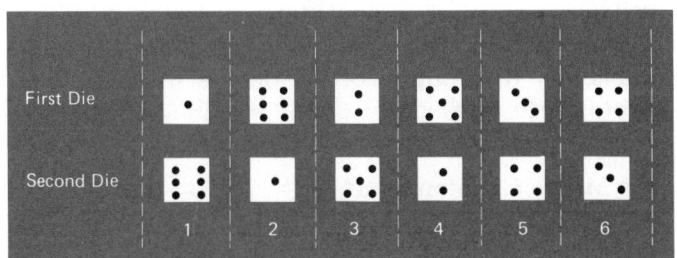

FIGURE 14.2
Six ways to get the number 7 with two dice

To find the chances of getting 7 in one roll of two dice, the player may use one of the following methods.

Analytical solution With the knowledge of some statistics the answer can be reached quickly. There is a chance of $1/6$ for any of the numbers, 1 through 6, to show up on one die. The chance for any two numbers to show up with two dice is $1/6 \times 1/6 = 1/36$. Since there are six different ways of getting seven with two dice (see Figure 14.2), then there is a chance of $1/36 \times 6 = 6/36 = .1667$ or 16.67 percent of getting the number 7 in each roll of the two dice.

Experimentation with the dice   It does not take very long to roll two dice, say, 1,000 times; doing so, the player may find that he or she rolled 7s 167 times. That is, the proportion is $167/1,000$ or a probability of 16.7 percent of getting a 7. The experimentation with the dice will take maybe half an hour. The answer will rarely be as exact as the analytical solution; it will probably be somewhere between 16.0 and 17.5 percent. However, greater accuracy may be achieved if the player rolls the dice 10,000 times.

Simulation with a physical analog model   Instead of experimenting with the dice the player can experiment with *a model* of the dice. A simple model can be constructed by taking six pieces of paper, each with the face of one side of a die (see Figure 14.3). Now, the pieces of paper

FIGURE 14.3
Simulated die

Papers in a hat

are placed into a hat. Without looking, pick one piece of paper.[5] This activity *simulates* one roll of a die. With another six pieces of paper and another hat the roll of two dice can be simulated. To simulate the experiment described in (*b*) above, all the player has to do is to return the pieces of paper into the hats and repeat the process 1,000 times.

The simulation just described may, in this case, be slower than the experimentation with the real dice. In general, it is usually faster. The big advantage, however, is that there is no need to have dice.

Simulation with a mathematical model   To speed up the simulation a mathematical model can be used. Each side of the die is represented by a number equal to the number of dots on that side (1 to 6). Then, instead of writing each number on a piece of paper, putting it in a hat and drawing numbers at random, a mechanism based on the probability distribution of the dots is used. This is the basis for the *Monte Carlo* method.

Monte Carlo

The Monte Carlo method

Monte Carlo is a technique that enables a simulation experiment in order to determine some probabilistic property of an event. This determination is executed by the use of *random sampling* applied to the components of the event.

---

[5] This procedure illustrates *random sampling* which is the selection of a sample from a population in a random manner.

Example: The Monte Carlo simulation of a dice game   Suppose that a Monte Carlo simulation is used to find out the chance of getting 7 in one roll of two dice. This is done as follows:

Step 1. Determine the probability distribution for the variable of interest   A distribution may be obtained by sampling the actual process, or through prior knowledge of the process. In this case the distribution is known to be ⅙ (16.67 percent) for each number of dots from 1 to 6. This information is given in the form of a table (Table 14.1).

TABLE 14.1
Probability of each side of a die

Number of dots on one die	Probability (percent)	Cumulative probability
1	16.67	16.67
2	16.67	33.34
3	16.67	50.00
4	16.67	66.67
5	16.67	83.34
6	16.67	100.00
Total	100.0	

Step 2. Convert the distribution to a cumulative distribution   In Table 14.1 the cumulative distribution is computed in the last column. This is done by adding the corresponding percentage, in the probability column, to the previous cumulative probability in the cumulative column. The information in the cumulative probability distribution column of Table 14.1 is plotted in Figure 14.4. The cumulative probabil-

Cumulate the distribution

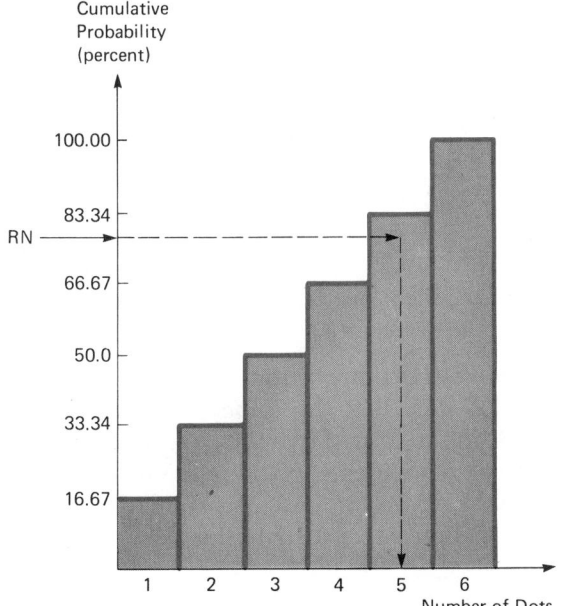

FIGURE 14.4
Cumulative distribution

ity is used for expedient assignment of "representative numbers," as shown next.

Step 3. Assign representative numbers to describe the various dots on a die Using the cumulative distribution as a guide, representative numbers are assigned to describe the number of dots on the die. This is done as follows: Since this case involves four-digit data (including the decimals), the numbers 0000 to 9999 shall be used (all four-digit numbers).

The assignment of representative numbers must be such that the *proportion* of the various states of nature (the number of dots in this case) be maintained. For example, the assignment of one dot on a die requires 1667 four-digit numbers. This is because the proportion of one dot is .1667 and out of *all* existing four-digit numbers (10,000), .1667 translates into 1667 (10,000 × .1667). The numbers to be used in each category are somewhat arbitrary. *Any* 1667 four-digit numbers can be used. For the sake of uniformity one can start with 0000. Starting with 0000 and counting 1667 numbers, one will end with the number 1666. However, since it does not make any difference which numbers are used, one can also use the numbers 0001 to 1667.

In assigning the representative numbers it is common to use, as an auxiliary instrument, the *cumulative* probability distribution. This is especially convenient if one starts with 0001, leaving the 0000 to be the last number assigned (*not* 10,000, which is a *five*-digit number.)

With one-digit numbers it is possible to start assignments with either 0 or 1; similarly with two-digits one can start with 00 or 01; in this text we start with 1, 01, 001, 0001, and so on, and end with 0, 00, 000, and 0000 because of the correspondence to the cumulative probability distribution. For example, Table 14.2 shows the cumulative probability

TABLE 14.2
The assignment of
representative numbers

Dots on a die	Cumulative distribution (%)	Assigned representative numbers
1	16.67	0001–1667
2	33.34	1668–3334
3	50.00	3335–5000
4	66.67	5001–6667
5	83.34	6668–8334
6	100.00	8335–0000

which is transferred from Table 14.1 together with the assigned numbers. Notice that the *upper limit* of the representative numbers (say 3334, in the case of two dots) corresponds to the cumulative distribution of two dots which is 33.34 percent. If one starts with 0, 00, and the like, then the upper limit of the assigned numbers is one less than the reading in the cumulative distribution.

Step 4. Generate random numbers (RN)[6] To generate random Generate RNs
numbers in this case means to select, at random, a sequence of four-digit
numbers from all four-digit numbers. These may be chosen through any
random process. For example, one can write each number between 0000
and 9999 on a piece of paper, mix them up in a container and draw one
piece of paper, read the number and return the paper to the container,
mix it up again and draw another number. A more convenient way,
however, is to use *a table of random numbers* (see Table C2 in
Appendix C). Another alternative is to generate such numbers with the
aid of a computer.

In any event the sequence of random numbers may look like this:
3422, 8153, 2597, 4650, 8341, and so on. Each number will be used to
simulate the roll of a die. To simulate 1,000 rolls of two dice a list of
2,000 four-digit random numbers is required.

Step 5. Predict a specific value of the variable of interest Each
random number (RN) corresponds to a unique value for the variable of
interest. The first random number 3422 is in the range 3335–5000 in
Table 14.2 and therefore represents three dots on the die. The second
RN 8153 is in the range 6668–8334 and corresponds to 5. The correspondence of some other random numbers is shown in Table 14.3. The same
procedure is illustrated graphically in Figure 14.4 for the random
number 8153, shown in Table 14.3.

Random numbers	3422	8153	2597	4650	8341
Dots on the die	3	5	2	3	6

TABLE 14.3
Correspondence of
random numbers

Step 6. The experiment Thus, instead of rolling a die 1,000 times,
one can look at a table of random numbers and find the corresponding
number of dots on a die. With a second set of random numbers the
results of 1,000 rolls of a second die can be simulated and the total dots
in a roll of two dice, for 1,000 rolls, can be computed by combining the
individual results (see Table 14.4).

All that is left is to count the number of 7s in the last row and find its
proportion in the 1,000 simulated rolls (each simulated roll is called a
run). A trial or a *run*

To perform this process manually may take as much time as rolling
the dice. However, a high-speed computer can simulate even one
million rolls of two dice in seconds.

---

[6] A random number is a number picked, at random, from a population of uniformly
distributed numbers. That is, each number in the population has an equal probability of
being selected.

TABLE 14.4
Simulation of two dice

Run number	1	2	3	4	5	$\cdots$	1,000
Die 1							
RN	3422	8153	2597	4650	8341	$\cdots$	
Dots	3	5	2	3	6	$\cdots$	
Die 2							
RN	7448	0012	4256	5119	6414	$\cdots$	
Dots	5	1	3	4	4	$\cdots$	
Total dots on two dice	8	6	5	7	10	$\cdots$	

The Monte Carlo steps—a summary

The steps in building a Monte Carlo simulation are as follows:

1. Describe the system and obtain the probability distributions of the relevant probabilistic elements of the system. This is a crucial step requiring intimate familiarity with the system. Frequently incorrect assumptions are made at this point which invalidate the rest of the simulation.
2. Define the appropriate measure(s) of system performance. If necessary, write it in the form of an equation(s).
3. Construct cumulative probability distributions for each of the stochastic elements.
4. Assign representative numbers in correspondence with the cumulative probability distributions.
5. For each probabilistic element, take a random sample (generate a number at random or pick one from a table of random numbers). This number points out what is happening in the system (what the measures of performance are) during a selected period of time, under assumed conditions.
6. Repeat step 5 until the measure of system performance "stabilizes" (discussed below).
7. Repeat steps 1–6 for various managerial policies. Decide on the appropriate managerial policy.

The above procedure will be demonstrated with an inventory control example.

An inventory control example

Marin's Service Station sells gasoline to boat owners. The demand for gasoline depends on weather conditions and fluctuates according to the following distribution:

Weekly demand (gallons)	Probability
2,000	.12
3,000	.23
4,000	.48
5,000	.17

Shipments arrive once a week. Since Marin's Service Station is located in a remote place, it must order and accept a fixed quantity of gasoline every week. Joe, the owner, faces the following problem: If he orders too small a quantity, he will lose, in terms of lost business and goodwill, 12 cents per gallon demanded and not provided. If he orders too large a quantity, he will have to pay 5 cents per gallon shipped back due to lack of storage. For each gallon sold he makes 10 cents profit. At the present time Joe receives 3,500 gallons at the beginning of each week before he opens for business. He feels that he should receive more, maybe 4,000 or even 4,500 gallons. The problem is to find the best order quantity.

This problem can be solved by trial and error. That is, the service station can actually order each quantity for, say, ten weeks, then compare the results. However, simulation can give an answer in a few minutes and a simulated loss is only a loss on paper.

Solution by simulation   To find the best ordering quantity it is necessary to compute the net profit (loss) for the existing order quantity (3,500 gallons) and for other possible order quantities. For example, 4,000 and 4,500 as suggested by Joe or any other desired figure (e.g., 3,600, 3,750, 3,800, and so on) may be tried. Each quantity is a proposed solution, and the first six out of seven steps must be executed for each; the seventh step then concludes the analysis.

Step 1. Describe the system and determine the probability distributions   Assume that today is the first day of the week, a shipment has just arrived, and there is now an inventory of 3,800 gallons. The tank's capacity is 5,500 gallons. The equations describing the system will be discussed later. At this point, it would be wise to check that the system does indeed operate as described above.

There is only one probability distribution in this case. It describes the demand. In more complicated Monte Carlo simulations there are several distributions involved.

Step 2. Decide on the measures of performance   The primary measure of performance is the *average daily profit* which is computed as (all quantities are in gallons):

10¢ × (sales) − 12¢ × (unsatisfied demand) − 5¢ × (quantity shipped back)

Several less important measures such as the average shortage are discussed at the end of this example.

Step 3. Compute cumulative probabilities   The cumulative probabilities are computed in Table 14.5.[7]

(A) Weekly demand	(B) Probability	(C) Cumulative probability	(D) Representative numbers (range)
2,000	.12	.12	01–12
3,000	.23	.35	13–35
4,000	.48	.83	36–83
5,000	.17	1.00	84–00

The cumulative probability column indicates the chance for a certain demand or less to occur. For example, there is a .35 chance for a demand of 3,000 or less.

Step 4. Assign representative ranges of numbers   For each possible demand a range of representative numbers is assigned in proportion to the probability distribution. For example, there is a chance of .12 for a demand of 2,000 to occur. Therefore, out of 100 numbers (all two-digit numbers),[8] 12 will be assigned to represent a demand of 2,000. An easy way of doing this is to assign the numbers 01, 02, 03, . . . , 12. (This information is entered in Table 14.5.) However, *any* 12 two-digit numbers can be assigned. Next, the demand of 3,000 is represented by 23 numbers, since it has a .23 chance of occurring. Since the numbers 01–12 have already been used it is logical to use the next 23 two-digit numbers 13–35.

Step 5. Generate random numbers and compute the system's performance   The first inventory system that will be considered is the current order policy of 3,500 gallons per week. For purposes of demonstration, step 5 is repeated here only ten times to simulate ten weeks. In reality it should continue until the measure of performance (average weekly profit) achieves *stability* as will be explained later. The detailed computations are shown in Table 14.6 and are executed as follows:

Column 1 designates the simulated week. In this example only ten weeks are simulated.

Column 2 is a list of random numbers (RN), taken from the right-hand side[9] of Table C2 in Appendix C. Here we are interested in two-

---

[7] Columns A and B are given; column C is computed from column B, and column D is assigned according to column C.

[8] In this case a two-digit random number is used. If the probability of demand were given by three-digit figures, for example, .115, then three-digit random numbers would have to be used.

[9] The table of RNs is entered at some random location, not necessarily the top-left corner, and the digits read in *any* direction: horizontally, downwards, diagonally, and so on. This procedure results in a set of random numbers because the table is generated in

TABLE 14.6
The simulation for ten weeks

(1)	(2)	(3) Inventory at beginning of week $I_1 = I_2 + 3{,}500$	(4) D Demand	(5) S Sold	(6) $I_2 = I_1 - S$ Inventory at end of week	(7) $U = D - I_1$ Unsatisfied demand	(8) B Shipped back	(9) Weekly profit	(10) Average weekly profit
Week number	RN								
1	32	3,800	3,000	3,000	800			300.00	300.00
2	08	4,300	2,000	2,000	2,300			200.00	250.00
3	46	5,500	4,000	4,000	1,500		300	385.00	295.00
4	92	5,000	5,000	5,000	0			500.00	346.25
5	69	3,500	4,000	3,500	0	500		290.00	335.00
6	71	3,500	4,000	3,500	0	500		290.00	327.50
7	29	3,500	3,000	3,000	500			300.00	323.57
8	46	4,000	4,000	4,000	0			400.00	333.12
9	80	3,500	4,000	3,500	0	500		290.00	328.33
10	14	3,500	3,000	3,000	500			300.00	325.50
Total	—	40,100	36,000	34,500	5,600	1,500	300	3,255.00	—
Avg./ week	—	4,010	3,600	3,450	560	150	30	325.50	325.50

digit numbers so the first and second of the four-digit numbers are used, starting with 32, then the next two, 08, and so on.

Column 3 represents the inventory at the beginning of each week (I_1). The column is computed by adding the 3,500-gallon shipment to the inventory at the end of the previous week (I_2). The *maximum inventory is 5,500* gallons, due to limited storage capacity. Thus, $I_1 = I_2 + 3{,}500$ (up to 5,500 as an upper limit).

Column 4 represents the forecast demand D based on Table 14.5. For example, the first RN, 32, falls in the representative range of 13–35, which is equivalent to a weekly demand of 3,000. Once the second column (RN) is generated, the entire fourth column can be computed quickly.

Column 5 represents the amount sold. Two cases may occur.

1. The demand D is equal to or smaller than the inventory on hand, I_1. In this case, sales equal demand (i.e., $S = D$ as in weeks 1, 2, 3, and 4).
2. Demand is *larger* than the inventory on hand. In this case, sales are limited to the inventory on hand I_1 (i.e., $S = I_1$). The difference between the demand and the inventory on hand $D - I_1$ is thus the unsatisfied demand, U (column 7). For example, in week 5 there is a

---

such a manner that every numeric location has the same chance (10 percent) of being occupied by a zero, or a one, or . . . or a nine. That is, no digit has a preferred chance of being included in the table *or* of occupying any particular location. The table thus represents a *uniform distribution* of the digits 0 through 9.

demand of 4,000 but an inventory of 3,500. Therefore, the sales are 3,500 and there is an unsatisfied demand of 500.

In column 6 the inventory at the end of each week, I_2, is listed. It is computed by subtracting the amount sold (column 5) from the beginning inventory (column 3), $I_2 = I_1 - S$.

Column 7 designates the unsatisfied demand, U. This column shows the difference between the demand and the beginning inventory whenever demand is larger (e.g., in week 5). Thus, $U = D - I_1$.

Column 8 designates the amount shipped back, B. Such a situation occurs when the "end-of-the-week inventory" plus the shipment (3,500 gallons in the system under study) exceed the 5,500-gallon tank capacity. In this case the excess supply is shipped back and the beginning inventory is 5,500. For example, in week 3 the shipment of 3,500 added to the weekend inventory of week 2 of 2,300 gives a total of 5,800 gallons. Therefore, 5,800 − 5,500 = 300 gallons are shipped back.

Column 9. The measure of performance in this problem is profit. The profit is calculated, every week, according to the formula:

$$\$ \text{ profit} = .10S - .12U - .05B$$

For example:

In week 1: $S = 3,000, U = 0, B = 0$. Profit = $.1(3,000) = \$300$.
In week 3: $S = 4,000, U = 0, B = 300$. Profit = $.1(4,000) - .05(300) = \$385$.

Column 10. The *average* weekly profit at any week is computed by totaling the weekly profits up to that week (cumulative profit) and dividing it by the number of weeks.

For example:

In week 3: Cumulative profit = $300 + $200 + $385 = $885.
Weekly average: $885/3 = $295.

Step 6. Stabilization of the simulation process Examination of column 10 in Table 14.6 indicates that the process, although close to stabilizing, has not yet stabilized (see Figure 14.5). That is, the *average* weekly profit is still fluctuating. Therefore, the simulation of ten weeks (labeled ten *runs*) is insufficient. Notice, however, that after seven weeks the differences are becoming very small. When the difference between consecutive average weekly profits becomes insignificant, the process is said to have "stabilized."

When to stop?

If there exist several measures of performance, then the stabilization analysis must be performed for *each* measure. Only after stabilization is achieved in *all* measures of performance (or at least in *all important* measures) should the simulation be stopped.

Computing the measures of performance The simulation performed thus far indicated an average weekly profit of $325.50 in a

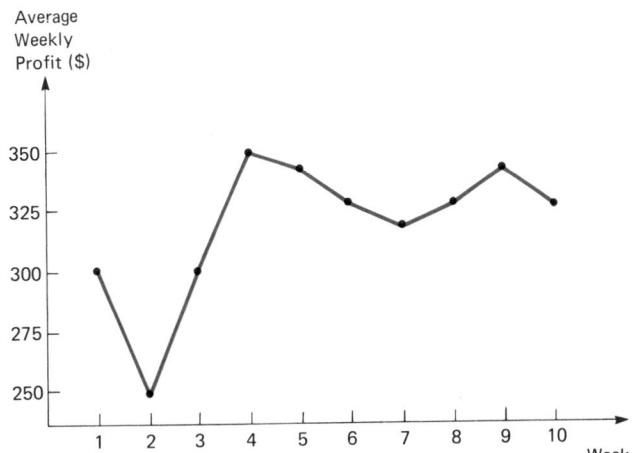

FIGURE 14.5
Stabilization of the
simulation process

process which had not yet completely stabilized. In addition to total profit, some other measures of performance can be computed.[10]

a. *The probability of running short and the average shortage.* In three out of the ten weeks there was an unsatisfied demand. Therefore, there is a 3/10 = 30 percent chance of running out of stock. The average shortage, per week, is 1,500/10 = 150 gallons.

b. *The probability of shipping back and the average quantity shipped back.* In one out of the ten weeks some gasoline was shipped back. On the average there is a 1/10 = 10 percent chance of shipping back an average amount of 300/10 = 30 gallons per week.

Multiple measures of performance

c. *The average demand.* The average weekly demand is computed as 3,600 which is close to the expected value of the demand (from Table 14.5) of 3,700. (In a stabilized process these two numbers will be very close.)

d. *The average beginning inventory* is computed as 4,010 gallons.

e. *The average weekly sales* are computed as 3,450 gallons.

f. *The average ending inventory* is computed as 560 gallons.

Step 7. Find the best ordering policy Steps 5 and 6 are now repeated for other ordering policies in order to find the best. In the example just presented the ordered quantity Q was 3,500; other values of Q (e.g., 3,300; 3,700; 4,000) should next be considered. Each Q constitutes an independent system for which the various measures of effectiveness such as average profit, average sales, and unsatisfied demand are computed.

In this case, the most important measure of performance has been assumed to be the average profit and therefore the system with the

---

[10] The number of simulation runs, which was close to sufficient for the average profit, is still too small for the other measures of performance.

highest average profit will be selected (lack of space prevents us from conducting the computations). In other systems, two or more measures of performance may have to be compared using a multiple objective method such as presented in Chapter 4.

A waiting line example

The city of Miami Beach is studying their Tourist Information Center. At the present time the center is manned by one employee and is open from 9:00 A.M. to 5:00 P.M. The time now is 9:00 A.M. and one tourist has just stepped in.

The length of service required by tourists vary according to the following probability distribution:

Length of service (minutes)	Probability (percent)
3	15.6
4	28.7
5	36.2
6	19.5

Tourists arrive at the center according to the following probability distribution:

Time between two consecutive arrivals (inter-arrival time, minutes)	Probability (percent)
3	20.2
4	23.6
5	31.2
6	18.4
7	6.6

Find:
a. The average waiting time per tourist, in minutes.
b. The percentage of time that the employee is busy (the utilization).
c. The average number of tourists in the center.
d. The probability of finding two tourists in the center.

Analysis

This is a waiting line problem, but it cannot be solved by the models of Chapter 13 because the assumptions of Poisson arrivals and exponential service times do not hold.

For illustrative purposes we will simulate ten[11] arriving tourists using the following random numbers for arrivals: 826, 058, 489, 643, 781, 321, 590, 187, 962, 608, and the following random numbers for service: 242, 318, 876, 408, 630, 027, 716, 203, 130, 297.

---

[11] The simulation *should* continue until stabilization of the measures of performance is achieved.

The simulation

Step 1. Assign representative numbers for the two distributions:

For arrivals:

Inter-arrival time	Probability	Representative numbers
3	20.2	000–201
4	23.6	202–437
5	31.2	438–749
6	18.4	750–933
7	6.6	934–999

For service:

Time in minutes	Probability	Representative numbers
3	15.6	000–155
4	28.7	156–442
5	36.2	443–804
6	19.5	805–999

Step 2 Generate arrival and service times (in minutes). This is done in Table 14.7.

TABLE 14.7
Simulation of tourist information center

Tourist number	Arrivals			Service				Measures of performance		
	RN (1)	Inter-arrival time (2)	Time arriving (3)	RN (4)	Length (min.) (5)	Start (6)	End (7)	Wait (8)	Idle (9)	No. in center (10)
1	—	—	9:00	242	4	9:00	9:04	—	—	1
2	826	6	9:06	318	4	9:06	9:10	—	2	1
3	058	3	9:09	876	6	9:10	9:16	1	—	2
4	489	5	9:14	408	4	9:16	9:20	2	—	2
5	643	5	9:19	630	5	9:20	9:25	1	—	2
6	781	6	9:25	027	3	9:25	9:28	—	—	1
7	321	4	9:29	716	5	9:29	9:34	—	1	1
8	590	5	9:34	203	4	9:34	9:38	—	—	1
9	187	3	9:37	130	3	9:38	9:41	1	—	2
10	962	7	9:44	297	4	9:44	9:48	—	3	1

Total (performance):   5
Average per tourist: 5/10

Explanation

Table 14.7 is divided into 11 columns: The first 4 deal with arrivals, the next 4 with service, and the last 3 with measures of performance. The time of the first arrival is given as 9:00. Next a random number is picked to predict the length of service (242 is in the 156–422 range, meaning four minutes of service). The second tourist is predicted to arrive six minutes after the first one since the first RN of 826 is in the range of 750 to 933 which corresponds to six minutes inter-arrival time.

In a similar manner we compute all arrival and service times. Next, we compute the starting time for service (column 6). If the employee is busy with the previous customer, the tourist will have to wait, as happened to tourist #3 who waited from 9:09 until 9:10. If no one is in the center the employee is idle, as is the situation between 9:04 and 9:06.

Analysis of the measures of performance

The average waiting time For the 10 arriving tourists only 5 minutes of waiting were recorded. Thus, the average waiting time per tourist was 0.5 minutes.

The utilization of the service facility The center was simulated during 48 minutes (from 9:00 to 9:48). During this period there were 6 minutes of idle time; thus, $48 - 6 = 42$ minutes of utilization or $42/48 = 87.5$ percent utilization.

The average number of tourists in the center During 6 minutes there were no tourists in the center, while during 5 minutes there were two (during times of waiting). During the remaining 37 minutes ($48 - 6 - 5 = 37$) there was 1 tourist.

On the average, there were:

$$\frac{0(6) + 1(37) + 2(5)}{48} = .98 \text{ tourists}$$

This is a weighted average that corresponds to L in Chapter 13.

The probability of finding two tourists in the center This situation happened in 5 out of the 48 minutes, or 10.4 percent.

The role of computers and flowcharts in simulation

Since simulation models involve as few simplifications of the real system as possible, then the function expressing the internal relationships is frequently quite complex. In addition, each simulation study involves large numbers of runs, as required for stabilization. On top of that, the entire simulation must be repeated each time a change is made in some of the input data. As a descriptive tool it is necessary to frequently check dozens of different system configurations. The end result of all the above is the necessity of a huge computational effort. Therefore computers are desired and frequently necessary for conducting simulation studies.

Simulation problems can be programmed for computers with relative ease, since there is no need to develop algorithms or optimize functions. In order to help the programming task, a flowchart of a simulation problem can be developed. A flowchart is a schematic

The need for a
computer

presentation of all computational activities used in the simulation but
written in symbolic language. Its major objective is to help the computer
programmer in writing the computer program. Figure 14.6 shows a
flowchart for the inventory problem simulated earlier.

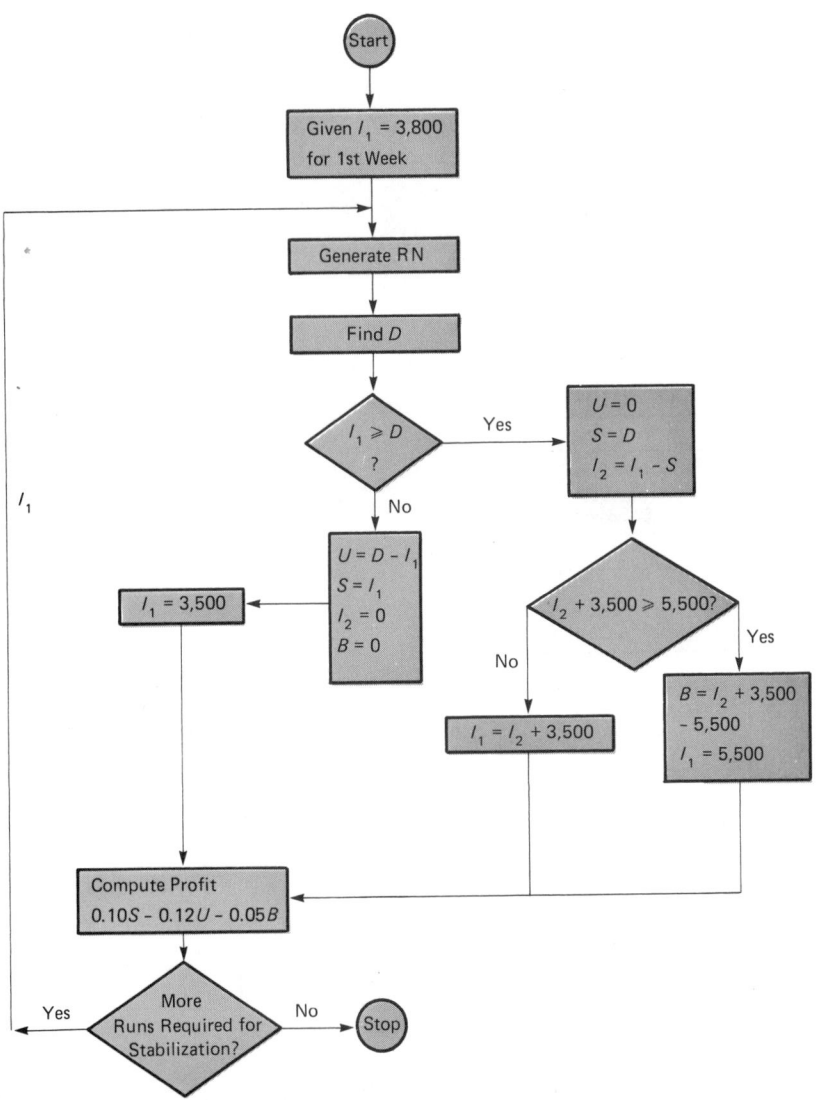

FIGURE 14.6
Flow diagram for the
inventory example

Summary

The basic idea of simulation is to utilize a mechanism that will
enable experimentation on a mathematical model that closely
resembles the real-life system.

Simulation is used mainly in places where normative models cannot be used. Either they cannot be used because the managerial problem is so complex that it is impossible to build a normative mathematical model that will adequately describe it, or the complexity may prevent us from solving the model.

Monte Carlo is a type of simulation where experiments are conducted through randomly selected events which exhibit predetermined probabilistic properties. Using random sampling, Monte Carlo generates chance outcomes which then are used to determine

FIGURE 14.7
Monte Carlo simulation process

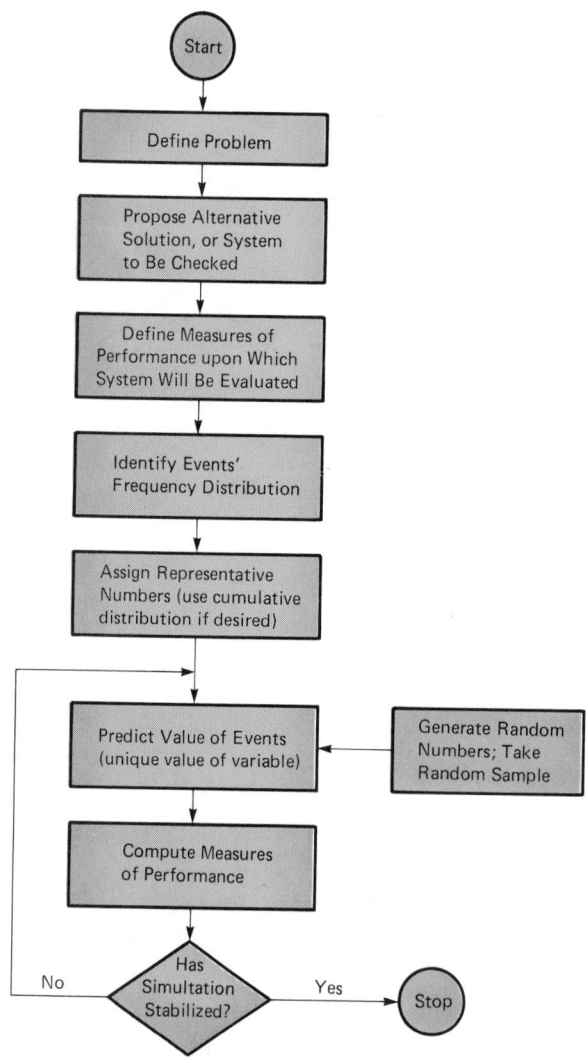

measures of performance. The Monte Carlo simulation process is summarized in Figure 14.7.

In addition to Monte Carlo, which is the main subject of this chapter, there exist four other types of simulation: artificial intelligence, heuristic programming, operational games, and system simulation.

14.7   PROBLEMS FOR PART A

1. Identify which types of simulation can be used in each of the following tasks.
   a. Writing poetry.
   b. Analyzing biblical passages to determine the author.
   c. Determining the effect of monetary policy on a national economy.
   d. Locating the most profitable sites for a chain of restaurants.
   e. Learning how to run a blast furnace.
   f. Imitating a controller's bond purchasing decision.

2. Distinguish between artificial intelligence and heuristics.

3. Give some examples of heuristics.

4. How can a "hospital game" make a nurse aware of interdependencies in her hospital which she never knew existed?

5. You are looking for syrup in a new grocery store. What heuristics do you employ?

6. You have the following weekend jobs facing you:

   Hanging a picture.
   Mowing a lawn.
   Walking a dog.
   Tuning up the car.
   Cleaning out the garage.

   In what order would you choose to do these? What heuristic decision rules did you employ to choose this order?

7. The community in South Miami is composed of 15 percent blacks, 40 percent Cubans, and 45 percent "others." Use random numbers to indicate the races of the first ten people from the community to enter a room. Use the following RNs: 23, 74, 50, 96, 82, 79, 40, 06, 67, 31.

8. There is a 30 percent chance that a company will sell 100 units, 50 percent that they will sell 110 units, and 20 percent chance they will sell 120 units. The profit per unit is $14.
   a. Use simulation to find the average profit. (Use 15 trials: random numbers are: 4, 7, 3, 6, 0, 9, 8, 2, 1, 1, 8, 6, 5, 7, 3, 0, 9, 4, 6, 8. Start the representative numbers from 1.)
   b. Compare it to the results of the expected value.

9. The U.S. Department of Agriculture estimates that the yearly yield of limes per acre is distributed as follows:

Yield in bushels/acre	Probability
350	.10
400	.18
450	.50
500	.22

   The estimated average price per bushel is $7.20.
   a. Find the expected per acre lime crop yield generated over the next ten years. (Use simulation; compare to the theoretical expected value results. Use RNs: 37, 23, 92, 01, 69, 50, 72, 12, 46, 81, 31, 89. Start the representative numbers from 00.)
   b. Find the average yearly revenue.

10. The following information is known to you:

    A rainy day in Miami has a 40 percent chance of being followed by a rainy day. A nonrainy day has an 80 percent chance of being followed by a nonrainy day.
    a. Use simulation to predict what the weather is going to be over the next 20 days. (Today is a nonrainy day.) Use two-digit RNs from Table C2 in Appendix C. Start at the top

left and go down the columns. Start the representative numbers from 01.

b. Based on the information collected in part (a), estimate the number of rainy days in Miami in one year (365 days).

11. A company has two cars. Car 1 is in use 40 percent of the time, and car 2, 30 percent of the time. The president wishes to go somewhere; what is the chance he will have a car available?

a. Draw a simulation flowchart.

b. Manually simulate for 20 periods. (Use the following RNs: 7, 4, 9, 8, 4, 8, 8, 2, 0, 1, 5, 5, 0, 1, 4, 7, 0, 3, 2, 2, 7, 1, 0, 9, 8, 1, 4, 5, 4, 8, 6, 1, 2. Start the representative numbers from 0.)

c. Find the theoretical answer (use conditional probabilities) and compare with the simulation results.

d. Show graphically the stabilization process for 20 runs. What are your conclusions?

e. If a company car is unavailable, a cab is used with an average cost of $15 per ride. Find the annual cost if the president makes 100 trips per year.

12. The B & T car dealership has a salesperson that sells 13 cars, on the average, each week. The sales statistics show that of all cars sold, 20 percent are small, 45 percent are of medium size, and the remainder are large. The profit from the sale of the cars and the commission paid are shown in the following table:

Type of car	Price per car ($)	Per car profit to dealership	Per car commission paid to salesperson
Small	5200	$310	$62
Intermediate	6050	425	70
Large	7800	500	80

Find, with the aid of simulation (simulate for 1 week):

a. The size of the last car sold during the week.

b. The commission the salesperson will make in an average week.

c. The total dollar sales volume generated in 1 month (4 weeks).

d. The chance of selling two large cars in a row.

e. The weekly profit to the car dealership.

Use the following RNs:
08, 48, 16, 78, 37, 91, 82, 31, 54, 25, 69, 94, 41. Start the representative numbers from 00.

13. A newscarrier sells newspapers and tries to maximize profit. The exact number of papers purchased daily by customers can't be predicted. An elaborate time study was performed on the demand each day, and the following table was developed (for 125 days):

Demand per day	Number of times
15	10
16	20
17	42
18	31
19	12
20	10
Total	125

The following ordering policy was used by the newscarrier: The amount ordered each day is equal to the quantity demanded the preceding day. Assume that demand the previous day was 18.

A paper costs the carrier 15 cents; the carrier sells it for 30 cents. Unsold papers are returned, and the carrier is credited 8 cents per paper out of the 15 cents paid. An unsatisfied customer is estimated to cost 7 cents in goodwill.

Determine the average daily profit if the newscarrier follows the ordering policy. Also, determine the average loss of goodwill. Simulate for 15 days; use three-digit RNs: 782, 430, 922, 871, 477, 838, 872, 276, 198, 520, 076, 452, 702, 042, 297. Start the representative numbers from 00.

14. ABC Corporation stocks small motors for their textile machines. The weekly demand for the motors is according to the following distribution:

Demand	5	6	7	8
Probability	.2	.3	.4	.1

Motors arrive at the end of each week (after the plant is closed for the weekend) either six in a package (60 percent chance) or ten in a package (40 percent chance).

Simulate 15 weeks of operation to find:

a. The average inventory on hand (at the beginning of the week).
b. The probability of stockout (in terms of number of times).
c. The inventory at the end of 15 weeks (before the last shipment arrives).
d. Is the process stabilized (check for the inventory level situation)?
e. Comment on the existing inventory policy.

Assume:
1. The current inventory, at the beginning of week 1, is 5.
2. Unsatisfied demand is provided from stock whenever a supply arrives.
3. Use RN for demand: 7, 8, 1, 6, 9, 0, 5, 9, 3, 2, 5, 4, 0, 4, 1, 7, 9, 3, 8, 2

For arrivals: 3, 1, 8, 0, 6, 7, 2, 4, 9, 0, 2, 8, 3, 5, 1, 9, 5, 7, 0, 4

Start the representative numbers from 1.

15. Customers arrive at a service facility according to the following distribution:

Number of arrivals per hour	Probability
4	.22
5	.68
6	.10

The service time is always exactly 11 minutes. The facility opens for service at 8:00 A.M. At the opening time the first customer is there, waiting.

Simulate for 15 customers. Start the representative numbers with 00. RNS: 73, 06, 62, 45, 93, 15, 69, 54, 37, 81, 26, 18, 81, 96, 31.
Find:
a. Average waiting time, W_q.

b. Average time in the system, W.
c. Average number of customers in the system.
d. The utilization ratio.

16. An airline has 15 daily flights from Miami to New York. The average profit per flight is $6,000. Each flight requires one pilot. Flights that do not have a pilot are cancelled (passengers are transferred to other airlines). Since pilots get sick from time to time, the airline has a policy of keeping 3 reserve pilots on stand-by to replace sick pilots. The probability distribution of sick pilots on any given day is given as:

Number sick in one day	Probability
0	.20
1	.25
2	.20
3	.15
4	.10
5	.10

Use Monte Carlo simulation to simulate ten days. Use the following random numbers:
24, 57, 77, 68, 64, 88, 98, 50, 91, 55.
Start assigning representative numbers from 01.

Note: The answers to the questions must be derived by *simulation* and not by statistics. The reserve pilots are drawn from a pool (so they cannot be considered to be sick).
Find:
a. The average daily utilization of the reserve pilots (in percent).
b. The average daily lost revenue due to cancelled flights caused by lack of pilots (in dollars).
c. The chance that one or more flights will be cancelled in a day.
d. The utilization of the aircraft (in percent).

PART B: EXTENSIONS

14.8 HEURISTIC SEQUENCING OF JOBS THROUGH A MACHINE

An interesting sequencing problem occurs when several different jobs must be processed through a single production facility such as a printing press, boring mill, or a computer. The facility must be shut down after finishing each job in order to prepare it for the next job. The time periods that the facility is shut down are frequently referred to as "setup" or "changeover" times. While the processing time of the jobs is usually independent of the sequence used, the setup times may depend on both the job being removed and the job being introduced. The setup times depend on the physical similarities between the jobs; similar jobs require less changeover time. Management desires to sequence the jobs that are required to be processed in such a way that the total setup time will be minimized.

The cost of setups

The difficulty in solving such a problem is that the sequencing can be done in many different ways; to be exact, n different jobs can be sequenced in $n!$ different ways.[12] For example: If there are only ten jobs, there will be $10! = 3,628,800$ different sequencing alternatives.

Unfortunately there is no simple analytical model that can tell us which sequence is the best. One way to find the best sequence is to compare all alternatives (complete enumeration). The complete enumeration of as few as 20 jobs may take, even with the aid of computers, a long time. Heuristic rules, although they do not guarantee an optimal solution, can usually identify a satisfactory solution very quickly.

Example

Assume the following situation.[13] A manager has three jobs assigned to a printing press in a certain day. The press is currently empty. The setup times for the jobs are indicated in Table 14-8. In this

TABLE 14.8
Setup times in minutes

From job	To job 1	2	3
Empty	25	20	30
1	0	35	20
2	50	0	45
3	45	10	0

---

[12] $n!$ (called n factorial) means $1 \times 2 \times 3 \ldots \times n$. For example, $4! = 1 \times 2 \times 3 \times 4 = 24$.

[13] The example is based on Gavett [3].

simplified case there are only six possible alternatives, therefore, it is possible to enumerate all of them rather easily. The results are given in Table 14.9.

TABLE 14.9
Enumeration results

Sequence job number	Setup times	Total (minutes)	
1 – 2 – 3	25 + 35 + 45	105	
1 – 3 – 2	25 + 20 + 10	55	←Minimum
2 – 3 – 1	20 + 45 + 45	110	
2 – 1 – 3	20 + 50 + 20	90	
3 – 1 – 2	30 + 45 + 35	110	
3 – 2 – 1	30 + 10 + 50	90	

By complete enumeration it is shown that the sequence 1 – 3 – 2 is the best, with a minimum total setup time of 55 minutes.

The next best rule

In many practical cases workers do not enumerate the alternatives, even when only a small number of jobs is involved. Instead they use an interesting rule of thumb, called the next best rule. According to this rule, the worker sorts all jobs and selects, as the first job to be processed, the job that requires the least setup time from the "empty" condition (job 2 in the example with only 20 minutes setup time). Then, the employee searches for that job which will require the *least* setup time from job 2 (job 3 in this case) and so on, until all jobs are sequenced.

In this case the selected sequence 2 – 3 – 1 will result in 110 minutes of setup time, a solution which is far from the best. On the average, however, as studies by Gavett [3] show, a savings of 8 percent to 76 percent, over a random selection, can be realized. Much *better results* were achieved by using another rule: the next best with adjustments.

The next best with adjustments

According to this rule, the original setup time matrix is modified in such a way that the minimum setup time in each column is subtracted from all other setup times in that column. (The zero values from a job to itself are not considered.) This calculation is shown in Figure 14.8.

Once the reduced matrix is constructed, the regular next-best rule is employed on it. Thus, from "empty" the least setup time to 1 now becomes 0. From 1 the least setup time is to number 3, from 3 one goes to 2. The solution is sequence 1 – 3 – 2 with 55 minutes of setup time (the optimal solution).

Both rules are relatively simple and can be used manually by the employees themselves.

FIGURE 14.8

Decision matrix using "next best with adjustments" rule

From	To 1	2	3		To 1	2	3		To 1	2	3
Empty	25	20	30		$25 - 25 = 0$	$20 - 10 = 10$	$30 - 20 = 10$		0	10	10
Job 1	0	35	20		X	$35 - 10 = 25$	$20 - 20 = 0$		X	25	0
Job 2	50	0	45		$50 - 25 = 25$	X	$45 - 20 = 25$		25	X	25
Job 3	45	10	0		$45 - 25 = 20$	$10 - 10 = 0$	X		20	0	X

Original matrix ⟶ Reduction process ⟶ Resultant (reduced) matrix

14.9   A BUSINESS GAME

A business game typically uses an electronic computer to simulate an industry in which there are a few companies (oligopoly) manufacturing and selling one product. Participants are organized into teams which manage their hypothetical companies in competition with each other. Decisions are made at regular intervals (e.g., "quarterly" decisions require 45 minutes in the game) and the outcome is determined by the interactions between the teams and the framework of the economic structure programmed into the computer. The models are basically deterministic, but the results may also be affected by probabilistic elements since chance events and luck are also sometimes programmed into the process.

Teams usually make the following types of decisions:

- Price of product.
- Marketing budget.
- Research and development budget.
- Maintenance budget.
- Production volume scheduled.
- Investment in plant and equipment.
- Purchase of materials.
- Dividends declared.
- Financing decisions.

A typical decision sheet, filled out by each of the firms each decision period (usually simulating a quarter of a year) is shown in Figure 14.9. When decisions have been made, they are punched on

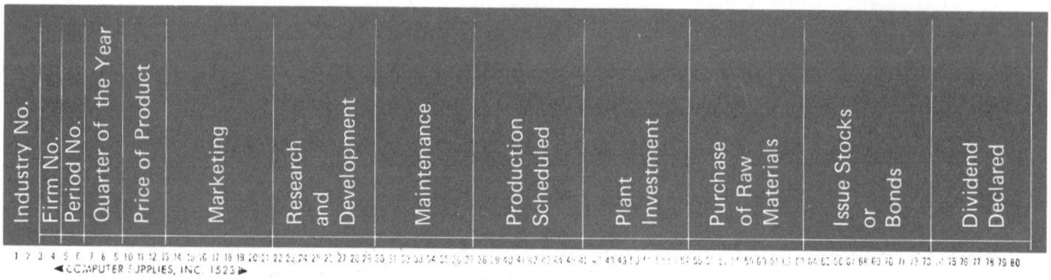

FIGURE 14.9
Decision sheet
(80-column punch card)

FIGURE 14.10
Typical game printout

```
                          EXECUTIVE GAME
MODEL 2 PERIOD  3 JFM PRICE INDEX 101.2 FORECAST,ANNUAL CHANGE  5.5 O/O
SEAS.INDEX   90 NEXT QTR.  100  ECON.INDEX  110 FORECAST,NEXT QTR.  113
```

```
                INFORMATION      ON      COMPETITORS
            PRICE          DIVIDEND   SALES VOLUME        NET PROFIT
```

	PRICE	DIVIDEND	SALES VOLUME	NET PROFIT
FIRM 1	$ 6.19	$ 100000	794383	$ 150120
FIRM 2	$ 6.30	$ 200000	950000	$ 335424
FIRM 3	$ 6.20	$ 0	350091	$ -53503
FIRM 4	$ 6.15	$ 200000	1314660	$ 275325
FIRM 5	$ 6.10	$ 100000	741021	$ 39519
FIRM 6	$ 6.15	$ 100000	462704	$ 53713
FIRM 7	$ 6.15	$ 150000	522485	$ -34884
FIRM 8	$ 6.10	$ 70000	519704	$ 22190
FIRM 9	$ 6.15	$ 100000	830413	$ 179052

```
                    FIRM 7 5
             OPERATING STATEMENTS
MARKET POTENTIAL                       741021
SALES VOLUME                           741021
PERCENT SHARE OF INDUSTRY SALES            11
PRODUCTION,THIS QUARTER                820000
INVENTORY,FINISHED GOODS               147336
PLANT CAPACITY,NEXT QUARTER            431593
                    INCOME STATEMENT
RECEIPTS,SALES REVENUE                             $   4520230
EXPENSES,MARKETING                 $    900000
  RESEARCH AND DEVELOPMENT               200000
  ADMINISTRATION                         419762
  MAINTENANCE                            120000
  LABOR(COST/UNIT EX.OVERTIME $ 1.43)   1176310
  MATERIALS CONSUMED(COST/UNIT  1.55)   1269597
  REDUCTION,FINISHED GOODS INV.         -239218
  DEPRECIATION(2.500 O/O)                221630
  FINISHED GOODS CARRYING COSTS          74218
  RAW MATERIALS CARRYING COSTS           67590
  ORDERING COSTS                         50373
  SHIFTS CHANGE COSTS                   100747
  PLANT INVESTMENT EXPENSES                   0
  FINANCING CHARGES AND PENALTIES             0
  SUNDRIES                               90348    4447357
PROFIT BEFORE INCOME TAX                            72873
INCOME TAX(IN.TX.CR.  7 O/O,SUP.TAX   0 O/O)        33354
NET PROFIT AFTER INCOME TAX                         39519
DIVIDENDS PAID                                     100000
ADDITION TO OWNERS EQUITY                          -60481
                    CASH FLOW
RECEIPTS,SALES REVENUE                             $   4520230
DISBURSEMENTS,CASH EXPENSE         $   3195348
  INCOME TAX                             33354
  DIVIDENDS PAID                        100000
  PLANT INVESTMENT                            0
  MATERIALS PURCHASED                   1350000    4678702
ADDITION TO CASH ASSETS                           -158472
                    FINANCIAL STATEMENT
NET ASSETS,CASH                                    $   204863
INV. VALUE,FINISHED GOODS                              445307
INVENTORY VALUE,MATERIALS                             1352205
PLANT BOOK VALUE(REPLACE.VAL.$   8912324)            8643557
OWNERS EQUITY(ECONOMIC EQUITY  10914699)           10645932
```

Source: Reprinted from R. C. Henshaw and J. R. Jackson, *The Executive Game*, 3d ed. (Homewood, Ill.: Richard D. Irwin, 1978). © 1978 by Richard D. Irwin, Inc.

cards which are fed into a computer or they are typed directly into an "on-line" computer system. The computer, having been programmed to simulate the industry's operations, computes the financial and operational results and prints this information, as well as other useful reports, for each firm, each quarter, as in Figure 14.10. In addition there is an "annual report" after every four quarters.

After a certain number of periods have been simulated, the game is stopped and the instructor discusses the policies used by the firms, their results, the techniques of analysis employed or employable, and so on. A number of specialized games exist for financial management, banking, marketing management, production management, and maintenance, to name just a few.

14.10   SIMULATION OF WAITING LINE PROBLEMS

Simulation for waiting lines

One of the most useful roles of Monte Carlo simulation is for solving waiting line problems. Analytical solutions, such as demonstrated in Chapter 13, become extremely difficult, or even impossible, when the waiting line system increases slightly in complexity; for example, when the arrival or the service rate does not follow a standard distribution (such as the Poisson), or when priorities are considered. As an example, consider a tool crib problem.

The tool crib problem

Manufacturing firms use a central tool crib to lend out tools to employees. Consider a typical situation with one clerk in the tool crib. Two different types of employees are served by it: production employees and maintenance employees. Each has a different rate of arrival, as shown in Table 14.10. Note that the arrival rates do not follow standard distributions. The table also shows the assigned numbers which are required for the simulation. The number of employees in both groups is large enough so that the source may be assumed infinite.

TABLE 14.10
The arrival rates

Production Employees:			Maintenance Employees:		
Time between arrivals (in hours)	*Probability*	*Assigned numbers*	*Time between arrivals (in hours)*	*Probability*	*Assigned numbers*
.2	.1	0	.4	.25	01–25
.3	.1	1	.6	.60	26–85
.5	.4	2–5	1.0	.15	86–00
.8	.3	6–8			
1.0	.1	9			

The production employees have priority over the maintenance employees; that is, a production employee will always be placed at the head of the waiting line. However, if a maintenance employee is being served, the service will continue uninterrupted (i.e., the production employee has a regular priority and not a "preemptive" priority over the maintenance employee).

Table 14.11 gives the distribution of service times, assuming that service can take only three time values: .1, .2, and .3 hours. The table also includes the assigned numbers required for the simulation.

Length of service time (in hours)	Probability	Assigned numbers
.1	⅓	001–333
.2	⅓	334–666
.3	⅓	667–999

TABLE 14.11
Service times

Note that an *exact* duplication of the ⅓ to ⅓ to ⅓ ratio is achieved by assigning only 999 out of all 1000 3 digit numbers.[14] The assignment of 3 digits was arbitrary in this case (one digit is actually sufficient).

The tool crib clerk earns $4 per hour. A production employee earns $5 per hour, and a maintenance employee earns $6 per hour. The problem is to find the optimal number of clerks in the tool crib. Management also wishes to know if the existing priority system should be maintained.

Solution

Simulating the arrivals   For the purpose of presentation, the time between arrivals of 15 employees of each type is simulated, using random numbers from Table C2 in Appendix C. The results are shown in Table 14.12. The table also indicates the clock time of arrivals.

For example, assume that employee 1 arrived upon opening at 7:00 A.M. Then, for arrival 2 the one-digit RN 5 is selected as the first RN from Table C2. According to Table 14.10 for production employees, an RN of 5 is in the assigned numbers 2–5 which corresponds to .5 hours between arrivals. Since the process starts at 7:00 then the clock time is 7:30. The generation of arrivals then continues. For the third production employee an RN of 2 is selected. The equivalent time between arrivals is again .5 hours, and the clock time is therefore 7:30 + 30 minutes = 8:00. The process continues for as many arrivals as desired (15 in the example). Once the generation of the production employees is completed, the

---

[14] If we do not assign some numbers (such as 000 in this case), then when such numbers appear as RNs they are skipped over.

TABLE 14.12
Generating arrivals
(number 1 arrives at time
zero)

| Arrival number | Production employees | | | Maintenance employees | | |
	Random number	Time between arrivals (hours)	Clock time	Random number	Time between arrivals (hours)	Clock time
2	5	.5	7:30	52	.6	7:36
3	2	.5	8:00	02	.4	8:00
4	0	.2	8:12	73	.6	8:36
5	2	.5	8:42	48	.6	9:12
6	7	.8	9:30	06	.4	9:36
7	3	.5	10:00	15	.4	10:00
8	4	.5	10:30	94	1.0	11:00
9	8	.8	11:18	12	.4	11:24
10	0	.2	11:30	95	1.0	12:24
11	6	.8	12:18	87	1.0	1:24
12	1	.3	12:36	04	.4	1:48
13	5	.5	1:06	99	1.0	2:48
14	9	1.0	2:06	40	.6	3:24
15	4	.5	2:36	98	1.0	4:24

generation of the maintenance employee arrivals is conducted. The only difference in the process is the use of two-digit RNs instead of one-digit RNs.

Simulating the length of service The lengths of service are generated using three-digit RNs and Table 14.11. The process is similar to the generation of arrivals. The results are shown in Table 14.12 where 30 services are generated. A different set of random numbers is used this time.

Simulating the process Figure 14.11 presents what happened during the first six hours of operation. Assume that at 7:00 a production

FIGURE 14.11
The first six hours

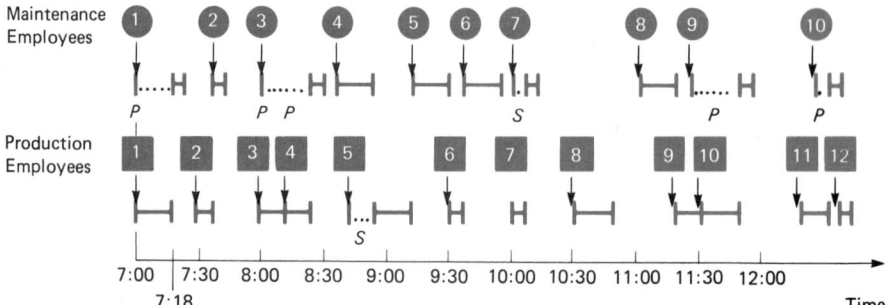

O = Maintenance Employee
□ = Production Employee
.... = Wait
— = Being Served
P = Wait Due to Priority
S = Wait Due to Service (busy)
| = Beginning or End of Service, or Arrival

employee and a maintenance employee are waiting at the crib. The production employee is served first (has priority). Table 14.13 indicates (based on the first random number of 782) a service of .3 hours (18 minutes) from 7:00 to 7:18. During this time the maintenance employee waits. The second production employee arrives after .5 hours at 7:30 (according to Table 14.12).

TABLE 14.13
Generating 30 services

Service number	RN	Length of service (hours)
1	782	.3
2	309	.1
3	194	.1
4	308	.1
5	421	.2
6	392	.2
7	283	.1
8	682	.3
9	871	.3
10	744	.3
11	244	.1
12	773	.3
13	264	.1
14	283	.1
15	879	.3
16	978	.3
17	477	.2
18	752	.3
19	016	.1
20	579	.2
21	260	.1
22	241	.1
23	643	.2
24	056	.1
25	861	.3
26	565	.2
27	029	.1
28	970	.3
29	958	.3
30	713	.3

The first maintenance employee will start receiving service at 7:18. This service will be completed at 7:24 (random number of 309 for a service time of .1 hours = 6 minutes, in Table 14.13). The second production employee arrives at 7:30 and is served from 7:30 to 7:36. The second maintenance employee arrives at 7:36 (random number 52 indicates that the second maintenance employee arrives .6 hours after the first one, Table 14.12). Since the tool crib is free he (or she) is served immediately (length of service is .1 hours as per Table 14.13). The third production employee and the third maintenance employee arrive at 8:00

(check Table 14.12 for computed time of arrival). Due to priority the production employee is served first. Production employee 3 is served for .2 hours, 8:00 to 8:12 (according to Table 14.13). Then production employee 4 arrives (check Table 14.12) and due to priority he (or she) is served before maintenance employee 3. Figure 14.11 shows the process for the first six hours. (This process could also be shown in an equivalent tabular form.)

Computing the characteristics and the effectiveness of the system

The process which was simulated for six hours should be continued until stabilization is achieved. However, for the purpose of demonstration, let us examine the results of the six hours of simulation.

Arrivals   Ten maintenance employees arrived, or 10/6 = 1.67 each hour, on the average. Twelve production employees arrived, or 12/6 = 2 per hour.

Service   All 22 arrivals were served. The total service time was 4.2 hours. This means that the tool crib clerk was busy 4.2/6 = 70 percent of the time. The average service time was 4.2/22 = .19 hours.

Probability of waiting   Five out of the ten maintenance workers had to wait for service. Thus, the probability of a maintenance worker having to wait is 5/10 = 50 percent. There was only one production employee out of 12 (8.34 percent probability) who had to wait.

Length of wait   Total waiting time was 1.5 hours. Thus, on the average, an employee waited 1.5/22 = .068 hours (about four minutes). However, the average waiting time for a maintenance employee was 1.3/10 = .13 hours versus .2/12 = .017 hours for a production employee.

The total cost of waiting

For production employees   = .2 hours × $5 = $1.0, for the 6-hour period
For maintenance employees = 1.3 × $6   = $7.8
Total.......................... $8.8

Waiting cost per hour = $\frac{8.8}{6}$ = $1.47

Priorities   In four cases (40 percent of all maintenance employees) priorities were utilized by the production employees.

Conclusion   In this case the system seems to be efficient. The cost of waiting is only $1.47 per hour. There is no sense in adding a second clerk to the tool crib at a cost of $4 an hour since the maximum possible saving is only $1.47. The priority for the production employees is questionable. A second simulation run on a "first-come, first-served" basis should be taken to compare the results. Also, a third simulation, giving priority to maintenance employees could be run. (They earn more!) Results should then be compared.

Under a different system it could have been possible for the waiting line to be longer, and the cost of waiting very high. In such a system a simulation run should be conducted to check if two or even three clerks were justified. Also, if one or more clerks are added, they could operate in various configurations. For example, each clerk could serve one group only, or both could serve one customer at one time (one doing the paperwork, one doing the material handling), and so on. Simulation can handle all such cases readily.

14.11   SIMULATION WITH CONTINUOUS PROBABILITY DISTRIBUTIONS

When the probability distributions are not discrete, as in the preceding Monte Carlo examples, but continuous instead, the process of "assigning" random numbers is somewhat modified. The cumulative probability distribution is again used however. The procedure is as shown in Figure 14.12.

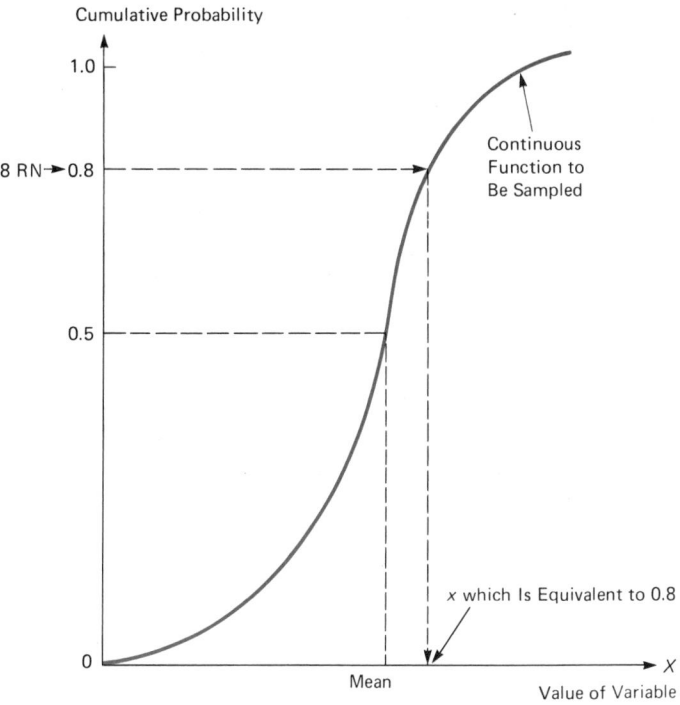

FIGURE 14.12
A continuous distribution

The procedure

A random number between 0 and 1.0 is first obtained from Table C2 by selecting a one-digit number, say 8, and putting a decimal point in front of this number. The result (.8 in Figure 14.12) represents the *cumulative probability* that a value of the variable is less than a number X. The number X can either be found graphically (follow the arrow in Figure 14.12) or from a table. For greater accuracy a three- or even four-digit RN could be selected.

Use of tables: Normal distribution

To illustrate, consider a variable which is normally distributed with mean $\mu = 100$ and standard deviation $\sigma = 10$.

Step 1 Generate RN. Let us assume that the three-digit random number 695 is selected.

Step 2 Put the decimal point in front of the RN; that is, the 695 is changed to .695.

Step 3 Use Table C1 in Appendix C, the "area under the normal curve." Since it is known that:

$$Z = \frac{X - \mu}{\sigma} \qquad (14.1)$$

then

$$X = \mu + Z\sigma \qquad (14.2)$$

The number .695 when spotted in the middle of Table C1 is equivalent to $Z = .51$. Using Equation 14.2 with $\mu = 100$ and $\sigma = 10$:

$$X = \mu + Z\sigma = 100 + .51 \times 10 = 105.1$$

Since Table C1 includes only numbers larger than .5, it is necessary to subtract any RN which is less than .5 (after the decimal point is added) from 1.0. For example, the RN of 273 is changed to .273 and then $1.0 - .273$ results in .727.

The corresponding value of Z is then found in Table C1 ($Z = .605$ is equivalent to .727), and then Equation 14.3 is used to find X,

$$X = \mu - Z\sigma \qquad (14.3)$$

That is, $X = 100 - .605 \times 10 = 93.95$.

For other distributions (e.g., binomial or exponential) a similar procedure may be used with the aid of the appropriate charts or tables. For details see Meier et al. [22].

14.12 PROBLEMS FOR PART B

17. Heuristic problem: Little Billie is famous as the best junior burglar in Beverly Hills. He only robs from the "filthy" rich and is very selective in what he is willing to "lift" (because his "goodies sack" will only hold 27 cubic feet). Also, being small, he can only carry up to 92 pounds in his pack. On this particular night he has the following items from which to choose:

Item	Value, $	Volume, Ft.³	Weight, lb.
A	300	2	25
B	100	1	10
C	500	3	20
D	900	5	30
E	600	5	15
F	400	1	35
G	200	2	10
H	300	3	15
I	500	4	15
J	700	8	10
K	200	4	20
L	800	7	20

Clearly, he wishes to maximize his "haul" but isn't sure which items to choose first. Test each of the following heuristic rules and advise Little Billie on their soundness:

1. If smaller items are chosen first, after they are gone, there might not be enough room for the bigger, more valuable items and the sack may have to be left partly empty. Therefore, since value is somewhat proportional to volume, fill the sack with the largest items first, tucking in the smaller items as space allows.
2. By the same reasoning perhaps the heaviest items should be chosen first.
3. Choose the items in order of their value.
4. Choose the items in order of their value per unit volume.
5. Choose the items in order of their value per unit weight.
6. Choose the items in order of their value per unit volume per unit weight.

18. Find the best sequence by using "next best" and "next best with adjustments" rules. The times are setup times.

To From	1	2	3	4	5	6	7	8
Initial condition	9	29	9	14	29	34	18	16
1	0	23	30	15	18	17	11	24
2	24	0	22	8	22	10	24	16
3	7	7	0	8	33	26	20	25
4	7	18	11	0	27	18	6	34
5	4	15	22	10	0	22	30	35
6	26	33	26	9	22	0	35	15
7	23	19	29	33	7	24	0	30
8	31	24	19	28	10	21	19	0

19. A doctor has the following patients waiting to see him (or her) with the corresponding projected treatment times. The doctor wishes to schedule them to minimize average waiting time. Formulate two heuristic rules and compare them with taking the patients in the order given.

Patient	Treatment time (hours)
A	1.0
B	.2
C	2.0
D	1.5
E	.1
F	.7

20.[15] People arrive at an elevator in groups once every three minutes (there is a pedestrian crossway in front of the building with a traffic light which switches every three minutes), with the following frequencies:

Number of people in group	Probability $P(x)$
3	.10
4	.15
5	.35
6	.25
7	.15

The elevator can accommodate at most five persons. It takes the elevator an average of two

---
[15] Developed by Professor Dieter Klein.

minutes to go and return to the ground floor if it doesn't go beyond the eighth floor. If it goes beyond the eighth floor, it takes an average of four minutes to return. In 75 percent of the trips, the elevator does not go beyond the eighth floor.

If a person waits for an elevator and the elevator returns, he takes it *without* waiting for the next group to arrive.

Simulate for ten arriving groups until all people are accommodated. The elevator is at the ground floor at the beginning of the simulation and should return to the ground floor at the end of the simulation.

Find (by simulation):

a. The average number of people arriving each time.
b. The average number in an elevator ride.
c. The average time a person had to wait for the elevator.
d. The probability that a person will have to wait for the elevator.
e. The utilization of the elevator.
f. How many trips the elevator will make in *one hour.*

Use the following RNs:

I. For arrivals: 15, 81, 22, 55, 91, 48, 06, 58, 37, 74, 26, 87.

II. For the elevator: 09, 28, 93, 65, 31, 71, 42, 18, 68, 80, 52, 22, 60, 03.

Assign representatives number from 01.

21. Of all the customers entering ABC National Bank, 20 percent go to the receptionist, 15 percent to the loan department, 55 percent to the cashier windows, and 10 percent to the credit card department.

Of all who see the receptionist, one half then go to the loan department, one fourth go to the credit card department, and one fourth leave the bank.

Of all those who go to the cashier windows, 80 percent leave the bank and 20 percent go the loan department.

Of all those who go to the credit card department, 50 percent will leave the bank and 50 percent will go to the cashier windows.

Of all those who go to the loan department, 50 percent will go to the cashier win-

dows, 15 percent will go to the credit department, and 35 percent will leave the bank.

Simulate the paths of five customers going through the bank. Assume that a customer may return to a service area more than once. Use the following random numbers: 78, 54, 16, 24, 58, 03, 90, 88, 48, 42, 59, 94, 80, 86, 14, 29, 36, 63, 12, 37, 89, 41 (start the first customer with the first random number, the second customer with the second random number, and so on).

Find:

a. In how many service areas each of the customers will stop.
b. How many times the first customer will show up at the cashier windows.
c. The average time at the receptionist desk is two minutes, at the cashier windows it is three minutes, and at the loan and credit card department it is ten minutes. Estimate how the *work load*, in terms of minutes of service, is divided among the four service areas.
d. How many visits were paid, in total, to the cashier windows.
e. The floor area of the bank is 5,000 square feet. How would you allocate this area to the various service areas if the area needed is considered proportional to the number of visits?

22. Pump-It-Yourself, Inc., is an independently owned and operated service station. As such, it does not receive regular deliveries from the local wholesale gasoline distributorship, which is controlled by a major oil company. Instead, the station has the opportunity of purchasing any or all of the excess gasoline remaining on the distributor's truck after all regular deliveries have been made each day. The delivery truck stops each day *after* the station has closed for business. The amount of gasoline remaining on the truck is a random variable with the following distribution:

Gallons remaining	Probability
0	.20
500	.25
1,500	.30
2,500	.15
3,500	.10

The station has a 3,000-gallon storage capacity, and the demand for gasoline varies according to the following distribution:

Gallons demanded	Probability
660	.10
1,200	.20
1,800	.30
2,400	.25
3,000	.15

Assume that unsatisfied demand is lost (customer goes to a competitor). Simulate the activities involving the supply and demand of gasoline for 12 days. Start with an inventory on hand of 2,100 gallons. Use the following random numbers:

RNs for demand: 79, 25, 03, 19, 28, 91, 58, 52, 68, 13, 46, 67

RNs for supply: 69, 07, 95, 41, 49, 76, 08, 37, 83, 57, 12, 29

Given:
Profit from a gallon sold = 20¢
Cost of ill-will = 5¢/gallon
Cost of shipping back = 2¢/gallon.

Determine:
a. The average daily demand for gasoline (compare to the "expected value").
b. The percentage of time that storage capacity will not be sufficient for taking all gasoline from the truck.
c. The percentage of time that demand can not be met.
d. The average daily beginning inventory.
e. The average daily ending inventory.
f. The average daily loss of unmet demand.
g. The percentage of times that sales equaled demand.
h. The daily net profit.

23. Given an inventory system with the following information:

- Replenishment arrives at the beginning of the week (Monday).
- Demand occurs during the week.
- Inventory is taken at the end of the week (Friday) and orders are placed at that time.
- Lead time: Orders are placed at the *end* of a week and are delivered at the beginning of the week after next (nine days lead time).

Ordering policy:
If inventory on hand at the end of a week is I (can be negative for shortage) and replenishment due in the beginning of the following week is R, then: If $I + R \leq 5$, order so that $I + R + Q = 10$, where Q is the size of the order. If $I + R > 5$, do not order.

The probability of demand in each given week is shown below:

Number of units	Probability
3	.05
4	.20
5	.35
6	.25
7	.15

Start with an inventory of six at the beginning of the first week (after replenishment arrived).

Then:
1. Write a simulation flowchart.
2. Manually simulate for 20 weeks (use RNs from Problem 22).

Find:
a. The percent of times the system will be in a stockout.
b. The average number of units stocked out per week.
c. The percent of times the system will have a zero inventory at the end of the week.
d. The frequency of placing replenishment orders.
e. The average inventory on hand.

24. Assume that in Problem 23 the cost of a stockout is $50 per unit, per occurrence, and the storage (holding) cost is $5 per unit, per week. Explain how you would simulate to find if a different inventory policy is more profitable.

25. Dr. X has an appointment schedule where patients are scheduled to come every 20 minutes. The office is open from 9:00 A.M. to noon, four days a week. The last patient is scheduled at 11:40 A.M. each day. Assume that patients arrive exactly on time. The time required for treatment or examination is distributed as follows:

Minutes	Percent
10.	14
15.	25
20.	41
25.	20

The doctor will see all patients that are scheduled. Simulate for *two days* to find:

a. The average waiting time (prior to treatment) per patient (in minutes).
b. The average utilization of the physician (the percentage that working time is of the total time in his office).

Note: If the physician completes his examination before noon, he will stay in the office until noon.

c. The average overtime (*in hours*) worked by the physician each week. Overtime is considered any time beyond noon.
d. The length of the last treatment on the second day (in minutes).
e. The average number of breaks the physician will have in a day, between seeing patients.
f. The exact time the doctor will finish the treatment of the last patient on the second day.

RN for the simulation: 52, 02, 73, 48, 06, 15, 94, 12, 95, 87, 04, 99, 40, 98, 58, 68, 08, 81

Start assigning RN with 00.

26. Northwestern, Inc., produces valves on a weekly schedule. Shipments are made to two customers, A and B. The customers enter orders, by phone, every Friday, after their weekly maintenance inspection is completed and they want immediate delivery. Past experience indicated the following demand pattern: customer A orders either 15 valves (35 percent of the cases) or 20 valves (65 percent of the cases). Customer B orders 25 valves in 20 percent of the cases, 30 valves in 40 percent of the cases, and 35 valves in the remaining cases.

The company would like to be able to meet all demand at least 95 percent of the time. The production manager thinks that he can do it with a weekly production schedule of 48 valves. Valves not demanded on Friday are used as safety stock, which currently stands at

5 units. Demand that cannot be met from production is met from the safety stock. Demand that cannot be met at all is considered a lost opportunity.

Simulate for 12 weeks.

RN for customer A: 63, 87, 06, 51, 33, 93, 15, 75, 26, 68, 41, 58

RN for customer B: 34, 66, 12, 87, 43, 04, 53, 92, 27, 72, 49, 81

Start assigning RNs from 00.

Find:

a. Is the production level of 48 sufficient to meet the company's service policy? Why?
b. What is the average weekly profit if one valve brings $27.50?
c. What will be the safety stock at the end of the twelfth week?
d. The average weekly number of valves demanded that are considered as a lost opportunity.

27. A certain service time is normally distributed averaging 15 minutes with a standard deviation of 2. Three RNs were generated: 386, 628, 953. Find the length of service time of the first three services.

28. Demand for a perishable liquid product is known to be normally distributed with an average daily demand of 23 gallons and a standard deviation of 4 gallons.

a. Generate demand for ten days. Use RNs: 783, 430, 922, 871, 477, 838, 872, 276, 198, 520
b. Round the average daily demand found in part *a* to one decimal point (e.g., 25.2). Assume that an inventory of 23.6 gallons is being kept daily. If demand in a given day is more than the inventory on hand, the company incurs a loss of $100 for each gallon short (proportion of $100 for fraction of a gallon). If there is some left over, the company's demurrage is $120 per gallon (proportion for a fraction). Find the average daily profit (loss) if each gallon sold contributes $50 to profit.
c. Based on the result of part *b*, estimate the chance of not meeting the demand on any specific day.

14.13 CASE

EXPRESS A.G.[16]

In early October, Mr. Hans Huber, operations manager of Express A.G., received a request from Mr. Max Retter, the traffic manager at Stuttgart, for an increase in the number of dispatchers assigned to the Stuttgart operation from two (the present number) to four. Mr. Retter claimed that with only two dispatchers the delivery-van drivers were spending too much idle time waiting to report in and to receive new instructions. When Mr. Huber asked Retter how he had arrived at "four dispatchers" as the appropriate number, Retter replied, "Based on my observations, four dispatchers should clear up most of the waiting time." Mr. Huber then promised to look into the matter and to advise Retter of his decision.

The delivery-van operations of Express A.G.

Express A.G. was an integrated transportation company operating throughout western Germany. Its headquarters were at Frankfurt, and other major operations centers were at München, Stuttgart, Hamburg, Bremen, and Aachen. An important segment of Express's business was the delivery-van operation. In each major center, Express operated a fleet of delivery vans that served the metropolitan area around the center. The delivery vans made home deliveries for many of the large department stores. In addition, the vans delivered goods locally that were brought into the metropolitan area warehouses by the large transcontinental trucking firms.

For each trip, the driver of the delivery van received instructions from the dispatcher as to the particular requirements of the assignment. Upon return to the motor pool, the driver reported to the dispatcher either the successful completion of his assignment or any difficulties that he may have encountered. At the completion of the "trip report," the dispatcher would assign the driver to a new job.

The operation at Stuttgart

Following the receipt of Mr. Retter's request, Mr. Huber became quite concerned. He felt that Retter's request should not be looked upon in isolation—if, as Retter claimed, the number of dispatchers at Stuttgart was inadequate, then it was probable that most of the other delivery-van centers were also understaffed. Therefore, he decided to send Felix Stamm, a staff operations analyst, to Stuttgart to investigate the problem.

EXHIBIT 1
Information about delivery-van operation at Stuttgart

Number of dispatchers	2
Number of delivery vans . . .	30
Average length of trip	2 hours
Arrival rate per hour at dispatcher's office	Random, approximately normally distributed, with mean = 15 and standard deviation = 4.*
Time with dispatcher	Random, approximately normally distributed, with mean = 8 minutes and standard deviation = 3 minutes. Minimum service time = 1 minute.
Wage rate per hour— dispatchers	12 D.M.†
Wage rate per hour—drivers	10 D.M.
Billing rate (revenue) per hour for van with driver	30 D.M.

* Within the hour, the arrivals appear to follow a completely random pattern.
† D.M. stands for the German currency Deutsche Mark.

---

[16] This case was prepared by Professor A. A. Robichek, Stanford University, Graduate School of Business. Copyright 1967, by l'Institut pour l'Etude des Méthodes de Direction de l'Entreprise (IMEDE), Lausanne, Switzerland. Reproduced by permission.

Mr. Stamm spent several days at Stuttgart and then returned to Frankfurt. He showed Mr. Huber the data he had gathered about the Stuttgart operation (see Exhibit 1) and promised to prepare a report within the next few days.

Questions:

1. What is the optimal number of dispatchers for Stuttgart under each of the following assumptions:

   a. While the driver is waiting to see a dispatcher, the van is being serviced by the service department;

   b. The van and the driver are both idle during the waiting period?

   (In resolving this problem, make any additional assumptions you consider necessary.)

2. What additional information would have been of assistance in resolving this problem?

Notes:

a. Simulate for two hours. Use the waiting times for the second hour to arrive at a decision (waiting time for the first hour is too far from a stabilized condition).

b. Round the time to whole minutes.

c. Simulate the exact minute of arrival by using the formula: random number $\times (60/100)$. After computing the average number of arrivals within an hour, arrange by the "order of arrivals."

d. Use Table C2 for estimated service time and arrival rate values.

14.14. GLOSSARY

Artificial intelligence   The behavior of a computer programmed to react to situations in much the same manner as a human being would.

Business games   Operational games that deal with decision making at the top of a business corporation.

DYNAMO   A special computer programming language.

Flowchart   A schematic presentation of all computational activities used in the simulation written in a symbolic language.

GPSS   A special computer programming language.

Heuristic programming   A step-by-step procedure using heuristics which, in a finite number of steps, arrives at a satisfactory solution.

Heuristics   Decision rules which are developed on the basis of logical problem analysis and, possibly, designed experimentation.

Industrial dynamics   A computerized system simulation of a whole company or industry.

Monte Carlo simulation   Simulation that uses a random number mechanism to describe the behavior of systems with probabilistic elements.

Oligopoly   A market where only a small number of sellers operate.

Operational (management) games   Simulation of a competitive situation arranged in the form of a game. Participants make periodic decisions and the results are then analyzed. Such games are used mainly for training purposes.

Random number   Numbers sampled from a uniform distribution. Each number has the same chance of being drawn.

Random number generation   A process of generating random numbers, usually by a computer. Can be done manually by drawing pieces of papers with numbers from a hat or from a specially constructed table.

Representative range of numbers   A range of numbers with the same number of digits (e.g., 00–19) that corresponds to the frequency distribution of the factor under consideration.

Rules of thumb   Rules of decision making which are based on trial and error and which yield acceptable solutions for managerial problems.

SIMSCRIPT   A special computer programming language.

Simulation A procedure that involves the use of a mathematical model that imitates reality for the purpose of conducting experiments on the model. These trial and error type experiments intend to *predict* the behavior of the system under different situations.

Simulation runs A simulation run is one simulation experiment with one set of input data.

System simulation Simulation of very large systems such as the national economy, usually computerized.

Time compression The ability to simulate years of operations in seconds or minutes of computer time.

14.15   REFERENCES AND BIBLIOGRAPHY

Heuristic programming

1. Findler, N., and Meltzer, B. *Artificial Intelligence and Heuristic Programming.* New York: American Elsevier Publishing Co., Inc., 1971.

2. Fuller, J. A. "Optimal Solutions vs. 'Good' Solutions: An Analysis of Heuristic Decision Making". *Omega* 6 (1978):479.

3. Gavett, J. W. "Three Heuristic Rules for Sequencing Jobs to a Single Production Facility." *Management Science* 11 (1965):B166–76.

4. Slage, J. *Artificial Intelligence, the Heuristic Programming Approach.* New York: McGraw-Hill Book Co., 1972.

Artificial intelligence

5. Dreyfus, H. L. *What Computers Can't Do: A Critique of Artificial Reason.* Scranton, Penn.: Harper & Row, Publishers, 1972.

6. Minsky, M. L. "Artificial Intelligence." *Scientific American,* vol. 215, September 1966.

7. Simon, H. A., and Newell, A. *Human Problem Solving.* Englewood Cliffs, N.J.: Prentice-Hall, Inc., 1971.

Gaming

8. Bartion, R. F. *The Imaginit Game A Creative Business Decision Simulation.* Lubbock, Tx: Active Learning Pub., 1978.

9. _____. *Primer on Simulation and Gaming.* Englewood Cliffs, N.J.: Prentice-Hall, Inc., 1972.

10. Carlson, J. G., and Misshauk, M. J. *Introduction to Gaming: Management Decision Simulations.* New York: John Wiley & Sons, Inc., 1972.

11. Graham, Robert G., and Gray, Clifford F. *Business Games Handbook.* New York: American Management Association, Inc., 1969.

12. Meredith, J. *The Hospital Game.* Cincinnati, Ohio: Shasta Publications, 1978.

Simulation

13. Edge, A. G. et al. *The Multinational Management Game.* Dallas, Tx: Business Publications, Inc., 1980.

14. Forrester, J. W. *Industrial Dynamics.* Cambridge, Mass.: Massachusetts Institute of Technology Press, 1961.

15. _____. *World Dynamics.* Cambridge, Mass.: Write-Allen Press, 1971.

16. Frazer, J. *Introduction to Business Simulation.* Englewood Cliffs, N.J.: Prentice-Hall, Inc., 1978.

17. Gordon, G. *System Simulation.* Englewood Cliffs, N.J.: Prentice-Hall, Inc., 1978.

18. Graybeal, W. and Pooch, U. W. *Simulation: Principles and Methods.* Cambridge Mass.: Winthrop Publishers, 1980.

19. Guetzkow, H., et al. *Simulation in Social and Administrative Science.* Englewood Cliffs, N.J.: Prentice-Hall, Inc., 1972.

20. House, W. C. *Business Simulation for Decision Making.* New York: PBI, 1977.

21. Jacoby, S. L. S. and Kowalik, J. S. *Mathematical Models with Computers.* New York: Prentice-Hall, Inc., 1980.

22. Meier, Robert C.; Newell, William T.; and Pazer, Harold L. *Simulation in Business and Economics.* Englewood Cliffs, N.J.: Prentice-Hall, Inc., 1969.

23. Naylor, T. H. *Computer Simulation Experiments and Models of Economic Systems.* New York: John Wiley & Sons, Inc., 1971.

24. _____. *Simulation Models in Corporate Planning.* New York: Praeger, 1979.

25. Pritsker, A. B., and Pegden, D. *Introduction to Simulation and SLAM.* West Lafayette, Ind.: Systems Publishing Corp., 1979.

26. Reitman, J. *Computer Simulation Applications.* New York: John Wiley & Sons, Inc., 1971.

27. Thierauf, R. J. *Systems Analysis and Design of Real-Time Management Information Systems.* Englewood Cliffs, N.J.: Prentice-Hall, Inc., 1975.

PART III

Up to this point the foundations and tools of management science have been presented. In this third part of the text, attention is directed to applying the results of the analysis. This aspect of management science (MS) is probably the most difficult, in practice.

The first chapter in this part deals with implementation of the MS recommendations as related to both the specific project itself and to the factors which are independent of any individual project.

To give the reader an opportunity to grapple with real-world issues, nebulous goals, and data problems, a case analysis, solved by three different MS models, is included in Chapter 16. The text then ends with a discussion of the outlook for applications of management science in the future and the general direction of development and growth of the field.

APPLICATIONS

15

The success of implementation depends first of all on the value of the project itself. The factors, or particulars, that determine the value of the project are discussed in the first half of this chapter.

The project particulars that are discussed in this chapter are:

1. The economic viability of the project.
2. Its priorities and timing.
3. The availability of financing (cash flow).
4. The organization of the project and the operations involved.

The second half of the chapter discusses those organizational factors relating to implementation which are independent of the particular project at hand. The organizational aspects are divided into three parts: those relating solely to the organization, those relating to operations, and behavioral factors. Together, these constitute what is called "the implementation climate." The chapter ends with a brief case illustrating some of the real-life difficulties in implementation.

Implementation

15.1 WHAT IS IMPLEMENTATION?

Machiavelli astutely noted over 400 years ago that there was "nothing more difficult to carry out, nor more doubtful of success, nor more dangerous to handle, than to initiate a new order of things." The implementation of a proposed MS solution is, in effect, the initiation of a new order of things, or in modern language—*the introduction of a change.* The difficulties pointed out by Machiavelli are the major concern of this chapter.

The introduction of change

The definition of implementation is somewhat complicated since implementation is a long and involved process whose boundaries are vague. In a simplistic manner, implementation can be defined as putting a recommended solution to work. Implementation can also be defined as "the manner in which the results of scientific effort may come to be used by the manager."

There is a distinction between two classes of implementation. First, there are the routine, programmed problems for which prototype models exist. These include, for example, certain allocation problems which are solvable with the aid of linear programming. For such problems, implementation means a commitment to routine and frequent use of the model, or *institutionalization.*

Institutionalization.

Second, for ill-structured, one-shot type decisions, implementation means simply the one-time use of the recommended solution.

One way to treat implementation is to view it not as an independent topic but as a *continuing step* in the MS approach to decision making and problem solving; that is, the activities performed from the time a study is begun by the management scientist, to the time the recommendation is executed.

Is implementation a problem?

Several researchers (e.g., Huysmanns [18]) believe that managers often receive little or no benefit from management science. One reason is that there exists a significant gap between MS recommendations and their actual execution.

Not all analysts share this view. Some believe that there is no real problem. Wagner, for example, believes that implementation is much easier now than it was in 1960 ([35]) and that the only factor really needed for successful MS applications is the joint exercise of good judgment by both executives and analysts.

There is very little evidence to substantiate the real extent and magnitude of the implementation problem. Actual information on the subject is a closely held secret in organizations, especially when thousands of dollars have been spent on unimplemented projects.

Of the available evidence, the results published by Turban [34] in his study of corporate headquarters, indicated that 35.4 percent of all projects were completely implemented, 21.4 percent were mostly implemented, 20.4 percent had some parts implemented, 4.4 percent had very few implemented parts, 11.4 percent were not implemented, and 7 percent were not yet clear. These findings show that one should talk in terms of *degree* of implementation rather than complete success or failure.

The degree of implementation

Whose problem is implementation?

Is implementation a problem of the management scientist or the manager? Implementation may not appear to be of direct concern to the scientist, but it should be. As Churchman et al. point out ([7]): adjustments, frequently essential for implementation of MS solutions, should not be entrusted to those who do not have a thorough understanding of the problem and its mode of solution.

Implementation should be important to scientists for another reason. The lower the rate of successful implementation, the smaller the chances are for the scientist to develop or even to survive. For this reason, implementation is an integral part of many MS/OR projects, even in the initial stages.

Approaches to the study of implementation

The major difficulty of studying implementation is its dependence on a multiplicity of interrelated factors. The majority of the studies of implementation deal with only one or, at most, with a few of these factors, which can be classified into two groups:

1. Those aspects directly related to an individual project or problem (labeled "project particulars").
2. The general conditions surrounding implementation in an organization. These conditions are termed the *implementation climate*.

Two groups of factors

In general, the degree and/or probability of implementation is a function of both. The major elements of each of these two perspectives are shown in Figure 15.1.

Project particulars

Of the various project particulars that are discussed in this chapter the project viability (Section 15.2) is probably the most important. Other factors, discussed in Section 15.3 are: timing and priority, availability of financing, and operations.

The implementation climate

Implementation climate, as viewed in this text, includes all those factors that determine the success of implementation but which are not

FIGURE 15.1
The implementation
process

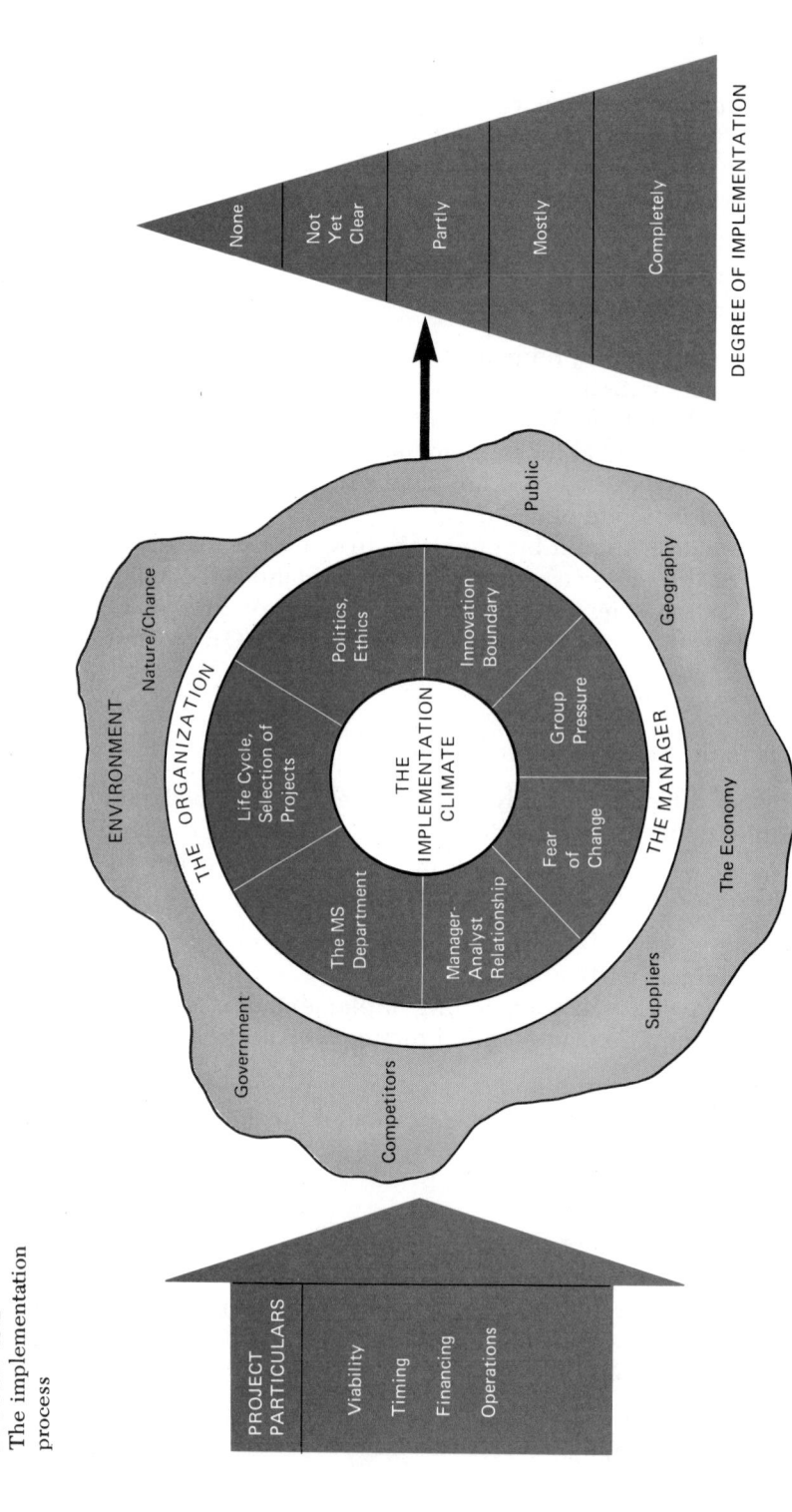

related to a *particular* project. These factors are divided into three classes:

Organizational factors (Section 15.4)

1. The support of top management.
2. The place of MS in the organizational structure.
3. The size of the MS unit.
4. The internal structure of the unit.
5. The information system and the availability of computers.

Operational factors (Section 15.5)

1. The selection of projects—life cycle.
2. The selection of projects—organizational validity.
3. Organizational politics.
4. Values and ethics.

Behavioral factors (Section 15.6)

1. The analyst-manager relationship.
2. The fear of change.
3. The pressure of the work group.
4. Individual innovation.

The characteristics of the implementation climate are much broader than those of the usual *organizational climate*. Organizational climate can be viewed as a *part* of the implementation climate; it is basically the expression of behavioral factors and can be defined as:

A set of properties of the work environment perceived directly[1] or indirectly[2] by the employees therein. Climate appears to be an influential force.

15.2 PROJECT VIABILITY

An MS proposal can be viewed as a course of action recommended by the analyst for implementation. As such, it should show a clear advantage over any other alternative including that of "doing nothing." Therefore, implementation is greatly dependent on the ability to show such advantage.

Each alternative requires an investment of resources (including money), which can be viewed as the costs in the system, in exchange for some expected benefit(s) yielded.

The *viability* of a project is determined by comparing the costs with anticipated outputs. This comparison is termed a *cost-benefit* or *cost-*   Cost-benefit analysis

---

[1] This can be measured through attitudes; for example, by questionnaires (see Litwin and Stringer [22]).

[2] Examples of indirect measures of climate are: turnover rate, absenteeism rate, and number of complaints.

effectiveness analysis. In practice, such an analysis may become rather complicated. One or more of the following reasons may account for this.

1. Cost valuation   The cost of a project seems, at least at first sight, easy to identify and quantify. In practice, it is often difficult to relate costs to projects in an exact way. Allocation of overhead cost is an example. Should it be allocated by volume, activity level, or value? What about future costs? A well-known "game" is to show the advantages of a certain alternative "neglecting" future costs. There are additional accounting complications such as the impact of taxation and the selection of a proper interest rate.

Neglecting future costs

2. Benefit valuation   The assessment of costs is not easy, but the assessment of benefits is even more difficult. First, benefits may be nebulous. Also, one frequently cannot precisely relate a benefit to a single cause. Second, results of a certain action may be felt over a long period showing up in different times and quantities. Third, a valuation of benefits includes the assessment of both quantity and quality. The latter is difficult to measure, especially when services are involved. Fourth, the multiplicity of consequences can pose a major problem for quantification. Also, some consequences, such as goodwill, inconvenience, waiting time, and pain are extremely difficult to valuate. (What is the cost of a trouble that "ages you by a year" overnight?).

3. Partial implementation   Lastly, decisions are frequently made on the basis of the return shown if *total* implementation is achieved rather than the more likely 90, or even 70, percent effective implementation. Clearly this will be misleading to management. The general reason for less than 100 percent implementation is that a change introduced at one point in a system usually precipitates compensatory change(s) elsewhere. This may thus force management to drop some parts of the proposal.

70 percent effective

15.3   OTHER PROJECT PARTICULARS

Timing and priorities

Two important factors in implementation are the timing and the priority of the project. For example, the analyst may find that an issue of prime importance at the time the study was undertaken is not as important at implementation time for several reasons. First, changes in the surrounding environment may have an impact on the importance of the problem, the costs, or the benefits involved. Secondly, errors could have been made in an initial assessment. Finally, other studies may indicate that more urgent or more profitable projects should be considered first.

Timing and priority are almost uncontrollable factors as far as the analyst is concerned. However, the analyst may be able to predict some of the problems and defer or adjust the implementation of the project.

On the other hand, timing may help implementation. For example, a project to increase the capacity of a refinery which was rejected in 1973 was implemented in 1974 due to the energy crisis.

Availability of financing

All required financing, cash flows, identification of sources, and assurances of funds should be planned in advance. Commitments should be secured so that money will be available when needed. Lack of appropriate financing is cited by many analysts as a major obstacle to implementation.

Operations and resources

Several practical questions should be answered regarding the project prior to its implementation. For example:

- Who will be responsible for executing each portion of the project?
- When must each part be completed?   Some questions
- What resources (in addition to money) will be required?
- What information is needed?

In brief, a complete planning document for implementation should be prepared. Based on the answers to these questions, operating procedures can be designed and any necessary training and transitions can be planned beforehand so that they do not become problems to implementation later.

15.4 ORGANIZATIONAL FACTORS

The aware organization may well ask "What's the best way of organizing our MS department to aid in achieving successful implementation?" Certain areas can be identified that will help provide an answer. Some such areas are:

The support of top management

Top management support is demonstrated by the status and backing given by the president and senior officers to the MS unit, their willingness to wait for results, and by the resources allocated to the MS operation. Without sufficient support the cooperation of the operating managers is difficult to obtain and the fate of MS is questionable.

The place of MS in the organizational structure

The management science unit is usually a staff unit. The higher the status accorded it, the better the chances for successful implementation.

One possibility is to organize MS with data processing as a systems department that reports to a senior vice president or to the president.[3] It could also be included in the research and development department, in the industrial engineering department, or in the finance and control department.

The size of the department

A few at first

A safe rule for the size of the department is "a few at first." Too large a group appears a luxury to budget-minded managers. Growth should come with success, but before either occurs, a natural flow of communication and a proper allocation of work should be decided within the group.

For many companies starting an MS unit, an experienced employee supervising one or perhaps two other employees would constitute an effective group. A one-person MS group is probably too small for effective action since one usually lacks the interdisciplinary expertise required.

The internal structure of the MS unit and its mode of operation

The leader of the MS unit and the way the unit is organized and operates are of utmost importance. In a study conducted in large U.S. corporations [34] it was found that about one third of all the directors of MS units hold a doctorate degree. Competency and high educational level are necessary not only for the directorship. Management science should be viewed as a unit of experts. Internally, the unit should be flexible with an organized communication system and a clear delegation of authority and responsibility. The mode of operations should be efficient, planning and control procedures should be clear, and customers should receive first-class treatment.

The relationship to the information system and computers

The MS unit could be integrated into the organization's *information system*. The information system must be capable of providing current as well as historical data to the analyst. By continuously monitoring the information flow to detect changes in basic model assumptions, managerial priorities, environmental constraints, and other pertinent information, the analyst can increase the likelihood of implementation significantly.

The nature of the information system is also important to imple-

---

[3] A study [34] of MS units in the headquarters of large corporations showed that 10 percent of the MS directors report directly to the president and 75 percent to vice presidents. The study also indicated that 23.4 percent of all MS departments in large U.S. corporations are part of the information systems division.

mentation; typically, an accounting information system does not provide sufficient data for MS purposes. Of more use are *decision support systems* (DSS), discussed in Chapter 17, and *management information systems* (MIS) whose purpose is to generate, collect, store, process, retrieve, and report data on demand by management. An important part of DSS and MIS, especially to the MS analyst, is the computer.

Tied in to the MIS

The computer allows the analyst to quickly solve very large problems which were previously impossible (or impractical) to solve by hand. In addition, many general computer packages are available either from the manufacturer or through SHARE[4] for such models as linear programming, inventory control, and PERT. To facilitate model building, some specialized codes are also available. The best known of these are the simulation languages: GPSS, SIMSCRIPT, and DYNAMO.

For all the advantages of computers, there are shortcomings. If the input data is inaccurate, the output data will also be—a phenomenon responsible for the acronym GIGO (garbage-in, garbage-out). This becomes particularly important in view of the human tendency to believe anything on a computer printout. Furthermore, the superior capabilities of the computer do sometimes result in correspondingly super mistakes. Thus the large likelihood of a person making a small error has been replaced with the smaller likelihood of a computer making a gigantic one[5] (as evidenced by the occasional clerk whose weekly payroll check suddenly jumps to $175,000).

GIGO

15.5   OPERATIONAL FACTORS

The selection of projects—life cycle

Proper *project selection* can be an important determinant of implementation. In many cases MS units have a certain degree of freedom in selecting and/or soliciting problems for study. Researchers at Northwestern University (see Radnor et al. [28]) have described the relationship between the selection of projects and the integration of an MS unit into the organization in terms of the three phases of a "life cycle," as explained below.

Life cycle

Introductory phase In this phase the MS unit is accepted by management only on a "trial" basis. It is apparent that success is a "must" in this critical phase if the unit is to survive. As a result, only projects with a high probability of success should be selected. That is, projects which take a relatively short time to complete, are technologically simple, and demonstrate high potential cost savings. The primary objective is to impress both top managment (the sponsors) and line

---

[4] SHARE is a national library of computer programs.

[5] Computers actually do not make mistakes. The mistakes are made by the programmers or by the operators.

management (the users) with results which are immediate and highly visible. Another motivation for selecting relatively small problems is that these usually require a smaller task force and fewer demands for management, thus facilitating the establishment of initial communications.

Transitional phase Based on initial success, the MS unit can continue on a full-scale basis. No formal commitments have been made yet, although the attitude toward it is somewhat less skeptical than in the previous phase. This time, however, the expectations are higher and small results will not be sufficient to provide the necessary "push" toward the third phase of the life cycle. Since somewhat larger and possibly less visible projects are involved, the group must educate both users and sponsors in what to expect. By working together with the MS unit, line and top managers learn about different ways of thinking about problems and may begin to appreciate some of the MS concepts being used. In turn, the joint work benefits the analysts in assessing management's needs. If significant results are obtained and functional channels of communication have been established, a further gain in status results.

Permanent phase At the successful completion of the transitional phase, the MS group is now established as a formal, permanent part of the organization. The immediate pressure to perform is off, and more difficult projects may be attempted. However, it is advisable to maintain a "portfolio concept"; that is, have a balance of projects which require various amounts of time and resources and are visible and difficult to different degrees. Only then will the group always have a "recent success" on hand to help justify longer term projects.

Portfolio concept

The selection of projects—organizational validity

The concept of organizational validity developed by Schultz and Slevin [30] implies that for an MS project to be implemented, it must be compatible with, or "fit," that organization. This fit *must* occur at three levels: individual, small group, and organizational. If an MS project requires an extraordinary amount of change in individual attitudes, small group dynamics, or organizational structure (i.e., there is no fit), then the probability of successful implementation will be reduced. Of the three, individual attitudes are the most difficult to measure, but this can be done, in part, with the aid of a special questionnaire which Schultz and Slevin developed.

Organizational fit

Organizational politics

Of all the factors that determine implementation, the most interesting and, in many cases, the most important one, is organizational politics—present in any organization.

This is often underestimated or ignored. The Research Institute of America [29] reports that office politics is on the increase today, at a tremendous cost to the individual as well as the organization. Chew [6] notes that "surveys show that organizational politics are becoming more and more ruthless—and backstabbing an accepted hazard of an executive's life." Backstabbing

Organizational growth usually results in an initial allocation of power, influence, and authority followed by a temporary stability (similar to "detente"). The implementation of an MS project often threatens this equilibrium by giving some individual(s) and/or group(s) greater power or status. Therefore, those who think that the balance of power will be changed to their disfavor will oppose the project.

This is where "politics" frequently enters the picture. The most insidious and detrimental, but best camouflaged, politics are typically played at the upper levels of management. The reasons are usually to maintain divisions of power or cover the fact that the executive has become incompetent in a position where the job has outgrown him or her. Politics are also employed at lower levels of the organization of course. Here, however, the younger employees are typically involved for reasons of self-interest such as money, prestige, or job security.

To some extent it thus appears that the analyst may be well advised to become involved, learn the rules, and find where the power centers and cliques are in order to gain support. An important question the analyst may eventually have to face is whether or not he or she can remain neutral.

In summary, politics, due to established managers' natural resistance to change, may be the greatest force opposing the implementation of any MS project. However, such politics appear to be minimal in hard-driving, low-overhead companies since less time is available and power positions are less solidified. There is also the possibility that some managers will play politics to *help* implement a project because they see it as an opportunity to fulfill their own interests. Playing politics is always a dangerous tactic however.

Values and ethics

The researcher, as a human being, should consider the ethics and values that are involved in implementing an MS project. The following points are of importance:

1. Goals of the MS project Since the process of implementation is an attempt to attain certain goals, the analyst should decide in his (or her) own mind whether the ultimate goals desired are ethical. For example, the authors are familiar with an analyst who was deeply involved in an implementation process until he learned he was helping make napalm for use in Vietnam. The analyst should also check if the goals are ethical to those people crucial to the implementation process.

2. *Implementation process* Another question the analyst should address is whether he or she considers it ethical to effect the implementation. That is, the goals may be ethical while the implementation process itself is not. A possible example is attempting to attain a sales goal via violation of government antitrust law.

3. *Possible impact on the system and on other systems* The probable results on other systems should also be ethical. That is, the goals and process may both be ethical, but the probable outcome of the implemented project on the system of interest, or on another system, may not be. For example, consider the possibility that a public transit system will drive a railroad company out of business.

Before undertaking a project, the analyst should be certain he or she understands what the manager's goal *really* is and whether the project involved will actually fulfill that. For example, if the proposed project is a new rapid transit system for a city, is the mayor motivated by a desire to improve the traffic flow in the city or is the mayor really interested in bringing a "progressive" image to the administration? Assuming the former is indeed the case, could the traffic flow be improved by merely rerouting certain streets or is the proposed project in order?

15.6 BEHAVIORAL FACTORS

Analyst-manager relationships

Churchman and Schainblatt [8] have laid out a matrix which helps to explain the type of relationship that may exist between the analyst and the manager. Four possibilities represented by the four cells of the matrix in Table 15.1 may be considered.

TABLE 15.1
Relationship types

Manager is— \ *Analyst is—*	*Responsible* **B**	*Not responsible* **B'**
Responsible **A**	Mutual understanding	Communication
Not responsible **A'**	Persuasion	Separate function

Separate function

Position *A'B'* is called the *separate function position*. This position represents the approach that it is up to the analyst to present a project (or a change) with detailed instructions on how to implement it. The manager then takes the analyst's plan and should be able to apply it if the instructions given are adequate. The functions of the parties are entirely separate; the job of one begins where that of the other ends.

Position $A'B$ is called the *persuasion position*. It holds that implementation rests to a great extent on the skill of the analyst in understanding the problems of the manager. That is, the obligation is on the analyst who must understand the essence of the manager's personality and overcome *resistance* using basically a persuasion approach. This position stresses the psychological and social factors of implementation.

Cell AB' is called the *communication position*. This position holds that the solutions suggested by the analyst are not accepted because the manager does not "understand" them.

The fourth position, AB, is called the *mutual understanding position*. Here implementation is considered to be a function of the type of relationship which exists between two responsible parties, and this position represents the *most desirable* kind of relationship. The ingredients of the relationship have been summarized in the concept of "trust" discussed by Churchman and Schainblatt [8]:

- The two parties have faith in each other's recommendations.
- Each party is sensitive to the motivation, aspirations, and values of the other.
- Each party understands his or her own decision-making process as well as that of the other.
- The party responsible for implementation is also involved in the formulation of goals in order that his or her recommendations bear a relationship to the needs of the recipients. For continuity, the same party is involved in formulation and implementation.
- The recipients are involved in the preparation of plans and programs so that they bear a relation to their own needs and values. This assures input of the recipients' values and needs.

The implementation matrix has been profitable in focusing attention on particular aspects of the relationship between the manager and the analyst. Some of these aspects are outlined below:

Communication   One frequently hears people say that "if only management scientists could learn to talk in a language that managers could understand, their recommendations would be accepted more readily." This relates to the fact that the quantitative nature of management science does not appear to be understood by most managers who, therefore, have to accept such recommendations as an act of faith.

However, experimentation conducted by Churchman ([8], [9]) indicates that lack of communication per se *does not* appear to be a major barrier to implementation. He found that no matter how the necessary information was communicated to the manager, there was no evidence that the *mode of communication* made any significant difference. Of

(margin notes) Persuasion position

Communication position

Mutual understanding

Mode of
communication
irrelevant

course, poor communication did not help implementation; but even when the project recommendations were made in terms which the manager could apparently understand, the project was still frequently not implemented. It seems, therefore, that lack of communication is used as an excuse, in most cases, and the real reasons for resistance are different.

Differences in cognitive styles Frequently, the so-called "communication barrier" is symptomatic of a more basic reason for nonimplementation: a difference in *cognitive styles* between the manager and the analyst. *Cognitive style* refers to the fact that people differ in the approach they take in solving problems. The differences in style may reflect underlying differences in personality, education, culture, or combinations of such traits. Two basic styles are distinguished: some people are *analytically oriented* and tend to solve problems by seeking out cause-effect relationships in a step-by-step manner. Others are *intuitively oriented* and tend to utilize common sense and subconscious feelings in arriving at solutions.

Analytical vs.
intuitive style

While it is difficult to generalize, it is probably true that, on the whole, MS analysts tend to be analytically oriented, while managers incline toward the intuitive end of the scale. This being the case, one would imagine that the manager and the analyst would have a great deal of difficulty working together, not because of a difficulty in understanding each other's language but because the way in which they analyze and solve problems is different.

Huysmans [18] has carried out a series of experiments which were designed to test the impact of cognitive style differences on proposal implementation. He labeled the two classes of cognitive styles as *analytical* and *heuristic*. Analytical reasoning is defined as being directed toward detecting underlying causal relationships and manipulating quantifiable variables so that some "optimal" solution is reached with respect to the objectives. On the other hand, heuristic reasoning is based upon common sense and intuition.

The results of Huysmans' experiments strongly suggest that cognitive style may operate as an important constraint on implementation. In particular, he found that heuristic subjects, with few exceptions, rejected—completely or in part—the MS recommendations when they were supported by an analysis of the technical problems, even though the recommendations were supported by persuasive arguments as well.

The analytical subjects, on the other hand, responded much more favorably to the MS proposals if the more technical approach was used. Furthermore, when the heuristic subjects received their recommendations from the analyst utilizing the more intuitive approach, they generally reached a level of implementation just as high as analytical subjects who received their recommendations via the technical approach.

Thus, to foster implementation, proposals should be couched in the manager's style.

Participation   One of the best ways to encourage implementation is via participation of the people involved. The importance of participation has been demonstrated by the classic Coch and French experiment [10].

The researchers worked with four comparable groups of clothing factory operators. Each was exposed to a change in work procedures. The groups differed mainly in the method by which they were exposed to this change.

Group 1   The change was introduced by a "no participation" method. The operators *were notified* about the nature of the change, as well as the reasons for the change.

No participation

Group 2   This group was introduced to the work change by a "participation through representation" method. In this variation, the operators elected representatives who were allowed to participate with the scientists in determining the nature of the change.

Group 3 and 4   The third and fourth groups were introduced to the work change through a "total participation" procedure. All the members of these groups met with the scientists, who in turn demonstrated the need for cost reduction. The operators were then given an opportunity to influence the formulation of new work methods. Groups 3 and 4 were identical in nature.[6]

Coch and French reported a marked difference between the results achieved by the methods of introducing the change. The most striking difference was between group 1 (the "no participation" group) and groups 3 and 4 (the "total participation" groups). Immediately after the change was implemented, the output of group 1 dropped to about two thirds of its previous level and resistance developed almost immediately after the change occurred. Marked expressions of aggression against management occurred such as conflict with the methods engineer, hostility toward the supervisor, deliberate restriction of production, and lack of cooperation with the supervisor. Seventeen percent of the group quit in the first 40 days.

In contrast, the output in groups 3 and 4 showed a smaller initial drop followed by a very rapid recovery to a level which exceeded that prior to the change. The researchers found no sign of hostility toward the staff or toward the supervisors in these groups, and no one quit during the experimental period.[7]

Findings such as these suggest that participation is helpful for overcoming resistance to at least certain types of change.

---

[6] The reason for having two identical groups was to increase the reliability of the results by showing that the results for the two groups were the same.

[7] The results for group 2 were between group 1 and groups 3 and 4.

The fear of change

The implementation of an MS project can be viewed as an introduction of change into an organization. The change can be social, technical, psychological, or structural (or a combination).

When the manager (or employee) resists the logical arguments presented in defense of an MS proposal, he or she may not be resisting the technical aspects of the proposed change as much as the perceived social ramifications. Managers often feel threatened by modern techniques of analysis and sense that a proposed project, with the help of high-speed computers, may take over or jeopardize their job. This fear of change may originate from various sources: that the job will be eliminated, that previous performance will be proven inefficient relative to the new technique, or that the new technique will result in a downgrading in the status or intrinsic satisfaction of the job.

Of course, the analyst may think that such beliefs are absurd. The important point, however, is that what governs the manager's behavior is not so much the real threat as the *perceived* threat.

Perceived threat

The best way for the analyst to cope with the fear of change is to eliminate the perceived threat. The problem is that some of the perceived threat is probably real (e.g., workers may be laid off and the importance of certain managers may be reduced). Furthermore, some of the consequences of the change are uncertain.

Managers sometimes are not afraid of the organizational and social ramifications as much as the changes in the actual job responsibilities. If the job's content and meaning are changed, managers may not be too sure of how they will perform. They may foresee more responsibility (which many like to avoid), more control, and more accountability than they are used to. While managers may not like their job more challenging, they may not like it more routinized than what they were used to either.

The apparent solution here is retraining. However, this may not be an easy task. For example, some managers think of themselves as complete failures in mathematics, just because they had problems with it 30 years ago in school.

Overcoming resistance to change Many theories of overcoming resistance to change have been developed by behavioral scientists. For example, one of the best known theories regarding organizational change comes from Lewin [16] who identifies the various organizational forces resisting change. In order to overcome this resistance and ensure long-term effectiveness, the implementation process must be considered

Unfreezing

as a three-step procedure consisting of unfreezing, changing, and refreezing. "Unfreezing" refers to overcoming resistance to change by introducing disequilibrium into the present stable equilibrium. "Changing" refers to the exposure and acceptance of new information, attitudes, and theories in order to achieve new perceptions and learn new behavioral patterns. "Refreezing" refers to the reinforcement, confirmation, and support of new behavior based on the implementation. The Lewin theory stresses the sequential nature of these activities.

Sorensen and Zand [32] conducted an empirical investigation in which the Lewin theory was used to explain the variability in the success of 280 MS projects. Their major hypothesis (which was supported by the experiment) was that, in general, high levels of unfreezing, changing, and refreezing caused high implementation success and low levels were less successful.

The pressure of the work group

Few factors have a more pronounced influence on an employee's behavior than the pressures of formal and informal work groups. This is as true at the managerial level, where these groups tend to take on the characteristics of political coalitions, as it is in the lower echelons of the organization.

Work groups can influence employee behavior in a variety of ways. Asch [4] has found, for example, that groups can influence the perception of their members. In one of his experiments five out of six group members were told to insist that two lines drawn on a blackboard were of *unequal* size, when in fact they were not. In more than half of the cases, the sixth member, when asked to compare the length of the lines, although he insisted for several minutes that the lines were of *equal* size, gradually conformed to the group consensus, even though it was obviously incorrect.

Peer pressure

Furthermore, group pressure is an important determinant of its members' output.[8] In particular, group pressure generally results in the reduction in variation in members' output; that is, there is a significant amount of pressure for conformity.

Individual Innovation

For several decades, scientists from psychology, economics, marketing, and organization theory have studied the conditions under which an individual chooses to try something new. One result is Slevin's theory of the *innovation boundary* [31] which suggests that two zones of innovation exist. In one zone individuals will choose to innovate or try new things while in the other they will not. Between the two zones lies the innovation boundary.

Innovation boundary

Slevin developed a mathematical model that describes the formation of the boundary as a function of four variables: current success level

---

[8] An important aspect here is the role of unions which frequently determine the methods, quality, and speed of work.

(S), target aspiration level (T), the cost of innovation (C), and the reward of successful performance (R).

Through experimentation and questionnaires it is possible to predict the location of individuals in the zones; it is also possible to analyze means of transforming an individual from the "no innovation" zone to the "innovation" zone. Figure 15.2 shows such situations with: (1) a potential move from point A (no innovation) to point B (innovation), and (2) a potential move of the innovation boundary in such a way that location A, which was previously in the no innovation zone, is now in the innovation zone.

FIGURE 15.2

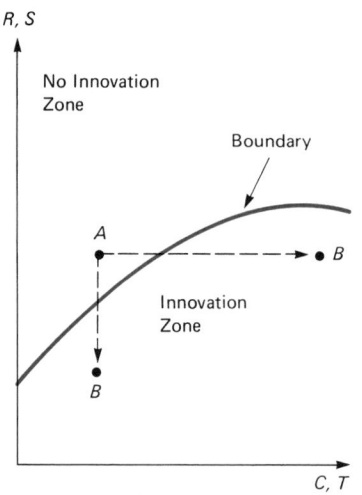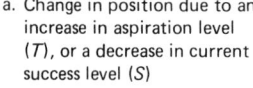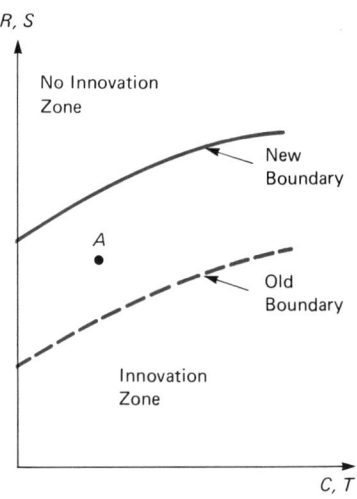

a. Change in position due to an increase in aspiration level (T), or a decrease in current success level (S)

b. Change in the boundary due to a decreased cost (C), or an increased reward (R)

15.7 IMPLEMENTATION FAILURE: A CASE STUDY

Several months ago a community hospital was approached with a proposed MS project that could have reduced the hospital's operating cost by about $4 per patient-day (about $365,000 a year). The administrator of the hospital was very candid in explaining the objections to the project, which were:

1. The hospital would gain nothing from the saving; the operating budget of the hospital would simply be reduced (this was a public hospital).

2. Showing lower cost than other community hospitals might be interpreted as either low health care quality rendered in the hospital or an inability of the administrator to use the budget effectively.

3. If the hospital could operate on a budget reduced by 10 percent, then the administrator might be viewed as incompetent since the previous situation was allowed to last for four years.
4. The administrator had no faith in the model since the analyst was unable to show the administrator a similar situation (in a hospital in a similar condition) that was successful.
5. The proposed project required the use of a computer which the hospital did not have. Under no circumstances would the administrator bring the "monster" in. The use of an outside computer was out of the question. How could the administrator trust an outsider when many insiders could not be trusted?

This case illustrates some of the implementation aspects discussed in this chapter. The problem for management scientists is to consider all the implementation aspects together to improve the chances of success.

15.8   CONCLUDING REMARKS

Implementation is the process of translating the models' results into operating instructions and carrying them out. Many management analysts see this as the major part of their task; it certainly is one of the most difficult aspects of the profession.

The tendency of some researchers to leave the "dirty" work of implementation to the manager, as well as the tendency of some managers to try to keep the management analyst out of the field during this final phase, may lead to the failure of implementation. Churchman, Ackoff, and Arnoff ([7], p. 616) conclude that it is *necessary* that the researcher be actively involved throughout.

This chapter has identified several aspects of projects which may pose a problem for implementation: the participants involved, the cost involved, the benefits accruing and their utility to management, the timing and priority of the project, the financing of the project, and operational difficulties that may develop as the project unfolds.

A positive climate is essential to the success of implementation. While the project particulars can be viewed as "seeds," the implementation climate can be viewed as the "weather." The better the seeds and the weather, the better is the chance for success.

However, good seeds and weather, although necessary, are not the only criteria. The management analyst and the methods of "cultivation" used also will affect implementation.

15.9   REVIEW QUESTIONS

1. In what way can implementation be viewed as "institutionalization"?
2. Propose some measures of cost and benefit for:

    a. Automating a production line.
    b. Introducing a laborsaving machine in a hospital.

c. Scheduling visits of welfare agency employees.

3. How might the analyst attempt to circumvent timing and priority difficulties?

4. Explain the concept of "degree of implementation" through an example and differentiate it from "probability of implementation."

5. What are the major reasons given for analysts *not* participating in implementation? Why is it important for them to participate?

6. How would one assess the benefits of installing a computerized inventory system?

7. Why is the availability of financing considered by some as the *most important* condition for implementation?

8. What implementation difficulties may be encountered if a complete operational plan of implementation is not prepared beforehand?

9. What is the danger of an MS group reporting to a line manager? Are there any advantages?

10. This chapter concerned the implementation climate of the entire organization. What points would be relevant concerning the internal organizational climate of the MS group itself?

11. What other parts of the "information flow" should the MS group be integrated into besides the management information system (MIS)? How important are they?

12. Give an example of an MS project that is incompatible with an organization.

13. Describe your own cognitive style; what type of reasoning is most persuasive to you?

14. Participation is considered to be one of the strongest factors to aid in implementation. Explain why this might be so.

15. Describe a project where the following would not be ethical to you:
    a. The goal.
    b. The implementation.
    c. The results.

16. Are group pressures stronger at lower levels of an organization or at higher levels? Why?

17. Give some examples of how to move a manager into the innovation zone by changing:
    a. S.
    b. T.
    c. C.
    d. R.

18. How would you argue with the hospital administrator's reasons for not implementing the project (Section 15.7)?

15.10 CASE

SUNRISE ELECTRONICS

Sunrise Electronics manufactures CB radios which are sold both through the company's retail outlets and in department stores. The company's policy for the past several years has been to emphasize sales and advertising with one goal in mind: increasing their share of the expanding market. During 1975 and 1976 the company's earnings were soaring. However, in the last quarter of 1976 the company incurred a loss; its first in the last eight years. Although the change in profitability was attributed in part to the change in CB radios from 23 to 40 channels, the company also realized that quality control and cost control had become extremely important. In addition, large inventories and high interest rates contributed to increased expenses.

The president of the company had been considering the idea of initiating a management science (MS) department because he had heard favorable reports on cost reductions achieved with the aid of management science techniques. In the weekly meeting of the executive committee he suggested starting an MS department on an experimental basis. Most of the vice presidents, especially the old timers, rejected the idea, claiming that such an experiment was not justified at this time.

After long deliberation the president decided to form an MS group within the existing industrial engineering department. Thus far, this department had been primarily engaged in methods improvements, work studies, and incentive schemes. John Green, the director of the department, had been pushing for years to get additional personnel to expand activities into management science.

The first step in the organization of the MS group was the recruitment of Bill Swan. Bill had a Master of Science degree in Management Science from a leading university and work experience of three years in an established MS department with a large oil company.

The first project that John and Bill conceived was in the materials management area. They felt that the company's mode of operations was heavily dependent upon proper inventories of raw materials, semifinished components, and finished goods. The materials management department was headed by Dave Wilkes who had been running the department for more than 15 years and had been with the company for 22 years, since its inception. Dave was considered a competent, hard working department head. Although he had only a high school education, he had taken some management development courses and had considerable experience. The latest changes in the company's CB models caused tremendous inventory problems and Dave had been working 12 hours a day or more to straighten things out. Dave did not like the idea of the MS group "poking into" *his* department and suggested they start in "any other place." He believed Bill to be a "good, sincere man" but that he did not understand the realities. Furthermore, Bill had never dealt with materials management of CB radios. "Inventories of oil differ from inventories in electronics; there is too much complexity in our inventories for mathematical models."

It was obvious that without top management's support the project would not move. Finally, John and Bill talked with the president who then called Dave and requested that he cooperate.

In the initial stages of the study Bill found that Dave ran the department in a very autocratic manner. Most decisions regarding purchasing, inventory level, storage, and usage were made by Dave, usually on the spot.

The only documentation that Bill found was in the finance and the accounting departments for billing and tax purposes. This documentation was not suitable for the data needs of an inventory model. When Dave was approached for the necessary information, he seemed to have trouble remembering. The more Bill attempted to extract the information, the more defensive Dave became.

After spending three months on the project, Bill suggested scrapping it and moving on to another department. "I am sure that some of the more up-to-date managers will be only too glad to participate."

Questions

1. What were the major factors that determined the failure of the MS project?
2. What steps could have been taken in the early stages that might have improved the chances of success for the project?
3. What alternatives are open to John now? Analyze all of them and recommend one.

15.11   GLOSSARY

Cognitive style   The manner in which people solve problems. Can be either *analytical* or *intuitive*.

Cost-benefit analysis   A comparison of the costs and benefits of each project or alternative, often expressed as a ratio.

Implementation Putting a recommended solution into effect. The manner in which the results of scientific effort may come to be used by the manager.

Implementation climate The environmental factors which impact the chance of implementing an MS project. This is in contrast to the specific factors ("project particulars") that impact the specific project.

Innovation boundary A line or a graph that divides those who are willing to try a change from those who resist it.

Institutionalization A permanent change. Routine and frequent use of the change.

Organizational validity The fitness between a project and an organization and its people.

Project viability Projects whose benefits are larger than their cost and which have a clear advantage over other alternatives.

15.12 REFERENCES AND BIBLIOGRAPHY

1. Abrams, John W. "Implementation of Operational Research: A Problem in Sociology." *The Journal of the Canadian Operational Research Society* 3 (1965):152–60.

2. Anderson, J. C. and Hoffmann T. R. "A Perspective on the Implementation of Management Science." *Academy of Management Review,* July 1978.

3. Arnofoky, J. S. *Relationship between Operations Research and the Computer.* New York: John Wiley & Sons, Inc., 1968.

4. Asch, E. "Effects of Group Pressure on the Modification and Distortion of Judgment," in *Readings in Social Psychology.* Edited by E. E. Maccoby et al. New York: Holt, Rinehart and Winston, Inc., 1958.

5. Berman, P. "The Study of Macro- and Micro-Implementation." *Public Policy,* Spring, 1978.

6. Chew, Peter T. "New Rules for Office Politics." *The Miami Herald,* February 24, 1974.

7. Churchman, C. W.; Ackoff, R. L.; and Arnoff, E. L. *Introduction to Operations Research.* New York: John Wiley & Sons, Inc., 1957.

8. ———, and Schainblatt, A. H. "The Researcher and the Manager: A Dialectic of Implementation." *Management Science* 11 (1965):B-69–B-87.

9. ———. "Commentary on 'The Researcher and the Manager: A Dialectic of Implementation.'" *Management Science* 12 (1965):B2–B39.

10. Coch, L., and French, J. R. P. Jr. "Overcoming Resistance to Change." *Human Relations* 1 (1948):512–32.

11. Doktor, R. et al. (eds) *The Implementation of Management Science* Amsterdam: North Holland Publishing Co. (in press).

12. Drucker, P. F. "The Performance Gap in Management Science." *Organizational Dynamics,* Fall 1973.

13. Gibson, H. L. "Determining User Involvement." *Journal of Systems Management,* Aug., 1977.

14. Ginzberg, M. J. "Steps Toward More Effective Implementation of MS and MIS." *Interfaces,* May, 1978.

15. Graham, R. J. "The First Step to Successful Implementation of Management Science." *Columbia Journal of World Business,* Fall. 1977.

16. Grayson, C. J. Jr. "Management Science and Business Practice." *Harvard Business Review,* July–August 1973.

17. Hammond, J. S. "The Role of the Manager and Analyst in Successful Implementation." *Sloan Management Review,* Winter 1974.

18. Huysmans, Jan H. B. M. *The Implementation of Operations Research: An Approach to the Joint Consideration of Social and Technological Aspects.* New York: John Wiley & Sons, Inc., 1970.

19. Konczal, E. D. "New Demands for Managing Management Science." *Journal of Systems Management,* November 1979.

20. Levitt, T. "A Heretical View of Management Science." *Fortune,* December 18, 1978.

21. Lewin, K. "Group Decision and Social Change," in *Readings in Social Psychology.* Edited by E. E. Maccoby et al. New York: Holt, Rinehart and Winston, Inc., 1958.

22. Litwin, G. H., and Stringer, R. A. Jr. *Motivation and Organizational Climate*. Cambridge, Mass.: Graduate School of Business, Harvard University, 1968.

23. Lockett, A. G. and Polding, E. "OR/MS Implementation—A Variety of Processes." *Interfaces*, Nov. 1978.

24. Lucas, H. C., Jr. "Unsuccessful Implementation: The Case of a Computer-Based Order Entry System." *Decision Sciences*, October 1978.

25. Mason, Richard O., and Mitroff, Ian I. "A Program for Research on Management Information Systems." *Management Science* 19 (1973):475–87.

26. Mitroff, I. I., et al. "On Managing Science in the Systems Age: Two Schemes for the Study of Science as a Whole System Phenomenon." *Interfaces*, vol. 4, no. 3, 1974.

27. Morris, W. T. *Implementation Strategies for Industrial Engineers*. Columbus, Ohio: Grid Publishing, Inc., 1979.

28. Radnor, Michael; Rubenstein, Albert H.; and Tansik, David A. "Implementation in Operations Research and R & D in Government and Business Organizations." *Operations Research* 18 (1970):967–97.

29. Research Institute of America. *Coping with Office Politics*. New York: Selectron Report, 1971.

30. Schultz, R. L., and Slevin, D. P., eds. *Implementing Operations Research/Management Science*. New York: American Elsevier Publishing Co., Inc., 1975.

31. Slevin, D. P. "The Innovative Boundary" (two articles). *Administrative Science Quarterly* 16 (1971):515–31 and 18 (1973):71–75.

32. Sorensen, R. E., and Zand, D. E. *Improving Implementation of OR/MS Models by Applying the Lewin-Schein Theory of Change*. A paper presented at the National Research Conference on Implementation Pittsburgh, Penn.: University of Pittsburgh, November 15–17, 1973.

33. Tarnowieski, Dale. *The Changing Success Ethic*. New York: American Management Association, 1973.

34. Turban, E. "A Survey Sample of Operations Research Activities at the Corporate Level." *Operations Research*, May–June 1972.

35. Wagner, H. M. *Principles of Operations Research*. 2d ed. Englewood Cliffs, N.J.: Prentice-Hall, Inc., 1975.

36. Zmud, R. W. and Cox, J. F. "The Implementation Process: A Change Process." *MIS Quarterly*, June, 1979.

16

In learning management science, it is necessary to spend the great majority of time studying the techniques. Of equal, and perhaps even greater, importance is obtaining experience in applying these techniques to real-world problems, which are usually more complex than the examples given in the textbook. Unfortunately, the techniques must come before the applications and most curricula simply cannot devote that much time to the latter.

The case in this chapter is included specifically to help alleviate this problem and fill the gap between theory and reality. It communicates a sense of reality for practicing MS applications. Moreover, it illustrates the fact that there are typically several ways to solve the same problem, though some are easier than others. The case also points up the importance of having the appropriate data and how often data is incomplete, or even contradictory.

A case application

16.1   BRUNSWICK CORPORATION[1]

Part (A)

In mid-April 1967, Gerry O'Keefe, vice president for marketing of Brunswick Products, was trying to decide how many Snurfers he should request the manufacturing plant to produce for the 1967–68 winter season.

The Snurfer was a new item, first introduced to the consumer market by Brunswick during July and August 1966; but because of the difficulty of predicting the actual sales requirements, the factory had produced more Snurfers than were eventually sold. Mr. O'Keefe was anxious to avoid the same situation occurring in the 1967–68 selling season.

EXHIBIT 1
Standard Snurfer

Source: Company sales brochure.

The Snurfer   The Snurfer was a surfboard-like device designed for use on snow. It consisted of a molded wooden plank 48 inches long by 7 inches wide upon which the rider stood and skiied/surfed down snow-covered slopes. The company in its specification brochure described the Snurfer:

[1] This case was made possible by the cooperation of the Brunswick Corporation. It was prepared by Richard G. C. Hanna, research assistant, under the supervision of Associate Professor Paul A. Vatter. Copyright © 1967 by the President and Fellows of Harvard College. Rev. 1/73. Reproduced by permission.

> Snurfing is the all-new and exciting winter fun sport. Children, teens, and young adults can now combine the many thrills and skills of surfing and skiing on the new Brunswick Snurfer. It's really maneuverable, fun-filled, and easy to learn. Goes on a minimum of snow—where saucers and sleds won't go. The Snurfer is just the thing for action-packed snow outings! Also fun for sand surfing.[2]

The Snurfer was produced in two types, the regular and the super. Exhibit 1 shows the regular model. The regular model consisted of a molded laminated wood shell, painted yellow with black stripes, which used metal staples as foot grips. The super Snurfer was the same basic shape as the regular but incorporated a metal keel for greater maneuverability. In place of the painted finish the super had a genuine natural wood surface, included deluxe metal traction button-type Snurf treads (foot grips), was decorated with an official red racing stripe and was sold complete with Snurf-Wax. The wax allowed the bottom surface to be polished for even greater speeds.

The development of the Snurfer, January 1966–March 1967   The idea for the Snurfer had originated in Muskegon, Michigan, in early 1966. A plumbing supply salesman had converted a water ski for his children to use in the snow. The idea interested him, and he experimented with different sizes and shapes and coined the name Snurfer.

During February the product came to the notice of a Brunswick employee who felt that the item might be of interest to the corporation. On April 1, 1966, after some negotiation, Brunswick bought both the rights to the design and the registered name from the Muskegon salesman. The contract involved a lump-sum payment and a royalty that was based on Brunswick's gross sales of the product. The royalty was not to become effective, however, until a set number of Snurfers had been sold.

Following the signing of the contract the Brunswick engineers commenced a careful study aimed at optimizing the shape of the Snurfer. Many samples were made, and field tests were conducted on the rapidly disappearing snow fields. By the end of April the design had been finalized and the engineers were ready to turn the project over to the production personnel.

While the engineers had been working on the design, Noel Biery, a product manager, and Mr. O'Keefe, the marketing vice president, had been attempting to determine the size of the potential market and to settle upon channels of distribution. Because the product had been proved to be more readily usable by children than adults, Brunswick had decided to distribute the product through toy channels. After making rather slow progress with the local toy stores and jobbers, the decision was made to show the Snurfer at the New York Toy Show in late March.

---

[2] 1967 sales brochure.

Only one prototype Snurfer was available at that time, yet the response at the show was encouraging. During the show, manufacturers' representatives covering 38 states were appointed. The product at this time, which consisted of only a single model (which later became the regular), was sold at a factory price of $3.60 with a suggested retail price of $5.95. During the second week in April engineering prototypes together with specification sheets were sent to all representatives and Brunswick asked them to sound out the market and push for orders during the remainder of April.

By the end of April, Mr. O'Keefe had to make the decision whether or not to continue with the Snurfer and, if so, to decide how many units he would order from the factory. The Brunswick production people were insistent that if the units were to be produced in time for the winter selling season, they must have the firm annual production requirements for the Snurfer by the end of April. With only one firm order for 3,000 units, Mr. O'Keefe decided to go ahead with the project and ordered 60,000 units from the factory for delivery during the 1966–67 winter season. Fifty thousand units were to be the regular Snurfer and 10,000 units the super.

The tooling, capable of producing up to 150,000 units, was ordered at a cost of $50,000, and production scheduled to commence in early September.

By June no further orders of note had been received and both Mr. Biery and Mr. O'Keefe became concerned as to what action should be taken. Brunswick's own full-time representative in New York was asked to investigate the reasons why the Snurfer was not being sold. With this assignment, and a Snurfer in hand, he visited several sporting good stores, as distinct from toy shops, and found the reaction to be very good. By July, Mr. Biery realized that the original decision to sell through toy jobbers and manufacturers' representatives had probably been a mistake; consequently the original distribution channels were closed down and Brunswick made an all-out effort to generate interest through their own dealer salespersons. However, by this time most sporting good stores had completed their winter buying; and although a good reaction was forthcoming, many stores were unwilling to order in quantity for the current season because of the late date. During August the decision was made to retrench, and the factory managed to cut back production from 60,000 to just over 50,000 units. In addition they agreed to change the product mix between regulars and supers.

The total number of Snurfers sold during the 1966–67 season only reached 35,000 units, with the ratio between supers and regulars being approximately 40:60. By mid-March 1967 there were nearly 17,000 Snurfers in inventory, consisting of 12,000 regulars and 5,000 supers.

The production decision—April 1967 Because of the difficulties and setbacks that they had experienced during 1966, Mr. O'Keefe and

Mr. Biery were anxious to ensure that the plans for 1967 were firmly based on what they had already learned.

In reviewing the situation they had reason to believe that most of the early problems had arisen from their decision to class the Snurfer as a toy. Experience had shown that a considerable degree of skill could be developed by Snurfer enthusiasts and that speeds in excess of 30 miles per hour were attainable. This fact coupled with the good, although somewhat late, response received from the sporting good shops suggested that by careful distribution and promotion 1967 sales were potentially well in excess of the 1966 predictions. Although both Mr. Biery and Mr. O'Keefe were convinced that the immediate prospects for the Snurfer were excellent, they were uncertain as to the actual market demand for the coming year and as to the share of this market that would be taken by the super Snurfer. They were certain, however, that in order to maximize the overall profitability of the product they would have to estimate the size of the production order in a careful and systematic manner. The factory order for the 1967–68 production run had to be in the hands of the production people by the end of April.

As a first step in determining this quantity Mr. Biery decided to review the new cost estimates for the two Snurfer models. The production department advised him that the existing tooling, which had been purchased at a cost of $50,000, was in good shape and would be capable of producing a total of 150,000 units per year in any mix of models. To produce anywhere between 150,000 and 200,000 units would require an additional $15,000 of tooling. To increase the production above 200,000 units per year would require yet another $55,000 in addition to the extra $15,000 already mentioned. This latter step-up in tooling would allow the factory to produce up to 500,000 Snurfers a year. In calculating costs Mr. Biery planned to amortize tooling completely during the year in which it was ordered.

After consultation with the salespersons it had been decided to sell the Snurfers in 1967 at an average price from the factory (quantity discounts were involved) of $4.30 for the standard and $5.50 for the super. Brunswick's direct costs for these items were $2.50 and $3.20 respectively. In addition to direct costs Mr. Biery estimated that 9 percent of the gross margin for both models would be required for selling expenses, royalties, and discounts, while a further 3 percent would be allocated to advertising and promotion. Also, there would be a penalty for overproduction in the form of an inventory-carrying cost that was charged at the rate of 2 percent per month based on Brunswick's direct costs. Mr. Biery estimated that any excess inventory could be considered as being carried for an average of six months.

Having outlined the costs involved, Mr. Biery turned his attention to the question of demand. Although he was uncertain as to what figure he should choose, he believed that it was unlikely that there would be any major intrusion into the 1967 market from competitive manufacturers. In addition he realized that the Snurfer was something of a novelty item, and as such, might follow the trend of the skate board or hoola-hoop with sales rising extremely rapidly for one or two years and then tailing off just as quickly. Because of the extreme uncertainty arising from these factors, he determined to concentrate solely on the demand for the 1967–68 season.

To help in ascertaining the demand he called on Mr. O'Keefe, and together they considered the possible sales figures for Brunswick's Snurfers. They finally decided that the median demand was 150,000 units. They were certain that the demand would not be below 50,000 or above 300,000 units, and they believed that there was one chance in four that demand would be at least 190,000 units, and three chances in four that the demand would be at least 125,000 units.

In order to decide on what quantity of units to order from the factory Mr. O'Keefe felt that they should estimate how this demand would be broken down between the super and standard model Snurfers. This was necessary because the factory had to order raw materials well in advance, and Mr. O'Keefe didn't want to be left carrying standard Snurfers in inventory while the market was demanding supers, or vice versa. Both Mr. Biery and Mr. O'Keefe believed that this breakdown of demand between models was independent of the overall level of demand. They reasoned that the consumer would purchase either the standard or the super entirely on each one's distinctive selling features, and this decision as to which to purchase would in no way be influenced by the total number of Snurfers being sold.

Mr. Biery and Mr. O'Keefe felt that the super Snurfer would most likely account for 40 percent of the total Brunswick demand, although it might rise to as high as 60 percent of the demand. In no circumstances, they believed, would it fall below 30 percent. In addition they considered there was a 75 percent chance that the share would be 45 percent of demand and a 25 percent chance that the supers would account for 36 percent of the total demand for Snurfers.

Possible production quantities   Mr. Biery now felt that he had all the information necessary to decide how many standard and super Snurfers he should order.

Part (B)

To help in determining what production quantities he should consider, Mr. Biery decided to look at the suggestions he had received from the various people associated with the project. He prepared the following summary of recommendations from letters and memos that he had in his files:

> Field sales personnel argued that the gross margins on both standard and super Snurfers far outweighed the storage costs if some were left

unsold. They requested that a total quantity of 225,000 be ordered. This was to be made up of 130,000 regulars and 95,000 supers.

On the other hand the production manager advised total production of 150,000 units split 70,000 super and 80,000 regulars. He argued that until the Snurfer caught on, there was no point in incurring an additional investment cost. Realizing the super sales contributed a higher gross margin, he had suggested raising the proportion of supers to around 47 percent rather than at the level of 40 percent which was more in line with previous selling experience.

Mr. Biery himself felt that each of these arguments had its merits but suspected that a production quantity of 200,000 units, split 85,000 supers and 115,000 regulars, might decrease the cost of lost sales without incurring too high an investment cost in tooling. To ensure that he made the correct decision, however, he decided that he would analyze all three alternatives in order to determine which suggestion formed the best course of action.

16.2   ANALYSIS

Review of the case

The vice president of marketing and the product manager of a new product must decide upon the production levels for two versions of the product. Sales of the new product in the previous year were less than anticipated but finally encouraging, given a new distribution network. The vice president had overproduced in the previous year and did not want to repeat that mistake. However, the product was of a type similar to hoola-hoops—in that it might suddenly "catch on," then boom for two seasons or so, and die. In those circumstances, the company certainly did not want to be caught short on inventory of finished product in the midst of a boom they had created themselves.

The estimate of the proportion mix between the two versions was in considerable error the previous year, and also had to be reconsidered. Profit margins on each version were known but depended on production levels. (Of course, production levels depended on profit margins as well.) Assuming the product was not of the boom-bust type, some feel for the distribution of demand for each version was available.

Overview points of note

1. Mr. O'Keefe desired to avoid overproducing as he had done in 1966–67; such a situation would have cast him in a bad light.
2. Factory price increased between 1966–67 and 1967–68 from $3.60 to $4.30, or about 20 percent.
3. We do not find out what the New York representative learned about

toy store sales. Since response at the toy show was good, it seems there may exist an unexploited opportunity here.

4. Distribution through sporting goods stores allowed the firm to use their own full-time representatives instead of outsiders.

5. Based on (4) above, Biery and O'Keefe estimated that 1967–68 sales could be "well in excess of the 1966 predictions." Normally, this phrase would probably be interpreted to mean "anywhere between 20 to 100 percent over the 60,000 value," or therefore 72–120,000 units.

6. Even if the equipment is amortized in the year it is ordered, it would still be useful in following years, or at least have a significant salvage value.

7. If inventory is carried an average of six months, then the assumption is that it *will* be sold in the next snow season.

8. The "no competition" assumption appears reasonable.

9. The boom-bust possibility is a serious assumption. If this is indeed that type of product, all demand projections could be extremely low for 1967–68. Following any final conclusion, this possibility should be checked.

10. The demand distribution given is not symmetric and hence not normal. Based on the figures given and the interpretation of the case (boom-bust possibility), a Beta distribution appears more reasonable.

11. The same comments as in (10) hold for the proportion of supers. Here, however, we have a definite market result to go by (40 percent).

Cost data

	Regular	Super
Inventory cost:		
.02 × 6 × DC		
(if overproduced)	$ .300	$ .384
Factory price.	4.300	5.500
Direct cost (DC)	2.500	3.200
Gross margin.	$1.800	$2.300
Selling expenditures,		
royalty, discount (9%)	.162	.207
Promotion, ads (3%)	.054	.069
Net margin*	$1.584	$2.024

    * Net margin is used throughout this case rather than the more common "profit." The difference is that the net margin can be applied toward fixed costs and is a more meaningful term to managers than profit where some unknown allocation has already been made for fixed costs.

Probability distributions

Regardless of what method is selected to analyze this case, the probability distributions of demand and fraction of supers (or regulars) must be determined. The data in the case are as follows:

Demand, D

Median: 150,000.
Lower limit: 50,000.
Upper limit: 300,000.
$P(D \geq 190,000) = .25.$
$P(D \geq 125,000) = .75.$
1967 sales: 14,000 supers; 21,000 regulars.
Inventory: 5,000 supers; 12,000 regulars.

Fraction supers, F (independent of demand)

Mode (most likely):   40 percent
Upper limit: 60 percent
Lower limit: 30 percent
$P(F \leq .45)^* = .75$
$P(F \leq .36)^* = .25$

From the above data the demand and fraction distributions can now be approximated. Because of the given form of the data (upper and lower limits) and the fact that the distributions are nonsymmetrical, a Beta distribution (see Chapter 8) appears to be a reasonable form to try. Other possibilities are a Gamma or a lognormal distribution. Each of these could be checked with a statistical goodness-of-fit test to see how close they matched the given data at the upper and lower quartile points and, if acceptable, the best fit taken.

Such a procedure is beyond the scope of this textbook, however, and a simpler approximation will be used here instead. Exhibits 2 and 3

Beta, Gamma or lognormal distribution?

EXHIBIT 2
Demand

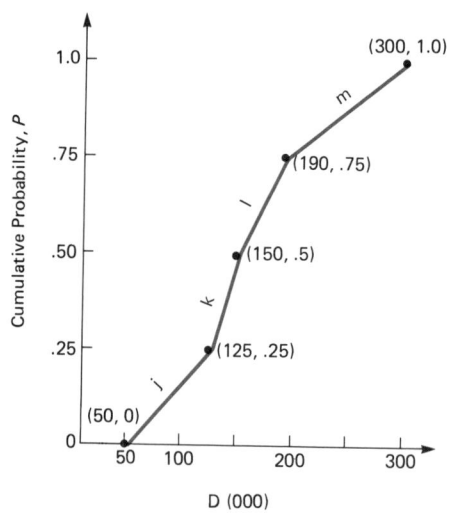

---

* Notice Mr. Biery's poor phrasing of these probabilities in the case. Literally the case states that $P(F = .45) = .75$ and $P(F = .36) = .25$. If true, these would be the *only* values that F could attain and the "most likely" value of .40 could never occur.

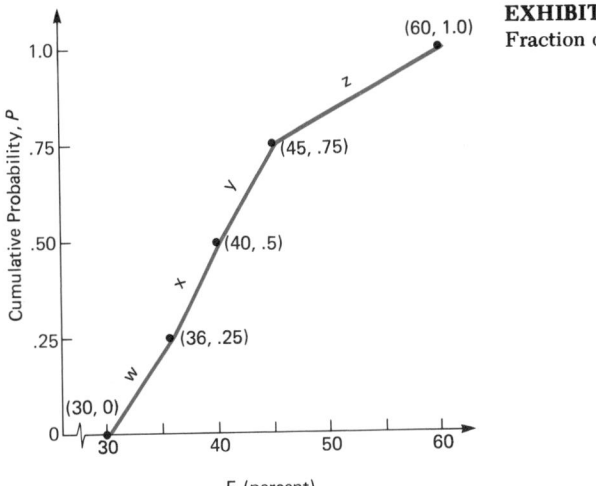

EXHIBIT 3
Fraction of supers

display the cumulative probability functions for the demand and fraction, with the given data marked by the dots. (The mode is used here as an estimate of the median for the fraction distribution.) The approximation will be to simply join the dots with a straight line of the form $P = a + bR$, where R is either demand D or fraction F, depending on which distribution is being approximated.

Invoking a piecewise linear approximation

For a straight line the values of a and b are given by:

$$b = \frac{P_1 - P_2}{R_1 - R_2}; \quad a = P_1 - bR_1.$$

Let us now calculate each of the line segments j, k, l, m, w, x, y, z in Exhibit 4.

Segment	$b = \dfrac{P_1 - P_2}{R_1 - R_2}$	$a = P_1 - bR_1$
j	.25/75 = .00333 per 1,000	.25 − .00333 (125) = − .16625
k	.25/25 = .010 per 1,000	.50 − .010 (150) = −1.0
l	.25/40 = .00625 per 1,000	.75 − .00625 (190) = − .4375
m	.25/110 = .00227 per 1,000	1.0 − .00227 (300) = .319
w	.25/6 = .04167 per 1%	.25 − 4.167 (.36) = −1.25
x	.25/4 = .06250 per 1%	.50 − 6.25 (.40) = −2.0
y	.25/5 = .0500 per 1%	.75 − 5.0 (.45) = −1.5
z	.25/15 = .01667 per 1%	1.0 − 1.667 (.60) = 0

EXHIBIT 4
Line segment coefficients

Now that the distributions have been approximated, analyses of the case may be conducted. Three different approaches are illustrated here: incremental analysis, decision tree analysis, and simulation.

16.3 SOLUTION BY INCREMENTAL ANALYSIS (see Chapter 12)

The net margin at median demand

The median expected demand was 150,000 units with a most likely split of 40 percent supers/60 percent regulars. At this production level no additional tooling would be necessary. The total net margin to the company (assuming all were sold and the 17,000 inventory maintained) would therefore be:

$$.4(150,000)(2.024) + .6(150,000)(1.584) = \$264,000$$

Sensitivity analysis

Before proceeding to the optimal production level analysis, we might look at the sensitivity of the margin to product mix demand.

a. Assuming the products will *not* substitute for each other, a 1 percent demand *decrease* in proportion of supers *reduces* the year's margin calculated above by:

$$\begin{pmatrix} \text{Reduction in super net margin} \\ (.01)(150,000)(2.024) \end{pmatrix}$$

$$+ \begin{pmatrix} \text{Overproduction inventory cost} \\ (.01)(150,000)(.384) \end{pmatrix} = \$3,612$$

and a 1 percent *increase* would reduce the margin by:

$$\begin{pmatrix} \text{Reduction in regular net margin} \\ (.01)(150,000)(1.584) \end{pmatrix}$$

$$+ \begin{pmatrix} \text{Overproduction inventory cost} \\ (.01)(150,000)(.300) \end{pmatrix} = \$2,826$$

b. If the products *will* substitute for each other, the corresponding reductions are:

$$(.01)(150,000)(2.024) - (.01)(150,000)(1.584)$$
$$= 3,036 - 2,376 = \$660 \text{ and } -\$660$$

respectively. This latter figure of $-\$660$ means that if customers buy supers when regulars are out of stock our "reduction" is really an *increase* in net margin (per 1 percent change in product mix).

The expected value of producing one more unit

Incremental analysis is also known by many other names, such as "critical fractile," "newsboy problem," and "marginal analysis." The idea is to see if increasing the production by *one unit* will improve or hurt the present situation. At the median demand:'

Expected increase in margin = (probability of sale, $1 - P$) (average net margin) $- P$ (avg. "loss" from carrying in inventory)
$$= (.5)[.4(2.024) + .6(1.584)] - .5[.4(.384)$$
$$+ .6(.300)]$$
$$= .5(1.76) - .5(.333)$$
$$= .88 - .167$$
$$= .713$$

where P is the cumulative probability in Exhibit 2 of demand *not* reaching the level D; i.e., not selling one more unit and then having to carry it in inventory until the following season.

Thus, the expected rewards of having one more Snurfer available for sale are considerably greater than the expected losses, when we are starting at the median demand figures. Note that the calculations assumed a hypothetical Snurfer that exhibited the margin and inventory cost characteristics of the super and regular models in the 40/60 proportion expected. Also note that the loss figures assumed no substitutability between the two models, and thus the loss was in holding the Snurfer in inventory for the next season (when it would be sold).

Clearly, at some point in the demand distribution, the probability of not selling the next unit is so large that the expected return (M) doesn't compensate for the probable loss (L). Calling this critical probability P^*:

The critical probability

$$(1 - P^*)M = P^*L$$

or

$$P^* = \frac{M}{M + L} = \frac{1.76}{1.76 + .333} = .84$$

Using the line segment m in Exhibit 2, with P given and solving for D, results in:

$$.84 = .319 + .00227D$$

or

$$D = 229 \text{ (thousand units)}$$

Since there are 17,000 units in inventory already, this then implies a *production* level of 229 − 17, or 212 thousand units. But will the expected increase in returns at this production level justify the cost of the additional tooling? To reach 200,000 production units from 150,000 requires \$15,000 in extra tooling. To go beyond 200,000 units requires another \$55,000. It certainly seems doubtful that it would be worth the extra \$55,000 to produce 12,000 more units since the net margin is only about \$2, but the \$15,000 investment might be worthwhile.

Justifying the extra tooling

This can be checked by calculating how much extra return the \$15,000 tooling can generate. *Without* the tooling, demand (sales) up to 150,000 + 17,000 = 167,000 units could be satisfied. *With* the tooling, an extra 50,000 units could be produced, or a maximum of 217,000 *sold*. Both line segments *l* and *m* in Exhibit 2 will have to be used to calculate the expected increase in net margin. This would be the probability of a sale $(1 - P_D)$ times the margin (M_D) less the probability of not making the sale (P_D) times the loss (L_D) for every thousand units (D) from 167 to 217. Average margins and losses based on the 40/60 product mix are again assumed.

Expected increase in margin

$$= \sum_{D=167}^{190} [(1 - P_D)M_D - P_D L_D] \quad \text{(segment } l\text{)}$$

$$+ \sum_{D=191}^{217} [(1 - P_D)M_D - P_D L_D] \quad \text{(segment } m\text{)}$$

$$= \sum_{167}^{190} [(1 + .4375 - .00625 D)1.76 - (-.4375 + .00625 D).333]$$

$$+ \sum_{191}^{217} [(1 - .319 - .00227 D)1.76 - (.319 + .00227 D).333]$$

$$= \sum_{167}^{190} (2.6757 - .01308 D)$$

$$+ \sum_{191}^{217} (1.0923 - .00475 D)$$

$$= (2.6757)24 - .01308 \sum_{167}^{190} D$$

$$+ (1.0923)(27) - .00475 \sum_{191}^{217} D$$

$$= 64.217 - .01308 \left(\frac{167 + 190}{2} \right) 24$$

$$+ 29.492 - .00475 \left(\frac{191 + 217}{2} \right) 27$$

$$= 11.51 \text{ thousand dollars.}$$

It is, therefore, concluded that the extra tooling is *not* worth the cost. However, it is *almost* worth the cost and faith in the probability distribution of demand is not strong, particularly if the Snurfer becomes a fad item. Thus, for another $3,500 Brunswick can obtain "insurance" that they aren't left out in the cold if the Snurfer "catches on."

Qualitative considerations and risk

The optimal product mix

Still to resolve is the question of the best production mix, because it is clear that the demand will not be *exactly* 40 percent–60 percent. Since each product results in different net margins, an *optimal* mix between the two models will give the highest expected yield. Again, marginal analysis can be used to find this mix. Since Brunswick expects to lose more, at the median mix, by a 1 percent decrease in proportion of supers available for customers ($3,612 versus $2,826 for regulars) the proportion of supers should be *increased* until the expected loss from each model is the same:

$$(1 - P^*)3,612 = (P^*)2,826$$

$$P^* = \frac{3,612}{3,612 + 2,826} = .56$$

where P^* is the probability of not selling at least one more super model. Using line segment y from Exhibit 3 results in the optimal product mix:

$$.56 = -1.5 + .05F$$

or

$$F = 41.2 \text{ percent supers}$$

Therefore, Brunswick should have available for sale:

$$.412(167,000) = 68,804 \text{ supers}$$
$$.588(167,000) = 98,196 \text{ regulars}$$

Since Brunswick already has 5,000 supers and 12,000 regulars in stock, they should *produce*:

63,804	supers
86,196	regulars
150,000	total

Note: previous calculations based on the median 40/60 mix should now be "corrected"; but since the correction is small (.2 percent for the margin), it is treated as not significant here.

16.4   SOLUTION BY DECISION TREE (see Chapters 3 and 4)

Here the approach is to handle the variability of demand by "discretizing" it into branches of a decision tree. If the number of branches is sufficiently large, the discrete approximation will be accurate enough for practical purposes. The method is illustrated with only a few branches.

The joint probabilities of the bivariate level/mix distribution are formed from the marginal probabilities. We work with only four branches, each with a probability of $(.5)(.5) = .25$:

A bivariate distribution

1. Demand of 125,000; fraction of supers of .36.
2. Demand of 125,000; fraction of supers of .45.
3. Demand of 190,000; fraction of supers of .36.
4. Demand of 190,000; fraction of supers of .45.

This simplification assumes that the given values properly represent the range of values they replace. For example, that 190,000 units with a probability of .5 represents from 150,000 to 300,000. A better approximation would have been to use all four segments of Exhibit 2 with each of the four segments of Exhibit 3, resulting in 16 branches.

Four or sixteen branches?

The decisions to consider are almost infinite: a production level anywhere between 0 and 500,000, and a mix from 0 percent supers to 100 percent. Let us consider the three alternatives of Part (B) since they generally fall at natural break points in demand. Then the decision tree appears as shown in Exhibit 5, assuming no costs for shortage (such as ill-will). The tree assumes the use of the available existing inventory.

Three policies to consider

The outcomes listed in the far right column of Exhibit 5 are calculated in the following manner. Consider the first outcome where

Calculating the first outcome.

EXHIBIT 5   Decision tree

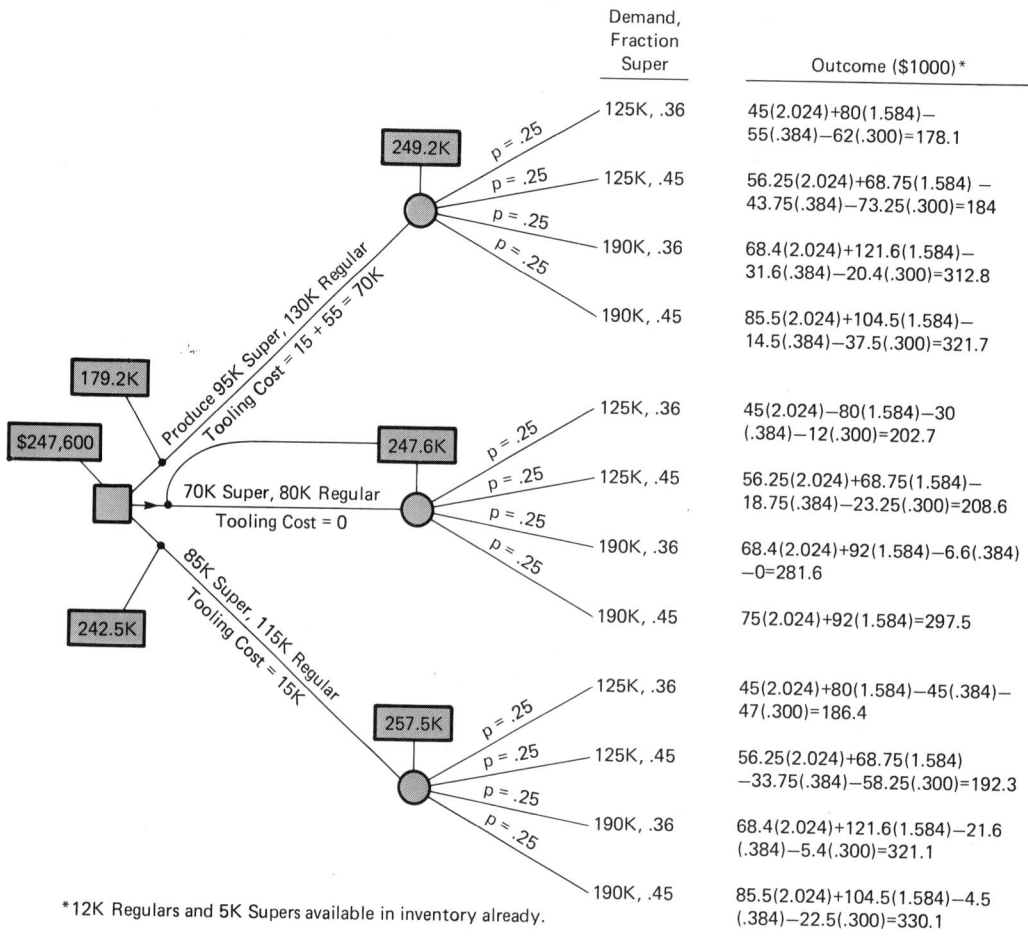

Demand,
Fraction
Super

Outcome ($1000)*

125K, .36	45(2.024)+80(1.584)−55(.384)−62(.300)=178.1
125K, .45	56.25(2.024)+68.75(1.584)−43.75(.384)−73.25(.300)=184
190K, .36	68.4(2.024)+121.6(1.584)−31.6(.384)−20.4(.300)=312.8
190K, .45	85.5(2.024)+104.5(1.584)−14.5(.384)−37.5(.300)=321.7
125K, .36	45(2.024)−80(1.584)−30(.384)−12(.300)=202.7
125K, .45	56.25(2.024)+68.75(1.584)−18.75(.384)−23.25(.300)=208.6
190K, .36	68.4(2.024)+92(1.584)−6.6(.384)−0=281.6
190K, .45	75(2.024)+92(1.584)=297.5
125K, .36	45(2.024)+80(1.584)−45(.384)−47(.300)=186.4
125K, .45	56.25(2.024)+68.75(1.584)−33.75(.384)−58.25(.300)=192.3
190K, .36	68.4(2.024)+121.6(1.584)−21.6(.384)−5.4(.300)=321.1
190K, .45	85.5(2.024)+104.5(1.584)−4.5(.384)−22.5(.300)=330.1

Boxes and labels on tree: 249.2K; 179.2K; $247,600; 242.5K; 247.6K; 257.5K

Produce 95K Super, 130K Regular Tooling Cost = 15 + 55 = 70K
70K Super, 80K Regular Tooling Cost = 0
85K Super, 115K Regular Tooling Cost = 15K

p = .25 (all branches)

*12K Regulars and 5K Supers available in inventory already.

95,000 supers and 130,000 regulars are produced; 100,000 supers and 142,000 regulars are available for sale; and (125,000) .36 = 45,000 supers and 80,000 regulars are demanded and, since they are available, are sold (in some cases the number demanded are not available, so sales are limited). On each super the margin is $2.024, and on each regular $1.584. There remains unsold 100,000−45,000 = 55,000 supers and, similarly, 62,000 regulars, each at a storage cost of $.384 and $.300, respectively. The outcome is $178,100.

Same answer as before

The result of the decision tree is the same as that by incremental analysis—by keeping the current tooling and only producing 150,000 units, the expected outcome is $5,100 better than spending the $15,000 and producing 200,000 units. The incremental analysis showed $3,500 better; but the product mix was quite different also: 41 percent supers instead of the 46.6 percent here (70,000/150,000 = .466).

The pros and cons of the three proposals are as follows. The extra tooling cost for the 225,000-unit proposal simply cannot be justified on the basis of the 25,000 extra units produced. On the other hand, if this is a hoola-hoop type product, then O'Keefe would certainly be glad they had the extra capacity. The advantage of the 150,000-unit proposal is the lack of a necessity to put more money into tooling without something definite to show for it. Up to now, they have only sold 35,000 units. In addition, O'Keefe didn't wish to repeat his previous overproduction mistake. However, with the high profit potential of the units and low costs of storage of any overproduction, it would appear a greater mistake on O'Keefe's part to underorder. In that case he would look even more foolish than just being an optimist—he would have overordered when the demand *wasn't* there, and then underordered when the demand *was* there. The last proposal may be the best compromise. It requires a small additional investment but generates a sufficient amount of extra capacity to minimize risk if high demand should occur.

The pros and cons of the three policies

16.5   SOLUTION BY SIMULATION

The procedure here would be to try several different policies (such as the three alternatives Mr. Biery is considering) with a computerized simulation. Each trial would constitute one possible reaction of the market. Repeating the process many many times would then give distributions for the variables of interest: net margin, shortages, sales mix, remaining inventory to carry over, and the like.

Determining the actual distributions of net margin, stockouts, and so on

Such a simulation was programmed in PL/I for an IBM 370 computer and run for 500 trials. The three policies described in Part (B) of the case were then tested:

A PL/I simulation

Alternative	Production strategy
I.	70K super, 80K regular, no extra tooling
II.	85K super, 115K regular, $15K tooling
III.	95K super, 130K regular, $70K tooling

It was also assumed that there was no substitution by customers of regulars for supers and vice versa. This assumption is relaxed later.

The stabilization history of three measures of performance are illustrated in Exhibit 6. In the lower section of the figure the average net margins of the three alternatives jump around quite a bit for the first 40 runs. The graphs only show every twentieth run, so the true variation can't be seen; but the average net margin for Alternative III goes from $144,000 (as shown) to $133,000 to $208,000 to $228,000. Thus, between runs 2 and 4 the average ranged through $95,000. Note in the figure that between runs 100 and 120 the difference shown is only $7,000. By run 140 the variations are almost completely damped out for all three alternatives (the purpose of the "fence" at run 140).

Stabilization of the measures

Stable by run 140

EXHIBIT 6
Stabilization of the
simulation

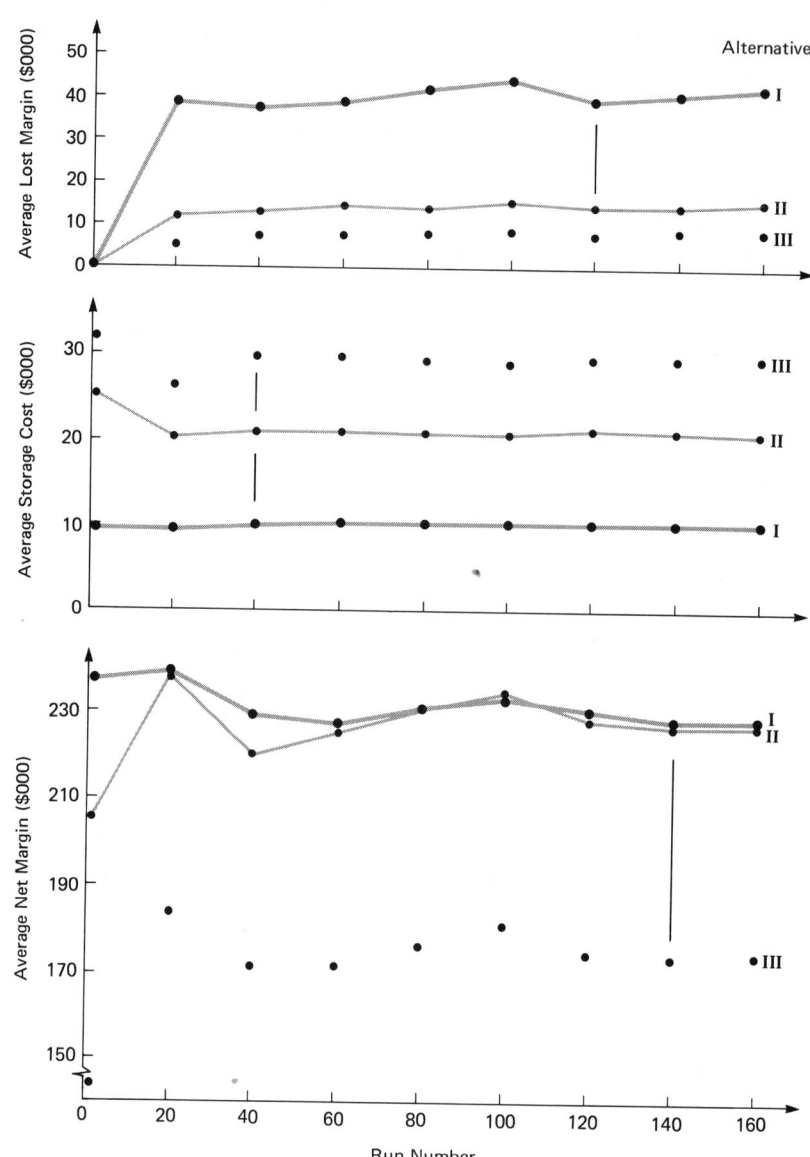

Average storage cost has much less variation and is essentially stable for all three alternatives in Exhibit 6 by run 40. At the top of the exhibit the average lost margin (by not having specific Snurfer models available when demanded) stabilizes for Alternatives II and III by run 40, but Alternative I doesn't stabilize until about run 120.

Plotting the distributions

Considering all three measures of performance, the number of trials needed was probably only 140 or so. Using 500 trials, however, allowed plotting more accurate frequency distributions of the three measures of performance for each of the alternatives, as shown in Exhibits 7, 8, and 9.

The most important measure, net margin, is graphed first. On a run-by-run basis, 64 percent of the time Alternative I had the highest net margin, and 36 percent of the time II was best. Alternative III was never

Net margin: I is best, III is never best

EXHIBIT 7
Distributions of net margins

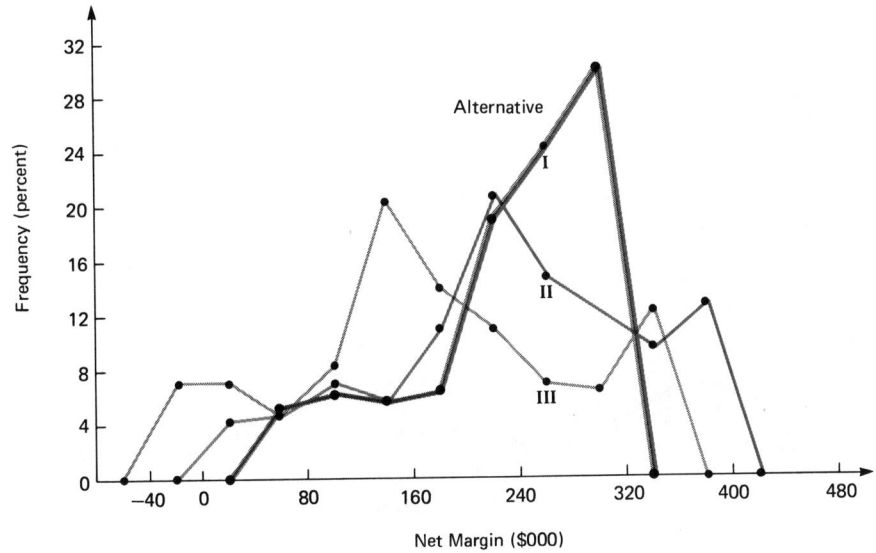

EXHIBIT 8
Storage cost distributions

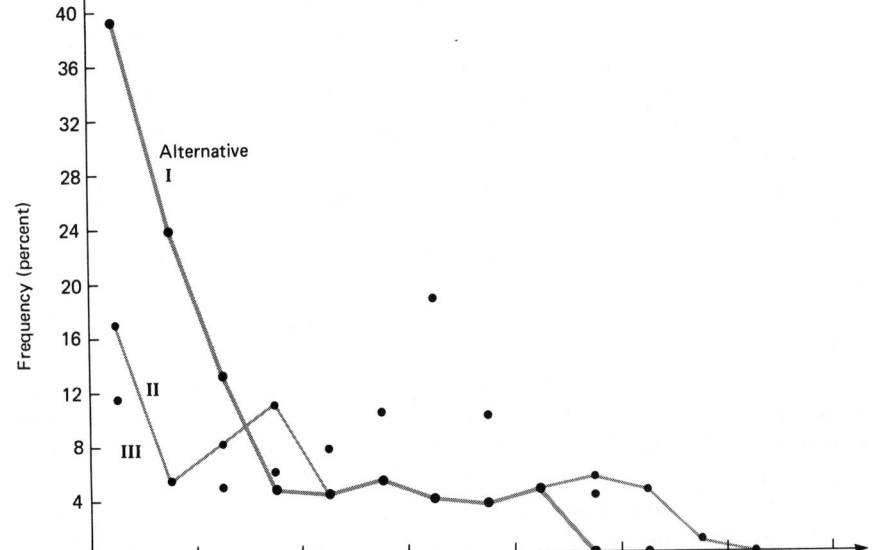

EXHIBIT 9
Distributions of lost
margins

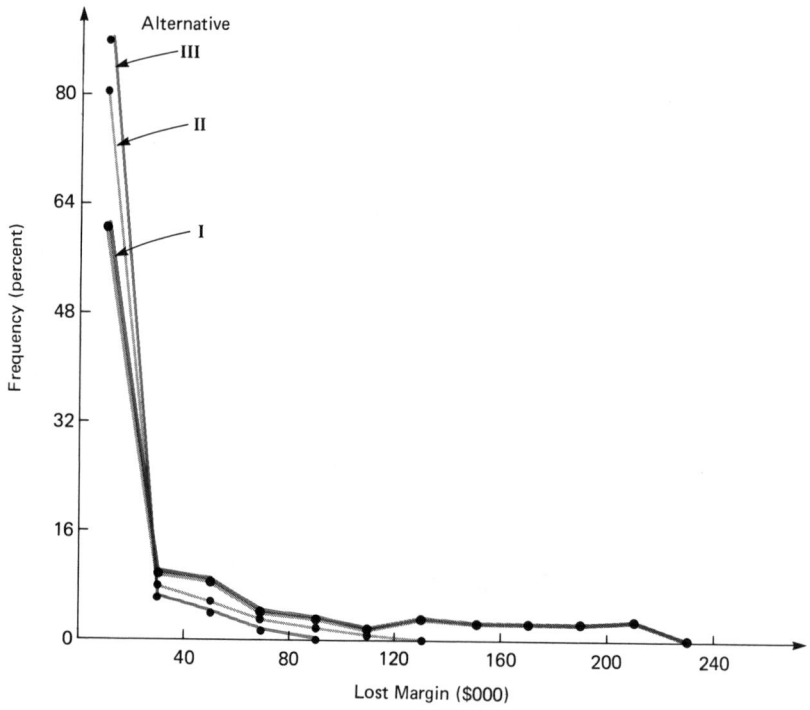

best—the $70,000 tooling investment for Alternative III was always a heavy penalty at the demand levels that were observed.

As can be seen in Exhibit 7, Alternative I has a distribution whose mode is at a significantly higher net margin than II, which is itself higher than III. Furthermore, fully 30 percent of I's margins are at this mode ($280,000–$320,000), whereas only 20 percent of II's and III's margins are at their modes. The result is that the mean and median margins are highest for I, then II, and lastly III.

The assumption of no substitution between Snurfer models was also relaxed. When this was done, Alternative I was even more superior, being favored in 71 percent, rather than 64 percent, of the runs. Again, Alternative III was never best.

Storage cost: I is best
again

Exhibit 8 illustrates the storage cost distributions of the three alternatives. As shown in the exhibit, Alternative I's highest frequency is near zero storage cost. Alternative II is the more even of the three distributions, with a lesser downward trend than I. And III's highest frequency is beyond $30,000 cost. In terms of storage cost the preferred order of alternatives is, again, I, II, and III.

Exhibit 9 illustrates the distributions of margins lost due to insufficient production. The majority of the time very little is ever lost, and all three alternatives look much the same up to about $35,000. Beyond this, Alternative I, which produces only 150,000 Snurfers, has a fairly constant (3 percent) distribution of loss up to $220,000. Alternative II drops off quickly, with no loss beyond $130,000, and III drops off even faster.

Lost margin: III is best

In summary, the simulation verifies the conclusion reached by the other two procedures: that Alternative I is the best of the three. The incremental analysis indicates Brunswick could increase their expected margin somewhat by reducing the number of supers in Alternative I from 70,000 to 64,000 and substituting the difference with regulars. It is seen from the net margin distributions in Exhibit 7 that Alternative I is superior for the majority of possible outcomes of demand, except for very high demands. At 175,000 total demand, Alternative II is about equivalent to Alternative I and, at 300,000 demand, II is $70,000 better than I. There is about a 37 percent chance of demand exceeding 175,000 (see Exhibit 2). The question then becomes: Is it worthwhile to spend $15,000 to try to gain this amount (computed earlier as an expected value of $11,510)? The answer: No, unless the money is important for some other reason (such as not looking like a fool again), or unless there is a good chance of this becoming a boom product. Then the $15,000 tooling is "insurance."

Use II for "insurance"

To conclude, all three analyses gave essentially the same answers. Some of the analyses were more direct, some required more approximations, and some took more effort. Yet, the model results in all cases could not be applied unthinkingly or uncritically. Other factors played important roles as well, such as regret, behavioral considerations, resource constraints, risk propensities, and the like. Probably the most important contribution of the model in a case such as this is to identify the poor alternatives and quantify the tradeoffs among the better alternatives so management can make a choice based on other relevant criteria.

16.6 REVIEW QUESTIONS

1. How would you respond to the arguments of field sales and the production manager in Part (B) of the case, given the quantitative analyses just presented?

2. Given the price of the Snurfer, how substitutable do you feel the two models are for each other?

3. What are the important nonquantitative factors in this case?

4. Which quantitative approach is most conceptu- ally straightforward? Which is simplest? Which is the most difficult? Which is the most accurate? Which do *you* prefer?

5. What are the key elements in this case that make the decision abnormally difficult?

6. How does the "boom or bust" aspect of the product complicate Mr. Biery's decision?

7. What decision is best for Brunswick? For Mr. O'Keefe? What would you decide in this situation?

16.7 REFERENCES AND BIBLIOGRAPHY

1. Aggarwal, R. and Khera, I. *Management Science, Cases and Applications.* San Francisco: Holden- Day, 1979.

2. Berczi, A. *Problems in Managerial Operations Re- search.* Englewood Cliffs, N.J.: Prentice-Hall, Inc., 1969.

3. Berry, W. L., et al. *Management Decision Sciences: Cases and Readings.* Homewood, Ill.: Richard D. Irwin, Inc., 1980.

4. Cabell, R. W., and Phillips, A. *Problems in Basic Operations Research Methods for Management.* New York: John Wiley & Sons, Inc., 1961.

5. Harris, R. D.; Maggard, M. J.; and Lesso, W. G. *Computer Models in Operations Research: A Computer-Augmented Approach.* New York: Harper & Row, Publishers, 1974.

6. Marshall, P., et al. *Operations Management: Text and Cases.* Homewood, Ill.: Richard D. Irwin, Inc., 1975.

7. Martin, M. J. C., and Denison, R. A. *Case Exercises in Operations Research.* New York: John Wiley & Sons, Inc., 1971.

8. McKenney, J. L. and Rosenbloom, R. S. *Cases in Operations Management.* New York: John Wiley & Sons, Inc., 1969.

9. Newson, P. *Management Science and the Manager: A Casebook.* Prentice-Hall, 1980.

17

This chapter assesses the growth and trends in the field of management science. The stages in the field's development are discussed, and it is concluded that the field is currently in a "maturing" stage—solidifying its areas of usefulness and moving into the realm of delivering human services where problems are more nebulous and ill-structured.

It appears that linear programming is still the most useful normative technique but that simulation is receiving increasing attention for two reasons. One reason is that simulation is a good tool for tackling the more prevalent ill-structured problems. Secondly, simulation is easier for the manager to understand and, due to its nature, tends to reinforce implementation of the study results.

Of all the new developments in management science, the most promising seems to be that of decision support systems. These systems bring together the manager, the management scientist, and the information systems analyst for a significant improvement in the managerial decision process.

The future of management science

MS—a newcomer

Management science, as a field, is about 35 years old, a relative newcomer. The early years of development have witnessed significant growth and changes in the field. Magee [14] identifies three separate stages of this development.

The *Primitive* stage (1950s)

Small problems—outside experts

The earliest stage of management science was characterized by a focus on small, well-defined "tactical" problems which could be "optimally" solved by consideration of only quantitative aspects. Typical model examples were economic-order-quantity inventory models and linear programming. The experts in the field were often from other disciplines such as economics and mathematics; academic programs in management science and operations research were very limited.

The *Academic* stage (1960s)

Growth of theory and techniques

The emphasis in this intermediate stage was on the "technical," rather than any managerial, aspects of problems. Thus the theory behind the models blossomed. Solid progress in techniques of analysis was being made as a foundation for further growth. An appreciation was being gained for the proper role of management science and its strengths and weaknesses. As a result the number of formal academic programs at major universities increased and trained management scientists as well as students exposed to the techniques were entering the business world and making firms aware of the emergence of a new discipline.

The *Maturing* stage (1970s)

This stage witnessed the expansion of some trends of the 60s, such as:

1. An interest in the nature of real-life managerial problems and their environments.
2. A more realistic appreciation of the strengths and limitations of management science.
3. More emphasis on the nonquantitative aspects: behavioral, functional, interrelationships, assumptions.
4. More of a "systems" orientation with integration of the quantitative and qualitative problem aspects.

More problem orientation

Additionally, more emphasis has been placed on the problem rather than on the theory. This more realistic perspective, in turn, led analysts to think in terms of dynamic, continually evolving solutions to on-going problems.

Fuzzy problems

There has also been a trend toward analyzing more ill-structured ("fuzzy") problems, such as exist in the public service area (urban development, transportation, health, education) as well as at top corporate levels. Such problems involve nonquantitative elements and thus indicate a possible expansion of management science toward other disciplines such as psychology and anthropology. This trend may herald a rift in the field, a possibility which will be addressed a bit later.

17.1 THE PAST: REQUIREMENTS FOR GROWTH

In 1961, Magee and Ernst [15] set out some general requirements for the growth of management science:

1. A need for it must exist.
2. Management must perceive their problems as potentially amenable to management science techniques.
3. Management science must prove itself in the eyes of the manager.

Requirements for growth

The assumption inherent in the requirements above is that, to survive as a discipline, management science must have a sponsor in the "real world." Magee and Ernst warn that the field must not turn inwards, continually finding better and better answers to a set of ever narrowing problems or else it will stop growing and occupy only a niche in the manager's sphere of acquaintance as have "time and motion study" and "quality control" in previous eras.

Their advice is of extreme importance because it is only too obvious from a cursory examination of the journals in management science that entire tomes could be written on such topics as: "A Hundred Different Types of EOQ Models" or "The Thousand Variations of the Queuing Problem." This would clearly be a continuation of the "academic stage" described earlier. However, if management science were to completely adopt this orientation, it could well become a field of esoterics talkling to themselves. Fortunately, this appears quite unlikely.

A field of esoterics?

It should be mentioned that the first two requirements of Magee and Ernst appear currently to be fulfilled; progress on the third item is slow. After an initial "oversell" to management, with the naturally resulting failures and disappointments, both sides are taking a more realistic view of the potentials (and limitations) of management science. Thus, a foundation for further growth appears to be forming.

17.2 THE PRESENT: EXTENSIONS OF MS/OR

Radnor and Neal [18] have closely studied the use of management science in business firms and have come to the following conclusions:

1. Management science (MS) capabilities are diffusing throughout firms.

MS is spreading

2. At the same time, a "core" MS group is establishing itself within firms as a separate entity.
3. MS is spreading into smaller organizations as well.
4. MS is still in a transitional state.

Outside of the industrial firm, it appears that MS is spreading into several other disciplines as well: economics, public affairs, sociology, engineering, and all areas of business [16]. This expanded base of operations appears to confirm Magee's contention that management science is currently in a "maturing stage."

Thus it appears that management science is finally being accorded some recognition by management, but probably not to the extent envisioned by scientists. Dearden and Lastanica [8] summarize studies which show that linear programming is still, in general, the only really useful normative technique for solving problems with a large number of variables. Such techniques as game theory and dynamic programming, about 20 years old, have had virtually no evidence of significant practical application. Management apparently views such techniques as useful *aids* to decision making but not of overwhelming importance. This may not hold for some other techniques however (such as interactive modeling and simulation), as will be discussed later.

17.3 THE FUTURE: EFFECTIVENESS AND FUZZY PROBLEMS

And what of the future? It seems clear that the "maturing" stage will continue for some time. As younger managers, whose education has included management science techniques, take over higher positions and as computers become more powerful and less expensive, it seems

A larger role for MS?

assured that management science will play an even larger role in private and public firms.

Clearly, management science will play a substantial role in the various functional business areas (such as production, marketing, accounting and finance) where routine planning, organizing, directing, and controlling are performed. This would amount to an expansion of MS on an already existing base. As Dearden and Lastanica [8] point out, most of the techniques are primarily useful for operational problems in business. Thus, one may expect to see increasing formation of optimal policies in problems such as inventories, staffing, scheduling, and allocation.

In the theoretical realm, Zeleny [25] points out the task:

> . . . As managerial concerns advance from simple, well-structured, static and deterministic problems toward more complex, fuzzy, dynamic and stochastic problems, the optimal working framework of the human mind changes from logical, rational, sequential, and qualitative, to perceptive, intuitive, simultaneous and qualitative. . . .

A *new* task for MS

The development of new tools, aimed at the enhancement of *intuitive* powers of managers, is the main task for management science today.

An accelerating factor in broadening the management science base may possibly be an enlarging role for interactive modeling on the computer terminal to help solve complicated sequencing and scheduling problems of lower and middle management:

> Most of the really important problems are complex and messy and thus their systematic treatment requires substantial subjective inputs: value judgments, opinions, personal goals and feelings. The decision maker's mind becomes an integral part of an analytical algorithm, its main interactive subroutine. This symbiotic, intricate and elegant cooperation of manager and management scientist leads to a stagewise, adaptive procedure where mutual learning helps to understand what the solutions should be and why. Men and machines cooperate rather than compute. [25].

Symbiotic cooperation

Just as important is the trend in management science toward the tackling of ill-structured problems. This trend is an outgrowth of the increasing problem orientation, rather than technique orientation, among management scientists. And this has been fostered, in large part, by the development of simulation.

Simulation, which goes hand in hand with advances in computer capabilities (at lower cost), has been a primary management science development with great potential beyond the operational level of business firms. The acceptance of simulation at the higher managerial levels is probably due primarily to the three following factors:

The importance of simulation

- Simulation, being descriptive, requires the manager to interact with the model by asking "what-if" type questions and then directing modifications in the model.
- To build the model accurately, the management scientist must constantly communicate with the manager.
- The model is built from the manager's perspective, rather than from the management scientist's.

Thus, as a model, simulation *requires* that the analyst act in a manner as if he were trying to guarantee implementation of his results: *involve those responsible and work with them on the problem.*

The expansion of management science outside the industrial firm will probably occur in several ways. To some extent, multiple-firm projects will undoubtedly appear, such as cooperation between producers, wholesalers, and retailers or, at least, information sharing as now exists among the airlines.

MS outside the firm

The movement into the services and the public sectors will significantly increase. Problem areas such as pollution, transportation, health, social services, fire/police/rescue services, insurance, education, and labor relations are typically ill-structured; but the solution of problems in these areas can also be much more rewarding. Again, simulation appears to be making the most headway on these types of problems. Government agencies are also utilizing management science techniques

The service and public sectors

throughout their areas of responsibility. In these areas it is imperative that the management scientist maintain a problem orientation since much of what must be dealt with cannot be addressed from a technique perspective.

17.4   DECISION SUPPORT SYSTEMS (DSS)

The tools and techniques presented in this book are structured around prototypal managerial problems. These problems are first identified and classified, and then tools such as linear programming prescribed for their solution. For more complex problems, simulation is advocated. In either case, the manager, or the decision maker, is often ignored. Questions such as; How are decisions made? What problem solving process does a manager really use? How will a manager use the "answers" these models provide? and Is the choice completely rational? are not raised. In addition, the examples and problems presented earlier were intentionally simplified for ease of understanding.

In reality, however, life is complicated and unclear. Although some cases involve simple problems which can be treated by the methods proposed, there are often other problems much more complex and unstructured which managers must solve.

Decision support systems (DSS) explore systematic approaches to improving the effectiveness of decision processes in complicated situations where the other tools, and their specific "answers" to specific "models," fail.

The basic philosophy of DSS centers around the following points:

a. An online interactive computer which enables a dialogue between man and machine is an integral part of decision making.
b. Managerial judgment is supported, rather than replaced; that is, judgment is essential.
c. Attempts are made to improve the *effectiveness* of decision making rather than its efficiency. Thus, instead of attempting to make faster, more accurate, or cheaper decisions, the emphasis is on improving the results of the decisions, or making *better* decisions.
d. The decision process is not automated with predefined problems, objectives, and solutions supported by *standard* management science tools. Rather, DSS creates *specialized* tools that are under the control of the specific decision maker in his or her own environment.

A key concept of DSS is Simon's bounded rationality [20]. Simon criticizes the classical model of rational decision making by claiming that it has an overrationalistic view of managerial behavior.

Simon claims that the manager's capacity for formulating and solving complex problems is very small when compared with the size of the problems needing solutions. The human brain is subject to two limitations: (1) it has limited information-storing capacity and (2) it has limited retention capacity. Therefore, people making decisions with bounded (or limited) rationality very seldom look for optimal solutions; instead, they search for "good-enough" solutions—they try to "satisfice" rather than to optimize. DSS attempts to broaden managers' limited rationality by adding the computer's capacity to that of the limited human brain.

The structure of DSS

DSS focuses on supporting decision making rather than on the system of information flows and reports.[1] DSS is composed of three major subsystems: *a data base, a model base,* and *the decision maker* (see Figure 17.1).

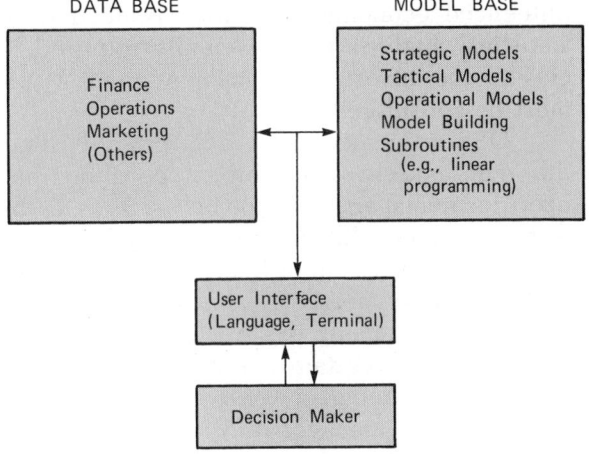

FIGURE 17.1
The structure of DSS

a. The data base subsystem includes data from both internal and external sources. The data are organized in logical form so they can be retrieved easily in response to the decision maker's inquiries or commands. The data base is organized with the appropriate software as a *data based management system* (DBMS).

b. The model-based subsystem includes several mathematical models. These can be specific models that were developed for a specialized purpose such as plant location or media selection, or a standard model such as linear programming or EOQ.

---

[1]For a complete description see Sprague and Watson [21].

c. The decision maker interfaces with the model and data base via an on-line terminal through a special command language. The command languages are human-oriented and sufficiently English-like to accommodate top managers unfamiliar with the standard computer languages. The language helps the manager grow competent in building and solving models in an interactive, exploratory manner. One well-known such language is *interactive financial planning system* (IFPS).

As an example of DSS let us look at a *portfolio management system* (PMS). Such a system supports investment managers in their daily decisions regarding their clients' portfolios. The traditional MS/OR approach provides a decision table for selecting the appropriate investments, or a linear programming model to optimally allocate the clients' funds. In reality, however, the decisions are much more complicated. To begin with, the required decision system is considerably more complex and must include an exhaustive analysis of stocks and other investment alternatives. In addition, the manager needs updated information about account performance. Forecasting of influencial economic indicators is needed continuously, and even a statistical analysis is occasionally required. On top of this, the policies of the investment manager and the preferences of the clients must be considered.

DSS recognizes that different investment managers operate in different models. Therefore, a portfolio management system developed for manager A cannot be used, as is, by manager B (in contrast to tools such as linear programming which are constant and universal). However, a system like PMS, once developed, can be adapted to fit the specific needs of almost any investment manager. It allows subjective judgment by the decision maker, such as assessment of probabilities of certain events and determination of clients' attitudes toward risk through a series of questions by the computer and answers by the manager and vice versa. This broad applicability is possible even though the entire protfolio management can be defined as an unstructured decision because there is sufficient structure in it for analytic aids and computers to be of value to the manager.

What-if analysis

One of the major features of DSS is the user's ability to conduct almost any type of "what-if" analysis. Standard models provide a very limited kind of such analysis, usually in their *sensitivity analysis* portion. Simulation provides an ample opportunity for such an analysis, but it must be preprogrammed in the computer. This may take time since the manager needs a computer programmer who will write and "debug" the changes. With DSS the manager can conduct a what-if dialogue with the computer, and, if necessary, write changes or additions in the computer program personally while interacting with the computer. Here is where judgment plays an important role. The manager may change the input data, add or delete assumptions, change the desired accuracy level of the analysis, or establish aspiration levels for the results. The entire dialogue is done on a what-if basis. That is, the manager may ask such a question as: What if the demand is 10 percent higher and the interest rate 2 percent lower? the computer may give an answer or it may direct the manager to program the necessary equations. This feature significantly increases both the flexibility of the analysis and the chances of implementing quantitative analysis in organizations.

Implementation of analytical models

One of the most important properties of DSS is its ability to translate complex analytical models into usable techniques for the decision maker. This is done through:

a. The interactive structure of DSS which allows the manager to ask questions.
b. The ability to graphically display results and conduct the sensitivity analysis on the screen.
c. The *participation* of the manager in the decision process through dialogue between the user and the system.

There are now dozens of different decision support systems used in organizations. They range from computerized maps used to assign school district boundaries to marketing models for product promotion, pricing, and advertising decisions to product design, modification, and scheduling to hospital rate setting and equipment replacement. Many of the systems deal with planning and financial analysis in organizations ranging in size from small hospitals to giant multinational corporations.

While the application of DSS has been executed by hundred of practitioners, its theoretical development has been conducted mainly at Carnegie Institute of Technology and at Massachusetts Institute of Technology (M.I.T.). The scientists of M.I.T. should be credited with the dissemination of information regarding DSS in a special series published by Addison-Wesley Publishing Company. (See Keen and Morton [13], Johansen et al. [11], and S. Alter [4]).

DSS can be considered an extension of simulation. Most of the DSS's perform some type of simulation ranging from Monte Carlo to heuristic programming, but DSS is much more than that. It may include a linear programming model or an EOQ in one of its elements; plus, it involves computer sciences, data processing, and management information systems. It relies on behavioral sciences and management theories and it may use economic theory and concepts, organizational procedures, or political views.

It has been predicted that sometime in the future computers will be used in every home. The computer will provide people with information about their bank accounts, stocks, football game schedules, and investment opportunities. However, even before that the computer will be found in every manager's office, as the most essential tool for supporting decision making activities.

17.5 CONCLUDING REMARKS

It appears that the broad industrial sponsorship of management science in the operational areas will continue to grow from an already well-established base. Additionally, interactive modeling may begin to play a much more important role in that growth.

Continuing a trend from the 1970s, management science will make further inroads in the services and public areas as public agencies and governmental units adopt MS techniques.

There is currently strong pressure within the field itself to emphasize applications and implementation instead of development of new and extended models. The use of decision support systems further supports this trend. This thrust is a healthy sign; it indicates that the field will continue growing and not become an esoteric endeavor. Those following the "applications" orientation will have to "get their hands dirty" trying to solve social issues, juggle political constraints, and deal with other such nonmathematical details. Those with a theoretical bent will also continue to advance that side, considering "fuzzy" managerial problems and qualitative and intuitive aspects of issues. Indeed, each fraction may well be very interested in the other, and there will undoubtedly be some few individuals who can embrace both cramps.

Finally, the rate of expansion of management science will depend on successful implementation. This text is intended to help in closing the gap between the sponsor-managers and the management scientists, in order to increase the successful implementation of MS projects, thus advancing management science as a discipline.

17.6 REFERENCES AND BIBLIOGRAPHY

1. Ackoff, R. L. "The Future of Operational Re- Is Past." *Journal of the Operational Research Society*, 30 (no. 2, 1979).

2. ———. "Resurrecting the Future of Operational Research." *Journal of the Operational Research Society*, 30 (no. 3, 1979).

3. Alberts, D. S. *A Plan for Measuring the Performance of Social Programs: The Applications of Operations Research Methodology*. New York: Praeger Publishers, Inc., 1970.

4. Alter, S. L. *Decision Support Systems: Current Practice and Continuing Challenges*. Reading, Mass.: Addison-Wesley, 1980.

5. Byrd, Jack. *Operations Research Models for Public Administration*. Lexington, Mass.: Lexington Books, 1975.

6. Charnes, A., and Cooper, W. W. "Management Sciences and Management: Some Requirements for Future Development." *Management Science* 13 (1966):C3–9.

7. Dantzig, G. D. "Operations Research in the World of Today and Tomorrow." ORC 65–67, Operations Research Center, University of California, Berkeley, January 1965.

8. Dearden, J., and Lastanica, J. "New Directions in Operations Research." *Financial Executive* **38** (1970):24–33.

9. Gray, P. "Is OR/MS Everywhere?" *Interfaces* (Bulletin of the Institute of Management Sciences) 9 (November 1979):129–34.

10. Hall, J. R., Jr. and Hess, S. W. "OR/MS Dead or Dying? RX for Survival." *Interfaces* (Bulletin of the Institute of Management Sciences) 8 (May 1978):42–44.

11. Johansen, R., et al. *Electronic Meetings: Technical Alternatives and Social Choices*. Reading, Mass: Addison-Wesley, 1979.

12. Keen, P. G. W. "Decision Support Systems: Translating Analytical Techniques into Useful Tools". *Sloan Management Review*, Spring, 1980.

13. Keen, P. G. W. and Morton, S. S. *Decision Support Systems: An Organizational Perspective*. Reading, Mass: Addison-Wesley, 1978.

14. Magee, J. F. "Progress in the Management Sciences." *Interfaces* (Bulletin of the Institute of Management Sciences) 3 (1973):35–41.

15. Magee, J. F., and Ernst, M. L. "The Challenge of the Future." Edited by R. L. Ackoff. *Progress in Operations Research*. New York: John Wiley & Sons, Inc., 1961.

16. Marmor, N. "Laying the Groundwork for the Future Success of Management Science." *Interfaces* (Bulletin of the Institute of Management Sciences) 3 (1973):54–56.

17. Rader, L. T. "Roadblocks to Progress in the Management Sciences and Operations Research." *Management Science* 11 (1965):C1–C5.

18. Radnor, M., and Neal, R. D. "The Progress of Management Science Activities in Large U.S. Industrial Corporations." *Operations Research* 21 (1973):427–50.

19. Saaty, T. L. "The Future of Operations Research in the Government." *Interfaces* (Bulletin of the Institute of Management Sciences) 2 (1972):1–9.

20. Simon, H. A. *The New Science of Management Decisions*, 3d ed. Englewood Cliffs, NJ: Prentice-Hall, 1977.

21. Sprague R. H. Jr., and Watson, H. J. "Bit by Bit: Toward Decision Support Systems." *California Management Review*, Fall, 1979.

22. Turban, E. "A Sample Survey of Operations Research Activities at the Corporate Level." *Operations Research* 20 (1972):708–21.

23. Weingartner, H. M. "What Lies Ahead in Management Science and Operations Research in Finance in the Seventies." *Interfaces* (Bulletin of the Institute of Management Sciences) 1 (1971):5–12.

24. Zeleny, Milan. "Notes, Ideas, and Techniques: New Vistas of Management Science." *Computers and Operations Research*, 2 (1975):121–25.

25. _____. "The last Mohicans of OR: Or, It Might be in the Genes." *Interfaces* (Bulletin of the Institute of Management Sciences) 9 (November 1979):135–41.

APPENDIXES

A—Mathematics

The purpose of this appendix is to review the mathematical concepts which are used in this text.

A1 DEFINITIONS

Some notation is used throughout the text, independent of subject, and the student should be intimately familiar with these symbols:

! . . . . "factorial": $n! = n(n-1)(n-2) \cdots (1)$
For example: $5! = 5 \cdot 4 \cdot 3 \cdot 2 \cdot 1 = 120$

Σ . . . . summation

$\sum_i$ . . . . sum over all values of the index i:

$$\sum_i x_i = x_1 + x_2 + \cdots + x_n, \quad \text{if} \quad i = 1, 2, \cdots, n.$$

Alternatively, the symbol $\sum_{i=1}^{n} x_i$

can be used.

$\Sigma\,\Sigma$ . . . . double summation

Example:

$$\sum_{i=1}^{3} \sum_{j=1}^{2} x_{ij} = x_{11} + x_{12} + x_{21} + x_{22} + x_{31} + x_{32}$$

Constant: A constant is a quantity that always maintains a fixed value.

Parameter: A parameter is usually constant throughout a problem but may change from problem to problem.

Variable: A variable is a quantity whose value may change throughout a problem.

Continuous variable: The variable may assume *any* value (e.g., 14.7638 . . .) within its acceptable range.

Discrete variable: The variable may only take on certain (countable) values (e.g., 1/7, 2/7, 3/7, etc.), but usually the integers (1, 2, 3, . . .).

Independent variable: In an equation, this variable is known. It is usually shown on the X axis in graphs.

Dependent variable: In an equation, this variable, whose value is desired, is unknown. It is usually shown on the Y axis in graphs.

Example:

In the equation for a circle's circumference, $C = \pi D$

C: A continuous dependent variable.

π: A constant (3.14159).

D: A continuous independent variable (the diameter).

A2 CONCEPTS

Functions

A function is a mathematical expression that states a relationship between at least two variables. The expression $y = f(x)$ is read as follows: y is a function of x. This means that given a value for x, then y can be determined, although $y = f(x)$ does not tell us how. It states that some relationship exists. This relationship may take the form of a table or an equation. For example, $C = \pi D$ means that C is a function of D. That is: given D, it is possible to determine C. This example demonstrates a *single-valued* function because for each value of D there exists only one value of C. Similarly, the equation $y = 4 + x^2$ is a single-valued function. However, the equation $y^2 = 4 + x$ is an example of a *multiple-valued* function because y, *the dependent variable,* may take on more than one value for each value of the *independent variable x* (if $x = 0$, then $y = 2$ or -2).

In the above examples, y was a function of the single variable x. However, in expressions like $y = f(x, z) = x^2 + 3z$, y is a function of *several variables.* Again, x and z would be the independent variables and y the dependent variable.

The *slope* of a function measures how much the dependent variable changes for a small amount of increase in each of the independent variables. If the function is a straight line, then the slope of the function is the same everywhere. However, for functions which are not straight lines, it is necessary to specify *where* the slope is to be measured and in what direction, because it may be different at different values of the independent variables. If the dependent variable *increases (decreases)* with small increases in the independent variables, then we say that the function is *positively (negatively) sloped.*

Continuous and discrete functions

In a manner similar to continuous and discrete variables, there exist continuous and discrete functions also. Examples of continuous functions are:

$$y = x^2 + 2x$$
$$y = 5$$

Some examples of discrete functions are:

$$y = 5x \qquad \text{where } x = 0, 1, 2, \ldots$$

$$y = \begin{cases} 10 + 3x \\ 14 + x \end{cases} \qquad \text{for} \qquad \begin{array}{c} 0 \le x \le 2 \\ x \ge 2 \end{array} \text{ and } x \text{ integer.}$$

Equalities

Functional relationships where the value of the dependent variable *equals* certain values of the independent variable are termed equations. For example, $y = 4x$.

Inequalities

If functional relationships cannot be written as equations but it is known that one exceeds the other, then they must be unequal and can be expressed as inequalities.

Such relationships can be designated by the symbols $\ne$. For example $y \ne 5x$ means that y is *not* equal to $5x$.

When relationships are not equal they can take *one* of four possible forms:

Form	*Symbol*	*Example*
Smaller than	$<$	$y < 6x + 2$
Smaller than or equal to	$\le$	$y \le 4x - 1$
Larger than	$>$	$y > 2x + 9$
Larger than or equal to	$\ge$	$y \ge 5x$

A3 LINEAR EQUATIONS

One of the most important functional relationships is the *linear equation* due to its simplicity and wide range of applicability. A linear equation of two variables (one dependent, one independent) is a straight line. A linear equation of three variables is a plane, in three dimensions. The general form of a linear equation is:

$$y = a_1x_1 + a_2x_2 + \cdots + a_nx_n + b = \sum_i a_ix_i + b \qquad (A1)$$

where the a_i and b are constants and the x_i are different variables. A linear equation always satisfies the following rule:

If kV_i is substituted for each variable V_i in the original equation,[1] $y = f(V_i)$, where k is a constant, then the result will be ky.

---

[1] V_i designates each variable; that is, $x_1, x_2, \ldots, x_n$.

Mathematically:

$$\text{If } y = f(V_i) \text{ is linear, then } f(kV_i) = ky \qquad \text{(A2)}$$

Example Is the function $y = 5x + 3(w - 4z)$ linear?
Solution. Substitute k times each variable in the equation and find:

$$5(kx) + 3[kw - 4(kz)] = 5kx + 3k(w - 4z) = ky$$

Thus, the equation is linear.

The slope of a linear equation

The slope of a linear equation is constant at all points of the function.

In general, the equation of a straight line is given as:

$$y = ax + b \qquad \text{(A3)}$$

where a and b are constants. The slope of such a line is always a. The constant b also has a special name: the *intercept*. This is because when x is set to 0 (which is where the line "intercepts" the y axis), the value of y equals b. The slope and intercept for the equation $y = 2x + 2$ are shown in Figure A1. Also shown in the figure are parts of the linear functions $y = 2$ and $y = 2x$, both of which differ from $y = 2x + 2$. The slope of $y = 2$ is 0, and its intercept is 2. The slope of $y = 2x$ is 2 and its intercept is 0.

FIGURE A1
Slope of linear functions

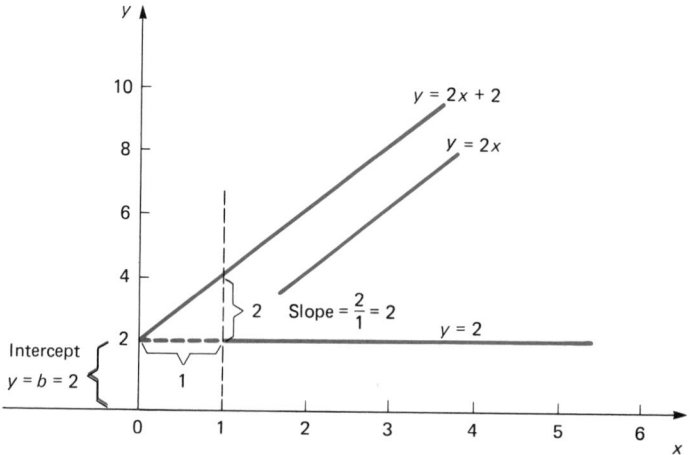

Nonlinear functions

Any function that does not meet the linearity requirement is considered *nonlinear*.

A4   RULES OF MANIPULATION

Inequalities

The rules of manipulation of inequalities are the same as for equations with one exception: when multiplying or dividing the inequality by a negative number, the inequality sign is reversed. For example, given:

$$3 \geq -5$$

Multiplying by -1:

$$-3 \leq 5$$

As another example:

$$-4y + 10x \geq 2x - 8$$

Dividing by -2:

$$2y - 5x \leq -z + 4.$$

Exponents

The definition of x^n (called x to the nth power) is x multiplied together n times, where n is called the *exponent*. The rules for manipulating exponents are:

1. *Rule of multiplication:*

$$x^a \cdot x^b = x^{a+b} \tag{A4}$$

For example, $x^2 \cdot x^3 = x^5$

2. *Rule of division:*

$$x^a/x^b = x^{a-b} \tag{A5}$$

The second rule holds for cases where $b > a$ as well. This states, for example, that $x^3/x^4 = x^{3-4} = x^{-1}$. Invoking rule 1, it is possible to work backwards through cross-multiplication to obtain:

$$x^4 \cdot x^{-1} = x^{4-1} = x^3$$

3. *Implications:*

    a.

$$x^n/x^n = x^0 = 1 \tag{A6}$$

for any nonzero value of x.

    b. *Example:* It can be seen that $1/x^2 = x^0/x^2 = x^{0-2} = x^{-2}$; that is, in general:

$$x^{-a} = 1/x^a \qquad \text{(A7)}$$

c.
$$(x^a)^b = x^{a \cdot b} \qquad \text{(A8)}$$

Example: $(x^2)^3 = (x \cdot x)(x \cdot x)(x \cdot x) = x^{2 \cdot 3} = x^6$.

d.
$$\sqrt[b]{x^a} = x^{a/b} \qquad \text{(A9)}$$

Example: $\sqrt[3]{x^6} = x^{6/3} = x^2$

A5   SIMULTANEOUS EQUATIONS

Frequently, in management science, sets of simultaneous equations are encountered which must be solved in order to determine the optimal answer to a problem. Sets of *linear* equations are particularly frequent, as in linear programming. A general set of *simultaneous linear equations* is indicated below where there are m equations and n unknown variables x_i.

$$
\begin{aligned}
a_{11}x_1 + \cdots + a_{1n}x_n &= b_1 \\
&\ \ \vdots \\
\cdots + a_{ij}x_j + \cdots &= b_i \\
&\ \ \vdots \\
a_{m1}x_1 + \cdots + a_{mn}x_n &= b_m
\end{aligned}
\qquad \text{(A10)}
$$

This system can be written as:

$$\sum_{j=1}^{n} a_{ij}x_j = b_i \qquad \text{for } i = 1, \ldots, m$$

The a_{ij} terms are the *coefficients* (constants) of the x variable in the ith row and jth column, x_j. Note that there are only n unknown x variables, one for each of j columns. There are also m right-hand constants, b_i. If all the b_i are zero, the linear system is called *homogeneous*.

There are a number of techniques for solving a system of linear equations if, indeed, a solution exists. On the other hand, sometimes more than one solution exists.

Solution methods

A common method is the *Gauss-Jordan* technique. Consider the following set of linear equations:

1.
$$3x_1 + x_2 = 6$$
2.
$$x_1 - 2x_2 = -1$$

The Gauss-Jordan solution procedure aims to eliminate x_i from all equations except the ith equation and to give x_i a coefficient of unity in that equation. Starting with x_1, Equation 1 is divided by 3:

1'. $$x_1 + \frac{1}{3} x_2 = 2$$

Next, the new Equation 1' is subtracted from Equation 2 (a rule of algebra states that a multiple of one equation can be added to, or subtracted from, another equation without affecting the functional relationship):

2. $$x_1 - 2x_2 = -1$$

1'. $$-\left(x_1 + \frac{1}{3} x_2 = 2 \right)$$

The result is:

2'. $$0 - 2\frac{1}{3} x_2 = -3$$

The new set of equations is thus:

1'. $$x_1 + \frac{1}{3} x_2 = 2$$

2'. $$-2\frac{1}{3} x_2 = -3$$

Now consider the variable x_2. In order to have a coefficient of 1 for x_2, Equation 2' is divided by $-2\frac{1}{3}$. The result is Equation 2″:

2″. $$x_2 = \frac{9}{7}$$

Next, one third of Equation 2″ is subtracted from 1' to eliminate x_2 in Equation 1':

1'. $$x_1 + \frac{1}{3} x_2 = 2$$

$$-\left(\frac{1}{3} x_2 = \frac{3}{7} \right)$$

The result is:

1″. $$x_1 \qquad = \frac{11}{7}$$

Thus, the answer is:

$$x_1 = \frac{11}{7} \qquad \text{and} \qquad x_2 = \frac{9}{7}$$

Other solution methods involve the use of matrices or determinants. For discussion see any text in the bibliography.

A6   MATRIX ALGEBRA

Matrices

A *matrix* is a rectangular (or square) array of numbers in m rows and n columns. Matrices are typically designated by capital letters. Alternately, small bracketed letters with two subscripts (the first refers to the row and the second to the column) to indicate elements of the matrix can be used. The general format of a matrix is:

$$A = [a_{ij}] = \begin{bmatrix} a_{11} & a_{12} & \cdots & a_{1n} \\ a_{21} & a_{22} & \cdots & a_{2n} \\ \cdot & \cdot & & \cdot \cdot \\ \cdot & \cdot & & \cdot \\ \cdot & \cdot & & \cdot \\ a_{m1} & \cdot \cdot & \cdots & a_{mn} \end{bmatrix} \tag{A11}$$

A is a matrix with m rows and n columns, or a matrix of $m \times n$ *dimension*. If $m = n$, the matrix is said to be a *square* matrix of *order* n. Each element in the matrix has an address designated by its row and its column. For example, a_{36} means a number in the third row and the sixth column.

Row and column vectors

If a matrix has only one row and two or more, say n, columns, it is called an n-dimensional *row vector;* if there is one column and two or more rows, it is called a *column vector.* Vector's elements are also designated by brackets [ ].
Examples:

Three-dimensional row vector:
$$S = [a_1 \quad a_2 \quad a_3] = [3 \quad 1 \quad -2]$$

Three-dimensional column vector:
$$T = \begin{bmatrix} a_1 \\ a_2 \\ a_3 \end{bmatrix} = \begin{bmatrix} 5 \\ 2 \\ 6 \end{bmatrix}$$

A matrix can be represented as a set of row or column vectors.
Example:

Given:
$$V = \begin{bmatrix} a_{11} \\ a_{21} \\ a_{31} \end{bmatrix}; \quad W = \begin{bmatrix} a_{12} \\ a_{22} \\ a_{32} \end{bmatrix}$$

and

$$X = [a_{11}\ a_{12}];\quad Y = [a_{21}\ a_{22}];\quad Z = [a_{31}\ a_{32}]$$

then:

$$A = [VW] = \begin{bmatrix} X \\ Y \\ Z \end{bmatrix} = \begin{bmatrix} a_{11} & a_{12} \\ a_{21} & a_{22} \\ a_{31} & a_{32} \end{bmatrix}$$

The null (zero) vector and unit vector

Two special vectors of importance are the *null vector*, with all elements zero; that is, [0 0 0 0], and the *unit vector*, with all elements zero except one which is unity (1); that is, [0 0 1 0].

The null matrix and unit matrix

Similar to the null vector and unit vector there also exist the *null matrix*, with all elements zero, and the *unit (or identity) matrix*, denoted by *I*, with all elements zero except for ones along the main (top-left to bottom-right) diagonal:

$$I = \begin{bmatrix} 1 & 0 & 0 \\ 0 & 1 & 0 \\ 0 & 0 & 1 \end{bmatrix} \tag{A12}$$

The transpose of a matrix

The *transpose* of a matrix, A^T, is the matrix obtained by interchanging the rows and columns of the original matrix, A.

$$\text{If:}\quad A = \begin{bmatrix} a_{11} & a_{12} & a_{13} \\ a_{21} & a_{22} & a_{23} \\ a_{31} & a_{32} & a_{33} \end{bmatrix} \quad \text{Then:}\quad A^T = \begin{bmatrix} a_{11} & a_{21} & a_{31} \\ a_{12} & a_{22} & a_{32} \\ a_{13} & a_{23} & a_{33} \end{bmatrix} \tag{A13}$$

Matrix manipulations

Addition and subtraction   In order to add or subtract matrices they must be exactly of the same size. Then the corresponding elements in each matrix are added or subtracted. For example in a 2 × 2 matrix:

$$\begin{bmatrix} a_{11} & a_{12} \\ a_{21} & a_{22} \end{bmatrix} + \begin{bmatrix} b_{11} & b_{12} \\ b_{21} & b_{22} \end{bmatrix} = \begin{bmatrix} a_{11} + b_{11}, & a_{12} + b_{12} \\ a_{21} + b_{21}, & a_{22} + b_{22} \end{bmatrix} \tag{A14}$$

Example:

$$\begin{bmatrix} 4 & 2 \\ 3 & 1 \end{bmatrix} + \begin{bmatrix} 5 & 3 \\ 0 & 4 \end{bmatrix} = \begin{bmatrix} 9 & 5 \\ 3 & 5 \end{bmatrix}$$

Multiplication To multiply a matrix by a constant (called a scalar) it is necessary to multiply every element of the matrix by the constant. For example:

$$kA = \begin{bmatrix} ka_{11} & ka_{12} \\ ka_{21} & ka_{22} \end{bmatrix} \qquad \text{(A15)}$$

Multiplying a matrix by a matrix is somewhat more complex. Let us use an example to demonstrate. Suppose that it is desired to multiply matrix A by matrix B where:

$$A = \begin{bmatrix} a_{11} & a_{12} \\ a_{21} & a_{22} \\ a_{31} & a_{32} \end{bmatrix} \qquad B = \begin{bmatrix} b_{11} & b_{12} \\ b_{21} & b_{22} \end{bmatrix}$$

Note that the number of columns of matrix A must equal the number of rows of matrix B. Otherwise they are not "conformable" for multiplication.

The product of $A \times B$ is:

$$C = \begin{bmatrix} a_{11} & a_{12} \\ a_{21} & a_{22} \\ a_{31} & a_{32} \end{bmatrix} \times \begin{bmatrix} b_{11} & b_{12} \\ b_{21} & b_{22} \end{bmatrix} = \begin{bmatrix} a_{11}b_{11} + a_{12}b_{21} & a_{11}b_{12} + a_{12}b_{22} \\ a_{21}b_{11} + a_{22}b_{21} & a_{21}b_{12} + a_{22}b_{22} \\ a_{31}b_{11} + a_{32}b_{21} & a_{31}b_{12} + a_{32}b_{22} \end{bmatrix} = \begin{bmatrix} c_{11} & c_{12} \\ c_{21} & c_{22} \\ c_{31} & c_{32} \end{bmatrix} \qquad \text{(A16)}$$

In general:

An element in the resultant matrix C is the sum of the products of the elements of the ith row of A and the jth column of B. A simple way to derive the solution of a matrix multiplication is as follows. First, represent the left matrix (A) by *row* vectors:

$$A = \begin{bmatrix} A_1 \\ A_2 \\ A_3 \end{bmatrix}$$

where A_1, A_2, and so on, are each a row vector: $(A_1 = [a_{11}\ a_{12}\ a_{13}\ .\ .\ .])$. Then represent the right matrix (B) by column vectors:

$$B = [B_1 \quad B_2]$$

where B_1, B_2, and so on, are each column vestors:

$$B_1 = \begin{bmatrix} b_{11} \\ b_{21} \\ . \\ . \\ . \end{bmatrix}$$

Then combine the matrices by forming the appropriate products:

$$A \times B = \begin{bmatrix} A_1 \times B_1 & A_1 \times B_2 \\ A_2 \times B_1 & A_2 \times B_2 \\ A_3 \times B_1 & A_3 \times B_2 \end{bmatrix} \qquad \text{(A17)}$$

Note that this final matrix has as many rows as matrix A and as many columns as matrix B. The remaining step is to multiply each of the A_iB_j vectors together, element by element, and sum.
Examples:

a.
$$\begin{bmatrix} 2 & 3 \\ 4 & 1 \\ 1 & 5 \end{bmatrix} \times \begin{bmatrix} 6 & 7 \\ 8 & 0 \end{bmatrix} = \begin{bmatrix} 2 \times 6 + 3 \times 8 = 36, & 2 \times 7 + 3 \times 0 = 14 \\ 4 \times 6 + 1 \times 8 = 32, & 4 \times 7 + 1 \times 0 = 28 \\ 1 \times 6 + 5 \times 8 = 46, & 1 \times 7 + 5 \times 0 = 7 \end{bmatrix} = \begin{bmatrix} 36 & 14 \\ 32 & 28 \\ 46 & 7 \end{bmatrix}$$

b.
$$\begin{bmatrix} 2 \\ 4 \end{bmatrix} \times [6 \quad 7] = \begin{bmatrix} 2 \times 6 = 12, & 2 \times 7 = 14 \\ 4 \times 6 = 24, & 4 \times 7 = 28 \end{bmatrix} = \begin{bmatrix} 12 & 14 \\ 24 & 28 \end{bmatrix}$$

c.
$$[2 \quad 3] \times \begin{bmatrix} 6 \\ 8 \end{bmatrix} = \qquad [2 \times 6 + 3 \times 8 = 36] = 36$$

d.
$$\begin{bmatrix} 2 \\ 4 \end{bmatrix} \times \begin{bmatrix} 6 \\ 8 \end{bmatrix} = \text{not conformable for multiplication}$$

In general, $A \times B$ does not give the same result as $B \times A$. That is, the cumulative law of algebra *does not* hold with matrices. However, the *associative law* holds; that is:

$$(A \times B) \times C = A \times (B \times C) \qquad \text{(A18)}$$

Also the *distributive law* holds:

$$A \times (B + C) = A \times B + A \times C \qquad \text{(A19)}$$

The inverse of a matrix

If square matrices A and D exist such that $AD = DA = I$ (the identity matrix), then D is said to be the inverse of A.[2]

$$D = A^{-1} \qquad \text{(A20)}$$

---

[2] A matrix whose determinant (to be presented soon) equals zero is called a *singular* matrix and it does not have an inverse.

Inverse matrices are important in solving systems of simultaneous linear equations. A simultaneous linear equation set, such as that of Equation A17, may be expressed in matrix form as follows:

1. All the coefficients a_{ij} are described in a matrix A

$$A = \begin{bmatrix} a_{11} & \cdots & a_{1n} \\ & \cdot & \\ \cdot & & \cdot \\ & \cdot & \\ a_{m1} & \cdots & a_{mn} \end{bmatrix}$$

2. All the unknown variables x_j are expressed as a column vector X

$$X = \begin{bmatrix} x_1 \\ \cdot \\ \cdot \\ \cdot \\ x_n \end{bmatrix}$$

3. The right-hand-side constants, b_i, are expressed as a column vector B

$$B = \begin{bmatrix} b_1 \\ \cdot \\ \cdot \\ \cdot \\ b_n \end{bmatrix}$$

4. The entire system is expressed as:

$$AX = B \tag{A21}$$

With matrix algebra it is possible to solve for the vector X by multiplying the inverse of the vector A times B:

$$X = A^{-1}B$$

Finding the inverse

Several methods are available for finding the inverse of a matrix but one which works for *any* sized matrix utilizes the Gauss-Jordan system: *Example:*

Given a matrix

$$A = \begin{bmatrix} a_{11} & a_{12} \\ a_{21} & a_{22} \end{bmatrix}$$

find the inverse.

Step 1   Append an identity matrix to the right side of the original matrix, A.

$$\begin{bmatrix} a_{11} & a_{12} & 1 & 0 \\ a_{21} & a_{22} & 0 & 1 \end{bmatrix}$$

Step 2   Manipulate the rows via the Gauss-Jordan method such that the identity matrix appears on the left side:

$$\begin{bmatrix} 1 & 0 & d_{11} & d_{12} \\ 0 & 1 & d_{21} & d_{22} \end{bmatrix}$$

The resulting right-hand matrix

$$D = \begin{bmatrix} d_{11} & d_{12} \\ d_{21} & d_{22} \end{bmatrix}$$

will then be the inverse of A:

$$D = A^{-1}$$

As an example, let us use the Gauss-Jordan coefficients of Section A5.

$$A = \begin{bmatrix} 3 & 1 \\ 1 & -2 \end{bmatrix}$$

Step 1

$$\begin{bmatrix} 3 & 1 & 1 & 0 \\ 1 & -2 & 0 & 1 \end{bmatrix}$$

Step 2   Divide the first row by 3:

$$\begin{bmatrix} 1 & 1/3 & 1/3 & 0 \\ 1 & -2 & 0 & 1 \end{bmatrix}$$

Subtract row 1 from row 2:

$$\begin{bmatrix} 1 & 1/3 & 1/3 & 0 \\ (1-1=0) & (-2-1/3 = -2^{1}/_3) & (0-1/3 = -1/3) & (1-0 = 1) \end{bmatrix}$$

Divide row 2 by $-2^{1}/_3$:

$$\begin{bmatrix} 1 & 1/3 & 1/3 & 0 \\ 0 & 1 & 1/7 & -3/7 \end{bmatrix}$$

Subtract one third of row 2 from row 1:

$$\begin{bmatrix} (1-0=1) & (1/3 - 1/3 = 0) & (1/3 - 1/21 = 2/7) & (0 + 1/7 = 1/7) \\ 0 & 1 & 1/7 & -3/7 \end{bmatrix}$$

The inverse is thus: $\begin{bmatrix} 2/7 & 1/7 \\ 1/7 & -3/7 \end{bmatrix}$

Check: $\begin{bmatrix} 3 & 1 \\ 1 & -2 \end{bmatrix}\begin{bmatrix} 2/7 & 1/7 \\ 1/7 & -3/7 \end{bmatrix} = \begin{bmatrix} 1 & 0 \\ 0 & 1 \end{bmatrix}$

A7 PRESENT VALUE

Many managerial decisions must reflect the value of time: "time is money." Thus, a dollar today is worth more than a dollar in the future (especially with inflation). This time value is accounted for by an interest rate (or, equivalently, a discount factor). The following formulas present the basic mathematical notions of annuities, compound interest, and present value.

Formulas for value and compound interest factors

Let:

F = future worth.
P = present value.
A = annuity, equal payments, of \$A each payment.
n = number of years.
i = interest rate.

1. *To find P, given F, single payment.* The present worth of a single sum F, payable n years from now.

$$P = \frac{F}{(1 + i)^n} \tag{A22}$$

2. *To find P, given A.*

$$P = A\left[\frac{(1 + i)^n - 1}{i(1 + i)^n}\right] \tag{A23}$$

This is the present value of a series of uniform end-of-year payments, each A, for n years.

This information is usually given in the form of tables in many finance, economics, and accounting texts.

A8 BIBLIOGRAPHY

1. Adams, B. *Fundamentals of Mathematics for Business, Social, and Life Sciences.* Englewood Cliffs, N.J. Prentice Hall, 1979.

2. Churchman, C. W.; Auerbach, L.: and Sadan, S. *Thinking for Decisions: Deductive Quantitative Methods.* Chicago: Science Research Associates, Inc., 1975.

3. Draper, J., and Klingman, J. S. *Mathematical Analysis.* New York: Harper & Row, Publishers, 1967.

4. Hohn, F. E. *Elementary Matrix Algebra.* 2d ed. New York: Macmillan, Inc., 1964.

5. Kemeny, J. G., et al. *Finite Mathematics with Business Applications.* 2d ed. Englewood Cliffs, N.J.: Prentice-Hall, Inc., 1972.

6. Mason, R. D. *Programmed Learning Aid for College Mathematics.* Homewood, Ill.: Learning Systems Co., 1971.

7. Owen G. *Finite Mathematics.* Philadelphia: W. B. Saunders Co., 1970.

8. Peck, L. C. *Basic Mathematics for Management and Economics.* Cleveland: Scott, Foresman and Co., 1970.

9. Theodore, C. A. *Applied Mathematics: An Introduction.* 3d ed. Homewood, Ill.: Richard D. Irwin, Inc., 1975.

10. Vazsonyi, A. *Finite Mathematics, Quantitative Analysis for Business,* New York: John Wiley & Sons, 1977.

B—Statistics

This appendix includes a condensed presentation of the basic concepts of statistics and probability theory as related to this text. For more detailed explanations, the reader is referred to the bibliography. Material here is divided into three main categories: probability, statistics, and distributions.

B1   PROBABILITY

The essence of probability is estimating the "odds," "risks," or "the long-run chances" of certain events occurring. An *event* is an *uncertain outcome*. The probability of a given event occurring is designated on a scale of 0 to 1. If the event *cannot* occur, then its probability is zero. If, on the other hand, the event is certain to occur, then its probability is one. Probability values other than 0 or 1 (expressed as a decimal fraction) represent an estimate of the random effect of chance. They measure the degree of belief that an event will occur. For example, a probability of .4 of showers today means that there is a .4 chance (or 40 percent chance) of rain.

Whenever probabilities are stated, a time frame must be specified. There is a certain chance for showers *today* which may differ from the chances tomorrow, or over a week's duration. The classical definition of probability is given below.

The probability of an occurrence is the relative frequency of an event when a situation is repeated many times under identical circumstances.

Formally, it is expressed as:

$$P(\text{event } A) = \frac{\text{Number of Occurrences of the Event } A}{\text{Total Number of Occurrences}} \qquad \text{(B1)}$$

Basic concepts

Range   Probabilities range between 0 and 1 and can never assume a negative value. Formally: $0 \leq P(A) \leq 1$, where $P(A)$ is the probability of event A.

Frequency and probability   The terms frequency and probability express the same idea in slightly different ways. For example, it can be said that the *frequency* of a "head" in a coin toss is one out of two. The same information is given by saying that the *probability* of a "head" in a coin toss is .5, or 50 percent. The two terms are used interchangeably.

Example. Suppose you are in a hurry driving on a crowded street. You have driven down this street 80 times before. Out of these 80 times, you estimate, as best you can recall, the relative frequency of occurrence of different speeds of traffic (events) on this street, as shown in Table B1.

TABLE B1
Probability distribution of traffic speeds

Speed MPH (event)	Number of times observed	Relative frequency, percent	Cumulative probability, percent
20	6	6/80 = 7.5	0 + 7.5 = 7.5
25	14	14/80 = 17.5	7.5 + 17.5 = 25.0
30	25	25/80 = 31.3	25 + 31.3 = 56.3
35	18	18/80 = 22.5	56.3 + 22.5 = 78.8
40	11	11/80 = 13.7	78.8 + 13.7 = 92.5
45	5	5/80 = 6.3	92.5 + 6.3 = 98.8
50	1	1/80 = 1.2	99.8 + 1.2 = 100.0
Total	80	80/80 = 100.0	100.0

Table B1 shows the frequency of the seven events. The table also shows the cumulative probability.

Cumulative probability   The last column of Table B1 shows the probability of two or more events occurring on a cumulative basis. For example, the probability of traveling at 25 miles per hour or less is: 7.5 percent + 17.5 percent = 25.0. The *cumulative probability for all the events* is 100 percent, by definition. This property helps us to compute cumulative probabilities. For example, let us compute the cumulative probability of traveling faster than 40 MPH. Since the cumulative probability of traveling 40 MPH or less is 92.5 percent, then the probability of going faster than 40 MPH is 100 percent − 92.5 percent = 7.5 percent. The same result is achieved if the probability of 45 MPH is added to that of 50 MPH: 6.3 percent + 1.2 percent = 7.5 percent.

Assessment of probabilities   Probabilities may be assessed in two ways, subjectively and objectively.

1. Subjective probability   If the chances of an event occurring are estimated by an individual, based on his or her beliefs and experience, but without hard data to back this belief, then the probability is termed *subjective*.

2. *Objective probability*   If the probability is based on hard facts, then it is termed objective. Three cases are distinguished:

i.   Probability which is *based on logic*. For example, the probability of a "head" in a coin toss is reasoned to be 50 percent.

ii.   Probability which is *based on historical data*. For example, if 17 of the last 100 years had more than 3 inches of rain in April, then the probability of having more than 3 inches of rain in April is assessed as 17/100 = 17 percent.

iii.   Probability which is *based on experimentation*. For example, in order to find out the reliability of a new product one may test 100 units of the new product to find out how many of these will work.

Random variable   A variable whose value is determined by chance is referred to as a random variable. For example, the traffic speed in Table B1 is a random variable.

Event relationships

Independent and dependent events   Events are classified as *independent* if the occurrence of one has no effect on the probability of others and vice versa. Events are considered *dependent* if the occurrence of one of them *does* affect the probability of the others.

Mutually exclusive events   If the occurrence of an event *precludes* the occurrence of another event (that is, the two *cannot* occur together) then the events are said to be mutually exclusive.

Collectively exhaustive events   A set (collection) of events is called *collectively exhaustive* if one of them *must* occur.

Union of events   An outcome that occurs whenever *any* event in a set of events happens is called the *union* of those events. It is expressed, for the case of two events, as:

$$(A \text{ or } B)$$

Such a situation occurs when the occurrence of either A, or B, or both together result in the same outcome (e.g., a successful product).

Joint (intersection of) events   An outcome that occurs only whenever *all* events occur (together) is called the *intersection* of events. These are referred to as *joint* events. For the case of two events this situation is written as:

$$(A \text{ and } B)$$

Probability relationships

Designations   Let:

$P(A)$ = probability of A occurring.
$P(B)$ = probability of B occurring.
And so on.

Conditional probabilities   The probability of two mutually exclusive events A and B occurring at the same time is zero, by definition. However, if A and B are *not mutually exclusive*, then it is possible to talk about the probability of A occurring *given* that B *has occurred* and vice versa. That is, if B happens first, what is the chance of A happening? The probability of A occurring, given that B has occurred, is called the *conditional* probability of A, given B, and is denoted $P(A|B)$. Similarly $P(B|A)$, denotes the conditional probability of B, given that A has occurred.

Joint probabilities   The probability of two or more events occurring jointly is labeled the *joint probability* of the events and is designated as $P(A \text{ and } B)$ for the case of two events.[1]

Laws of probability[2]

Multiplication   The multiplication rule is used to find the probability of the *joint occurrence* of two or more events. Two cases are distinguished:

1.   Dependent events   For the case of two events:

$$P(A \text{ and } B) = P(A) \times P(B|A) = P(B) \times P(A|B) \qquad \text{(B2)}$$

The Relationship between Conditional and Joint Probabilities

It is possible to compute the conditional probability of two events if the probability of each event and their joint probability are given.

$$P(A|B) = \frac{P(A \text{ and } B)}{P(B)} \qquad \text{(B3)}$$

2.   Independent events   If the events are independent, then the outcome of one has no effect on the outcome of the other and therefore the conditional probabilities are identical. For two events this can be expressed as:

$$P(A|B) = P(A) \qquad \text{and} \qquad P(B|A) = P(B) \qquad \text{(B4)}$$

Inserting these values in Equation B2 we get a simplified multiplication law for independent events:

$$P(A \text{ and } B) = P(A) \times P(B) \qquad \text{(B5)}$$

---

[1] Also written as $P(A, B)$.

[2] These laws are given here for two events. They can be extended, as shown in some cases, to any number of events.

This law can be extended to any number of independent events; that is:

$$P(A \text{ and } B \text{ and } C \text{ and } . . .) = P(A) \times P(B) \times P(C) \times . . . \quad \text{(B6)}$$

Addition This law predicts the chances of a *union* of events occurring. Three cases are distinguished:

1. Nonexclusive joint events In such a case the formula is (for two events):

$$P(A \text{ or } B) = P(A) + P(B) - P(A \text{ and } B) \quad \text{(B7)}$$

2. Mutually exclusive events The joint occurrence of mutually exclusive events is impossible (by definition). Thus, $P(A \text{ and } B) = 0$.

Therefore Equation B7 becomes:

$$P(A \text{ or } B) = P(A) + P(B) \quad \text{(B8)}$$

3. Mutually exclusive and collectively exhaustive events. If a of events is both mutually exclusive and collectively exhaustive, then the *union* of these events *must occur* (by definition); that is, the probability of (A or B or . . .) is certain (equal to one). This property can be expressed as:

$$P(A \text{ or } B \text{ or } . . .) = P(A) + P(B) + . . . = 1 \quad \text{(B9)[3]}$$

B2 STATISTICS

Definitions

Statistics "*Statistics are like miniskirts. They cover up the essentials but give you ideas.*" The word statistic generally is taken to mean an estimate of a population characteristic or a summarized presentation of a mass of data. There are two subtopics of statistics: *descriptive* and *inferential*.

Descriptive statistics is the methodology which reduces a large mass of data into a few summary statistics. The most common are: the *central tendency*, the *dispersion*, and the *frequency distribution*.

Inferential statistics is the methodology for inferring the characteristics of a large mass of data based upon the examination of a sample.

---

[3] Probabilities of events can be designated as p_i = probability of event i. Then Equation B9 is written as:

$$\sum_{1}^{n} p_i = 1$$

Population and samples   The description of data depends on what type of measurement is used. In general, two approaches exist: (1) measuring the entire population and (2) measuring a sample.

Population   A population is a complete set of individuals, objects, or measurements, having some common observable characteristics. The observation of the entire population is normally more expensive and takes more time than the observation of a sample. On the other hand, observing the population generally yields more accurate results.

Samples   A sample is a small portion of data drawn from a larger group (the population). If properly drawn it is possible to make reasonably accurate conclusions about the entire population from the study of the sample. This ability provides a powerful device for getting the information required for decision making cheaply and quickly.

Frequency distribution   A frequency distribution is a function telling how many times each of a set of random events, x_i, occurred. In other words, given a set of mutually exclusive and collectively exhaustive events (such as shown in Table B1), then the set of relative frequencies of all events, is called the *frequency distribution function*. Frequency distribution functions can be shown graphically as histograms (such as Figure B1) or curves (Figure B2). A detailed discussion of the most common frequency distribution functions used in this text is given in Section B3 of the appendix.

Measures of central tendency

The most common statistic is the central tendency or the average. The purpose of the average is to represent a group of individual values in a concise manner. The most common measures of central tendency are: the *mean*, the *median*, and the *mode*.

The population mean   The population mean is given as:

$$\mu = \sum_i x_i \, P(x_i) \qquad (B10)$$

where:

x_i is the value of the variable.

$P(x_i)$ is the probability of obtaining the value x_i (or the relative frequency of x_i in the population).[4]

μ = a Greek letter (pronounced mu) that designates the mean.

The expected value   The mean and expected value of a random variable are conceptually and numerically the same. The two are

---

[4] If the frequency of all values is the same, the formula is:

$$\mu = \frac{\Sigma x_i}{n} \qquad (B11)$$

completely interchangeable. An expected value is designated by $E(x)$ (read as: the expected value of x).

The median   The *median* is the middle value of the distribution. That is, if the number of observations is odd, then 50 percent of the observed data is smaller than the median and 50 percent is larger than the median. If the number of observations is even, then we average the middle two. For example, in Table B1, both the 40th and the 41st observation (which are 50 percent of the total of 80 observations) are 30 mph. Thus 30 mph is the median speed.

The mode   The *mode* is that data value with the highest frequency (there may be more than one). In Table B1, it is 30 mph (25 observations). In this distribution the median and mode fell in the same speed value, but that need not necessarily be true in other cases. Also, although the mode is always physically a realizable integer data point, the mean and the median may *not* be. For example, the mean family size in the United States is about 4.3 people. The mean, median, and mode apply both to populations and to samples.

Measures of dispersion

Measures of dispersion are measures of scatter about an average, or how data are scattered around the mean. the most important measure of dispersion in the context of this book is the standard deviation.

Standard deviation and variance of the population   The standard deviation is designated by the Greek letter sigma (σ).

The formula for populations involving frequency distributions is:[5]

$$\sigma = \sqrt{\sum_i (x_i - \mu)^2 P(x_i)} \tag{B12}$$

The value σ^2 is known as the population *variance*.

Sample distributions

The mean   Data such as those presented in Table B1 (a sample of 80 observations) can be described by a sample mean (denoted by $\bar{x}$) according to the following formula:

$$\bar{x} = \sum_i x_i \frac{f_i}{n} \tag{B14}$$

---

[5] If the frequency of all values is the same, the formula simplifies to:

$$\sigma = \sqrt{\frac{\sum (x_i - \mu)^2}{n}} \tag{B13}$$

where n is the population size.

The meaning of this notation can be explained by using the data of Table B1: x_i is the ith speed, f_i is the number of occurrences of that speed, and n is the sample size (80 in this case). The term f_i/n is the frequency of speed i.

The standard deviation and variance The sample standard deviation s, is calculated from Equation B15.

$$s = \sqrt{\sum_i (x_i - \bar{x})^2 \frac{f_i}{n-1}} \tag{B15}$$

The value s^2 is known as the sample *variance*.

Sample error Once $\bar{x}$ has been determined, it is possible to estimate the population mean. The difference between μ and $\bar{x}$ is termed the sampling error.

The law of large numbers Sampling is governed by the following law:

> As the size of a sample increases toward infinity, the difference between the true population mean and the sample mean tends toward zero.

Thus, it may be assumed that the sample mean is a good estimate of the population mean if the sample is "large enough" (30 is often considered the dividing point between a "small" and a "large" sample).

The central limit theorem It is possible to assess the *error* in estimating the population mean, indirectly, with the aid of the *central limit theorem*. The *central limit theorem* tells us that if one continues to take random samples of size n, from *any population distribution* with a standard deviation of σ, then the distribution of the *means of the samples* will tend to be normally distributed (the normal distribution is discussed in the next part of the appendix), with mean μ and standard deviation $\sigma/\sqrt{n}$, as n approaches infinity. Again, for practical purposes, if $n \geq 30$ ("large enough") then a normal distribution of the samples' means can be assumed.

B3 PROBABILITY DISTRIBUTIONS

Discrete and continuous probability distributions

If a random variable may take only certain specific numerical values, such as integer numbers, then the probability distribution that characterizes the process which generated that random variable is called a *discrete distribution*. However, if the random variable may take *any* value (within a specified interval), then the probability distribution is labeled *continuous*. In this appendix the following distributions will be discussed: the Poisson (a discrete distribution) and the normal and exponential (continuous distributions).

The Poisson distribution

The Poisson distribution describes situations where the number of occurrences per unit of time is constant; however, the timing of occurrence is random. In other words, occurrences have an equal chance of happening during any moment in the time interval under study.

The distribution is shown in Figure B1.

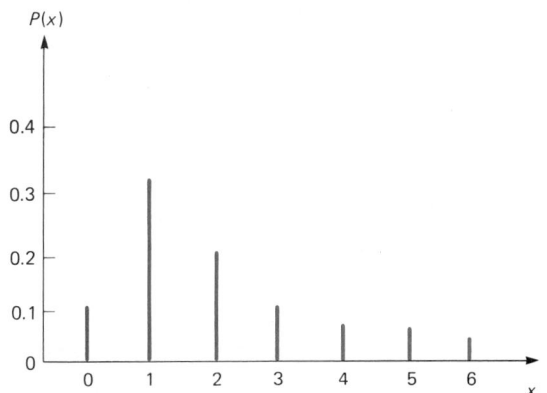

FIGURE B1
The Poisson probability distribution

The formula for the Poisson distribution is:

$$P(x) = \frac{\lambda^x e^{-\lambda}}{x!} \tag{B16}$$

where:

λ = the average number of occurrences per unit of time.
e = 2.718 (the base of the natural logarithms), approximately.
x = a variable that assumes integer values such as ($x = 0, 1, 2, \ldots$).
$P(x)$ = relative frequency of each value of x.

The mean and standard deviation of this distribution are:

$$\text{Mean} = \lambda \tag{B17}$$

$$\text{Standard Deviation} = \sqrt{\lambda} \tag{B18}$$

The normal distribution

The normal distribution is a continuous distribution discovered over 200 years ago. It was then considered to be the law governing distributions of natural phenomena. This belief has been modified as other distributions were discovered; however, the distribution is still the most common in statistics.

FIGURE B2
The normal distribution

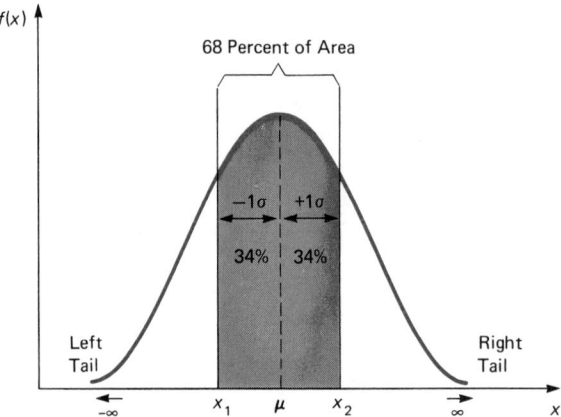

The normal distribution is shown in Figure B2 and its formula is:

$$f(x) = \frac{1}{\sigma \sqrt{2\pi}} \left[e^{-1/2} \left(\frac{x - \mu}{\sigma} \right)^2 \right]$$

(B19)

where:

$f(x)$ is the relative frequency of variable x,
μ = the mean of the distribution.
σ = the standard deviation of the distribution.
π = 3.14 (approximately).

Note that in contrast to the Poisson distribution we talk here about $f(x)$ being the relative frequency of point x, in the range of $-\infty$ to ∞. (In contrast, the $P(x)$ in the Poisson was the *probability* of x having a *particular value.*)

Note also that the values of μ and σ are necessary and sufficient to describe the normal curve.

The area under the normal curve   Since the normal distribution is symmetrical, its midpoint is the mean. All x values (on the x axis) are measured as deviations from the mean in standard deviation units.

The area under the normal curve describes the proportion of the total distribution between two points on the x axis. For example, in Figure B2, the shaded area between point x_1 (which is one standard deviation to the left of the mean) and point x_2 (which is one standard deviation to the right of the mean) is 68 percent of the total area. The area from point $-\infty$ (left side) to point x_2 is 84 percent (34 percent plus the mean which is exactly at 50 percent). It is known that 95.4 percent of the curve lies between $\pm 2\sigma$ around the mean and 99.7 percent lies between $\pm 3\sigma$.

The standard normal distribution A normal distribution whose mean is zero and whose standard deviation is one is called a *standard normal distribution*. Such a distribution was used for the construction of Table C1, in Appendix C, which lists the area under the curve as a function of the number of standard deviations, Z. This table is extremely useful since it enables one to find the probabilities for *any* given normal distribution, using the relationship:

$$Z = \frac{x - \mu}{\sigma} \qquad \text{(B20)}$$

where x is the value of the measured variable. Note that *if* in Equation B20, $\mu = 0$ and $\sigma = 1$, then $z = x$.

The use of the table of the area under the normal curve (Table C1) Tables that give the area under the normal curve appear in two alternative forms (Figure B3).

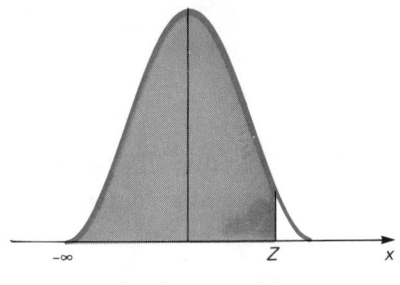

a. Area from $-\infty$ to Z

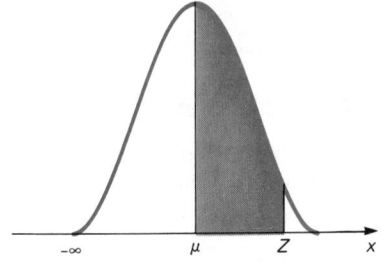

b. Area between μ and Z

FIGURE B3
Alternative presentation of the area under the normal curve

Alternative a. The entries in a table of this type represent the proportion of the total area under the normal curve (shaded) which falls between $-\infty$ and Z standard deviations to the right of the mean.

Alternative b. The entries in a table of this type represent the proportion of the total area under the normal curve (shaded) which falls between the mean and Z standard deviations to the right of the mean.

The difference between the same entry in the two tables is .5; that is, each entry in table type *a* is exactly .5 larger than that of type *b*. In this text, Table C1 is a type *a* table.

Use of the table

Example 1 Find the area between $-\infty$ and $Z = 1.43$ standard deviations to the right of the mean. First find the entry in row $Z = 1.4$

that intersects with column .03; the reading is .9236 (that is, 92.36 percent of the area is covered).

Example 2   Find the area between the mean and .45 standard deviations to the *left of the mean.*

Solution   Find the entry equivalent to $Z = .45$ (row $Z = .4$, column .05) which is .6736. Then subtract .5 from this value. The result .6736 − .5 = .1736 means that the solution is 17.36 percent of the area.

See Figure B4 for a graphical presentation of these two examples.

FIGURE B4
Graphical presentation of
the two examples

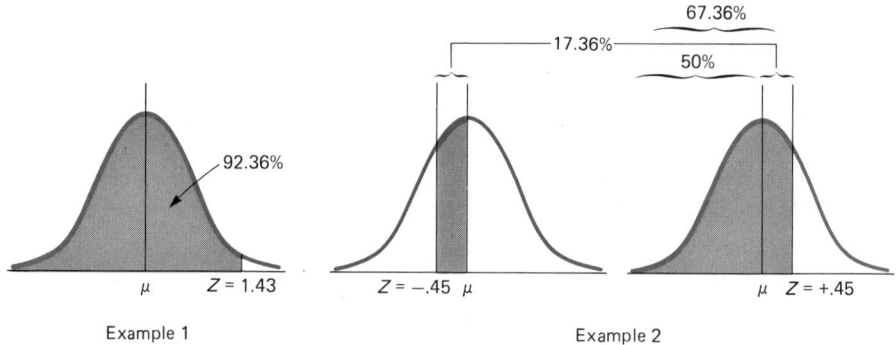

Example 1   Example 2

The negative exponential distribution

The negative exponential distribution describes the probability "that it will take x time before the first occurrence of an outcome."

The formula for the distribution is:

$$f(x) = \lambda e^{-\lambda x} \qquad \text{for } \lambda \geq 0 \tag{B21}$$

where λ = the average number of occurrences per unit of time (e.g., service rate).

The statistics of this distribution are:

$$\text{Mean} = \frac{1}{\lambda} \tag{B22}$$

$$\text{Standard Deviation} = \frac{1}{\lambda} \tag{B23}$$

The distribution is shown in Figure B5.

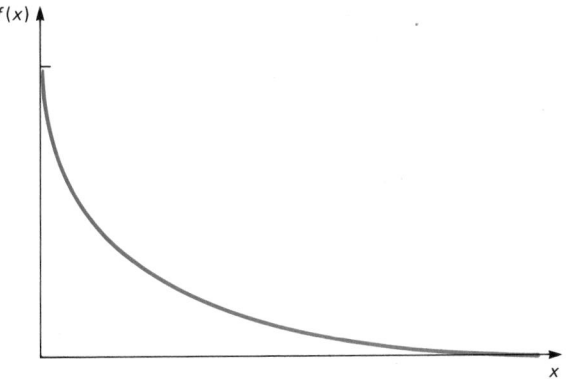

FIGURE B5
The negative exponential distribution

B4   BIBLIOGRAPHY

1. Clelland, R. C.; deCani, J. S.; and Brown, F. F. *Basic Statistics with Business Applications.* 2d ed. New York: John Wiley & Sons, Inc., 1973.

2. Daniel, W. W., and Terrell, J. D. *Basic Statistics.* Boston: Houghton Mifflin Co., 1975.

3. Gulezion, R. C. *Elements of Business Statistics.* Philadelphia: W. E. Saunders, 1979.

4. Madsen, R. W. and Mueschberger, M. L. *Statistical Methods for Business and Economics.* Englewood Cliffs, NJ: Prentice-Hall, 1980.

5. Mason, R. D. *Programmed Learning Aid for Business and Economic Statistics.* Homewood, Ill.: Richard D. Irwin, Inc. (Learning Systems Co.), 1974.

6. Mullen, K., and Malik, H. J. *Applied Statistics for Business and Economics.* Reading, Mass.: Addison-Wesley Publishing Co., Inc., 1975.

7. Sanders, D. H., et al. *Statistics—A Fresh Approach.* 2d ed. New York: McGraw-Hill Book Co., 1980.

8. Spirer, H. F. *Business Statistics.* Homewood, Ill.: Richard D. Irwin, Inc., 1975.

9. Spurr, W. A., and Bonini, C. P. *Statistical Analysis for Business Decision.* Homewood, Ill.: Richard D. Irwin, Inc., 1973.

10. Stockton, J. R., and Clark, C. T. *Introduction to Business and Economic Statistics.* 5th ed. Cincinnati: South-Western Publishing Co., 1975.

11. Wonnacott, T. H., and Wonnacott, R. J. *Introductory Statistics for Business and Economics.* New York: John Wiley & Sons, Inc., 1972.

C—Tables

TABLE C1
Cumulative probabilities of the normal probability distribution (areas under the normal curve from $-\infty$ to z)

Z	.00	.01	.02	.03	.04	.05	.06	.07	.08	.09
.0	.5000	.5040	.5080	.5120	.5160	.5199	.5239	.5279	.5319	.5359
.1	.5398	.5438	.5478	.5517	.5557	.5596	.5636	.5675	.5714	.5753
.2	.5793	.5832	.5871	.5910	.5948	.5987	.6026	.6064	.6103	.6141
.3	.6179	.6217	.6255	.6293	.6331	.6368	.6406	.6443	.6480	.6517
.4	.6554	.6591	.6628	.6664	.6700	.6736	.6772	.6808	.6844	.6879
.5	.6915	.6950	.6985	.7019	.7054	.7088	.7123	.7157	.7190	.7224
.6	.7257	.7291	.7324	.7357	.7389	.7422	.7454	.7486	.7517	.7549
.7	.7580	.7611	.7642	.7673	.7704	.7734	.7764	.7794	.7823	.7852
.8	.7881	.7910	.7939	.7967	.7995	.8023	.8051	.8078	.8106	.8133
.9	.8159	.8186	.8212	.8238	.8264	.8289	.8315	.8340	.8365	.8389
1.0	.8413	.8438	.8461	.8485	.8508	.8531	.8554	.8577	.8599	.8621
1.1	.8643	.8665	.8686	.8708	.8729	.8749	.8770	.8790	.8810	.8830
1.2	.8849	.8869	.8888	.8907	.8925	.8944	.8962	.8980	.8997	.9015
1.3	.9032	.9049	.9066	.9082	.9099	.9115	.9131	.9147	.9162	.9177
1.4	.9192	.9207	.9222	.9236	.9251	.9265	.9279	.9292	.9306	.9319
1.5	.9332	.9345	.9357	.9370	.9382	.9394	.9406	.9418	.9429	.9441
1.6	.9452	.9463	.9474	.9484	.9495	.9505	.9515	.9525	.9535	.9545
1.7	.9554	.9564	.9573	.9582	.9591	.9599	.9608	.9616	.9625	.9633
1.8	.9641	.9649	.9656	.9664	.9671	.9678	.9686	.9693	.9699	.9706
1.9	.9713	.9719	.9726	.9732	.9738	.9744	.9750	.9756	.9761	.9767
2.0	.9772	.9778	.9783	.9788	.9793	.9798	.9803	.9808	.9812	.9817
2.1	.9821	.9826	.9830	.9834	.9838	.9842	.9846	.9850	.9854	.9857
2.2	.9861	.9864	.9868	.9871	.9875	.9878	.9881	.9884	.9887	.9890
2.3	.9893	.9896	.9898	.9901	.9904	.9906	.9909	.9911	.9913	.9916
2.4	.9918	.9920	.9922	.9925	.9927	.9929	.9931	.9932	.9934	.9936
2.5	.9938	.9940	.9941	.9943	.9945	.9946	.9948	.9949	.9951	.9952
2.6	.9953	.9955	.9956	.9957	.9959	.9960	.9961	.9962	.9963	.9964
2.7	.9965	.9966	.9967	.9968	.9969	.9970	.9971	.9972	.9973	.9974
2.8	.9974	.9975	.9976	.9977	.9977	.9978	.9979	.9979	.9980	.9981
2.9	.9981	.9982	.9982	.9983	.9984	.9984	.9985	.9985	.9986	.9986
3.0	.9987	.9987	.9987	.9988	.9988	.9989	.9989	.9989	.9990	.9990
3.1	.9990	.9991	.9991	.9991	.9992	.9992	.9992	.9992	.9993	.9993
3.2	.9993	.9993	.9994	.9994	.9994	.9994	.9994	.9995	.9995	.9995
3.3	.9995	.9995	.9995	.9996	.9996	.9996	.9996	.9996	.9996	.9997
3.4	.9997	.9997	.9997	.9997	.9997	.9997	.9997	.9997	.9997	.9998

TABLE C2
Random numbers

7823	9505	7863	2976	4536	0062	2757	3281
4308	3826	1329	8318	5829	0986	2765	0874
9228	9903	9793	6938	9344	2120	1306	4629
8717	5407	0187	3141	7651	9415	2893	9213
4773	8866	4966	3964	8718	9311	5954	6955
8387	4641	6280	4467	4578	2349	7635	7109
8728	4950	9218	2101	8320	1526	8462	2968
2768	3615	2529	2812	3783	0934	3126	4600
1988	5102	1837	3864	1161	8517	7101	8024
5202	0158	0715	9539	4229	3874	6042	1437
9763	5760	9080	5720	1216	7843	5890	2789
7025	2332	6238	8043	1373	5162	6336	7402
6020	5070	7485	5620	3081	4854	8759	8005
0526	8974	8545	8541	6886	5014	2012	1843
5078	8581	1215	2189	8128	9536	5357	5770
5801	3622	6441	5059	8871	3844	7643	8809
8691	0747	7648	9165	7648	5068	5216	9526
6272	9181	7511	3217	8037	9114	8365	3502
9208	4589	5428	8676	3424	2940	7001	0478
0693	0665	0855	7396	5297	4919	1061	3722
0363	1856	9196	6949	6230	9456	9558	5963
5238	3367	2373	5890	6273	4141	4451	6709
1907	6029	5227	6050	2698	8500	1478	5049
3057	3784	1807	2634	8159	3015	9813	0030
2926	0519	2181	5244	1046	5367	5901	7474
0456	0663	0756	4094	4418	7953	4044	7590
4124	4389	1198	5571	6119	6540	7273	2009
9376	3496	0902	9923	2789	4477	6797	1870
1543	7954	9548	1232	4219	0236	6777	0342
2739	5811	1642	5979	2059	8088	3391	3480
0682	0604	2051	1375	8191	2566	3162	2572
0535	0605	6357	8278	3078	6929	5224	9124
7782	3184	4504	5879	3238	4159	5676	0418
0805	5265	6536	6506	9487	6087	9420	9063
6262	7289	3310	8731	3921	2095	5837	4218
8508	3313	2976	5658	3616	3361	9396	5188
6248	3796	5543	2582	2832	1983	4747	9837
5220	0327	3268	4413	3040	6358	8106	0776
5193	3007	3666	8084	1389	5026	2680	1549
2652	1375	4799	8832	3241	0752	5649	3029

D—Answers to even-numbered problems

CHAPTER 2

2.   *a.*   A ≤ 400
     b.   A + B ≥ 540
     c.   A + B ≤ 720
     d.   800A + 1150B ≤ 50,000

CHAPTER 3

2. Insure, 50,000 deductible: Expected cost = $825

4. *b.*   2.75 cars per day
   c. $195,525

6. Do not play; expected loss of playing is $0.167 per play.

8. *a.*   Select a_1: Expected profit 6.1, EOL = 1.1
   b.   Select a_2: Expected profit 4.5, EOL = 1.6
   c.   Select a_1: Expected profit 2.0, EOL = .3

10. Choose alternative c for a cost of $7300

12. Order 11 crates; average daily profit $15.60

14. Convert now; expected cost $2500

16. *a.*   EVPI = 1.1
    b.   EVPI = 1.6
    c.   EVPI = 0.3

18. EVPI = $83.40

20. If $p(s_2) > p(s_3)$, select a_1.
    If $p(s_2) < p(s_3)$, select a_2.

22. User of maximin will select "bonds."
    User of other criteria will select "land."

CHAPTER 4

2. U(1000) = 25

4. Since U(3000) is about 31 and the expected utility of the investment is 26.50, she should *not* invest.

6. *a.*   A = 20 percent, B = 20 percent, C = 33 percent, D = 27 percent
   b.   A = 15 percent, B = 20 percent, C = 39 percent, D = 26 percent

8. The best year was 1978 with the highest index of 250.

10. Do not insure: expected cost = $80

12. Do not repair: expected cost = $1370

14. Attend at random: expected value is 1.74

16. Expand: expected present value = $695,000

18. Use no preparation: expected cost = $130.20

20. *a.* $P(D_1/T+) = 0.667$
        $P(D_1/T-) = 0.250$
    b.   0.64

22. *a.*   Select a_2: Expected value = $19,500
    b.   EVPI = $750
    c. $P(R/A) = 0.947$; $P(R/B) = 0.26$; $P(U/A) = 0.053$; $P(U/B) = 0.74$
    d.   If test predicts receptive market, select B (expected value = 23,837). If test predicts unfavorable, then select A (expected value = 9640).
    e.   EVPI = $255

CHAPTER 5

2. Two optimal solutions give $z = 95$; $x_1 = 12.6$, $x_2 = 6.4$; $x_1 = 8$, $x_2 = 11$

4. c. $x_1 = 9$, $x_2 = 7.5$
   d. $z = 117$
   e.

Constraint	Slack	Surplus
#1	5	0
#2	0	0
#3	0	12
#4	15	0

   f. $x_1 = 10.67$, $x_2 = 3.33$, $z = 105.34$

6. a. 600 shirts, 1200 pants, $z = \$4200$/day
   b. The price of shirts must exceed $6/unit

8. 37.5 hours (150 units) on line #1
   170 hours (850 units) on line #2
   Total cost = $1150

10. Max $z = 5x_1 + 4x_2 + 7x_3$
    s.t. $7x_1 + 10x_2 + 13x_3 \le 10,000$
    $2x_1 + 2.5x_2 + 3x_3 \le 18,000$
    $30x_1 + 40x_2 + 60x_3 \le 225,000$
    Solution: $x_1 = 1428.6$, $x_2 = 0$, $x_3 = 0$, $z = 7142.85$

12. a. Max $z = 16x_1 + 8x_2 + 11x_3 + 6x_4 + 10x_5$
    b. Max $z = x_1 + x_2 + x_3 + x_4 + x_5$
    The constraints in both cases are:
    $200x_1 + 120x_2 + 150x_3 + 80x_4 + 100x_5 \le 10,000$
    $20x_1 + 15x_2 + 16x_3 + 10x_4 + 14x_5 \le 1000$

14. Max $z = 75x_1 + 99x_2 + 72.5x_3$
    s.t. $5x_1 + 7x_2 + 10x_3 \le 1000$
    $10x_1 + 8x_2 + 5x_3 \le 800$

16. 10 each of A, B, D; $251\frac{2}{3}$ of C. $z = \$25,448.23$

18. $1,940,000 in Treasury bonds; $0 in corporate bonds; $1,940,000 in loans; $1,120,000 in stock; $564,312.50 return on investment.

20.
	Case a	Case b
1.	#1	#6
2.	#4, #1	#4, #5
3.	None	#1

22. b. 5 (the number of constraints)
    c. If degenerate.
    d. Bread 750.9 grams; carrots 135.8 g.; halibut 111.6 g.; eggs 325.4 g. Cost: 92¢ per day.
    e. 56.36 grams of protein
    f. Beef 169.6 grams; butter 62.8 g.; bread 500 g.; carrots 130.4 g.; halibut 70.1 g.; eggs 200 g. Cost: $1.085. 52.5 grams of protein.

24. a. $x_1 = 10$, $x_2 = 8$, $z = 82$
    b. Solution is degenerate.
    e. Additional solution: $x_1 = 11.45$, $x_2 = 6.18$, $z = 82$

26. $x_1 = 1$, $x_2 = 3$, $z = 14$

28. $x_1 = 1$, $x_2 = 3$, $z = 14$

30. Unbounded solution in x_2

CHAPTER 6

2. $u_1 = 1\frac{2}{3}$, $u_2 = \frac{1}{3}$, $u_3 = u_4 = 0$, $w = 132$

4. a. Min. $50u_1 - 20u_2 + 26u_3 - 26u_4$
      s.t. $5u_1 + 2u_3 - 2u_4 \ge 5$
      $3u_1 - 2u_2 + 3u_3 - 3u_4 \ge 3$
      $- 1u_2 - 1u_3 + 1u_4 \ge 1$
   b. Min. $-50u_1 + 20u_2 - 20u_3 + 45u_4$
      s.t. $-3u_1 + 1u_2 - 1u_3 + 2u_4 \ge -6$
      $-4u_1 + 2u_2 - 2u_3 + 3u_4 \ge 2$

6. a. $x_1 = .4$, $x_2 = .1$, $z = 200$
   b. The first, third, and fourth.
   c. 1. None 4. None
      2. None 5. Reduce cost by $50(.5)$ $= \$25$
      3. None 6. Infeasible

8. a. $2666.67 \le x_1 \le 8000$
      $2500 \le x_2 \le 7500$
   b. No non-basic variables.
   c. $-\infty \le b_1 \le 11.50$
      $-16.50 \le b_2 \le \infty$
      $102.86 \le b_3 \le 240$
      $120 \le b_4 \le 233.33$
      $60 \le b_5 \le \infty$

10. a. $x_1 = 0.5$, $x_2 = 0$, $z = 350$
    b. Coefficient of x_2 must exceed 35.
    c. Can decrease by 3.5
    d. Coefficient can increase up to $2\frac{1}{3}$
    e. Infeasible solution

12. $x_1 = x_2 = 400$, priorities 1, 2, and 3 are achieved; underachievement of $28,000 on priority $4 and 200 hours on priority 5.

14. a. Either $x_1 = 1$, $x_2 = 2$ or $x_1 = 2$, $x_2 = 1$; $z = 3$
    c. LP solution $x_1 = \frac{5}{3}$, $x_2 = \frac{5}{3}$, $z = \frac{10}{3}$
       Rounding gives the two solutions in a.
    d. $\frac{1}{3}$
    e. Min. $w = 5u_1 + 5u_2$
       s.t. $2u_1 + u_2 \ge 1$
       $u_1 + 2u_2 \ge 1$
       Solution: $u_1 = \frac{1}{3}$, $u_2 = \frac{1}{3}$, $w = 3\frac{1}{3}$

16. Min. $600x_1$ (M-1 flights) $+ 8000x_2 + 10,000x_3$

s.t. $100x_1 \qquad + 180x_2 + 270x_3 \geq 3200$

$\qquad 4x_1 \qquad + 12x_2 + 17x_3 \leq 140$

$\qquad x_1 \qquad\qquad\qquad \leq 15$

$\qquad\qquad x_2 \qquad\qquad \leq 12$

$\qquad\qquad\qquad x_3 \leq 6$

x_i integer

18. *a.* $x_1 = 13\frac{1}{3},\ x_2 = 23\frac{1}{3},\ z = \$9250$

b. $x_1 = 13,\ x_2 = 23,\ z = \$9075$

20. See Problem 14 solution.

CHAPTER 7

2. *a.* Cost = \$700

b. Cost = \$560

c. Optimal solution cost = \$560

d. Yes, many.

4. *a.* Optimal profit = \$1260

b. Max. $6x_{11} + 4x_{12} + 3x_{21} + 5x_{22} + 8x_{31}$
$\qquad + 7x_{32} + 5x_{41} + 9x_{42}$

s.t. $\quad x_{11} + x_{12} \leq 50$

$\qquad x_{21} + x_{22} \leq 80$

$\qquad x_{31} + x_{32} \leq 60$

$\qquad x_{41} + x_{42} \leq 40$

$\qquad x_{11} + x_{21} + x_{31} + x_{41} = 80$

$\qquad x_{12} + x_{22} + x_{32} + x_{42} = 100$

6. *b.* Several optimal solutions with a distance of 885 miles.

8. *b.* Optimal minimum cost = \$11,200; $x_{AC} = 1000$; $x_{BD} = 1300$

c. Min.

$6x_{AC} + 7x_{AD} + 9x_{AE} + 9x_{BC} + 4x_{BD} + 6x_{BE}$

s.t. $\quad x_{AC} + x_{AD} + x_{AE} = 1000$

$\qquad x_{BC} + x_{BD} + x_{BE} = 1300$

10. *a.* A–O, B–N, C–P, Min. cost = \$16

12. *a.* Several optimal solutions with minimum complaints of 21

14. *a.* $x_{AI} = 60,\ x_{AII} = 80,\ x_{BII} = 40,\ x_{BIII} = 80$, Cost = \$8500

16. $x_{A1} = 3000,\ x_{B1} = 2000,\ x_{C1} = 200,\ x_{C2} = 1600,$ $x_{D3} = 6000$, Profit = \$555,000

18. See answer to Problem 2.

20. *a.* Degenerate, cost = 6400

b. $x_{1A} = 200,\ x_{2A} = 400,\ x_{3C} = 500,\ x_{3D} = 100,$ $x_{4B} = 400,\ x_{4E} = 300$, Cost = 6000

22. $x_{AE} = 40,\ x_{CD} = 20$, minimum mileage = 3800

24. See Problem 10.

CHAPTER 8

2. *a.*

Event	T_E	T_L	Slack
1.........	0	0	0
2.........	3	3	0
3.........	5	8	3
4.........	10	10	0
5.........	16	16	0
6.........	19	19	0

b. (See *a.* also).

Activity	Slack
a.............	0
b	3
c.............	0
d	3
e.............	0
f.............	7
g.............	6
h	5

c. Critical path: a–c–e–i

d. 3 on b–d

3 on b–f

3 on b–g

e. Total slack: $3 + 7 + 6 + 5 = 21$

4. *a.* a–d–e–g–i–j

b. 20 days

c. 61 days

d. 20 days

6. *b.* b–f–h

c. 9 weeks

d. a–c; 6 weeks

e. 1 extra week: No effect

2 extra weeks: Second critical path b–e–g

3 extra weeks: One week delay and new critical path b–e–g

8. *b.* b–e–g–h

c. new critical path a–d–g–h

d. From c and f to d, then to g, lastly to h

10. *a.* and *b.*

Event	T_E	T_L	Slack
1.........	0	0	0
2......	10	10	0
3.......	10	11	1
4......	5	8	3
5......	17	17	1
6......	12	13	0
7......	21	21	0

c. (See a. and b. above.) Critical path 1–2–6–7
d. 1–3–5
e. New critical path 1–4–5–7 and project completion in 22 weeks
f. 3 weeks

12. P(completion within 14 days) = 15.87 percent. Expected bonus of $3174 > Expected penalty of $2944. Therefore, *accept* the contract.

14. *a.* 31 weeks; $31,000
b. 14 weeks; $53,000
c. $22,000
d. $47,100
e. $42,100

16. 15 days, $1540

CHAPTER 9

2. P→A→H→LA, cost = $380

4.
Year	Price
1	$110
2	100
3	100
4	110

6. *a.* 1 to A, 2 to B, 1 to C; $33,000/month
b. 2 to A, 1 to B, 1 to C; $32,000/month
c. 1 to each; $29,000/month

8. *a.* Sell on any day (except the fifth) if the price is ≥ 22; otherwise, wait. On the fifth day, sell at any price.
b. Net return = $21,526

10. Mon: Wait.
Tues.: Sell if 350, otherwise wait.
Wed.: Sell if 400, otherwise wait.
Thurs.: Sell.

12. *a.* Min. $z = 20A + 15B + 23C + 18D$
s.t. $\quad 4A + 2B + 5C + 3D \geq 14$
$A, B, C, D \geq 0$ and integer
b. 1A and 2C; Cost = $66

CHAPTER 10

2. $Q(3) = [.456 \quad .544]$

4. *a.* 75 good; 74 fair; 32 poor
b. 52.68 good; 83.42 fair; 43.90 poor

6. *a.* P(A operates) = .948; P(B operates) = .977; lease B
b. If the lease for A is less than $(948 \div .977) \times$ lease for B, then A should be leased; otherwise, lease B.

8. *a.* 21.74 in checking; 8.53 in loans; 9.72 in savings.

10. 42.3 percent to A; 19.8 percent to B; 36.9 percent to C

14.
Level	Days
1	7.01
2	10.50
3	24.05
4	40.15
5	50.50
6	51.47
7	77.35
8	59.80
9	44.17
Total	365.00

16. *b.* 39 at airport, 61 at beach
c. $458.80
d. 27 percent

18. *a.* 3.37 weeks
b. $5/3$ weeks in good condition; 1 week in fair condition; $19/27$ weeks in poor condition.
c. In the long run, 100 percent. Within a week, 10 percent if in good condition, 20 percent if fair, and 90 percent if poor.

CHAPTER 11

2. *b.* A should advertise; B should cut prices; game value = -1

4. *a.* A use a_1 one-sixth of the time, a_2 five-sixths of the time
B use b_1 one-half of the time, b_2 one-half of the time
b. 0.5 percent increase to A at B's expense
c. Yes

6.
	b_1	b_2	b_3
a_1	−3	4	3
a_2	2	1	4
a_4	1	6	−4

8. *a.* A: Advertise in evening.
B: Advertise once in the evening and once in the afternoon or else twice in the evening.

b.   25 percent to A; 75 percent to B

10. *b.*   Farmer should plant on a large scale to guarantee at least $2500

 c.   Everyone plant on a small scale and each make $10,000

12. *a.*   B play b_1 only for a gain of 1 to B

 b.   B play b_2 only for a gain of 0.6 to B

14. *a.*   Min. $z = x_1 + x_2$
  s.t. $7x_1 + x_2 \geq 1$
                    $8x_2 \geq 1$
  For A: a_1 $^4/_7$ of the time, a_2 $^3/_7$
  For B: b $^1/_2$ of the time, b_2 $^1/_2$
  Game value = 1

 b.   Min. $z = x_1 + x_2 + x_3$
  s.t. $3x_1 + 2x_2 + 5x_3 \geq 1$
             $4x_2 + x_3 \geq 1$
             $2x_1 + 5x_2 \geq 1$
  For A: a_1 three-fourths of the time, a_2 one-fourth of the time
  For B: b_1 three-fourths of the time, b_2 one-fourth of the time
  Value of the game = $^7/_4$

CHAPTER 12

2.   4000 bags, 1.2 month's worth

4.   800 bags, 0.8 month's worth

6.   No, the cost would be $1530 compared to $1464 by ordering only 150 units (for which space is available).

8. *a.*   Order $10,000 worth 20 times per year

 b. $2000

 c. $3200 more per year

 d.   Order $10,488 worth

 e. $266.67 more per year

10. $.32 per unit per year

12. *a.* $11,100

 b.   1200 units; $3,600

 c.   6

16. *b.*   40

 c.   10 days

 d.   40 days
  30 units maximum inventory

 e.   Increases the cost from $750 to $812.50

18. *a.*   20 days

 b.   400

 c.   40 days

 d. $30,000 per year

20. *a.*   15

 b.   No, total cost is $1470 higher.

 c.   7 percent

24. *a.*   32

 b. $1600 per cycle

 c.   12

 d.   Every 16 days (.533 months)

26. *a.* $3280

 b.   30

28.   7

30.   106

32.   Order 150 in week 10, 145 in week 13, and 155 in week 15

CHAPTER 13

2. *a.*   2.545 hours

 b.   9.44 repairs

6. *a.*   50 percent

 b.   3.12 percent

 c.   6.25 percent

 d.   2.22 percent

 e.   93.75 percent

8.

μ	L_q	W_q
3.1	29.04	9.68
3.5	5.13	1.71
4	2.25	.75
6	0.5	.167

10.   10.33 truckloads per hour

12. $60

14. *a.*   No, only 60 percent of the time

 b.   Yes, since the system will reduce the total hourly cost of the system from $9.17 to $8.50

16.   Line 1 utilization is best : 73.9 percent

18.   Unpooled W = 1 hour; pooled W = 35 minutes

20.   Use 2 forklifts: Total cost = $21.92 per hour

22. *a.*   No, an explosive queue forms for tools.

 b.   Yes, a savings of $2.62 per hour.

24. *a.*   3.68

 b.   1.32

 c.   73.6 percent

 d.   48 percent

 e. $127

26. *a.*   0.8

 b.   2.5 minutes

   c. 36.5 percent
   d. 11 percent
   e. No, the savings is only 0.6¢

28. *a.* 2.235 days
   b. 0.383 days
   c. No, since the savings of $45.89 per day doesn't justify the daily cost of $48.
   d. Not in this case.

CHAPTER 14

8. *a.* 108 units for $1512 average profit
   b. 109 units

10. *b.* 109.5 days

12. *a.* Intermediate
   b. $944
   c. $342,800
   d. 15.4 percent
   e. $5,670

14. *a.* 13.27 units
   b. 20 percent
   c. 17 units
   d. No, inventory is increasing.

16. *a.* 80 percent
   b. $3000
   c. 30 percent
   d. 96.6 percent

18. *NB* rule: 3–2–4–7–5–1–6–8 for total of 73
   NBWA rule: Same as above.

20. *a.* 5 people
   b. 3.846 people
   c. 0.94 minutes
   d. 54 percent
   e. 97 percent
   f. 25.2 trips

22. *a.* 1755 compared to $E(V) = 1890$
   b. 8.33 percent
   c. 41.67 percent
   d. 1816.67 gallons
   e. 441.67 gallons
   f. $22.75 due to ill-will; $91.00 due to opportunity loss of 20¢ gallon
   g. 66.6 percent
   h. $260.00 − 0.83 (shipped back) = $259.13. Opportunity loss of $22.75 might also be deducted.

26. *a.* Unit demand was met (97.6%) but weekly demand was not (66.7%).
   b. $1331.45
   c. Zero
   d. 1.16 valves per week

28. *b.* $830.50 profit per day
   c. 50 percent

Index

This book has been set VIP, in 10 and 9 point Caledonia, leaded 2 points. Part number and title and chapter number and title are 36 point Caledonia bold. The size of the type page is 37 picas (28 pica text & 8 pica margin) by 48 picas.